interact with it.

SOUND BYTES

See key concepts demonstrated through multimedia lessons that include video, sound, or animation. Also includes Sound Byte Labs featuring multiple choice quizzing.

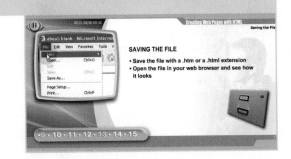

GO!

Technology in Action

Third Edition

Alan Evans • Kendall Martin
Mary Anne Poatsy

PEARSON

Prentice
Hall

Upper Saddle River, New Jersey

Technology in Action
Complete Edition/Alan Evans, Kendall Martin, Mary Anne Poatsy

Vice President and Publisher: Natalie E. Anderson
Executive Acquisitions Editor, Print: Stephanie Wall
Executive Acquisitions Editor, Media: Richard Keaveny
Product Development Manager: Eileen Bien Calabro
Editorial Project Manager: Sarah Parker McCabe
Development Editor: Shannon LeMay-Finn
Editorial Supervisor: Brian Hoehl
Editorial Assistants: Alana Meyers, Kaitlin O'Shaughnessy
Executive Producer: Lisa Strite
Media Development Manager: Cathi Profitko
Senior Media Project Manager: Steve Gagliostro
Senior Marketing Manager: Jason Sakos
Marketing Assistant: Ann Baranov
Sr. Sales Associate: Joseph Pascale
Managing Editor: Lynda J. Castillo
Senior Production Project Manager: April Montana
Manufacturing Buyer: April Montana
Production/Editorial Assistant: Sandra K. Bernales
Art Director: Blair Brown
Cover Photo: Co Rentmeester Inc.
Composition and Project Management: Prepare Inc.
Cover Printer: Phoenix Color
Printer/Binder: Courier

Credits and acknowledgments borrowed from other sources and reproduced, with permission, in this textbook appear on appropriate page within text (or on pages 641–649).

Microsoft® and Windows® are registered trademarks of the Microsoft Corporation in the U.S.A. and other countries. Screen shots and icons reprinted with permission from the Microsoft Corporation. This book is not sponsored or endorsed by or affiliated with the Microsoft Corporation.

Pearson Education LTD.
Pearson Education Singapore, Pte. Ltd
Pearson Education, Canada, Ltd
Pearson Education–Japan

Pearson Education Australia PTY, Limited
Pearson Education North Asia Ltd
Pearson Educación de Mexico, S.A. de C.V.
Pearson Education Malaysia, Pte. Ltd

10 9 8 7 6 5 4 3 2 1

ISBN 0-13-187886-7

Dedication

For my wife Patricia, whose patience, understanding, and support continue to make this work possible. And for my father, Dean, who blazed the author trail so I could follow in his footsteps!

Alan Evans

For all the teachers, mentors, and gurus who have popped in and out of my life.

Kendall Martin

For my husband Ted, who unselfishly continues to take on more than his fair share to support me throughout this process; and for my children, Laura, Carolyn, and Teddy, whose encouragement and love have been inspiring.

Mary Anne Poatsy

About the Authors

Alan Evans, MS, CPA

aevans@mc3.edu
Alan is currently the director of computer science for Montgomery County Community College. Alan's parents instilled in him a love of education at an early age. After a successful career in business, Alan finally realized his true calling was education. He has been a teacher and an administrator at the collegiate level for the past six years.

Alan makes presentations at technical conferences and meets regularly with computer science faculty and administrators from other colleges to discuss curriculum development. Currently, he is researching computer literacy standards for first-year college students.

Kendall Martin, PhD

kmartin@mc3.edu
Kendall has been teaching since 1988 at a number of institutions, including Villanova University, DeSales University, Arcadia University, Ursinus College, County College of Morris, and Montgomery County Community College, at both the undergraduate and master's degree level.

Kendall's education includes a B.S. in Electrical Engineering from the University of Rochester and an M.S. and Ph.D. in Engineering from the University of Pennsylvania. She has industrial experience in research and development environments (AT&T Bell Laboratories) as well as experience from several start-up technology firms.

At Ursinus College, Kendall developed a successful faculty training program for distance education instructors, and she makes conference presentations during the year.

Mary Anne Poatsy, MBA, CFP

mpoatsy@mc3.edu
Mary Anne is an adjunct faculty member at Montgomery County Community College, teaching various computer application and concepts courses in face-to-face and online environments.

Mary Anne holds a B.A. in Psychology and Elementary Education from Mount Holyoke College and an MBA in Finance from Northwestern University's Kellogg Graduate School of Management. Mary Anne has more than 10 years of educational experience, ranging from elementary and secondary education to Montgomery County Community College, Muhlenberg College, and Bucks County Community College, as well as training in the professional environment. Before teaching, Mary Anne was a vice president at Shearson Lehman Hutton in the Municipal Bond Investment Banking department.

 **Acknowledgments**

First, we would like to thank our students. We constantly learn from them while teaching, and they are a continual source of inspiration and new ideas.

We could not have written this book without the loving support of our families. Our spouses and children made sacrifices (mostly in time not spent with us) to permit us to make this dream into a reality.

Our heartfelt thanks go to Shannon LeMay-Finn, our developmental editor. Shannon took three authors and helped them become a cohesive team. She continues to go above and beyond the requirements of her job in a quest to make this book special.

Although working with the entire team at Prentice Hall was a truly enjoyable experience, a few individuals deserve special mention. The constant support and encouragement we receive from Stephanie Wall, Executive Editor, continue to make this book grow and change. Jodi Bolognese, our editorial project manager, can juggle more balls in the air at one time than anyone on the planet! She really kept the book moving along toward completion. And Sarah Parker McCabe, who took over for Jodi midway through this edition, is doing an admirable job filling Jodi's large shoes! As Media Development Manager, Cathi Profitko worked tirelessly to ensure that the media accompanying the text was professionally produced and delivered in a timely fashion. Despite the inevitable problems that always crop up when producing multimedia, she handled all challenges with a smile. She is absolutely one of the hardest-working individuals we have ever known. And we can't forget Natalie Anderson, Vice President of Information Technology Business Publishing, who is our publisher. Natalie has a wonderful sense of humor, which helps smooth over the inevitable bumps in the road encountered on a project of this magnitude. Our heartfelt appreciation also goes to April Montana, Senior Project Manager of Production, who continues to work tirelessly to ensure our book is always published on time and looks fabulous. The timelines are always short, the art is complex, and there are many people with whom she has to coordinate tasks. She makes it look easy. Her dedication and hard work help make this book a reality.

There were many people we did not meet in person at Prentice Hall, and elsewhere, who made significant contributions by designing the book, illustrating, composing the pages, producing multimedia, and securing permissions. We thank them all, particularly supplement authors LeeAnn Bates, Lynn Bowen, Gina Bowers-Miller, Diane Coyle, Bob Litzenberger, and Patricia Rahmlow.

Also deserving of thanks are the many experienced textbook authors who provided invaluable advice and encouragement to three neophytes at the start of this project.

Many of our colleagues at Montgomery County Community College made suggestions and provided advice during this project. We appreciate all the help everyone provided, but we would particularly like to thank John Mack, Jerri Williams, Diane Coyle, and Dianne Meskauskas, who worked directly on the supplements to the book.

And finally, we would like to thank the reviewers and the many others who contributed their time, ideas, and talents to this project. We appreciate the time and energy that you put into your comments because they helped us turn out a better product.

Reviewers

Prentice Hall and the authors would like to thank the following people for their help and time in making this book what it is. We couldn't publish this book without their contributions.

Reviewers of the Third Edition.

Nazih Abdallah	University of Central Florida
Joan Alexander	Valencia Community College—West
LaDonna Bachand	Santa Rosa Junior College
Linda Belton	Springfield Technical Community College
Jeff Burton	Daytona Beach Community College
Kristen Callahan	Mercer County Community College
Judy Cestaro	California State University—San Bernardino
Deborah Chapman	University of Southern Alabama
Gerianne Chapman	Johnson & Wales University
Beverly Fite	Amarillo College
Sherry Green	Purdue University—Calumet Campus
Terry Hanks	San Jacinto College
Jim Hendricks	Pierce College
Stephanie Jones	South Plains College
Norma Marler	Catawba Valley Community College
Evelynn McCain	Boise State University
Dana McCann	Central Michigan University
Helen McFadyen	Mass Bay Community College—Framingham
Rebecca Mundy	University of Southern California
Margaret Nedreberg	Youngstown State University
Omar Nooraldeen	Cape Fear Community College
Claudia Orr	Northern Michigan University
Woody Pekoske	North Carolina State University
Russell Sabadosa	Manchester Community College
Peg Saragina	Santa Rosa Junior College
Judy Scheeren	Westmoreland County Community College
Samuel Scott	Pierce College
Kriss Stauber	El Camino College
Janet Towle	New Hampshire Community Technical College—Nashua
Goran Trajkovski	Towson University

Reviewers of Active Helpdesk, Third Edition.

Susan Birtwell	Kwantlen University College
Annette Duvall	Albuquerque Technical-Vocational Institute
Donna Madsen	Kirkwood Community College
Russell Sabadosa	Manchester Community College
Judy Scheeren	Westmoreland County Community College
Neal Stenlund	Northern Virginia Community College

Reviewers of the Second Edition.

Wilma Andrews	Virginia Commonwealth University
LeeAnn Bates	
Susan Birtwell	Kwantlen University College
Jeff Burton	Daytona Beach Community College
Gerianne Chapman	Johnson & Wales University
Gail Cope	Sinclair Community College
Doug Cross	Clackamas Community College
Susan N. Dozier	Tidewater Community College
Annette Duvall	Albuquerque Technical Vocational Institute
Laurie Eakins	Eastern Carolina University
Susan Hanson	Albuquerque Technical Vocational Institute
Marie Hartlein	Montgomery County Community College
Catherine Hines	Albuquerque Technical Vocational Institute
Mary Carole Hollingsworth	Georgia Perimeter College

Norm Hollingsworth ....Georgia Perimeter College
Glen Johansson ....Spokane Community College
David Kight ....Brewton-Parker College
Yvonne Leonard ....Coastal Carolina University
Toni Marucco ....Lincoln Land Community College
Lisa Nademlynsky..Johnson & Wales University
Judy Ogden ....Johnson County Community College
Connie O'Neill ....Sinclair Community College
Brenda Parker...Middle Tennessee State University
Patricia Rahmlow ....Montgomery County Community College
Mirella Shannon ....Columbia College
John Taylor ....Hillsborough Community College—Brandon Campus
Dennie Templeton...Radford University
Catherine Werst ....Cuesta College
Barbara Yancy...Community College of Baltimore County—Essex Campus
Mary Zajac..Montgomery County Community College

Reviewers of the First Edition.

Wilma Andrews ....Virginia Commonwealth University
Linda Belton ....Springfield Technical Community College
Julie Boyles
Gerald U. Brown Jr. ....Tarrant County College
Judy Cestaro...California State University—San Bernardino
Debra Chapman ....The University of South Alabama
Françoise Corey ....California State University, Long Beach
Thad Crews ....Western Kentucky University
John Cusaac ....Fullerton College
Susan N. Dozier ....Tidewater Community College
Annette Duvall...Albuquerque Technical Vocational Institute
Catherine L. Ferguson ....University of Oklahoma
Beverly Fite ....Amarillo College
Richard A. Flores ....Citrus College
Sherry Green...Purdue University—Calumet
Debra Gross ....The Ohio State University
Judy Irvine..Seneca College
Kathy Johnson ....DeVry Chicago
Stephanie Jones...South Plains College
Robert R. Kendi ....Lehigh University
Jackie Lamoureux ....Albuquerque Technical Vocational Institute
Judith Limkilde ....Seneca College—King Campus
Richard Linge ....Arizona Western College
Joelene Mack ....Golden West College
Dana McCann ....Central Michigan University
Lee McClain ....West Washington University
Daniela Marghitu ....Auburn University
Laura Melella...Fullerton College
Josephine G. Mendoza ....California State University—San Bernardino
Rebecca A. Mundy ....University of Southern California
Linda Mushet ....Golden West College
Omar Nooraldeen...Cape Fear Community College
Woody Pekoske ....North Carolina State University
Paul Quan ....Albuquerque Technical Vocational Institute
Kriss Stauber ....El Camino College
Neal Stenlund ....Northern Virginia Community College
Song Su ....East Los Angeles College
Goran Trajkovski..Towson University
Linda Foster-Turpen ....Albuquerque Technical Vocational Institute
Bill VanderClock ....Bentley Business University
Mary Ann Zlotow ....College of DuPage

Letter from the Authors

Why We Wrote This Book

Our 17 years of teaching computer concepts have coincided with sweeping innovations in computing technology that have affected every facet of society. From ATMs to the Web, computers are more than ever a fixture of our daily lives—and the lives of our students. But although today's students have a greater comfort level with their digital environment than previous generations, their textbooks haven't caught up. Even the best books spend too much time introducing hardware that students already know and not enough time explaining all the fun and productive things that same hardware can do.

We wrote *Technology in Action* to address this problem by focusing on today's student. Instead of a history lesson on the microchip, we focus on what tasks students can accomplish with their PC and what skills they can apply immediately in the workplace and at home. The result is a book that sparks student interest by focusing on the material they want to learn (such as how to set up a home network), while teaching the material they need to learn (such as how networks work). The sequence of topics is carefully set up to mirror the typical student learning experience.

As they read through this text, your students will progress through stages of increasing difficulty.

1. Examining why it's important to be computer fluent and how computers affect our society
2. Examining the basic components of the computer
3. Connecting to the Internet
4. Exploring software
5. Learning the operating system and personalizing the computer
6. Evaluating and upgrading the PC
7. Exploring home networking and keeping the computer safe from hackers
8. Going mobile with cell phones, PDAs, tablet PCs, and laptops
9. Going behind the scenes, looking at hardware in more detail

We have written this book in a "spiraling" manner, intentionally introducing on a basic level in the earlier chapters those concepts that students have troubles with and then later expanding on those concepts in more detail when students have become more comfortable with them. Thus, the focus of the early chapters is on practical uses for the computer, with real-world examples to help students place computing in a familiar context. For example, we introduce basic hardware components in Chapter 2, and then go into increasingly more detail on some hardware components in Chapters 6, 8, and 9.

The BEHIND THE SCENES chapters venture deeper into the realm of computing through in-depth explanations of how elements of the system unit (CPU, motherboard, RAM) work. They are specifically designed to keep more experienced students engaged and challenge them with interesting research assignments.

We have also developed a comprehensive multimedia program to reinforce the material taught in the text and support both classroom lectures and distance learning. New HELPDESK training content, created specifically for *Technology in Action*, enables students to take on the role of a helpdesk operator and work through common questions asked by computer users. Exciting SOUND BYTE multimedia—fully integrated with the text—accelerates student mastery of complex topics.

Now that the computer has become a ubiquitous tool in our lives, a new approach to computer concepts is warranted. This book is designed to reach the students of the 21st century.

Visual Walk-Through

TOPIC SEQUENCE

Concepts are covered in a spiraling manner between chapters in order to mirror the typical student learning experience.

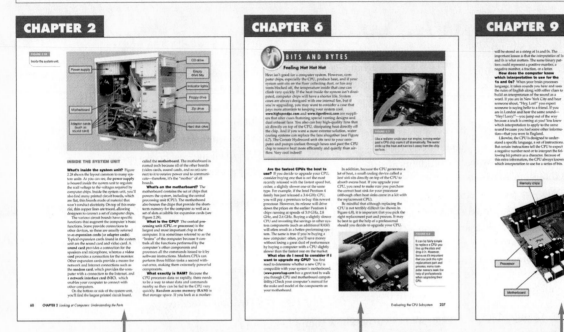

CHAPTER 2

CHAPTER 6

CHAPTER 9

Hardware First Introduced
Chapter 2 is the first time students read about introductory hardware. It is covered at the beginning level because this is their experience level at this point of the book.

Hardware Taught in More Depth in Additional Chapters
In later chapters, students are taught hardware in greater depth because they are more experienced and comfortable working with their computer.

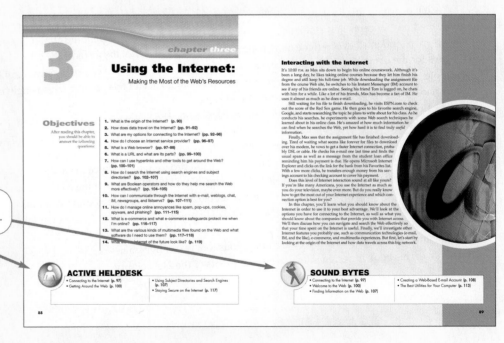

Multimedia Cues
Visual integration of multimedia.

Trends in IT explore newer topics involved in computing.

Dig Deeper boxes cover technical topics in depth to challenge advanced students.

Bits and Bytes teach good habits for safe computing.

Question/Answer Format
Written in an engaging and easy-to-read format.

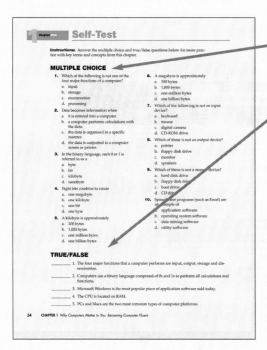

NEW

Multiple Choice and True and False

Technology in Focus
Five special features that teach key uses of technology today.

Student CD
The launch pad to the multimedia.

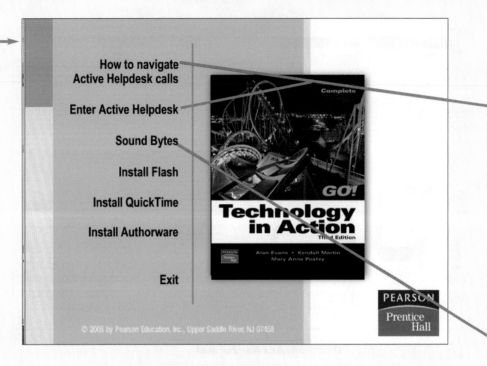

How to navigate
Active Helpdesk calls

Enter Active Helpdesk

Sound Bytes

Install Flash

Install QuickTime

Install Authorware

Exit

© 2005 by Pearson Education, Inc., Upper Saddle River, NJ 07458

PEARSON
Prentice
Hall

Complete

GO!
**Technology
in Action**
Third Edition

Alan Evans • Kendall Martin
Mary Anne Poatsy

Companion Website
Includes an interactive study guide,
online end-of-chapter material,
additional Internet exercises, and
much more.

Welcome to the Companion Website for *Technology in
Action, Third Edition.*

This interactive site was designed to reinforce and
help you test your understanding of the concepts
in your textbook. Key features are:

Online Study Guide offers a concise review of each
chapter including hints and feedback.

Sound Bytes are interactive multimedia labs
written specifically to the text, designed to
demystify even the most complex topics.

Quick links to downloadable resources:
Student!
Instructors!

Browser Tuneup
"Check your computer for a report on the current
browser you are using and plug-ins installed."

Copyright © 1995-2006, Pearson Education, Inc., publishing as Pearson Prentice Hall | Legal and Privacy Terms

www.prenhall.com/techinaction

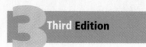

Active Helpdesk
Interactive training that puts the student in the role of a helpdesk staffer fielding questions from callers.

Supervisor available to assist students.

NEW Assessment at the end of each call.

Textbook page references within each call.

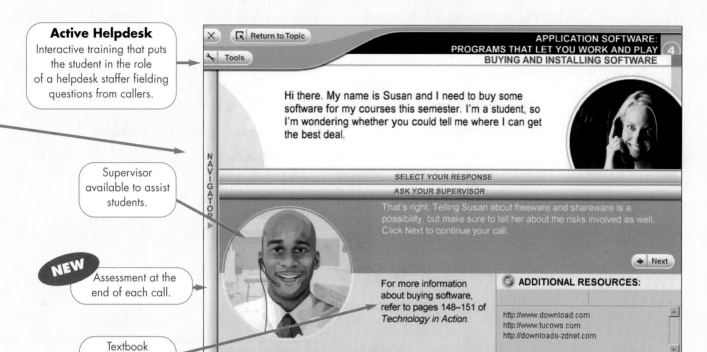

Audio on or off.

Related Bits and Bytes referenced and Sound Bytes.

NEW Transcript now available in Spanish.

Sound Bytes
Multimedia lessons with video, audio, or animation and corresponding labs featuring multiple-choice quizzing.

Video or animation teaches key concepts.

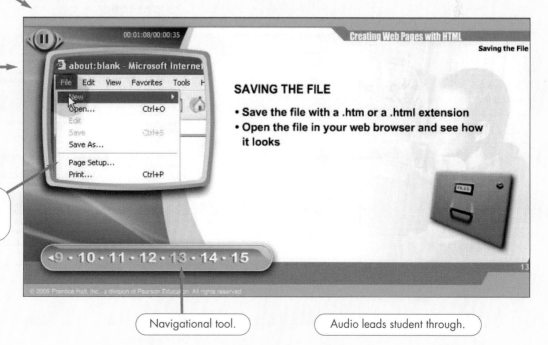

Navigational tool.

Audio leads student through.

NEW Annotated Instructor Edition

Provided with each chapter are divider pages like the one shown here. These pages are created by the author team and list the activities they like to complete in the classroom, assign for homework, or use for assessment.

These activities are divided into seven types and are made easy to identify with unique icons. These seven types are:

PowerPoint Presentations

Discussion Exercises

Active Helpdesk Calls

Sound Bytes

Writing Exercises

Preparing for the Next Chapter

Test Bank

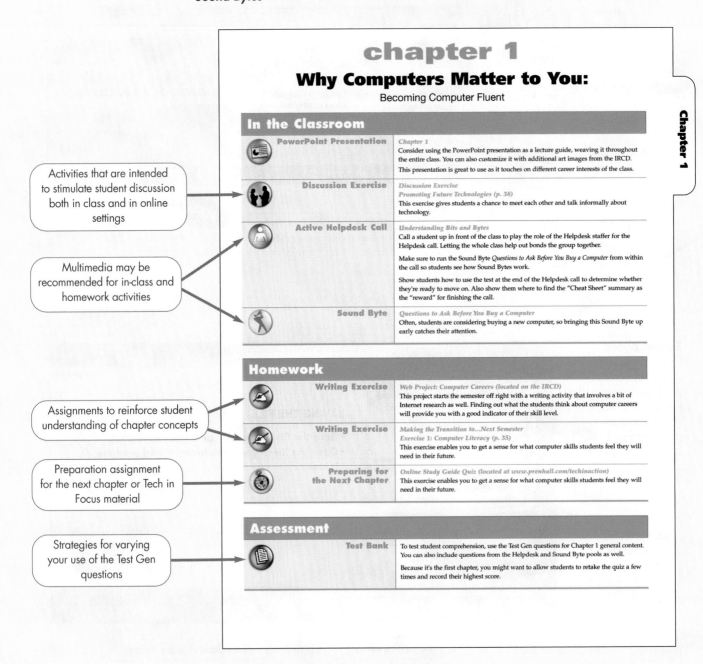

chapter 1
Why Computers Matter to You:
Becoming Computer Fluent

In the Classroom

PowerPoint Presentation
Chapter 1
Consider using the PowerPoint presentation as a lecture guide, weaving it throughout the entire class. You can also customize it with additional art images from the IRCD. This presentation is great to use as it touches on different career interests of the class.

Discussion Exercise
Discussion Exercise
Promoting Future Technologies (p. 38)
This exercise gives students a chance to meet each other and talk informally about technology.

Active Helpdesk Call
Understanding Bits and Bytes
Call a student up in front of the class to play the role of the Helpdesk staffer for the Helpdesk call. Letting the whole class help out bonds the group together.

Make sure to run the Sound Byte *Questions to Ask Before You Buy a Computer* from within the call so students see how Sound Bytes work.

Show students how to use the test at the end of the Helpdesk call to determine whether they're ready to move on. Also show them where to find the "Cheat Sheet" summary as the "reward" for finishing the call.

Sound Byte
Questions to Ask Before You Buy a Computer
Often, students are considering buying a new computer, so bringing this Sound Byte up early catches their attention.

Homework

Writing Exercise
Web Project: Computer Careers (located on the IRCD)
This project starts the semester off right with a writing activity that involves a bit of Internet research as well. Finding out what the students think about computer careers will provide you with a good indicator of their skill level.

Writing Exercise
Making the Transition to...Next Semester
Exercise 1: Computer Literacy (p. 35)
This exercise enables you to get a sense for what computer skills students feel they will need in their future.

Preparing for the Next Chapter
Online Study Guide Quiz (located at www.prenhall.com/techinaction)
This exercise enables you to get a sense for what computer skills students feel they will need in their future.

Assessment

Test Bank
To test student comprehension, use the Test Gen questions for Chapter 1 general content. You can also include questions from the Helpdesk and Sound Byte pools as well.

Because it's the first chapter, you might want to allow students to retake the quiz a few times and record their highest score.

Chapter 1

Activities that are intended to stimulate student discussion both in class and in online settings

Multimedia may be recommended for in-class and homework activities

Assignments to reinforce student understanding of chapter concepts

Preparation assignment for the next chapter or Tech in Focus material

Strategies for varying your use of the Test Gen questions

GREATLY ENHANCED

Instructor Resource CD
- **NEW! Interactive Course builder** to help you integrate all the instructor resources.
- **NEW! Recommended chapter lectures** written by the authors that you can customize.
- All resources included with the Technology in Action Instructional System, including the Testgen.

Instructor Resource Center
on CD-ROM

Complete

GO!

Technology
in Action
Third Edition

PEARSON
Prentice
Hall

Alan Evans • Kendall Martin
Mary Anne Poatsy

Contact your local Prentice Hall sales rep to learn more about the
Technology in Action instructional system.

Contents at a Glance

Third Edition

Contents

CHAPTER 4

Application Software:
Programs That Let You Work and Play 130

TECHNOLOGY IN FOCUS

CHAPTER 5

CHAPTER 6

Understanding and Assessing Hardware: Evaluating Your System

TECHNOLOGY IN FOCUS

CHAPTER 11

Behind the Scenes:
Databases and Information Systems

CHAPTER 12

CHAPTER 13

GO!
Technology
in Action
Third Edition

Why Computers Matter to You:

Becoming Computer Fluent

Objectives

After reading this chapter, you should be able to answer the following questions:

1. What does it mean to be "computer fluent"? **(p. 3)**

2. How does being computer fluent make you a savvy computer user and consumer? **(pp. 4–5)**

3. How can becoming computer fluent help you in a career? **(pp. 5–17)**

4. How can becoming computer fluent help you understand and take advantage of future technologies? **(pp. 17–20)**

5. What kinds of challenges do computers bring to a digital society and how does becoming computer fluent help you deal with these challenges? **(pp. 20–22)**

6. What exactly is a computer and what are its four main functions? **(p. 22)**

7. What is the difference between data and information? **(p. 22)**

8. What are bits and bytes and how are they measured? **(pp. 22–24)**

9. What hardware does a computer use to perform its functions? **(pp. 24–25)**

10. What are the two main types of software you find in a computer? **(pp. 25–26)**

11. What different kinds of computers are there? **(pp. 26–27)**

ACTIVE HELPDESK

• Understanding Bits and Bytes **(p. 24)**

How Do You Become Computer Fluent?

It's safe to say that computers are nearly everywhere in our society. You find them in schools, cars, airports, shopping centers, toys, medical devices, homes, and in many people's pockets. If you're like most Americans, you interact with computers almost every day, sometimes without even knowing it. Whenever you buy something with a credit card, you interact with a computer. And, of course, most of us can't imagine our lives without e-mail. If you don't yet have a home computer and don't feel comfortable using one, you still can't have escaped the impact of technology: countless ads for computers, cell phones, digital cameras, and an assortment of Web sites surround us each day. We're constantly reminded of the ways in which computers, the Internet, and technology are integral parts of our lives.

So, just by being a member of our society you already know quite a bit about computers. But why is it important to learn more about computers, becoming what is called **computer fluent**? Being computer fluent means being familiar enough with computers that you understand their capabilities and limitations and know how to use them. But being computer fluent means more than just knowing about the parts of your computer. The following are some other benefits: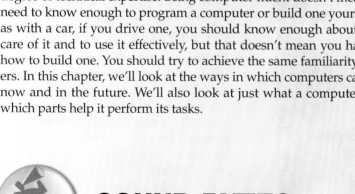

- As a computer-fluent individual you can use your computer more wisely and be a more knowledgeable consumer.

- Computer-fluent employees are sought after in most every vocation.

- Becoming computer fluent will help you better understand and take advantage of future technologies.

In addition, understanding computers and their ethical, legal, and societal implications will make you a more active and aware participant in society.

Anyone can become computer fluent—no matter what your degree of technical expertise. Being computer fluent doesn't mean you need to know enough to program a computer or build one yourself. Just as with a car, if you drive one, you should know enough about it to take care of it and to use it effectively, but that doesn't mean you have to know how to build one. You should try to achieve the same familiarity with computers. In this chapter, we'll look at the ways in which computers can affect your life, now and in the future. We'll also look at just what a computer does as well as which parts help it perform its tasks.

SOUND BYTES

- Virtual Computer Tour **(p. 25)**
- Questions to Ask Before You Buy a Computer **(p. 26)**

Becoming a Savvy Computer User and Consumer

One of the benefits of becoming computer fluent is being a savvy computer user and consumer. What does this mean? The following are just a few examples of what it may mean to you:

- **Avoiding hackers and viruses.** Do you know what hackers and viruses are? Both can pose threats to computer security. Being aware of how hackers and viruses operate and knowing the damage they can do to your computer can help you avoid falling prey to them.

- **Protecting your privacy.** You've probably heard of identity theft—you see and hear news stories all the time about people whose "identities" are stolen and whose credit ratings are ruined by "identity thieves." But do you know how to protect yourself from identity theft when you're online?

- **Understanding the *real* risks.** Part of being computer fluent means being able to separate the *real* privacy and security risks from things you don't have to worry about. For example, do you know what a cookie is? Do you know whether it poses a privacy risk for you when you're on the Internet? What about a firewall? Do you know what one is? Do you really need one to protect your computer?

- **Using the Internet wisely.** Anyone who has ever searched the Web can attest that finding information and finding *good* information are two different things. People who are computer fluent make the Internet a powerful tool and know how to find the information they want effectively. How familiar with the Web are you and how effective are your searches?

- **Avoiding online annoyances.** If you have an e-mail account, chances are you've received electronic junk mail, or spam. How can you avoid being overwhelmed by spam? What about adware and spyware—do you know what they are? Do you know what software you should install on your computer to avoid online annoyances?

- **Being able to maintain, upgrade, and troubleshoot your computer.** Learning how to care for and maintain your computer (see Figure 1.1) and knowing how to diagnose and fix certain problems can save you a lot of time and hassle. Do you know how to upgrade your computer if you want more memory, for example? Do you know which software and computer settings can help you keep your computer in top shape?

- **Making good purchasing decisions.** Everywhere you go you see ads like the one in Figure 1.2 for computers and other devices: laptops, printers, monitors, cell phones, digital cameras, and personal digital assistants (PDAs). Do you know what all the words in the ads mean? What is RAM? What is a CPU? What are MB, GB, GHz, and cache? How fast do you need your computer to be and how much memory should you have? Understanding computer "buzz words" and keeping up-to-date with technology will help you better determine which computers and devices match your needs.

FIGURE 1.1

Although you may not need to repair or construct a computer, being computer fluent means being able to perform basic upgrades and maintaining your computer.

FIGURE 1.2

Do you know what all the words in a computer ad mean? Can you tell whether all the necessary information is listed in this ad?

Type:	Personal computer/Mini tower
Dimensions (WxDxH)/Weight:	6.6 in x 16.8 in x 17.6 in/26 lbs
Processor:	Intel® Pentium® 4 with Hyper-Threading Technology
Cache Memory:	2 MB L2 Cache
RAM:	1 GB (installed) / 4 GB (max) PC3200 DDR2 SDRAM
Storage Floppy Drive:	1.44 MB - 3.5" HD
Storage Hard Drive:	200 GB Serial ATA (7200 rpm)
Optical Storage:	1 x CD-RW - 48x (read), - internal
Optical Writer:	1 x DVD-RW - 16x (read), 8x (write) - internal
Video Output:	Graphics card - ATI Radeon 9800 256 MB DDR
Audio Output:	Sound Blaster Audigy 4 Pro Sound Card
Ports:	6 USB 2.0 (2 front, 4 back) - 2 IEEE 1394 (1 front, 1 back)
OS Provided:	Microsoft Windows XP Media Center Edition

NEW!

- **Knowing how to integrate the latest technology with your equipment.** Finally, becoming computer fluent means knowing which technologies are on the horizon and how to integrate them into your home setup when possible (see Figure 1.3). Can you connect your laptop to a wireless network? What is "Bluetooth" and does your computer "have" it? Can a device with a USB 2.0 connector be plugged into an old USB 1.0 port? (For that matter, what is a USB port?) How much memory should your cell phone have? Knowing the answers to these and other questions will help you make better purchasing decisions.

FIGURE 1.3

Can you identify all of these devices? Do you know how to get them all to work well together?

Being Prepared for Your Career

Regardless of which profession you pursue, if computers are not already in use in that career, they most likely will be soon. In fact, the U.S. Department of Labor predicts that by 2010, 70 percent of the U.S. workforce will be using computers at work. Meanwhile, the U.S. Department of Agriculture has found that employees who use a computer on the job earn about 10 percent more than those who don't.

So becoming truly computer fluent—understanding the capabilities and limitations of computers and what you can do with them—will undoubtedly help you perform your job more effectively. Let's look at some ways in which computers are used in different careers.

COMPUTERS IN BUSINESS: WORKING IN A DATA MINE?

Businesses accumulate a lot of data, but just how do they manage to make meaning of all of it? How do they separate the anomalies from the trends? They use a process known as *data mining*. For example, large retailers often study the data gathered from register terminals to determine which products are selling on a given day and in a specific location. This helps managers figure out how much merchandise they need to order to replace stock that is sold. Managers also use mined data to determine that for a certain product to sell well, they must lower its price—especially if they cut the price at one store and saw sales increase, for example. Data mining thus allows retailers to respond to consumer buying patterns.

In the music business, managers can use data mining to keep track of which music people are downloading and the geographic areas in which they live. This provides marketing personnel in the music companies with information that they can use to drive sales. If the latest 50 Cent single is being downloaded like crazy in Phoenix yet local record stores are failing to order significant quantities of the CDs, record executives can use this information to convince record stores that demand will increase for the CD

and to up their orders. Using data-mining techniques such as this is music to management ears!

COMPUTERS IN RETAIL: LET ME LOOK THAT UP FOR YOU

Many students have part-time jobs in retail stores and restaurants. These jobs are often far from glamorous, but they do provide employees with experience using a host of computers, from the mundane to the complex. Most retail employees use simple computers when they process a transaction. These point-of-sale (POS) terminals (formerly known as cash registers) are in turn often connected to complex inventory and sales computer systems that provide immediate data to retail store managers and customers (see Figure 1.4). Sales clerks can perform searches for customers to determine which stores might have an item in stock that the customer couldn't find. Restaurant servers place orders on touch-screen POS systems that not only generate a customer's bill, but also are linked to food and beverage ordering systems to assist management in estimating and placing supply orders.

Before computers, if managers wanted to know how well a certain style of shoes was selling, for example, they would have to take inventory physically (count the remain-

FIGURE 1.4

Point-of-sale terminals not only update sales and inventory databases, but also enable retail clerks to search databases based on customer inquiries.

ing shoes). However, when a POS terminal records sales as they are made, it's easy for managers to query a sales database and determine how products are performing.

COMPUTERS IN SHIPPING: UPS DATA ON THE GO

Did you know that United Parcel Service (UPS) handles over 14 million packages *per day*? That's a lot of packages. But just how does the "brown" company ensure all its customers' packages get from Point A to Point B without ending up forever at Point C? The company uses a sophisticated database and a very efficient package-tracking system that follows the packages as they move around the world.

For UPS, package tracking starts when the sender drops off a package and the company creates a "smart label" for the package (see Figure 1.5a). In addition to the standard postal bar code and a bar code showing UPS customer numbers, this smart label contains something called a MaxiCode. The MaxiCode is a specially designed scannable sticker that resembles an inkblot and contains all the important information about the package (class of service, destination, etc.). When the package is handled in processing centers, UPS workers scan the MaxiCode using wearable scanners (see Figure 1.5b). Worn on the employee's hands, these scanners use Bluetooth technology to transmit

the scanned data through radio waves to a terminal the workers wear. This terminal then sends the data across a wireless network, where it is recorded in the UPS database.

To track package delivery, UPS carriers use delivery acquisition devices (see Figure 1.5c) that feature wireless networking capability, infrared scanners (to scan the smart labels and transmit the information back to the UPS database), and an electronic pad to capture customer signatures. By capturing all of this data and making it available on its Internet database, UPS enables its customers to track their packages through the delivery process. UPS is also able to make informed decisions about staffing and deploying equipment (trucks, airplanes, etc.) based on the volume and type of packages in the system at any given time. Today, even something as seemingly simple as package delivery makes use of sophisticated computer devices.

COMPUTERS IN THE ARTS: SHALL WE DANCE?

Some art students think that because they're studying art, there is no reason for them to study computers. However, unless you plan on being a starving artist (!), you'll probably want to sell your work. To do so, you'll need to advertise to the public and/or contact art galleries to convince them to purchase or

FIGURE 1.5

(a) Package tracking starts at the point of sending by the generation of a smart label for the package. (b) Scanning is accomplished by wearable scanners. (c) Delivery personnel carry delivery acquisition devices that feature wireless networking capability, internal modems, infrared scanners, Global Positioning System (GPS) capabilities, and an electronic pad to capture customer signatures.

FIGURE 1.6

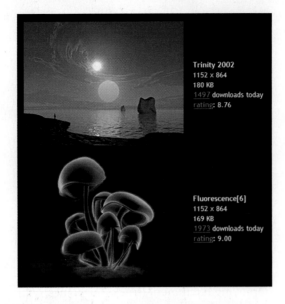

Trinity 2002
1152 × 864
180 KB
1497 downloads today
rating: 8.76

Fluorescence[6]
1152 × 864
169 KB
1973 downloads today
rating: 9.00

display your work. Wouldn't it be helpful if you knew how to create a Web site like the one shown in Figure 1.6?

But using computers in the arts goes way beyond using the Internet. For example, the Atlanta Ballet, in conjunction with the Georgia Institute of Technology, is using computers to create virtual dancers and new performances for audiences. As shown in Figure 1.7, live dancers are wired with sensors that are connected to a computer that captures the dancers' movements. Based on the data it collects, the computer generates a

virtual dancer on a screen. The computer operator can easily manipulate this virtual dancer as well as change the dancer's costume with a click of a mouse. This allows the ballet company to create new experiences for the audience by pairing virtual dancers with live dancers.

Of course, not all artwork is created using traditional materials such as paint and canvas. Many artists today work exclusively with computers to create digital art. Mastery of software programs such as Adobe Illustrator, Photoshop, and Macromedia Flash are essential to creating such digital art. Other artists are pushing the envelope of creating art with computers even more. For example, artist Camille Utterback used a computer and video clips of pedestrians in Tokyo to create a visual art piece entitled *Liquid Time* (see Figure 1.8). When no one is near the visual art piece, the screen displays a static image. However, as onlookers in the gallery move closer to the work, a camera mounted on the ceiling of the art gallery captures the movements and dimensions of the onlookers in the gallery. A computer with specialized software then uses this captured data and causes the video playing in the *Liquid Time* piece to ripple. Because the rippling effect is based on the movement and size of the gallery patrons, the work looks different to each person looking at it.

FIGURE 1.7

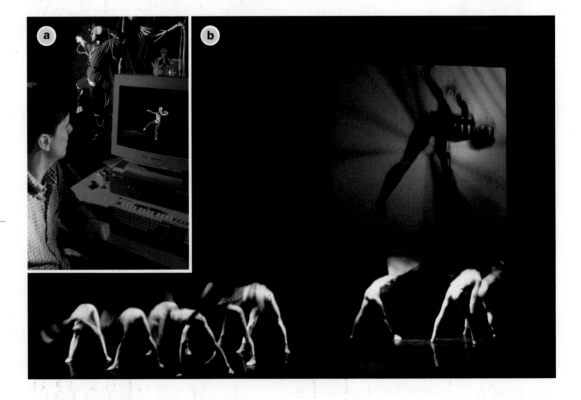

As viewers move away from the work, the video returns to a static display.

COMPUTERS IN THE MEDICAL FIELD: FACT OR SCIENCE FICTION?

In movies set in the distant future, humans can sometimes interface with computers just by thinking at them. Until recently, such scenes took place only in movies. However, *Wired* magazine recently reported that a company called Cyberkinetics has designed a human neural interface system, known as BrainGate, capable of translating a person's thoughts into cursor movements. As the first person to test this revolutionary device, quadriplegic Matthew Nagle has had a tiny array of microelectrodes implanted in his brain. The computer equipment receiving data from his neural activity identifies the impulses that the brain associates with physical movement (of, say, his arm) and translates the instructions into cursor movements on his computer (see Figure 1.9). Therefore, just by thinking "move paddle down," the paddle on Nagle's game of Pong moves down. This revolutionary device is the result of decades of research and sophisticated computing devices.

In addition to being an integral part of many medical research projects, computers are helping doctors and nurses learn their trades. Training for physicians and nurses can be difficult at best. Often, the best way for medical students to learn is to experience a real emergency situation. The problem is that students are then confined to watching as the emergency unfolds while trained personnel actually care for patients. Students rarely get to train in real-life situations, and when they do, a certain level of risk is involved.

FIGURE 1.8

Computers even figure directly into the development of artworks. Camille Utterback used video clips of pedestrians in Tokyo in her work entitled *Liquid Time*.

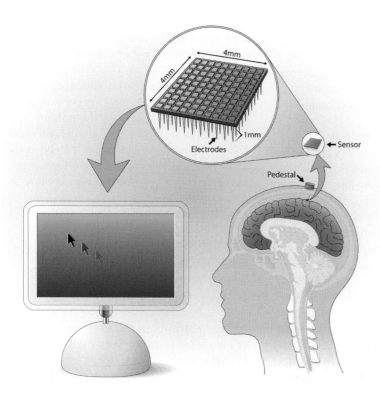

FIGURE 1.9

Quadriplegic Matthew Nagle is the first person to have the BrainGate Neural Interface implanted in his body. A silicon chip studded with microelectrodes is embedded in his brain and is connected to a signal converter, which is in turn connected to his computer. The converter sees how his neurons fire when he thinks certain thoughts and begins to recognize patterns, which are then translated into cursor movements on his computer.

FIGURE 1.10

Patient simulators (made by Medical Education Technologies, Inc.) allow health care students to practice medical procedures without risk of injury or death to the patient.

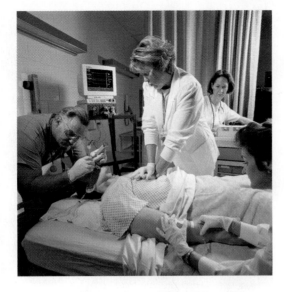

Medical students are now getting access to better training opportunities thanks to a computer technology called a **patient simulator** (shown in Figure 1.10). Patient simulators are life-sized mannequins that can speak, breathe, and blink (their eyes respond to external stimuli). They have a pulse and a heartbeat and respond just like humans to procedures such as the administration of intravenous drugs.

Medical students can train on patient simulators and experience firsthand how a human would react to their treatments without any risk to a live patient. The best thing about these "patients" is that if they "die," students can restart the computer simulation and try again. Teaching hospitals, universities, and medical schools are currently deploying patient simulators. In addition, the U.S. military is using patient simulators to train medics to respond to terrorist attacks that employ chemical and biological agents.

FIGURE 1.11

The Physiome Project has developed a working computer model of the human lungs, including 300 million air sacs.

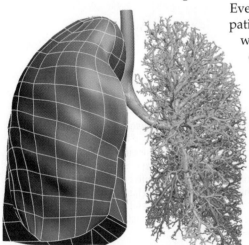

Even more exciting than patient simulators is the work progressing on modeling complete human biological systems. The Physiome Project is the brainchild of the Bioengineering Institute in Auckland, New Zealand. In this project, bioengineers are creating realistic computer simulations of all systems and features of the human anatomy. They have recently completed a digital re-creation of the human heart and lungs (shown in Figure 1.11).

Although the current system models a *theoretical* human's lungs, researchers hope to one day use computers to simulate a *specific* person's anatomical systems. With such a system, imaging scans (CTs, MRIs, etc.) of your body and a sample of your DNA would be fed into a computer, which would create an *exact* computer model of your body. This would allow doctors to experiment with different therapies to see how you would react to specific treatments and to then choose the best option. There is a great deal of work to be done before this becomes a reality, but computer-literate medical professionals will be needed to make it happen.

Surgeons are even using computer-guided robots to perform surgery. Surgeons are often limited by their manual dexterity and can have trouble making small, precise incisions. So how can robots help? Robotic surgery devices can exercise much finer control when making delicate incisions than can a human guiding a scalpel. To use the robots, doctors look into a surgery control device where they manipulate controls that move robotic devices hovering over the patient (see Figure 1.12). One robot control arm contains a slender imaging rod that allows the doctor to see inside the patient when the rod is inserted into the patient. Doctors can now perform a coronary bypass by making two small incisions in the patient and inserting the imaging rod in one incision and another robotic device with a scalpel into the other. The ability to make small incisions instead of the large ones required by conventional surgery means less trauma and blood loss for the patient. Although it hasn't been done yet, theoretically, doctors do not even have to be in the same room as the patient to perform surgery. They could be thousands of miles away controlling the movements of the robotic devices from a control station.

COMPUTERS IN LAW ENFORCEMENT: PUT DOWN THAT MOUSE—YOU'RE UNDER ARREST!

Today, wearing out shoe leather to solve crimes is far from the only method available to investigators trying to catch criminals. Just like on *CSI*, computers are being used in

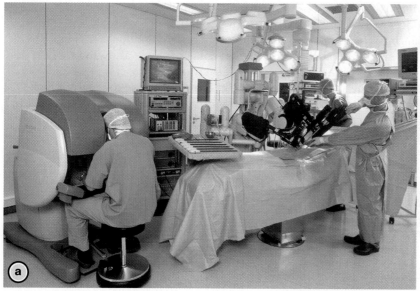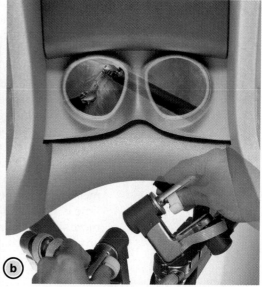

FIGURE 1.12

Surgeons use computer-guided robots, such as the da Vinci Surgical System from Intuitive Surgical, to perform surgery. (a) Here, a doctor looks into the control device where he manipulates controls that move the robotic devices hovering over the patient. (b) This is what surgeons see as they operate on the patient.

police cars and crime labs to solve an increasing number of crimes.

One technique modern detectives are using to solve crimes is to employ computers to search the vast number of databases on the Internet. Proprietary law enforcement databases such as the FBI's National Crime Information Center database enable detectives to track down a wealth of information about individuals and businesses to help them solve crimes. Detectives are also using their knowledge of wireless networking to intercept and read suspects' e-mail or chat sessions when they're online, all from the comfort of a car parked outside the suspect's home (where legally permissible, that is).

As detective work goes more high tech, so, too, does crime. To fight such high-tech crime, a law enforcement specialty called **computer forensics** is growing. Already being used to send criminals behind bars, computer forensics is the application of computer systems and techniques to gather potential legal evidence. The ability to recover and read deleted or damaged files from a criminal's computer is already providing evidence for trials. The tried and true techniques of personally interviewing and observing suspects are still crucial to investigative work, but using computers can make the entire process more efficient.

Do you think there will ever be a day when crime can actually be predicted? Every day, businesses across the world use complicated forecasting models to make predictions about their sales, inventory lev-

els, and so on. Thanks to recent technological advancements, law enforcement officials might soon have access to specialized computer software that can forecast criminal activity, allowing police officers hopefully to take preventative measures to stop crime before it occurs.

Don't believe it? Criminologist Jacqueline Cohen and computer scientist Andreas Olligschlaeger received funding from the U.S. Department of Justice to study police reports from Rochester, New York, and Pittsburgh, Pennsylvania. After entering the data about criminal offenses, precinct staffing, and patrol routes, the two researchers used trend-spotting programs developed for business data mining to analyze the data. The result: the program was able to predict criminal activity before it happened an astounding 80 percent of the time. The key to the analysis was identifying and studying leading indicators that trigger crime sprees. Whereas consumer researchers may look at consumer spending patterns and levels of disposable income, criminologists study soft crime statistics such as disorderly conduct and trespassing. Increases in these types of crimes indicate that serious crimes may soon be on the rise. When a trend is identified, patrols in the area can be stepped up to try to head off crimes before

FIGURE 1.13

(a) Smart parking meters, such as the one made by the Australian company Reino shown here, let you pay with cash, credit card, or cell phone and can send a text message to your phone when your time is almost up.
(b) Handheld devices help parking enforcement officers issue tickets faster and record the data from them more accurately.

they occur. Building, analyzing, and fine-tuning the models will keep law enforcement officials busy for years.

Even something as simple as parking enforcement uses computers today. Smart meters, such as the one shown in Figure 1.13, are being installed in major cities around the globe and can manage up to 10 parking spaces each. When you park in a space, you go to the meter and pay with cash, credit card, or your cell phone. The meter can even send a text message to your cell phone when your time is almost up so you can pay for more. The meter reports revenue and any malfunctions to the parking authority's central computer on a regular basis. Parking officials can access the meter remotely and change parking rates in response to usage patterns, scheduling of special events, or time of day. Parking enforcement officers have special PDAs that communicate wirelessly with the meters to determine when parked cars are in violation. The meters send information (such as the time, date, and location of the violation) to the PDAs, which makes generating tickets quicker and more accurate.

Beating the meter maid just became a lot harder!

COMPUTERS IN THE LEGAL FIELDS: WELCOME TO THE VIRTUAL COURTROOM

In courtrooms today, video of crimes in progress (often captured by cameras at convenience stores or gas stations) are sometimes displayed to the jury to help them understand how the crime unfolded. But what happens if no surveillance camera recorded the crime? Paper diagrams, models, and still photos of the crime scene used to be the only choice for attorneys to illustrate their case. Now there is a much more exciting and lively alternative: computer forensics animations.

Computer forensics animations are extremely detailed (and often lifelike) re-creations that have been generated with computers based on forensic evidence, depositions of witnesses, and the opinions of experts. Using sophisticated animation

programs, similar to the ones used to create movies such as *Finding Nemo*, forensic animators can depict one side's version of how events occurred, allowing the jury to watch it unfold.

Of course, being able to view sophisticated multimedia, televise trials, or record witness testimony for archiving requires modern courtrooms to be wired. Courtrooms such as Florida's Ninth Judicial Circuit Court (see Figure 1.14) are on the cutting edge, complete with robot-controlled video cameras that pivot to record whomever is speaking on the microphone at the time. Video images can be streamed directly to a Web site for immediate viewing or stored for archival purposes. Meanwhile, the judge has a touch-screen terminal to control the action in the courtroom, including turning on real-time closed-captioning by linking in the court reporter's transcription terminal. Lawyers have access to wireless touch-screen handheld devices that allow them to access and display evidence they have stored on the courtroom's multimedia systems. Attorneys can also connect their own laptops to the system, and audio recordings of all proceedings are captured and can be played back immediately, if needed.

Outside the courtroom, lawyers and other legal professionals use vast online legal libraries and databases (such as LexisNexis) to research cases and prepare for court. Legal professionals just don't travel without a computer any more.

COMPUTERS IN EDUCATION: AND ON THE LEFT, YOU SEE THE *MONA LISA*

When teaching today, you need to be at least as computer savvy as your students. Computers are part of most schools, even preschools. And in many colleges, students are required to have their own computers. So, teachers must have a working knowledge of computers to integrate computer technology effectively into the classroom.

The Internet has obvious advantages in the classroom as a research tool for students, and effective use of the Internet allows teachers to expose students to places they otherwise could not. Many museums have virtual tours on their Web sites that allow students to examine objects in the museum

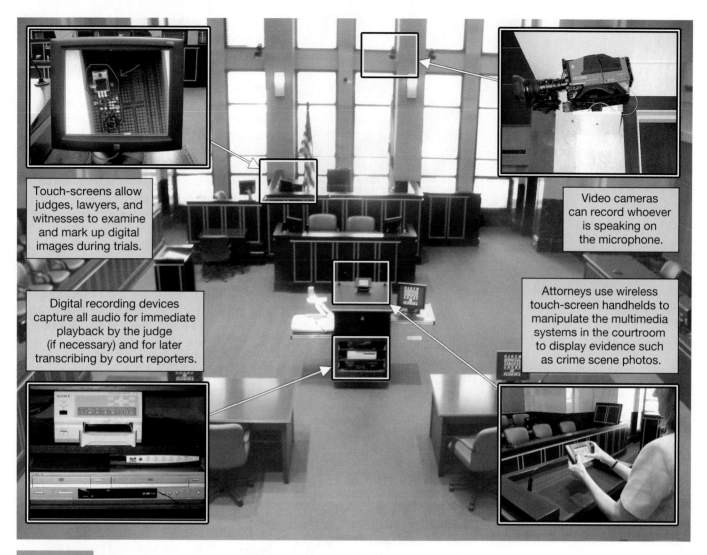

Touch-screens allow judges, lawyers, and witnesses to examine and mark up digital images during trials.

Digital recording devices capture all audio for immediate playback by the judge (if necessary) and for later transcribing by court reporters.

Video cameras can record whoever is speaking on the microphone.

Attorneys use wireless touch-screen handhelds to manipulate the multimedia systems in the courtroom to display evidence such as crime scene photos.

FIGURE 1.14

Courtrooms such as Florida's Ninth Judicial Circuit Court are on the cutting edge.

collections. Often, these virtual tours include three-dimensional photos that can be viewed from all angles. So, even if you teach in Topeka, Kansas, you can take your students on a virtual tour of the Smithsonian Institution in Washington, D.C., for example (see Figure 1.15); no field trip expenses or permission slips needed.

FIGURE 1.15

Can't fit in a field trip to Washington, D.C., this semester? As a teacher, you can still conduct a virtual field trip for your students using the Internet.

FIGURE 1.16

Multimedia tours using PDAs and wireless technology are now commonplace in museums and galleries. Aside from providing additional contextual material to visitors (such as displaying similar works by other artists), such multimedia tours enable patrons to participate in opinion polls and to send messages to other museum visitors.

using a PDA, you can listen to music that the artist listened to when he or she was creating the work or look at other works that are not contained in the museum that reflect similar techniques or themes to the one you're viewing. For more modern artists, you can watch interviews with the artist explaining his or her motivation for the work. You can even use the PDA to contact other members of your group and direct them to specific works you want them to see. Knowing how to use a PDA effectively may help make a museum tour even more memorable.

Computers in the classroom will become more prevalent as prices continue to fall and parents demand that their children be provided with the necessary computer skills they need to be successful in the workplace. Therefore, as an educator, being computer fluent will help you plan constructive computerized lessons for your students and use technology to interact with them.

But what about when you actually want to take your students to visit museums first-hand? Today, technology is often used to enhance visitors' experiences at museums. London's Tate Modern Museum , for example, offers PDA tours that provide visitors with additional information about the art they're viewing (see Figure 1.16). By simply

COMPUTERS AND THE SCIENCES: PROGRAMMING THE PERFECT STORM

As we all know, weather forecasting is not an exact science. Who hasn't had a trip to the beach ruined by rain? But thanks to a partnership between the National Severe Storms Lab and the National Center for Supercomputing Applications (NCSA), tornado forecasting may be getting more accurate. Using data collected during a tornado in South Dakota, scientists have been able to create the most advanced color-coded digital storm model known to date (see Figure 1.17). The model is so detailed it takes *nine days* for a supercomputer (the most powerful computer on earth) to generate the simulation, even though the computer is executing four billion operations *a second*. By studying the data produced by this simulation, forecasters hope to improve their predictions about where tornadoes will form and touch down.

Other technological applications in the sciences are being used on some of the oldest sites on earth. The ancient site of Pompeii has been under the intense scrutiny of tourists and archaeologists for decades. Sadly, all the foot traffic and exposure to the elements is eroding portions of the ruins.

BITS AND BYTES

Detailed Maps Just a Few Clicks Away

As you read this, hundreds of satellites are orbiting the globe taking wonderfully detailed pictures of the earth. Until recently, these photos weren't available to the general public. However, thanks to NASA (and U.S. taxpayer dollars) and some savvy software developers, an application called World Wind is now making some 10 trillion bytes of imagery available to you. Need a picture of Mt. Fuji for your science project? An aerial picture of your house for your PowerPoint presentation? Just download the software from **http://worldwind.arc.nasa.gov/** and you're ready to go. With a few clicks you can zoom in on an object at up to one square meter resolution. You can even click on an image and obtain the GPS coordinates for that location. Geography was never so easy or interactive!

A color-coded digital model of a tornado forming. The red balls in the center forming the tornado funnel will change to yellow as the storm's intensity decreases.

Today scientists are using three-dimensional scanners and imaging software to capture a detailed record of the current condition of the ruins (see Figure 1.18). The virtual re-creation of the ruins is so lifelike that archaeologists can study the ruins on-screen instead of at the actual site. Using the scans as well as satellite imagery, aerial photography, and other data, scientists will eventually be able to re-create missing portions of the ruins in a virtual model. And scientists won't stop at Pompeii: this method will soon be used to make records of other decaying sites. Archaeologists of tomorrow, get set for a different sort of fieldwork!

COMPUTERS IN SPORTS: BEND YOUR ELBOW ANOTHER TWO DEGREES?

Want to be a world-class swimmer or baseball player? Getting an Olympic-caliber coach and training for hours every day isn't enough any longer. To get that competitive edge, you really need to use a computer.

That's right, computers are now being used to help athletes analyze their performance and improve their game. How does this work? First, video recordings are made of athletes in action. The video is then transferred into special motion analysis software on a computer. This software measures the exact angles of the athlete's body parts as

Digital re-creation of the ruins of Pompeii allows archaeologists to study the ruins without even being there, as well as extrapolate missing portions of the structures.

they progress through ranges of motion, such as the angle of a baseball player's left arm relative to his body as he swings the bat. Minor adjustments can be made on the computer regarding positioning of body parts and the force used in performing various movements. This helps baseball players, for example, enhance their performance by determining what adjustments they should make to hit the ball harder and farther.

The United States Olympic Training Center in Colorado makes extensive use of computers in training athletes such as swimmers. The major objective of training swimmers to swim faster is to reduce drag from the water and minimize turbulence (which can also slow a swimmer down). Software has been developed for the center that simulates the way water flows around the parts of a swimmer's body when he or she is in motion. Coaches can use the software to experiment with small changes in the position of a swimmer's arms or legs to determine whether turbulence and drag are reduced. The coaches can then train the swimmers to use the new techniques to improve their strokes and speed.

Aren't planning on competing in the next Olympics or playing in the major leagues? How about improving your weekend golf game? Employees in golf shops are now using sophisticated motion capture equipment to improve golfers' swings. To have your golf swing analyzed, golf shop personnel hook you up into shoulder, leg, and hip harnesses containing motion sensors (see Figure 1.19). As you swing away at a variety of shots (drives, chips, etc.), computers capture information about the motion of your

swing. Your swing is then compared to a database of the ideal positions of pro golfers. Trainers then suggest adjustments you can make so that your swing more closely emulates successful golfers. So even weekend warriors can benefit from high-tech analysis of their game.

COMPUTER GAMING CAREERS: NOW BIGGER THAN HOLLYWOOD!

It's amazing but true: revenues from computer gaming in the United States have surpassed revenues from the Hollywood film industry. In fact, computer gaming is now a $10 billion industry in the United States and is projected to continue to grow rapidly over the next decade. If you're a gamer, you know games must be creative to grab their audience. Large-scale games are impossible to create on your own—you must be part of a team. These creative teams have to meet face-to-face on a daily basis to swap ideas. The good news is that because computer games are best developed for a local market by people native to that market, game development will most likely stay in the United States instead of being outsourced to other countries (as many programming jobs have been).

Obviously, you'll need an in-depth knowledge of computers to pursue a career in game programming or as a gaming artist. Mastering software animation tools such as 3ds Max, shown in Figure 1.20, will enable you to create the characters and scenery you need to populate game worlds.

FIGURE 1.19

Software like cSwing can allow you to analyze and correct your golf swing using a camcorder and a computer.

COMPUTERS AT HOME: JUST PROGRAM IT AND FORGET IT

Sick of cleaning your home or mowing the lawn? Robots are not just found in science labs and industrial settings anymore. Robotic "maintenance workers" are now emerging for the home market. Why should you have to waste time mowing the lawn or vacuuming the floors when robots can do these tasks for you? Is security a concern in your home? Why not have a robot customized to patrol your home as a security guard? Figure 1.21 shows a few popular home robots.

Meanwhile, so-called smart devices— devices such as temperature controls, lights, and security devices that contain computer chips and can control functions in the home without human intervention—are becoming widely available for the home. And although attempts have been made to launch Internet-connected appliances (such as refrigerators that order food over the Internet when you're running low), these have not yet met with widespread success. Will your oven one day prepare your food without your supervision? Only time will tell. You can keep tabs on the latest products available at sites such as **www.smarthome.com**.

Getting Ready for the Technology of Tomorrow

If you're computer fluent, you'll be a smarter computer user and you'll be prepared to handle the technological challenges in your chosen career. But what are the other benefits? By understanding computers and how they work today, you'll be better able to take advantage of and understand the technologies of tomorrow. Let's take a look at some emerging technologies and how they may affect your life.

NANOSCIENCE: THE NEXT "BIG" THING

Have you ever heard of *nanoscience*? Developments in computing based on the principles of nanoscience are being touted as the next big wave in computing. Ironically, this realm of science focuses on very small objects. In fact, **nanoscience** involves the study of molecules and structures (called *nanostructures*) whose size ranges from one to 100 nanometers.

How big is this? The prefix *nano* stands for one-billionth. Therefore, a nanometer is one-billionth of a meter. To put this in perspective, a human hair is approximately 50,000

FIGURE 1.20

Using powerful tools such as 3ds Max 7 from Discreet, game developers can create complex worlds and characters to satisfy the most demanding gamer.

FIGURE 1.21

(a) White Box Robotics' 912 robot acts as a home security device equipped with webcams, facial-recognition software, and wireless communications (for contacting authorities if it detects unauthorized persons). (b) The RoboMower from Friendly Robotics mows your lawn. (c) The iRobot Roomba vacuums your floors.

FIGURE 1.22

Composed of vapor-ized gallium nitrate condensed on a sili-con wafer, this beauti-ful grouping of "nanoflowers" is com-posed of tiny silicon carbide wires. Each "flower" is about one-hundredth the size of a human hair. These "flowers" show a remarkable ability to repel water, which may make them useful for material coatings.

nanometers wide. Put side by side, 10 hydrogen atoms (the simplest atom) would measure approximately one nanome-ter. Anything smaller than a nanometer is just a stray atom or particle floating around in space. Therefore, nanostructures repre-sent the smallest human-made structures that can be built.

Nanotechnology is the science revolving around the use of nanostructures to build devices on an extremely small scale. Right now, nanoscience is limited to improving existing products such as enhancing fibers

used in clothing with coatings so they repel stains or don't wrinkle (see Figure 1.22). However, someday scientists hope to use nanostructures to build computing devices too small to be seen by the naked eye. Nanowires, which are extremely small con-ductors, could be used to create extremely small pathways in computer chips. Developments such as this could lead to computers the size of a pencil eraser that are far more powerful than today's desktop computers.

If you watch *Star Trek*, you know that "nanoprobes" (tiny machines that can be injected into the bloodstream) have already been envisioned on the TV series' 24th-century world. But nanotechnology is a relatively new field (less than 15 years old). Although we can create a carbon nanotube (see Figure 1.23), we are still a long way from developing nanoscale machines—and some scientists don't think this will ever be possible. However, researchers are investi-gating the use of nanostructures to deliver precise doses of drugs on a molecule-by-molecule basis within the human blood-stream. Universities and government labora-tories are investing billions of dollars in nanotechnology research every year. If you have an interest in science and engineering, this is the time to pursue an education in nanoscience, because you could be on the forefront of the next big technological break-through.

BIOMEDICAL CHIP IMPLANTS: COMBINING HUMANS WITH MACHINES?

Mention implanting technology into the human body and some people conjure up images of the Terminator, a cybernetic life form from the future that looks human but is mostly machine. Unlike the *Terminator* movies, however, the goal of modern-day biomedical chip research is not to change humans into machine-like cyborgs. Rather, the goals are to provide technological solu-tions to physical problems (see Figure 1.24) and to provide a means for positively identi-fying individuals.

One potential application of biomedical chip implants is to provide sight to the blind. Macular degeneration and retinitis pigmentosa are two diseases that account for the majority of blindness in developing

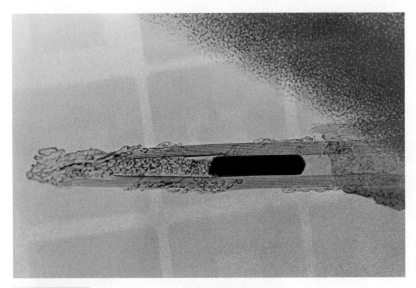

FIGURE 1.23

A carbon nanotube developed in a laboratory. Nanotubes have approximately 60 times the tensile strength of steel. Although they can't be manufactured on a large scale yet, scientists envision using nanotubes to construct extremely durable goods and structures.

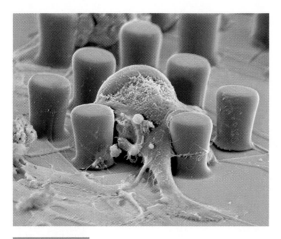

FIGURE 1.24

Researchers are experimenting with implantable chips such as this one. Here, we see a nerve cell on a silicon chip. The cell was cultured on the chip until it formed a network with nearby cells. The chip contains a transistor that stimulates the cell above it, which in turn passes the signal to neighboring neurons. Chips such as these could be used to repair nerve damage and restore movement or sensation to parts of the body.

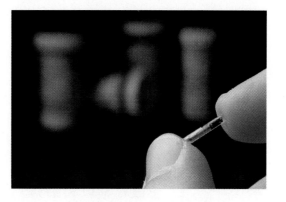

FIGURE 1.25

The VeriChip is a small device implanted directly under the skin. A special scanner is able to read the personal information stored on it.

nations. Both diseases result in damage to the photoreceptors contained in the retina of the eye. (Photoreceptors convert light energy into electrical energy that is transmitted to the brain, allowing us to see.) Researchers are experimenting with chips that contain microscopic solar cells and are implanted in the damaged retina of patients. The idea is to have the chip take over for the damaged photoreceptors and transmit electrical images to the brain. Although these chips have been tested in patients, they have not yet restored anyone's sight. But uses of biomedical chips such as these illustrate the type of medical devices you may "see" in the future.

Though using a biomedical chip to restore a person's sight is not yet a reality, one type of chip is already being implanted in humans as a means of verifying a person's identity. Called the VeriChip, this "personal ID chip" is about the size of a grain of rice and is implanted underneath the skin (see Figure 1.25). When exposed to radio waves from a scanning device, the chip emits a signal that transmits its unique serial number to the scanner. The scanner then connects to a database that contains the name, address, and medical conditions of the person in whom the chip has been implanted.

The creators of the Verichip, Applied Digital Solutions, envision the VeriChip speeding up airport security and being used together with other devices (such as electronic ID cards) to provide tamperproof security measures. If someone stole your credit card, that person couldn't use it if a salesclerk had to verify your identity by scanning a chip before authorizing a transaction. Chips could eventually be developed so that they contain a vast wealth of information about the person in whom they are implanted. However, it remains to be seen whether the general public will accept having personal data implanted into their bodies.

ARTIFICIAL INTELLIGENCE: WILL COMPUTERS BECOME HUMAN?

Science fiction shows and movies such as *Star Wars* have always been populated with robots that emulate humans, seemingly effortlessly. So, when will we have C-3PO, R2-D2, or the Terminator helping us in our home or office?

The answer is not anytime soon, although advances are being made. **Artificial intelligence (AI)** is the science that attempts to produce machines that display the same type of intelligence that humans do. Current computers can perform both calculations and the tasks that are programmed into them much faster than humans. As mentioned earlier, there are already robots on the market that can be programmed to do tasks such as lawn mowing. In addition, industrial robots are commonly used to perform tasks such as welding and painting in factories. NASA is currently working on a line of robots (see Figure 1.26) to be used in deep

FIGURE 1.26

NASA is developing robots such as the scorpion bot shown here that are truly designed to go where no human has gone before. The flexible legs allow the robot to move over rough terrain or wiggle under ledges where traditional roving vehicles can't go.

FIGURE 1.27

With cameras becoming smaller, you could be under surveillance at any time and not even know it. Should the government be allowed to install cameras to monitor sensitive sites for criminal or terrorist activity, or should your privacy be respected?

space exploration (perhaps on the next mission to Mars) to collect mineral specimens.

The performance of tasks by current robots is based on preprogrammed algorithms. Currently, no computers can emulate the human thought process completely. The human brain is superior to computers in a very important way: it is capable of processing almost a limitless number of tasks at the same time. Just to write an e-mail on your computer, your brain coordinates thousands of nerve impulses that control your hands, eyes, and thought processes. Although computers can multitask, not even the most powerful computers can handle the multitasking load of a human brain.

The reason computers can't emulate human thought yet is because no one fully understands how the human brain works. Scientific studies have confirmed that electrical activity between neurons somehow coalesces into thoughts, but scientists aren't quite sure how that happens. Until the human brain is fully understood, progress in the area of artificial intelligence is likely to proceed quite slowly, but you'll no doubt experience artificial intelligence breakthroughs in your lifetime.

Understanding the Challenges Facing a Digital Society

Part of becoming computer fluent is also being able to understand and form knowledgeable opinions on the challenges facing a digital society. Although computers offer us a world of opportunities, they also pose ethical, legal, and moral challenges and questions. For example, how do you feel about the following:

- Since the tragic events of September 11, 2001, various nationwide surveillance programs have been proposed. Some programs include installing surveillance cameras in public places that could be considered attractive areas to stage terrorist activities. These cameras would be monitored via the Internet, possibly by volunteers. Should the government be allowed to monitor your activities in public places àla George Orwell's famous book *1984* to help keep the country secure?

- Advances in technology in surveillance devices (see Figure 1.27) are allowing these devices to become smaller and less noticeable. In certain jurisdictions, courts have upheld the rights of employers to install surveillance devices in the workplace (sometimes without needing to notify employees) for the purposes of cutting down on theft and industrial espionage. Do you know if your employer is watching you? Do you think your employer should have this right?

- Many employees don't know that employers have the right to monitor e-mail and network traffic on the systems they use at work as they are provided at the employer's expense for the sole purpose of allowing employees to do their jobs. Have you visited Web sites that you don't want your employer to know about (such as employment sites as part of a new job search)? Been sending personal e-mail through your company e-mail system? Does your employer know about these activities? Should they have the right to know?

TRENDS IN IT

Ethics: Knowledge Is Power: Bridging the Digital Divide

What would your life be like if you had never touched a computer because you simply couldn't afford one? What if there were no computers in your town? If you're like most people in the United States, access to computers is a given. But for many people, access to the opportunities and knowledge computers and the Internet offer is an impossibility.

The discrepancy between the "haves" and "have-nots" with regards to computer technology is commonly referred to as the *digital divide*. This discrepancy is a growing problem. People with access to computers and the Internet (that is, those who can afford it) are poised to take advantage of the many new developments technology offers, whereas poorer individuals, communities, and school systems that can't afford computer systems and Internet access are being left behind.

For example, in the United States, more teachers are using the Internet to communicate with parents than ever before. E-mail updates on student progress, Web sites with homework postings that allow parents to keep tabs on assignments, and even online parent/teacher conferences are becoming popular. Unwired parents and students are left out of the loop. In the United States, children who do not have access to the Internet and computers won't be prepared for future employment, contributing to the continuing cycle of poverty.

But the digital divide isn't always caused by low income. Terrain can be a factor that inhibits connectivity (see Figure 1.28). In Nepal's mountainous terrain, even though a village might only be a few miles away "as the crow flies," it might take two days to hike there because of the lack of roads. Volunteers, funded by a generous donor, have installed twelve outdoor access points complete with directional antennas to connect a series of villages to the Internet via a wireless network. The last access point in the connectivity chain connects to an Internet service provider

FIGURE 1.28

Terrain (such as mountains) and remote locations (like the Sahara desert) can present barriers to conquering the digital divide.

22 miles away. The villagers are now able to hold meetings, school classes, and access the Internet without trekking across miles of mountainous terrain. Unfortunately, this solution isn't available throughout Nepal . . . nor even throughout some areas of the United States.

So the United States must be the most wired country in the world with the smallest gap in the digital divide, right? Guess again. Although 30 percent of American households have broadband connections (either cable or DSL), a whopping two thirds of South Korean households have high-speed connections. This widespread connectivity is changing the face of Korean society. Government agencies, once known for long lines and mind-numbing paperwork, have installed efficient Web sites to streamline processes.

And although we're still in the test-marketing phase of video-on-demand in a few markets in the United States, South Koreans routinely download movies and watch them whenever they want.

So what is being done to bridge the digital divide in rural and poor areas of the world? Some organizations are attempting to increase local and global Internet and computer access, whereas community organizations such as libraries and recreation centers are providing free Internet access to the public. Meanwhile, others are sponsoring referendums that increase Internet capacity in schools or are e-mailing their local and state representatives, urging them to back legislation to provide funding for computer equipment in struggling school systems. Others suggest computer users donate their old computers to a charity that refurbishes and distributes them to needy families. To help bridge the digital divide, you can start by supporting such programs and institutions (such as your local library) in your area that are attempting to increase Internet and computer access.

These are just a few examples of the kind of questions active participants in today's digital society need to be able to think about, discuss, and, at times, take action on. Being computer fluent enables you to form *educated* opinions on these issues and to take stands based on accurate information rather than media hype and misinformation. Here are a few other questions you, as a member of our digital society, may be expected to think about and discuss:

- What privacy risks do biomedical chips such as the VeriChip pose? Do the privacy risks of such chips outweigh the potential benefits?

- Should companies be allowed to collect personal data from visitors to their Web site without their permission?

- Should spam be illegal? If so, what penalties should be levied on people who send spam?

- Is it ethical to download music off the Web without paying for it? What about copying a friend's software onto your computer?

- What are the risks involved with humans attempting to create computers that can learn and become more human?

- Should we rely solely on computers to provide security for sensitive areas such as nuclear power plants?

As a computer user, you must consider these and other questions to define the boundaries of the digital society in which you live.

Becoming Computer Fluent

By now you can see why becoming computer fluent is so important. But where do you start? As mentioned in the introduction, you glean some knowledge about computers just from being a member of our society. However, although you certainly know what a computer *is*, do you really understand how it works, what all its parts are, and what these parts do? In this section, we'll discuss what a computer does that makes it such a useful machine.

COMPUTERS ARE DATA PROCESSING DEVICES

Strictly defined, a **computer** is a data processing device that performs four major functions:

1. It *gathers* data (or allows users to input data).
2. It *processes* that data into information.
3. It *outputs* data or information.
4. It *stores* data and information.

To understand these four functions, you need to understand the distinction between the terms *data* and *information*. People often use these terms interchangeably. Although in a simple conversation they may mean the same thing, when discussing computers, the distinction between *data* and *information* is an important one.

In computer terms, **data** is a representation of a fact or idea. Data can be a number, a word, a picture, or even a recording of sound. For example, the number 6125553297 and the names Derek and Washington are pieces of data. But how useful are these chunks of data to you? **Information** is data that has been organized or presented in a meaningful fashion. When your computer provides you with a contact listing that indicates Derek Washington can be reached by phone at (612) 555-3297, the data mentioned earlier suddenly becomes useful—that is, it is *information*.

Computers are very good at processing data into information. When you first arrived on campus, you probably were directed to a place where you could get an ID card. You most likely provided a clerk with personal data (such as your name and address) that was entered into a computer. The clerk then took your picture with a digital camera (collecting more data). This information was then processed appropriately so that it could be printed on your ID card (see Figure 1.29). This organized output of data on your ID card is useful information. Finally, the information was probably stored as digital data on the computer for later use.

BITS AND BYTES: THE LANGUAGE OF COMPUTERS

How do computers process data into information? Unlike humans, computers work exclusively with numbers (not words). In

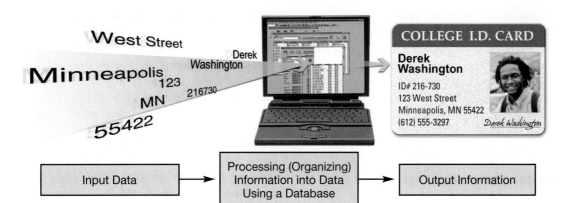

FIGURE 1.29

Computers process data into information.

| Input Data | → | Processing (Organizing) Information into Data Using a Database | → | Output Information |

order to process data into information, computers need to work in a language they understand. This language, called **binary language**, consists of just two digits: 0 and 1. Everything a computer does (such as process data or print a report) is broken down into a series of 0s and 1s. Each 0 and 1 is a **binary digit**, or **bit** for short. Eight binary digits (or bits) combine to create one **byte**. In computers, each letter of the alphabet, each number, and each special character (such as the @ sign) consists of a *unique* combination of eight bits, or a string of eight 0s and 1s. So, for example, in binary (computer) language, the letter K is represented as 01001011. This equals eight bits, or one byte. (We'll discuss binary language in more detail in Chapter 9.)

You've probably heard the terms kilobyte (KB) and megabyte (MB) before. But how do these fit into the bit and byte discussion here? Not only are bits and bytes used as the language that tells the computer what to do, they are also what the computer uses to *represent* the data and information it inputs and outputs. Word processing files, digital pictures, and even software programs are all represented inside a computer as a series of bits and bytes. These files and applications can be quite large, containing many millions of bytes. To make it easier to measure the size of these files, we need larger units of measure than a byte. Kilobytes, megabytes, and gigabytes are therefore simply amounts of bytes. As shown in Figure 1.30, a **kilobyte (KB)**

FIGURE 1.30 How Much Is a Byte?

Name	Abbreviation	Number of Bytes	Relative Size
Byte	B	1 byte	Can hold one character of data.
Kilobyte	KB	1,024 bytes	Can hold 1,024 characters or about half of a typewritten page double-spaced.
Megabyte	MB	1,048,576 bytes	A floppy disk holds approximately 1.4 MB of data, or approximately 768 pages of typed text.
Gigabyte	GB	1,073,741,824 bytes	Approximately 786,432 pages of text. As 500 sheets of paper is approximately 2 inches, this represents a stack of paper 262 feet high.
Terabyte	TB	1,099,511,627,776 bytes	This represents a stack of typewritten pages almost 51 miles high.
Petabyte	PB	1,125,899,906,842,624 bytes	The stack of pages is now 52,000 miles high, or about one-fourth the distance from the Earth to the moon.

is approximately 1,000 bytes, a **megabyte (MB)** is about a million bytes, and a **gigabyte (GB)** is about a billion bytes. As our information processing needs have grown, so too have our storage needs. Today, some computers can store up to a petabyte of data—that's more than one quadrillion bytes!

COMPUTER HARDWARE

You've no doubt heard the term *hardware* used in reference to computers. An anonymous person once said that **hardware** is any part of a computer that you can kick when it doesn't work properly. A more formal definition of hardware is any part of the computer you can physically touch. All hardware on the computer helps the computer to perform its various tasks (see Figure 1.31).

Most computer systems have hardware devices that you use to enter, or input, data (text, images, and sounds) into your computer. These devices, such as a keyboard and a mouse, are called **input devices**. In addition to the keyboard and the mouse, input devices include scanners (which input text and photos), microphones (which input sounds), and digital cameras (which input photos and video).

You also use input devices to provide the steps and tasks the computer needs to process data into usable information. These steps and tasks are called **instructions**. Instructions may be in the form of a user response to a question posed when working in a software application or in the form of a command in which you instruct the computer what to do (such as clicking an icon with your mouse).

As noted earlier, once data is entered into a computer, the computer processes that data. Those components that process data are located inside the **system unit**. The system unit is the metal or plastic case that holds all the physical parts of the computer

FIGURE 1.31

Each part of the computer serves a special function.

Input

Storage

Processing

Output

together. The part of the system unit that is responsible for the processing (or the "brains" of the computer) is called the **central processing unit**, or **CPU**.

Another component inside the system unit that helps process data into information is **memory**. Memory chips hold (or store) the instructions or data that the CPU processes. The most common type of memory that a computer uses for processing data is random access memory, or RAM.

The CPU and memory are located on a special circuit board in the system unit called the **motherboard**. Once this data has been processed, it is classified as information.

In addition to input devices and the system unit, a computer includes devices that let you see your processed information. These devices, called **output devices**, include monitors and printers. Because they output sound, speakers are also considered output devices.

Finally, when your data has been input, processed, and output, you may want to store the data or information so that you can access and use it again. Specialized **storage devices** such as hard disk drives, floppy disk drives, and CD drives allow you to store your data and information.

We'll discuss all the hardware you find on a computer in much more detail in Chapter 2.

COMPUTER SOFTWARE

A computer needs more than just hardware to work: it also needs some form of software. Think of a book without words or a CD without music. Without words or music, these two common items are just shells that hold nothing. Similarly, a computer without software is a shell full of hardware components that can't do anything. **Software** is the set of computer programs that enables the hardware to perform different tasks. There are two broad categories of software: application software and system software.

When you think of software, you are most likely thinking of application software. **Application software** is the set of programs you use on a computer to help you carry out tasks. If you've ever typed a document, created a spreadsheet, or edited a digital photo, for example, you've used a form of application software (see Figure 1.32).

SOUND BYTE

Virtual Computer Tour

In this Sound Byte, you'll take a video tour of the inside of a system unit. From opening the cover to locating the power supply, CPU, and memory, you'll become more familiar with what's inside your computer.

System software is the set of programs that enables your computer's hardware devices and application software to work together. The most common type of system software is the **operating system (OS)**, the program that controls the way in which your computer system functions. It manages the hardware of the computer system, including the CPU, memory, and storage devices, as well as input and output devices such as the mouse, keyboard, and printer. The operating system also provides a means by which users can interact with the computer. We'll cover software in greater depth in Chapters 4 and 5.

COMPUTER PLATFORMS: PCs AND MACs

The kind of operating system software you have depends on your computer's **platform**. The two most common platform types are the PC (short for personal computer, named after the original IBM personal computer)

and the Apple Macintosh (or Mac). Macs and PCs use different CPUs, and therefore, each system processes information very differently. Correspondingly, their operating systems are also different. Macintosh computers use the Macintosh operating system (or Mac OS), whereas PCs generally run on the Microsoft Windows operating system. But that's where their differences end. You can still use both PCs and Macs to perform the same types of tasks (word processing and so on). The PC is not necessarily better than the Mac (or vice versa), but PCs have by far the larger market share (see Figure 1.33). Although the vast majority of consumers use PCs, Macs are the platform of choice for professions such as graphic design and animation.

SPECIALTY COMPUTERS

PCs and Macs (whether desktop or laptop units) are obviously not the only computers you may encounter. There are smaller, more mobile computers that you can carry around, such as PDAs. In addition, there are computers you may never come in direct contact with but that are important to our society nonetheless:

- **Servers** are computers that provide resources to other computers connected in a network. When you connect to the Internet, for example, your computer is communicating with a server at your Internet service provider (ISP). This server provides your computer with ser-

FIGURE 1.33

Ever since the early 1980s, PCs and Macs have been gunning for each other's market share. Although PCs have a much larger market share, Macs are still the platform of choice for many professions, such as graphic design.

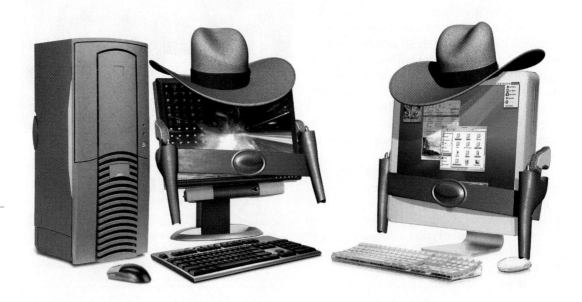

vices that allow it to access the Internet. One server can provide services to many computers.

- **Mainframes** are large, expensive computers that support hundreds or thousands of users simultaneously. Mainframes excel at executing many different computer programs at the same time. Although many large companies still use mainframes, smaller and cheaper PC-based servers have replaced mainframes in many companies.

- **Supercomputers** are specially designed computers that can perform complex calculations extremely rapidly. They are used in situations in which complex models requiring intensive mathematical calculations are needed (such as weather forecasting or atomic energy research). Supercomputers are the fastest and most expensive computers. The main difference between a supercomputer and a mainframe is that supercomputers are designed to execute a few programs as quickly as possible, whereas mainframes are designed to handle many programs running at the same time (but at a slower pace).

- **Embedded computers** are specially designed computer chips that reside inside other devices such as your car or your electronic thermostat in your home. These are self-contained computer devices that have their own programming and typically do not receive input from you nor do they interact with other systems. They usually perform preprogrammed functions such as temperature control for your house.

No matter what the size, computers are an integral part of our lives, and they are constantly changing. Whether you're a novice or an experienced computer user or fall somewhere in between, you need to learn as much as you can about computers so that you can use them wisely.

What Can You Do with a Digital Home?

You're probably already using your computer in many different ways to fit your lifestyle. Perhaps you're ripping your CD collection to MP3 files so you can transfer them from your computer to your iPod. Maybe you're burning a CD of all your favorite songs for a party you're having. But wouldn't it be great if you could manage the music for your party from the iPod iTunes software straight from your computer? And what about that video of your friend's birthday party you shot last week? You've already imported it to your computer, edited it, and added a music track. But when your friends come over for the party this weekend, wouldn't it be fun to be able to show them the video on the TV in the living room instead of having them crowd around your computer monitor?

So when in the future will you do all this? Right now, if you set up a digital home. Setting up a digital home means having an appropriate computer and digital devices that are all connected to a home network. Let's look at the key components you need to have to have a digital home, some of which are shown in Figure 1.34:

1. **A Computer:** A computer is the nerve center of any digital home, allowing you to interface with all the different digital devices you have connected to the network. For a Windows-based computer (see Figure 1.35), you should opt for a computer running the current version of Microsoft Windows XP Media Center Edition (MCE) as its operating system. (We'll discuss operating systems in more detail in Chapter 5.) MCE is installed on specially constructed "Media Center" PCs. A typical Media Center PC includes the following components:

   a. **A TV Tuner:** A TV tuner allows your computer to receive television channels from a cable connection and display them on your computer monitor. In fact, you can install more than one TV tuner in your computer (MCE supports up to three tuners), which allows you to receive multiple television channels at the same time.

   b. **Digital Video Recorder Software:** In combination with a TV tuner, digital video recorder software allows you to turn your computer into a digital video recorder (like TiVo). Digital video recorders record TV programs like VCRs, but they use a hard drive (in this case, the computer's hard drive) to store the video instead of a video cassette tape. If you have multiple TV tuners installed in your computer, you can record several programs onto your computer's hard drive at the same time.

   c. **A Radio Tuner:** A radio tuner allows you to tune into Internet radio stations and record their broadcasts as digital files on your computer.

   d. **DVD and CD Players/Recorders:** To make it easy to transfer your audio or video files from one device to another, DVD and CD players/recorders allow you to record files onto DVDs and CDs instead of your hard drive.

   e. **A Web Browser:** In order to surf the Web and acquire digital content online (at music sites such as iTunes or Napster), your computer needs to have Web browser software such as Internet Explorer installed.

   f. **A Network Adapter:** A network adapter is a special device that is installed in your computer that

FIGURE 1.34

You can create a digital home with only a few devices.

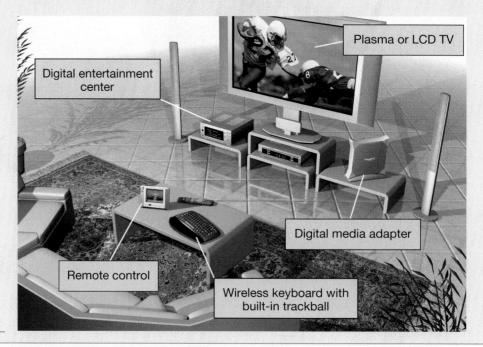

Digital entertainment center

Plasma or LCD TV

Digital media adapter

Remote control

Wireless keyboard with built-in trackball

allows it to communicate with other devices on a network. (You'll learn more about network adapters in Chapter 7.) For digital devices to communicate with each other, they need to be connected to a network.

g. **Video and Music Players:** This special software (such as iTunes or Windows Media Player) enables you to playback or view digital content on your computer.

2. **A Network (Preferably Wireless):** Unless you're going to view digital and audio files on your computer only, you need a network to transfer such files easily to other devices (such as televisions) in your home. A wireless network is preferable to a wired network, as it is easier to relocate devices. For example, suppose you rearrange your living room and need to move your TV to the opposite end of the room. If your TV was connected to a wired network, you might have to run a new cable or relocate the existing one. With a wireless network, you'd just move the TV and be done with it. (You'll learn all about wired and wireless networks in Chapter 7.)

3. **A Digital TV:** Newer plasma and liquid crystal display (LCD) televisions (see inset, Figure 1.34) or High Definition TVs (HDTVs) are an important part of any digital home as they enable you to best show off all your digital entertainment (digital photos, DVDs, and so on). Note that even if you don't have a plasma or LCD television, so long as you bought it within the last five years or so, you can probably use it to display digital content as well. However, televisions are not usually ready to be integrated into a network right out of the box. For this you need a digital media adapter.

4. **A Digital Media Adapter:** A digital media adapter (see inset, Figure 1.34) allows you to transfer media (such as video, digital photos, or MP3s) from your computer to your other media devices (such as your plasma TV). These devices are also known as media center extenders. Essentially, a digital media adapter allows you to integrate your TV into your home network. The digital media adapter is a device that you connect to your computer network

(either wired or wirelessly) and then to your TV through specially designed audio-visual connectors.

5. **A Digital Entertainment Center:** Although not a requirement, a digital entertainment center (see inset, Figure 1.34) is a device that makes your digital system much more manageable as it incorporates the functionality of a DVD player, a CD player/changer, an FM tuner, and a digital video recorder (DVR) all into one device. Instead of having individual devices cluttering up the living room, a digital entertainment center provides a compact solution for managing your digital media.

6. **Remote Controls:** Remote controls that work with your computer, digital media adapters, and digital devices allow you to control the digital devices and access your digital media (such as MP3 files) no matter what device in the house the media is stored on. Such remote controls also allow you to access the Internet directly so you can download your favorite movies, surf the Web, or even view your e-mail on your TV. Devices such as the iPronto from Philips (see inset, Figure 1.34) come with software that allows you to program your own custom interface for the remote. You can even program macros that perform multiple commands with the press of a button.

With these devices installed, you can get the maximum benefit from your computer and all your digital entertainment devices. When you're in your living room, you can play digital music files stored on your computer (in the den) for the party you're throwing. You can also display the video of your friend's birthday party (downloaded to your computer) on the TV for your friends to see. And when you're in your room, you can watch the latest episode of *Law and Order* that you recorded on your computer's hard drive, while your sister is simultaneously listening to MP3 files stored on your computer on the TV in the living room. For more information on creating a digital home check out **www.intel.com/ personal/digital_home/**.

FIGURE 1.35

Microsoft Windows XP Media Center Edition (MCE) is an operating system that allows you to manage all your media entertainment from your computer.

1. What does it mean to be "computer fluent"?

Computer fluency goes way beyond knowing how to use a mouse and send e-mail. If you are computer fluent, you understand the capabilities and limitations of computers and know how to use them wisely. Being computer fluent also enables you to make informed purchasing decisions, use computers in your career, understand and take advantage of future technologies, and understand the many ethical, legal, and societal implications of technology today.

2. How does being computer fluent make you a savvy computer user and consumer?

By understanding how a computer is constructed and how its various parts function, you'll be able to get the most out of your computer. Among other things, you'll be able to avoid hackers, viruses, and Internet headaches; protect your privacy; separate the real risks from those you don't have to worry about; be able to maintain, upgrade, and troubleshoot your computer; and make good purchasing decisions.

3. How can becoming computer fluent help you in a career?

As computers become more a part of our daily lives, it is difficult to imagine any career that does not use computers in some fashion. Understanding how to use computers effectively will help you be a more productive and valuable employee, no matter which profession you choose.

4. How can becoming computer fluent help you understand and take advantage of future technologies?

The world is changing every day, and many changes are a result of new computer technologies. Understanding how today's computers function should help you utilize technology effectively now. And by understanding computers and how they work today, you can contribute to the technologies of tomorrow.

5. What kinds of challenges do computers bring to a digital society and how does becoming computer fluent help you deal with these challenges?

Although computers offer us a world of opportunities, they also pose ethical, legal, and moral challenges and questions. Being computer fluent enables you to form *educated* opinions on these issues and to take stands based on accurate information rather than media hype and misinformation.

6. What exactly is a computer and what are its four main functions?

Computers are data processing devices. They help organize, sort, and categorize data to turn it into information. The computer's four major functions are (1) it gathers data (or allows users to input data); (2) it processes that data (performs calculations or some other manipulation of the data); (3) it outputs data or information (displays information in a form suitable for the user); and (4) it stores data and information for later use.

7. What is the difference between data and information?

Data is a representation of a fact or idea. The number 3 and the words *televisions* or *Sony* are pieces of data. Information is data that has been organized or presented in a meaningful fashion. An inventory list that indicates that "3 Sony televisions" are in stock is processed information. It allows a retail clerk to answer a customer query about the availability of merchandise. Information is more powerful than raw data.

8. What are a bit and a byte and how are they measured?

To process data into information, computers need to work in a language they understand. This language, called binary language, consists of two numbers: 0 and 1. Each 0 and 1 is a binary digit, or bit. Eight bits create one byte. In computers, each letter of the alphabet, each number, and each special character consists of a unique combination of eight bits (one byte), or a string of eight 0s and 1s. For describing large amounts of storage capacity, the terms kilobyte (approximately 1,000 bytes) megabyte (approximately one million bytes), and gigabyte (approximately one billion bytes) are used.

9. What hardware does a computer use to perform its functions?

Hardware is any part of the computer you can touch. Most computers have input devices that you use to input data into your computer. Those components that process that data are located inside the system unit. They include the CPU (central processing unit), memory, and motherboard. Output devices (such as monitors and printers) are used to display information (after processing) in a format suitable for users. Finally, storage devices (such as hard disk drives) are used to preserve data and information for future use.

10. What are the two main types of software you find in a computer?

The two broad categories of software are application software and system software. Application software is the set of programs you use on a computer to help you carry out tasks (such as writing a letter). System software is the set of programs that enables your computer's hardware devices and application software to work together. The most common type of system software is the operating system.

11. What different kinds of computers are there?

Aside from PCs and Macs, you'll find mobile computing devices (such as laptops and PDAs), as well as servers, mainframes, and supercomputers. Servers are computers that provide resources to other computers connected in a network. Mainframes are large, expensive computers specifically designed to provide services to hundreds (or thousands) of users at the same time. Supercomputers are designed to perform a small number of calculations as rapidly as possible.

Buzz Words

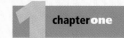

Word Bank

- biomedical chips
- bit
- byte
- computer forensics
- CPU

- data
- gigabyte
- information
- input
- megabyte

- nanotechnology
- output
- processing
- server
- storage

Instructions: Fill in the blanks using the words from the Word Bank above.

Because of the integration of computers into business and society, many fields of study are available now that were unheard of a few years ago. (1) _____ , the study of very small computing devices built at the molecular level, will provide major advances in the miniaturization of computing. (2) _____ is already taking criminologists beyond what they could accomplish with conventional investigation techniques. And as (3) _____ become widespread, individuals may benefit from having computing devices implanted in their bodies.

At the lowest level, computers manipulate data in units called (4) _____ s. Because these units are too small to define data on their own, they are grouped together to form (5) _____ s. (6) _____ represents raw facts or ideas. (7) _____ represents facts or ideas that have been organized or processed in some fashion to make them more meaningful. When storing data, large quantities of space are needed. The capacity of most hard drives today is measured in (8) _____ s, which represents over 1 billion bytes of information.

For a computer to use data, various components of the computer must interact with the data. Mice and keyboards are (9) _____ _input_ _____ devices used to enter data into the computer. The CPU is an example of a (10) _____ device that helps turn data into information. (11) _____ _out_ _____ devices, such as monitors and printers, enable computers to provide information in a usable format. To save information and data for later use, (12) _____ _stor_ _____ devices such as hard disk drives are used.

Becoming Computer Fluent

Using the key terms and ideas you learned in this chapter, write a paragraph or two for your computer illiterate grandfather explaining how a computer works. Make sure you cover input, processing, output, and storage and explain how computers and peripherals handle each of these areas.

Self-Test

Instructions: Answer the multiple choice and true/false questions below for more practice with key terms and concepts from this chapter.

MULTIPLE CHOICE

1. Which of the following is not one of the four major functions of a computer?
   a. input
   b. storage
   c. enumeration
   d. processing

2. Data becomes information when
   a. it is entered into a computer.
   b. a computer performs calculations with the data.
   c. the data is organized in a specific manner.
   d. the data is outputted to a computer screen or printer.

3. In the binary language, each 0 or 1 is referred to as a
   a. byte
   b. bit
   c. kilobyte
   d. nanobyte

4. Eight bits combine to create
   a. one megabyte
   b. one kilobyte
   c. one bit
   d. one byte

5. A kilobyte is approximately
   a. 100 bytes
   b. 1,000 bytes
   c. one million bytes
   d. one billion bytes

6. A megabyte is approximately
   a. 100 bytes
   b. 1,000 bytes
   c. one million bytes
   d. one billion bytes

7. Which of the following is not an input device?
   a. keyboard
   b. mouse
   c. digital camera
   d. CD-ROM drive

8. Which of these is not an output device?
   a. printer
   b. floppy disk drive
   c. monitor
   d. speakers

9. Which of these is not a storage device?
   a. hard disk drive
   b. floppy disk drive
   c. boot drive
   d. CD drive

10. Spreadsheet programs (such as Excel) are an example of
    a. application software
    b. operating system software
    c. data mining software
    d. utility software

TRUE/FALSE

_____ 1. The four major functions that a computer performs are input, output, storage, and dissemination.

_____ 2. Computers use a binary language composed of 0s and 1s to perform all calculations and functions.

_____ 3. Microsoft Windows is the most popular piece of application software sold today.

_____ 4. The CPU is located on RAM.

_____ 5. PCs and Macs are the two most common types of computer platforms.

Making the Transition to... Next Semester

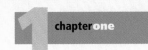

1. Computer Literacy

In your college career, you'll be spending time understanding the requirements of the degree program you choose. At many schools, computer literacy requirements exist, either as incoming requirements (skills students must have before they are admitted) or outgoing requirements (skills students must prove they have before graduating). Does your program require specific computer skills? Should these be required? How can students efficiently prove that they have these skills?

2. Future Hardware/Software Needs

Think about the schedule of courses you will be taking next semester. How many courses will require you to produce papers in electronic format? How many will require you to use course management software, such as Blackboard or WebCT? Will any require you to use some specialty software product such as a nutrition monitoring program or a statistics training application? Do any courses require specialized hardware for your computer?

3. Future System Needs

Consider the number of years you are planning to continue your studies. Will you be purchasing a computer system? Will you need to upgrade your existing system? If you do buy a new system today, might you need to buy/upgrade another system before the end of your collegiate career?

4. Using New Technologies

Do you think you are taking advantage of the latest technologies for learning? Can you record lectures on a cell phone, laptop, or PDA? Can you read posted lecture notes from a PDA? Can you copy files you need to take home from the school network to an iPod MP3 player?

5. Using Biomedical Implants

If having such a chip implanted meant you would never need to carry cash or a credit card to the bookstore with you because your financial information was encoded on the chip, would you want one? If it could help instructors take attendance automatically in your class by reading your personal information, would that be an acceptable use? Would you consider using such a chip if it could be disabled whenever you wanted it to be or if only individuals you authorized had access to the information?

6. Campus Policing

In the section "Computers in Law Enforcement: Put Down that Mouse—You're Under Arrest!" the use of trend-spotting programs to predict criminal activity was discussed. If existing criminal statistics are used to help identify trouble spots (such as wild parties) on your campus and the potential for serious criminal activity, is this the same as profiling? Does your campus police force have the right to take proactive steps to prevent crime based solely on developing trends? Should someone be held accountable if such information is not acted upon and a crime occurs?

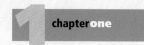

Making the Transition to...
The Workplace

1. Computer-Free Workplaces?

In this chapter we listed a number of careers that demand computer skills. How are computers used in the profession you are in or plan to enter? Can you think of any careers in which people do not use computers? Can you imagine computers being used in these careers in the future? How?

2. Medical Computing Applications

In their training and their work, doctors and nurses rely on computers. What about patients? Does having access to a computer and computer skills help a patient create better health care options? Does having access to a computer help with filing an insurance claim? Does it help with finding the best doctor or hospital for a specific procedure? Explain your answers.

3. Preparing for a Job

An office is looking for help and needs an employee able to manipulate data on Excel spreadsheets, to coordinate the computer file management for the office, and to conduct backups of critical data. How could you prove to the interviewer that you have the skills to handle the job? How could you prove you have the ability to learn the job?

4. Career Outlook

Which career fields are growing the fastest? (Suggestion: Try asking Jeeves at **www.ask.com**.) What computer skills and knowledge do the top 10 of these career paths demand?

5. IT Careers

Information technology (IT) careers are suited to a wide range of people at different points in their lives.

a. Would an IT career have advantages for a single parent? How?

b. Would an IT career be able to help someone pursue a later career in a nontechnical field?

c. How might an IT career assist someone in completing a college degree?

6. Job Skills Assessment

Frequently, job seekers are asked about their computer fluency when applying for a job.

a. How do you think computer skill levels are determined by employers? How should they be determined?

b. If your interpretation of "expert" doesn't match your prospective employer's version, does that make you wrong?

Critical Thinking Questions

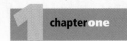

Instructions: Albert Einstein used "Gedanken experiments," or critical thinking questions, to develop his theory of relativity. Some ideas are best understood by experimenting with them in our own minds. The following critical thinking questions are designed to demand your full attention but require only a comfortable chair—no technology.

1. Rating Your Computer Fluency

This chapter lists a number of ways in which knowing about computers (or becoming computer fluent) will help you. How much do you know about computers? What else would you like to know? How do you think learning more about computers will help you in the future?

2. Data Mining

This chapter briefly discusses data mining, a technique companies use to study sales data and gather information from it. Have you heard of data mining before? How might a company like Wal-Mart or Target use data mining to better run their business? Can you think of any privacy risks data mining might pose?

3. Nanotechnology

As you learned in the chapter, nanotechnology is the science revolving around the use of nanostructures to build devices on an extremely small scale. What applications of tiny computers can you think of? How might nanotechnology impact your life?

4. Biomedical Chips

This chapter discusses various uses of biomedical chips. Many biomedical chip implants that will be developed in the future will most likely be aimed at correcting vision loss, hearing loss, or other physical impediments. But chips could also be developed to improve physical or mental capabilities of healthy individuals. For example, chips could be implanted in athletes to make their muscles work better together, thereby allowing them to run faster. Or, your memory could be enhanced by providing additional storage capacity for your brain.

a. Should biomedical implant devices that increase athletic performance be permitted in the Olympics?
b. What about devices that repair a problem (such as blindness in one eye) but then increase the level of visual acuity in the affected eye so that it is better than normal vision?
c. Would you be willing to have a chip implanted in your brain to improve your memory?
d. Would you be willing to have a VeriChip implanted under your skin?

5. Artificial Intelligence

Artificial intelligence is the science that attempts to produce machines that display the same type of intelligence that humans do. Do you think humans will ever create a machine that can think? In your opinion, what are the ethical and moral implications associated with artificial intelligence?

Problem:

People are often overwhelmed by the relentless march of technology. Accessibility of information is changing the way we work, play, and interact with our friends, family, and coworkers. In this Team Time, we consider the future and reflect on how the advent of new technologies will affect our daily lives 10 years in the future.

Task:

Your group has just returned from a trip in a time machine 10 years into the future. Amazing changes have taken place in just a short time. To a large extent, consumer acceptance of technology makes or breaks a new technology. Your mission is to create a creative marketing strategy to promote the technological changes you observed in the future and accelerate their acceptance.

Process:

Divide the class into three or more teams.

1. With the other members of your team, use the Internet to research up-and-coming technologies (**www.howstuffworks.com** is a good starting point). Prepare a list of innovations that you believe will occur in the next 10 years. Determine how they will be integrated into society and the effect they will have on our culture.

2. Present your group's findings to the class for debate and discussion. Note specifically how the rest of the class reacts to your reports on the innovations. Are they excited? Skeptical? Incredulous? Did they laugh off your ideas or become wildly enthusiastic?

3. Write a marketing strategy paper detailing how you would promote the technological changes that you envision for the future. Also note some barriers for acceptance the technology may have to overcome, as well as any legal or ethical challenges or questions you see the new technology posing.

Conclusion:

The future path of technology is determined by dreamers. If not for innovators such as Edison, Bell, and Einstein, we would not be as advanced a society as we are today. Innovators come from all walks of life and our creative energies must be exercised to keep them in tune. Don't be afraid to suggest technological advancements that seem outrageous today. In 1966, when the original *Star Trek* series was on television, handheld communicators seemed astounding and beyond our reach. Yet the dreamers who created those communication devices for a science fiction series spawned a multi-billion-dollar cell phone industry in the 21st century. The next technological wave may be started in your imagination!

Multimedia

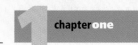

In addition to the review materials presented here, you'll find additional materials featured with the book's multimedia, including the *Technology in Action* Student Resource CD and the Companion Web site (**www.prenhall.com/techinaction**), which will help reinforce your understanding of the chapter content. These materials include the following:

ACTIVE HELPDESK

In Active Helpdesk calls, you'll assume the role of a Helpdesk operator taking calls about the concepts you've learned in this chapter. You'll apply what you've learned and receive feedback from a supervisor to review and reinforce those concepts. The Active Helpdesk calls for this chapter are listed here and can be found on your Student Resource CD:

- Understanding Bits and Bytes

SOUND BYTES

Sound Bytes are dynamic multimedia tutorials that help demystify even the most complex topics. You'll view video clips and animations that illustrate computer concepts, and then apply what you've learned by reviewing with the Sound Byte Labs, which include quizzes and activities specifically tailored to each Sound Byte. The Sound Bytes for this chapter are listed here and can be found on your Student Resource CD and on the Companion Web site (**www.prenhall.com/techinaction**):

- Virtual Computer Tour
- Questions to Ask Before You Buy a Computer

COMPANION WEB SITE

The *Technology in Action* Companion Web site includes a variety of additional materials to help you review and learn more about the topics in this chapter. The resources available at **www.prenhall.com/techinaction** include:

- **Online Study Guide.** Each chapter features an online true/false and multiple-choice quiz. You can take these quizzes, automatically check the results, and e-mail the results to your instructor.
- **Web Research Projects.** Each chapter features a number of Web research projects that ask you to search the Web for information on computer-related careers, milestones in computer history, important people and companies, emerging technologies, and the applications and implications of different technologies.

Looking at Computers:

Understanding the Parts

Objectives

After reading this chapter, you should be able to answer the following questions:

1. What devices do you use to get data into the computer? **(pp. 42–47)**

2. What devices do you use to get information out of the computer? **(pp. 48–54)**

3. What's on the front of your system unit? **(pp. 55–58)**

4. What's on the back of your system unit? **(pp. 58–59)**

5. What's inside your system unit? **(pp. 60–61)**

6. How do you set up your computer to avoid strain and injury? **(pp. 62–63)**

ACTIVE HELPDESK

- Using Input Devices **(p. 47)**
- Using Output Devices **(p. 54)**

Setting Up Your System

Jillian has just bought a new computer and is setting it up. She spent more than she had planned to buy a flat-panel monitor, which she places on her small desk. It takes up far less room than her old monitor, which was big and bulky. Next she pulls out her system unit, which she knows is the component she'll connect all the other pieces of her system to. Although she was tempted to buy the most powerful computer on the market, she bought one that best met her needs and was slightly less expensive. Still, it came with a CD-RW/DVD combo player, a 100-GB hard drive, and what the computer salesperson said was enough memory and power to do almost anything. She sets it on the floor next to her desk and attaches the monitor to it.

Next she pulls out her keyboard. She looked into buying a wireless keyboard, but because her budget was tight, she bought a standard keyboard instead. The box tells her it is a "USB" keyboard, so she finds what looks to be the right port on the back of her system unit and plugs it in. Her mouse also needs a USB port. Finding another USB port, she attaches the mouse there. She's glad that her system has plenty of USB ports and sees there are even several on the front of the tower.

She sets up her speakers next. Although the salesperson told her she'd probably want to upgrade them, she decided to wait until she can afford it. She arranges them on her desk, and inserts the speakers into the "speaker out" port on the back of her tower.

Last is her printer. She debated over which type of printer to buy, but decided to buy an ink-jet because she prints a lot of color copies and photos. She finds the right port on her system unit and connects it. She then plugs the power cables of the monitor, speakers, printer, and system unit into the surge protector, which the salesperson told her would protect her devices from power surges. All that's left is to make sure her setup is comfortable, and she's ready to go.

What kind of computer setup do you have? Do you know all the options available and what the different components of your system do? In this chapter, we'll take a look at your computer's basic parts. You'll learn about input devices (such as the mouse and keyboard), output devices (such as monitors and printers), storage devices (such as the hard drive), as well as components inside the computer that help it to function. Finally, you'll learn how to set up your computer so that it's safe from power surges and comfortable to work on.

SOUND BYTES

- Port Tour: How Do I Hook It Up? **(p. 59)**
- Virtual Computer Tour **(p. 61)**
- Healthy Computing **(p. 63)**

FIGURE 2.1

Do you know what all of the hardware in your system is for?

Your Computer's Hardware

Considering the amount of amazing things computers can do, they are really quite simple machines. You learned in Chapter 1 that a basic computer system is made up of software and hardware. In this chapter, we look more closely at your computer's **hardware**, the parts you can actually touch (see Figure 2.1). Hardware components consist of the **system unit**, the box that contains the central electronic components of the computer, and **peripheral devices**, those devices such as monitors and printers that are connected to the computer. Other devices, such as routers, help a computer communicate with other computers to facilitate sharing documents and other resources. Together the system unit and peripheral devices perform four main functions: they enable the computer to *input* data, *process* that data, and *output* and *store* the data and information. We begin our exploration of hardware by taking a look at your computer's input devices.

Input Devices

An **input device** enables you to enter data (text, images, and sounds) and instructions (user responses and commands) into the computer. The most common input devices are the **keyboard** and the **mouse**. You use keyboards to enter typed data and commands, whereas you use the mouse to enter user responses and commands. There are other input devices as well: microphones input sounds, whereas scanners and digital cameras input nondigital text and digital images, respectively.

FIGURE 2.2

(a) The first six keys in the top-left row of alphabetic keys give the QWERTY keyboard its name. QWERTY is the standard keyboard that comes with most computers. (b) With a Dvorak keyboard, you can type most of the more commonly used words in the English language with the letters found on "home keys," the keys in the middle row of the keyboard.

KEYBOARDS

Aren't all keyboards the same? Most desktop computers come with a standard keyboard, which uses the **QWERTY keyboard** layout, as shown in Figure 2.2a. This layout gets its name from the first six letters in the top-left row of alphabetic keys on the keyboard. Over the years, there has been some debate over what is the best layout for keyboards. The QWERTY layout was originally designed for typewriters, not computers, and was meant to slow typists to prevent typewriter keys from jamming. The QWERTY layout is therefore considered inefficient because it slows typing speeds. Now that technology can keep up with faster typing, other keyboard layouts are being considered.

The **Dvorak keyboard** is the leading alternative keyboard, although it is not nearly as common as the QWERTY. The Dvorak keyboard puts the most commonly used letters in the English language on "home keys," the keys in the middle row of the keyboard, as shown in Figure 2.2b. The Dvorak keyboard's design reduces the distance your fingers travel for most keystrokes, increasing typing speed.

How can I use my keyboard most efficiently? All keyboards have the standard set of alpha and numeric keys that you regularly use when typing. As shown in Figure 2.3, there are also other keys on a keyboard that have special functions. Knowing how to use these special keys will help you improve your efficiency:

- The **numeric keypad** allows you to enter numbers quickly.

- **Function keys** act as shortcut keys you press to perform special tasks. They are sometimes referred to as the "F" keys because they start with the letter *F* followed by a number. Each software appli-

BITS AND BYTES

Keeping Your Keyboard Clean

To keep your computer running at its best, it's important that you occasionally clean your keyboard. To do so, follow these steps:

1. Turn off your computer.
2. Disconnect the keyboard from your system.
3. Turn the keyboard upside down and *gently* shake out any loose debris. You may want to spray hard-to-reach places with compressed air (found in any computer store) or use a vacuum device made especially for computers. Don't use your home vacuum because the suction is too strong and may damage your keyboard.
4. Wipe the keys with a cloth or cotton swab lightly dampened with a diluted solution of dishwashing liquid and water or isopropyl alcohol and water. Don't spray or pour cleaning solution directly onto the keyboard. Make sure you hold the keyboard upside down or at an angle to prevent drips from running into the circuitry.

cation has its own set of tasks assigned to the function keys, although some are more universal. For example, the F1 key is usually the Help key in software applications. However, the F4 key performs a different shortcut in Microsoft Word than it does in Microsoft Excel.

- The **Control key** is used in combination with other keys to perform shortcuts and special tasks. For example, holding down

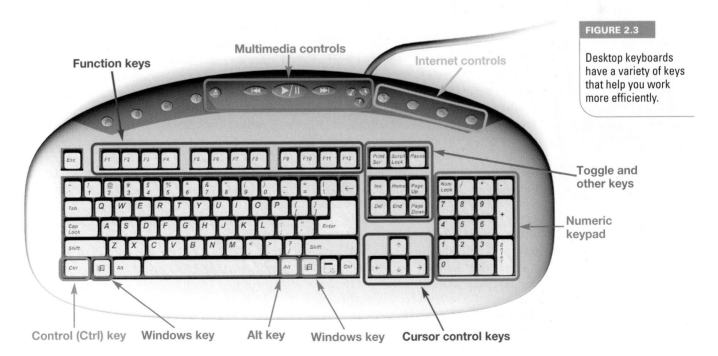

Function keys
Multimedia controls
Internet controls

FIGURE 2.3

Desktop keyboards have a variety of keys that help you work more efficiently.

Toggle and other keys

Numeric keypad

Control (Ctrl) key   Windows key   Alt key   Windows key   Cursor control keys

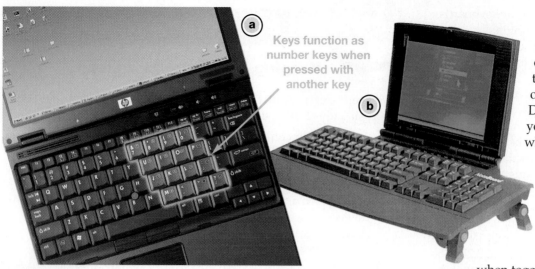

Keys function as number keys when pressed with another key

FIGURE 2.4

(a) Laptop keyboards are more compact than traditional desktop keyboards, and usually don't include extra keys such as the numeric keypad. However, on many laptops, certain letter keys function as number keys when pressed in combination with another key. (b) This full-size keyboard is designed to work with a laptop. With its special folding legs, it sits right on top of your laptop keyboard, allowing you to have all the functionality of a standard keyboard.

the Control key while pressing the letter *B* adds bold formatting to selected text. Similarly, you use the **Alt key** with other keys for additional shortcuts and special tasks. (On Macintosh computers, the Control key is the Apple or Command key and the Alt key is the Option key.)

- The **Windows key** is specific to the Windows operating system. Used alone, it brings up the Start menu; however, it's used most often in combination with other keys as shortcuts. For example, pressing the Windows key plus the letter *E* starts Windows Explorer.

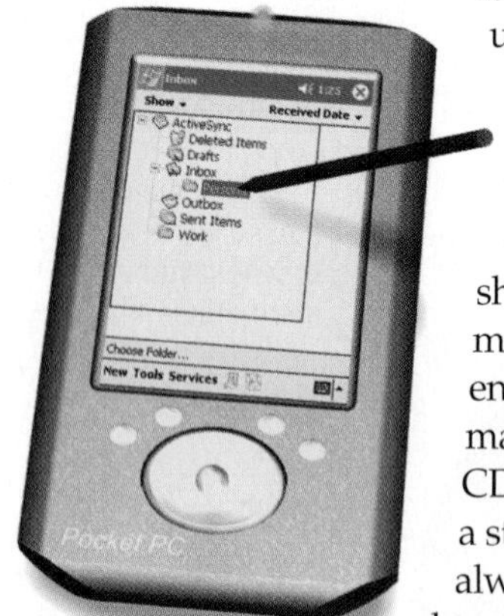

Some keyboards (such as the one shown in Figure 2.3) also include multimedia and Internet keys or buttons that enable you to open a Web browser, view e-mail, access Help features, or control your CD/DVD player. Unlike the other keys on a standard keyboard, these buttons are not always in the same position on every keyboard, but the symbols on top of the buttons generally help you determine their function.

Another set of controls on standard keyboards are the **cursor control keys** that move your **cursor**, the flashing | symbol on the monitor that indicates where the next character will be inserted. The arrow keys move the cursor one space at a time in a document, either up, down, left, or right.

FIGURE 2.5

The stylus is the PDA's primary input device. You use it by tapping or writing on the PDA's touch-sensitive screen.

Above the arrow keys, you'll usually find keys that move the cursor up or down one full page or to the beginning (Home) or end (End) of a line. The Delete (Del) key allows you to delete characters, whereas the Insert key allows you to insert or overwrite characters within a document. The Insert key is a **toggle key** because its function changes each time you press it: when toggled on, the Insert key inserts new text within a line of existing text. When toggled off, the Insert key *replaces* (or overwrites) existing characters with new characters as you type. Other toggle keys include the Num Lock key and the Caps Lock key, which toggle between an on/off state.

Are keyboards different on laptops? Laptop keyboards obviously need to be more compact than standard keyboards and therefore have fewer keys. Still, a lot of the laptop keys have alternate functions so that you can get the same capabilities from the limited keys as you do from the special keys on standard keyboards. For example, many laptop keyboards do not have separate numeric keys. Instead, the letter keys function as number keys when they are pressed in combination with another key (every laptop will be different). The keys you use as numeric keys on laptops have number notations on them so you can tell which keys to use (see Figure 2.4a). You can also hook up traditional keyboards to most laptops, or you can use a specially designed keyboard, shown in Figure 2.4b, that fits on top of the laptop.

What about keyboards for PDAs? Generally, you enter data and commands into a personal digital assistant (PDA) by using a **stylus**, a pen-shaped device that you use by tapping or writing on the PDA's touch-sensitive screen, as shown in Figure 2.5. However, some PDAs have built-in keyboards that allow you to type in text just as you would with a normal keyboard. If your PDA doesn't include a built-in keyboard, you can buy keyboards that attach to the PDA. We'll discuss PDA keyboards in more detail in Chapter 8.

Are there wireless keyboards? As its name indicates, a wireless keyboard doesn't

Keystroke Shortcuts

You may know that you can combine certain keystrokes to take shortcuts within the Windows operating system. The following are a few of the most helpful shortcuts to make your time at the computer more efficient. For more shortcuts for Windows-based PCs, visit **http://support.microsoft.com**. For a list of shortcuts for Mac computers, see **www.apple.com/support**.

Text Formatting	File Management	Cut/Copy/Paste	Windows Controls
CTRL+B Applies (or removes) **bold** formatting to selected text	**CTRL+O** Opens the Open dialog box	**CTRL+X** Cuts (removes) selected text from document	**Alt+F4** Closes the current window
CTRL+I Applies (or removes) *italic* formatting to selected text	**CTRL+N** Opens a new document	**CTRL+C** Copies selected text	**Ctrl+Esc** Opens the Start menu
	CTRL+S Saves a document	**CTRL+V** Pastes selected text (previously cut or copied)	**Windows Key+F1** Opens Windows Help
CTRL+U Applies (or removes) underlining to selected text	**CTRL+P** Opens the Print dialog box		**Windows Key+F** Opens the Search (Find Files) dialog box

use cables to connect to your computer. Rather, it's powered by batteries and sends data to the computer using a form of wireless technology. Infrared wireless keyboards communicate with the computer using infrared light waves (similar to how a remote control communicates with a TV). The computer receives the infrared light signals through a special infrared port. The disadvantage to infrared keyboards is that you need to point the keyboard directly at the infrared port on the computer for it to work.

What are the best wireless keyboards? The best wireless keyboards send data to the computer using radio frequency (RF). These keyboards contain a radio transmitter that sends out radio wave signals. These signals are received by a small receiver device that sits on your desk and is plugged into the back of the computer where the keyboard would normally plug in. Unlike infrared technology, RF technology doesn't require that you point the keyboard at the receiver for it to work. RF keyboards used on home computers can be placed as far as 6 to 30 feet from the computer, depending on their quality. RF keyboards used in business conference rooms or auditoriums can be placed as far as 100 feet away from the computer, but they are far more expensive than traditional wired keyboards.

MICE AND OTHER POINTING DEVICES

What kinds of mice are there? The mouse you're probably most familiar with, like the one shown in Figure 2.6a, has a rollerball on the bottom, which moves when you drag the mouse across a mousepad. The movement of the rollerball controls the movement of your **mouse pointer**, the I-beam or arrow

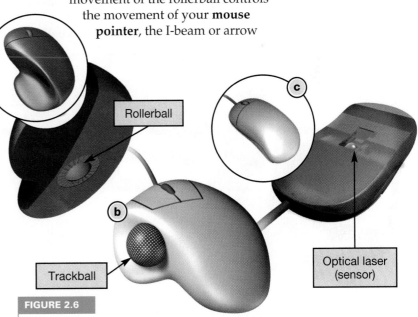

Rollerball
Trackball
Optical laser (sensor)

FIGURE 2.6

(a) A traditional mouse has a rollerball on the bottom, which moves when you drag the mouse across a mousepad. (b) A trackball mouse turns the traditional mouse on its back, allowing you to control the rollerball with your fingers. (c) An optical mouse has an optical laser (or sensor) on the bottom that detects its movement.

Keeping Your Mouse Clean

It's amazing what kind of dirt and grime your rollerball mouse can pick up, even in the cleanest environment. You know your mouse needs cleaning when it becomes sluggish, nonresponsive, or jerky in its motion. To clean your rollerball mouse, follow these steps:

1. Turn your mouse over and remove the rollerball by first turning and removing the surrounding disk.
2. Take a dry cotton swab and remove any loose dust that has accumulated in the ball area.
3. Run a fresh cotton swab lightly dampened in rubbing alcohol over the inside of the ball cavity, concentrating on the rollers.
4. Clean the mouse ball with rubbing alcohol to remove any oil and grime.
5. Let the components dry before putting them back together.

that appears on the screen. Mice also have two or three buttons that enable you to execute commands and open shortcut menus. (Mice for Macintoshes sometimes have only one button.) Some newer mice have additional programmable buttons and wheels that let you quickly scroll through documents or Web pages.

Do I always need a mousepad? It's best to use a mousepad with a traditional rollerball mouse because the mousepad creates the friction needed to move the mouse's rollerball. But you don't need to use a mousepad with every mouse. A **trackball**

mouse, shown in Figure 2.6b, is basically a traditional mouse that has been turned on its back. The rollerball sits on top or on the side of the mouse and you move the ball with your fingers, allowing the mouse to remain stationary. A trackball mouse doesn't demand much wrist motion, so it's considered healthier for the wrists than a traditional mouse.

Another mouse that doesn't use a mousepad is the **optical mouse**, shown in Figure 2.6c. Instead of a rollerball, the optical mouse uses an internal sensor or laser to detect the mouse's movement. The sensor sends signals to the computer, telling it where to move the pointer on the screen. Optical mice are often a bit more expensive than traditional mice, but because they have no moving parts on the bottom, they have small advantages over traditional mice: there is no way for dirt to interfere with the mechanisms and less chance of parts breaking down.

Are there wireless mice? Just as there are wireless keyboards, there are wireless mice, both traditional and optical. Wireless mice are similar to wireless keyboards in that they use batteries and send data to the computer by radio or light waves. If you also have an RF wireless keyboard, your RF wireless mouse and keyboard can share the same RF receiver.

What about mice for laptops? Some laptops incorporate a trackball-like mechanism as a mouse. Others incorporate a **trackpoint**, a small, joystick-like nub that allows you to move the cursor with the tip of your finger.

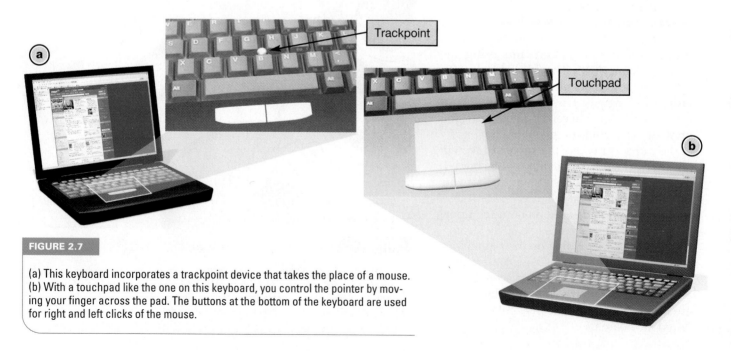

FIGURE 2.7

(a) This keyboard incorporates a trackpoint device that takes the place of a mouse. (b) With a touchpad like the one on this keyboard, you control the pointer by moving your finger across the pad. The buttons at the bottom of the keyboard are used for right and left clicks of the mouse.

Other laptops have a **touchpad**, a small, touch-sensitive screen at the base of the keyboard. To use the touchpad, you simply move your finger across the pad. Some touchpads are also sensitive to taps, interpreting them as mouse-button clicks. Figure 2.7 shows some of the mouse options you'll find in laptops. Of course, if you prefer, you can always hook up a traditional mouse to your laptop as well.

Are game controls considered mice? Game controls (such as joysticks and steering wheels) are not mice per se, but they are considered input devices because they send data to the computer. Force-feedback joysticks and steering wheels deliver data in both directions: they translate your movements to the computer and translate its responses as forces on your hands, creating a richer simulated experience. If you like to move around a lot when you play games, you can purchase wireless game controllers at most computer stores.

Can I use a mouse with a PDA? As we mentioned earlier, the input device you use with PDAs is a *stylus*. You don't use a traditional mouse. However, some PDAs with built-in keyboards do include touchpads and trackpoint controls similar to those found in laptops. Although you can't hook

up a traditional desktop mouse to a PDA, there are micelike devices made especially for PDAs that eliminate the need for a stylus, as shown in Figure 2.8.

INPUTTING SOUND

What's the best microphone to have?
A **microphone** allows you to capture sound waves (such as your voice) and transfer them to digital format on your computer. Microphones come with most computers, but if you didn't get a microphone with your computer, you may want to buy a desktop microphone if you plan to record your own audio files (see Figure 2.9).

A headset microphone is the best type of microphone for videoconferencing and speech-recognition uses. *Videoconferencing technology* allows a person sitting at a computer equipped with a personal video camera and a microphone to transmit video and audio across the Internet (or other communications medium). All computers participating in a videoconference need to have a microphone and speakers installed so that participants can speak to and hear one another.

In *speech-recognition systems*, you operate your computer through a microphone, telling it to perform specific commands (such as to open a file) or to translate your spoken words into data input. Speech recognition has yet to truly catch on, but its popularity is growing. In fact, it's included in the software applications found in Office 2003. We discuss speech-recognition software in more detail in Chapter 4.

Are expensive microphones worth the money? Microphone quality varies widely. For personal use, an inexpensive microphone is probably sufficient. However, if you plan to create professional products and sell them to others, you'll most likely need a more expensive professional recording studio microphone. Speech-recognition software requires a high degree of voice clarity, so it's best to have a headset-style microphone for this application.

ACTIVE HELPDESK

Using Input Devices

In this Active Helpdesk call, you'll play the role of a Helpdesk staffer, fielding calls about different input devices, such as the different mice and keyboards on the market, what wireless input options are available, and how to best use these devices.

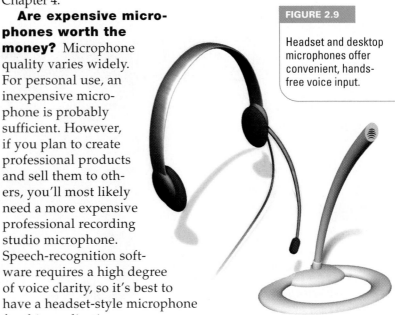

FIGURE 2.9

Headset and desktop microphones offer convenient, hands-free voice input.

FIGURE 2.8

This PDA "mouse" is a stick-on device that offers mouselike controls and eliminates the need for a stylus.

Output Devices

As you learned in Chapter 1, **output devices** enable you to send processed data out of your computer. This can take the form of text, pictures (graphics), sounds (audio), and video. One common output device is a **monitor** (sometimes referred to as a **display screen**), which displays text, graphics, and video as *soft copies* (copies you can see only on-screen). Another common output device is the **printer**, which creates tangible or hard copies (copies you can touch) of text and graphics. Speakers are obviously the output devices for sound.

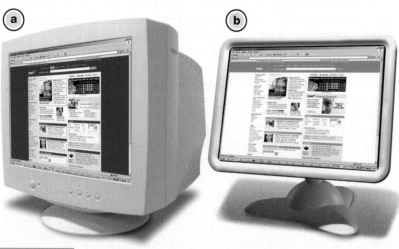

FIGURE 2.10

(a) CRT monitors are big and bulky and look like television sets. (b) LCDs (flat-panel monitors) save precious desktop space and weigh considerably less than CRT monitors.

MONITORS

What are the different types of monitors?
There are two basic types of monitors: CRTs and LCDs. If your monitor looks like a traditional television set, it has a picture tube device called a **cathode-ray tube (CRT)** like the one shown in Figure 2.10a. If your monitor is flat, such as those found in laptops, it's using **liquid crystal display (LCD)** technology (see Figure 2.10b), similar to that used in digital watches. LCD monitors (also called *flat-panel monitors*) are lighter and more energy efficient than CRT monitors, making them perfect for portable computers such as laptops. The sleek style of LCD monitors also makes them a favorite for users with small workspaces.

CRT Monitors

How does a CRT monitor work? A CRT screen is a grid made up of millions of **pixels**, or tiny dots (see Figure 2.11). Simply put, illuminated pixels are what create the images you see on your monitor. There are three pixel colors: red, blue, and green. The pixels are illuminated by an electron beam that passes back and forth across the back of the screen very quickly so that the pixels appear to glow continuously. The various combinations of red, blue, and green make up the components of color we see on our monitors. Figure 2.12 shows in more detail how a CRT monitor works.

What factors affect the quality of a CRT monitor? A couple of factors affect the quality of a CRT monitor. One is the monitor's

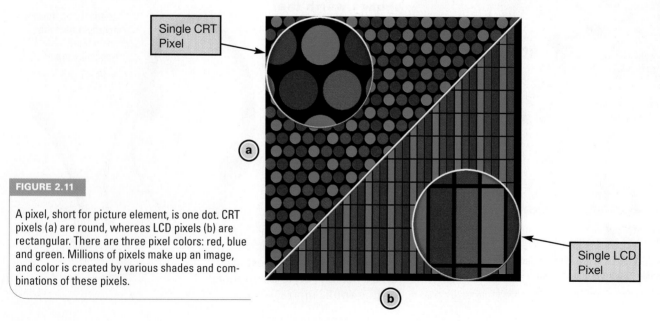

FIGURE 2.11

A pixel, short for picture element, is one dot. CRT pixels (a) are round, whereas LCD pixels (b) are rectangular. There are three pixel colors: red, blue and green. Millions of pixels make up an image, and color is created by various shades and combinations of these pixels.

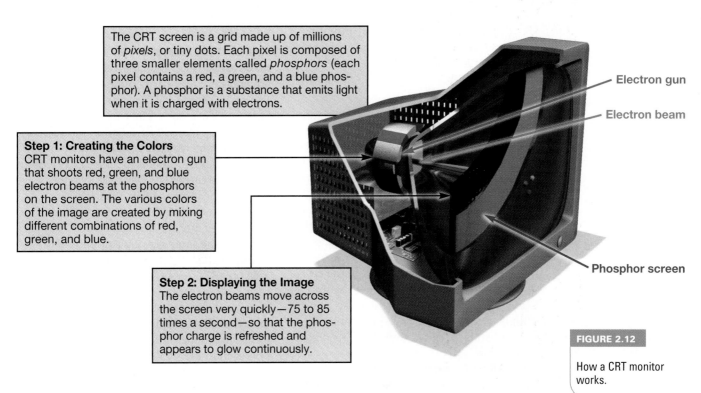

The CRT screen is a grid made up of millions of *pixels*, or tiny dots. Each pixel is composed of three smaller elements called *phosphors* (each pixel contains a red, a green, and a blue phosphor). A phosphor is a substance that emits light when it is charged with electrons.

Step 1: Creating the Colors
CRT monitors have an electron gun that shoots red, green, and blue electron beams at the phosphors on the screen. The various colors of the image are created by mixing different combinations of red, green, and blue.

Step 2: Displaying the Image
The electron beams move across the screen very quickly—75 to 85 times a second—so that the phosphor charge is refreshed and appears to glow continuously.

Electron gun

Electron beam

Phosphor screen

FIGURE 2.12

How a CRT monitor works.

refresh rate. **Refresh rate** (sometimes referred to as *vertical refresh rate*) is the number of times per second the electron beam scans the monitor and recharges the illumination of each pixel. Common monitors have refresh rates that range between 75 and 85 hertz (Hz). Although some monitors have higher refresh rates, they do not offer any significant benefits. Hertz is a unit of frequency indicating cycles per second, in this case meaning the electron beam scans the monitor 75 to 85 times each second. The faster the refresh rate, the less the screen will flicker, the clearer the image will be, and the less eyestrain you'll experience.

The clearness or sharpness of the image—its **resolution**—is controlled by the number of pixels displayed on the screen. The higher the resolution, the sharper and clearer the image. Monitor resolution is listed as a number of pixels. A high-end monitor may have a maximum resolution of $1,600 \times 1,200$, meaning it contains 1,600 vertical columns with 1,200 pixels in each column. Note that you can adjust a monitor's resolution to either make the screen display larger (reducing the resolution) or to fit more on your screen (increasing the resolution). (We discuss setting your monitor's resolution in more detail in Chapter 6.)

Dot pitch is another factor that affects monitor quality. **Dot pitch** is the diagonal distance, measured in millimeters, between pixels of the same color on the screen. A smaller dot pitch means that there is less blank space between pixels, and thus a sharper, clearer image. A good CRT monitor has a dot pitch of 0.28 mm or less.

BITS AND BYTES

Cleaning Your Monitor

Have you ever noticed how quickly your monitor attracts dust? It's important to keep your monitor clean because dust buildup can act like insulation, keeping heat in and causing the electronic components to wear out much faster. To clean your monitor, follow these steps:

1. Shut off the monitor.
2. For a CRT monitor, wipe the monitor's surface using a sheet of fabric softener or a soft cloth dampened with window cleaner or water. Never spray anything directly onto the monitor. (Check your monitor's user manual to see if there are cleaning products you should avoid using.) For an LCD (flat-panel) monitor, use a 50/50 solution of isopropyl alcohol and water on a soft cloth and wipe the screen surface gently.
3. In addition to the screen, wipe away the dust from around the case.

Finally, don't place anything on top of the monitor because the items may block air from cooling it, and avoid placing magnets (including your speaker system's subwoofer) anywhere nears the monitor because they can interfere with the mechanisms inside the monitor.

So, if you're buying a new CRT monitor, choose the one with the highest refresh rate, the highest maximum resolution, and the smallest dot pitch.

LCD Monitors

How does an LCD monitor work? Like a CRT screen, an LCD screen is composed of a grid of pixels. However, instead of including a cathode-ray tube, LCD monitors are made of two sheets of material filled with a liquid crystal solution. A fluorescent panel at the back of the LCD monitor generates light waves. When electric current passes through the liquid crystal solution, the crystals move around, either blocking the fluorescent light or letting the light shine through. This blocking or passing of light by the crystals causes images to be formed on the screen.

Are all LCD monitors the same? You'll generally find two types of LCD monitors on the market: **passive-matrix displays** and **active-matrix displays**. Less expensive LCD monitors use passive-matrix displays, whereas more expensive monitors use active-matrix displays. Passive-matrix technology uses an electrical current passed through the liquid crystal solution to charge groups of pixels, either in a row or a column. This causes the screen to brighten with each pass of electrical current and subsequently fade. With active-matrix displays, each pixel is charged individually, as needed. The result is that an active-matrix display produces a clearer, brighter image with better viewing angles. As the price of active-matrix displays continues to drop, passive-matrix displays will soon become a thing of the past.

LCD vs. CRT

Are LCD monitors better than CRT monitors? LCD monitors have a number of advantages over CRT monitors, as shown in Figure 2.13. Certainly, size is an advantage, because LCD monitors take up far less space on a desktop than a CRT monitor. Additionally, LCD monitors weigh less, making them the obvious choice for mobile devices. LCD technology also causes less eyestrain than the refreshed pixel technology of a CRT.

Because of their different technologies, you can see more of an LCD screen than you can with the same size CRT monitor. For example, there are 17 inches of viewable area on a 17-inch LCD monitor but only 15 inches of viewable area on a 17-inch CRT monitor. LCDs are also more environmentally friendly, emitting less than half the electromagnetic radiation and using less power than their CRT counterparts.

One of the few disadvantages of LCD monitors is their limited viewing angle. Even with the most expensive models, you may have a hard time seeing the screen image clearly from an angle. Additionally, the resolution on a LCD screen is fixed and cannot be modified to the same degree as that of a CRT. CRT monitors also have better color accuracy than LCD monitors.

PRINTERS

What are the different types of printers? There are two primary categories of printers: *impact* and *nonimpact*. **Impact printers** have tiny hammer-like keys that strike the paper through an inked ribbon, thus making a mark on the paper. The most common impact printer is the dot-matrix printer.

FIGURE 2.13 CRT Monitors Versus LCD Monitors

CRT Monitor Advantages	LCD Monitor Advantages
Images viewable from all angles (LCD monitors often have limited viewing angle)	Take up less space and weigh less than CRT monitors
Resolution can be adjusted more completely	Cause less eyestrain than CRT monitors
Better color accuracy and clarity	Are more environmentally friendly than CRT monitors
Better for gaming and watching DVDs due to quicker pixel response time and higher color accuracy	Larger viewable area compared with similar sized CRT (17-inch viewable area on 17-inch LCD monitor compared with 15-inch viewable area on a 17-inch CRT monitor)

In contrast, **nonimpact printers** don't have mechanisms that strike the paper. Instead, they spray ink or use laser beams to transfer marks onto the paper. The most common nonimpact printers are ink-jet printers and laser printers. Such nonimpact printers have replaced dot-matrix printers almost entirely. They tend to be less expensive, quieter, faster, and offer better print quality than dot-matrix printers.

What were dot-matrix printers used for? You may remember the printers that used paper with perforated edges and track-feed holes down the side. Those were **dot-matrix printers**, the first computer printers. They were revolutionary at the time because they allowed users to print a copy of the information displayed on their computer screens—something that hadn't been possible before. In addition to being slow and noisy, the output of the first dot-matrix printers wasn't nearly as good as that produced by typewriters.

Do people still use dot-matrix printers? Although ink-jet and laser printers have replaced dot-matrix printers for everyday use, dot-matrix printers are still used for printing multipart forms such as invoices or contracts. This is because the pressure of the hammer-like keys can penetrate the multiple layers of paper.

What are the advantages of ink-jet printers? Compared with dot-matrix printers, **ink-jet printers** (see Figure 2.14) are quieter, faster, and offer higher-quality printouts. In addition, even high-quality ink-jet printers are affordable. Ink-jet printers work by spraying tiny drops of ink onto paper. The first ink-jet printers suffered from clogged ink jets, but over time, that problem was resolved. Their initial advantage, which continues today, is that ink-jets print color images. In fact, when

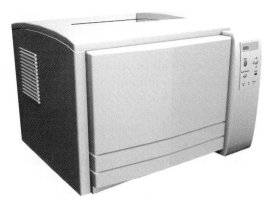

Laser printers print quickly and offer high-quality printouts.

using the right paper, higher-end ink-jet printers print images that look like professional-quality photos. Because of their high quality and low price, ink-jet printers are the most popular printer for color printing.

Why would I want a laser printer? **Laser printers** are often preferred for their quick and quiet production and high-quality printouts (see Figure 2.15). Because they

BITS AND BYTES

Does It Matter What Paper I Print On?

The quality of your printer is only part of what controls the quality of a printed image. The paper you use and the printer settings that control the amount of ink used are equally important. If you're printing text-only documents for personal use, using low-cost paper is fine. You may also want to consider selecting "Draft" mode in your printer setting to conserve ink. However, if you're printing documents for more formal use, such as résumés, you may want to adjust your print settings to "Normal" or "Best" and choose a higher-quality paper. Paper quality is determined by the paper's weight, whiteness, and brightness.

The *weight* of paper is measured in pounds, with 24 pounds being standard. A heavier paper may be best for projects such as brochures, but be sure to check that your printer can handle the added thickness. It is a matter of personal preference as to the degree of paper *whiteness*. Generally, the whiter the paper, the brighter colors appear. However, in some more formal printings such as résumés, you may want to use a creamier color. The *brightness* of paper usually varies from 85 to 94. The higher the number, the brighter the paper and the easier it is to read printed text. Opacity, or thickness of the paper, is especially important if you're printing on both sides of the paper.

If you're printing photos, paper quality can have a big impact on the results. Photo paper is more expensive than regular paper and comes in a variety of textures ranging from matte to high gloss. For a photo-lab look, high-gloss paper is the best choice. Semigloss (often referred to as satin) is good for portraits, whereas a matte surface is often used for black-and-white printing.

Ink-jet printers are popular for home users, especially for color printing.

print quickly, laser printers are often used in schools and offices where multiple computers share one printer. Although more expensive to buy than ink-jet printers, over the long run, for high-volume printing, laser printers are more economical than ink-jets (they cost less per printed black-and-white page) when you include the price of ink and special paper in the overall cost.

What kind of printer could I use for my laptop? Although any printer that is suitable for your desktop is appropriate to use with your laptop, you may want to consider a portable printer for added mobility and flexibility (see Figure 2.16). Portable printers are compact enough to fit in a briefcase, are lightweight, and run on battery power.

Are there wireless printers? Infrared-compatible or wireless printers allow you to print from your handheld device, laptop, or camera. These printers work using Bluetooth, a wireless short-range radio technology we'll discuss in more detail in Chapter 8.

Are there any other types of specialty printers? A **multifunction printer**, or an all-in-one printer, is a device that combines the functions of a printer, scanner, copier, and fax into one machine. Popular for their space-saving convenience, all-in-one printers can be either ink-jet or laser-based.

Plotters are large printers used to produce oversize pictures that require precise

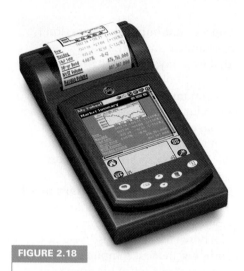

FIGURE 2.18

Thermal printers are ideal for mobile computing because they are compact, lightweight, and require no ink cartridges. Here you see a PDA set into a thermal printer.

continuous lines to be drawn, such as maps or architectural plans (see Figure 2.17). Plotters use a computer-controlled pen that provides a greater level of precision than the series of dots that laser or ink-jet printers are capable of making.

Thermal printers, such as the one shown in Figure 2.18, are another kind of specialty printer. These printers work by either melting wax-based ink onto ordinary paper (in a process called *thermal wax transfer printing*) or by burning dots onto specially coated paper (in a process called *direct thermal printing*). They are used in stores to print receipts and in airports for electronic ticketing, among other places. Thermal printers are also emerging as a popular technology for mobile and portable printing, for example, in conjunction with PDAs. Many models feature wireless infrared technology for complete portability.

Choosing a Printer

How do I select the best printer? There are several factors to consider when choosing a printer:

- **Speed.** A printer's speed determines how many pages it can print per minute (called pages per minute, or ppm). The speed of ink-jet printers has improved over the years so that many ink-jet printers now print as fast as laser printers. Printing speeds vary by model and range from 8 to 30 ppm for both laser and ink-jet printers. Text documents printed in black and white print faster than those documents with color.

FIGURE 2.16

Portable printers are compact and lightweight, allowing you to take them with you when you travel.

FIGURE 2.17

Plotters are large printers used to print oversize images, maps, or architectural plans.

How Ink-Jet and Laser Printers Work

Ever wonder how a printer knows what to print, and how it puts ink in just the right places? Most ink-jet printers use *drop-on-demand* technology in which the ink is "demanded" and then "dropped" onto the paper. Two separate processes use drop-on-demand technology: thermal bubble, used by Hewlett-Packard and Canon, and piezoelectric, used by Epson. The difference between the two processes is how the ink is heated within the print cartridge reservoir (the chamber inside the printer that holds the ink).

In the thermal bubble process, the ink is heated in such a way that it expands (like a bubble) and leaves the cartridge reservoir through a small opening, or nozzle. Figure 2.19 shows the general process for thermal bubble. In the piezoelectric process, each ink nozzle contains a crystal at the back of the ink reservoir that

receives an electrical charge, causing the ink to vibrate and drop out of the nozzle.

Laser printers use a completely different process. Inside a laser printer is a big metal cylinder (or drum) that is charged with static electricity. When you ask the printer to print something, it sends signals to the laser in the laser printer, telling it to "uncharge" selected spots on the charged cylinder, corresponding to the document you wish to print. Toner, a fine powder that is used in place of liquid ink, is attracted to only those areas on the drum that are not charged. (These uncharged areas are the characters and images you want to print.) The toner is then transferred to the paper as it feeds through the printer. Finally, the toner is melted onto the paper. All unused toner is swept away before the next job starts the process all over again.

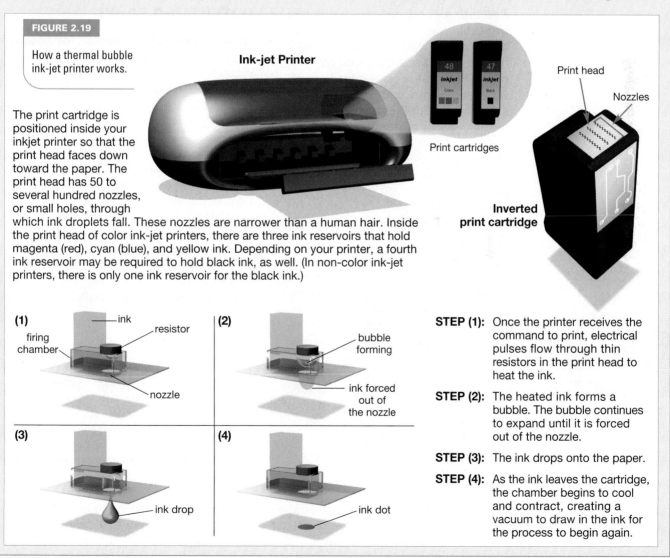

FIGURE 2.19

How a thermal bubble ink-jet printer works.

Ink-jet Printer

Print cartridges

Print head

Nozzles

Inverted print cartridge

The print cartridge is positioned inside your inkjet printer so that the print head faces down toward the paper. The print head has 50 to several hundred nozzles, or small holes, through which ink droplets fall. These nozzles are narrower than a human hair. Inside the print head of color ink-jet printers, there are three ink reservoirs that hold magenta (red), cyan (blue), and yellow ink. Depending on your printer, a fourth ink reservoir may be required to hold black ink, as well. (In non-color ink-jet printers, there is only one ink reservoir for the black ink.)

(1) ink — resistor
firing chamber
nozzle

(2) bubble forming
ink forced out of the nozzle

(3) ink drop

(4) ink dot

STEP (1): Once the printer receives the command to print, electrical pulses flow through thin resistors in the print head to heat the ink.

STEP (2): The heated ink forms a bubble. The bubble continues to expand until it is forced out of the nozzle.

STEP (3): The ink drops onto the paper.

STEP (4): As the ink leaves the cartridge, the chamber begins to cool and contract, creating a vacuum to draw in the ink for the process to begin again.

Maintaining Your Printer

In general, printers require very little maintenance. Occasionally, it's a good idea to wipe the case of the printer with a damp cloth to free it from accumulated dust. However, do not wipe away any ink residue that has accumulated inside the printer. If you are experiencing streaking or blank areas on your printed paper, your print head nozzles may be clogged. To fix this, run the printer's cleaning cycle. (Check your printer's manual for instructions, because every printer is different.) If this doesn't work, you may want to use a cleaning sheet to brush the print head clean. These sheets often come with printers or with reams of photo paper. If you still have a problem, try a cleaning cartridge. Cleaning cartridges contain a special fluid that scrubs the print head. Such cartridges can be found where most ink cartridges are sold (just make sure you buy one that is compatible with your printer).

on an ink-jet printer, 1 to 2 megabytes (MB) of memory should be enough. You need about 4 MB of memory if you expect to print large text-only documents and 8 MB if you print graphic-intense files. Unlike ink-jet printers, laser printers won't print at all without sufficient memory. To ensure your laser printer meets your printing needs, buy one with 16 MB of memory. Some printers allow you to add more memory later.

- **Use and cost.** If you will be printing mostly black-and-white, text-based documents or will be sharing your printer with others, a laser printer is best because of its printing speed and overall economies for volume printing. If you're planning to print color photos and graphics, an ink-jet is the better, more economical choice.

- **Resolution.** A printer's resolution (or printed image clarity) is measured in dots per inch (dpi), or the number of dots of ink in a one-inch line. The higher the dpi, the greater the level of detail and quality of the image. You'll sometimes see dpi represented as a horizontal number multiplied by a vertical number, such as 600×600, but you may also see the same resolution simply stated as 600 dpi. For general-purpose printing, 300 dpi is sufficient. If you're going to print photos, 1,200 dpi is better. The dpi for professional photo-quality printers is twice that.

- **Color output.** If you're using an ink-jet printer to print color images, buy a four-color (cyan, magenta, yellow, and black) or six-color printer (four-color plus light cyan and light magenta) for the highest-quality output. Some printers come with one ink cartridge for all colors, whereas others have two ink cartridges, one for black and one for color. The best setup is to have individual ink cartridges for each color so you can replace only the specific color cartridge that is empty. Color laser printers have separate toner cartridges for each color.

- **Memory.** Printers need memory in order to print. Ink-jet printers run slowly if they don't have enough memory. If you plan to print small text-only documents

ACTIVE HELPDESK

Using Output Devices

In this Active Helpdesk call, you'll play the role of a Helpdesk staffer, fielding calls about different output devices, including the differences between LCD and CRT monitor technologies and between ink-jet and laser printers and the advantages and disadvantages of each.

OUTPUTTING SOUND

What is the output device for sound?

As noted earlier, most computers include inexpensive speakers as an output device for sound. These speakers are sufficient to play the standard audio clips you find on the Web and usually enable you to participate in tele-conferencing. However, if you plan to digitally edit audio files or are particular about how your music sounds, you may want to upgrade to a more sophisticated speaker system, such as one that includes subwoofers (special speakers that produce only low bass sounds) and surround-sound capability (speaker systems set up in such a way that they surround you with sound). We discuss how to evaluate and upgrade your speaker system in more detail in Chapter 6.

The System Unit

We just looked at the components of your computer that you use to input and output data in some form. But where does the processing take place and where is the data stored? The *system unit* is the box that contains the central electronic components of the computer, including the computer's processor (its brains), its memory, and the many circuit boards that help the computer function. You'll also find the power source and all the storage devices (CD/DVD drive, Zip drive, and hard drive) in the system unit.

FIGURE 2.20

System units come in several different designs. (a) A standard tower configuration takes up more room than (b) the Apple iMac G5. However, the closed iMac cannot be easily upgraded.

Which is the best system unit style? Most system units on desktop computers are *tower configurations*, which typically stand vertically (see Figure 2.20a). Some creatively designed desktop system units, such as the Apple iMac (see Figure 2.20b), house not just the computer's processor and memory, but its monitor as well. Although the all-in-ones like the Apple iMac take up less desktop space than the towers, tower configurations make it easier for you to expand your computer. This is because most tower configurations have empty areas that allow you to install additional storage drives such as an additional DVD or CD drive that didn't come with your system.

ON THE FRONT PANEL

What's on the front panel of my computer? No matter whether you choose a desktop or tower design, the front panel of your computer provides you with access to power controls as well as to the storage devices on your computer. Figure 2.21 shows the front panel of a typical system. Although your system might be slightly different, chances are it includes many of the same features.

Power Controls

What's the best way to turn my computer on and off? Your system has a power-on button on the front panel. (You may also find power-on buttons on some keyboards.) Although you use this button to turn *on* your system, you *don't* want to use it to turn *off* (or power off) your system. Modern operating systems want control over the shutdown procedure, so you turn off the power by clicking on a shutdown

icon on the desktop, *not* by pushing the main power button.

If you do shut off the power using the main power button without shutting down your operating system first, nothing on your system will be permanently damaged. However, some files and applications may not close properly, so the operating system may need to do some extra work the next time you start your computer.

Should I turn off my computer every time I'm done using it? Some people say you should leave your computer on at all times. They argue that turning your computer on and off throughout the day

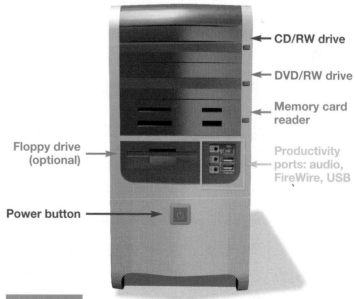

CD/RW drive

DVD/RW drive

Memory card reader

Productivity ports: audio, FireWire, USB

Floppy drive (optional)

Power button

FIGURE 2.21

The front panel of your computer provides you with access to power controls as well as to the storage devices on your computer.

subjects its components to stress as the heating and cooling process forces the components to expand and contract repeatedly. Other people say you should shut down your computer when you're not using it. They claim that you'll end up wasting money on electricity to keep the computer running all the time. However, modern operating systems include power-management settings that allow the most power-hungry components of the system (the hard drive and monitor) to shut down after a short idle period.

So, if you use the computer sporadically throughout the day, it may be best to keep it on when you're apt to use it and power it down when you're sure you won't be using it for long periods. However, if you only use your computer for a little while each day, you'll be paying electricity charges during long periods of nonuse. If you're truly concerned about the stresses incurred from powering on and off your computer, you may want to buy a warranty with the computer, which will undoubtedly cost less than the extra power you'd use to keep your computer constantly running.

Can I "rest" my computer without turning it off completely? As mentioned earlier, your computer has power-management settings that help it conserve energy. These settings are called *standby mode* and *hibernation*. When your computer is in **standby mode**, its more power-hungry components, such as the monitor and hard drive, are put in idle. In essence, the computer is

FIGURE 2.23

When you select Turn Off Computer from the Start Menu in Windows XP, you have three options. For a warm boot, choose Restart. To power down the computer completely, choose Turn Off. You can also choose to put your computer in standby mode to rest the computer without shutting it down completely.

napping. To wake it up, you tap a key on the keyboard or move the mouse.

When the computer is in **hibernation**, it saves an image of your desktop and powers down. When you wake the computer from hibernation (by pushing the power button), the computer reloads everything to your desktop so that it is exactly as it was before it went into hibernation. In Windows XP, you can find the settings for standby and hibernation modes in the Performance and Maintenance option in the Control Panel menu (see Figure 2.22).

What's the restart option in Windows for? If you're using Windows XP, you have the option to *restart* the computer when you select Turn Off Computer from the Start menu (see Figure 2.23). Restarting the system when it's powered on is called a **warm boot**. You might need to perform a warm boot if the operating system or other software application stops responding. It takes less time to perform a warm boot than to power down completely and then restart all of your hardware. You can also perform a warm boot by pressing the Ctrl, Alt, and Delete keys at the same time.

Starting your computer when it has been completely powered down, such as first thing in the morning, is a **cold boot**.

Drive Bays: Your Access to Storage Devices

What else is on the front panel?

Besides the power button, the other features that can be seen at the front of your system

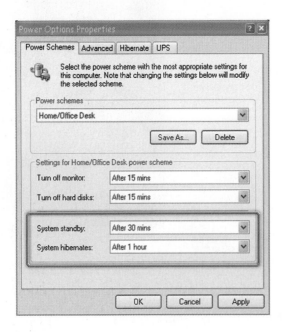

FIGURE 2.22

Using the hibernation and standby settings is not only good for the environment, but it is also good for your pocketbook.

unit are **drive bays**. These bays are special shelves reserved for storage devices, those devices that hold your data and applications when the power is shut off. There are two kinds of drive bays:

1. Internal drive bays cannot be seen or accessed from outside the system unit. Generally, internal drive bays are reserved for the **hard disk drive** (or just **hard drive**). The hard drive holds all permanently stored programs and data.

2. External drive bays can be seen and accessed from outside the system unit. External drive bays house floppy disk and CD drives, for example. Empty external drive bays are covered by a faceplate.

By looking at the front panel of your system unit, you can tell which devices have been installed, and often how many bays remain available for expansion.

What kind of data is saved on the hard disk drive? The hard disk drive is a **nonvolatile storage** device, meaning it holds the data and instructions your computer needs *permanently*, even after the computer is turned off. Today's hard drives, with capacities of up to 500 GB, can hold hundreds of billions of pieces of data.

The hard disk drive is generally installed inside the system unit with all the other drive bays (see Figure 2.24). However, unlike the other drive bays, you can't access the hard disk drive from the outside of the system unit, making it a form of *nonportable* permanent storage.

What kinds of external drive bays do most PCs have? On the front panel, you'll see one or two bays for other storage devices such as CD drives. **CD-ROM drives** read CDs, whereas **CD-RW drives** can both read from and write data to CDs. Some computers may also come with a separate **DVD drive**, which allows them to play DVDs and CDs, or a **DVD-RW drive**, which allows them to both read and write DVDs. DVDs are the same size and shape as CDs but can hold more than 25 times as much data. DVD-RW drives are especially useful if you're creating digital movies. Today, many computers come with a "combo" CD-RW/DVD drive, a device that can read and write CDs and play DVDs.

Some PCs still have a bay for a **floppy disk drive**, which reads and writes to eas-

FIGURE 2.24

The hard disk drive holds all the data and instructions that the computer needs, even after the power is turned off. Although the photo here shows an open hard disk drive, hard disk drives are actually enclosed within the system unit in a hermetically sealed protective case to prevent contamination. In fact, a smoke or dust particle is enough to crash a hard drive.

ily transportable floppy disks, which hold a limited amount of data. Some computers also feature a **Zip disk drive**, which resembles a floppy disk drive but has a slightly wider opening. Zip disks work just like standard floppies but can carry much more data. These storage devices are fast becoming so-called "legacy" technologies and are not standard on many new computers.

Flash drives, sometimes referred to as *jump drives* or *thumb drives*, are the new alternative to storing portable data. These devices are not much larger than your thumb, and can hold upwards of 4 GB of data. Flash drives conveniently plug into universal serial bus (USB) ports.

Several manufacturers now also include slots on the front of the system unit in which you can insert portable **flash memory cards** such as Memory Sticks and CompactFlash cards. Many laptops also include slots for flash memory cards. Flash memory cards let you transfer digital data between your computer and devices such as digital cameras, PDAs, video cameras, and printers. Although incredibly small—some are just the size of a postage stamp—these memory cards have capacities that match or exceed that of a CD. We discuss flash memory in more detail in Chapter 8.

Figure 2.25 shows the storage capacities of the various portable storage media (such as floppy disks and CD-ROMs) used in your computer's drive bays. As you learned in Chapter 1, storage capacity is measured in bytes. A kilobyte (KB) equals about 1,000 bytes, a megabyte (MB) equals about a million bytes, and a gigabyte (GB) equals about a billion bytes.

FIGURE 2.25 **Storage Media Capacities**

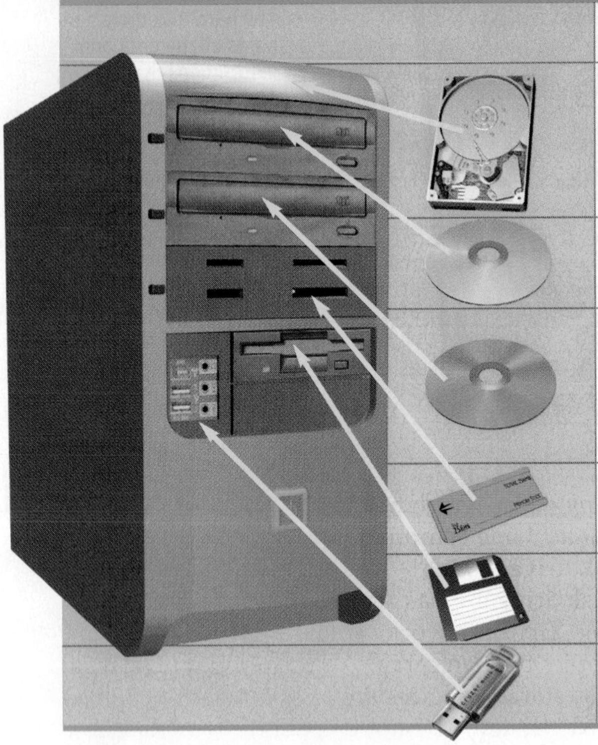

	Storage Medium	Capabilities	Storage Capacity

	Hard Drive	Read and Write	External:
			    Up to 2 TB (Terabyte)
			Internal:
			    Up to 500 GB

	CD CD-RW	Read-only Read and write	700 MB

	DVD
	DVD+RW
		Read-only
		Read and write
			4.7 GB (for single-sided
			    single layered DVDs)
			9.4 GB (for single-sided
			    dual layered DVDs)

	Flash Memory Cards	Read and write	16 MB to 8 GB
	Floppy Disk	Read and write	1.44 MB
	USB Drive	Read and write	Up to 4 GB

Ports

What are the ports on the front of my computer for? Ports are the place on the system unit where peripheral devices attach to the computer so data can be exchanged between them and the operating system. Traditionally, ports have been located on the back of the system unit. However, in many new computer models, some commonly-used ports are placed on the front of the computer for easier access when connecting

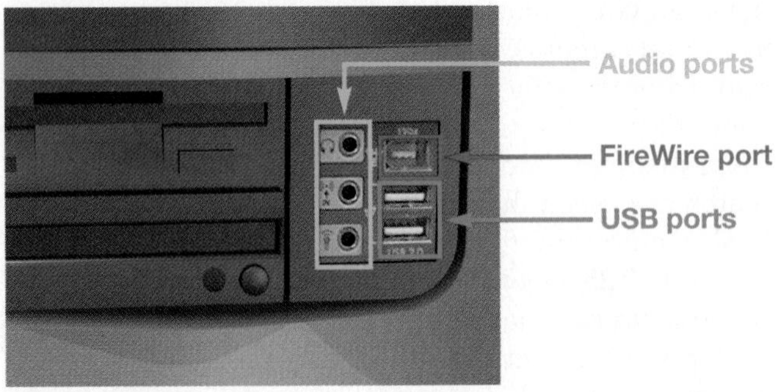

FIGURE 2.26

Front-panel ports allow you to connect easily to your devices.

portable devices such as digital cameras, MP3 players, and PDAs to the computer (see Figure 2.26).

ON THE BACK

What's on the back of my system unit? Peripheral devices, such as monitors, printers, keyboards, and mice, connect to the system unit through ports. Because peripheral devices exchange data with the computer in various ways, a number of different ports have been created to accommodate these devices (see Figure 2.27). Serial ports and parallel ports have long been used to connect input and output devices to the computer. Traditional **serial ports** send data one bit (or piece of data) at a time and are often used to connect modems to the computer. Sending data one bit at a time is a slow way to communicate. Data sent over serial ports is transferred at a speed of 115 kilobits per second (Kbps), or 115,000 bits per second. A **parallel port** sends data between devices in *groups* of bits at speeds of 500 Kbps and is therefore much faster than a traditional serial port.

Parallel ports are often used to connect printers to computers.

Universal serial bus (USB) ports are fast replacing traditional serial and parallel ports as the means to connect input and output devices to the computer. This is mainly because of their ability to transfer data quickly. USB 1.1 ports transferring data at approximately 12 megabits per second, or Mbps (that's 12,000 Kbps), are quickly being replaced by their speedier successor, **USB 2.0** ports. USB 2.0 ports transfer data at 480 Mbps and are approximately 40 times faster than the original USB port. USB ports can connect a wide variety of peripherals to the computer, including keyboards, printers, mice, and digital cameras. Devices with USB 1.1 port connections can connect to USB 2.0 ports and vice versa, but they operate at the USB 1.1 speed.

Which ports help me connect with other computers? Another set of ports on your computer helps you communicate with other computers. Called **connectivity ports**, these ports give you access to networks and the Internet and enable your computer to function as a fax machine. To find connectivity ports, look for a port that resembles a standard phone jack. This jack is the **modem port**. It uses a traditional telephone signal to connect two computers.

Most computers now come configured with a second connectivity port called an **Ethernet port**. This port is slightly larger than a standard phone jack and transfers data up to 100 Mbps. You use it to connect your computer to a DSL/cable modem or a network.

What are the fastest ports available? Newer interfaces such as **FireWire** (or IEEE 1394) and the latest **FireWire 800** are the fastest ports available. The FireWire interface moves data at 400 Mbps, whereas the newer FireWire 800 doubles the rate to 800 Mbps. Devices such as digital video cameras, MP3 players, and digital media players all benefit from the speedy data transfer of FireWire.

What are the other ports on the back? Other ports on the back of the computer include the audio and video ports. The VGA (video graphics array) monitor port is the standard port to which monitors (both CRT and LCD) connect. Audio ports or jacks are where you connect headphones, micro-

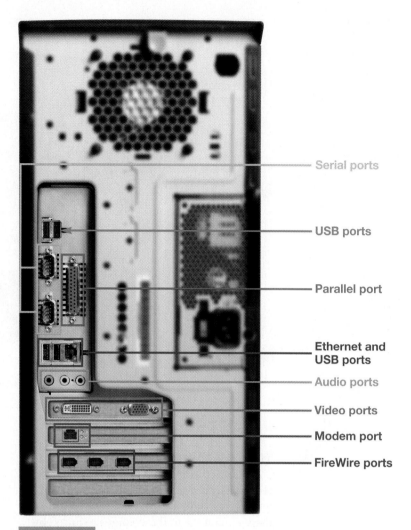

FIGURE 2.27

The back of your computer probably has many or all of these ports, although they may not be in the same places. There are several different ports because many devices exchange data with the computer in various ways. Color coding helps identify the correct device to connect to each port.

phones, and speakers to the computer. We'll explore all the ports on your system unit in more detail in Chapter 6.

SOUND BYTE

Port Tour: How Do I Hook It Up?

In this Sound Byte, you'll take a tour of both a desktop system and a laptop system to compare the number and variety of available ports. You'll also learn about the different types of ports and compare their speed and expandability.

FIGURE 2.28

Inside the system unit.

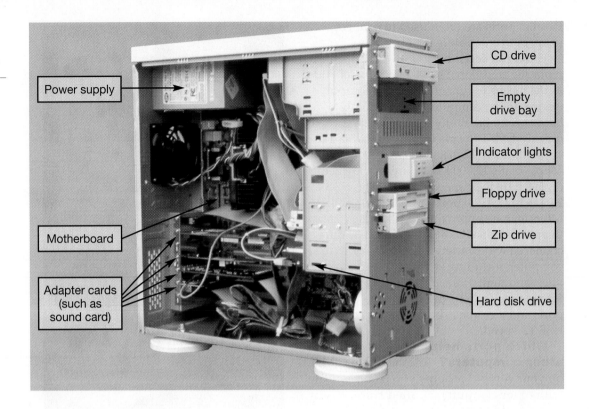

Power supply

Motherboard

Adapter cards
(such as
sound card)

CD drive

Empty
drive bay

Indicator lights

Floppy drive

Zip drive

Hard disk drive

INSIDE THE SYSTEM UNIT

What's inside the system unit? Figure 2.28 shows the layout common to many system units. As you can see, the **power supply** is housed inside the system unit to regulate the wall voltage to the voltages required by computer chips. Inside the system unit, you'll also find many printed circuit boards, which are flat, thin boards made of material that won't conduct electricity. On top of this material, thin copper lines are traced, allowing designers to connect a set of computer chips.

The various circuit boards have specific functions that augment the computer's basic functions. Some provide connections to other devices, so these are usually referred to as **expansion cards** (or **adapter cards**). Typical expansion cards found in the system unit are the sound card and video card. A **sound card** provides a connection for the speakers and microphone, whereas a **video card** provides a connection for the monitor. Other expansion cards provide a means for network and Internet connections such as the **modem card**, which provides the computer with a connection to the Internet, and a **network interface card (NIC)**, which enables your computer to connect with other computers.

On the bottom or side of the system unit, you'll find the largest printed circuit board, called the **motherboard**. The motherboard is named such because all of the other boards (video cards, sound cards, and so on) connect to it to receive power and to communicate—therefore, it's the "mother" of all boards.

What's on the motherboard? The motherboard contains the set of chips that powers the system, including the central processing unit (CPU). The motherboard also houses the chips that provide the short-term memory for the computer as well as a set of slots available for expansion cards (see Figure 2.29).

What is the CPU? The **central processing unit** (**CPU**, or **processor**) is the largest and most important chip in the computer. It is sometimes referred to as the "brains" of the computer because it controls all the functions performed by the computer's other components and processes all the commands issued to it by software instructions. Modern CPUs can perform three billion tasks a second without error, making them extremely powerful components.

What exactly is RAM? Because the CPU processes data so rapidly, there needs to be a way to store data and commands nearby so they can be fed to the CPU very quickly. **Random access memory (RAM)** is that storage space. If you look at a mother-

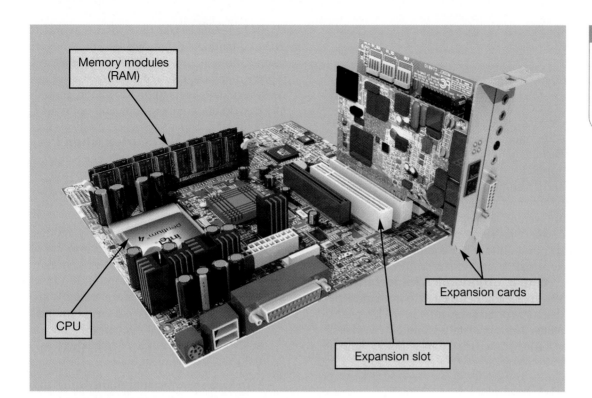

FIGURE 2.29

A motherboard contains the CPU, the memory (RAM) cards, and slots available for expansion cards.

Memory modules (RAM)

CPU

Expansion cards

Expansion slot

board, you'll see RAM as a series of small cards (called *memory cards* or *memory modules*) plugged into slots on the motherboard. The CPU can request the contents of RAM, which can be located, opened, and delivered to the CPU for processing in a few billionths of a second (or *nanoseconds*).

Sometimes RAM is referred to as *primary storage* for this reason, but it should not be confused with other types of *permanent* storage devices. Because all the contents of RAM are erased when you turn off the computer, RAM is the *temporary* or **volatile storage** location for the computer. To save data more permanently, you need to save it to the hard drive or to another permanent storage device such as a floppy disk, CD, or flash drive. A more complete discussion on the CPU and RAM is in Chapter 6.

Does the system unit contain any other kinds of memory besides RAM? In addition to RAM, the motherboard also contains a form of memory called **read-only memory (ROM)**. ROM holds all the instructions the computer needs to start up. Unlike data stored in RAM, which is volatile storage, the instructions stored in ROM are permanent, making ROM a *nonvolatile storage* location. As is the case with the hard disk drive, this means it does not get erased when the power is turned off.

SOUND BYTE

Virtual Computer Tour

In this Sound Byte, you'll take a video tour of the inside of a system unit. From opening the cover to locating the power supply, CPU, and memory, you'll become more familiar with what's inside your computer.

BITS AND BYTES

Opening Up Your System Unit

Many people use a computer for years without ever needing to open their system unit. But there are two reasons you might want or need to do so: to replace a defective expansion card or device or to upgrade your computer. If your hard drive or CD-ROM drive fails, with a bit of guidance, you can open the system unit yourself and replace it. Adding additional memory or adding a DVD-RW drive are upgrade procedures that you can do safely at home. However, it's important that you follow the device's specific installation instructions. These instructions will detail any safety procedures you'll need to observe, such as unplugging the computer or grounding yourself to avoid static electricity, which can damage internal components. It's also important to check with the manufacturer of your system to see if opening up the case will void the system's warranty.

Setting It All Up: Ergonomics

It's important that you understand not only your computer's components and how they work together, but also how to set up these components safely. *Merriam-Webster's Dictionary* defines **ergonomics** as "an applied science concerned with designing and arranging things people use so that the people and things interact most efficiently and safely." In terms of computing, ergonomics refers to how you set up your computer and other equipment to minimize your risk of injury or discomfort.

Why is ergonomics important? Workplace injuries related to musculoskeletal disorders occur frequently in the United States. Approximately 1.8 million workers experience such disorders annually, with 600,000 needing to take time off from work. The Occupational Safety and Health Administration, or OSHA (**www.osha.gov**), reports that these types of injuries cost businesses and taxpayers up to $20 billion annually in workers' compensation and up to $40 billion in other expenses such as medical care.

How can I avoid injuries when I'm working at my computer? The following are some guidelines that can help you avoid discomfort, eyestrain, or injuries when you're working at your computer:

- **Position your monitor correctly.** Studies suggest it's best to place your monitor at least 25 inches from your eyes. You may need to decrease the screen resolution to make text and images more readable at that distance. Also, experts recommend the monitor be positioned at eye level or so that it is at an angle 20 to 50 degrees below your line of sight.

- **Purchase an adjustable chair.** Adjust the height of your chair so that your feet touch the floor. (You may need to use a footrest to get the right position.) Back support needs to be adjustable so that you can position it to support your lumbar (lower back) region. You should also be able to move the seat or adjust the back so you can sit without exerting pressure on your knees. If your chair doesn't adjust, placing a pillow behind your back can provide the same support.

- **Assume a proper position when typing.** A repetitive strain injury (RSI) is a painful condition caused by repetitive or awkward movements of a part of the body. Improperly positioned keyboards are one of the leading causes of RSIs in computer users. Your wrists should be flat (unbent) with respect to the keyboard and your forearms parallel to the floor. You can either adjust the height of your chair or install a height-adjustable keyboard tray to ensure a proper position. Specially designed ergonomic keyboards and wrist rests like the ones shown in Figure 2.30 can help you achieve the proper position of your wrists.

- **Take breaks from computer tasks.** Remaining in the same position for long periods of time increases stress on your body. Shift your position in your chair and stretch your hands and fingers periodically. Likewise, staring at

FIGURE 2.30

(a) Ergonomic keyboards that curve and contain built-in wrist rests help you maintain proper hand position to minimize strain on your wrists. (b) If your keyboard does not come with a wrist rest, you can buy one separately. Wrist rests are positioned next to the keyboard and help support the wrists to keep them flat.

Wrist rest

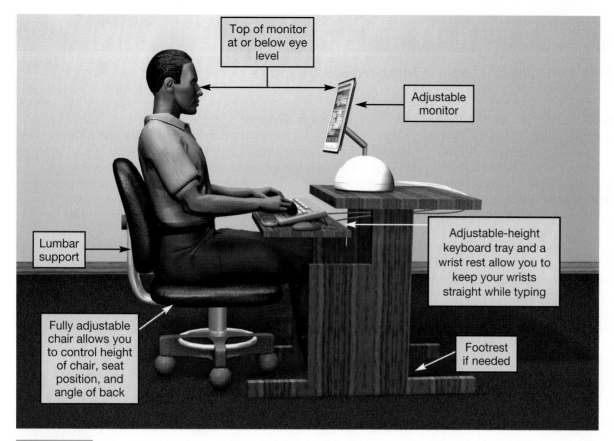

Top of monitor at or below eye level

Adjustable monitor

Lumbar support

Fully adjustable chair allows you to control height of chair, seat position, and angle of back

Adjustable-height keyboard tray and a wrist rest allow you to keep your wrists straight while typing

Footrest if needed

FIGURE 2.31

Achieving comfort and a proper typing position is the way to avoid repetitive strain injuries and other aches and pains when working at a computer. To achieve this, obtain equipment that boasts as many adjustments as possible. Every person is a different shape and size, requiring each workspace to be individually tailored. Additionally, look for ergonomically correct peripheral devices such as keyboards, wrist rests, and anti-glare screens to facilitate a safe working environment.

the screen for long periods of time can lead to eyestrain, so rest your eyes by periodically taking them off the screen and focusing them on an object at least 20 feet away.

- **Ensure the lighting is adequate.** Assuring proper lighting in your work area is a good way to minimize eyestrain. To do so, eliminate any sources of direct glare (light shining directly into your eyes) or reflected glare (light shining off the computer screen) and ensure there is enough light to read comfortably. If you still can't eliminate glare from your computer screen, you can purchase an anti-glare screen to place over your monitor. Look for ones that

are polarized or have a purplish optical coating for the greatest relief.

Figure 2.31 illustrates how you should arrange your monitor, chair, body, and keyboard to avoid injury or discomfort when you're working on your computer.

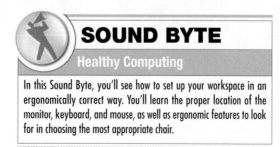

SOUND BYTE

Healthy Computing

In this Sound Byte, you'll see how to set up your workspace in an ergonomically correct way. You'll learn the proper location of the monitor, keyboard, and mouse, as well as ergonomic features to look for in choosing the most appropriate chair.

Emerging Technologies: Tomorrow's Displays

Until the early 2000s, CRT monitors were our only choice for monitors on our computers. Although large and heavy, they provide excellent resolution and clarity. Today, LCD screens have taken the desktop market by storm. First introduced in 2000, these monitors are now out-selling CRTs. Lighter and less bulky than CRT monitors, they can be easily moved and take up less real estate on a desk. Still, current LCD technology does have limitations. LCD screens are relatively fragile and viewing angles are limited. In addition, LCDs can't display full-motion video as well as CRT monitors, making them unpopular with gamers.

Despite their limitations, LCDs will continue to be the predominant display device in the next few years. But according to sources like *PC Magazine*, new technologies are being developed that take LCD displays to the next level.

Flexible Screens

The most promising displays currently under development are *organic light-emitting displays* (*OLEDs*). These displays, currently used in some Kodak cameras, use organic compounds that produce light when exposed to an electric current. OLEDs tend to use less power than other flat-screen technologies, making them ideal for portable battery-operated devices. However, most research is being geared toward *flexible OLEDs* (*FOLEDs*). Unlike LCDs and CRTs, which use rigid surfaces such as glass, FOLED screens would be designed on lightweight, inexpensive, flexible material such as transparent plastics or metal foils. As shown in Figure 2.32, the computer screen of the future might roll up into an easily transported cylinder the size of a pen!

FOLEDs would allow advertising to progress to a new dimension. Screens could be hung where posters

FIGURE 2.32

With FOLED technology, you'll be able to unroll a computer screen wherever you need it from a container the size of a pen. The prototype shown is currently being developed by Universal Display Corporation and may be available within a few years.

are hung now (such as on billboards). And wireless transmission of data to these screens would allow advertisers to display easily updatable full-motion images. Combining transparency and flexibility would also allow these displays to be mounted on windshields or eyeglasses.

There are some obstacles to be overcome before these screens will be widely available. Currently, the compounds that create blue hues age faster than the ones that produce reds and greens. This makes it difficult to maintain balanced colors over time. And the compounds used to form the OLEDs can be contaminated by exposure to water vapor or oxygen. However, once these problems are overcome, flexible displays should be popping up everywhere.

Wearable Screens

Who needs a screen when you can just wear one? Microdisplays are screens that, measured diagonally, are 1 inch or less in size. These displays are currently in use or in development and can be used in head-mounted displays, such as the glasses shown in Figure 2.33. Eventually, these displays could replace heavier screens on laptops, desktops, and even PDAs.

"Bistable" Screens

Your computer screen constantly changes its images when you are surfing the Internet or playing a game. Because PDA and cell phone screens don't necessarily change that often, something called a "bistable" display may one day be used in these devices. A *bistable display* has the ability to retain its image even when the power is turned off. In addition, bistable displays are lighter than LCD displays and reduce overall power consumption, resulting in longer battery life. As the market for portable devices continues to explode, you can expect to see bistable technologies in mobile computer screens.

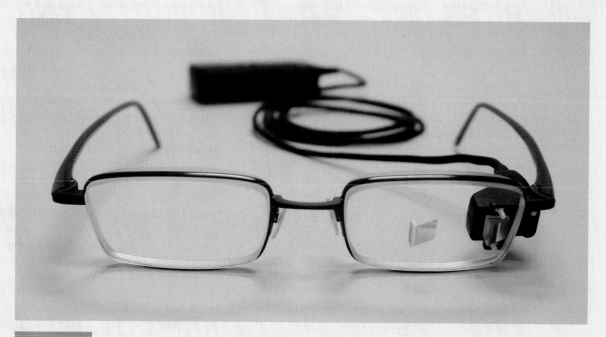

FIGURE 2.33

A prototype developed by MicroOptical Corporation features a microdisplay embedded in a pair of glasses. To users, it appears as though the display is projected right in front of them. Within a few years, you'll be able to buy a microdisplay when you buy glasses.

1. What devices do you use to get data into the computer?

An input device enables you to enter data (text, images, and sounds) and instructions (user responses and commands) into the computer. You use keyboards to enter typed data and commands, whereas you use the mouse to enter user responses and commands. Keyboards are distinguished by the layout of the keys as well as the special keys found on the keyboard. The most common keyboard is the QWERTY keyboard. However, over the years, there has been some debate over what is the best layout for keyboards. The Dvorak keyboard is a leader in alternative keyboards. The Dvorak keyboard puts the most commonly used letters in the English language on "Home Keys," the keys in the middle row of the keyboard.

Laptop keyboards are more compact and have fewer keys than standard keyboards. Still, a lot of the laptop keys have alternate functions so that you can get the same capabilities from the limited number of keys as you do from the special keys on standard keyboards. PDAs use the stylus instead of a keyboard.

Most computers come with a standard rollerball mouse, but you can also find optical mice, trackball mice, and wireless mice. In a trackball mouse, the rollerball sits on top or on the side of the mouse so you can move the ball with your fingers. An optical mouse uses an internal sensor or laser to control the mouse's movement. Wireless mice use batteries and send data to the computer via radio or light waves.

Laptops incorporate the mouse into the keyboard area. Laptop mice include trackball mice, trackpoints, and touchpads.

Microphones are the devices used to input sounds, whereas scanners and digital cameras input nondigital text and images.

2. What devices do you use to get data out of the computer?

Output devices enable you to send processed data out of your computer. This can take the form of text, pictures, sounds, and video. Monitors display soft copies of text, graphics, and video, whereas printers create hard copies of text and graphics.

There are two basic types of monitors: CRTs and LCDs. If your monitor looks like a TV set, it has a picture tube device called a CRT (cathode ray tube). If it is flat, it's using LCD (liquid crystal display) technology. LCD monitors take up less space and are lighter and more energy efficient than CRT monitors, making them perfect for portable computers. However, CRT monitors are less expensive, have higher resolutions, can be viewed at an angle, and offer better color quality.

There are two primary categories of printers: impact and non-impact. Impact printers have hammer-like keys that strike the paper through an inked ribbon. Non-impact printers spray ink or use laser beams to transfer marks on the paper. The most common nonimpact printers are inkjet printers and laser printers. Specialty printers are also available. These include multifunction printers, plotters, and thermal printers. When choosing a printer, you should be aware of factors such as speed, resolution, color output, memory, and cost.

Speakers are the output devices for sound. Most computers include speakers. However, you may want to upgrade to a more sophisticated speaker system, such as one that includes subwoofers and surround-sound.

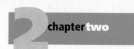

3. What's on the front of your system unit?

The system unit is the box that contains the central electronic components of the computer. On the front of the system unit, you'll find the power source as well as access to the storage devices in your computer. Most PCs include one or two bays for storage devices such as CD drives and DVD drives. Zip drives and floppy disk drives are becoming legacy technologies and are not found on new computers. Most computers include access to USB and other ports on the front panel, and several manufacturers now also include slots on the front of the system unit into which you can insert portable flash memory cards such as Memory Sticks and Compact Flash cards.

4. What's on the back of your system unit?

On the back of the system unit you'll find a wide variety of ports that allow you to hook up peripheral devices (such as your monitor and keyboard) to your system. The most common ports found on the back of the system unit are serial ports, parallel ports, USB, and connectivity ports.

Traditional serial ports send data one bit (or piece of data) at a time at speeds of 56 Kbps and are used to connect modems to the computer.

Parallel ports send data between devices in *groups* of bits at speeds of 92 Kbps.

USB 1.1 and 2.0 ports are fast replacing serial and parallel ports. At 12 Mbps and 480 Mbps, respectively, they transfer data more quickly than their predecessors.

Firewire 400 and 800 ports provide even faster data transfer at approximately 400 and 800 Mbps, respectively.

Connectivity ports give you access to networks and the Internet and enable your computer to function as a fax machine. Connectivity ports include modem ports and Ethernet ports.

5. What's inside your system unit?

The system unit contains the main electronic components of the computer. On the motherboard, the main circuit board of the system, is the computer's central processing unit (CPU), which coordinates the functions of all other devices on the computer.

RAM, the computer's volatile memory, is also located on the motherboard. RAM is where all the data and instructions are held when the computer is running. ROM, a permanent type of memory, is responsible for housing instructions to help start up the computer.

The hard drive (the permanent storage location) and other storage devices (CD/DVD drives, floppy drives) are also located inside the system unit, as are expansion cards (such as sound, video, modem, and network interface cards) that help the computer perform special functions.

6. How do you set up your computer to avoid strain and injury?

Ergonomics refers to how you arrange your computer and equipment to minimize your risk of injury or discomfort. This includes positioning your monitor correctly, buying an adjustable chair that ensures you have good posture when using the computer, assuming a proper position when typing, and making sure the lighting is adequate. Other good practices include taking frequent breaks as well as using other ergonomically designed equipment such as keyboards.

Buzz Words

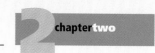

Word Bank

- CPU
- CRT
- Dvorak
- ergonomics
- ink-jet printer
- laser printer

- LCD
- microphone
- monitor
- mouse
- optical
- parallel

- QWERTY
- RAM
- ROM
- speakers
- system unit
- USB

Instructions: Fill in the blanks using the words from the Word Bank above.

Austin had been getting a sore back and stiff arms when he sat at his desk, so he redesigned the (1) _____ of his computer setup. He placed the (2) _____ so that it was 25 inches from his eyes and bought an adjustable chair. He also decided to improve his equipment in other ways. His (3) _____ was old, so he replaced it with a(n) (4) _____ mouse that didn't need a mousepad. To plug in the mouse, he used a(n) (5) _____ port on the back of his (6) _____ . He considered buying an alternative keyboard to replace the (7) _____ keyboard he got with his computer, but he didn't know much about alternative keyboards like the (8) _____ keyboard, so he decided to wait.

Because he often printed flyers for his band, Austin decided to buy a printer that could print text-based pages quickly. Although he decided to keep his (9) _____ to print photos, he decided to buy a new (10) _____ to print his flyers faster. When looking at printers, Austin also noticed (11) _____ monitors that would take up less space on his desk than the (12) _____ monitor he had. Unfortunately, he couldn't afford to buy a new monitor. However, he decided he could afford new (13) _____ , because the ones that came with his computer didn't have subwoofers. He bought a professional (14) _____ a while back so he could record music at home. Finally, knowing his system could use more memory, Austin checked out prices for additional (15) _____ .

Becoming Computer Fluent

Your parents live a day's drive from your school and have just called asking you for help in setting up their new computer.

  Instructions: Because you can't help them in person, prepare a setup guide for your parents as either a Word document or slide presentation. Your setup guide should have all the components of a computer system illustrated and defined. In addition, you should describe with illustrations and words the various ports your parents will need to use to attach various peripheral devices to the system unit. You may use the Internet for information, device pictures, and illustrations, but remember to credit all sources at the end of your guide.

Instructions: Answer the multiple choice and true/false questions below for more practice with key terms and concepts from this chapter.

MULTIPLE CHOICE

1. Which devices below are considered input devices?
   a. mouse and monitor
   b. scanner and printer
   c. monitor and scanner
   d. keyboard and microphone

2. Which is a true statement?
   a. The function keys perform the same special tasks in all applications.
   b. The Windows key may be used alone or in combination with other keys as shortcuts.
   c. The Control key when used alone is a shortcut to bring up the Start menu.
   d. All of the above

3. Which is NOT an advantage of an LCD monitor?
   a. has better color accuracy and clarity
   b. causes less eyestrain
   c. has a larger viewable area
   d. None of the above

4. Higher refresh rate of a monitor
   a. controls the clarity of the image
   b. improves color brightness
   c. reduces eyestrain
   d. only a and b
   e. only a and c

5. Restarting the system when it's powered on is called
   a. a cold boot
   b. a warm boot
   c. hibernation
   d. stand-by

6. The modem port and the Ethernet port are considered
   a. connectivity ports
   b. universal serial bus ports
   c. FireWire ports
   d. parallel ports

7. Which of the following are the fastest ports?
   a. USB 2.0 and parallel ports
   b. USB 1.1 and Ethernet ports
   c. USB 2.0 and FireWire ports
   d. FireWire and parallel ports

8. Which of the following devices is considered the "brains" of the computer?
   a. random access memory
   b. motherboard
   c. central processing unit
   d. read-only memory

9. The type of device that plugs into a slot on a motherboard is a(n)
   a. accessory card
   b. processing card
   c. expansion card
   d. extension card

10. Which of the following is important to consider when setting up a computer?
    a. ensure the lighting is adequate
    b. position the monitor about 2 feet from your face
    c. adjust the chair for proper support
    d. All of the above
    e. None of the above

TRUE/FALSE

_____ 1. The optical mouse is basically like a rollerball mouse, but the rollerball is on the side or top of the mouse.

_____ 2. Random access memory is permanent storage that is located on the motherboard.

_____ 3. Some flash devices can hold as much information as a CD ROM.

_____ 4. Traditional serial ports are becoming legacy technology.

_____ 5. Ink-jet printers are faster and quieter than laser printers.

Making the Transition to... Next Semester

1. Choosing the Best Keyboard

Once you become more familiar with software products such as Microsoft Office, you may want to migrate to a customized keyboard design. Although keyboards have similar setups, some keyboards provide special keys and buttons to support different users. For example, some keyboards are designed specifically for multimedia use, Internet use, and office use. Which one is best for you?

a. Examine the various keyboard setups at the Microsoft Web site (**www.microsoft.com/hardware/keyboard**). Which keyboard would best suit your needs and why? What features would be most useful to you? How would you evaluate the additional costs vs. the benefits?

b. What advantages would a wireless keyboard give you? How much do wireless keyboards cost? What price would you be willing to pay to go wireless?

c. When would you need a keyboard for your PDA? What is the current price for a portable folding PDA keyboard?

2. Choosing the Best Mouse

On the Web, research the different kinds of mice available and list their special features, functions, and costs. Of these mice, which do you think would be most useful to you? Why?

3. Pricing Computer Upgrades

Investigate the following on the Internet:

a. How much would it cost to add a CD or DVD drive to your computer? Does your system have an extra drive bay to install an extra CD/DVD drive?

b. How much would it cost to buy new 17-inch CRT and LCD monitors? What kind of monitor would be best to view DVDs?

c. How much do various computer speaker systems cost? What speakers would be best to listen to CDs?

d. Do you know whether your current sound card and video card support the new devices? How could you find this out?

4. Exploring Scanners

One input device you did not explore in the text is a scanner. Conduct research on the Web to find out about scanners.

a. What are the different kinds of scanners on the market?

b. What qualities do good scanners have?

c. How much do scanners cost?

d. Create a table comparing all the specifications listed earlier for several different scanners. Highlight the scanner you would be most interested in purchasing.

Making the Transition to... The Workplace

1. PCs vs. Macs

There are two main types of computers in the workplace: PC-style computers (manufactured by a variety of companies) and Apple Macintosh and G Series computers (manufactured by Apple Computer).

a. What system are you used to using?

b. What questions would you need to ask if you walked into a new job and found a different system on your desk?

2. What System Will You Use?

When you arrive at a new position for a company, you'll most likely be provided with a computer. Based on the career you are in now or are planning to pursue, answer the following questions:

a. What kind of computer system would you most like to use (PC, Macintosh, tower configuration, desktop configuration, laptop, PDA, etc.)?

b. What kind of keyboard, mouse, monitor, and printer would you like to have?

c. Would you need any additional input or output devices to perform your job?

3. What Hardware Will You Use?

What types of computer hardware would make your work life more efficient? What adjustments would you need to make on your current system to accommodate those hardware devices? (For example, does your computer have the right kind of port or enough ports to support additional hardware devices?)

4. Choosing the Best Printer

You are looking for a new printer for your home business. You have always had an ink-jet printer, but now that costs for laser printers are dropping, you're considering buying a laser printer. However, you're still unsure because they're more expensive than ink-jet printers, although you've heard that there is an overall cost savings with laser printers when the cost of toner/ink and paper is taken into consideration.

a. Using the Internet, investigate the merits of different ink-jet and laser printers. Narrow in on one printer in each category and note the initial cost of each.

b. Research the cost of ink/toner for each printer. Calculate the cost of ink/toner supplies for each printer, assuming you will print 5,000 black-and-white pages per year. How much will it cost per page of printing, not including the initial cost of the printer itself?

c. Investigate the multipurpose printers that also have faxing, scanning, and copying capabilities. How much more expensive are they than a traditional ink-jet or laser printer? Are there any drawbacks to these multipurpose machines? Do they perform each function as well as their stand-alone counterparts?

d. Based on your research, which printer would be the most economical?

5. Office Ergonomics

Your boss has designated you "ergonomics coordinator" for the department. She has asked you to design a flyer to be posted around the office informing your coworkers of the proper computer setup as well as the potential risks if such precautions are avoided. Create an ergonomics flyer, making sure it fits on an 8.5 × 11 piece of paper.

Critical Thinking Questions

Instructions: Albert Einstein used "Gedanken experiments," or critical thinking questions, to develop his theory of relativity. Some ideas are best understood by experimenting with them in our own minds. The following critical thinking questions are designed to demand your full attention but require only a comfortable chair—no technology.

1. **Keyboard of the Future**

   What do you think the keyboard of the future will look like? What capabilities will it have that keyboards currently don't have? Will it have ports? Cables? Special communications abilities?

2. **Mouse of the Future**

   What do you think the mouse (or other pointing device) of the future will look like? What sorts of improvements on the traditional mouse can you imagine? Do you think there will ever be a day when we won't need mice and keyboards to use our computers?

3. **Storage Devices of the Future**

   How do you think storage devices will change in the future? Will increased storage capacity and decreased size affect the ways in which we use computers?

4. **Computers Decreasing Productivity?**

   Can you think of any situations in which computers actually decrease productivity? Why? Should we always expect computers to increase our productivity? What do you think the impact of using computers would be:

   a. in a third-grade classroom?
   b. in a manager's office for a large chain supermarket?
   c. for a retired couple who purchase their first PC?

5. **"Smart" Homes**

   The Smart Medical Home project of the University of Rochester's Center for Future Health is researching how to use technology to monitor many aspects of your health. The Smart Medical Home is the creation of a cross-disciplinary group of scientists and engineers from the college, the Medical Center, and the university's Center for Future Health. This particular "smart home" includes a sophisticated computer system that helps keep track of items such as eyeglasses or keys, and the kitchen is equipped with a new kind of packaging to signal the presence of dangerous bacteria in food. Spaces between ordinary walls are stuffed with gadgetry, including banks of powerful computers.

   a. What abilities should a smart home have to safeguard and improve the quality of your life?
   b. Could there be potential hazards of a smart home?

6. **Toy or Computer?**

   When do you think a toy becomes a computer? The Microsoft Xbox has a hard disk drive, a CD-ROM, internal RAM, and a built-in Ethernet port. Is this a computer or a toy?

Problem:

As you learned in Chapter 1, there are two major classes of computer systems in the marketplace today: PCs and Apple computers. Many people have chosen one camp with an almost religious fervor. In this exercise, each team will explore the trade-offs between a PC and an Apple computer and defend their allegiance to one system or the other.

Task:

Split your class into two teams:

Team A   is a group of PC diehards. They believe these computers perform as well as Apple systems and cost less, providing better value.

Team B   is a group of hard-working Apple-loving software developers. They believe there are no systems as user friendly and reliable as those made by Apple.

Look at the following list of settings for computer labs. Each team should decide why their particular system would be the best choice in each of these settings.

1. An elementary school considering incorporating more technology into the classroom
2. A small accounting firm expanding into new offices
3. A video production company considering producing digital video
4. A computer system for a home office for an aspiring author

Process:

STEP 1: Form the two teams. Think about what your goals are and what information and resources you need to tackle this project.

STEP 2: Research and then discuss the components of each system you are recommending. Are any components better suited for each particular need? Consider all the input, output, processing, and storage devices. Are any special devices or peripherals required?

STEP 3: Write a summary position paper. For each of the four settings, support your system recommendation for

Team A   Some kind of PC computer system

Team B   An Apple system

Conclusion:

There are a number of competing designs for computer systems. Being aware of the options in the marketplace and knowing how to analyze the trade-offs in different designs allows you to become a better consumer as well as a better computer user.

Multimedia

In addition to the review materials presented here, you'll find additional materials featured with the book's multimedia, including the *Technology in Action* Student Resource CD and the Companion Web site (**www.prenhall.com/techinaction**), which will help reinforce your understanding of the chapter content. These materials include the following:

ACTIVE HELPDESK

In Active Helpdesk calls, you'll assume the role of a Helpdesk operator taking calls about the concepts you've learned in this chapter. You'll apply what you've learned and receive feedback from a supervisor to review and reinforce those concepts. The Active Helpdesk calls for this chapter are listed here and can be found on your Student Resource CD:

- Using Input Devices
- Using Output Devices

SOUND BYTES

Sound Bytes are dynamic multimedia tutorials that help demystify even the most complex topics. You'll view video clips and animations that illustrate computer concepts, and then apply what you've learned by reviewing with the Sound Byte Labs, which include quizzes and activities specifically tailored to each Sound Byte. The Sound Bytes for this chapter are listed here and can be found on your Student Resource CD and on the Companion Web site (**www.prenhall.com/techinaction**):

- Port Tour: How Do I Hook It Up?
- Virtual Computer Tour
- Healthy Computing

COMPANION WEB SITE

The *Technology in Action* Companion Web site includes a variety of additional materials to help you review and learn more about the topics in this chapter. The resources available at www.prenhall.com/techinaction include:

- **Online Study Guide.** Each chapter features an online true/false and multiple-choice quiz. You can take these quizzes, automatically check the results, and e-mail the results to your instructor.

- **Web Research Projects.** Each chapter features a number of Web research projects that ask you to search the Web for information on computer-related careers, milestones in computer history, important people and companies, emerging technologies, and the applications and implications of different technologies.

The History *of* THE PC

Do you ever wonder how big the first personal computer was, or how much the first portable computer weighed? Computers are such an integral part of our lives that we don't often stop to think about how far they've come or where they got their start. But in just 30 years, computers have evolved from expensive, huge machines that only corporations owned to small, powerful devices found in millions of homes. In this Technology in Focus feature, we look at the history of the computer. Along the way, we discuss some developments that helped make the computer powerful and portable, as well as the people who contributed to its development. But first, we start with the story of the personal computer and how it grew to be as integral to our lives as the automobile.

The First Personal Computer: The Altair

Our journey through the history of the personal computer starts in 1975. At that time, most people were unfamiliar with the mainframes and supercomputers that large corporations and the government owned. With price tags exceeding the cost of buildings, and with few if any practical home uses, these monster machines were not appealing or attainable to the vast majority of Americans. But that began to change when the January 1975 cover of *Popular Electronics* announced the debut of the **Altair 8800**, touted as the first personal computer (see Figure 1). For just $395 for a do-it-yourself kit or $498 for a fully assembled unit (about $1,000 in today's dollars), the price was reasonable enough so that computer fanatics could finally own their own computers.

The Altair was a very primitive computer, with just 256 bytes (not *kilo*bytes, just bytes) of memory. It didn't come with a keyboard, nor did it include a monitor or printer. Switches on the front of the machine were used to enter data in unfriendly machine code (strings of 1s and 0s). Flashing lights on the front indicated the results of a program. User-friendly it was not—at least not by today's standards.

Despite its limitations, computer "hackers" (as computer enthusiasts were called then) flocked to the machine. Many who bought the Altair had been taught to program, but until that point had access only to big, clumsy computers. They were often hired by corporations to program "boring" financial, statistical, or engineering programs in a workplace environment. The Altair offered these enthusiasts the opportunity to create their own programs. Within three months, Micro Instrumentation and Telemetry Systems (MITS), the company behind the Altair, received more than 4,000 orders for the machine.

The release of the Altair marked the start of the personal computer (PC) boom. In fact, two men who would play large roles in the devel-

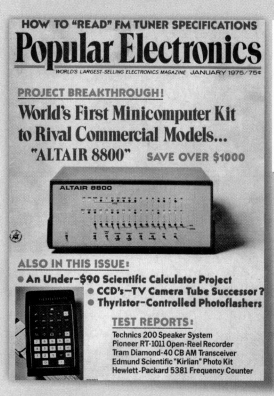

FIGURE 1
In 1975, the Altair was touted as the "world's first minicomputer" in the January issue of *Popular Electronics*.

opment of the PC were among the first Altair owners. Recent high school grads Bill Gates and Paul Allen were so enamored by this "minicomputer," as these personal computers were called at the time, that they wrote a compiling program (a program that translates user commands into those that the computer can understand) for the Altair. The two friends later convinced its developer, Ed Roberts, to buy their program. This marked the start of a small company called Microsoft. But we'll get to that story later. First, let's see what their future archrivals were up to.

Why Was It Called the "Altair"?

For lack of a better name, the Altair's developers originally called the computer the PE-8, short for Popular Electronics 8-bit. However, Les Soloman, the *Popular Electronics* writer who introduced the Altair, wanted the machine to have a catchier name. The author's daughter, who was watching *Star Trek* at the time, suggested the name Altair (that's where the *Star Trek* crew was traveling that week). The first star of the PC industry was born.

The Apple I and II

Around the time the Altair was released, **Steve Wozniak**, an employee at Hewlett-Packard, was becoming fascinated with the burgeoning personal computer industry and was dabbling with his own computer design. He would bring his computer prototypes to meetings of the Homebrew Computing Club, a group of young computer fans who met to discuss computer ideas in Palo Alto, California. **Steve Jobs**, who was working for computer game manufacturer Atari at the time, liked Wozniak's prototypes and made a few suggestions. Together, the two built a personal computer, later known as the **Apple I**, in Wozniak's garage (see Figures 2 and 3). In that same year, on April 1, 1976, Jobs and Wozniak officially formed the **Apple Computer Company**.

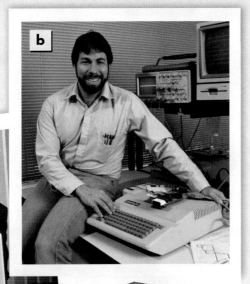

No sooner had the Apple I hit the market than Wozniak was working to improve it. A year later, in 1977, the **Apple II** was born (see Figure 4). The Apple II included a color monitor, sound, and game paddles. Priced around $1,300 (quite a bit of money in those days), it included 4 kilobytes (KB) of random access memory (RAM) as well as an optional floppy disk drive that enabled users to run additional programs. Most of these programs were games. However, for many users, there was a special appeal to the Apple II: the program that made the computer function when the power was first turned on was stored in read-only memory (ROM). Previously, such routine-task programs had to be rewritten every time the computer was turned on. This automation made it possible for the least technical computer enthusiast to write programs.

An instant success, the Apple II would be the most successful in the company's line, outshining even its successor, the **Apple III**, released in 1980. Eventually, the Apple II included a spreadsheet program, word processing, and desktop publishing software. These programs gave personal computers like the Apple functions beyond just gaming and special programming, leading to their increased popularity. We talk more about these advances later. For now, other players were entering the market.

FIGURE 2

Steve Jobs (a) and Steve Wozniak (b) were two computer hobbyists who worked together to form the Apple Computer Company.

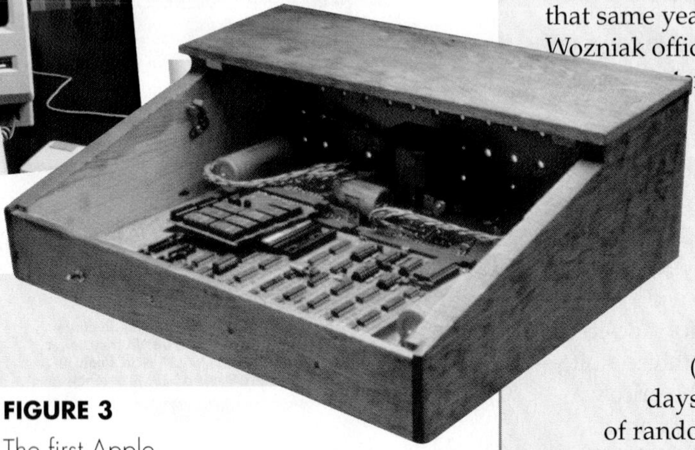

FIGURE 3

The first Apple computer, the Apple I, looked like a typewriter in a box. It was one of the first computers to incorporate a keyboard.

Original Apple II

FIGURE 4

The Apple II came with the addition of a monitor and an external floppy disk drive.

Why Is It Called "Apple"?

Steve Jobs wanted Apple Computer to be the "perfect" computer company. Having recently worked at an apple orchard, Jobs thought of the apple as the "perfect" fruit—it was high in nutrients, came in a nice package, and was not easily damaged. Thus, he and Wozniak decided to name their new computer company Apple.

Enter the Competition

Around the time Apple was experiencing success with its computers, a number of competitors entered the market. The largest among them were Commodore, RadioShack, and IBM. As Figure 5 shows, just years after the introduction of the Altair, the market was filled with personal computers from a variety of manufacturers.

The Commodore PET and TRS-80

Among Apple's strongest competitors were the **Commodore PET 2001**, shown in Figure 6, and Tandy RadioShack's **TRS-80**, shown in Figure 7. Commodore introduced the PET in January 1977. It was featured on the cover of *Popular Science* in October 1977 as the "new $595 home computer." Tandy RadioShack's home computer also garnered immediate popularity. Just one month after its release in 1977, the TRS-80 Model 1 sold approximately 10,000 units. Priced at $599.95, the easy-to-use machine included a monochrome display and 4 KB of memory. Many other manufacturers followed suit over the next decade, launching new desktop products, but none were as successful as the TRS-80 and the Commodore.

FIGURE 5
Personal Computer Development

YEAR	APPLE	IBM	OTHERS
1975			MITS Altair
1976	Apple I		
1977	Apple II		Tandy RadioShack's TRS-80 Commodore PET
1980	Apple III		
1981		IBM PC	Osborne
1983	Lisa		
1984	Macintosh	286-AT	IBM PC clones

FIGURE 6
The Commodore PET was well received because of its all-in-one design.

FIGURE 7
The TRS-80 hid its circuitry under the keyboard. The computer was nicknamed "trash-80," which was more a play on its initials than a reflection of its capabilities.

The Osborne

The Osborne Company introduced the **Osborne** in April 1981 as the industry's first portable computer (see Figure 8). Although portable, the computer weighed 24.5 pounds, and its screen was just 5 inches wide. In addition to its hefty weight, it came with a hefty price tag of $1,795. Still, the Osborne included 64 KB of memory, two floppy disk drives, and preinstalled software programs (such as word processing and spreadsheet software). The Osborne was an overnight success, with sales quickly reaching 10,000 units per month. However, despite the Osborne's popularity, the release of a successor machine, called the **Executive**, reduced sales of the Osborne significantly, and the Osborne Company eventually closed. Compaq bought the Osborne design and later produced its first portable in 1983.

IBM PCs

By 1980, IBM recognized it needed to get its feet wet in the personal computer market. Up until that point, the company had been a player in the computer industry, but primarily with mainframe computers, which it sold only to large corporations. It had not taken the smaller, personal computer seriously. In August 1981, however, IBM released its first personal computer, appropriately named the **IBM PC**. Because many companies were already familiar with IBM mainframes, they readily adopted the IBM PC. The term *PC* soon became the term used to describe all personal computers.

The IBM PC came with 64 KB of memory, expandable to 256 KB, and started at $1,565. IBM marketed its PC through retail outlets such as Sears and Computerland in order to reach the home market, and it quickly dominated the playing field. In January 1983, *Time* magazine, playing on its annual "man of the year" issue, named the computer "1982 machine of the year" (see Figure 9).

FIGURE 8

The Osborne was introduced as the first portable personal computer. It weighed a whopping 24.5 pounds and contained just 64 KB of memory.

FIGURE 9

The IBM PC was the first (and only) nonhuman object chosen as "man of the year" (actually, "machine of the year") by *Time* magazine in its January 1983 issue. This designation indicated the impact the PC was having on the general public.

Other Important Advancements

It was not just the *hardware* of the personal computer that was developing during the 1970s and 1980s. At the same time, advances in programming languages and operating systems and the influx of application software were leading to more useful and powerful machines.

The Importance of BASIC

The software industry began in the 1950s with the development of programming languages such as FORTRAN, ALGOL, and COBOL. These languages were used mainly by businesses to create financial, statistical, and engineering programs for corporate enterprises. But the 1964 introduction of **Beginners All-Purpose Symbolic Instruction Code (BASIC)** revolutionized the software industry. BASIC was a programming language that the beginning programming student could easily learn. It thus became enormously popular—and the key language of the PC. In fact, **Bill Gates** and **Paul Allen** (see Figure 10) used BASIC to write the program for the Altair. As we noted earlier, this program led to the creation of **Microsoft**, a company that produced software for the microcomputer.

The Advent of Operating Systems

Because data on the earliest personal computers was stored on audiocassettes (not floppies), many programs were not saved or reused. Rather, programs were rewritten as needed. Then Steve Wozniak developed a floppy disk drive called the **Disk II**, which he introduced in July 1978. With the introduction of the floppy drive, programs could be saved with more efficiency, and operating systems (OSs) developed.

OSs were (and still are) written to coordinate with the specific processor chip that controlled the computer. Apples ran exclusively on a Motorola chip, while PCs (IBMs and so on) ran exclusively on an Intel chip. **Disk Operating System (DOS)**, developed by Wozniak and introduced in December 1977, was the OS that controlled the first Apple computers. The **Control Program for Microcomputers (CP/M)**, developed by Gary Kildall, was the first OS designed for the Intel

FIGURE 10
Bill Gates and Paul Allen are the founders of Microsoft.

8080 chip (the processor for PCs). Intel hired Kildall to write a compiling program for the 8080 chip, but Kildall quickly saw the need for a program that could store computer operating instructions on a floppy disk rather than on a cassette. Intel wasn't interested in buying the CP/M program, but Kildall saw a future for the program and thus founded his own company, Digital Research.

In 1980, when IBM was considering entering the personal computer market, it approached Bill Gates at Microsoft to write an OS program for the IBM PC. Although Gates had written versions of BASIC for different computer systems, he had never written an OS. He therefore recommended IBM investigate the CP/M OS, but no one from Digital Research returned IBM's call. Microsoft reconsidered the opportunity and developed **MS-DOS** for IBM computers. (This was one phone call Digital Research certainly regrets not returning!)

MS-DOS was based on an OS called **Quick and Dirty Operating System (QDOS)** developed by Seattle Computer Products. Microsoft bought the nonexclusive rights to QDOS and distributed it to IBM. Eventually, virtually all personal computers running on the Intel chip used MS-DOS as their OS. Microsoft's reign as one of the dominant players in the PC landscape had begun. Meanwhile, many other software programs were being developed, taking personal computers to the next level of user acceptance.

The Software Application Explosion: VisiCalc and Beyond

Inclusion of floppy disk drives in personal computers not only facilitated the storage of operating systems, but also set off a software application explosion, because the floppy disk was a convenient way to distribute software. Around that same time, in 1978, Harvard Business School student Dan Bricklin recognized the potential for a spreadsheet program that could be used on PCs. He and his friend Bob Frankston (see Figure 11) thus created the program **VisiCalc**. VisiCalc not only became an instant success, it was also one of the

main reasons for the rapid increase in PC sales. Finally, ordinary home users could see how owning a personal computer could benefit their lives. More than 100,000 copies of VisiCalc were sold in its first year.

After VisiCalc, other electronic spreadsheet programs entered the market. **Lotus 1-2-3** came on the market in 1982, and **Microsoft Excel** entered the scene in 1985. These two products became so popular that they eventually put VisiCalc out of business.

Meanwhile, word processing software was gaining a foothold in the PC industry. Up to this point, there were separate, dedicated word-processing machines, and the thought hadn't occurred to anyone to enable the personal computer to do word processing. Personal computers, it was believed, were for computation and data management. However, once **WordStar**, the first word processing application, came out in disk form in 1979 and was available on personal computers, word processing became another important use for the PC. In fact, word processing is now one of the most common PC applications. Competitors such as **Word for MS-DOS** (the precursor to Microsoft Word) and **WordPerfect** soon entered the market. Figure 12 lists some of the important dates in software application development.

The Graphical User Interface

Another important advancement in personal computers was the introduction of the **graphical user interface (GUI)**, which allowed users to interact with the computer more easily. Until that time, users had to use complicated command- or menu-driven interfaces to interact with the computer. Apple was the first company to take full commercial advantage of the GUI, but competitors were fast on its heels, and soon the GUI became synonymous with personal computers. But who developed the idea of the GUI? You'll probably be surprised to learn that a company known for its photocopiers was the real innovator.

Xerox

In 1972, a few years before Apple had launched its first PC, photocopier manufacturer **Xerox** was hard at work in its Palo Alto Research Center (PARC) designing a personal computer of its own. Named the **Alto** (shown in Figure 13), the computer included

FIGURE 11
Dan Bricklin and Bob Frankston created VisiCalc, the first business application developed for the personal computer.

FIGURE 12
Software Application Development

YEAR	APPLICATION
1978	**VisiCalc:** First electronic spreadsheet application. **WordStar:** First word processing application.
1980	**WordPerfect:** Thought to be the best word processing software for the PC. WordPerfect was eventually sold to Novell, then later acquired by Corel.
1982	**Lotus 1-2-3:** Added integrated charting, plotting, and database capabilities to spreadsheet software.
1983	**Word for MS-DOS:** Introduced in *PC World* magazine with the first magazine-inserted demo disk.
1985	**Excel:** One of the first spreadsheets to use a graphical user interface. **PageMaker:** First desktop publishing software.

a word processor, based on the What You See Is What You Get (WYSIWYG) principle, that was a file management system with directories and folders. It also had a mouse and could connect to a network. None of the other personal computers of the time had any of these features. Still, for a variety of reasons, Xerox never sold the Alto commercially. Several years later, it developed the Star Office System, which was based on the Alto. Despite its convenient features, the Star never became popular, because no one was willing to pay the $17,000 asking price.

The Lisa and the Macintosh

Xerox's ideas were ahead of their time, but many of the ideas of the Alto and Star would soon catch on. In 1983, Apple introduced the **Lisa**, shown in Figure 14. Named after Apple founder Steve Jobs's daughter, the Lisa was the first successful PC brought to market to use a GUI. Legend has it that Jobs had seen the Alto during a visit to PARC in 1979 and was influenced by its GUI. He therefore incorporated a similar user interface into the Lisa, providing features such as windows, drop-down menus, icons, a hierarchical file system with folders and files, and a point-and-click device called a mouse. The only problem with the Lisa was its price. At $9,995 ($20,000 in today's dollars), few buyers were willing to take the plunge.

A year later, in 1984, Apple introduced the **Macintosh**, shown in Figure 15. The Macintosh was everything the Lisa was and then some, and at about a third of the cost. The Macintosh was also the first personal computer to introduce 3.5-inch floppy disks with a hard cover, which were smaller and sturdier than the previous 5.25-inch floppies.

The Internet Boom

The GUI made it easier for users to work on the computer. The Internet provided another reason for consumers to buy computers. Now they could conduct research and communicate with each other in a new and convenient way. In 1993, the Web browser **Mosaic** was introduced. This browser allowed users to view multimedia on the

FIGURE 13
The Alto was the first computer to use a graphical user interface, and it provided the basis for the GUI that Apple used. However, because of marketing problems, the Alto never was sold.

FIGURE 14
The Lisa was the first computer to introduce a GUI to the market. Priced too high, it never gained the popularity it deserved.

Macintosh in 1984

FIGURE 15
The Macintosh became one of Apple's best-selling computers, incorporating a graphical user interface along with other innovations such as the 3.5-inch floppy disk drive.

Web, causing Internet traffic to increase by nearly 350 percent.

Meanwhile, companies discovered the Internet as a means to do business, and computer sales took off. IBM-compatible PCs became the personal computer system of choice when, in 1995, Microsoft (the predominant software provider to PCs) introduced Internet Explorer, a Web browser that integrated Web functionality into Microsoft Office applications, and **Windows 95**, the first Microsoft OS designed to be principally a GUI OS, although it still was based on the DOS kernel.

About a year earlier, in mid-1994, Jim Clark, founder of the computer company Silicon Graphics Inc., Marc Andreessen, and others from the Mosaic development team developed the commercial Web browser Netscape. Netscape's popularity grew quickly, and it soon became a predominant player in browser software. However, pressures from Microsoft became too strong. In the beginning of 1998, Netscape announced it was moving to the open source market, no longer charging for the product and making the code available to the public.

Making the PC Possible: Early Computers

Since the first Altair was introduced in the 1970s, more than a billion personal computers have been distributed around the globe. Because of the declining prices of computers and the growth of the Internet, it's estimated that a billion more computers will be sold within the next decade. But what made all this possible? The computer is a compilation of parts, all of which are the result of individual inventions. From the earliest days of humankind, we have been looking for a more systematic way to count and calculate. Thus, the evolution of counting machines has led to the development of the computer we know today.

The Pascalene Calculator and the Jacquard Loom

The **Pascalene** was the first accurate mechanical calculator. This machine, created by the French mathematician **Blaise Pascal** in 1642, used revolutions of gears to count by tens, similar to odometers in cars. The Pascalene could be used to add, subtract, multiply, and divide. The basic design of the Pascalene was so sound that it lived on in mechanical calculators for more than 300 years.

Nearly 200 years later, **Joseph Jacquard** revolutionized the fabric industry by creating a machine that automated the weaving of complex patterns. Although not a counting or calculating machine, the **Jacquard Loom** (shown in Figure 16) was significant because it relied on stiff cards with punched holes to automate the process. Much later this process would be adopted as a means to record and read data by using punch cards in computers.

Babbage's Engines

Decades later, in 1834, **Charles Babbage** designed the first automatic calculator, called the **Analytical Engine** (see Figure 17). The machine was actually based on another

FIGURE 16

The Jacquard Loom used holes punched in stiff cards to make complex designs. This technique would later be used in the form of punch cards to control the input and output of data in computers.

machine called the **Difference Engine**, which was a huge steam-powered mechanical calculator Babbage designed to print astronomical tables. Babbage stopped working on the Difference Engine to build the Analytical Engine. Although it was never developed, Babbage's detailed drawings and descriptions of the machine include components similar to those found in today's computers, including the store (RAM), the mill (central processing unit), as well as input and output devices. This invention gave Charles Babbage the title of the "father of computing."

Meanwhile, Ada Lovelace, the daughter of poet Lord Byron and a student of mathematics (which was unusual for women of that time), was fascinated with Babbage's Engine. She translated an Italian paper on Babbage's machine, and at the request of Babbage added her own extensive notes. Her efforts are thought of as the best description of Babbage's Engines.

The Hollerith Tabulating Machine

In 1890, **Herman Hollerith**, while working for the U.S. Census Bureau, was the first to take Jacquard's punch card concept and apply it to computing. Hollerith developed a machine called the **Hollerith Tabulating Machine** that used punch cards to tabulate census data. Up until that time, census data had been tabulated in a long, laborious process. Hollerith's tabulating machine automatically read data that had been punched onto small punch cards, speeding up the tabulation process. Hollerith's machine became so successful that he left the Census Bureau in 1896 to start the Tabulating Machine Company. His company later changed its name to International Business Machines, or IBM.

The Z1 and Atanasoff-Berry Computer

German inventor **Konrad Zuse** is credited with a number of computing inventions. His first, in 1936, was a mechanical calculator called the **Z1**. The Z1 is thought to be the first computer to include features that are integral to today's systems, including a control unit and separate memory functions, noted as important breakthroughs for future computer design.

FIGURE 17
The Analytical Engine, designed by Charles Babbage, was never fully developed, but included components similar to those found in today's computers.

In late 1939, John Atanasoff, a professor at Iowa State University, and his student, Clifford Berry, built the first electrically powered digital computer, called the **Atanasoff-Berry Computer (ABC)**, shown in Figure 18. The computer was the first to use vacuum tubes to store data instead of the mechanical switches used in older computers. Although revolutionary at its time, the machine weighed 700 pounds, contained a mile of wire, and took about 15 seconds for each calculation. (In comparison, today's personal computers can calculate more than 300 billion operations in 15 seconds.) Most important, the ABC was the first to use the binary system. It was also the first to

FIGURE 18
The Atanasoff-Berry Computer laid the design groundwork for many computers to come.

have memory that repowered itself upon booting. The design of the ABC would end up being central to that of future computers.

The Harvard Mark I

From the late 1930s to the early 1950s, **Howard Aiken** and **Grace Hopper** designed the Mark series of computers at Harvard University. The U.S. Navy used these computers for ballistic and gunnery calculations. Aiken, an electrical engineer and physicist, designed the computer, while Hopper did the programming. The **Harvard Mark I**, finished in 1944, could perform all four arithmetic operations (addition, subtraction, multiplication, and division).

However, many believe Hopper's greatest contribution to computing was the invention of the **compiler**, a program that translates English language instructions into computer language. The team was also responsible for a common computer-related expression. Hopper was the first to "debug" a computer when she removed a moth that had flown into the Harvard Mark I. The moth caused the computer to break down. After that, problems that caused the computer to not run were called "bugs."

The Turing Machine

Meanwhile, in 1936, the British mathematician **Alan Turing** created an abstract computer model that could perform logical operations. The **Turing Machine** was not a real machine but rather a hypothetical model that mathematically defined a mechanical procedure (or algorithm). Additionally, Turing's concept described a process by which the machine could read, write, or erase symbols written on squares of an infinite paper tape. This concept of an infinite tape that could be read, written to, and erased was the precursor to today's RAM.

The ENIAC

The Electronic Numerical Integrator and Computer (ENIAC), shown in Figure 20, was another U.S. government-sponsored machine developed to calculate the settings used for weapons. Created by **John W. Mauchly** and **J. Presper Eckert** at the University of Pennsylvania, it was placed in operation in June 1944. Although the ENIAC is generally thought of as the first successful high-speed electronic digital computer, it was big and clumsy. The ENIAC used nearly 18,000 vacuum tubes and filled approximately 1,800 square feet of floor space. Although inconvenient, the ENIAC served its purpose and remained in use until 1955.

FIGURE 19

Grace Hopper coined the term *computer bug*, referring to a moth that had flown into the Harvard Mark I, causing it to break down.

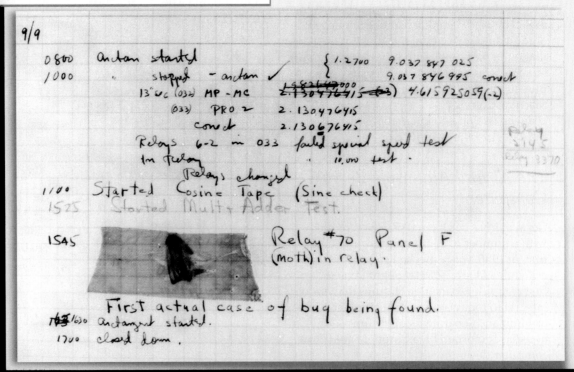

The UNIVAC

The **Universal Automatic Computer**, or **UNIVAC**, was the first commercially successful electronic digital computer. Completed in June 1951 and owned by the company Remington Rand, the UNIVAC operated on magnetic tape (as opposed to its competitors, which ran on punch cards). The UNIVAC gained notoriety when, in a 1951 publicity stunt, it was used to predict the outcome of the Stevenson-Eisenhower presidential race. By analyzing only 5 percent of the popular vote, the UNIVAC correctly identified Dwight D. Eisenhower as the victor. After that, the UNIVAC soon became a household name. The UNIVAC and computers like it were considered **first-generation computers** and were the last to use vacuum tubes to store data.

FIGURE 20

The ENIAC took up an entire room and required several people to manipulate it.

Transistors and Beyond

Only a year after the ENIAC was completed, scientists at the Bell Telephone Laboratories in New Jersey invented the **transistor** as a means to store data. The transistor replaced the bulky vacuum tubes of earlier computers and was smaller and more powerful. It was used in almost everything, from radios to phones. Computers that used transistors were referred to as **second-generation computers**. Still, transistors were limited as to how small they could be made.

A few years later, in 1958, **Jack Kilby**, while working at Texas Instruments, invented the world's first **integrated circuit**, a small chip capable of containing thousands of transistors. This consolidation in design enabled computers to become smaller and lighter. The computers in this early integrated circuit generation were considered **third-generation computers**.

Other innovations in the computer industry further refined the computer's speed, accuracy, and efficiency. However, none were as significant as the 1971 introduction by the Intel Corporation of the **microprocessor chip**, a small chip contain-

ing millions of transistors. The microprocessor functions as the central processing unit (CPU), or brains, of the computer. Computers that used a microprocessor chip were called **fourth-generation computers**. Over time, Intel and Motorola became the leading manufacturers of microprocessors. Today, the Intel Pentium 4 chip, shown in Figure 21, contains more than 42 million transistors.

As you can see, personal computers have come a long way since the Altair and have a number of inventions and people to thank for their amazing popularity. What will the future bring? If current trends continue, computers will be smaller, lighter, and more powerful. The advancement of wireless technology will also certainly play a big role in the development of the personal computer.

FIGURE 21

The Pentium 4 chip contains more than 42 million transistors.

3

Using the Internet:

Making the Most of the Web's Resources

Objectives

After reading this chapter, you should be able to answer the following questions:

1. What is the origin of the Internet? **(p. 90)**

2. How does data travel on the Internet? **(pp. 91–92)**

3. What are my options for connecting to the Internet? **(pp. 92–96)**

4. How do I choose an Internet service provider? **(pp. 96–97)**

5. What is a Web browser? **(pp. 97–98)**

6. What is a URL and what are its parts? **(pp. 99–100)**

7. How can I use hyperlinks and other tools to get around the Web? **(pp. 100–101)**

8. How do I search the Internet using search engines and subject directories? **(pp. 102–107)**

9. What are Boolean operators and how do they help me search the Web more effectively? **(pp. 104–105)**

10. How can I communicate through the Internet with e-mail, weblogs, chat, IM, newsgroups, and listservs? **(pp. 107–111)**

11. How do I manage online annoyances like spam, pop-ups, cookies, spyware, and phishing? **(pp. 111–115)**

12. What is e-commerce and what e-commerce safeguards protect me when I'm online? **(pp. 116–117)**

13. What are the various kinds of multimedia files found on the Web and what software do I need to use them? **(pp. 117–118)**

14. What will the Internet of the future look like? **(p. 119)**

ACTIVE HELPDESK

- Connecting to the Internet **(p. 97)**
- Getting Around the Web **(p. 100)**

- Using Subject Directories and Search Engines **(p. 107)**
- Staying Secure on the Internet **(p. 117)**

Interacting with the Internet

It's 10:00 P.M. as Max sits down to begin his online coursework. Although it's been a long day, he likes taking online courses because they let him finish his degree and still keep his full-time job. While downloading the assignment file from the course Web site, he switches to his Instant Messenger (IM) account to see if any of his friends are online. Seeing his friend Tom is logged on, he chats with him for a while. Like a lot of his friends, Max has become a fan of IM. He uses it almost as much as he does e-mail.

Still waiting for his file to finish downloading, he visits ESPN.com to check out the score of the Red Sox game. He then goes to his favorite search engine, Google, and starts researching the topic he plans to write about for his class. As he conducts his searches, he experiments with some Web search techniques he learned about in his online class. He's amazed at how much information he can find when he searches the Web, yet how hard it is to find truly *useful* information.

Finally, Max sees that the assignment file has finished downloading. Tired of waiting what seems like forever for files to download over his modem, he vows to get a faster Internet connection, probably DSL or cable. He checks his e-mail one last time and finds the usual spam as well as a message from the student loan office reminding him his payment is due. He opens Microsoft Internet Explorer and clicks on the link for the bank from his Favorites list. With a few more clicks, he transfers enough money from his savings account to his checking account to cover his payment.

Does this level of Internet interaction sound at all like yours? If you're like many Americans, you use the Internet as much as you do your television, maybe even more. But do you really know how to get the most out of your Internet experience and which connection option is best for you?

In this chapter, you'll learn what you should know about the Internet in order to use it to your best advantage. We'll look at the options you have for connecting to the Internet, as well as what you should know about the companies that provide you with Internet access. We'll then discuss how you can navigate and search the Web effectively so that your time spent on the Internet is useful. Finally, we'll investigate other Internet features you probably use, such as communication technologies (e-mail, IM, and the like), e-commerce, and multimedia experiences. But first, let's start by looking at the origin of the Internet and how data travels across this big network.

SOUND BYTES

- Connecting to the Internet **(p. 97)**
- Welcome to the Web **(p. 100)**
- Finding Information on the Web **(p. 107)**

- Creating a Web-Based E-mail Account **(p. 108)**
- The Best Utilities for Your Computer **(p. 113)**

Internet Basics

You've no doubt been on the Internet countless times. According to the Nielsen/Net Ratings, as of early 2005, nearly 70 percent of American homes were connected to the Internet, a number that grows each day. But what exactly *is* the Internet? The **Internet** is the largest computer network in the world, actually a network of networks, connecting millions of computers from more than 65 countries. Today, most people use the Internet to communicate with others, although online shopping and entertainment activities follow close behind. Yet these uses are a far cry from the original intention of the Internet.

THE ORIGIN OF THE INTERNET

Why was the Internet created? To understand why the Internet was created, you need to understand what was happening in the early 1960s in the United States. In the midst of the Cold War with Russia, military leaders and civilians alike were concerned about a Russian nuclear or conventional attack on the United States. Meanwhile, the U.S. armed forces were becoming increasingly dependent on computers to coordinate and plan their activities. For the U.S. armed forces to operate efficiently, computer systems located in various parts of the country needed to have a reliable means of communication—one that could not be disrupted easily. Thus, the U.S. government funded much of the early research into the Internet to facilitate computer communications for the military.

At the same time, researchers also hoped the Internet would address the problems involved with getting different computers to communicate with each other. Although computers had been networked together since the early 1960s, there was no reliable way to connect computers from different manufacturers because these computers used different proprietary methods of communication. What was lacking was a common communications method that *all* computers could use, regardless of the differences in their individual designs. The Internet was therefore created to respond to these two concerns: to establish a secure form of military communications and to create a means by which all computers could communicate.

Who invented the Internet? The modern Internet evolved from an early "internetworking" project called the **Advanced Research Projects Agency Network (ARPANET)**. Funded by the U.S. government for the military in the late 1960s, ARPANET began as a four-node network involving UCLA, Stanford Research Institute, the University of California at Santa Barbara, and the University of Utah in Salt Lake City. The first real communication occurred in late 1969 between the computer at Stanford and the computer at UCLA. Although the system crashed after the third letter was transmitted, it was the beginning of a revolution that has grown into millions of computers connected to the Internet today.

Although many people participated in the creation of the ARPANET, two men who worked on the project, Vinton Cerf and Robert Kahn, are generally acknowledged as the "fathers" of the Internet. They earned this honor because they were primarily responsible for developing the communications protocols (or standards) in the 1970s that are still in use on the Internet today.

THE WEB VERSUS THE INTERNET

So are the Web and the Internet the same thing? Because the **World Wide Web (WWW** or the Web)** is what we use the most, we sometimes think of the "Net" and the "Web" as being interchangeable. However, the Web is the means we use to access information over the Internet. What distinguishes the Web from the rest of the Internet is (1) its use of common communication protocols (such as TCP/IP) and special languages (such as the Hypertext Markup Language, or HTML) that enable different computers to talk to each other and display information in compatible formats and (2) its use of special links (called *hyperlinks*) that enable users to jump from one place to another on the Web. Other ways to disseminate information over the Internet include communications systems such as e-mail and instant messaging and information exchange technologies such as File Transfer Protocol (FTP) and newsgroups, all of which we discuss later in this chapter.

THE INTERNET'S CLIENTS AND SERVERS

How does the Internet work?

Computers connected to the Internet communicate (or "talk") to each other in a similar fashion as we do when we ask a question and get an answer. Thus, a computer connected to the Internet acts in one of two ways: it is either a **client**, a computer that asks for data, or a **server**, a computer that receives the request and returns the data to the client. Because the Internet uses clients and servers, it is referred to as a **client/server network**. (We'll discuss such networks in more detail in Chapter 7.)

How do computers talk to each other? Suppose you want to access the Web to check out snow conditions at your favorite ski area. As Figure 3.1 illustrates, when you type the Web site address of the ski area in your **Web browser** (software such as Internet Explorer that allows you to access the Web), your computer acts as a *client computer* because you are asking for data from the ski area's Web site. Your browser's request for this data travels along several pathways, similar to interstate highways. The largest and fastest pathway is the main artery of the Internet, called the **Internet backbone**, to which all intermediary pathways connect. All data traffic flows along the backbone and then on to smaller pathways until it reaches its destination, which is the *server computer* for the ski area's Web site. The server computer returns the requested data to your computer by using the most expedient pathway system (which may be different from the pathway the request took). Your Web browser then interprets the data and displays it on your monitor.

How does the data get sent to the correct computer? Each time you connect to the Internet, your computer is assigned a unique identification number.

FIGURE 3.1

How the Internet's client/server network works.

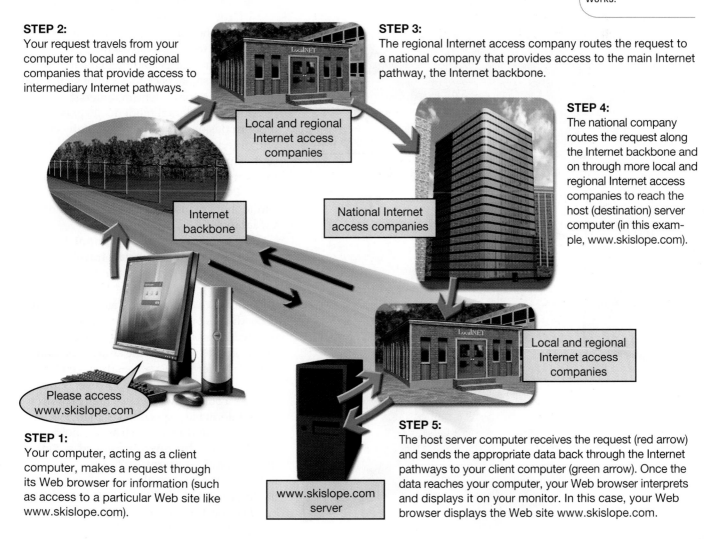

STEP 2:
Your request travels from your computer to local and regional companies that provide access to intermediary Internet pathways.

Local and regional Internet access companies

STEP 3:
The regional Internet access company routes the request to a national company that provides access to the main Internet pathway, the Internet backbone.

STEP 4:
The national company routes the request along the Internet backbone and on through more local and regional Internet access companies to reach the host (destination) server computer (in this example, www.skislope.com).

Internet backbone

National Internet access companies

Local and regional Internet access companies

Please access www.skislope.com

www.skislope.com server

STEP 1:
Your computer, acting as a client computer, makes a request through its Web browser for information (such as access to a particular Web site like www.skislope.com).

STEP 5:
The host server computer receives the request (red arrow) and sends the appropriate data back through the Internet pathways to your client computer (green arrow). Once the data reaches your computer, your Web browser interprets and displays it on your monitor. In this case, your Web browser displays the Web site www.skislope.com.

This number, called an **Internet Protocol (IP) address**, is a set of four numbers separated by dots, such as 123.45.245.91. IP addresses are the means by which all computers connected to the Internet identify each other.

Similarly, each Web site is assigned an IP address that uniquely identifies it. However, because the long strings of numbers that make up IP addresses are difficult for humans to remember, Web sites are given text versions of their IP addresses. So, the ski area Web site mentioned earlier may have an IP address of 234.59.180.37 and a text name of **www.skislope.com**. When you type **www.skislope.com** into your browser window, your computer (with its own unique IP address) looks for the ski area's IP address (234.59.180.37). Data is exchanged between the ski area's server computer and your computer using these unique IP addresses.

CONNECTING TO THE INTERNET

To take advantage of the resources the Internet offers, you need a means to connect your computer to it. Home users have several connection options available. One common method is a **dial-up connection**. With dial-up connections, you connect to the Internet using a standard telephone line. Other connection options, collectively called **broadband connections**, offer faster means to connect to the Internet. Broadband connections include cable, satellite, and DSL.

DIAL-UP CONNECTIONS

How does a dial-up connection work?
A dial-up connection is the least costly method of connecting to the Internet, needing only a standard phone line and a modem (see Figure 3.2). A **modem** is a device that converts (*mod*ulates) the digital signals the computer understands to the analog signals that can travel over phone lines. In turn, the computer on the other end must also have a modem to translate (*dem*odulate) the received analog signal back to a digital signal that the receiving computer can understand.

Although external modems do exist, modern desktop computers generally come with internal modems built into the system unit. Laptops usually use either internal modems or small credit card-sized devices called **PC cards** (sometimes called **PCMCIA cards**) that are inserted into a special slot on the laptop.

Data transfer rate, or **throughput**, is the measurement of how fast data travels between computers. It is also informally referred to as *connection speed*. Current modems have a maximum data transfer rate of 56 kilobits per second (Kbps), usually referred to as 56K. A kilobit is 1,000 bits, normally used to represent the amount of data that is transferred in a second between two telecommunication points. However, when you use a 56K modem, you actually connect to the Internet at a speed lower than 56 Kbps because of interference such as line noise.

What are the advantages of a dial-up Internet connection?
A dial-up connection is the least costly way to connect to the Internet. Although slower than broadband connections, dial-up connections, with today's 56K modems, are often fine for

FIGURE 3.2

Dial-up connection modem options. (a) A dial-up Internet connection uses a standard phone cord that connects a phone jack and your computer's internal modem, which is an expansion card located inside the system unit. (b) Laptops often use small credit-card-sized devices called PC cards to connect to the Internet.

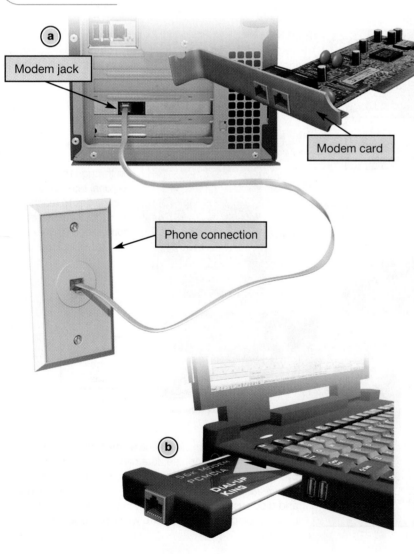

Modem jack

Modem card

Phone connection

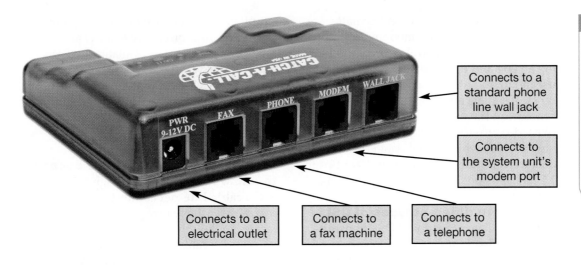

FIGURE 3.3

Connects to a standard phone line wall jack

Connects to the system unit's modem port

Connects to an electrical outlet

Connects to a fax machine

Connects to a telephone

Devices such as Catch-A-Call temporarily place your Internet connection on hold while you answer incoming calls or receive faxes. This makes sharing one phone line for Internet access and phone service less inconvenient.

casual Internet users who do not need a very fast connection.

What are the disadvantages of dial-up? In a word: speed. Even at 56 Kbps, moving through the Internet with a dial-up connection can be a slow and frustrating experience. Web pages can take a long time to load, especially if they contain multimedia. Similarly, if you visit many Web sites at the same time or receive or send large files through e-mail, you'll find that a dial-up connection is very slow. Another disadvantage to dial-up is that when you're on the Internet, you tie up your phone line if you don't have a separate line.

Can I avoid tying up my phone line when I use a dial-up connection? One solution to this problem is to install an additional phone line for your Internet connection. However, this can be costly. Alternatively, if you have a call-waiting feature with your phone service, you can use a device such as Catch-A-Call, shown in Figure 3.3. These devices enable you to receive incoming phone calls without disconnecting from the Internet. When you receive a call, the device displays a flashing red light. To accept the call, you pick up your phone and the device automatically puts your Internet connection on hold.

If neither of these options works for you, you may want to pursue other means of connecting to the Internet besides a dial-up connection, such as broadband connections.

BROADBAND CONNECTIONS

What broadband options do I have?
The two leading broadband home Internet connection technologies are *DSL*, which uses

a standard phone line to connect your computer to the Internet, and *cable*, which uses your television's cable service provider to connect to the Internet. Some users, especially those located in rural areas, connect to the Internet by *satellite*.

DSL

How does DSL work? Similar to a dial-up connection, **DSL** (short for **Digital Subscriber Line**) uses telephone lines to connect to the Internet. However, unlike dial-up, DSL allows phone and data transmission to share the same line, thus eliminating the need for an additional phone line. Phone lines are made of twisted copper wires known as *twisted-pair wiring*. Think of this twisted copper wiring as a three-lane highway with only one lane being used to carry voice data. DSL uses the remaining two lanes to send and receive data separately, at much higher frequencies. Thus, although it uses a standard phone line, a DSL connection is much faster than a dial-up connection.

Can anyone with a phone line have DSL? Just because you have a traditional phone line in your house doesn't mean that you have access to DSL service. Your local phone company must have special DSL technology to offer you the service. Although more phone companies are acquiring DSL technology, many areas in the United States, especially rural ones, still do not have DSL service available.

You also need a special **DSL modem**, like the one shown in Figure 3.4. Although it's called a

FIGURE 3.4

You need a special DSL modem to connect to the Internet using DSL.

modem, a DSL modem doesn't actually function like the dial-up modems described earlier. Rather than modulating/demodulating analog and digital data, DSL modems use modulation techniques to separate the types of signals into voice and data signals so they can travel in the right "lane" on the twisted-pair wiring. Voice data is sent at the lower speed, while digital data is sent at data transfer rates ranging from 500 Kbps to 1.5 megabits per second (Mbps), which is 1,500 Kbps.

Are there different types of DSL service? The more typical DSL transmissions download (or receive) data from the Internet faster than they can upload (or send) data. Such transmissions are referred to as **Asymmetrical Digital Subscriber Line (ADSL)**. Other DSL transmissions, called **Symmetrical Digital Subscriber Line (SDSL)**, upload and download data at the same speed. If you upload data to the Internet often (if you design and update your own Web site, for example), you may want to investigate the range of sending-speed capabilities of your DSL connection, or check to see if your DSL provider offers SDSL service.

What are the advantages to DSL? With data transfer rates that reach 1.5 Mbps, DSL beats the slow speeds of dial-up by a great deal, and with DSL service, you can connect to the Internet without tying up your phone line. In addition, unlike cable and satellite, DSL service does not share the line with other network users in your area. Therefore, in times of peak Internet usage, DSL speed is not affected, whereas cable and satellite hookups often experience reduced speeds during busy times. Additionally, bad weather does not affect DSL service as it can with satellite, and DSL service is less susceptible to the radio frequency interference that hinders cable.

Are there drawbacks to DSL? As mentioned earlier, DSL service is not available in all areas. If you do have access to DSL service, the quality and effectiveness of your service depend on your proximity to a phone company central office (CO). A CO is the place where a receiving DSL modem is located. Data is sent through your DSL modem to the DSL modem at the CO. For the DSL service to work correctly, you must be within approximately three miles of a CO because the signal quality and speed weaken drastically at distances beyond 18,000 feet. A

simple call to your local phone company can determine your proximity to a CO and whether DSL service is available. You can also find out whether DSL is available in your area by checking **www.dsl.com** or **www.getconnected.com**.

Cable

If I have cable TV, do I have access to cable Internet? Although cable TV and a **cable Internet connection** both use *coaxial cable*, they are separate services. In fact, even though you may have cable TV in your home, cable Internet service may not be available in your area. Cable TV is a one-way service in which the cable company feeds your television programming signals. In order to bring two-way Internet connections to homes, cable companies must upgrade their networks for two-way data transmission capabilities and with fiber-optic lines, which transmit data at close to the speed of light along glass or plastic fibers or wires. Because data sent through fiber-optic lines is transmitted at the speed of light, transmission speeds are much faster than are those along other conventional copper wire technologies.

What do I need to hook up to cable Internet? Cable Internet connection requires a **cable modem**, as shown in Figure 3.5. Generally, the modem is located somewhere near your computer. The cable modem is then connected to an expansion (or adapter) card called a **network interface card (NIC)**, located inside your system unit. The cable modem works similarly to a traditional dial-up modem in that it modulates/demodulates the cable signal into digital data and back again. Because the cable TV signal and Internet data can share the same line, you can watch cable TV and be on the Internet at the same time.

Why would I choose a cable connection? The speed of a cable Internet connection is slightly better than the speed of a DSL connection. With cable Internet, you can receive data at speeds up to 4 Mbps and send data at approximately 500 Kbps. As technology improves, these transfer rates also will improve, and some cable companies are already offering data transfer rates of up to 6 Mbps. However, the availability of cable Internet compared to DSL may be the main reason you choose cable. Although cable service is not available in all areas, it is quickly

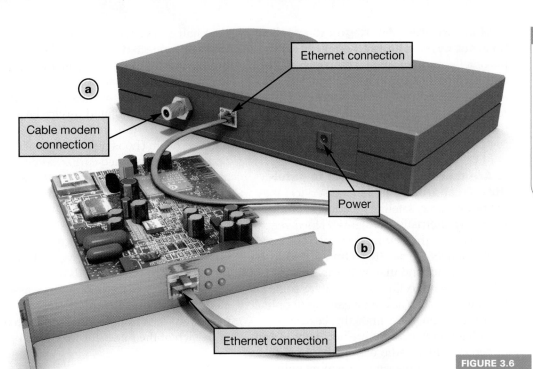

(a)

Ethernet connection

Cable modem
connection

Power

(b)

Ethernet connection

FIGURE 3.5

A cable Internet connection. (a) In order to gain cable Internet access, you need a cable modem. (b) This modem connects to a network interface card located inside your computer's system unit.

rolling out and may be available where DSL is not. Check your local cable TV provider to determine whether cable Internet is available where you live and what the transfer rates are in your area.

Are there any disadvantages to cable Internet? Because you share your cable Internet connection with your neighbors, you may experience periodic decreases in connection speeds during peak usage times. Although your cable Internet connection speeds are still faster than the dial-up alternative, your ultimate speed depends on how many other users are trying to transmit data at the same time as you are.

Satellite

What is satellite all about? Satellite Internet is another way to connect to the Internet. Most people choose satellite Internet when other high-speed options are not available. To take advantage of satellite Internet, you need a satellite dish, which is placed outside your home and connects to your computer with coaxial cable, the same type of cable used for cable TV. As shown in Figure 3.6, data from your computer is transmitted between your personal satellite dish and the satellite company's receiving satellite dish by a satellite that orbits the earth. A major provider for satellite Internet is DirecWay, the same company that offers satellite television.

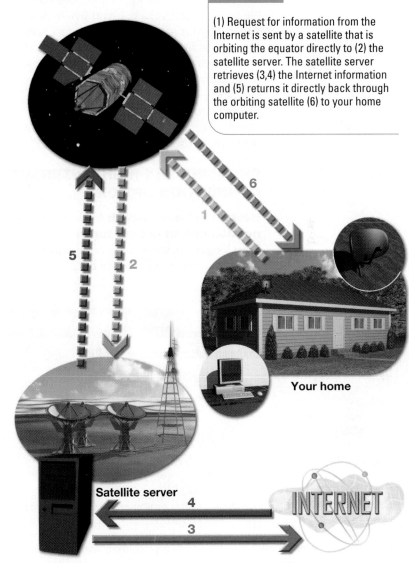

FIGURE 3.6

(1) Request for information from the Internet is sent by a satellite that is orbiting the equator directly to (2) the satellite server. The satellite server retrieves (3,4) the Internet information and (5) returns it directly back through the orbiting satellite (6) to your home computer.

Your home

Satellite server

INTERNET

What are the advantages to satellite Internet connections? Because several major telecommunications companies maintain satellites in orbit above the equator, almost anyone in the United States can receive satellite service. It is therefore a particularly popular choice for those who live in rural areas of the country where neither cable nor DSL service is available.

Are there any drawbacks to satellite? Because other broadband services may not be available, satellite broadband may be your only alternative to dial-up. However, restrictions to this service do apply. Because it takes longer for data to be transferred with satellite broadband than with cable or DSL, this type of connection is not best for some Internet uses such as online gaming or online securities trading. Additionally, because download transmissions are not "wired," but rather are sent as radio waves, the strength and reliability of the signal are more vulnerable to interference. Last, if you live in North America, your satellite dish must face south for the best line of sight to the satellites circling the earth's equator. If high buildings, mountains, or other tall objects obstruct your southern exposure, your signal may be blocked. Unfavorable weather conditions can also block or interfere with the satellite transmission signal.

CHOOSING THE RIGHT INTERNET CONNECTION OPTION

How do I choose which Internet connection option is best for me? Dial-up is no longer the most common means of Internet connection. Already by 2004, more than half of all Americans connecting to the Internet connected with some form of broadband connection. If you are considering switching to broadband, you'll need to consider several factors before deciding which type of broadband service best meets your needs. To start, your location plays the biggest role in choosing among broadband options. As mentioned earlier, some areas aren't able to offer DSL and/or cable Internet service. Additionally, you may need to consider which other services you want bundled into your payment, such as cable or satellite TV, and which service inconveniences you are willing to live with, such as the slower peak time speeds associated with cable and the weather interference associated with satellite. Figure 3.7 shows the maximum data transfer rates associated with each of the Internet connection options.

Finding an Internet Service Provider

Once you have chosen the method by which you'll connect to the Internet, whether it's dial-up or broadband, you need a way to *access* the Internet. **Internet service providers (ISPs)** are national, regional, or local companies that connect individuals, groups, and other companies to the Internet. EarthLink, for example, is a well-known national ISP.

As mentioned earlier, the Internet is a network of networks, and the central component of the Internet network is the *Internet backbone*. The Internet backbone is the main pathway of high-speed communications

FIGURE 3.7	Comparing Residential Internet Connection Options	
Connection Option	Maximum Upload Data Transfer Rate (approximate)	Maximum Download Data Transfer Rate (approximate)
Dial-up	56 Kbps	56 Kbps
DSL (ADSL)	300 Kbps	1 Mbps
DSL (SDSL)	1.5 Mbps	1.5 Mbps
Cable	500 Kbps	6 Mbps
Satellite	100 Kbps	500 Kbps

Note: The data transfer rates listed in this table are approximations. As technologies improve, so too do data transfer rates.

lines through which all Internet traffic flows. Large communications companies, such as AT&T, Quest, and Sprint, are backbone providers that control access to the main lines of the Internet backbone. These backbone providers supply Internet access to ISPs, which, in turn, supply access to other users.

Large businesses and educational facilities connect to the Internet through one of the *regional* ISPs that then connect to the backbone. Local cable and telephone companies fit into this category of regional ISPs.

Home or small business users connect to the Internet through *local* ISPs or through **online service providers (OSPs)**, which are Internet access providers such as America Online (AOL) that have their own proprietary online content.

Where do I find an ISP? If you have a broadband connection, your broadband provider *is* your ISP. If you're accessing the Internet from a dial-up connection, you need to determine which ISPs are available in your area. Look in the phone book, check ads in the newspaper, or ask friends which ISP they use. You're no doubt familiar with many of them already. Additionally, you can go to sites such as **www.thelist.com** or **www.all-free-isp.com** for listings of national and regional ISPs.

How exactly are OSPs different from ISPs? OSPs and ISPs both provide you with access to the Internet so you can visit Web sites and send e-mail. However, OSPs (such as CompuServe, AOL, and Microsoft's MSN) go a step further than standard ISPs by offering unique content and special services and areas that only their subscribers can access. Initially, when getting around the Internet was more cumbersome, the streamlined content and directory-like searching mechanisms OSPs offered were worth the higher monthly fees. Now, with efficient sites such as Yahoo!, many people find it is more cost-effective and equally convenient to connect to the Internet with a local or national ISP.

CHOOSING AN ISP

What factors should I consider in choosing an ISP? If you're in the market for an ISP, you'll need to consider the following:

- How much does the ISP cost for monthly Internet access and what other services does it offer?

- Does the ISP have a local access number so that you can avoid long-distance phone charges while you use the Internet?

- If you travel a lot, does the ISP have local access in the areas where you'll be traveling or an available 800 number to connect to?

- Does the ISP allow you to access your e-mail by using the Web?

- Will you need more than one e-mail account? If so, how many accounts does the ISP provide?

- How are services paid for and how are renewals handled? (For example, does the ISP automatically charge your credit card each month?)

- Are you planning on having a Web site? If so, does the ISP have space for your Web site on its server?

- Is there a trial period? Trial periods enable you to check out availability during peak and off-peak hours before committing to the ISP long-term.

- How is the ISP's customer service? The best ISPs provide customer service that is accessible by phone and the Web.

It's important that you carefully select the right ISP for your needs. Although one ISP may be perfect for your friends, their needs may be different from yours. Remember, too, that changing your ISP can be both time-consuming (you may need to change connections) and inconvenient (if your e-mail address changes, you'll need to notify everyone).

Navigating the Web: Web Browsers

Once you're connected to the Internet and have an ISP to access its services, you're free to explore the many features the Internet has to offer, including the Web. However, in order to explore the Web, you need more than an ISP—you also need a *Web browser*. As defined earlier, a Web browser is software installed on your computer system that allows you to locate, view, and navigate the Web. The most common browser in use today is Microsoft's **Internet Explorer (IE)**. IE is a graphical browser, meaning it can display pictures (graphics) in addition to text, as well as other forms of multimedia, such as sound and video.

SOUND BYTE

Connecting to the Internet

In this Sound Byte, you'll learn the basics of connecting to the Internet from home, including the various types of Internet connections as well as useful information on selecting the right ISP.

ACTIVE HELPDESK

Connecting to the Internet

In this Active Helpdesk call, you'll play the role of a Helpdesk staffer, fielding calls about various options for connecting to the Internet and how to choose an Internet service provider.

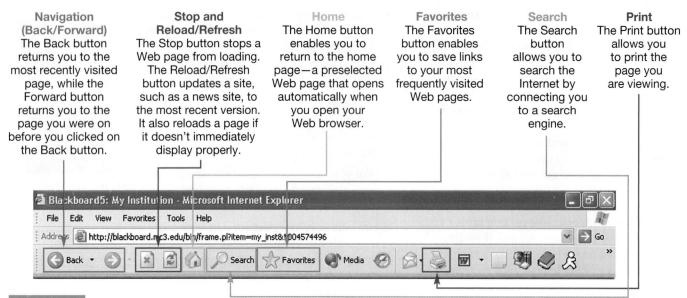

Navigation (Back/Forward)
The Back button returns you to the most recently visited page, while the Forward button returns you to the page you were on before you clicked on the Back button.

Stop and Reload/Refresh
The Stop button stops a Web page from loading. The Reload/Refresh button updates a site, such as a news site, to the most recent version. It also reloads a page if it doesn't immediately display properly.

Home
The Home button enables you to return to the home page—a preselected Web page that opens automatically when you open your Web browser.

Favorites
The Favorites button enables you to save links to your most frequently visited Web pages.

Search
The Search button allows you to search the Internet by connecting you to a search engine.

Print
The Print button allows you to print the page you are viewing.

FIGURE 3.8

Most browsers feature navigational tools, like those shown here for Internet Explorer, that help you find your way around Web pages more efficiently.

What features do browsers offer?
As you can see in Figure 3.8, a browser's toolbars provide convenient navigation and Web page management tools. Whether you are like most surfers using Internet Explorer or are using another Web browser, you will find similar toolbar navigation features on each of the browsers.

What other Web browsers are there?
Although Internet Explorer enjoys predominant market share, there are other browsers to choose from. Firefox, a free browser, and Safari, the default browser for Macs, are quickly gaining popularity. In addition to Internet Explorer, Firefox, and Safari, there are plenty of other browsers you might want to explore:

- Opera (**www.opera.com**) is a browser that has a small but dedicated following. Opera's advantage over IE is that it can preserve your surf sessions: When you launch Opera, it loads and opens all the Web sites you had open when you last used it.

- Lynx (**http://lynx.isc.org**) is an alternative text-only browser that you navigate by highlighting emphasized words on the screen with the up and down arrow keys, and then pressing Enter.

- Netscape Navigator (**www.netscape.com**) used to be one of the more popular browsers. In 1998, in response to pressures from IE, the Netscape Corporation decided to release the source code for the then popular browser and make it available to anyone for free.

- Mozilla (**www.mozilla.org**) began from Netscape's original code but has evolved to include not only browser features but also an e-mail client, an HTML editor, and a chat component. Because of the integration of these extra features, Mozilla is now called Mozilla Suite.

Getting Around the Web: URLs, Hyperlinks, and Other Tools

Unlike text in a Microsoft Word document, which is linear (meaning you read it from top to bottom, left to right, one page after another), the Web is anything but linear. As its name implies, the Web is a series of connected paths or links that connect you to different **Web sites**, or locations on the Web. You gain initial access to a particular Web site by typing in its unique address, or **Uniform Resource Locator** (**URL**, pronounced "you-are-ell"). For example, the URL of the Web site for *Popular Science* magazine is **http://www.popsci.com**. By typing in this URL for *Popular Science* magazine, you connect to the **home page**, or main page, of the Web site. Once in the home page, you can move all around the site by clicking on specially formatted pieces of text called *hyperlinks*. Let's look at these and other navigation tools in more detail.

URLs

What do all the parts of the URL mean? As noted earlier, a URL is a Web site's address. And, like a regular street address, a URL is composed of several parts that help identify the Web document for which it stands, as shown in Figure 3.9. The first part of the URL indicates the set of rules (or the **protocol**) used to retrieve the specified document. The protocol is generally followed by a colon, two forward slashes, *www* (indicating World Wide Web), and then the **domain name**. (Sometimes, the domain name is also thought to include the www.)

What's the protocol? For the most part, URLs begin with *http*, which is short for the **Hypertext Transfer Protocol (HTTP)**. The protocol allows files to be transferred from a Web server so that you can see them on your computer using a browser.

Another common protocol used to transfer files over the Internet is **File Transfer Protocol (FTP)**. FTP is used to upload and download files from one computer to another. FTP files use an FTP file server, whereas HTTP files use a Web server. In order to connect to most FTP servers, you need a user ID and a password. **ftp://ftp.uwp.edu** is a typical FTP address. (In this case, the site is used to transfer files to the University of Wisconsin at the Parkside campus.) To upload and download files from FTP sites, you can use a Web browser (such as Internet Explorer) or file transfer software, such as WS-FTP, Fetch, or CuteFTP.

What's in a domain name? Domain names consist of two parts: the first part indicates who the site's **host** is. For example, in the URL **www.berkeley.edu**, berkeley.edu is the domain name and berkeley is the host. The three-letter suffix in the domain name (such as .com or .edu) is called the **top-level domain (TLD)**. This suffix indicates the kind of organization the host is. Figure 3.10 lists the top-level domains that are currently approved and in use.

As shown in Figure 3.10, there are TLDs for each country in the world. These are two-letter designations such as .uk for the United Kingdom and .us for the United States. Within a country-specific domain, further subdivisions can be made for regions or states. For instance, the .us domain contains subdomains for each state, using the two-letter abbreviation of the state. For example, the URL for the state of Pennsylvania's Web site is **www.state.pa.us**.

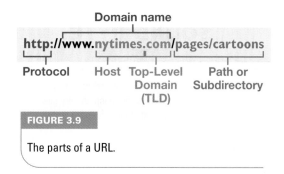

FIGURE 3.9

The parts of a URL.

FIGURE 3.10	Current Top-Level Domains and Their Authorized Users
Domain Name	**Who Can Use the Domain Name**
.aero	Members of the air transport industry
.biz	Businesses
.com	Originally for commercial sites, can be used by anyone now
.coop	Cooperative associations
.edu	Degree-granting institutions
.gov	United States government
.info	Information service providers
.jobs	Posting and recruiting job opportunities
.mil	United States military
.museum	Museums
.name	Individuals
.net	Originally for networking organizations, is no longer restricted
.org	Organizations (often nonprofits)
.pro	Credentialed professionals
.travel	Travel-related services
.uk	United Kingdom country code
.us	United States country code

Note: For a full listing of country codes, refer to **http://www.norid.no/domenenavnbaser/domreg.html**

SOUND BYTE

Welcome to the Web

In this Sound Byte, you'll visit the Web in a series of guided tours of useful Web sites. This tour serves as an introductory guide for Web newcomers as well as a great resource for more experienced users.

ACTIVE HELPDESK

Getting Around the Web

In this Active Helpdesk call, you'll play the role of a Helpdesk staffer, fielding calls about Web browsers, URLs, and how to use hyperlinks and other tools to get around the Web.

What's the information after the domain name that I sometimes see? When the URL is only the domain name (such as **www.nytimes.com**), you are requesting a site's home page. However, at times, a forward slash and additional text follow the domain name, such as **www.nytimes.com/pages/cartoons**. The information after the slash indicates a particular file or **path** (or **subdirectory**) within the Web site. In this example, you would connect to the cartoon pages in the *New York Times* site.

HYPERLINKS AND BEYOND

What's the best way to get around in a Web site? As mentioned earlier, once you've reached a Web site, you can jump from one location, or Web page, to another within the Web site or to another Web site altogether by clicking on specially coded text called **hyperlinks**, shown in Figure 3.11. Generally, text that operates as a

hyperlink appears in a different color (often blue) and/or is underlined. Sometimes images also act as hyperlinks. When you pass your cursor over a hyperlinked image, the cursor changes to a hand with a finger pointing upward. To access the hyperlink, you simply click on the image.

To get back to your original location or a Web page you viewed previously, you use the browser's Back and Forward buttons (shown previously in Figure 3.8). If you want to back up more than one page, click on the down arrow next to the Back button to access a list of most recently visited Web sites. By selecting any one of these sites in the list, you can return to that page without having to navigate back through other Web sites and Web pages you've visited.

The **History list** on your browser's toolbar is also a handy feature. The History list shows all the Web sites and pages that you've visited over a certain period of time. These Web sites are organized according to date and can go back as far as three weeks, depending on your usage.

As another way to retrace your steps, some sites also provide a **breadcrumb list**—a list of pages you've visited that usually appears at the top of a page. Figure 3.11 shows an example of a breadcrumb list. Breadcrumbs get their name from the Hansel and Gretel fairy tale in which the children dropped breadcrumbs on the trail to find their way back out of the forest.

FAVORITES AND BOOKMARKS

What's the best way to mark a site so I can return to it later? If you want an easy way to return to a specific Web page, you can use your browser's **Favorites** or **Bookmark** feature (shown previously in Figure 3.8). (IE and Safari call this feature Favorites; Firefox calls the same feature a Bookmark.) This feature places a marker of the site's URL in an easily retrievable list in your browser's toolbar. To add a Web page to your list of Favorites in IE, from within the site you wish to mark, click on the Favorites menu and select Add to Favorites. As shown in Figure 3.12, you can modify the name of

---

YAHOO! EDUCATION Directory

Search: ⦿ the Web | ○ the Directory | ○ this category

Yahoo! My Yahoo! Mail Welcome, **Guest** [Sign In]

U.S. Private Colleges and Universities

Directory > Education > Higher Education > Colleges and Universities > United States > **Private**

CATEGORIES

Breadcrumb list

- Alabama@
- Alaska@
- Arizona@
- Arkansas@
- California@
- Colorado@

Hyperlinks

- Montana@
- Nebraska@
- Nevada@
- New Hampshire@
- New Jersey@
- New Mexico@

FIGURE 3.11

When you click on a hyperlink, you jump from one location in a Web site to another. When you click on the links in a breadcrumb list, you can navigate your way back through a Web site.

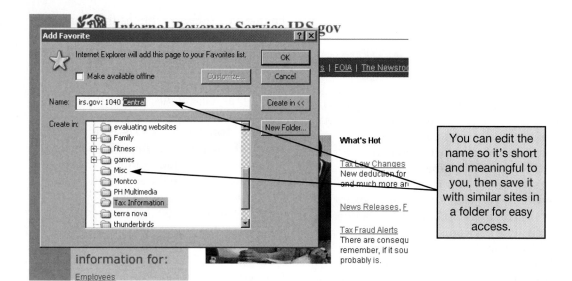

FIGURE 3.12

Using the IE Favorites feature makes returning to an often-used or hard-to-find Web page much easier.

You can edit the name so it's short and meaningful to you, then save it with similar sites in a folder for easy access.

the Web page on your Favorites list to make it more meaningful. (The process for adding and modifying a Bookmark in Firefox is similar.) If your list of Favorites becomes long, you can create folders to organize the sites into categories.

Safari offers a library feature you can use to edit and organize your Favorites. In addition, Safari and Firefox both enable you to import Favorites from IE. Or, to access your Bookmarks and Favorites from any computer, you can use **MyBookmarks.com**, a free Internet service that keeps your Bookmarks and Favorites stored online.

TABBED BROWSING

What can I do if I want to view many Web pages at the same time? Both Safari and Firefox offer tabbed browsing, a feature that is gaining popularity and is not found in Internet Explorer v6. With tabbed browsing, Web pages are loaded in "tabs" within the same browser window, as shown in Figure 3.13. Rather than having to switch between Web pages on several open windows, you can flip between the tabs in one window. You can even open several Favorites from one folder and choose to have them displayed as tabs.

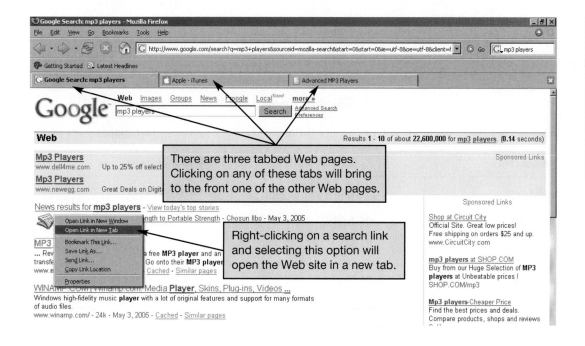

FIGURE 3.13

Tabbed browsing is one of the innovative features in Firefox and Safari. With tabbed browsing, multiple open Web pages are displayed as separate tabs allowing you to quickly switch between the pages.

There are three tabbed Web pages. Clicking on any of these tabs will bring to the front one of the other Web pages.

Right-clicking on a search link and selecting this option will open the Web site in a new tab.

Getting Around the Web: URLs, Hyperlinks, and Other Tools **101**

Searching the Web: Search Engines and Subject Directories

The Internet, with its billions of Web pages, offers its visitors access to masses of information on virtually any topic. There are two main tools you can use to find information on the Web: a **search engine** is a set of programs that searches the Web for specific words (or **keywords**) you wish to query (or look for) and then returns a list of the Web sites on which those keywords are found. Popular search engines include Google and AlltheWeb. You can also search the Web using a **subject directory**, which is a structured outline of Web sites organized by topics and subtopics. Yahoo! is a popular subject directory. Figure 3.14 lists popular search engines and subject directories and their URLs.

SEARCH ENGINES

How do search engines work? Search engines have three parts. The first part is a program called a **spider** (also known as a **crawler** or **bot**). The spider constantly collects data on the Web, following links in Web sites and reading Web pages. Spiders get their name because they crawl over the Web using multiple "legs" to visit many sites simultaneously. As the spider collects data, the second part of the search engine, an *indexer* program, organizes the data into a large database. When you use a search engine, you interact with the third part: the search engine software. This software searches the indexed data, pulling out relevant information according to your search. The resulting list appears in your Web browser as a list of *hits*, or sites that match your search.

Why don't I get the same results from all search engines? Each search engine uses a unique formula, or algorithm, to formulate the search and create the resulting index, as shown in Figure 3.15. In addition, search engines differ in how they rank the search results. Most search engines rank their results based on the *frequency* of the appearance of your queried keywords in Web sites as well as the *location* of those words in the sites. Thus, sites that include the keywords in their URL or site name most likely appear at the top of the hit list. After that, results vary because of differences in each engine's proprietary formula.

In addition, search engines differ as to which sites they search. For instance, Google and AlltheWeb search nearly the entire Web, whereas specialty search engines search only sites that are specifically relevant to the particular subject. Specialty search engines exist for almost every industry or interest. For example, **www.dailystocks.com** is a search engine used primarily by investors that searches for corporate information to help them make educated decisions. Search Engine Watch (**www.searchenginewatch.com**) has a list of many specialty search engines organized by industry.

FIGURE 3.14	**Popular Search Engines and Subject Directories**		
Search Engines		**Subject Directories**	
AlltheWeb	**www.alltheweb.com**	CompletePlanet	**www.completeplanet.com**
AltaVista	**www.altavista.com**	LookSmart	**www.looksmart.com**
Dogpile	**www.dogpile.com**	Lycos	**www.lycos.com**
Excite	**www.excite.com**	MSN	**www.msn.com**
Google	**www.google.com**	Open Directory Project	**www.dmoz.org**
Teoma	**www.teoma.com**	Yahoo!	**www.yahoo.com**

Note: For a complete list of search engines, go to **www.search-engines-megalist.com**.

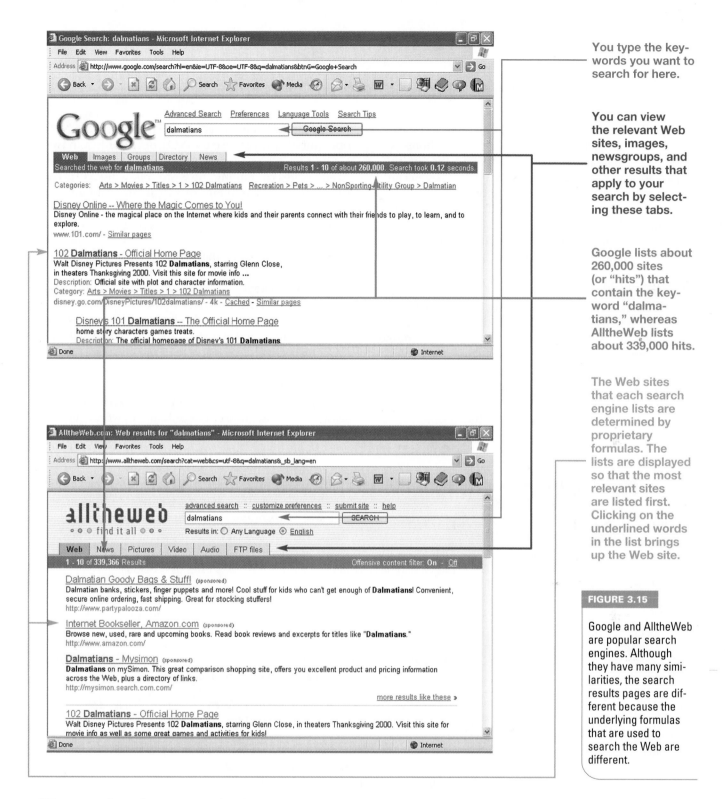

You type the keywords you want to search for here.

You can view the relevant Web sites, images, newsgroups, and other results that apply to your search by selecting these tabs.

Google lists about 260,000 sites (or "hits") that contain the keyword "dalmatians," whereas AlltheWeb lists about 339,000 hits.

The Web sites that each search engine lists are determined by proprietary formulas. The lists are displayed so that the most relevant sites are listed first. Clicking on the underlined words in the list brings up the Web site.

FIGURE 3.15

Google and AlltheWeb are popular search engines. Although they have many similarities, the search results pages are different because the underlying formulas that are used to search the Web are different.

What are the advantages of using the different kinds of search engines?

Using a search engine with a large index such as Google can be advantageous in conducting a search for hard-to-find information because it searches that many more indexed Web sites. However, if you're looking for only a few sites that have a high relevancy to your search, a search engine that has a smaller database, such as the search engine Teoma (**www.teoma.com**), may be more helpful.

If you can't decide which search engine is best, you may want to try a **meta search engine**, such as Dogpile (**www.dogpile.com**). Meta search engines search other search engines rather than individual Web sites.

Refining Your Web Searches: Boolean Operators

When you conduct Web searches, you often receive a list of hits that includes thousands—even millions—of Web pages that have no relevance to the topic you're trying to search. **Boolean operators** are words you can use to refine your searches, making them more effective. These words—AND, NOT, and OR—describe the relationships between keywords in a search. Figure 3.16 shows examples of these operators being used as well as the results the searches would produce.

Narrowing Searches

Using the Boolean AND operator helps you narrow (or limit) the results of your search. When you use the AND operator to join two keywords, the search engine returns only those documents that include *both* keywords (not just one). For example, if you type *Car AND Ford* into the search engine's search box, it will list only Web sites with pages that contain *both* the word *Car* and the word *Ford*, as shown in Figure 3.16.

You can also narrow your search by using the NOT operator. When you use the NOT operator to join two keywords, the search engine doesn't show the results of any pages containing the word following NOT. For example, as shown in Figure 3.16, if you want information on buying cars but you don't want any information on Fords, you could type *car NOT Ford* into the search box.

Be aware, however, that when you use the NOT operator, you may eliminate documents that contain the unwanted keyword but that also contain important information that may have been useful to you. Note that some search engines also let you use the plus sign (+) and minus sign (–) instead of the words AND and NOT, respectively.

Expanding Searches

The OR operator expands a keyword search so that the search results include either or both keywords. For

FIGURE 3.16 — Using Boolean Operators

Operator	Example	Results
AND	Car AND Ford	Only those documents that contain both the words **Car** AND **Ford**. Most search engines assume that the word AND is used as a default.
NOT	Car NOT Ford	Only those documents that contain the word **Car** but do NOT also contain the word **Ford**. This is the most restrictive of all searches and will return the smallest number of documents.
OR	Car OR Ford	All documents that contain either the word **Car** OR the word **Ford** OR **both** words. This results in the greatest number of documents.
Combinations	(Car AND Ford) NOT Gerald	Will give you all the documents referring to **Cars** and **Fords**, but no documents no documents relating to our 38th president, Gerald Ford.
Quotation Marks	"Lord of the Rings"	Will return only those documents that contain the string of words "Lord of the Rings" in that exact order. Without the quotation marks, you would get documents containing any of those words.
Wildcard*	Psych*	Stands in place of a series of letters. Good for those searches when you are searching for a term that can have several different endings, such as psychology, psychiatry, etc., and you want to research all of them.
Wildcard%	Goldsm%th	Stands in place of a single letter. Good to use when there are different spellings of the same word, such as Goldsmith and Goldsmyth.

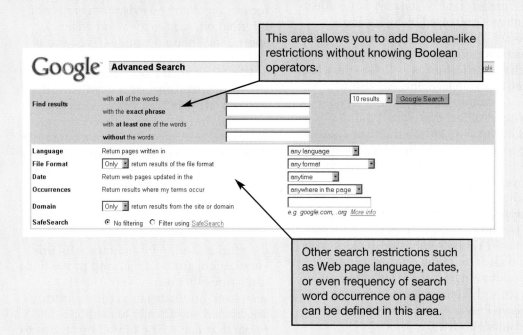

This area allows you to add Boolean-like restrictions without knowing Boolean operators.

Other search restrictions such as Web page language, dates, or even frequency of search word occurrence on a page can be defined in this area.

FIGURE 3.17

Most search engines have an Advanced Search form that you can fill out that uses the Boolean operators but in a more user-friendly format.

example, if you type *Car OR Ford* into the search box, it will list Web sites with pages that contain *either* the word *car* or the word *Ford or* both, as shown in Figure 3.16. Boolean OR searches are particularly helpful if there are a variety of synonymous keywords you could use in your search.

Other Helpful Search Strategies

Combining terms produces more specific results. To do so, though, you must use parentheses to add order to your search. For example, if you are looking for tutorials or lessons to better use the program Microsoft Excel, you can search for (Tutorials OR Lessons) AND Excel. Similarly, if you want to know how to better use the entire Microsoft Office suite with the exception of Access, you can search for (Tutorials OR Lessons) AND (Office NOT Access).

To search for an exact phrase, you simply place quotation marks around your keywords. The search engine will look for only those Web sites that contain the words in that *exact order*. For example, if you want information on the movie *Lord of the Rings* and you type in these words without quotation marks, your search results will contain pages that include any of the words *Lord, of, the*, and *Rings*, although not neces-

sarily in that order. Typing in *"Lord of the Rings"* in quotes *guarantees* search results will include this *exact* phrase.

Some search engines let you use an asterisk (*) to replace a series of letters and a percent sign (%) to replace a single letter in a word. These symbols, called **wildcards**, are helpful when you're searching for a keyword but are unsure of its spelling, or if a word can be spelled in different ways or may contain different endings. For example, if you're doing a genealogy project and are searching for the name *Goldsmith*, you might want to use *Goldsm&th* to take into consideration alternate spellings of the name (such as *Goldsmyth*). Similarly, if you're searching for sites related to psychiatry and psychology and you type *psych**, the search results will include all pages containing the words *psychology, psychiatry, psychedelic*, and so on.

Using Boolean search techniques can make your Internet research a lot more efficient. With the simple addition of a few words, you can narrow your search results to a more manageable and more meaningful list. Meanwhile, most search engines offer an Advanced Search page that provides the same type of strategies in a well-organized form (see Figure 3.17).

SUBJECT DIRECTORIES

How can I use a subject directory to find information on the Web? As mentioned earlier, a *subject directory* is a guide to the Internet organized by topics and subtopics. Yahoo! is one of the most popular subject directories, although it now has a search engine feature as well. Google, which started as a search engine, has also added a subject directory feature.

With a subject directory, you do not use keywords to search the Web. Instead, after selecting the main subject from the directory, you narrow your search by successively clicking on subfolders that match your search until you have reached the appropriate information. For example, to find previews on newly released movies in Yahoo's subject directory, you would click on the main category of Entertainment, select the subcategory Movies and Films, select the further subcategory Preview, and then open one of the listed Web sites.

Can I find the same information with a subject directory as I can with a search engine? Most subject directories are more commercial and consumer-oriented than academic- or research-based. The main categories in the subject directory of Yahoo!, for example, include Computers & Internet, Entertainment, and Recreation & Sports. Even within categories such as Reference, you find consumer-oriented subcategories such as Phone Numbers and Quotations.

Many subject directories, such as Yahoo! and MSN, are part of a larger Web site that focuses on offering its visitors a variety of information, such as the weather, news, sports, and shopping guides. This type of Web site is referred to as a **portal**.

When should I use a subject directory instead of a traditional search engine? Directory searches are great for finding information on general topics (such as sports and hobbies) rather than narrowing in on a specific or unusual piece of information. For example, conducting a search on the keyword *hobbies* on a search engine does not provide you with a convenient list of hobbies, as does a subject directory. And although most directories tend to be commercially oriented, there are academic and professional directories that use subject experts to select and annotate sites. These directories are created specifically to facilitate the research process. The Librarians' Index to the Internet (**www.lii.org**), in Figure 3.18, for example, is an academic directory whose index lists librarian-selected Web sites that have little if any commercially sponsored content.

EVALUATING WEB SITES

How can I make sure the Web site is appropriate to use for research? When you're using the Internet for research, you shouldn't assume that everything you find is accurate and appropriate to use. Before you use an Internet resource, ask yourself the following questions:

1. **Who is the author of the article or the sponsor of the site?** If the author is well known or the site is published by a reputable news source (such as the *New York Times*), you can feel more confident using it as a source than if you are unable to locate information about the author or do not know who sponsors the site. (Note: Some sites include a page with information about the author or the site's sponsor.)

2. **For what audience is the site intended?** Ensure that the content, tone, and style of the site match your needs. You probably wouldn't want to use information from a site geared

FIGURE 3.18

Subject directories are best for searches that are more general, or just for browsing within a topic. Some academic subject directories, such as **www.lii.org**, are annotated by experts.

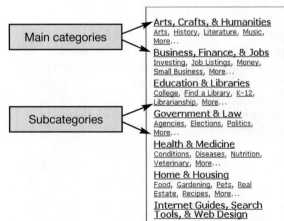

toward teens if you're writing for adults, nor use a site that has a casual style and tone for serious research.

3. **Is the site biased in any way?** The purpose of many Web sites is to sell you a product or service, or to persuade rather than inform. These sites, although useful in some situations, present a biased point of view. Look for sites that offer several sets of facts or consider opinions from several sources.

4. **Is the information in the site current for your needs?** Material can last a long time on the Web. Some research projects (such as historical accounts) depend on older records. However, if you're writing about cutting-edge technologies, you need to look for the most recent sources. Therefore, look for a date on information to make sure it is current.

5. **Are the links available and appropriate?** Check out the links provided on the site to determine whether they are still working and appropriate for your needs. Don't assume that the links provided are the only additional sources of information. Investigate other sites on your topic as well.

The answers to these questions will help you decide whether you should consider a Web site to be a good source of information.

Communicating Through the Internet: E-Mail and Other Technologies

For better or worse, **e-mail** (short for **electronic mail**) is fast becoming the primary means of communication in the 21st century. However, it is not the only form of Internet-based communication: *weblogs, chat rooms, instant messaging, newsgroups,* and *listservs* are also popular forms. Like any other means of communication, you need to know how to use these tools efficiently to get the best out of them.

E-MAIL

Why did e-mail catch on so quickly?
E-mail has quickly caught on as the primary method of electronic communication because it's fast and convenient and reduces the costs of postage and long-distance phone calls. In addition, with e-mail, the sender and receiver don't have to be available at the same time in order to communicate. Because of these and other reasons, more than 90 percent of Americans who access the Internet claim that their main activity is sending and receiving e-mail.

Are all e-mail accounts the same? To read, send, and organize your e-mail, you use some sort of **e-mail client**. In the early days of e-mail, when dial-up connections were the only way to access the Internet, e-mail client programs such as Microsoft Outlook, Outlook Express, or Eudora were the only way to receive and send e-mail. These e-mail clients are software programs running on your computer that access your ISP's server. However, with these e-mail clients, you are only able to view your e-mail from the computer on which the client program is installed, which can be less than convenient if you travel or want to view your e-mail when you're away from that computer.

Today, many ISPs offer the services of a Web-based e-mail client so users can look at their e-mail directly from the Web. Web-based e-mail uses the Internet as the client; therefore, you can access a Web-based e-mail account from any computer that has access to the Web—no special client software is needed. Free e-mail accounts such as Yahoo! or Hotmail use Web-based e-mail clients.

If you use a broadband connection, such as cable or DSL, your broadband provider will provide you with a Web-based e-mail account. Some e-mail clients, such as AOL, offer both client and Web access to e-mail. If you have a Web-based e-mail client, you can still choose to use an e-mail client program such as Outlook because these programs offer organizational features that most Web-based e-mail clients do not.

What are the advantages of a Web-based e-mail account? Unlike client based e-mail, which is only accessible from the computer on which it is installed, if you have a Web-based e-mail account, your e-mail is accessible from any computer as long as you have access to the Internet. A secondary Web-based e-mail account also provides you with a more permanent e-mail address. Your other e-mail accounts and addresses may change when you switch ISPs or change employers, so having a permanent

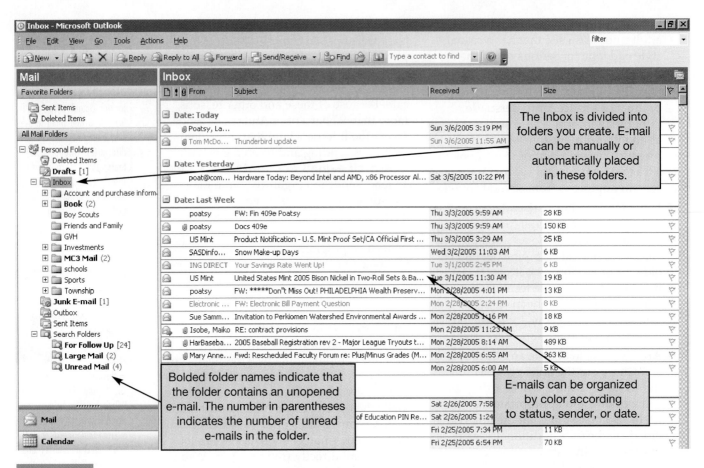

The Inbox is divided into folders you create. E-mail can be manually or automatically placed in these folders.

Bolded folder names indicate that the folder contains an unopened e-mail. The number in parentheses indicates the number of unread e-mails in the folder.

E-mails can be organized by color according to status, sender, or date.

FIGURE 3.19

You can organize your e-mail by color coding it and assigning messages to specific folders. Additionally, you can automatically filter out unwanted e-mail and sort the remaining e-mail into topic-specific folders.

e-mail address is important. Finally, if you need to send personal e-mail from work, using a Web-based e-mail account keeps your private e-mail off the company's system.

Why would I need client-based e-mail program? Many people have more than one e-mail account. You may have a personal account, a work account, and an account you use when filling out forms on the Internet. One of the benefits of using a client-based e-mail program such as Microsoft Outlook is that you can download your e-mail from many different e-mail accounts so that it all can be accessed in one location.

In addition, client e-mail programs offer several features to help you manage and

SOUND BYTE

Creating a Web-Based E-mail Account

In this Sound Byte, you'll see a step-by-step demonstration explaining how to create a free Yahoo! Web-based e-mail account. You'll also learn the options available with such accounts.

organize your e-mail and coordinate e-mail with your calendar, tasks, and contact lists. As you can see in Figure 3.19, you can choose to organize your e-mail by task, sender, or priority using color codes, or you can distribute your messages to designated folders within your inbox.

WEBLOGS (BLOGS)

What is a blog? Weblogs (or blogs) are personal logs, or journal entries, that are posted on the Web. The beauty of blogs is that they are simple to create, manage, and read. Although different types of blogs exist, there are some basic similarities: first, blogs are arranged as a listing of entries on a single page, with the most recent blog appearing on the top of the list. Second, blogs are public. Everyone who has a Web browser and access to the Internet can read the blog. Finally, blogs are searchable, making them user friendly.

What do people write in blogs? Many people use blogs as a sort of personal scrapbook. They just write a stream-of-conscious flow of thoughts or a report of their daily activities whenever the urge strikes. Many blogs, however, focus on a particular topic. For example, **www.rottentomatoes.com** is a blog site that contains reviews and opinions about movies. **www.gizmodo.com** is a blog site that devotes itself to discussing techno-gadgets (see Figure 3.20).

How do I create a blog? It is easy to write and maintain a blog, and you'll find many Web sites that provide the necessary tools for you to create your own blog. Two sites that offer blog hosting for free are **www.blogger.com** and **www.livejournal.com**. For a relatively small fee, you can add other features to your blog, such as pictures or subpages. Another alternative is to host your blog yourself. Hosting your own blog requires that you have an IP address (like 32.168.87.145) and a URL, such as **www.mydailydribble.org** in order for people to access it online.

CHAT ROOMS

What's a chat room? A **chat room** is an area on the Web where many people come together to communicate online. The conversations are in real time and are visible to everyone in the chat room. Usually, chat rooms are created to address a specific topic, and chances are you can find a chat room on any subject of interest to you. Yahoo.com is a good source to locate chat rooms.

Do people know who I am in a chat room? When you enter a chat room, you sign in with a username and password. It's best to not disclose your true identity but rather to "hide" behind a username, thus protecting your privacy. On the other hand, the people you are chatting with are also hiding their identities. Some chatters use this veil of privacy to cover dishonest intentions. Undoubtedly, you have heard stories of individuals, especially young teenagers, being deceived (and sometimes harmed) by someone they've met in a chat room. A number of Web sites, such as **www.chatdanger.com**, try to protect vulnerable people such as children from malicious chat room users (see Figure 3.21).

Netiquette

Are there special ways to behave in a chat room? General rules of etiquette (often referred to as **netiquette**) exist across chat rooms and other online forums, including obvious standards of behavior such as

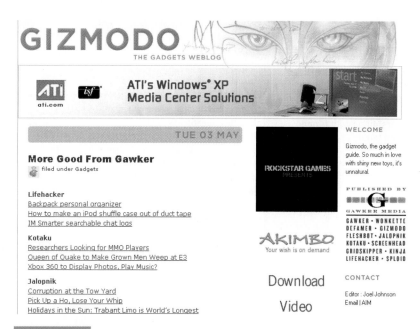

FIGURE 3.20

Blogs like the one shown here from **www.gizmodo.com** can be online reviews organized by category or personal journals recording the blogger's thoughts, viewpoints, and feelings.

introducing yourself when you enter the room and specifically addressing the person you are talking to. Chat room users are also expected to refrain from swearing, name calling, and using explicit or prejudiced language and are not allowed to harass other participants. In addition, chat room users cannot repeatedly post the same text with the intent to disrupt the chat. (This behavior is called *scrolling*.) Similarly, users shouldn't type in all capital letters, because this is interpreted as shouting.

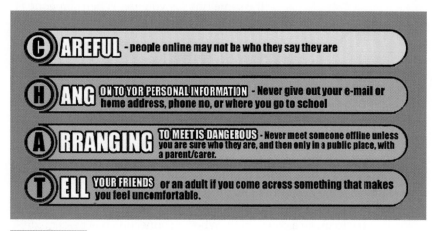

FIGURE 3.21

www.Chatdanger.com is produced by Childnet International, a nonprofit organization working to help make the Internet safe for children.

FIGURE 3.22

Instant messaging services such as AOL Instant Messenger enable you to have real-time online conversations with friends and family.

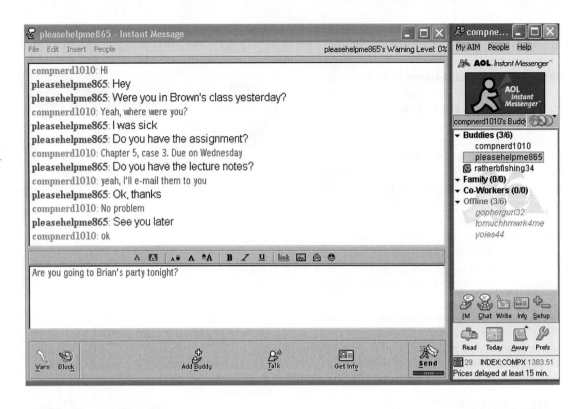

INSTANT MESSAGING

How does instant messaging work?
Instant messaging (IM) services are programs that enable you to communicate in real time with friends who are also online. AOL's Instant Messenger (AIM or IM), shown in Figure 3.22, is one of the most popular instant messaging services. Yahoo and MSN also host popular instant messaging services. When you use IM, you set up a list of contacts, often called a *Buddy List*. To communicate with someone from your Buddy List, that person must be online at the same time as you are. When someone is trying to communicate with you when you're online, you are notified and can then accept or reject the communication. If you want to chat with more than one person, you can either hold simultaneous individual conversations, or if you all want to talk together, you can create custom IM chat rooms.

What's the difference between a chat room and IM? When you use IM services, you have private conversations with people you know. With chat rooms, anyone who enters the chat room can take part in the conversation.

NEWSGROUPS

What's a newsgroup? A newsgroup (sometimes referred to as a **discussion group**) is an online discussion forum in which people post messages and read and reply to messages from other members of the newsgroup. Newsgroups exist for more than 30,000 topics, from games and hobbies to science and computers to current issues and debates. The best directory of newsgroups is the Tile.Net Usenet Newsgroups Directory, available at **www.tile.net**. You can also find newsgroups through Google Groups, which is a directory of newsgroups that appears as a separate tab when you log onto Google's home page.

BITS AND BYTES

Want to Call Your Buddies Over IM?

Would you rather talk to your Buddy than have a typed conversation? You each need only AOL IM or MSN Messenger and a microphone. After you have decided on the Buddy you want to talk to, right-click on the Buddy's screen name, select Connect to Talk from the drop-down menu, and then select Connect. The Talk box will contact your Buddy to see if he or she wants to talk, and then try to make a connection. When a connection has been made, you can begin to talk to each other. Talking over IM is like talking on a walkie-talkie. While you are talking, you need to hold down the Push to Talk button and release it to hear your Buddy.

LISTSERVS

What is a listserv? Listservs are electronic mailing lists of e-mail addresses of people who are interested in a certain topic or area of interest. They are used to share information with a common group of individuals. You can find thousands of lists to join by browsing **www.tile.net/lists** or **www.lsoft.com/catalist.html**. To subscribe to a specific listserv, you send an e-mail to the list address with a special message in the subject field. Each list has a slightly different format, and that information will be given in the list's description. You will then begin to receive e-mails from all the members of the list and can post to the list yourself. Unsubscribing involves sending an exit e-mail.

Listservs have been replaced to some extent by newsgroups. However, in a listserv, the messages are delivered only to members of the list, whereas newsgroups are most often open to public viewing.

Managing Online Annoyances

Surfing the Web, sending and receiving e-mail, and chatting online have become a common part of most of our lives. Unfortunately, the Web has become fertile ground for people who want to advertise their products, track our Web-browsing, or even con people out of personal information. In this section, we'll look at ways in which you can manage, if not avoid, these and other online headaches.

Spam

How can I best avoid spam?
Companies that send out **spam**, unwanted or junk e-mail, find your e-mail address either from a list they purchase or with software that looks for e-mail addresses on the Internet. If you've used your e-mail address to purchase anything online or to open up an online account, or if you've participated in a newsgroup or a chat room, your e-mail address will eventually appear on one of the lists spammers get.

One way to avoid spam in your primary account is to create a special, free Web-based e-mail address that you use when you fill out forms on the Web. For example, both Hotmail and Yahoo! allow you to set up free e-mail accounts. If your free Web-based e-mail account is saturated with spam, you can abandon that account with little inconvenience. It's much harder to abandon your primary e-mail address.

Another way to avoid spam is to filter it out. A **spam filter** is an option you can select in your e-mail account that places known spam messages into a folder other than your inbox. Most Web-based e-mail services, such as Hotmail and Yahoo!, offer spam filters (see Figure 3.23). Outlook 2003

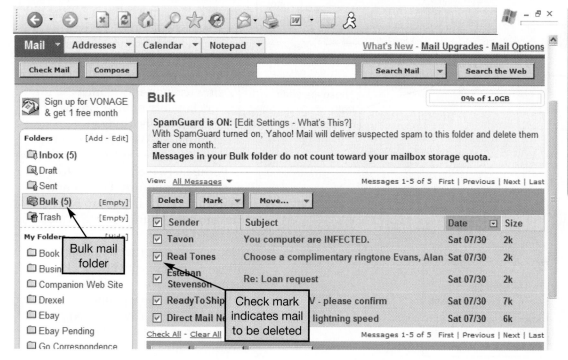

FIGURE 3.23

In Yahoo! Mail, turning on the SpamGuard feature alerts the Yahoo! Mail server to screen your incoming mail for obvious or suspected spam. This mail is then directed into a folder called "Bulk" where you can review the mail (to ensure it is really spam) and delete it.

BITS AND BYTES

Why Is It Called "Spam"?

Why and how unwanted e-mail has been dubbed "spam" is not really known, but one theory is that the name came from the Monty Python song that praises the canned processed meat product SPAM. The song is an endless repetition of the term spam, much like the endless repetition of useless text that constitutes the unwanted e-mail. Also, electronic spam, like its canned ham namesake, is rarely asked for but often served. When served, it's rarely eaten and generally pushed out of the way, similar to electronic spam that is often received but rarely read.

also features a spam filter, but what if you are still using a previous version of Outlook to manage your e-mail? Then you need to obtain special **spam filtering software** and install it on your computer. Programs that provide you with some control over spam include MailWasher Pro, Spam Alarm, and SpamButcher, all of which can be obtained at **www.download.com**.

How do spam filters work? Spam filters and filtering software can catch up to 95 percent of spam. They work by checking incoming e-mail subject headers and sending addresses against databases of known spam. Spam filters also check your e-mail for frequently used spam patterns and keywords (such as "Viagra" and "free"). E-mail that the filter identifies as spam does not go into your inbox but rather to a folder. Because spam filters aren't perfect, you should check the spam folder rather than just deleting its contents because legitimate e-mail might end up there.

How else can I prevent spam? There are several additional ways you can prevent spam:

1. Before registering on a Web site, read its privacy policy to see how it uses your e-mail address. Don't give the site permission to pass on your e-mail address to third parties.

2. Don't reply to spam to remove yourself from the spam list. By replying, you are confirming your e-mail address is active. Instead of stopping spam, you may receive more.

3. Subscribe to an e-mail forwarding service such as **www.emailias.com** or **www.sneakemail.com**. These services screen your e-mail messages, forwarding only those messages you designate as being OK to accept.

POP-UPS

How do I get rid of Pop-up windows? Pop-up windows are the billboards of the Internet. These windows pop up when you enter Web sites, sporting "useful" information or touting products. Although some sites use pop-ups to increase the functionality of their site (your account balance may pop up at your bank's Web site, for example), many pop-ups are just plain annoying.

Fortunately, there are ways to reduce or eliminate pop-ups. Firefox and Safari have built-in pop-up blockers. The most recent upgrade to Windows XP (Service Pack 2) includes a Pop-up Manager for Internet Explorer that allows you to selectively block pop-ups (see Figure 3.24).

Some of the more popular search engines (Google, Yahoo!, MSN) provide toolbars that, when installed in your Web browser, allow you to access the search

FIGURE 3.24

Internet Explorer's Pop-up Manager enables you to selectively block pop-up windows.

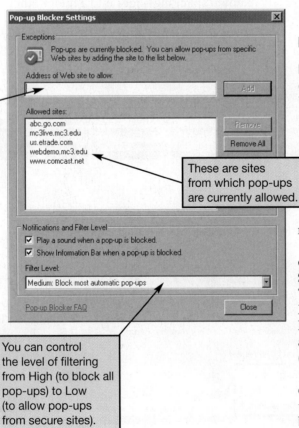

You can add Web sites to this list that would still be allowed to show pop-ups.

These are sites from which pop-ups are currently allowed.

You can control the level of filtering from High (to block all pop-ups) to Low (to allow pop-ups from secure sites).

engine from the Web browser without having to open it up directly. In addition to the immediate convenience, these toolbars also contain pop-up blockers. Generally, between the new pop-up provisions in your browser and your search engine toolbar, additional protection is not necessary. However, if you feel you need more protection, you can install anti-pop-up software. Two free anti-pop-up programs are Pop-Up Stopper and Pop-Up Defender, both of which are available at **www.download.com**.

COOKIES

What are cookies? Cookies are small text files that some Web sites automatically store on your computer's hard drive when you visit the site. When you log on to a Web site that uses cookies, a cookie file assigns an ID number to your computer. The unique ID is intended to make your return visit to a Web site more efficient and better geared to your interests. The next time you log on to that site, the site marks your visit and keeps track of it in its database.

What do Web sites do with cookie information? Cookies provide Web sites with information about your browsing habits, such as the ads you've opened, the products you've looked at, and the time and duration of your visits. Cookies also remember personal information you enter into Web site forms, such as your credit card information, name, mailing address, and phone number. Companies use this information to determine the traffic flowing through their Web site and the effectiveness of their marketing strategy and Web site placement. By tracking which pages you view, how long you stay on the site, and how many times you come back to the site, cookies enable companies to identify different users' preferences.

Can companies get my personal information when I visit their sites? Cookies do not go through your hard drive in search of personal information such as passwords or financial data. The only personal information a cookie obtains is the information you supply when you fill out forms online.

Do privacy risks exist with cookies? Some sites sell the personal information their cookies collect to Web advertisers that are building huge databases of consumer preferences and habits, collecting personal and business information such as credit card numbers, phone numbers, credit reports, and the like. The ultimate concern is that advertisers will use this information indiscriminately, thus infiltrating your privacy.

Should I delete cookies from my hard drive then? Because cookies pose no *security* threat (because it is virtually impossible to hide a virus in a cookie), take up little room on your hard drive, and offer you small conveniences on return visits to Web sites, there is no great reason for you to delete them. Deleting your cookie files could also cost you the inconvenience of reentering data you have already entered once into Web site forms. However, if you're uncomfortable with the accessibility of your personal information, you can periodically delete cookies or configure your browser to block certain types of cookies, as shown in Figure 3.25. Software programs such as Cookie Pal also exist to help monitor cookies for you.

SPYWARE

What is spyware? If you ever install software from a Web site, you may be installing something on your computer together with the software. Called **spyware** (or **adware**), these unwanted piggyback programs run in the background of your system and gather information about you, usually your Internet surfing habits, without your knowledge.

FIGURE 3.25

Tools are available, either through your browser or as a separate software application, to sort between cookies you want to keep and cookies that you don't want on your system.

They then transmit this information to the owner of the spyware program so that the information can be used for marketing purposes. Many spyware programs use cookies to collect information.

Can I prevent spyware? Most antivirus software doesn't detect spyware or prevent spyware cookies from being placed on your hard drive. However, you can obtain **spyware removal software** and run it on your computer to delete unwanted spyware. Because new spyware is created all the time, you should update your spyware removal software regularly. Ad-aware (available for free at **www.download.com**) and PestPatrol (available at **www.pestpatrol.com**) are programs that are easy to install and update. Figure 3.26 shows an example of PestPatrol in action.

PHISHING AND INTERNET HOAXES

What is phishing? One of the more recent scams involving the Internet is **phishing** (pronounced "fishing"). Phishing lures Internet users into revealing personal information such as credit card or social security numbers or other sensitive information that could lead to identity theft. The scammers send e-mails that look like

they are from a legitimate business the recipient deals with, such as an online bank. The e-mail states that the recipient needs to update or confirm his or her account information, and sends the recipient to a Web site that looks like a legitimate site but is really a fraudulent copy the scammer has created. Once the e-mail recipient confirms his or her personal information, the scammers capture it and can begin using it.

How can I avoid being caught by phishing scams? The best way to avoid falling for such scams is to avoid replying directly to any e-mail asking you for personal information. Check with the company asking for the information and only give the information if you are certain it is needed, and only over the phone. Never give personal information over the Internet unless you know the site is a secure one. We discuss ways you can make sure a site is secure later in this chapter.

What is an Internet hoax? Internet **hoaxes** contain information that is untrue. Hoax e-mail messages may request that you send money to cover medical costs for an impoverished and sick child or ask you to pass on bogus information, such as how to avoid a virus. Chain e-mail letters are also considered a form of Internet hoax.

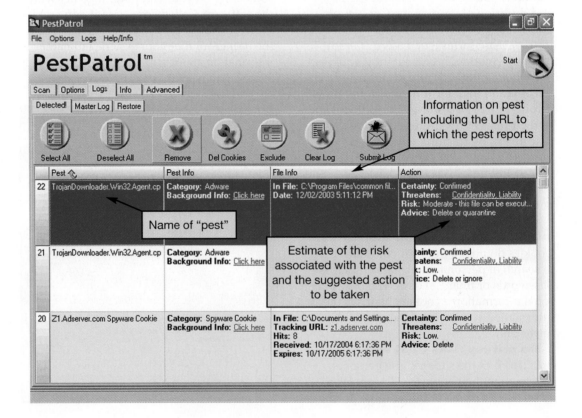

Ethics: What Can You Borrow from the Internet?

You've no doubt heard of *plagiarism*—taking another person's words as your own. And you've probably heard the term *copyright violation*, especially if you've been following the music industry's battle to keep "free" music off the Web. But what constitutes plagiarism and what constitutes copyright violation? And what can you borrow from the Web? Consider these scenarios:

1. You find a political cartoon that would be terrific in a PowerPoint presentation you're creating for your civics class. You copy it into your presentation.
2. Your hobby is cooking. You design a Web site that includes videos of you preparing recipes, as well as the recipes themselves. Some of these recipes you take from your favorite cookbooks, others you get from friends. You don't cite your sources, nor obtain permission from the originators of the recipes you post to your Web site.
3. You're pressed for time and need to do research for a paper due tomorrow. You find information on an obscure Web site and copy it into your paper without documenting the source.
4. You download a song from the Internet and incorporate it into a PowerPoint presentation for a school project. Because you figure everyone knows the song, you don't credit it in your sources.

Which of the preceding scenarios represent copyright violations? Which represent plagiarism? The distinctions between these scenarios are narrow in some cases, but it's important to understand the differences.

As noted earlier, plagiarism occurs when you use someone else's ideas or words and represent them as your own. In today's computer society, it's easy to copy information from the Internet and paste it into a Word document, change a few words, and call it your own. To avoid plagiarism, use quotation marks around all words you borrow directly and credit your sources for any ideas you paraphrase or borrow. Avoiding plagiarism means properly crediting *all* information you obtain from the Internet, including words, ideas, graphics, data, and audio and video clips.

Copyright violation is more serious because it is punishable by law. The law assumes that all original work including text, graphics, software, multimedia, audio or video clips, and even ideas is copyrighted, regardless of whether the work displays the copyright symbol (©). Copyright violation occurs when you use another person's material for your own personal *economic* benefit, or when you take away from the economic benefit of the originator. Don't assume that by citing a source you're abiding by copyright laws. In most cases, you need to seek *and receive* written permission from the copyright holder. There are exceptions to this rule. For example, there is no copyright on government documents; therefore, you can download and reproduce material from NASA, for example, without violating copyright laws. The British Broadcasting Corporation (BBC) is also beginning to digitize and make available its archives of material to the public without copyright restrictions.

Teachers and students also receive special consideration regarding copyright violations. This special consideration falls under a provision called *academic fair use*. As long as the material is being used for educational purposes only, *limited* copying and distribution is allowed. For example, an instructor can make copies of a newspaper article and distribute it to her class or a student can include a cartoon in a PowerPoint presentation without seeking permission from the artist. However, to avoid plagiarism in these situations, you still must credit your sources of information.

So, do you now know which of the four scenarios above are plagiarism or copyright violations?

1. You are not in violation because the use of the cartoon is for educational purposes and falls under the academic fair use provision.
2. If your Web site is for your economic benefit, you would be in violation of copyright laws because no credit was given for the recipes, and you are presenting them as your own.
3. You are in violation of plagiarism because you copied from another source and implied it was your own work.
4. Again, because it is for a school project, you are not in violation because of the academic fair use provision. However, it's always important to document your sources.

Why are hoaxes so bad? The sheer number of e-mails generated by hoaxes can cost millions in lost opportunity costs caused by time spent reading, discarding, or resending the message, and they can clog up the Internet system. If you receive an e-mail you think might be a hoax, don't pass it on. First determine whether it is a hoax by visiting the U.S. Department of Energy's Hoaxbusters site at **http://hoaxbusters.ciac.org**.

Conducting Business Over the Internet: E-Commerce

E-commerce, or **electronic commerce**, is the business of conducting business online for purposes ranging from fund-raising to advertising to selling products. A good example of an e-commerce business (or e-business) is **www.dell.com**. The company's online presence offers customers a convenient way to shop for computer systems. Its success is because of creative marketing, an expanding product line, and reliable customer service and product delivery—all hallmarks of traditional businesses as well. Traditional stores that have an online presence are referred to as **click-and-brick businesses**. These stores are able to provide a variety of services on Web sites. Customers can visit their sites to check the availability of items or to get store locations and directions.

A significant portion of e-commerce consists of **business-to-consumer (B2C)** transactions—transactions that take place between businesses and consumers, such as the purchases consumers make at online stores and online banking. There is also a **business-to-business (B2B)** portion of e-commerce; this consists of businesses buying and selling goods and services to other businesses. Finally, the **consumer-to-consumer (C2C)** portion of e-commerce consists of consumers selling to each other through online auction sites such as eBay.

What are the most popular e-commerce activities? According to **www.consumerreports.com**, consumers buy books, music and videos, movie and event tickets, and toys and games more often online than in retail stores. Auction sites such as eBay together with payment exchange services such as PayPal are becoming the online equivalent to the weekend yard sale and have dramatically increased in popularity.

But e-commerce encompasses more than just shopping opportunities. Today, anything you can do inside your bank you can do online, and over 25 percent of U.S. households do some form of online banking. Most people use online services to check their account balances, while checking stock and mutual fund performances is also popular. Credit card companies also allow you to view your credit card statement and conduct investment activities online, and you can also pay your bills online (although some companies charge a fee for this service).

E-COMMERCE SAFEGUARDS

Just how safe are online transactions? When you buy something over the Web, you most likely use a credit card; therefore, the exchange of money is done directly between you and a bank. Because online shopping eliminates a sales clerk or other human intermediary from the transaction, it can actually be safer than traditional retail shopping. Still, because users are told to be wary of online transactions and because the integrity of online transactions is the backbone of e-commerce, businesses must have some form of security certification to give their customers a level of comfort. Businesses hire security companies such as VeriSign to certify that their online transactions are secure. Thus, if the Web site displays the VeriSign seal, you can usually trust that the information you submit to the site is protected.

Another indication that a Web site is secure is the appearance of a small icon of a closed padlock (IE) or key (Netscape) on the status bar at the bottom of the screen, as shown in Figure 3.27. Additionally, the beginning of the URL of the site will change from http:// to https://, the s standing for "secure."

How else can I shop safely online? To ensure that your online shopping experience is a safe one, follow these guidelines:

- Shop at well-known, reputable sites. If you aren't familiar with a site, investigate it with the Better Business Bureau (**www.bbb.org**), or at **www.bizrate.com** or **www.webassured.com**.

- When you place an order, print a copy of the order and make sure you receive a confirmation number.

- Make sure the company has a phone number and street address in addition to a Web site.

When the beginning of the URL changes from http:// to https://, the Web site is secure.

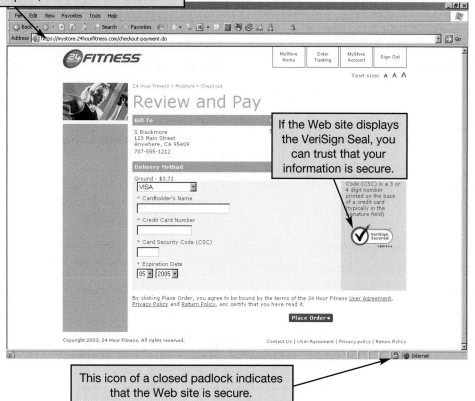

If the Web site displays the VeriSign Seal, you can trust that your information is secure.

This icon of a closed padlock indicates that the Web site is secure.

FIGURE 3.27

The VeriSign seal, a closed padlock icon, and *https* in the URL are indications that the site is secure.

- Always pay by credit card. The U.S. federal consumer credit card protection laws protect credit card purchases.
- Check the return policy. Print it out and save it in case the site disappears overnight.

Web Entertainment: Multimedia and Beyond

Internet radio, MP3 music files, streaming video, and interactive gaming are all part of a growing entertainment world available over the Internet. What makes the Web appealing to many people is its enriched multimedia content. **Multimedia** is anything that involves one or more forms of media in addition to text.

Many types of multimedia are used on the Web. Graphics—drawings, charts, and photos—are the most basic form of multimedia on the Web. Audio files are what give sound to the Web—the clips of music you hear when you visit certain Web sites, MP3 files that you download, or live broadcasts you can listen to through Internet radio. Video files on the Web range from the simple (such as short video clips) to the complex (such as hour-long live concerts). In addition to movies, you can watch live or prerecorded television broadcasts, movie trailers, and sporting events.

What is streaming audio and video? If you've been on the Web a lot, you've probably encountered streaming audio and video. Some Web sites, especially those offering live broadcasts, use **streaming audio** to enhance the listening process. Streaming audio continuously feeds an audio file to your browser so you avoid having to wait for the entire file to download completely before listening to it. Likewise, **streaming video** continuously feeds a video file to your browser so you can watch large files as they download instead of first having to download the files completely.

Do I need anything besides a browser to view or hear multimedia on the Web? Without any additional software, most graphics on the Web will

ACTIVE HELPDESK

Staying Secure on the Internet

In this Active Helpdesk call, you'll learn about e-commerce and what e-commerce safeguards protect you when you're online as well as what cookies are and what risks they pose.

FIGURE 3.28

Popular Plug-Ins/Players and Their Uses

	Plug-In/Player Name	Where You Can Get the Plug-In/Player	What the Plug-In/Player Does
	Adobe Acrobat Reader	www.adobe.com	Lets you view and print Portable Document Format (PDF) files
	Authorware Player	www.macromedia.com	Helps you view animations
	Flash Player	www.macromedia.com	Lets you play animation and other graphics files on the Web
	QuickTime® Player	www.apple.com/quicktime	Lets you play MP3 and AAC files, MPEG4 and H.264 video files, listen to live audio, and view live video broadcasts on Web
	RealPlayer	www.real.com	Lets you play streaming audio, video, animations, and multimedia presentations on the Web
	Shockwave Player	www.macromedia.com	Lets you play interactive games, multimedia, graphics, and streaming audio and video on the Web
	Windows Media Player	www.microsoft.com	Lets you play MP3 and WAV files, listen to music files and live audio, and view movies and live video broadcasts on the Web

appear in your browser when you visit a site. However, to view and hear some multimedia files on the Web, you need a special software program called a **plug-in** (or **player**). Figure 3.28 lists the most popular plug-ins.

If you've purchased your computer over the past several years, you'll find plug-ins already installed with your browser. For those you don't have, the Web site requiring the plug-in usually displays a message on the screen that includes links to a site where you can download the plug-in free of charge. For example, to use streaming audio on a Web site, your browser might send you to **www.macromedia.com**, where you can download Shockwave Player.

Do I need to update players and plug-ins? Like most technological resources, improvements and upgrades are available for players and plug-ins. Most plug-ins and players will alert you to check for and download upgrades when they are available. It is best to keep the players and plug-ins as current as possible so that you get the full effects of the multimedia running with these players.

Are there any risks with using plug-ins? When a browser requires a plug-in to display particular Web content, it usually automatically accesses the plug-in, generally without asking you for consent to start the plug-in. This automatic access can present security risks. To minimize such risks, update your plug-ins and browser software frequently so that you will have the most up-to-date remedies against identified security flaws.

Is there any way to get multimedia Web content to load faster? When you're on the Internet, your browser keeps track of the Web sites you've visited so it can load them faster the next time you visit them. This cache (or hiding place) of the HTML text pages, images, and video files from recently visited Web sites can make your Internet surfing more efficient, but it can also congest your hard drive. To keep your system running efficiently, delete your Temporary Internet Cache periodically. For Internet Explorer 6, select Tools, Internet Options, then in the Temporary Internet Files area, select Delete Files. For Netscape Navigator 6, select Edit, Preferences, Advanced, Cache, and then select Clear Disk Cache.

The Future of the Internet

What does the future have in store for the Internet? Certainly, the Internet of the future will have more bandwidth, offer increased services, and reach more of the world's population than it does today. One thing is sure: because of the prevalence of wireless technologies, the Internet will be more accessible, and we will become more dependent on it. With the increase of commerce and communication activities dominating the Internet, the concern is that there will be no bandwidth left for one of the Internet's original purpose: exchange of scientific and academic research.

Two major projects currently under way in the United States to develop advanced technologies for the Internet are the Large Scale Networking (LSN) program and Internet2.

What are the Large Scale Networking and Internet2 programs? Out of a project entitled the Next Generation Internet (which ended in 2002), the U.S. government created the **Large Scale Networking (LSN)** program. LSN's aim is to fund the research and development of cutting-edge networking and wireless technologies and to increase the speed of networks.

The **Internet2** is an ongoing project sponsored by over 200 universities (supported by government and industry partners) to develop new Internet technologies and disseminate them as rapidly as possible to the rest of the Internet community. The Internet2 backbone supports extremely high-speed communications (up to 9.6 gigabits per second, or Gbps) and provides an excellent test bed for new data transmission technologies. It is hoped that the Internet2 will solve the major problem plaguing the current Internet: lack of bandwidth. Once the Internet2 is fully integrated with the current Internet, greater volumes of information should flow more smoothly.

What new experiences will the Internet provide in the future? When using the Internet today, we use our senses of sight and hearing to view various multimedia. But what about our senses of smell and taste? In 2002, TriSenx (**www.trisenx.com**) launched the Sensory Enhanced Net Experience machine, or the "Senx device." This device reads embedded Web page commands and uses specialized software to generate fragrances and aromas. The desktop device plugs into a port on your computer and is priced at around $370. With smell technology conquered, can the sense of taste be far behind? Certainly not! Printer-like devices could generate printed flavor cards in the near future. Several companies are working on bringing these devices to market.

But why would I want to smell and taste the Internet? Imagine watching a *Star Wars* DVD on your computer and being able to smell the ozone when a laser cannon evaporates an Imperial TIE fighter. In addition, advertisers could increase sales by inducing consumers to buy products after they've had a whiff of them. For example, Internet banner ads could be embedded with the sweet aroma of cookies, which might make you want to dash off to the store to buy some. If the smell doesn't do it, you can just download and print an ice-cream flavor card from the Internet and be able to taste it before you buy any.

How else will the Internet become a more integral part of our lives? In the future, you can expect to use the Internet to assist you with many day-to-day tasks that you now do manually. No longer will PCs and mobile devices be our primary access to the Internet. As other less-obvious Internet-enabled devices become popular and more accessible to the common consumer, our lives will become more Internet dependent. For example, Internet-enabled appliances and household systems are now available that allow your home virtually to run itself. For example, refrigerators can monitor their contents and go online to order more diet soda when they detect that the supply is getting low. Meanwhile, Internet heating and cooling systems can monitor weather forecasts and order fuel deliveries when supplies run low or bad weather is expected. These appliances will become more widespread as the price of equipment drops.

The uses for the Internet are limited only by our imaginations and the current constraints of technology. But as you enter the workforce perhaps you will invent the next killer consumer application (the next eBay?) or contribute to the development of key technologies (nanotech circuits?) that will drive the speed of the Internet to new heights. Think about what you will want to use the Internet for tomorrow—then make it a reality.

three

Summary

1. What is the origin of the Internet?

The Internet is the largest computer network in the world, connecting millions of computers. Government and military officials developed the Internet as a reliable means of communications in the event of war. Eventually, scientists and educators used the Internet to exchange research. Today, we use the Internet and the Web (which is a part of the Internet) to shop, research, communicate, and entertain ourselves.

2. How does data travel on the Internet?

A computer connected to the Internet acts as either a client, a computer that asks for information, or a server, a computer that receives the request and returns the information to the client. Data travels between clients and servers along a system of communication lines, or pathways. The largest and fastest of these pathways is the Internet backbone. To ensure that data is sent to the correct computer along the pathways, IP addresses (unique ID numbers) are assigned to all computers connected to the Internet.

3. What are my options for connecting to the Internet?

Home users have many options for connecting to the Internet. A dial-up connection, in which you connect to the Internet using a standard phone line, was at one time the standard way to connect to the Internet. Now, other connection options, called broadband connections, are faster and will soon make dial-up a legacy connection technology. Broadband connections include cable, DDSL, and satellite.

4. How do I choose an Internet service provider?

Internet service providers (ISPs) are national, regional, or local companies that connect individuals, groups, and other companies to the Internet. Factors to con-

sider in choosing an ISP include cost, quality of service, and availability.

5. What is a Web browser?

Once you're connected to the Internet, in order to locate, navigate to, and view Web pages, you need special software called a Web browser installed on your system. The most common Web browsers are Microsoft Internet Explorer, Firefox, and Safari.

6. What is a URL and what are its parts?

You gain access to a Web site by typing in its address, or Uniform Resource Locator (URL). A URL is composed of several parts, including the protocol, the host, the top-level domain, and, occasionally, paths (or subdirectories).

7. How can I use hyperlinks and other tools to get around the Web?

One unique aspect of the Web is that you can jump from place to place by clicking on specially formatted pieces of text called hyperlinks. You can also use tools such as Back and Forward buttons, History lists, breadcrumb lists, and Favorites or Bookmarks to navigate the Web.

8. How do I search the Internet using search engines and subject directories?

A search engine is a set of programs that searches the Web for specific keywords you wish to query and then returns a list of the Web sites on which those keywords are found. A subject directory is a structured outline of Web sites organized by topics and subtopics.

9. What are Boolean operators and how do they help me search the Web more effectively?

Sometimes, search engines return lists with thousands or millions of hits. Boolean

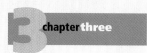

operators are words (AND, NOT, and OR) you can use to refine your searches, making them more effective.

10. How can I communicate through the Internet with e-mail, weblogs, chat, IM, newsgroups, and listservs?

Communication was one of the reasons the Internet was developed and is one of the primary uses of the Internet today. E-mail allows users to communicate electronically without the parties involved being available at the same time, while chat rooms are public areas on the Web where different people communicate. Weblogs are journal entries posted to the Web that are generally organized by a topic or area of interest and that are publicly available. Instant messaging enables you to communicate in real time with friends who are also online. Listservs are electronic mailings to groups of people, and newsgroups are online discussion forums in which people post messages and read and reply to messages from other newsgroup members. Both listservs and newsgroups are organized by topic or areas of interest. Listservs are private, whereas newsgroups are public.

11. How do I manage online annoyances like spam, pop-ups, cookies, spyware, and phishing?

The Web is filled with annoyances such as spam, pop-ups, cookies, spyware, and scams such as phishing that make surfing the Web frustrating and sometimes dangerous. Software tools help to prevent or reduce spam, pop-ups, and spyware, while exercising caution can prevent serious harm being done due to phishing and other Internet scams and hoaxes.

12. What is e-commerce and what e-commerce safeguards protect me when I'm online?

E-commerce is the business of conducting business online. E-commerce includes transactions between businesses (B2B), between consumers (C2C), and between businesses and consumers (B2C). Because more business than ever before is conducted online, numerous safeguards have been put in place to ensure transactions are protected.

13. What are the various kinds of multimedia files found on the Web and what software do I need to use them?

The Web is appealing because of its enriched multimedia content. Multimedia is anything that involves one or more forms of media in addition to text, including graphics, audio, and video clips. Sometimes you need a special software program called a plug-in (or player) to view and hear multimedia files. Plug-ins are often installed in new computers or are offered free of charge at manufacturers' Web sites.

14. What does the Internet of the future look like?

The Internet of the future will have higher bandwidth and will be able to provide additional services as a result of projects such as the Large Scale Networking (LSN) program and Internet2. Design enhancements to the Internet will engage more of our senses, including smell and taste. The Internet will become more ingrained into our daily lives as Internet-enabled appliances and household systems will provide more remote-control features for your home.

Buzz Words

Word Bank

- AOL 5
- Bookmark 9
- breadcrumb list 13
- browser 8
- Buddy List 7
- cable modem 2

- cookie(s) 12
- dial-up 1
- DSL 3
- hyperlink 11
- Internet service provider 6
- keyword 15

- newsgroup
- satellite 4
- search engine 14
- spam
- subject directory
- URLs 10

Instructions: Fill in the blanks using the words from the Word Bank.

The day finally arrived when Juan no longer was a victim of slow Internet access through a traditional (1) _____ connection. He could finally hook up to the Internet through his new high-speed (2) _____ . He had been investigating broadband access for a while and thought that connecting through his existing phone lines with (3) _____ would be convenient. Unfortunately, it was not available in his area. Where Juan lives, a clear southern exposure does not exist, so he did not even entertain the idea of a (4) _____ connection. Although Juan relished the speedy access, he was faced with changing from (5) _____ , his online service provider, to a different (6) _____ through his cable company. Although he needed to change his e-mail address, he was glad he didn't have to give up instant messaging, because his (7) _____ of online contacts had grown to be quite extensive. Juan knew he could access instant messaging through the (8) _____ Firefox.

Juan clicked on his list of favorite Web sites and found the movie review site he had saved as a (9) _____ the day before. He prefers to use this feature rather than entering in the (10) _____ of the sites he visits often. Juan navigated through the site, clicking on the (11) _____ that took him immediately to the page he was most interested in. Finding the movie he wanted to see, Juan ordered tickets online. The credit card information he input during an earlier visit to the site automatically appeared. Juan is glad that Web sites use (12) _____ to capture personal information.

Then, using the (13) _____ at the top of the Web site, he traced his steps back to his starting point. Juan next typed in the address for Google, his preferred (14) _____ , and typed in the (15) _____ to begin his search for a good restaurant in the area.

Becoming Computer Fluent

Instructions: Using keywords from the chapter, write a letter to your local cable company imploring it to bring cable modem service to your neighborhood. In the letter, include your dissatisfaction with dial-up as well as your opinion on why cable is better than DSL (which is currently being offered in your neighborhood) and satellite. Also include the activities on the Internet you think people in the community could benefit from by using high-speed cable access.

Self-Test

Instructions: Answer the multiple choice and true/false questions below for more practice with key terms and concepts from this chapter.

MULTIPLE CHOICE

1. The Internet was initially created for the purpose of
   a. online shopping
   b. military and educational communications
   c. personal and family communications
   d. e-commerce activities

2. The main artery, or largest and fastest pathway, of the Internet is called the
   a. TCP/IP line
   b. fiber optic network
   c. Internet backbone
   d. artery protocol

3. Which Internet connections use regular phone lines to connect to the Internet?
   a. dial-up and cable
   b. satellite and DSL
   c. cable and DSL
   d. dial-up and DSL

4. Which of the following Internet connection options is most likely to result in slower data transfer speeds due to users sharing the same lines?
   a. dial-up
   b. cable
   c. DSL
   d. None of the above

5. The software that is necessary to locate, view, and navigate the Web is called a(n)
   a. Internet service provider
   b. Web browser
   c. Web viewer
   d. Universal Resource Locator

6. Which of the following is not a way to search for information on the Web?
   a. spider directory
   b. search engine
   c. subject directory
   d. meta-search engine

7. An advantage of a Web-based e-mail account is that
   a. you have access to organizational tools to manage your e-mails
   b. your e-mail is more secure
   c. you are less subject to spam and other online annoyances
   d. you can access your e-mail from any computer with an Internet connection

8. Weblogs are
   a. private Web exchanges between two people
   b. online advertisements
   c. personal journal entries posted on the Web
   d. harmful Internet viruses

9. Phishing is
   a. a way to get useful information from a Web site
   b. a scam to obtain personal information
   c. a means to compliment another party via e-mail
   d. a type of chain letter sent over the Internet

10. To view and hear some multimedia files on the Web, you might need
    a. a browser
    b. a plug-in
    c. a player
    d. All of the above

TRUE/FALSE

_____ 1. The Web is a large network of networks, connecting millions of computers from around the world.

_____ 2. Satellite Internet connection is perfect for those users living in the city.

_____ 3. All search engines display the same results when the same keyword is used.

_____ 4. Cookies are small text files stored on your computer, intended to make your return visit to a Web site more efficient and better geared to your particular interests.

_____ 5. Internet2 is a project currently underway to explore expanding the capacity of the Internet.

Making the Transition to...
Next Semester

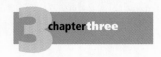

1. Online Support Facilities

Your school most likely has many online support facilities. Do you know what they are? Go to your school's Web site and search for online support.

a. Is there online tutoring?

b. Can you reserve a book from the library online?

c. Can you register for classes online? yes

d. Can you take classes online?

e. Can you buy books online?

2. Plagiarism Policies

Does your school have a plagiarism policy?

a. Search your school's Web site to find the school's plagiarism policy. What does it say?

b. How well do you paraphrase? Find some Web sites that help test or evaluate your paraphrasing skills.

3. Advanced Web Searches

Using search engines effectively is an important tool. Some search engines help you with Boolean-type searches using advanced search forms. Choose your favorite search engine and select the Advanced Search option. (If your favorite search engine does not have an advanced search feature, try Yahoo! or Google.)

a. Conduct a search for inexpensive vacation spots for spring break using Boolean search terms. Record your results along with your search queries.

b. Conduct the same search but use the advanced search form with your favorite search engine. Were the results the same? If there were any differences, what were they? Which was the best search method to use in this case and why?

4. Internet Connection Options

You are planning on moving to an apartment next semester and will be leaving behind the comforts of broadband access of the residence halls. Evaluate the Internet options available in your area.

a. Create a table that includes information on various dial-up ISPs, cable Internet, DSL, and satellite broadband service providers. The table should include the name of the provider, the cost of the service, the upload and download transfer rates, and the installation costs (service and parts). Also include whether a Web-based e-mail account will be available. Include the URL of each ISP or broadband service provider's Web site.

b. Based on the table you create, write a brief paragraph describing which service you would choose and why.

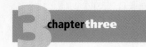

Making the Transition to... The Workplace

1. Online Résumé Resources

Using a search engine, locate several Web resources that offer assistance in writing a résumé. For example, the University of Minnesota (**www.umn.edu/ohr/ecep/resume**) has a résumé tutor that guides you as you write your résumé.

a. What other Web sites can you find that help you write a résumé?

b. Do they all offer the same services and have the same features?

c. Which Web site features do you think work best?

2. Online Cover Letter Resources

Your résumé will need to be accompanied by a cover letter. Research Web sites that offer advice for and samples of cover letters.

a. Which Web sites do you feel offer the best advice on how to write a cover letter?

b. Which style cover letter works best for you?

c. What do the Web sites say you should include in your cover letter and why?

3. Evaluating Web Content

You have noticed that your coworkers are using the Internet to conduct research. However, they are not careful to check the validity of the Web sites they find before using the information.

a. Research the Internet for Web site evaluation guidelines. Print out your sources and findings.

b. Using the material from Step (a), create a scorecard or set of guidelines that will help others determine whether a Web site is reliable.

4. Internet Connection Speed

You would like to know how fast your Internet connection speed is. Your coworker in the Information Technology (IT) department recommended the following sites for you to check out: **www.testmyspeed.com**, **www.bandwidthplace.com**, and **www.pcpitstop.com.**

a. List reasons why you would be interested in measuring your Internet connection speed.

b. List four factors that can affect your connection speed.

c. Discuss why "defragging" your hard drive may help improve your connection speed.

5. E-Mail Privacy

"An e-mail is no more private than a postcard."

a. Search the Internet for resources that can help you support and oppose the preceding statement. Print out sources for both sides of the argument.

b. Write a paragraph that summarizes your position.

Critical Thinking Questions

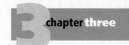

Instructions: Albert Einstein used "Gedanken experiments," or critical thinking questions, to develop his theory of relativity. Some ideas are best understood by experimenting with them in our own minds. The following critical thinking questions are designed to demand your full attention but require only a comfortable chair—no technology.

1. Internet and Society

The Internet was initially created in part to enable scientists and educators to share information quickly and efficiently. The advantages the Internet brings to our lives are evident, but does Internet access also cause problems?

a. What advantages and disadvantages does the Internet bring to your life?

b. What positive and negative effects has the Internet had on our society as a whole?

c. Some people argue that conducting searches on the Internet provides answers but does not inspire thoughtful research. What do you think?

d. Should use of the Internet be banned, or at least limited, for research projects in schools? Why or why not?

2. File Swapping Ethics

The original file-swapping site Napster's unprecedented rise to fame came to a quick halt because of accusations of copyright infringements. However, downloading music from the Internet still occurs.

a. What's your opinion on having the ability to download music files of your choice? Do you think the musicians who oppose online music sharing make valid points?

b. Discuss the differences you see between sharing music files online and sharing CDs with your friends.

3. The Power of Google

Google is the largest and most popular search engine on the Internet today. Because of its size and popularity, some people claim that Google has enormous power to influence a Web user's search experience solely by its Web site ranking processes. What do you think about this potential power? How could it be used in negative or harmful ways?

a. Some Web sites pay search engines to list them near the top of the results pages. These sponsors therefore get priority placement. What do you think of this policy?

b. What effect (if any) do you think that Google has on Web site development? For example, do you think Web site developers intentionally include frequently searched words in their pages so that they will appear in more hits lists?

c. When you "google" someone, you type their name in the Google search box to see what comes up. What privacy concerns do you think such "googling" could present? Have you ever googled yourself or your friends?

4. Charging for E-Mail?

Should there be a charge placed on sending e-mail or on having IM conversations? What would be an appropriate charge? If a charge is placed on e-mail and IM conversations, what would happen to their use?

Problem:

With millions of sites on the Internet, finding useful information can be a daunting—at times, impossible—task. However, there are methods to make searching easier, some of which have been discussed in this chapter. In this Team Time, each team will search for specific items or pieces of information on the Internet and compare search methodologies.

Task:

Split your group into three or more teams depending on class size. Each group will search for the same items.

Search Items:

- What was America's first penny candy to be individually wrapped?
- On which fraternity in which college was the movie *Animal House* based?
- What are the previous names for the American League baseball team the Anaheim Angels?
- What is the cheapest price to purchase a copy of the latest version of Microsoft Office Professional?
- Where can you go to buy the least expensive pink fuzzy bathrobe?

Process:

STEP 1. Teams are positioned at computers connected to the Internet.

STEP 2. Each team is given the list of search items. Each team should use a different search strategy from the following list: (1) use only a subject directory, (2) use only a search engine, or (3) use only the Advanced Search feature of a search engine. If more teams are allowed, you could also add a team that only uses a meta search engine. Other than these restrictions, teams can use whichever search strategies they feel will best reach the desired goal with the most accuracy in the least amount of time.

STEP 3. Print out the results from each search page. Teams compare printouts and notes to determine which search methods worked best for each item.

Conclusion:

Were subject directories better than search engines for certain searches? Which methods were used to narrow down choices? How were final answers determined?

Multimedia

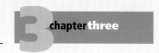

In addition to the review materials presented here, you'll find additional materials featured with the book's multimedia, including the *Technology in Action* Student Resource CD and the Companion Web site (**www.prenhall.com/techinaction**), which will help reinforce your understanding of the chapter content. These materials include the following:

ACTIVE HELPDESK

In Active Helpdesk calls, you'll assume the role of a Helpdesk operator taking calls about the concepts you've learned in this chapter. You'll apply what you've learned and receive feedback from a supervisor to review and reinforce those concepts. The Active Helpdesk calls for this chapter are listed here and can be found on your Student Resource CD:

- Connecting to the Internet
- Getting Around the Web
- Using Subject Directories and Search Engines
- Staying Secure on the Internet

SOUND BYTES

Sound Bytes are dynamic multimedia tutorials that help demystify even the most complex topics. You'll view video clips and animations that illustrate computer concepts, and then apply what you've learned by reviewing with the Sound Byte Labs, which include quizzes and activities specifically tailored to each Sound Byte. The Sound Bytes for this chapter are listed here and can be found on your Student Resource CD and on the Companion Web site (**www.prenhall.com/techinaction**):

- Connecting to the Internet
- Welcome to the Web
- Finding Information on the Web
- Creating a Web-Based E-mail Account
- Best Utilities for Your Computer

COMPANION WEB SITE

The *Technology in Action* Companion Web site includes a variety of additional materials to help you review and learn more about the topics in this chapter. The resources available at **www.prenhall.com/techinaction** include:

- **Online Study Guide.** Each chapter features an online true/false and multiple-choice quiz. You can take these quizzes, automatically check the results, and e-mail the results to your instructor.
- **Web Research Projects.** Each chapter features a number of Web research projects that ask you to search the Web for information on computer-related careers, milestones in computer history, important people and companies, emerging technologies, and the applications and implications of different technologies.

129

Application Software:

Programs That Let You Work and Play

Objectives

After reading this chapter, you should be able to answer the following questions:

ACTIVE HELPDESK

Using Application Software

Finals are this week. Jenna sits down to tackle the last project for her computer literacy class, a research assignment on "simulation" software. She's a fan of the *Sims* software games and is researching how different professions are using simulation software to train workers. Her instructor said the class can use any format for the project, so Jenna decides to do a PowerPoint presentation. With the Insert Slides from Outline feature, she transfers the outline she has already prepared in Word to PowerPoint slides. Using that as the basis for her presentation, she embellishes the slides with photographs and other illustrations, being careful to include references to her sources.

With the presentation complete, she burns it onto a CD using Roxio, then checks this project as "complete" in the Task Manager in Outlook. While in Outlook, Jenna turns to her calendar to check out tomorrow's activities, and answers a few e-mails that have accumulated in her Inbox. Last, she makes a note to balance her checkbook and to record her income and expenses from last month. Because she records all her banking transactions in the financial planning application Quicken, balancing her checkbook against the bank's records and monitoring her budget are a breeze. Later, she will download the information into TurboTax, a tax-preparation software program, so that she can do her taxes herself. She's saved a lot of money by doing her own taxes, and the programs were quite simple to learn.

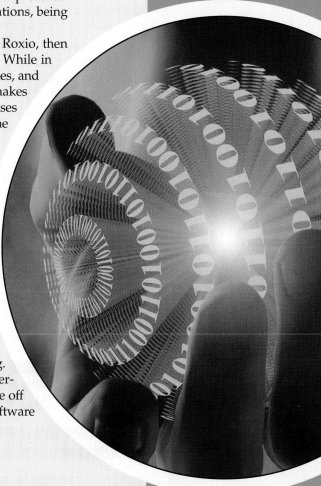

Before going to dinner, Jenna quickly checks into Blackboard, the course management software program her online class uses to manage assignments, homework, and discussions. Not seeing anything new to do, Jenna relaxes by playing a bit in *Sims*.

How often do you use software and what kinds of software are you familiar with? Do you know what software programs are on the market and what their most important features are? In this chapter, you'll learn about the kinds of software you can use to perform a variety of tasks, from simple word processing to digital image editing. We'll then discuss how you can buy software, what the different versions of software mean, and how you can legally get software for free off the Web. Finally, we'll look at how you can install and uninstall software safely on your system.

SOUND BYTES

- Creating Web Queries with Excel **(p. 134)**
- Using Speech-Recognition Software **(p. 141)**
- Enhancing Photos with Image-Editing Software **(p. 148)**

The Nuts and Bolts of Software

A computer without software is like a sandwich with no filling. Although the computer hardware is obviously critical, a computer system does nothing without software. What is software? Technically speaking, the term **software** refers to a set of instructions that tells the computer what to do. These instruction sets, also called **programs**, provide a means for us to interact with and use the computer, all without specialized computer programming skills. Your computer has two basic types of software, *system software* and *application software*:

- **System software** helps run the computer and coordinates instructions between application software and the computer's hardware devices. System software includes the *operating system* and *utility programs* (programs in the operating system that help manage system resources). We discuss system software in detail in Chapter 5.

- **Application software** is what you use to do tasks at home, school, and work. You can do a multitude of things with application software, such as writing letters, sending e-mail, balancing a budget, creating presentations, editing photos, and taking an online course, to name a few.

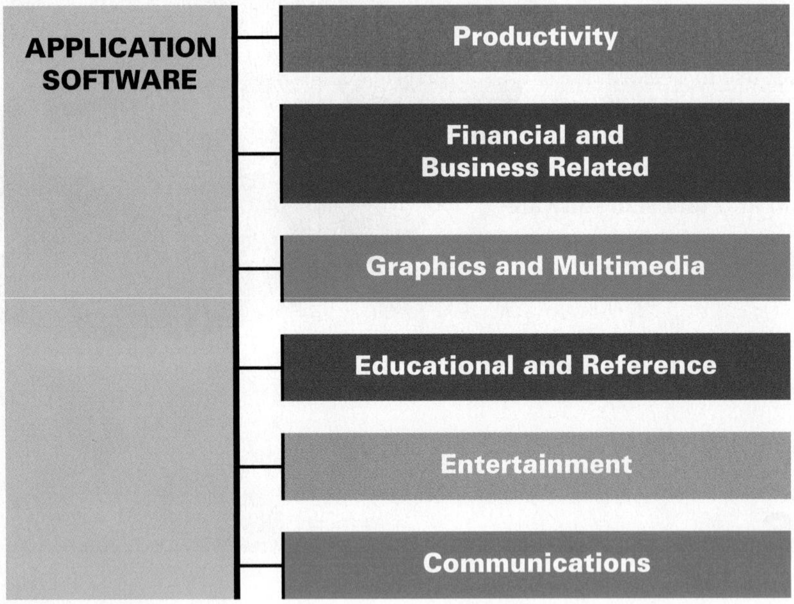

Figure 4.1 shows the various types of application software available. In this chapter, we look at all of these types in detail, starting with productivity software.

Productivity Software

It's safe to say you already regularly use some form of productivity software. **Productivity software** includes programs that enable you to perform various tasks generally required in home, school, and business. This category includes word processing, spreadsheet, presentation, database, and personal information manager (PIM) programs.

WORD PROCESSING SOFTWARE

What is the best software to use to create general documents? Most students use **word processing software** to create and edit written documents such as papers, letters, and résumés. Microsoft Word and Corel's WordPerfect are popular word processing programs. Writer, a word processing program from the OpenOffice suite, is gaining in popularity because it's available as a free download from the Internet. Writer has many of the same features as its higher-priced Word and WordPerfect competitors, making it a great choice for the cost-conscious.

Because of its general usefulness, word processing software is the most widely used software application. Word processing software has a key advantage over its ancestral counterpart, the typewriter: You can make revisions and corrections without having to retype an entire document. You can quickly and easily insert, delete, and move pieces of text. Similarly, you can remove and insert text from one document into another seamlessly.

How do I control the way my documents look? Another advantage of word processing software is that you can easily format, or change the appearance of, your document. As a result, you can produce sophisticated documents without having to send them to a professional printer. With formatting options, you can change fonts, font styles, and sizes; add colors to text; adjust the margins; add borders to portions of text or whole pages; insert bulleted and numbered lists; and organize your text into columns. You can also insert pictures from your own files or from a precreated gallery of images

FIGURE 4.1

Application Software Categories.

APPLICATION SOFTWARE

- Productivity
- Financial and Business Related
- Graphics and Multimedia
- Educational and Reference
- Entertainment
- Communications

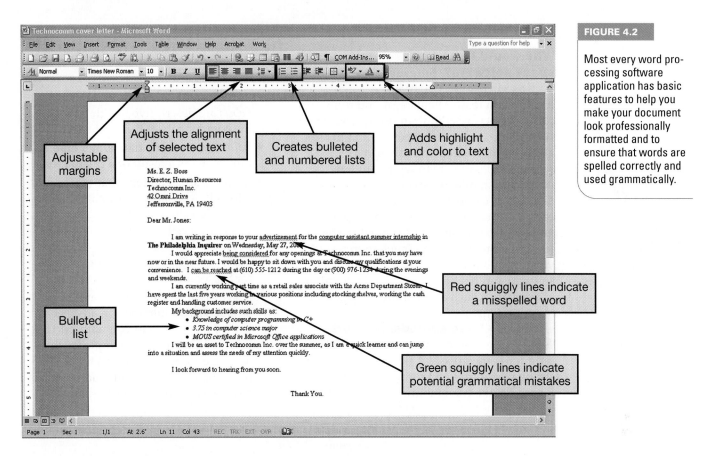

FIGURE 4.2

Most every word processing software application has basic features to help you make your document look professionally formatted and to ensure that words are spelled correctly and used grammatically.

Adjusts the alignment of selected text

Creates bulleted and numbered lists

Adds highlight and color to text

Adjustable margins

Ms. E. Z. Boss
Director, Human Resources
Technocomm Inc.
42 Omni Drive
Jeffersonville, PA 19403

Dear Mr. Jones:

I am writing in response to your advertizement for the computer assistant summer internship in **The Philadelphia Inquirer** on Wednesday, May 27, 20...

Red squiggly lines indicate a misspelled word

Bulleted list

Green squiggly lines indicate potential grammatical mistakes

called *clip art* that is included with the software. Using formatting tools, you can also spice up the look of your document by creating an interesting background or by adding a "theme" throughout your document with coordinated colors and styles. Figure 4.2 shows an example of some of the formatting options.

What special tools do word processing programs have?
You're probably familiar with the basic tools of word processing software. Most applications come with some form of spelling/grammar checker, for example. Another popular tool is the search/replace tool, which allows you to search for text in your document and automatically replace it with other text.

However, the average user is unaware of many interesting word processing software tools. For example, did you know that you could translate words or phrases to another language or automatically correct your spelling as you type? You can also automatically summarize key points in a text document. Writer, the word processing program in the OpenOffice Suite, has many of the same tools you're used to seeing in Microsoft Word, as well as some unique ones (see Figure 4.3).

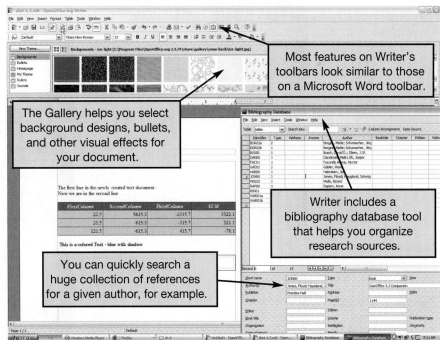

Most features on Writer's toolbars look similar to those on a Microsoft Word toolbar.

The Gallery helps you select background designs, bullets, and other visual effects for your document.

Writer includes a bibliography database tool that helps you organize research sources.

You can quickly search a huge collection of references for a given author, for example.

FIGURE 4.3

Writer, the word processing program in the OpenOffice Suite, has many of the same features as Word and WordPerfect as well as some unique ones.

SPREADSHEET SOFTWARE

Why would I need to use spreadsheet software? Spreadsheet software, such as Microsoft Excel or Lotus 1-2-3, enables you to do calculations and numerical analyses easily. You can use spreadsheet software to track your expenses and to create a simple budget. You can also use spreadsheet software to figure out how much you should be paying on your student loans, car loans, or credit card bills each month. You know you should pay more than the minimum payment to spend less on interest, but how much more should you pay and for which loan? Spreadsheet software can help you easily evaluate different scenarios such as planning the best payment strategy.

How do I use spreadsheet software? The basic element in a spreadsheet program is the *worksheet*, which is a grid consisting of columns and rows. As shown in Figure 4.4, the columns and rows form individual boxes called *cells*. Each cell can be identified according to its column and row position. For example, a cell in column A row 1 is referred to as cell A1. There are several types of data you can enter into a cell:

- *Labels* are descriptive text that identifies the components of the worksheet.
- *Values* are numeric data either entered in directly or as a result of a calculation.
- *Formulas* are equations that you build yourself using addition, subtraction, multiplication, and division, as well as values and cell references. For example, in Figure 4.4, you would type the formula =B8-B22 to calculate net income for September.
- *Functions* are formulas that are *preprogrammed* into the spreadsheet software. Functions help you with calculations ranging from the simple (such as adding groups of numbers) to the complex (such as determining monthly loan payments), without you needing to

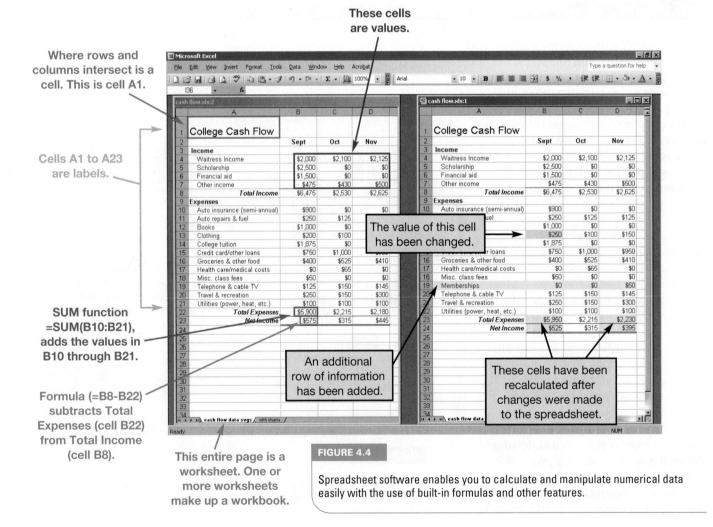

These cells are values.

Where rows and columns intersect is a cell. This is cell A1.

Cells A1 to A23 are labels.

SUM function =SUM(B10:B21), adds the values in B10 through B21.

Formula (=B8-B22) subtracts Total Expenses (cell B22) from Total Income (cell B8).

The value of this cell has been changed.

An additional row of information has been added.

These cells have been recalculated after changes were made to the spreadsheet.

This entire page is a worksheet. One or more worksheets make up a workbook.

FIGURE 4.4

Spreadsheet software enables you to calculate and manipulate numerical data easily with the use of built-in formulas and other features.

know the exact formula. So, in Figure 4.4, to calculate your average earned income in September, you could use the built-in AVERAGE function, which would look like this: =AVERAGE(B4:B7).

The primary benefit of spreadsheet software is its ability to recalculate all functions and formulas in the spreadsheet automatically when assumptions are changed. For example, in Figure 4.4, you can insert an additional row (Memberships) and change a value (September clothing expense), then recalculate the results for Total Expenses and Net Income without having to redo the worksheet from scratch.

Because automatic recalculation enables you to see immediately the effects that different options have on your spreadsheet, you can quickly test different assumptions in the same analysis. This is called a "what-if" analysis. Look again at Figure 4.4 and ask, "What if college tuition goes up another $100? What impact will such an increase have on my budget?" By adding another $100 to tuition shown in the budget in Figure 4.4, you will automatically know the impact a tuition increase will have on your expenses and net income.

How do I change the way my spreadsheets look? To make important data more apparent or an entire spreadsheet more readable, you may want to adjust the size of cells or add colors to text labels. Spreadsheet software offers similar formatting options to those found in word processing software, including the ability to change the font and style of text and numbers. In addition, you can add colored shading and borders, change the height and width of rows and columns, and apply symbols to currency ($) and percentage (%) values.

What kinds of graphs and charts can I create with spreadsheet software? Sometimes it's easier to see the meaning of numbers when they are shown in a graphical format, or a chart. As shown in Figure 4.5, most spreadsheet applications allow you to create a variety of charts, including basic column charts, pie charts, and line charts, with or without three-dimensional (3-D) effects. In addition to these basic charts, you can use stock charts (for investment analysis) and scatter charts (for statistical analysis), as well as create custom charts.

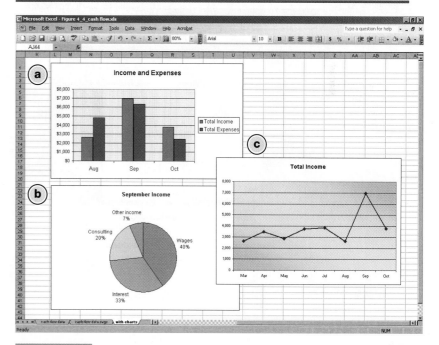

FIGURE 4.5

(a) Column charts show comparisons. (b) Pie charts show how parts contribute to the whole. (c) Line charts show trends over time.

Are spreadsheets used for anything besides financial analysis? Even if you never need to crunch a number, spreadsheets are good tools for keeping track of information such as addresses or for creating simple lists of your CD collection. Excel, for example, offers database-type features that enable you to sort through your address book quickly to find a particular contact or to filter a list to show a subset of contacts, perhaps only those people to whom you want to send party invitations. Spreadsheets also contain time and date functions, so you can use them as calendar and appointment files.

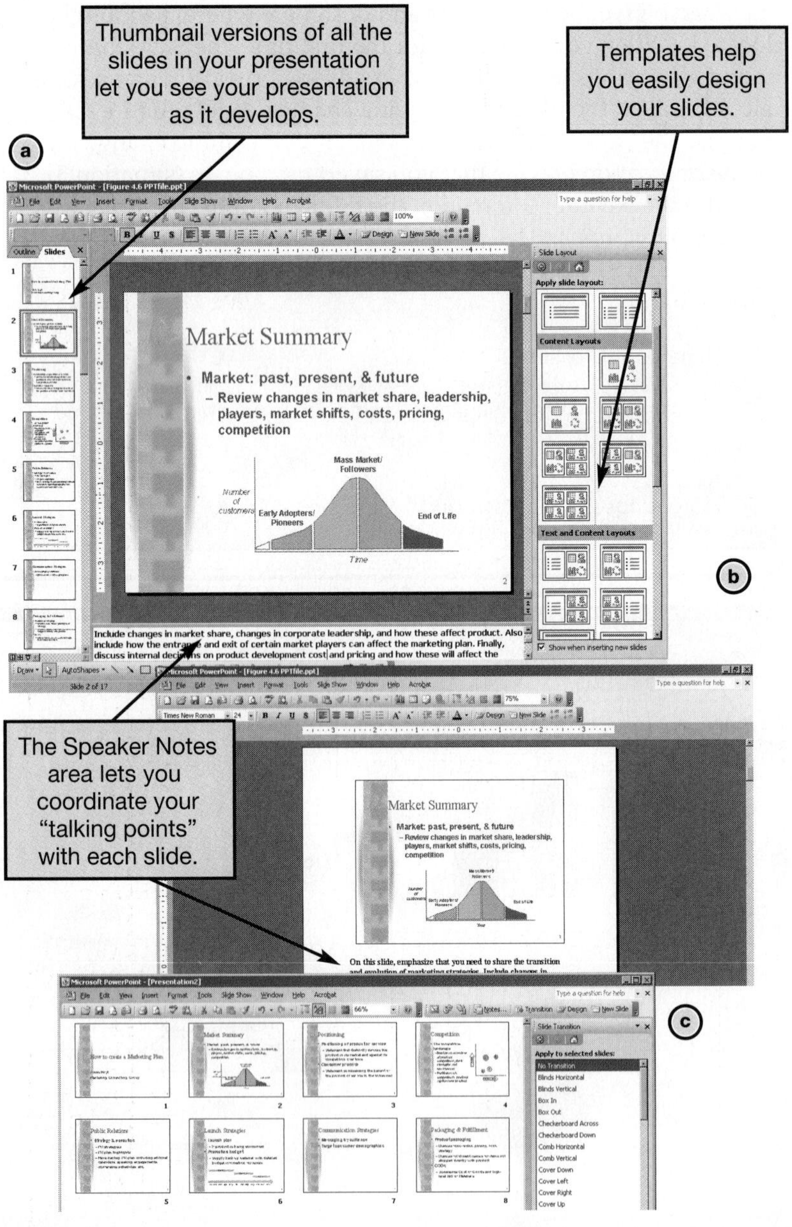

PRESENTATION SOFTWARE

What software do I use to create presentations? You've probably sat through presentations during which the speaker's dialogue is displayed in slides projected on a screen. These presentations can be very basic outlines, containing only a few words and simple graphics, or elaborate multimedia presentations with animated text, graphic objects, and colorfully formatted backgrounds. You use **presentation software** such as Microsoft PowerPoint or Corel Presentations to create these types of dynamic slide shows. Because these applications are so simple to use, you can produce high-quality presentations without a lot of training.

How do I create a presentation? Using the basic features included in presentation software, creating a slide show is very simple. To arrange text and graphics on your slides easily, you can choose from a variety of *slide layouts*. These layouts give you the option of using a single or double column of bulleted text as well as various combinations of bulleted text and other content such as clip art, graphs, photos, and even video clips.

You can also lend a theme to your presentation by choosing from different *design templates*. You can use animation effects to control how and when text and other objects enter and exit each slide. Similarly, slide transitions add different effects as you move from one to the next during the presentation.

Are there different ways to view my slides while I'm working on my presentation? There are several different formats with which you can view your presentation. The most common is Normal (or Slide) view (see Figure 4.6a). In recent versions of PowerPoint, this view consists of three panes: the left pane shows either small versions of the slides or an outline of the presentation; the middle pane shows the slide you are currently working on; and the bottom pane shows speaker notes. Speaker notes are helpful notes to yourself you use while you give your presentation; these notes can be seen and modified in Notes view (see Figure 4.6b) as well as in Normal view.

Finally, you can view the slides in Slide Sorter view (see Figure 4.6c). In this view, you can see thumbnail versions of your

Thumbnail versions of all the slides in your presentation let you see your presentation as it develops.

Templates help you easily design your slides.

The Speaker Notes area lets you coordinate your "talking points" with each slide.

FIGURE 4.6

Using PowerPoint, you can view your slides in three views: (a) Normal, (b) Notes, and (c) Slide Sorter.

FIGURE 4.7

In databases, similar information is organized by main topic into tables, and grouped into categories called fields. Each individual row of data is called a record. Some databases have multiple tables that "relate" to each other through common fields.

Microsoft Access - [SalesDeptContactInfo : Table]

File   Edit   View   Insert   Format   Records   Tools   Window   Help   Type a question for help

ContactID	First Name	Last Name	CompanyName	Street Address	City	State	Business Phone
1	Susan	Scantosi	eWidgetPlus	363 Rogue Street	St. Louis	MO	(612) 444-1236
2	Thomas	Mazeman	BooksRUs	2165 Piscotti Ave	Springfield	IL	(888) 234-6983
3	Douglas	Seaver	Printing Solutions	7700 First Ave	Topeka	KS	(888) 988-2678
4	Amir	Ramiv	TechStands	1436 Riverfront Place	St. Louis	MO	(877) 867-7656
5	Franklin	Scott	WorksSuite	8789 Ploughman Drive	Tulsa	OK	(800) 864-2390
6	Ronald	Komeika	Creekside Financial	1264 Pond Hill Road	Toledo	OH	(343) 333-3333
7	Barbara	Mitchell	Market Tenders	9823 Bridge Street	LaPorte	IN	(888) 238-2123
(AutoNumber)							

The category First Name is a field

All the information for Douglas Seaver represents one record

slides. It is easiest to rearrange slides and add transitions and other effects when you're in Slide Sorter view.

DATABASE SOFTWARE

How can I use database software?
Database software, such as Corel Paradox and Microsoft Access, is basically a complex electronic filing system. As mentioned earlier, spreadsheet applications include many database features and are easy to use for simple database tasks such as sorting, filtering, and organizing data. However, you need to use a more robust, full-featured database application to manage larger and more complicated groups of data that contain more than one table or when you need to group, sort, and retrieve data and to generate reports.

Traditional databases are organized into fields, records, and tables, as shown in Figure 4.7. A *field* is a data category such as "First Name," "Last Name," or "Street Address." A *record* is a collection of related fields, such as "Douglas Seaver, Printing Solutions, 7700 First Avenue, Topeka, KS, (888) 988-2678." A *table* groups related records together, such as "SalesDeptContactInfo."

How do businesses use database software?
Many online businesses use database applications because users can easily open, view, and update live data within a Web browser from anywhere. For example, many online companies have their inventory in a database that is automatically revised as each order is placed. Companies such as FedEx and UPS let customers search

their online databases for tracking numbers, allowing customers to get instant information on the status of their packages. Other businesses use databases to keep track of clients, invoices, or personnel information.

PERSONAL INFORMATION MANAGER (PIM) SOFTWARE

Which applications should I use to manage my time, contact lists, and tasks?
Most productivity software suites contain some form of **personal information manager (PIM) software**, such as Microsoft Outlook or Lotus Organizer. These programs strive to replace the management tools found on a traditional desk, such as a calendar, address book, notepad, and to-do list. Some PIMs contain e-mail management features so that you can not only receive and send e-mail messages, but also organize them into various folders, prioritize them, and coordinate them with other activities in your calendar (see Figure 4.8).

FIGURE 4.8

The Outlook Today feature in Microsoft Outlook includes common PIM features, such as a summary of your appointments, a list of your tasks, and how many new e-mail messages you have.

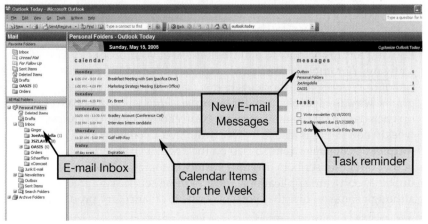

New E-mail Messages

E-mail Inbox

Calendar Items for the Week

Task reminder

If you share a common network and are using the same PIM software as others on the network (as is often the case in offices), you can use a PIM program to check people's availability before scheduling meeting times. If you are working on a team project, you can create and electronically assign tasks to group members using a PIM. You can even track each person's progress to ensure that the team finishes the project on time.

PRODUCTIVITY SOFTWARE TOOLS

What tools can help me work more efficiently with productivity software? Whether you are working on a word processing document, spreadsheet, database, or slide presentation, there are several tools you can use to increase your efficiency:

- **Wizards** are step-by-step guides that walk you through the necessary steps to complete a complicated task. At each step, the wizard asks you questions. Based on your responses, the wizard helps you complete that portion of the task. Many productivity software applications include wizards. For example, you can easily create charts in Excel using the Excel Chart Wizard.
- **Templates** are forms included in many productivity applications that provide the basic structure for a particular kind of document, spreadsheet, or presentation. Templates can include specific page layout designs, special formatting and styles relevant to that particular document, as well as automated tasks (macros).
- **Macros** are small programs that group a series of commands to run as a single

command. Macros are best used to automate a routine task or a complex series of commands that must be run frequently. For example, a teacher may write a macro to sort the grades in her grade book automatically in descending order and to highlight those grades that are below a C average. Every time she adds the results of an assignment or test, she can set up the macro to run through those series of steps automatically.

INTEGRATED SOFTWARE APPLICATIONS VS. SOFTWARE SUITES

Are there different ways to buy productivity software? You can buy productivity software as individual stand-alone programs, as integrated software applications, or as a suite of software applications.

Integrated Software Applications

What's an integrated software application? An **integrated software application** is a single software program that incorporates the most commonly used tools of many productivity software programs into one *integrated* stand-alone program. Microsoft Works is an example of an integrated software application. Note that integrated software applications are not substitutes for the full suite of applications they replace. Generally, because they don't include many of the more complex features of the stand-alone productivity software applications, they can be thought of as "software lite." To have access to the full range of functionality of word processing and spreadsheet software, for example, you should purchase the individual applications or a suite that includes each of these applications.

Figure 4.9 shows the Task Launcher for Microsoft Works (the Task Launcher is the first window that opens when you launch Microsoft Works). As you can see, this integrated software application includes word processing, spreadsheet, and database features as well as templates, calendar, encyclopedia, and map features.

Why would I use an integrated software application instead of individual stand-alone programs? Integrated software applications are perfect if you don't need the more advanced fea-

BITS AND BYTES

Productivity Software Tips and Tricks

Looking for tips on how to make better use of your productivity software? A number of Web sites send subscribers daily e-mails full of tips, tricks, and shortcuts to their favorite software programs. **www.NerdyBooks.com**, for example, sends subscribers a free tip each day to their e-mail account. NerdyBooks's free *Who Knew?* weekly newsletter is also full of software tips. *Dummies Daily* (**http://etips.dummies.com**), based on the *For Dummies* series of help books, offers subscribers tips on a variety of topics, including productivity software applications. Most of these services are free, although some require that you subscribe to an ancillary product.

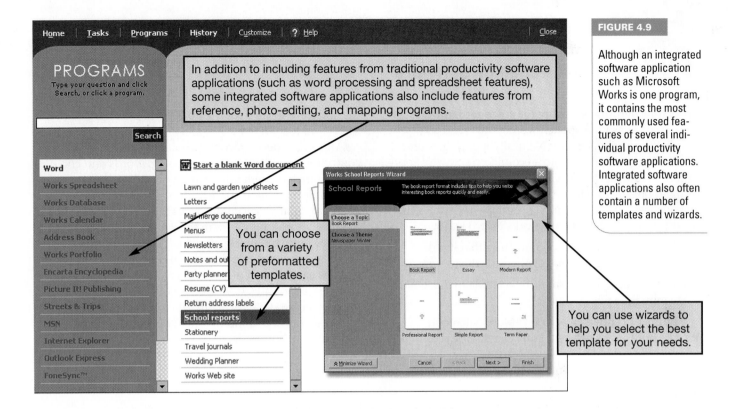

In addition to including features from traditional productivity software applications (such as word processing and spreadsheet features), some integrated software applications also include features from reference, photo-editing, and mapping programs.

You can choose from a variety of preformatted templates.

You can use wizards to help you select the best template for your needs.

FIGURE 4.9

Although an integrated software application such as Microsoft Works is one program, it contains the most commonly used features of several individual productivity software applications. Integrated software applications also often contain a number of templates and wizards.

tures found in the individual productivity software applications. Also, if you don't have the interest or time to learn how to use the features in a stand-alone application, integrated software programs are the better choice because they contain many templates. In addition to templates for frequently developed documents such as résumés, cover letters, and invoices, integrated software programs contain hundreds of nonstandard templates, such as fitness workout tracking worksheets, CD inventory databases, and mortgage payment schedules. Some of these templates enable you to accomplish tasks that would perhaps be too complicated to tackle without a template.

Integrated software programs are also less expensive than their full-featured counterparts. However, if you find your needs go beyond the limited capabilities of an integrated program, you might want to consider buying those individual programs that meet your particular requirements, or you may want to consider buying a software suite.

Software Suites

What's a software suite? A **software suite** is a group of software programs that have been bundled together as a package.

You can buy software suites for many different categories of applications, including productivity, graphics, and virus protection. Microsoft Office is just one example of the many types of software suites on the market today (see Figure 4.10). You can also buy different versions of the same suite, the difference being the combination of software applications included in each version.

FIGURE 4.10

Software suites provide users with a cheaper method of obtaining all of the software they want to buy in one bundle.

Speech-Recognition Software

Speech-recognition software (or **voice-recognition software**) translates your spoken words into typed text. ScanSoft's product, Dragon NaturallySpeaking, is one of the leading stand-alone voice-recognition software applications on the market. Microsoft has incorporated speech recognition software features into its word processing, spreadsheet, and presentation programs in Office 2003. Speech-recognition software works in two ways:

- It can perform dictation, meaning that it will "type" the words you speak into a document.

- It can execute the formatting and file management commands you give to it.

Figure 4.11 shows how you can use Microsoft Word's built-in speech-recognition software to instruct the software to carry out simple voice commands to select and format text.

Although speech recognition can be useful, getting a computer to understand your spoken words and correctly translate them into printed digital content are difficult. Improvements to the process continue to be made, and current accuracy rates for Dragon NaturallySpeaking v7 are in the 90 percent range. How does the software work? It's an extremely complicated process. As you speak, the speech-recognition software divides each second of your speech into 100 individual samples, or sounds. It then compares these individual sounds with a database (called a *codebook*) containing samples of every sound a human being can make. When a match is made, your voice sound is given a

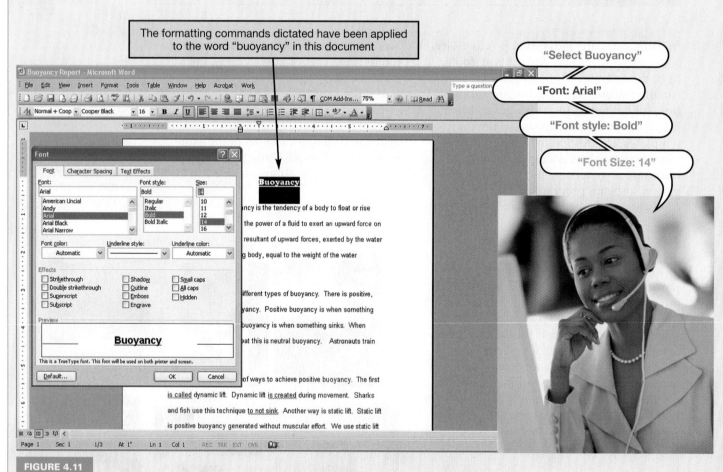

> The formatting commands dictated have been applied to the word "buoyancy" in this document

> "Select Buoyancy"

> "Font: Arial"

> "Font style: Bold"

> "Font Size: 14"

FIGURE 4.11

Speech-recognition software allows you to not only create documents through dictation, but also to edit and format the documents with simple voice commands.

number that corresponds to the number of the similar sound in the database.

Once your voice sounds are assigned values, these values are matched with another database containing *phonemes* for the language being spoken. A phoneme is the smallest phonetic unit that distinguishes one word from another. For example, "b" and "m" are both phonemes that distinguish the words *bad* and *mad* from each other in the English language. A typical language such as English is comprised of thousands of different phonemes. And because of differences in pronunciation, some phonemes may actually have several different corresponding matching sounds.

Once all the sounds are assigned to phonemes, word and phrase construction can begin. The phonemes are matched against a word list that contains transcriptions of all known words in a particular language. Because pronunciation can vary (for example, *the* can be pronounced so that it rhymes with *duh* or *see*), the word list must contain alternate pronunciations for many words. Each phoneme is worked on separately; the phonemes are then chained together to form words that are contained in the word list. Because a variety of sounds can be put together to form many different words, the software analyzes all the possible values and picks the one value that it determines has the best probability of correctly matching your spoken word. The word is then displayed on the screen or is acted upon by the computer as a command.

Why are there problems with speech-recognition software? We don't always speak every word the same way, and accents and regional dialects result in great variations in pronunciations. Therefore, speech recognition is not perfect and requires significant training. Training entails getting the computer to recognize your particular way of speaking, a process that involves reading prepared text into the computer so the phoneme database can be adjusted to your specific speech patterns.

Another approach to improve speech inconsistencies is to restrict the word list to a few key words or phrases and then have the computer guess the probability that a certain phrase is being said. This is how cell phones that respond to voice commands work. The phone doesn't really figure out you said "call home" by breaking down the phonemes. It just determines how likely it is that you said "call home" as opposed to "call office." This cuts down on the processing power

needed and reduces the chance of mistakes. However, it also restricts the words you can use to achieve the desired results.

Although not perfect, speech-recognition software programs can be of invaluable service for individuals who can't type very well or who have physical limitations that prevent them from using a keyboard or mouse. For those whose careers depend on a lot of typing, using speech-recognition software reduces the chances of their incurring debilitating repetitive strain injuries. Additionally, because most people can speak faster than they can write or type, speech-recognition software can help you work more efficiently. It can also help you to be productive during generally nonproductive times. For example, you can dictate into a digital recording device while doing other things such as driving, then later download the digital file to your computer and let the program type up your words for you.

Speech recognition should continue to be a hot topic for research over the next decade. Aside from the obvious benefits to persons with disabilities, many people are enamored with the idea of talking to their computers!

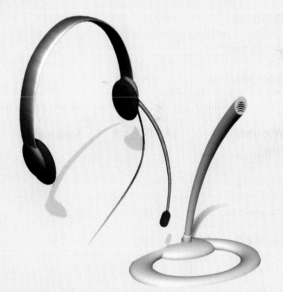

SOUND BYTE

Using Speech-Recognition Software

In this Sound Byte, you'll see a demonstration of the speech-recognition software included with Microsoft Office. You'll also learn how to access and train speech-recognition software so that you can create and edit documents without typing.

Which software applications do productivity software suites contain? Most productivity software suites contain the same basic software programs, such as word processing, spreadsheet, presentation, and PIM software. The Microsoft Office suite bundles together the word processing program Microsoft Word, the spreadsheet program Excel, the presentation program PowerPoint, and the PIM program Outlook. However, depending on the version and manufacturer, some suites also include other programs, such as database programs and speech-recognition software.

What are the most popular productivity software suites? As illustrated in Figure 4.12, there are three primary developers of productivity software suites: Microsoft, Corel, and Lotus. Microsoft and

Corel offer different bundled packages with different combinations of software applications, whereas Lotus offers only SmartSuite.

Why would I buy a software suite instead of individual programs? Most people buy software suites because suites are cheaper than buying each program individually. In addition, because the programs bundled together in a software suite come from the same developer, they work well together (that is, they provide for better integration) and share common features, toolbars, and menus. For example, say you use Corel's WordPerfect, a stand-alone word processing software application, and Microsoft's stand-alone spreadsheet program Excel. If you want to incorporate an Excel chart into a WordPerfect document, you may have trouble because the two programs come from different developers. However, with a

FIGURE 4.12   Software Suites

	Word Processing	Spreadsheet	Presentation	PIM	Database	Other Included Software
Microsoft Office 2003	**Word**	**Excel**	**PowerPoint**	**Outlook**	**Access**	**Publisher**
Professional	x	x	x	x	x	x
Standard	x	x	x	x		
Academic*	x	x	x	x		
Small Business	x	x	x	x		x

* Academic edition is priced lower than Standard edition and is for non-commercial use only.

WordPerfect Office 12	**WordPerfect**	**QuattroPro**	**Presentation**	**Address Book**	**Paradox**	**Other Included Software**
Standard	x	x	x	x		
Professional	x	x	x	x	x	
Student & Teacher	x	x	x	x	x	
Home	x	x				Personal Financial Essentials, Corel Photobook and Photo Album, and Pinnacle

Lotus SmartSuite	**Word Pro**	**Lotus 1-2-3**	**Freelance**	**Organizer**	**Approach**	
SmartSuite	x	x	x	x	x	

software suite such as Microsoft Office, you can easily incorporate an Excel chart into a Word document with a few simple clicks.

Financial and Business-Related Software

Financial and business-related software can be grouped into three main categories:

- Personal financial software that helps you perform businesslike tasks at home, such as preparing your taxes and managing your personal finances
- General business software used in different capacities across industries
- Specialized business software designed for particular industries

PERSONAL FINANCIAL SOFTWARE

What software can I use to do my taxes? Tax-preparation software such as Intuit's TurboTax and H&R Block's TaxCut enable you to prepare your state and federal taxes on your own rather than having to hire a professional. Each program offers a complete set of tax forms and instructions as well as expert advice on how to complete each form. Error-checking systems are built into the programs to help catch your mistakes. Furthermore, TurboTax offers you guidance on financial planning for the following year to help you effectively plan and manage your financial resources (see Figure 4.13).

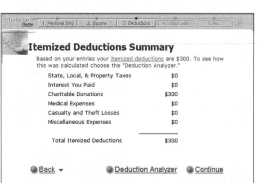

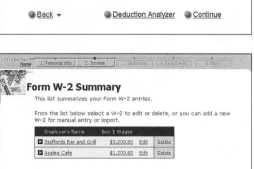

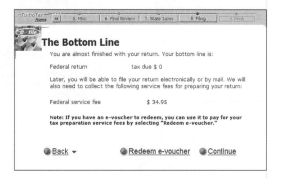

FIGURE 4.13

Tax-preparation software, such as Intuit's TurboTax, enables you to prepare your taxes on your own through a guided step-by-step process.

BITS AND BYTES

Need a Way to Share Files? Try PDF

Say you've created a file in Microsoft Excel, but the person to whom you want to send it doesn't have Excel, or any spreadsheet software, installed on his computer. Or say your sister owns a Mac and you own a PC. You are constantly running into file-sharing problems. What do you do in these situations? One solution is to create a PDF file. Portable Document Format (PDF) is a file format you can create with Adobe Acrobat. This program transforms any file, regardless of its application or platform, into a document that can be shared, viewed, and printed by anyone who has Adobe Reader. Adobe Acrobat is an expensive application, but if you are using Writer, the word processing application from OpenSource, or WordPerfect, you can create PDF files easily. Adobe Reader, the program you need to read all PDF files, is a free download available at **www.adobe.com**.

What software can I use to help keep track of my finances? Financial planning software helps you manage your daily finances. Intuit's Quicken and Microsoft Money are popular examples. These programs include electronic checkbook registers and automatic bill payment tools, as shown in Figure 4.14. With these features, you can print checks from your computer or pay your regular monthly payments such as rent and student loans with automatically scheduled online payments or printed checks. The software automatically records all transactions, even online payments, in your checkbook register. You assign categories to each transaction, use these categories to analyze your spending patterns, and can even compare your spending habits to a budget you set up.

Financial planning programs also coordinate with tax-preparation software. Quicken, for example, coordinates seamlessly with TurboTax so you never have to go through your checkbook and bills to find tax deductions and tax-related income or expenses. In addition, many banks and credit card companies offer online services that download into Quicken or Money. Quicken even offers a credit card. All your purchases are organized into categories and are downloaded easily to your Quicken file to further streamline your financial planning and record keeping. You can also purchase a Pocket PC version of Quicken to install on your personal digital assistant (PDA) so your financial records are always at your fingertips.

FIGURE 4.14

When you write checks with personal financial planning software, your transactions are entered automatically in an electronic checkbook.

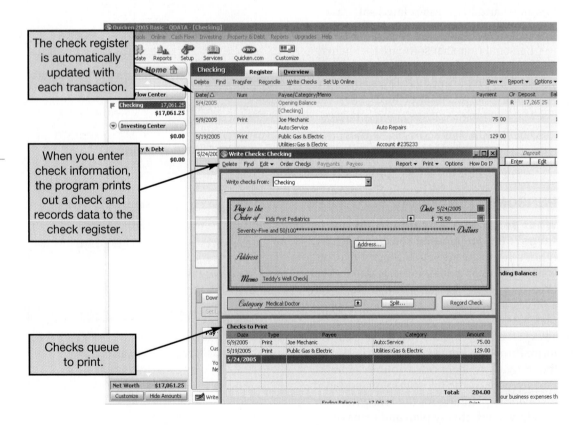

What programs are good for people with small businesses? If you have a small business or a hobby that produces income, you know the importance of keeping good records and tracking your expenses and income. **Accounting software** helps small business owners manage their finances more efficiently by providing tools for tracking accounts receivable and accounts payable. In addition, these applications also offer inventory management plus payroll and billing tools. Examples of accounting software applications include Intuit's QuickBooks and Peachtree Accounting. Both programs include templates for invoices, statements, and financial reports so that small business owners can create common forms and reports.

GENERAL BUSINESS SOFTWARE

What financial and business-related software do bigger businesses use?

As indicated earlier, some business software is task-specific and used across a variety of industries. This type of software includes programs such as Palo Alto Software's Business Plan Pro and Marketing Plan Pro, which help businesses write strategic and development plans.

Another good example of general business software is **project management software**, such as Microsoft Project. Such software helps project managers easily create and modify project management scheduling charts like the one shown in Figure 4.15. Charts like these help project managers plan and track specific project tasks as well as coordinate personnel resources.

What other kinds of software do businesses often use? Mapping programs such as Rand McNally's StreetFinder and Microsoft's Streets & Trips are perfect for businesses that require a lot of travel. These programs provide street maps and written directions to locations nationwide, and you can customize the maps so that they include landmarks and other handy traveling sites such as airports, hotels, and restaurants.

These programs are often available in versions for PDAs and for cars and work in conjunction with a Global Positioning System (GPS) device to help you navigate your way

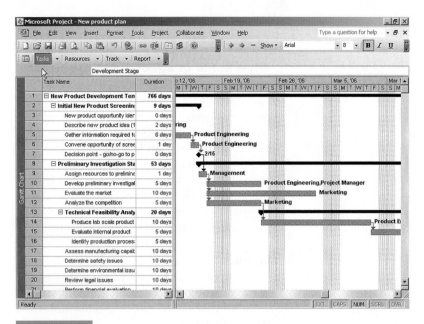

FIGURE 4.15

A Gantt chart in Microsoft Project provides project managers with a visual tool for assigning personnel and scheduling and managing tasks.

around. Mapping programs are essential for sales representatives or delivery-intensive businesses. Of course, mapping programs are also good for nonprofessionals traveling to unfamiliar locations.

Businesses also use **customer relationship management (CRM) software** to store sales and client contact information in one central database. Sales professionals use CRM programs to get in touch and follow up with their clients. These programs also include tools that enable businesses to assign quotas and to create reports and charts to document and analyze actual and projected sales data. CRM programs coordinate well with PIM software such as Outlook and can be set up to work with PDAs. GoldMine Business Contact Manager from FrontRange Solutions is an example of a CRM program.

CRM software deals directly with the customer. Other software products, such as **Enterprise Resource Planning (ERP) systems**, are used to control many "back office" operations and processing functions such as billing, production, inventory management, and human resources management. ERP systems are implemented by third-party vendors and matched directly to the specific needs of a company.

SPECIALIZED BUSINESS SOFTWARE

What kinds of specialized business software are there? Some software applications are tailored to the needs of a particular company or industry. Such software designed for a specific industry is called **vertical market software**. For example, the construction industry uses software such as Intuit's Master Builder, which features estimating tools to help construction companies bid on jobs. It also integrates project management functions and accounting systems that are unique to the construction industry.

Other examples of vertical market software include property management software for real estate professionals; ambulance scheduling and dispatching software for emergency assistance organizations; and library automation software for cataloging, circulation, inventory, online catalog searching, and custom report printing at libraries.

In addition to these specific business software applications that companies can buy off the shelf, programs are often custom developed to address the specific needs of a particular company. These custom applications are often referred to as **proprietary software** because they are owned and controlled by the company that uses them.

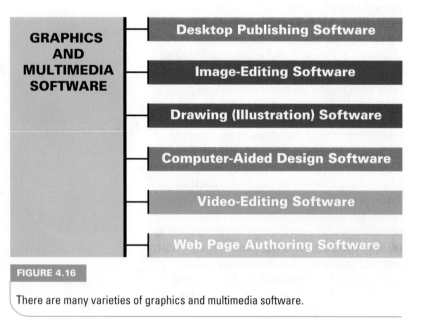

GRAPHICS AND MULTIMEDIA SOFTWARE

Desktop Publishing Software

Image-Editing Software

Drawing (Illustration) Software

Computer-Aided Design Software

Video-Editing Software

Web Page Authoring Software

FIGURE 4.16

There are many varieties of graphics and multimedia software.

Graphics and Multimedia Software

Graphics software encompasses a wide range of programs home users and professionals alike use to design and create attractive documents, images, illustrations, and Web pages. In addition, graphics software allows engineers and other professionals to create three-dimensional models and drawings to help them visualize construction plans. Graphics software is a part of a larger group of software: multimedia software. **Multimedia software** includes video and audio editing software, animation software, and other special software required to produce computer games. In this section, we look at a number of popular types of graphics and multimedia software, shown in Figure 4.16.

DESKTOP PUBLISHING SOFTWARE

What software can I use to lay out and design newsletters and other publications? Desktop publishing (DTP) software allows you to incorporate and arrange graphics and text in your documents in creative ways. Although many word processing applications allow you to use some of the features that are hallmarks of desktop publishing, specialized desktop publishing software such as QuarkXPress and Adobe PageMaker allows professionals to design books and other publications (see Figure 4.17) with complex layouts.

What tools do desktop publishing programs include? Desktop publishing programs offer a variety of tools with which you can format text and graphics. With text formatting tools, you can easily change the font, size, and style of your text as well as arrange text on the page in different columns, shapes, and patterns. You can import files into your documents from other sources, including elements from other software programs (such as an Excel chart or text from Word) or graphics files. You can readily manipulate graphics with tools that can crop, flip, or rotate images or modify the image's color, shape, and size. Desktop publishing programs also include features that allow you to publish to the Web.

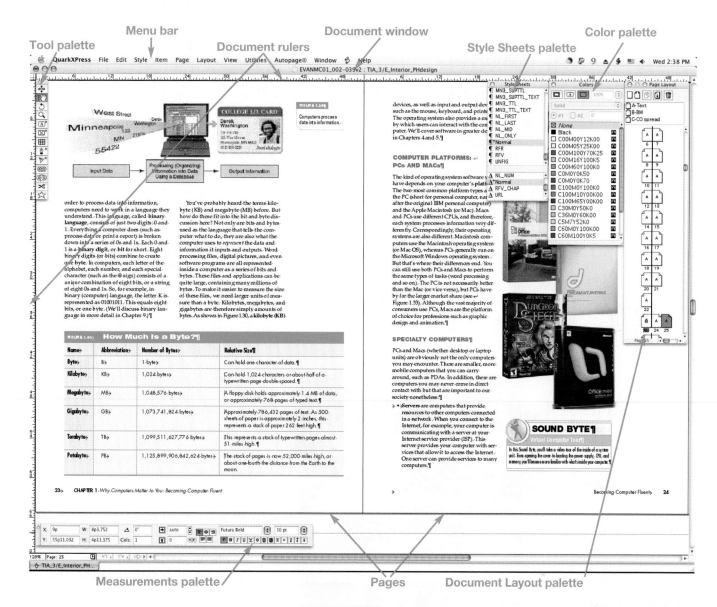

FIGURE 4.17

Major publishing houses use professional desktop publishing programs such as QuarkXPress to lay out the pages of textbooks.

IMAGE-EDITING SOFTWARE

What software do I use to edit my photos? As its name implies, **image-editing software** (sometimes called **photo-editing software**) enables you to edit photographs and other images. Image-editing software includes tools for basic modifications to digital images such as removing red-eye, modifying color hues, and removing scratches or rips from scanned images of old photos. Many of these software packages now also include an extensive set of painting tools such as brushes, pens, and artistic-type mediums (paints, pastels, oils) that allows you to create realistic-looking images as well. Often graphic designers use digital photos and images as a basis for their design and then modify these images within image-editing software to create their final product.

Adobe Photoshop and Jasc Paint Shop Pro 7 are full-featured image-editing software applications. They each offer sophisticated tools such as those for layering images (placing pictures on top of each other) and masking images (hiding parts of layers to create effects such as collages) (see Figure 4.18). Designers use these more sophisticated tools to create the enhanced digital images used commercially in logos, advertisements, and on book and CD covers.

Can a nonprofessional use image-editing software? Image-editing programs such as ArcSoft, Microsoft Picture It!, and Roxio PhotoSuite are programs geared to the casual home user and are often included with digital cameras. With these applications, you can perform the most common image-editing tasks, such as taking out red-eye and cropping and resizing pictures. These programs enable you to add creative effects such as borders and frames, and some have templates in which you can insert your favorite pictures into preformatted calendar pages or greeting cards. They may also have photo fantasy images that let you paste a face from your digital image

SOUND BYTE

Enhancing Photos with
Image-Editing Software

In this Sound Byte, you'll learn tips and tricks on how to best use image-editing software. You'll learn how to remove the red-eye from photos and incorporate borders, frames, and other enhancements to produce professional effects.

onto the body of a professional athlete or other famous person.

There are also many image-editing programs sold as stand-alone programs on the market that are designed specifically for the casual user and that are perfect for viewing or modifying a digital image. If you want to use a program that offers you more than basic features but that is still easy to use, Adobe Photoshop Elements is a good basic program for the novice (see Figure 4.19). With this program, you can improve the color balance of an image, touch up an image (by removing red-eye, for example), add creative effects to an image, or group images together to create montages.

DRAWING SOFTWARE

What kind of software should I use for simple illustrations? Drawing software (or **illustration software**) programs let you create or edit two-dimensional line-based drawings. You use drawing software to create technical diagrams or original non-photographic drawings, animations, and illustrations using standard drawing and painting tools such as pens, pencils, and paintbrushes. You can also drag geometric objects from a toolbar onto the canvas area to create images and use paint bucket, eyedropper, and spray can tools to add color and special effects to the drawings.

Are there different types of drawing software? Drawing software is used in both creative and technical drawings. Software applications such as Adobe Illustrator include tools that let you create professional-quality illustrations. The Illustrator image controls let you create complex designs and use special effects, and its warping tool allows you to bend, stretch, and twist portions of your image or text. Because of its many tools and fea-

FIGURE 4.18

With some image-editing software, you can take two individual pictures and combine them into one picture.

tures, Illustrator is one of the preferred drawing software programs of most graphic artists.

Microsoft Visio is a program used to create technical drawings, maps, basic block diagrams, networking and engineering flowcharts, and project schedules. Visio uses project-related templates with special objects that you drag onto a canvas. For example, using the Visio floor template and dragging furniture and other interior objects onto it, you can create an interior design like the one shown in Figure 4.20. In addition to these uses, Visio also provides mind-mapping templates that help you organize your thoughts and ideas.

COMPUTER-AIDED DESIGN SOFTWARE

What software is used to make 3-D models? Computer-aided design (CAD) programs are a form of 3-D modeling that engineers use to create automated designs, technical drawings, and model visualizations. Specialized CAD software is used in industries such as architecture, automotive, aerospace, and medical engineering.

With CAD software, architects can build virtual models of their plans and readily visualize all aspects of design prior to actual construction. Engineers use CAD software to design everything from factory components to bridges. The 3-D nature of these programs allows engineers to rotate the model and make adjustments to their designs where necessary, thus eliminating costly building errors.

CAD software is also being used in conjunction with GPS systems for accurate placement of fiber-optic networks around the country. The medical engineering community uses CAD to create anatomically accurate solid models of the human anatomy to develop medical implants quickly and accurately. The list of CAD applications keeps growing as more and more industries realize the benefits CAD can bring to their product development and manufacturing process.

VIDEO-EDITING SOFTWARE

What kind of software can I use to edit my digital videos? With the boom of digital camcorders and increasing graphics capabilities on home computers, many

FIGURE 4.19

Image-editing software like Adobe Elements enables you to easily create (a) calendars, (b) greeting cards and postcards, (c) slide shows, and (d) more from your digital photos.

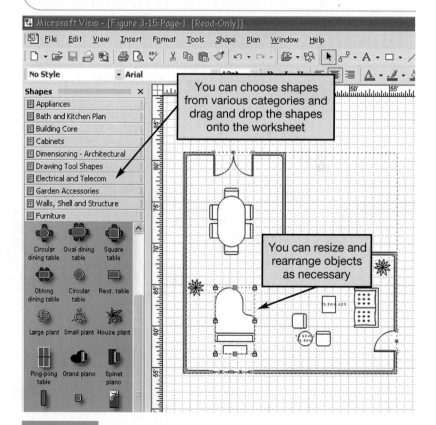

FIGURE 4.20

The drawing program Visio lets you create different types of diagrams easily with drag-and-drop options.

people are experimenting with **digital video–editing software**. There are quite a few video-editing software applications on the market at a wide range of prices. Although the most expensive products (such as Adobe Premiere) offer the widest range of special effects and tools, there are some moderately priced video-editing programs that have enough features to keep the casual user happy. Microsoft Movie Maker and Apple's iMovie HD have intuitive drag-and-drop features that makes it simple to create near-professional movies with little or no training (see Figure 4.21). Some software developers offer free trial versions for you to test run before buying them. For example, Microsoft Movie Maker can be downloaded for free from the Microsoft Web site for those running Windows XP.

Does video-editing software support all kinds of video files? Video files come in a number of formats. Many of the affordable video-editing software packages support only a few types of video files. For example, one application may support Windows Media Player video files, whereas another may support QuickTime or RealPlayer video files instead. Fortunately, software boxes list which types of video files the software supports. You should buy the least expensive application with the greatest number of supported file formats.

How do I incorporate or edit sound in digital videos? Adding music to or editing sounds in digital videos can change a standard video into a work of art. If you have Microsoft Windows on your computer, you already have Sound Recorder. With this program you can record simple sounds, adjust volume to fade in or fade out sounds, and even add echo and other special effects to your video. Sony's Sound Forge and other similar applications incorporate a variety of features that enable you to edit sounds and music by removing and rearranging sound clips in addition to adding special volume and sound effects. Professionals and real audio enthusiasts use higher-end products such as Adobe Premiere, but the high price of these programs tends to limit them from being used by nonprofessionals.

For more information on video-editing software, see the Technology in Focus feature "Digital Entertainment" on page 174.

WEB PAGE AUTHORING SOFTWARE

What software do I use to create a Web page? Web page authoring software allows even the novice user to design interesting and interactive Web pages, with-

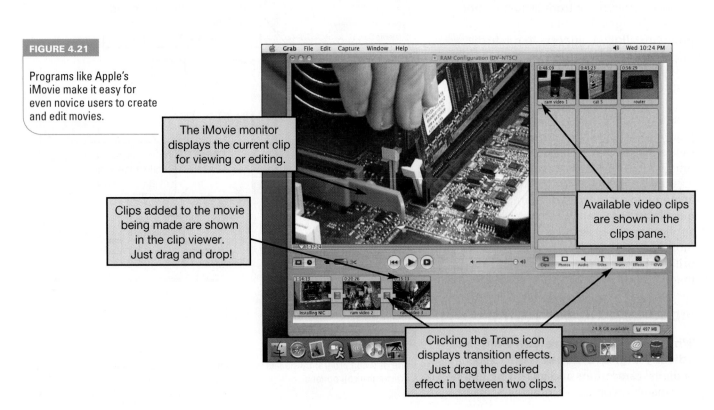

FIGURE 4.21

Programs like Apple's iMovie make it easy for even novice users to create and edit movies.

The iMovie monitor displays the current clip for viewing or editing.

Clips added to the movie being made are shown in the clip viewer. Just drag and drop!

Available video clips are shown in the clips pane.

Clicking the Trans icon displays transition effects. Just drag the desired effect in between two clips.

out knowing any Hypertext Markup Language (HTML) code. Web page authoring applications often include wizards, templates, and reference materials to help you easily complete most Web page authoring tasks. More experienced users can take advantage of the advanced features included in this software, including features that enable you to add headlines and weather information, stock tickers, and maps to make your Web content current, interactive, and interesting. Microsoft FrontPage and Macromedia Dreamweaver are two of the leading programs to which both professionals and casual Web page designers turn.

Are there other ways to create Web pages? If you need to produce only the occasional Web page and do not need a separate Web page authoring program, you'll find that many software applications include features that enable you to convert your document easily into a Web page. For example, in some Microsoft Office applications, you can choose to save the file as a Web page and the application will automatically convert the file to a Web-compatible format.

Educational and Reference Software

Educational software refers to the variety of software applications on the market that offer some form of instruction or training. Software applications that act as sources for reference materials, such as the standard atlases, dictionaries, and thesauri, are referred to collectively as **reference software**.

EDUCATIONAL SOFTWARE

What kinds of educational software applications are there? Although there is a multitude of educational software products geared to the younger set, software developers have by no means ignored adult markets. In addition to all the products relating to the younger audience, there are software products that teach users new skills such as typing, languages, cooking, or playing the guitar. Test preparation software is popular for students taking the SAT, GMAT, LSAT, or MCAT exams.

Is there software to train you to use special machines? There are plenty of programs with tutorial-like training for many popular computer software applications. These programs use illustrated step-by-step instructions to guide the user through unfamiliar skills. Some training programs use simulation techniques where the learning is done in a realistic environment. Such simulation training programs include commercial and military flight training, surgical instrument training, and machine operation training.

A benefit of these simulated training programs is they safely allow users to experience potentially dangerous situations. Consequently, users of these training programs are more likely to take risks and learn from their mistakes—something they could not afford to do in real-life situations. Simulated training programs save costly errors. Should something go awry, the cost of the error is only restarting the simulation program as opposed to the high costs of a real-life error.

Do I need special software to take courses online? Taking classes over the Internet is fast becoming a popular method of learning because it offers greater schedule flexibility for busy students. Although some courses are run from an individually developed Web site, many online courses are run through **course management software** programs such as Blackboard and WebCT. These programs provide traditional classroom tools such as calendars and grade books over the

BITS AND BYTES

What Is "Edutainment"?

Many educational programs for children disguise the learning process by combining it with interactive puzzles, games, and other fun activities. Because it combines education and entertainment, this software is referred to as *edutainment*. Often these programs include a theme or story that is carried throughout the program, and learners are rewarded with prizes when they've correctly answered questions. Edutainment software is most popular with preschool and early elementary-aged students, but adult edutainment programs exist to assist older learners in mastering certain skills such as typing or English as a second language.

Internet (see Figure 4.22). There are also special areas for students and their professor to exchange ideas and information in chat rooms, discussion forums, and e-mail messages. Of course, there are areas where assignments, lectures, and other pertinent class information can be posted.

REFERENCE SOFTWARE

How can I use software to research information? Encyclopedias are no longer those massive sets of books in the library. Now you can find full sets of encyclopedias on small CD-ROMs. In addition to containing all the information found in traditional paper encyclopedias, electronic encyclopedias include multimedia content such as interactive maps, video, and audio clips. When researching famous sports figures, for example, you not only can read

about Jackie Robinson, but also can view a video of Robinson in play. World Book, Britannica, and Grolier all offer their encyclopedias on CD. Many encyclopedias have online components, as well. Encarta, for example, can be found on the Web at **www.encarta.com**.

What other types of reference software are there? As with all other categories of software, reference software is a growing field. In addition to the traditional atlases, dictionaries, and thesauri available on CD, many other types of reference software are available. Medical and legal reference software is available for basic information you would have previously had to pay a professional to obtain. For example, medical references such as *Franklin Physicians' Desk Reference* enable you to access information on Food and Drug Administration (FDA)-approved drugs, whereas legal software packages such as Family Lawyer provide standard legal forms.

Entertainment Software

Entertainment software is, as its name implies, designed to provide users with entertainment. Computer games make up the vast majority of entertainment software. These digital games began with Pong, Pacman, and Donkey Kong and have evolved to include many different categories, including action, adventure, driving, puzzle, role-playing, card-playing, sports, strategy, and simulation. Entertainment software also includes other types of computer applications, such as **virtual reality programs**, which turn an artificial environment into a realistic experience.

How do I tell what computer games are appropriate for a certain user? The Entertainment Software Rating Board (ESRB) is a self-regulatory body established in 1994 by the Entertainment Software Association (see **www.esrb.org**). The ESRB rating system helps parents and other consumers choose the computer and video games that are right for their families by providing information about game content, so they can make informed purchase decisions. ESRB ratings have two parts: *rating symbols* suggest age appropriateness for the game, and *content descriptors* indicate

FIGURE 4.22

Course management software such as Blackboard provides traditional classroom features such as important classroom documents (syllabus, calendar), classroom discussions, and a grade book in an online environment.

FIGURE 4.23   **ESRB Ratings**

ESRB Rating	Description	Example
Adults Only	Titles rated **AO (Adults Only)** have content suitable only for adults. Titles in this category may include graphic depictions of sex and/or violence. Adults Only products are not intended for persons under the age of 18.	Riana Rouge
Everyone	Titles rated **E (Everyone)** have content that may be suitable for ages 6 and older. Titles in this category may contain minimal cartoon, fantasy, or mild violence and/or infrequent use of mild language.	Myst John Madden Football
Teen	Titles rated **T (Teen)** have content that may be suitable for ages 13 and older. Titles in this category may contain violence, suggestive themes, crude humor, minimal blood, and/or infrequent use of strong language.	Warcraft Deer Hunter Everquest
Mature	Titles rated **M (Mature)** have content that may be suitable for persons ages 17 and older. Titles in this category may contain mature sexual themes, more intense violence and/or strong language.	Halo/Halo 2 Doom Tom Clancy games Urban Runner

elements in a game that may have triggered a particular rating and/or may be of interest or concern.

To take full advantage of the ESRB rating system, it's important to check both the rating symbol (on the front of the game box) and the content descriptors (on the back of the game box). Figure 4.23 shows an example of the rating symbols and a content descriptor.

Can I make my own video games?
Creating video games is catching on as a new career opportunity for video game enthusiasts. Professionally created video games involve some careful programming and use fairly sophisticated software applications that are not recommended for the casual home enthusiast. However, if you should want to try your hand at creating your own video games, multimedia software applications such as Macromedia Flash RPG Maker will certainly provide you with enough tools to create games for your personal entertainment.

Do I need special equipment to run entertainment software? As with any computer software, you need to make sure your system has enough processing power, memory (RAM), and hard disk capacity to run the program. Because entertainment programs generally incorporate

sophisticated multimedia features, you need to ensure your system has the appropriate sound cards, video cards, speakers, monitor, and CD or DVD drives as well.

Some software may require a joystick to play the game. Virtual reality programs also require specialized equipment such as goggles or gloves (see Figure 4.24).

FIGURE 4.24

(a) You need a joystick to play some computer games. (b) Virtual reality games require special equipment such as goggles to deliver the three-dimensional effects.

DIGITAL AUDIO SOFTWARE

Why are MP3 files so popular? MP3 is the audio compression format that reduces the file size of traditional digital audio files so more files take up less storage capacity. For example, a typical CD holds between 10 and 15 songs in uncompressed format and between 100 and 180 songs in MP3 format. The smaller file size not only lets you store and play music in less space, but also distributes it swiftly and easily over the Internet. Hundreds of digital audio software applications are available to allow you to copy (or rip), play, edit, and organize MP3 files, as well as to record and distribute your own music online. Most digital audio software programs support one of the following functions. Some programs, like the popular iTunes, incorporate many of these capabilities into one multi-functional program:

- **MP3 recording:** Allows you to record directly from streaming audio and other software or microphone sources to MP3 format.

- **Ripping:** Allows you to copy CDs and encode them to MP3 format.

- **MP3 burning:** Allows you to record MP3 files onto a CD.

- **Encoding and decoding/format conversion:** Encoders are programs that convert files to MP3 format at varying levels of quality. Most ripping software has encoders built in to convert the files directly into MP3 format. Decoding/format conversion programs allow you to convert MP3 files to another audio format such as WAV, Windows Media Audio (WMA), or AIFF.

Can I modify or edit my MP3 files? Audio-editing software includes tools that make editing your MP3 files as easy as editing your text files. Such software enables you to do some basic editing such as cutting dead-air space from the beginning or end of the song or cutting a portion out in the middle. You can also add special sound effects or smooth abrupt starts and finishes on your MP3 files.

How can I manage all the MP3 files on my hard drive? Software such as MP3 File Editor and iTunes allow you to organize MP3 and other audio files so that you can sort, filter, and search your collection by artist, album, or category. Using these programs, you can manage individual tracks, generate play lists, and even export the files to a database or spreadsheet application for further manipulation (see Figure 4.25).

Communications Software

The advent of the computer and other technologies has broadened our ability to communicate with each other beyond the standard phone call and written letter. Today, we have other means of communications available that combine computer hardware and software. For example, e-mail and instant messaging, which are discussed in Chapter 3, are fast replacing more traditional means of communications. **Groupware**, software that helps people who are in different locations work together using e-mail and online scheduling tools, is fast becoming a popular means for communication. Lotus Notes from IBM and Novell's Groupwise are two popular groupware solutions that support the sharing of information within a company.

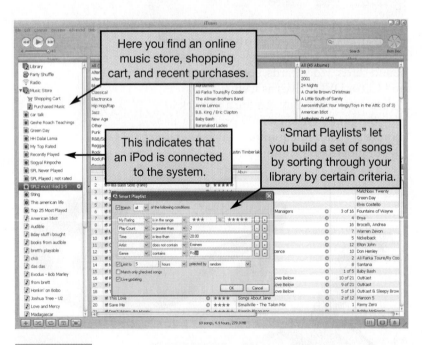

FIGURE 4.25

Software programs such as iTunes help you manage all the MP3 files on your computer. You can sort, filter, and search your collection by artist, album, or category, as well as create play lists.

TRENDS IN IT

Emerging Technologies: Is It Real or Is It Virtual?

The applications of virtual reality, beyond familiar video games, are almost endless. Three-dimensional environments created by computers are getting better and better at helping people experience new things, or experience familiar things in new ways.

Overcoming fear is a growing application for virtual reality programs. Dentists, for instance, are trying virtual reality headsets for their patients to help them reduce anxiety about getting their teeth cared for. And fear of flying can be treated with virtual reality therapy. Gradual exposure to takeoff and landing in a virtual environment allows would-be travelers to face their phobias and prepare to take the next step into a real flight. Fear of heights, spiders, thunderstorms, and even public speaking (which is many people's greatest fear) have been treated with virtual reality therapy.

Virtual reality programs provide the opportunity for people with disabilities to practice maneuvering wheelchairs or to become familiar with public transportation before venturing into a new city or town. Surgeons can practice difficult procedures on a virtual patient without risk. And therapy for burn patients that incorporates virtual reality seems to ease pain more when used with medication than does medication alone (see Figure 4.26). While being treated, patients wear virtual reality goggles and immerse themselves in a world apart from their pain. Psychologists say that patients are so absorbed in the virtual reality experience that they are not as aware of their pain.

You won't lose any weight or get in shape in a virtual gym. But you can get instant coaching feedback and see a replay of your performance. And you can do it without getting hurt, which is a big advantage for coaches in risky sports such as football and skiing. Swiss Olympic skier Simon Ammann used a virtual reality program to compare his jumps wearing two different pairs of skis to determine which was best. He and his coach believe the change in skis that resulted from the experiment was a factor in his gold-medal performance at the 2002 Winter Olympics.

Of course, if you'd rather travel, you can always use the virtual reality program created at UCLA to explore the world of ancient Rome in A.D. 400, through simulations of 22 temples, courts, and monuments. The ancient cityscape is loaded into a supercomputer with a special spherical screen that fills the viewer's field of vision. You can not only see the monuments, but you can also move around them and even levitate for a closer look. See you there!

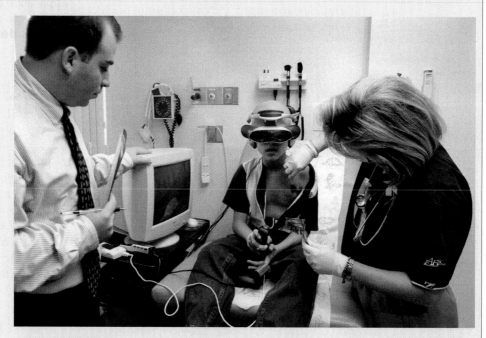

FIGURE 4.26

Burn patients who incorporate virtual reality into their therapy sometimes experience less pain.

What other kinds of group communications software exist? To enhance long-distance group communications, businesses often utilize videoconferencing technologies. **Videoconferencing** involves the transmission of audio (voice) and video (picture) data over computer networks. Videoconferencing systems can be quite complex or as simple as a computer setup enhanced with a camera on top of a monitor, microphone, and speakers. Improvements in videoconferencing technology have made this form of communication much more efficient and effective than it was when it was first introduced.

Web conferencing is another form of group communications that allows you to conference with anyone, anywhere over the Internet (see Figure 4.27). All you need to conduct or join an online meeting is a computer, an Internet connection, and a phone (for audio conference). With Web conferencing software, you have the ability to conduct meetings with audio, file transfer, streaming video, and whiteboard capabilities.

Do I need special software to have phone conversations over the Internet? **Telephony technology**, often referred to as Voice over Internet Protocol (VoIP), is the transmission of telephone calls over the Internet. VoIP can take place between two computers, between a computer and a phone with an adapter, or between two phones with adapters. If you are not using phones to make your phone calls, your computer system needs a microphone and speakers. In any case, the data from the phone call is sent over the Internet, so you'll need an Internet connection as well as a software client, a small software application that is provided by the VoIP provider to run on its server.

How do I make a phone call with VoIP? Depending on the service, there are two ways to make a phone call with VoIP. One is to use a traditional telephone and an adapter that connects to your cable/DSL Internet connection. The other is to use a microphone headset that is plugged into your computer. You dial the phone number using the number pad on your keyboard, and the call is then routed through the Internet connection. Either way, once dialed, the call goes through your local telephone company to a VoIP provider, over the Internet to the called party's local telephone company, and finally to the party you wish to speak to.

Getting Help with Software

If you need help while you work with software, there are several different resources you can access to find answers to your questions. For general help or information about the product, many Web sites offer **frequently asked questions (FAQs)** for answers to the most common questions.

Some programs also offer online help and support. Sometimes, online help is

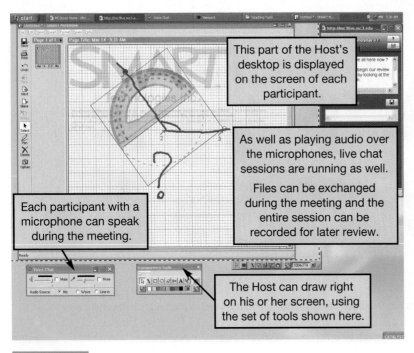

This part of the Host's desktop is displayed on the screen of each participant.

As well as playing audio over the microphones, live chat sessions are running as well.

Files can be exchanged during the meeting and the entire session can be recorded for later review.

Each participant with a microphone can speak during the meeting.

The Host can draw right on his or her screen, using the set of tools shown here.

FIGURE 4.27

Web Demo, a software product from Linktivity, enables users to conduct meetings online. Meeting participants need a computer, an Internet connection, and a telephone to have access to file exchange, audio, streaming video, and whiteboard capabilities during the online meeting.

comparable to a user's manual. However, many times, online help also allows you to chat (using the Internet) with a member of an online support team. Some applications are context-sensitive and offer help based on what task you're doing or ScreenTips to explain where your cursor is resting.

In Microsoft Office applications, on the far right of the menu bar, you'll find the Ask a Question box in which you can type your question. The Office Assistant, generally an animated paper clip (also known as Clippy or Clippit; see Figure 4.28), provides tips on tasks while you're working or answers your specific questions.

Finally, there is the Help menu on the menu bar of most applications where you can choose to search an index or content outline to find out the nature of almost any feature of a Microsoft application.

Where do I go for tutorials and training on an application? If you need help learning how to use a product, sometimes the product's developer offers online tutorials or program tours that show you how to use the software features. Often, you can find good tutorials simply by searching the Internet. **PCShowandTell.com**, for example, includes more than 40,000 multimedia help files and is accessible for a small annual fee. **Webnests.com**, an online company dedicated to online hosting products, offers free tutorials for many software applications.

Buying Software

These days, you no longer need to go to a computer supply store to buy software. You can find software in almost any retail environment. Additionally, you can purchase software online, through catalogs, or at auctions.

STANDARD SOFTWARE

What application software comes with my computer? Virtually every new computer comes with some form of application software, though the applications depend on the hardware manufacturer and computer model. You can usually count on your computer having some

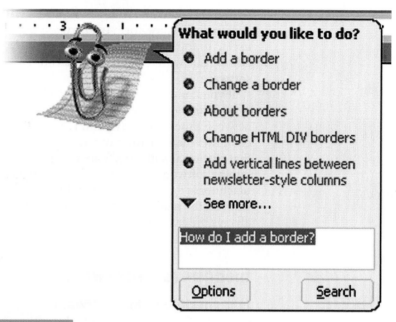

FIGURE 4.28

The Microsoft Office Assistant gives you tips on tasks you're working on or answers specific questions you have.

form of productivity software preinstalled, such as Microsoft Works or Corel OfficeSuite.

Multimedia-enriched computers may also offer graphics software or a productivity suite that includes Web page

BITS AND BYTES

Software 911

If your software problem is more technical, such as an error message, there are lots of resources available on the Web. Most software manufacturers have support on their Web sites that include FAQs, discussion boards monitored by employees of the company, and collections of tutorials and troubleshooting advice. For example, to resolve problems with Microsoft products, check the Microsoft Knowledge Base, located at **support.microsoft.com**. The Knowledge Base is a collection of more than 250,000 articles written by Microsoft support professionals reflecting their resolution of customer issues and problems. To search the Knowledge Base most effectively, use a search engine such as Google. To do so, go to Google (**www.google.com**) and select the Advanced Search option. Type in your search terms but specify *support.microsoft.com* as the domain to be searched.

authoring software. Many computers will also include some form of software that is useful to the home user, such as image editing software or financial planning software.

If you know you'll need a particular type of software not offered as standard on your new computer, you may want to see if the computer manufacturer has an offer to add that particular software. Sometimes, initially buying software through the hardware manufacturer is less expensive than buying software on the retail market, but this is not always the case so do some comparative pricing before you buy.

DISCOUNTED SOFTWARE

Is it possible to buy software at a discount? Software manufacturers understand that students and educators often need to use software for a short period of time because of a specific class or project. Additionally, software developers want to encourage you to learn with their product, hoping you'll become a long-term user of their software. Therefore, if you're a student or an educator, you can purchase software that is no different from regularly priced software at prices that are sometimes substantially less than general consumer prices. (Figure 4.11 shows what applications are included in the academic versions of productivity software suites.)

Sometimes, campus computer stores or college bookstores also offer discounted prices to students and faculty who possess a valid ID. Online software suppliers such as **JourneyEd.com, Edtech-cps.com**, and **AcademicSuperstore.com** also offer the same software applications available in the store to students at reduced prices. You can also find software through mail-order companies. Check out catalogs.google.com for an extensive listing of companies that offer software by mail order.

Can I buy used software? Often, you can buy software through online auction sites such as eBay. If you do so, you need to ensure you are buying licensed (legal) copies. Computer shows that display state-of-the-art computer equipment are generally good sources for software. However, here, too, you must exert a bit of caution to ensure you are buying licensed copies and not pirated versions.

Can I buy software directly from the Internet? Of course, you can buy and download software applications directly from many developers and retail store Web sites. You can also buy software on the Internet that is custom developed to your specific needs. Companies such as First Internet Software House (**www.fishouse.com**) act as intermediaries between you (the software user) and a software developer. With custom-developed software, the developer tweaks open-source software code to meet your particular needs.

Microsoft, through its .NET program, offers software over the Internet for *all* devices—not just computers—that have a connection to the Internet. Therefore, you can download software specifically for your PDA or wireless phone by using .NET. Additionally, if you have a Microsoft .NET account (available free of charge at the Microsoft Web site), you can connect to any other .NET-connected device.

FREEWARE AND SHAREWARE

Can I get software for free legally? **Freeware** is any copyrighted software that you can use for free. Plenty of freeware exists on the Web, ranging from games and screen savers to business, educational, graphics, home and hobby, and system utility software programs. To find freeware, simply type *freeware* in your search engine. One good source of freeware offering a large variety of programs is **FreewareHome.com**.

Although they do not charge a fee, some developers release free software and request that you mail them a postcard or send them an e-mail message to thank them for their time in developing the software and to give them your opinion of it. Such programs are called *postcardware* and *e-mailware*, respectively.

Can I try out new software before it is really released? Some software developers offer **beta versions** of their software free of charge. Beta versions are still under development. By distributing free beta versions, developers hope to have users report errors or bugs they find in the program. This helps the developers correct any errors before they launch the software on the market at retail prices.

Is it still freeware if I'm asked to pay for the program after using it for a while? Software that allows users to test software (run it for a limited time free of charge) is referred to as **shareware**. Shareware is not freeware. If you use the software after the initial trial period is over, you will be breaking the software license agreement.

Software developers put out shareware programs to get their products into users' hands without the added expense and hassle of marketing and advertising. Therefore, quite a few great programs are available as shareware that can compete handily with programs on retail shelves. For example, TechSmith.com offers screen capture and desktop recording software applications such as SnagIt and Camtasia as shareware. You can try these products for free for a 30-day period and then you must purchase the software to continue using it. For a listing of other shareware programs, visit **Download.com** or **Shareware.com**.

Can shareware programmers *make* me pay for the shareware once I have it? The whole concept of shareware assumes users will behave ethically and abide by the license agreement. However, to protect themselves, many developers have incorporated code into the program to stop it from working completely, or to alter the output slightly, after the 30-day trial period expires. On some Yahoo games, for example, a reminder that the product is not free appears on the screen after a certain number of days, like the one shown in Figure 4.29. CorelDRAW prevents you from using the product at all once the trial period is over.

Are there risks associated with installing or downloading from the Internet beta versions, freeware, and shareware? Not all files available as shareware and freeware will work on your computer. You can easily crash your system and may even need to reinstall your operating system as a result of loading a freeware or shareware program that was not written for your computer's operating system.

FIGURE 4.29

Many software programs, such as Diner Dash from Yahoo Games, are available to play free on the Web, or as an evaluation version that you download to your machine. If you choose Download Now, after a specified amount of "free" playtime, you're given the opportunity to purchase the full version of the game.

Of course, by their very nature, beta products are most likely not bug-free, so you always run the risk of something going awry with your system. Unless you're willing to deal with potential problems, it may be best to wait until the last beta version is released. By that time, most of the serious bugs have been worked out.

As a matter of precaution, you should be comfortable with the reliability of the software developer before downloading a freeware, shareware, or beta version of software. If it's a reliable developer whose software you are already familiar with, you can be more certain that a serious bug or virus is not hiding in the software. However, downloading software from an unknown source could potentially put your system at risk for contracting a virus. (We discuss viruses in detail in Chapter 7.)

A good practice to establish before installing any software on your system is to use the operating system's Restore feature and create a *restore point*. That way, if anything goes wrong during installation, you can always restore your system back to how it was before you started. (We discuss the System Restore utility in Chapter 5.) Also, make sure that your virus protection software is up-to-date.

SOFTWARE VERSIONS AND SYSTEMS REQUIREMENTS

What do the numbers after software names indicate? Software developers sometimes change their software programs to repair problems (or bugs) or to add new or upgraded features. Generally, they keep the software program's name but add a number to it to indicate it is a different version. Originally, developers used numbers only to indicate different software versions (major upgrades) and releases (minor upgrades). Today, however, software developers also use years (such as Office 2003) and letters (Windows XP) to represent a version upgrade.

When is it worth it to buy a newer version? Although software developers suggest otherwise, there is no need to rush out and buy the latest version of a software program every time one is released. Depending on the software, some upgrades are not significantly different from the previous version to make it cost-effective for you to buy the newest version. Unless the upgrade adds features that are important to you, you may be better off waiting to upgrade every other release. You should also consider how often you use the software to justify an upgrade, and whether your current system can handle the new system requirements of the upgraded version.

If I have an older version of software and someone sends me files from a newer version, can I still open them? Software vendors recognize that people work on different versions of the same software. Vendors therefore make the newest version backward compatible, meaning it can recognize (open) files created with older versions. However, many software programs are not forward compatible, meaning that older versions cannot recognize files created on newer versions.

How do I know whether the software I buy will work on my computer? Every software program has a set of system requirements that specify the minimum recommended standards for the operating system, processor, primary memory (RAM), and hard drive capacity. Sometimes there are other specifications for the video card, monitor, CD drive, and other peripherals. These requirements are generally printed on the software packaging or at the publisher's Web site. Before installing software on your computer, ensure your system setup meets the minimum requirements by having sufficient storage, memory capacity, and processing capabilities.

Installing/Uninstalling and Opening Software

Before you use your software, you must permanently place it, or install it, on your system. The installation process is slightly different depending on whether you've purchased the software from a retail outlet and have an installation CD or whether you are downloading it from the Internet. And deleting, or uninstalling, software from your system requires certain precautions to ensure you remove all associated programs from your system.

How do I install software? When you purchase software today, you insert the CD that contains the program files, and for most programs being installed on a PC, an installation wizard automatically opens, as shown in Figure 4.30. By simply following the steps indicated by the wizard, you can install the software application on your system. If for some reason the wizard

BITS AND BYTES

Keeping Your Software Up-to-Date

Bugs in software occur all the time. Software developers are constantly testing their product, even after releasing the software to the retail market, and users report errors they find. In today's environment where security is a large concern, companies test their products for vulnerabilities against hackers and other malicious users. Once a fix or patch to a bug or vulnerability is created, most software developers will put the repair in downloadable form on the Internet, available at no charge. You should check periodically for any software updates or service packs to ensure your software is up-to-date. For your convenience, many products have an automatic update feature that downloads and installs updates automatically.

doesn't open automatically, the best way to install the software is to go to the Add/Remove Programs icon located in Control Panel on the Start menu. This feature locates and launches the installation wizard.

How is the installation process different for software I download off the Web? Obviously, when you download software from the Internet, you do not get an installation CD. Instead, everything you need to install and run the downloaded program is contained in one file that has been compressed (or zipped) to make the downloading process quicker. For the most part, these downloaded files unzip themselves and automatically start or *launch* the setup program. During the installation and setup process, these programs select or create the folder on your computer's hard drive in which most of the program files will be saved. You can also usually select a different location if you desire. Either way, note the name and location of the files, because you may need to access them later.

What do I do if the downloaded program doesn't install by itself? Some programs you download do not automatically install and run on your computer. Although the compressed files may unzip automatically through the download process, the setup program may not run without some help from you. In this case, you need to locate the files on the hard drive (this is why you must remember the location of the files) and find the *Setup.exe* program. (Files ending with the .exe extension are executable files or applications. All other files in the folder are support, help, and data files.) Once the setup program begins, you will be prompted with the necessary actions to complete the installation.

What's the difference between a custom installation and a full installation? One of the first steps in the installation wizard is deciding between a full installation and a custom installation. A **full installation** will copy all the files and programs from the distribution CD to the computer's hard drive. By selecting **custom installation**, you can decide which features you want installed on the hard drive. By doing so, you can save space on your hard drive, installing only those features you know you want.

Can I just delete a program to uninstall it? A software application contains many different files such as library files, help files, and other text files in addition to

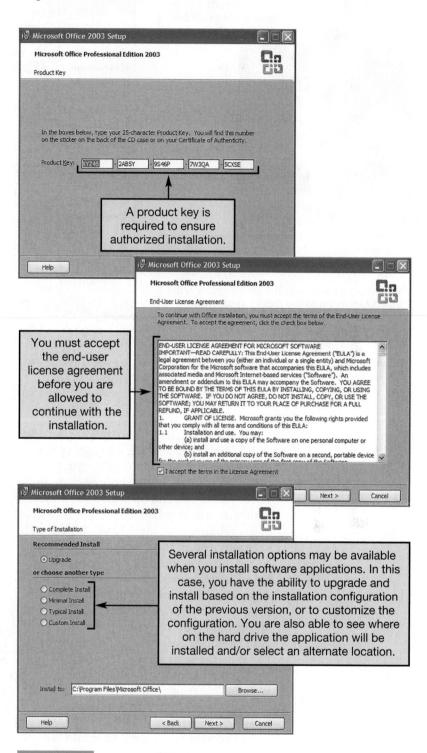

You must accept the end-user license agreement before you are allowed to continue with the installation.

A product key is required to ensure authorized installation.

Several installation options may be available when you install software applications. In this case, you have the ability to upgrade and install based on the installation configuration of the previous version, or to customize the configuration. You are also able to see where on the hard drive the application will be installed and/or select an alternate location.

FIGURE 4.30

Installation wizards guide you through the installation process and generally appear automatically when you install new software.

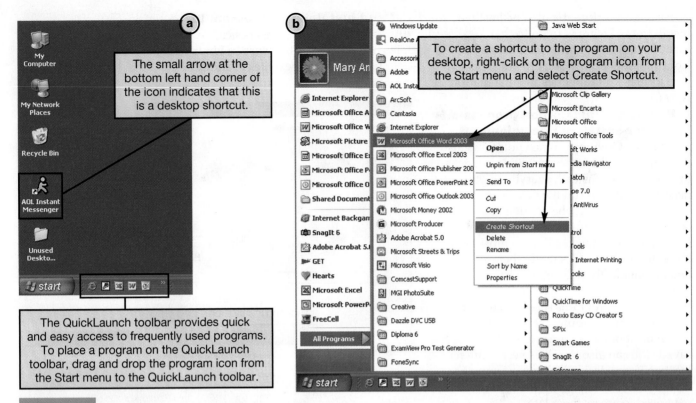

The small arrow at the bottom left hand corner of the icon indicates that this is a desktop shortcut.

The QuickLaunch toolbar provides quick and easy access to frequently used programs. To place a program on the QuickLaunch toolbar, drag and drop the program icon from the Start menu to the QuickLaunch toolbar.

To create a shortcut to the program on your desktop, right-click on the program icon from the Start menu and select Create Shortcut.

FIGURE 4.31

To quickly access an application you use often, you can place a shortcut in (a) the QuickLaunch toolbar or (b) on your desktop.

the main file you use to run the program. By just deleting the main file, you are not ridding your system of all the other ancillary programs. Although this is not harmful to your system, you end up with a lot of useless clutter on your hard drive.

Sometimes, programs have an Uninstall Program icon in the main program file. Using this icon will clear out most of the associated programs as well as the main program. If you can't locate the uninstall program for your particular software application, you can go to the Add/Remove Software icon in Control Panel on the Start menu. This feature will give you a list of software applications installed on your system, from which you choose the software application you would like to delete.

Is there a best way to open an application? The simplest way to open an application is by clicking its icon in All Programs from the Start menu. Every program that you install on your system is listed through the Start menu. However, if you find you use only a few programs

most often, you can place a shortcut to that program either on the QuickLaunch toolbar on the taskbar or on your desktop. To place a program in the QuickLaunch toolbar on the taskbar, simply open the QuickLaunch toolbar (right-click the taskbar and select QuickLaunch), then drag the selected program from the Start menu to the QuickLaunch toolbar (see Figure 4.31a).

To create a shortcut on the desktop, simply right-click the icon of the desired program and click "Send to" then select "Desktop." This places the shortcut icon directly on the Desktop. Alternatively, you can select "Create Shortcut" (see Figure 4.31b) and then drag the new shortcut icon to the desktop. You can identify a shortcut icon by the little black arrow in the lower-left corner of the icon, as shown in Figure 4.31a.

ACTIVE HELPDESK

Buying and Installing Software

In this Active Helpdesk call, you'll play the role of a Helpdesk staffer, fielding calls about how to best purchase software or get it for free, how to install and uninstall software, and where you can go for help when you have a problem with your software.

Ethics: Can I Borrow Software That I Don't Own?

Most people don't understand that unlike other items they purchase, software applications they buy don't belong to them. The only thing they're actually purchasing is a license that gives them the right to use the software for their own purposes as the *only* user of that copy. The application is not theirs to lend or copy for installation on other computers, even if it's another one of their own.

Software licenses are agreements between you, the user, and the software developer that you accept prior to installing the software on your machine. It is a legal contract that outlines the acceptable uses of the program and any actions that violate the agreement. Generally, the agreement will state who the ultimate owner of the software is, under what circumstances copies of the software can be made, or whether the software can be installed on any other machine. Finally, the license agreements will state what, if any, warranty comes with the software.

A computer user who copies an application onto more than one computer, if the license agreement does not permit this, is participating in **software piracy**. Historically, the most common way software has been pirated among computer users has been when they supplement each other's software library by borrowing CDs and installing the borrowed software on their own computers. Larger-scale illegal duplication and distribution by counterfeiters is also quite common. The Internet also provides a means of illegally copying and distributing pirated software.

Is it really a big deal to copy a program or two? As reported by the Business Software Alliance, 40 percent of all software is pirated. Not only is pirating software unethical and illegal, the practice also has financial impacts on all software application consumers. The reduced dollars from pirated software lessen the amount of money available for further software research and development while increasing the up-front cost to legitimate consumers.

To tell if you have a pirated copy of software installed on your computer at work or at home, you can download a free copy of GASP (a suite of programs designed to help identify and track licensed and unlicensed software and other files) from the Business Software Alliance Web site (**www.bsa.org/usa**). There is a similar program available at the Microsoft Web site (**www.microsoft.com/piracy/**). These programs check the serial numbers for the software installed on your computer against software manufacturer databases of official licensed copies and known fraudulent copies. Any suspicious software installations are flagged for your attention.

As of yet, there's no such thing as an official software police, but software piracy is so rampant that the U.S. government is taking steps to stop piracy worldwide. Efforts to stop groups that reproduce, modify, and distribute counterfeit software over the Internet are in full force. Software manufacturers also are becoming more aggressive in programming mechanisms into software to prevent repeated installations. For instance, with the launch of Microsoft Office 2003, installation requires the registration of the serial number of your software with a database maintained at Microsoft. Failure to register your serial number in this database or attempting to register a serial number that has been used previously results in the software failing to operate after the 50th time you use it.

Summary

1. What's the difference between application software and system software?

System software is the software that helps run the computer and coordinates instructions between application software and the computer's hardware devices. System software includes the operating system and utility programs. Application software is the software you use to do everyday tasks at home, school, and work. Application software includes productivity, financial and business, graphics and multimedia, educational and reference, entertainment, and communications software programs.

2. What kinds of applications are included in productivity software?

Productivity software programs include word processing, spreadsheet, presentation, personal information manager (PIM), and database programs. You use word processing software to create and edit written documents. Spreadsheet software enables you to do calculations and numerical and what-if analyses easily. Presentation software enables you to create slide presentations. Personal information manager (PIM) software helps keep you organized by putting a calendar, address book, notepad, and to-do lists within your computer. Database programs are electronic filing systems that allow you to filter, sort, and retrieve data easily.

3. What kinds of software do businesses use?

Many businesses, across a variety of industries, use general business software, such as Business Plan Pro and Marketing Plan Pro, to help them with tasks common to most businesses. In addition, businesses may use specialized business software (or vertical market software) that is designed for their specific industry. Individuals can also use software to help with business-like tasks such as preparing taxes or managing personal finances. These programs are called personal financial software programs.

4. What are the different kinds of graphics and multimedia software?

Graphics software encompasses a wide range of programs used to design and create attractive documents, images, illustrations, Web pages, and three-dimensional models and drawings. Graphics software is a part of a larger group of software called multimedia software. Multimedia software includes video and audio editing software, animation software, and other special software required to produce computer games.

5. What is educational and reference software?

Educational software refers to the variety of software applications on the market that offer some form of instruction or training. This ranges from simple tutorials to online course programs to complex simulation training programs. Software applications that act as sources for reference materials, such as the standard atlases, dictionaries, and thesauri, are referred to collectively as reference software. A lot of reference software on the market incorporates complex multimedia.

6. What are the different types of entertainment software?

Beyond the games that most of us are familiar with, entertainment software includes virtual reality programs that use special equipment to make users feel as though they are actually experiencing the program in a realistic 3-D environment. In addition, a wide variety of software programs are used to play, copy, record, edit, and organize MP3 files.

7. What kinds of software are available for communications?

E-mail and IM are two popular forms of electronic communications. Groupware, software that helps people who are in different locations work together, is also becoming popular. In addition, businesses use communications software such as telephony programs to add phone capabilities to computer systems and video and Web-conferencing software to enable people to meet without being physically present in the same room.

8. Where can I go for help when I have a problem with my software?

Most software programs have a Help menu built into the program with which you can search through an index or subject directory to find answers. Some programs group those most commonly asked questions in a single frequently asked questions (FAQ) document. Additionally, there are vast resources of free or fee-based help and training available on the Internet or at booksellers.

9. How can I purchase software or get it for free?

Almost every new computer system comes with some form of software to help you accomplish basic tasks. All other software

you need to purchase unless it is freeware, which you can download from the Internet for free. You can also find special software called shareware that lets you run it free of charge for a test period. Although you can find software in almost any store, as a student you can purchase the same software at a reduced price with an academic discount.

10. How do I install and uninstall software?

When installing and uninstalling software, it's best to use the specific Add/Remove Program feature that comes with the operating system. Most programs are installed using an installation wizard that steps you through the installation. Other software programs may require you to activate the setup program, which will begin the installation wizard. Using the Add/Remove Programs feature when uninstalling a program will help you ensure that all ancillary program files are removed from your computer.

Buzz Words

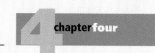

Word Bank

- application software
- beta versions
- freeware
- help
- illustration software
- image-editing software

- integrated software
- productivity software
- shareware
- software piracy
- software suite
- speech-recognition software

- spreadsheet
- system requirements
- system software
- templates
- wizards
- word processing

Instructions: Fill in the blanks using the words from the Word Bank.

Roxanne is happy. Her aunt is upgrading to a newer computer and is giving Roxanne her old one. Roxanne has just enrolled in college and knows she's going to need at least a(n) (1) _____ program to help her write papers and a(n) (2) _____ program to help her keep track of expenses while at school. Because both these software applications are part of a larger group of applications called (3) _____ , she knows she can buy them as a group. She's been told that it's cheaper to buy them as a(n) (4) _____ than to buy them individually. Because she knows she'll need the full versions, she cannot buy a(n) (5) _____ program.

Because she's not a great typist, Roxanne is interested in (6) _____ that will convert her dictated words into typed text. As a graduation present, Roxanne received a new digital camera. She needs to install the (7) _____ that came with her camera to edit and manage her digital pictures. Although she's used the software a couple of times on her parents' computer, she is still glad for the (8) _____ feature to assist her with specific feature questions and the (9) _____ that provide step-by-step guides to help her do things.

Roxanne especially likes the decorative preformatted (10) _____ she can use to insert pictures and make them seem professional. She also knows of some (11) _____ games she can download without cost from the Internet and other (12) _____ programs that she could try but eventually pay for. There are actually so many (13) _____ programs she'd like to install, she doesn't know what to pick first. It's tempting for her to borrow software from her friends, but she knows that it's considered (14) _____ . She also knows before installing any of the programs she must check the (15) _____ to see if the software is compatible with her system as well as whether the system has enough resources to support the software.

Becoming Computer Fluent

Using key terms from this chapter, write a letter to one of your friends or relatives about which software applications he or she may need to work more productively. Also include which software application(s) that individual may need to modify, review, and store the pictures from a digital camera he or she just purchased.

Instructions: Answer the multiple choice and true/false questions below for more practice with key terms and concepts from this chapter.

MULTIPLE CHOICE

1. Application software
   a. runs the computer and coordinates instructions
   b. helps maintain the resources of the operating system
   c. is only productivity software
   d. is used to perform everyday tasks

2. Which of the following is NOT an example of a software suite?
   a. Microsoft Office
   b. Microsoft Works
   c. WordPerfect 12
   d. None of the above are examples of a software suite

3. An integrated software program is
   a. a stand-alone program developed to work exclusively for one company
   b. an application designed specifically for a particular business or industry
   c. several individual application programs bundled together
   d. a program that includes tools of several applications that work together

4. Most editions of productivity software applications generally include
   a. word processing, spreadsheet, and Internet browser software
   b. spreadsheet, database, and virus protection software
   c. word processing, spreadsheet, and presentation software
   d. spreadsheet, personal information manager, and file compression software

5. The software you use to write checks and manage your budget is
   a. financial planning software
   b. database software
   c. spreadsheet software
   d. project management software

6. What software is used to layout and design publications?
   a. painting software
   b. desktop publishing software
   c. computer-aided design software
   d. all of the above

7. ESRB is responsible for providing
   a. licensing of entertainment software
   b. standards for educational software
   c. ratings for game software
   d. evaluations of edutainment software

8. Which of the following statements is true?
   a. MP3 music files sound almost the same as uncompressed originals
   b. MP3 files can be played using a variety of software programs
   c. MP3 files are smaller than other audio files
   d. Only a and b are true
   e. All of the above are true

9. A good practice before installing any software on your system is to
   a. defrag the system to make sure there is room for the new program
   b. create a restore point if you're using Windows XP
   c. contact technical support for the proper installation process
   d. All of the above are good practices

10. Once you buy a software program you can
    a. install it on only one computer
    b. install it on all computers in your home
    c. lend it to your friends as long as they are only using it for academic purposes
    d. both b and c

TRUE/FALSE

_____ 1. Microsoft Works is a bundled package of word processing, spreadsheet, database, and presentation software applications.

_____ 2. Groupware is a form of communications software.

_____ 3. The best way to delete a program you no longer want on your system is to delete the icon from the Start menu.

_____ 4. Shareware software is a form of open-source software.

_____ 5. FAQs are a good way to get help for common problems.

Making the Transition to... Next Semester

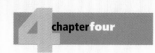

1. Software Training

You are most likely familiar with many software applications. Undoubtedly, you will use many more applications before your course work is done. Make two lists. In one list, itemize by category the software applications you are already familiar with. In the other list, identify at least three other software applications you think you may need, or would want to try, in the future. Research the types of on-campus or online training or help features that may be offered for those programs you have on your second list.

2. Installing Software

You have just spent $285 on a software package. You have a desktop you use at home and a laptop you use only at work.

a. Are you allowed to install the software on both computers? Should you be allowed to do that?

b. What if you wanted to install the software on two computers that you own and use exclusively at home?

c. Can you install the software on two computers if you use only one computer at a time?

d. Could you install the software package on your computer and also on a friend's computer if she is interested in buying her own copy but wanted to test it first?

3. Removing Software

You are trying to decide if you want to remove some software that you used this past semester from your system. How do the following items weigh into your decision to remove the software or to leave it on your system?

a. The amount of hard disk space available

b. How frequently you use the software

c. Licensing agreements

d. The amount of RAM installed on the system

4. More Than One Application?

Can you think of a situation that would make it useful for you to have multiple software applications for the same type of work? For example, two word processor packages or two tax software applications? What would the advantages and disadvantages be?

5. Choosing the Best Software

This past semester you spent a lot of time doodling and created a comic strip character that all your friends love. You've decided to start releasing a small newsletter, including some articles and a few comics each week. Which software applications would be the best fit for the following tasks:

a. Designing and laying out the newsletter

b. Creating the text articles

c. Creating the comic strip

d. After the first five issues it is clearly a smash, and you decide to expand it into a *zine*, an Internet-delivered magazine. Now which software applications are important to you for the same tasks?

Making the Transition to... The Workplace

1. **Software Training Needs**

   When applying for a new position, whether in your current company or in a different one, it's always good to indicate your experience with products or processes you will be required to use on the job. Research the types of software applications you will be required to use in your next position or in the job you'd like to have. Do you have any experience with these applications? If not, what kinds of training can you seek to familiarize yourself quickly with these applications? Are there resources within the company you can take advantage of, training manuals you can read, or courses you can take?

2. **Integrating Applications**

   Some software applications work well together and some do not. Certainly, all of the applications within a given suite such as Microsoft Office are well integrated. Give an example of a business office need that would benefit from the following:

   a. Integrating Excel with Word
   b. Integrating Access with Excel
   c. Integrating Access with Word

3. **Choosing the Best Software for the Job**

   For each of the following positions, describe the set of software applications you would expect to encounter if you were:

   a. A photographer opening a new business to sell your own photography
   b. An administrative assistant to a college president
   c. A graphic designer at a large publishing house
   d. A director in charge of publicity for a new summer camp for children
   e. A presenter to elementary students discussing your year living abroad
   f. A Web page designer for a small not-for-profit organization
   g. A construction site manager
   h. A person in the career you are pursuing

4. **The Right Productivity Suite**

   You are asked to research the cost and use of productivity software for your small company. Right now, the company has been getting by with Microsoft Works, but the need to expand to a full-fledged productivity suite is evident. Research the major productivity suites on the market. Look at cost, the ability to exchange files between customers and other employees easily (does file type make a difference?), and the various features within each version of software. Explore the major developer's products as outlined in Figure 4.12 on page 142 as well as the open-source option OpenOffice. Which productivity suite would you recommend? Be specific in your recommendation.

Critical Thinking Questions

Instructions: Albert Einstein used "Gedanken experiments," or critical thinking questions, to develop his theory of relativity. Some ideas are best understood by experimenting with them in our own minds. The following critical thinking questions are designed to demand your full attention but require only a comfortable chair—no technology.

1. Software Ethics

The cost of new software applications can be prohibitively high. You need to do a project for school that requires the use of a software application you don't own, but your roommate has a copy that her dad gave her from his work. She is letting you install it on your machine.

a. Is it okay for you to borrow this software?

b. Would your answer to the preceding question be different if you uninstalled the application after you were finished using it?

c. Would the answer to the preceding question be different if the software was on the school's network and you could copy it from there?

2. Software Ethics 2

Currently, there is no true system to check for illegal installations of software programs. What kind of program/system do you think could be developed to do this type of checking? Who would pay to develop, run, and maintain the program: the developers or the software users?

3. Categories of Software

This chapter has organized the many software applications into a variety of categories. Which category (or categories) of software do you feel has the need for a new, breakthrough product? What needs are there in your work or hobbies that existing software applications do not yet address?

4. The Pros and Cons of Software

Over the past 10 years many tasks have moved from professional, expensive environments to home desktops. Image editing and video editing were once available only to expensive professional studios but now can be done at home. Résumés were once taken to professional typesetters, but popular word processors can now do the work at home. What are the positive and negative impacts of this pattern for consumers? Does it offer consumers more power, opportunity, and control, or impose more pressures to purchase software and learn new skills?

5. Software for the Hearing and Visually Impaired

The World Wide Web Consortium (W3C) currently has an initiative to ensure that all Web pages are accessible to everyone, including those with visual and hearing impairments. Currently, software such as the freeware program Bobby (**bobby.watchfire.com**) can test Web pages to determine whether alternatives to auditory and visual Web content is available, such as closed captioning for auditory files and auditory files for visual content. Bobby generates a report that identifies and prioritizes Web site areas that do not meet the guidelines.

a. Can you think of any other unique uses of software that might make the world a better place for those with visual and hearing impairments?

b. Pick a favorite Web site and see how it checks out using the Bobby software. What changes would be necessary for that Web site to conform to W3C standards?

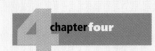

Problem:

Gizmos Inc. is a start-up company in the business of designing, building, and selling the latest gizmos. You have been hired as director of information systems. As such, one of your responsibilities is to ensure all necessary software applications are purchased and installed on the company's server.

Task:

Split your class into as many groups of four or five as possible. Each group is to perform the same activity and present and compare their results at the end of the project.

Process:

1. Identify a team leader who will coordinate the project and record and present results.

2. Each team is to identify the various kinds of software that Gizmos Inc. needs. Ensure that all activities and departments of the company have software to meet their needs. Consider communications software employees will need, software they can use to design the gizmos, productivity software they may need, and software the sales reps will need to help keep track of their clients. Also consider software that human resources personnel can use to keep track of employee data and that software product managers can use to track projects. In addition, think of other software that might be useful to Gizmos Inc.

3. Create a detailed and organized list of required software applications. If possible, include licensing fees, assuming the company has 50 users.

Conclusion:

Software applications help us do the simplest and most complex tasks every day. It's important to understand how dependent we are becoming on computers and technology. Compare your results with other team members. Were there software applications that you didn't think about that other members did? How expensive is it to ensure that even the smallest company has all the software to carry out daily activities?

Multimedia

In addition to the review materials presented here, you'll find additional materials featured with the book's multimedia, including the *Technology in Action* Student Resource CD and the Companion Web site (**www.prenhall.com/techinaction**), which will help reinforce your understanding of the chapter content. These materials include the following:

ACTIVE HELPDESK

In Active Helpdesk calls, you'll assume the role of a Helpdesk operator taking calls about the concepts you've learned in this chapter. You'll apply what you've learned and receive feedback from a supervisor to review and reinforce those concepts. The Active Helpdesk calls for this chapter are listed here and can be found on your Student Resource CD:

- Choosing Software
- Buying and Installing Software

SOUND BYTES

Sound Bytes are dynamic multimedia tutorials that help demystify even the most complex topics. You'll view video clips and animations that illustrate computer concepts, and then apply what you've learned by reviewing with the Sound Byte Labs, which include quizzes and activities specifically tailored to each Sound Byte. The Sound Bytes for this chapter are listed here and can be found on your Student Resource CD and on the Companion Web site (**www.prenhall.com/techinaction**):

- Creating Web Queries with Excel
- Using Speech-Recognition Software
- Enhancing Photos with Image-Editing Software

COMPANION WEB SITE

The *Technology in Action* Companion Web site includes a variety of additional materials to help you review and learn more about the topics in this chapter. The resources available at **www.prenhall.com/techinaction** include:

- **Online Study Guide.** Each chapter features an online true/false and multiple-choice quiz. You can take these quizzes, automatically check the results, and e-mail the results to your instructor.

- **Web Research Projects.** Each chapter features a number of Web research projects that ask you to search the Web for information on computer-related careers, milestones in computer history, important people and companies, emerging technologies, and the applications and implications of different technologies.

Digital Entertainment

When did everything go "digital"? It used to be that you'd only find analog forms of entertainment. Today, no matter what you're interested in—music, movies, television, radio—a digital version is popular (see Figure 1). MP3 files encode digital forms of music, while digital cameras and video camcorders are now commonplace. In Hollywood, some feature films are now being shot entirely with digital equipment.

FIGURE 1
Analog versus Digital Entertainment

	ANALOG	DIGITAL
MUSIC	Vinyl albums Cassette tapes	CDs MP3 files
PHOTOGRAPHY	35-mm single lens reflex (SLR) cameras Photos stored on film	Digital cameras Photos stored as digital files
VIDEO	8-mm, Hi8, or VHS camcorders Film stored on VHS tapes	Digital video (DV) camcorders Film stored as digital files; often distributedon DVDs
RADIO	AM/FM radio	HD Radio XM Radio
TELEVISION	Conventional broadcast TV	High-Definition Television (HDTV)

George Lucas, a great proponent of digital technology, filmed *Star Wars: Episode II Attack of the Clones* all the way back in 2002 completely in digital format. It played in special digital release at digital-ready theaters. And in January 2005, the digital film *RIZE*, by David LaChapelle, premiered at the Sundance Film Festival. It was streamed from computers in Oregon to a full-size cinema screen in Park City, Utah, beginning a new age of movie distribution. Digital entertainment is here to stay.

Meanwhile, satellite radio systems such as XM Radio and HD Radio are digital formats, and High-Definition Television (HDTV), a digital encoding of television signals, is scheduled to become the national standard sometime in 2006. In this Technology in Focus, we look at two popular forms of digital entertainment: digital photography and digital video. But first, let's consider what makes digital special.

What's So Special about Digital?

So, what *is* so special about digital? Think about the information captured in music and film: sounds and images. Sound is carried to your ears by sound waves, which are actually patterns of pressure changes in the air. Images are our interpretation of the changing intensity of light waves around us. These sound and light waves are called *analog* or continuous waves. They illustrate the loudness of the sound or the brightness of the colors in the image at a given moment in time. They are continuous signals because you would never have to lift your pencil off the page to draw them: they are just one long continuous line.

The first generation of recording devices (such as vinyl records and analog television shows) was designed to reproduce these sound and light waves. The needle in a groove of a vinyl record vibrates in the same pattern as the original sound wave. Television signals are actually waves that tell your TV how to display the same color and brightness as seen in the original studio. But it's difficult to describe a wave, even mathematically. Very simple sounds, like the C note of a piano, have a very simple shape, like that shown in Figure 2a. However, something like the word *hello* generates a very complex pattern, like that shown in Figure 2b.

Digital formats are descriptions of these signals as a long string of *numbers*. This is the main reason why digital recording has such

FIGURE 2

(a) This is an analog wave showing the simple, pure sound of a piano playing middle C. (b) This is the complex wave produced when a person says "hello."

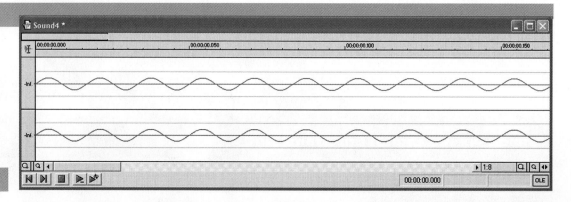

a

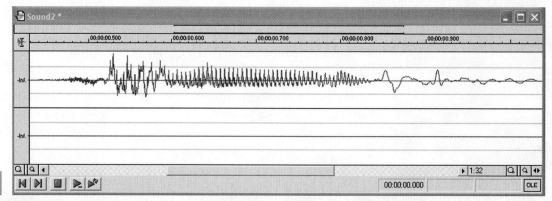

b

FIGURE 3

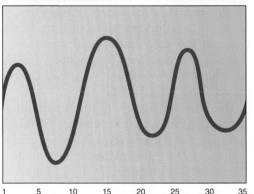

a Analog Sound Wave

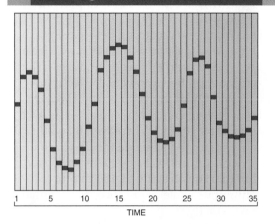

b Digitized Sound Wave

(a) Here you see a simple analog wave. (b) Here you see a digitized version of the same wave.

an advantage over analog. Digital gives us a simple way to describe sound and light waves *exactly*, so sounds and images can be reproduced perfectly each time. We already have easy ways to distribute digital information (on CDs, DVDs, or using e-mail, for example). But how could a digital format, a sequence of numbers, act as a convenient way to express these complicated wave shapes?

The answer is provided by something called **analog-to-digital conversion**. In analog-to-digital conversion, the incoming analog signal is measured many times each second. The strength of the signal at each

measurement is recorded as a simple number. The series of numbers produced by the analog-to-digital conversion process gives us the digital form of the wave. Figure 3 shows an analog and digital version of the same wave. In Figure 3a, you see the original continuous analog wave. You could draw the wave in Figure 3a without lifting your pencil from the page. In Figure 3b, the wave has been digitized and now is not a single line but rather is represented as a series of points or numbers.

So, how does this all work? Let's take music as an example. Figure 4 shows how

FIGURE 4

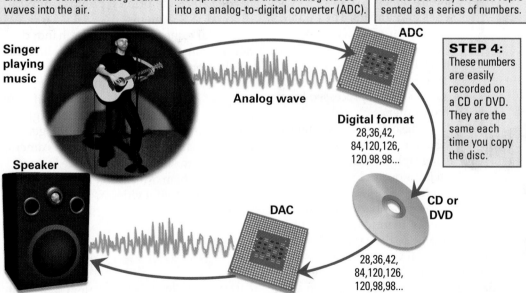

STEP 1: A singer plays music and sends complex analog sound waves into the air.

STEP 2: In the recording process, a microphone feeds these analog waves into an analog-to-digital converter (ADC).

STEP 3: The ADC digitizes the waves. They are now represented as a series of numbers.

During the complete recording process, information moves from analog form to digital data and then back again to analog sound waves.

Singer playing music

Analog wave

ADC

STEP 4: These numbers are easily recorded on a CD or DVD. They are the same each time you copy the disc.

Digital format
28,36,42,
84,120,126,
120,98,98...

Speaker

DAC

CD or DVD

28,36,42,
84,120,126,
120,98,98...

STEP 6: These analog waves tell your receiver how to move the speaker cones to duplicate the same sound waves as in the original music.

STEP 5: To play the CD, your CD player must have a digital-to-analog converter (DAC) to convert the numbers back to the analog wave.

the process of creating digital entertainment begins with the physical act of playing music, which creates analog waves. Next, a chip inside the recording device called an *analog-to-digital converter* (ADC) digitizes these waves into a series of numbers. This series of numbers can be recorded onto CDs and DVDs or sent electronically. On the receiving end, a playback device, such as a CD player or DVD player, is fed that series of numbers. Inside the playback device, a *digital-to-analog converter* (DAC), a chip that converts the digital numbers to a continuous wave, reproduces the original wave exactly.

More precisely, the digital wave will be *close* to exact. How accurate it is, how close the digitized wave is in shape to the original analog wave, depends on the **sampling rate** of the ADC. The sampling rate specifies the number of times the analog wave is measured each second. The higher the sampling rate, the more accurately the original wave can be re-created. However, higher sampling rates also produce much more data, and therefore result in bigger files. For example, sound waves on CDs are sampled at a rate of 44,000 times a second. This produces a huge list of numbers—44,000 of them each second!

So, when sounds or image waves are digitized, it means that analog data is changed into digital data—from a wave into a series of numbers. The digital data is perfectly reproducible and can be distributed easily on CDs and DVDs or through the airwaves. It can also be easily processed by a computer.

These digital advantages have revolutionized photography, music, movies, television, and radio. For example, digital television has a sharper picture and superior sound quality. However, there is a cost in the shift from analog to digital technologies. The Federal Communications Commission (FCC) has set a target date of December 31, 2006, when all over-the-air broadcasters must transmit in digital format. Consumers will be forced to choose between upgrading to digital HDTV sets or purchasing a converter for older sets. The digital revolution in television will bring better quality and additional conveniences, but at a cost, as the older analog equipment is phased out. (Visit **www.fcc.gov/dtv** for more information on when and how the FCC ruling will affect you.)

The same tension exists in the migration from analog to digital technology in photography. Let's take a look at this form of entertainment and explore the advantages and investment required in migrating from an analog to a digital format.

Digital Photography

Before digital cameras hit the market, most people used some form of 35-mm single lens reflex (SLR) camera. When you take a picture using a traditional SLR camera, a shutter opens, creating an aperture (a small window in the camera), which allows light to hit the 35-mm film inside. Chemicals coating the film react when exposed to light. Later, additional chemicals develop the image on the film and it is printed on special light-sensitive paper. A variety of lenses and processing techniques, special equipment, and filters are needed to create printed photos from traditional SLR cameras.

Digital cameras, on the other hand, do not use film. Instead, they capture images on electronic sensors called charge coupled device (CCD) arrays and then convert those images to digital data, a long series of numbers that represents the color and brightness of millions of points in the image. Unlike traditional cameras, digital cameras allow you to see your images the instant you shoot them. Most camera models can now record digital video as well as digital photos.

Digital Camera Quality

Part of what determines the quality of a digital camera is its **resolution**, or the sharpness of the images it records. A digital camera's resolution is measured in megapixels

FIGURE 5

Digital Camera
Resolutions.

Nikon SQ
(highest resolution 3.1 MP)

Minolta Dimage S414
(highest resolution 4 MP)

Canon EOS Rebel 300D
(highest resolution 6.3 MP)

Kodak DCS Pro
(highest resolution 14 MP)

(MP). The prefix *mega* is short for millions. The word *pixel* is short for picture element, or a single dot in a digital image. The higher the number of megapixels, the higher the quality of the camera and the images it takes.

Popular camera models come in a range of resolutions. An inexpensive pocket-sized camera like the Nikon CoolPix SQ is a 3.1-MP camera, which means that every photo it takes can contain up to 3.1 megapixels, or 3.1 million picture elements. Slightly more expensive consumer cameras such as the Canon EOS Digital Rebel 300D measure 6.3 MP. Professional photographers are moving to digital cameras as well. Professional digital cameras such as the Kodak DCS Pro 14 can take photos at resolutions up to 14 MP but sell for thousands of dollars. Figure 5 shows some popular digital camera models and the number of pixels they record at their maximum resolution.

If you're interested in an inexpensive digital camera and plan to make only 5 × 7" or 8 × 10" prints, a lower resolution camera is fine. However, low-resolution cameras do not record enough pixels to print larger-size prints. If you did print an 11 × 14" enlargement from a 2-MP shot, for example, the image would look grainy—you would see individual dots of color instead of a clear, sharp image.

Camera prices continue to drop as new models with higher resolutions are introduced, so 7-MP and 8-MP cameras are becoming affordable. With such resolutions, you can print larger photos (11 × 14"

and up) and still have sharp, detailed images.

Storage of Digital Images

When a digital camera takes a photo, it stores the images on a flash memory card inside the camera, as shown in Figure 6. Flash memory cards are very small and convenient, allowing you to easily transfer digital information between your camera and your computer or printer. Flash memory therefore takes the place of film used in traditional cameras.

To fit more photos on the same size flash memory card, digital cameras allow you to choose from several different file types in order to *compress*, or squeeze, the image data into less memory space. When you choose to compress your images, you will lose some of the detail, but in return you'll be able to fit more images on your flash card. Figure 7 shows the most common file types supported by digital cameras: the RAW uncompressed data type and the Joint Photographic Experts Group (JPEG) type. RAW files record all of the

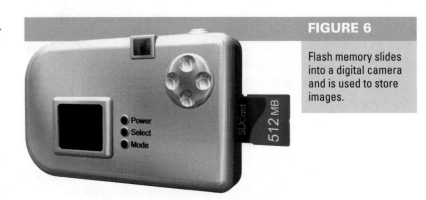

FIGURE 6

Flash memory slides into a digital camera and is used to store images.

FIGURE 7
File Types Commonly Used in Digital Cameras

FILE TYPE	COMPRESSED	SAMPLE QUALITY	FILE SIZE	NUMBER OF IMAGES THAT FIT ON A 128-MB FLASH CARD
RAW	No	High: Contains all the original data	6.0 MB	21
JPEG (at highest camera resolution)	Yes	Medium: Moderate compression; some lost quality	3.1 MB	41
JPEG (at lowest camera resolution)	Yes	Low: More compression; more lost quality	0.9 MB	142
		Note: The file sizes in this table refer to image storage on a Canon EOS Rebel 300D camera.		

original image information and so are larger than compressed JPEG files. JPEG files can be compressed just a bit, keeping most of the details, or compressed a great deal, losing some detail. Most cameras allow you to select from a few different JPEG compression levels.

Often cameras also support a very low-resolution storage option, creating files that you can easily attach to e-mail messages. This low-res setting typically provides images that are not useful for printing but that are so much smaller in size that it is easy to e-mail them. Even those with slow Internet connections are able to quickly download and view them on-screen.

Preparing Your Camera and Taking Your Photos

Preparing your camera includes ensuring that your camera's batteries are charged and the settings are correct. Digital cameras consume a great deal of power, so you might want to carry a spare charged battery pack. Also make sure the flash card is installed and that it has enough space for the number of photos you plan to take.

Next, set the resolution on your camera. Most cameras offer two or three different resolution settings. For example, a 6-MP camera might be able to shoot

images at 6 MP, 2.7 MP, or 1.5 MP. If you're taking a photo that will be enlarged and that needs to be at a very high quality, use the full power of your camera. Shoot the image at 6 MP and save the image as uncompressed data at the highest resolution. If you're planning to use the image for a Web page, where having a smaller file would be helpful, use a lower resolution and the space-saving compressed JPEG format. If you're unsure how you're going to use your images, record them with the maximum resolution your camera allows.

Most cameras include an autofocus feature and automatically set the aperture and correct shutter speed. This makes taking a digital photo as simple as pressing a button. The great thing about digital cameras, of course, is that they let you instantly examine your photos in a display window on the camera. If you don't like a certain photo, you can delete it immediately, freeing space on your flash card.

Transferring Your Photos to Your Computer

If you just want to print your photos, you may not need to transfer them to your computer. Many photo printers can make prints directly from your camera or from the flash memory card. However, transferring the photos to your computer allows you to store them and frees your flash card for reuse.

Transferring your photos to your computer is simple. All current model digital cameras have a built-in universal serial bus (USB) 2.0 port (some high-end models may also include a FireWire port). Using a USB 2.0 cable, you can connect the camera to your computer to store the converted images as uncompressed files or in a compressed format as JPEG files. Another option is to transfer the flash card from your camera to the computer. Some desktops have flash card slots on the front of the system unit. However, if yours does not, you can buy an external memory card reader like the one shown in Figure 8 and attach it to your computer using an available USB port.

When you connect your camera to your computer, with the Microsoft Windows XP operating system, the rest of the transfer is automatic. You'll hear a ding-dong sound telling you the computer and camera are connected and can communicate. Next, a

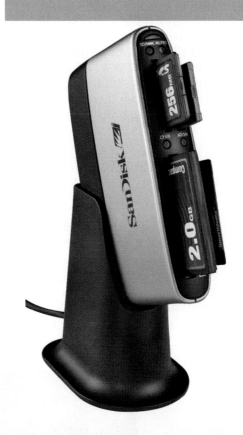

FIGURE 8

If your computer does not have a built-in flash card reader, you can buy an external reader that attaches to your computer using a USB cable and port.

How Do My Old Photos Become Digital?

Obviously, not every document or image you have is in an electronic form. What about all the photographs you have already taken? Or an article from a magazine or a hand-drawn sketch? How can these be converted into digital format?

Digital scanners like the one shown in Figure 9 convert paper text and images into digital formats. You can place any flat material on the glass surface of the scanner and then convert it into a digital file. Most scanner software allows you to store the converted images as RAW files or in compressed form as JPEG files. And some scanners include hardware that allows you to scan film negatives or slides as well or even to insert a stack of photos to be scanned in sequence.

Scanner quality is measured by its resolution, which is given in dots per inch (dpi). Most modern scanners can digitize a document at $2,400 \times 4,800$ dpi, in either color or gray-scale modes. You can easily connect a scanner to your computer using USB 2.0 or FireWire ports. Scanners also typically come with software supporting optical character recognition (OCR). OCR software converts pages of handwritten or typed text into electronic files. You can then open and edit these converted documents with traditional word processing programs. In addition, many scanners have a Copy button that allows you to scan and sometimes print documents, taking the place of a copy machine.

FIGURE 9

Scanners can convert paper documents, photo prints, or strips of film negatives into digital data.

series of prompts appears, asking you which images you'd like to transfer and where you'd like to store them. You now have TIFF or JPEG image files on your computer. If you're satisfied with the photos, you can send them to your friends as e-mail attachments, for example. If you're not satisfied with them, you can process them further.

Processing Your Photos and Adding Special Effects

Once you've taken your photos, you may want to process them, cropping them, for example, or adding special effects. Traditional photographers often invest in special equipment and chemicals needed to develop 35-mm film. The photographer can then resize or crop the photo, add different filtering effects, or combine photos.

With digital photography, you can do all of this using inexpensive image-editing software.

There are hundreds of image-editing programs available, from freeware to very sophisticated suites. Many times the manufacturer of your camera will include some image-editing program on a CD that comes with your camera. If you want to purchase a more powerful program, Adobe Photoshop and Jasc Paint Shop Pro are two well-reviewed packages. They allow you to remove flaws such as red-eye; crop images; correct poor color balance; apply filtering effects such as mosaics, charcoal, and impressionistic style; and merge components from multiple images. Figure 10 shows just a few examples of the filtering effects you can apply to an image. The exact set of filtering effects you will have depends on the software you're using.

FIGURE 10

Using image-editing software, you can add filtering effects such as color pencil, collage, and oil painting.

Original

Color Pencil

Collage

Oil Painting

FIGURE 11

Printing Your Photos

Once you've processed your photos, you can print them using a professional service or your own printer. Most photo printing labs, including the film-processing departments at stores such as Wal-Mart and Target, offer digital printing services, as do many high-end online processing labs. These sites accept original or edited image files and print them on professional photo paper with high-quality inks. The paper and ink used at processing labs are higher quality than what is available for home use and produce heavier, glossier prints that won't fade. In addition, Kodak and Sony have kiosks in department stores and photography stores that you can use yourself. They accept image files directly from your flash cards, allow you to do a small amount of editing such as cropping the image or correcting red-eye, and print the finished photos on the spot.

There are also online services, like Snapfish.com and Shutterfly.com, that let you upload your images to their Web site. You can organize them as an online photo album for others to view for free, and if you want hard copy prints, mugs, t-shirts, or calendars sporting your shot, you can order them directly from the site.

Photo printers for home use are available in two technologies: ink-jet and dye sublimation (see Figure 11). Most popular and inexpensive are ink-jet printers. As noted in Chapter 2, some ink-jet printers are capable of printing high-quality color photos, although they vary in speed and quality. Some include a display window so you can review the image as you stand at the printer, while others are portable, allowing you to print your photos wherever you are. Some printers even allow you to crop the image right at the printer, without having to use special image-editing software.

Unlike ink-jet printers, dye-sublimation printers produce images using a heating element instead of an ink-jet nozzle. The heating element passes over a ribbon of translucent film that has been dyed with bands of colors. By controlling the temperature of the element, dyes are vaporized from a solid into a gas. The gas vapors penetrate the photo paper before they cool again to solid form, producing glossy, high-quality images. If you're interested in a printer to use for printing only photographs, a dye-sublimation printer is a good choice. However, some models print only specific photo sizes, such as 4 × 6" prints, so be sure the printer you buy will fit your long-term needs.

Transferring images to a printer is similar to transferring them to your computer. If you have a direct-connection camera, you can plug the camera directly into the printer with a cable. Some printers have slots that accept different types of flash memory cards. Of course, you can also transfer your images to the printer from your computer if you have stored them there.

Some printers support a system known as Digital Print Order Format (DPOF). Using a combination of a DPOF camera and a DPOF printer, you can review all the shots on your camera and build an order of how many copies and what sizes you would like to print. You then just insert the flash card into the printer and your entire order is printed automatically.

You may decide not to print your photos. As noted earlier, online albums let you share your photos without having to print them. And portable devices like Apple's photo iPod and many PDAs enable you to carry and display your photos without printing them. The photo iPod, for example, can be connected to a TV and deliver slide shows of your photographs complete with musical soundtracks you have selected.

The Digital Advantage

Is a digital camera right for you? Figure 12 lists just a few of the advantages digital cameras have over traditional cameras. Digital cameras give you the power to create images that only professional photographers with expensive processing studios could produce a few years ago.

Digital Video

Personal video cameras have been popular for a long time. The first camcorders were analog video cameras, like the one shown in Figure 13a. These were large, heavy units that held a full-size VHS tape. The push to produce smaller, lighter models led to the introduction of compact VHS tapes and then to 8-mm and Hi8 formats. Still, all of these are analog formats, and each records to its own specific type of tape.

The newest generation of video equipment for home use is the *digital video,* or DV, format shown in Figure 13b. Introduced in 1995, the digital video standard led to a new generation of recording equipment. Today, digital video cameras offer many advantages over their VHS counterparts. They are incredibly small and light and use a tape format called MiniDV. These tapes can hold one to three hours of video but are just about two square inches in size, and they allow manufacturers to design stylish and sleek cameras. In addition to MiniDV, new formats are emerging all the time. For exam-

---

FIGURE 12
Digital Photography Advantages

	TRADITIONAL SLR CAMERA	DIGITAL ADVANTAGE
Developing	Send out or pay more for one-hour developing Forced to develop the entire roll Special equipment required for applying special effects before printing	Immediate processing Print only the shots you like Easy to apply filters and special effects using inexpensive software
Storage	Need to purchase and carry many rolls of film; temperature and x-ray sensitive Can be stored on hard drive, CD, or DVD only after scanning the negative or print Negatives must be protected in special sleeves	No need to purchase film; large flash memory cards provide room for many shots Can easily be stored on hard drive, CD, or DVD with no scanning necessary Images stored as data files; only need to back up these files to ensure they are protected
Distribution	Paper prints can be mailed; however, must be scanned into a digital format for electronic distribution	Images can be printed on home printers and professionally; easy to distribute image files as e-mail attachments or on CD; can also post images to Web easily
Quality	Sets the standard for quality	Excellent quality comparable to traditional photos

ple, a few Sony digital video cameras use an even more compact tape called MicroMV. If you're buying a digital video camera, look for a format that is popular enough that it will be simple to purchase new blank tapes if you are traveling.

By using digital video, you can easily transfer video files to your computer. Then, using simple video-editing software, you can edit the video at home, cutting out sections, resequencing segments, and adding titles. To do the same with analog videotape would require expensive and complex audio/video equipment usually seen only in video production studios. And with digital video, you can save (or *write*) your final product on a CD or DVD and play it in your home DVD system or on your computer.

Although you have terrific convenience and control with digital video, there are costs in making the move from analog to digital. Digital video cameras come in a wide range of prices, but they are more expensive than the analog models still available. This is reasonable because digitizing video and audio requires a lot of processing power. Video for motion pictures is recorded as high-resolution images at a rate of 30 frames per second (fps). This means 1,800 images must be digitized for each minute of video. In addition to the video, the audio also must be digitized. Digital video cameras do the analog-to-digital conversion right in the camera. They are equipped with FireWire and/or USB 2.0 ports so you can later send the digital data quickly from the camera directly to your computer.

For many people, the advantages of working with digital video are worth the extra cost. Let's look at how you would use a digital video camera and see if the investment would be worthwhile for you.

Preparing Your Camera and Shooting Your Video Footage

Preparing your digital video camera involves making sure you have enough battery power and tape capacity. Batteries for digital video cameras are rechargeable and can provide between one and nine hours of shooting time. Longer-lasting batteries cost and weigh more, so you'll want to think about how you use your camera before deciding which batteries to purchase. Most

videographers recommend carrying two spare batteries, though having one spare is fine if you can recharge it while you're using the second.

Digital video cameras record on tape, so make sure you have enough tape to cover the event. Many models also let you record segments directly onto a flash memory card. If you want to record a short clip that you can quickly transfer to your computer without having to hook up any cables, make sure you have a large enough flash memory card with you. Check the user guide for your particular camera to see how much flash memory you need to store video. For example, on the Sony DCR-TRV80, you can store about 80 minutes of video on a 512-MB Memory Stick.

Shooting video with a digital video camera is similar to shooting video with an analog camera. Automated programs control the exposure settings for different environments (nighttime shots, action events, and so on), while automatic focusing and telephoto zoom lens features are common as well. Many cameras include an antishake feature that stabilizes the image when you're using the camera without a tripod. Using these features, you can capture great footage by just pointing and hitting Record.

Transferring Your Video to Your Computer

Digital video cameras already hold your video as digital data, so transferring the data to your computer is simple. All you need to do is to make sure you have the correct cable to match the type of output port on the camera. Many cameras use a FireWire port and connect the camera to your computer with a FireWire cable. Although every FireWire port is the same, there are two different types of connectors used on FireWire cables: 4-pin and 6-pin. Digital video cameras usually have a port that matches the 4-pin connector, while desktop computers may have a port matching either the 4- or 6-pin connectors. Be sure to check both your camera and computer and use a cable with the matching connector on each end. Some digital video cameras now offer a USB 2.0 port; you can then connect the camera to any free USB 2.0 port on your computer.

Once you connect your camera to your computer, Microsoft Windows XP automatically identifies it, recognizing its manufacturer and model. The Windows operating system then scans the software on your system and presents a list of all the programs you can use to import your video. You may have received a video-editing program with your digital video camera. Install that and it will appear on this list. Windows Movie Maker is another video-editing program and is a feature of Windows XP Home Edition. Other digital video-editing programs such as Adobe Premiere and Pinnacle Studio DV can import video as well. These are more powerful, full-featured programs that you purchase separately. Figure 15a shows the list that pops up for a computer with Windows Movie Maker, Sonic Solutions, and Adobe Premiere installed.

The software allows you to fast-forward, pause, and rewind, moving to the segment you wish to transfer (or record) to your hard drive. In Figure 15b, both video and audio are chosen to record (transfer). You can use the digital video camera control arrows on the bottom right-hand side of the Record dialog box to locate the exact piece of footage you want to transfer. Click the Record button and the video file transfers to the hard drive.

One camcorder on the market today offers another option. Made by Sony, the DVD Handycam Camcorder DCR-DVD101 writes its digital data directly onto 3-inch DVDs. It can record up to 20 minutes of video when using the highest quality setting. You can then drop the DVD into most DVD players and view it immediately.

But What If I Already Have an Analog Camcorder?

If you have an older analog video camera, you can still begin to play with digital video if you purchase a special unit called a *video capture device*. A video capture device digitizes and compresses analog video and then passes it on to your computer. To use one, you connect your analog video camera to the video capture unit, which in turn connects to your computer. Your camera then feeds its video signals to the capture device, which then sends the video to the computer in a digitized form. You can use this device to convert and send existing analog tapes into your computer or to process new videos you shoot with your analog camcorder into digital computer files. Figure 14a shows an example of an external video capture device. Note that video capture devices also are available as expansion (adapter) cards that you install in an unused expansion slot inside your computer.

There are some other options available as well. If you want the ultimate in simplicity, devices such as the Iomega Super DVD QuickTouch Burner, shown in Figure 14b, allow you to transfer video from an analog camera or old tapes directly to DVD discs with just one button. Or you may want to purchase a new video card. Some video cards have a video-in port built into the design. You can connect an older analog camera directly to the video card and digitize from your analog camera.

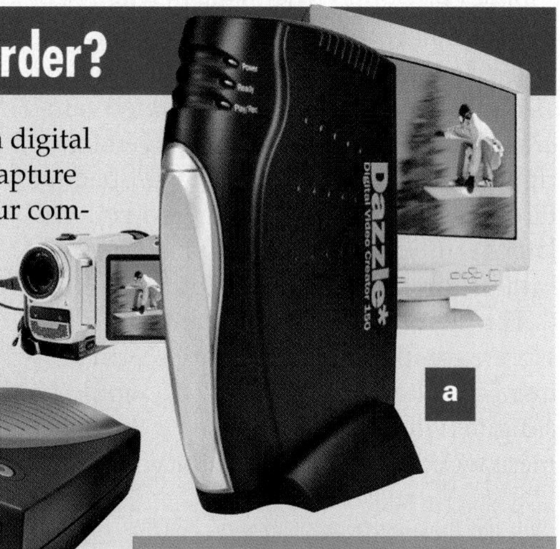

FIGURE 14

(a) You can still create digital video with an older analog camera by connecting your camera to a video capture device, which in turn connects to your computer. (b) Or, using a device such as the Iomega Super DVD QuickTouch Video Burner shown here, you can easily transfer your analog video to DVD. The burner plugs into your computer using a USB 2.0 port, and the burner has jacks that allow you to connect it to your analog camera.

Windows Movie Maker, Sonic Solutions, and Adobe Premiere are all installed on this computer

a

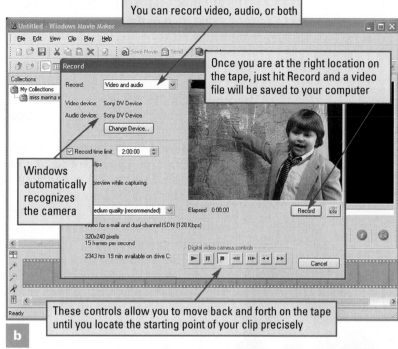

You can record video, audio, or both

Once you are at the right location on the tape, just hit Record and a video file will be saved to your computer

Windows automatically recognizes the camera

These controls allow you to move back and forth on the tape until you locate the starting point of your clip precisely

b

Editing Your Video and Adding Special Effects

Once the digital video data is in a file on your hard drive, the fun really begins. Video-editing software presents a storyboard or timeline with which you can manipulate your video file, as shown in Figure 16. Using this software, you can review your clips frame by frame or trim them at any point. You can order each segment on the timeline in whichever sequence you like and correct segments for color balance, brightness, or contrast.

FIGURE 15

The Windows XP operating system makes it simple to import digital video data to a file on your hard drive. (a) Windows first presents a list of all the software packages on your system that you can use to import video from your camera. (b) The software program you pick lets you move to any starting spot on the tape. Hit Record to create a video file on the hard drive.

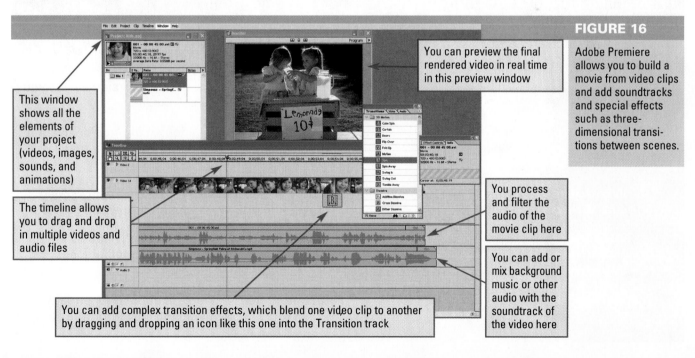

FIGURE 16

Adobe Premiere allows you to build a movie from video clips and add soundtracks and special effects such as three-dimensional transitions between scenes.

You can preview the final rendered video in real time in this preview window

This window shows all the elements of your project (videos, images, sounds, and animations)

The timeline allows you to drag and drop in multiple videos and audio files

You process and filter the audio of the movie clip here

You can add or mix background music or other audio with the soundtrack of the video here

You can add complex transition effects, which blend one video clip to another by dragging and dropping an icon like this one into the Transition track

In addition, you can add transitions to your video such as those you're used to seeing on TV—fades to black, dissolves, and so on. Figure 16 shows how easy it is to add transitions in Adobe Premiere: Just select the type of transition you want from the drop-down list and drag that icon into the timeline where you want the transition to occur.

Video-editing software also lets you add titles, animations, and audio tracks to your video, including background music, sound effects, and additional narration. In Figure 16 there are two audio tracks, the original voices on the video as well as an additional audio clip. You can adjust the volume of each audio track to switch from one to the other or have both playing together. Finally, you can preview all of these effects in real time.

Outputting (Exporting) Your Video

Once you're done editing your video file, you can save (or export) it in a variety of formats. Figure 17 shows some of the popu-lar video file formats in use today, along with the file extensions they use. (*File extensions* are the letters that follow the period in a file name, such as in Movie1.*mpg*. These extensions indicate the type of data inside the file.)

Your choice of file format for your finished video will depend on what you want to do with your video. For example, the RealMedia RM streaming file format is a great choice if your file is very large and you'll be posting it on the Web. The Microsoft AVI format is a good choice if you're sending your file to a wide range of users because it's very popular and commonly accepted as the standard video format on Windows machines.

When you export your video, you have control over every aspect of the file you create, including its format, window size, frame rate, audio quality, and compression level. You can customize any of these if you have specific production goals, but most often just using the default values works well.

When would you want to customize some of the audio and video settings? If you're trying to make the file as small as possible so it will download quickly or so it can fit on a single CD, you would select values that trade off audio and video

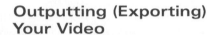

FIGURE 17
Typical File Formats for Digital Video

Format	File Extension	Notes
QuickTime	.mov .qt	You can download QuickTime player for free from **www.apple.com/quicktime**. The pro version allows you to build your own QuickTime files.
Moving Picture Experts Group (MPEG)	.mpg .mpeg	MPEG-4 video standard adopted internationally in 2000; recognized by most video player software.
Windows Media Video	.wmv	Microsoft file format recognized by Windows Media Player (included with Windows operating system).
Microsoft Video for Windows	.avi	Microsoft file format recognized by Windows Media Player (included with Windows operating system).
RealMedia	.rm	Format from RealNetworks is popular for streaming video. You can download the player for free at **www.real.com**.

FIGURE 18
Digital Video Advantages

	Analog Video Camera	Digital Advantage
Editing	Home users cannot edit their videos without expensive equipment.	Editing video is easy using inexpensive software.
Storage	Film is stored on analog tapes (VHS, 8-mm, or Hi8 tapes). Tapes have a limited lifetime and are sensitive to heat, magnetic fields, water damage, and mechanical breakdown.	Video is stored on smaller MiniDV tapes. Short video clips can be saved directly to flash memory cards. You can easily transfer and store video files onto a computer hard drive, CD, or DVD. There is no loss of information over time.
Distribution	You can make copies of tapes but only if you own multiple VHS VCRs or Hi8 players. To make digital versions of analog tapes, you need a separate video capture device.	You can make DVD copies using a simple DVD-RW drive. You can also post videos to Web sites or attach them to e-mail messages.
Quality	Excellent video and audio quality.	Excellent video quality and CD-quality audio.

quality for file size. For example, you could drop the frame rate to 15 fps, shrink the window size to 320 × 240 pixels, and switch to mono audio instead of stereo.

You can also try different compression choices to see which one does a better job of compressing your particular file. **Codecs** (**co**mpression/**dec**ompression) are rules implemented in either software or hardware that squeeze the same audio/video information into less space. Some information will be lost using compression, and there is a variety of different codecs to choose from, each claiming better performance than its competitors. Commonly used codecs include MPEG, Indeo, DivX, and Cinepak. There is no one codec that is always superior—a codec that works well for a simple interview may not do a good job compressing a live-action scene.

If you'd like to save your video onto a DVD, you can use special DVD authoring software such as Ulead's DVD Workshop or Adobe's Encore DVD. These programs create final DVDs that have animated menu systems and easy navigation controls, allowing the viewer to move quickly from one movie or scene to another. Home DVD players as well as gaming systems such as Playstation 2 and Xbox can read these DVDs, so your potential audience is even greater!

The Digital Advantage

Is a digital video camera right for you? Figure 18 lists just a few of the advantages of digital video cameras over traditional analog camcorders. Analog video changed how we communicate. It became possible to make a video and send it by mail to relatives all across the country. Digital video allows you even more creative control over the videos you produce, enabling you to edit them at home and share them with others even more easily.

Using System Software:

The Operating System, Utility Programs, and File Management

Objectives

After reading this chapter, you should be able to answer the following questions:

1. What software is included in system software? **(p. 192)**
2. What are the different kinds of operating systems? **(pp. 192–194)**
3. What are the most common desktop operating systems? **(pp. 194–198)**
4. How does the operating system provide a means for users to interact with the computer? **(pp. 198–200)**
5. How does the operating system help manage the processor? **(p. 200)**
6. How does the operating system manage memory and storage? **(p. 201)**
7. How does the operating system manage hardware and peripheral devices? **(pp. 201–202)**
8. How does the operating system interact with application software? **(pp. 202–203)**
9. How does the operating system help the computer start up? **(pp. 203–207)**
10. What are the main desktop and window features? **(pp. 207–209)**
11. How does the operating system help me keep my computer organized? **(pp. 209–214)**
12. What utility programs are included in system software and what do they do? **(pp. 214–223)**

ACTIVE HELPDESK

- Managing Hardware and Peripheral Devices: The OS **(p. 202)**
- Starting the Computer: The Boot Process **(p. 207)**
- Organizing Your Computer: File Management **(p. 214)**
- Using Utility Programs **(p. 216)**

Working with System Software

Franklin begins his workday as he does every morning, powering on his computer and watching it boot up. Once he sees the welcoming image of his desktop, he opens Microsoft Outlook to check his e-mail, Internet Explorer to access his company's Web site, and Microsoft Word to bring up the proposal he needs to finish. As he reads his e-mail, a warning pops up alerting him that one message may contain a file with a virus. He deletes the file without opening it, glad that his antivirus software had been automatically updated yesterday.

Clicking back to Word, Franklin searches for a proposal he worked on last year. Fortunately, he knows where to look because he has been creating folders for his projects and diligently saving his files in their proper folder. He learned the hard way that keeping his files organized in folders is worth the effort it takes to create them. Last year, his desktop was a complete mess. He was constantly losing time trying to find files because he couldn't remember where he saved them and he gave them names he easily forgot. His organized folders now make finding his files a snap.

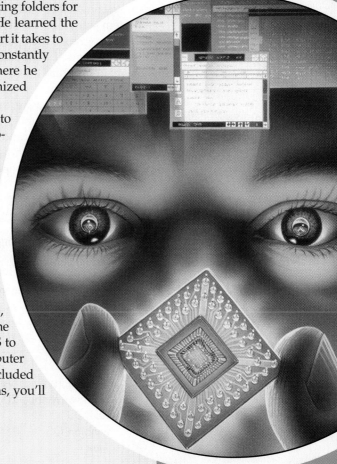

Later, at the end of the workday, Franklin has one more thing to do. Recently, his computer has been running sluggishly, so he is hoping to improve its performance. Last night, he ran Disk Cleanup, a utility program that removes unneeded files from the hard drive, as well as ScanDisk, a utility program that checks for disk errors. Although he had seen an improvement in his computer's performance, he decides to use the defrag utility to defrag his hard drive, hoping it will give him more space and allow his system to work more efficiently. As he's leaving work, Franklin hears the clicking of the hard drive as the defrag utility goes to work.

Are you as familiar with your system as Franklin is? In this chapter, you'll learn all about system software and how vital it is to your computer. We'll start by examining the operating system (OS), looking at the different operating systems on the market as well as the tasks the OS manages. We'll then look at how you can use the OS to keep your files and folders organized so that you can use your computer more efficiently. Finally, we'll look at the many utility programs included as system software on your computer. Using these utility programs, you'll be better able to take care of your system and extend its life.

SOUND BYTES

- Customizing Windows XP **(p. 208)**
- File Management **(p. 211)**
- File Compression **(p. 218)**
- Hard Disk Anatomy Interactive **(p. 219)**
- Letting Your Computer Clean Up After Itself **(p. 222)**

System Software Basics

As you learned in the last chapter, there are two basic types of software on your computer: application software and system software. **Application software** is the software you use to do everyday tasks at home and at work. It includes programs such as Microsoft Word and Excel. **System software** is the set of software programs that helps run the computer and coordinates instructions between application software and the computer's hardware devices. From the moment you turn on your computer to the time you shut it down, you are interacting with system software.

System software consists of two primary types of programs: the operating system and utility programs. The **operating system (OS)** is the main program that controls how your computer system functions. The OS manages the computer's hardware, including the processor (also called the central processing unit, or CPU), memory, and storage devices, as well as peripheral devices such as the monitor and printer. The operating system also provides a consistent means for software applications to work with the CPU. Additionally, it is responsible for the management, scheduling, and interaction of tasks as well as system maintenance. Your first interaction with the OS is the *user interface*.

System software also includes **utility programs**. These are small programs that perform many of the general housekeeping tasks for the computer, such as system maintenance and file compression.

Do all computers have operating systems? Every computer, from the smallest notebook to the largest supercomputer, has an operating system. Even tiny personal digital assistants (PDAs) as well as some appliances have operating systems. The role of the OS is critical; the computer cannot operate without it.

Operating System Categories

Although most computer users can name only a few operating systems, hundreds exist. As Figure 5.1 illustrates, these operating systems can be classified into four categories,

FIGURE 5.1	Operating System Categories	
Category of Operating System	**Examples of Operating System Software**	**Examples of Devices Using the Operating System**
Real-Time Operating System (RTOS)	There are no commercially available RTOS programs. Non-commercially available programs include QNX Neutrino and Lynx.	Scientific instruments Automation and control machinery Video games
Single-User, Single-Task Operating System	Palm OS Pocket PC (Windows CE) Windows Mobile 2003 MS-DOS Symbian OS Linux	PDAs Embedded computers in cell phones, cameras, appliances, and toys
Single-User, Multitask Operating System	Windows family (2003, XP, 2000, Me, 98, NT) Mac OS X Linux	Personal desktop computers Laptops
Multiuser Operating System	UNIX Novell NetWare Windows Server 2003 OS/2 Windows XP Linux	Networks (both home and business) Mainframes Supercomputers

depending on the number of users they service and the tasks they perform. Some operating systems coordinate resources for many users on a network (multiuser operating system), whereas other operating systems, such as those found in some household appliances and car engines, don't require the intervention of any users at all (real-time operating system). Some operating systems are available commercially, for personal and business use (single-user, multitask operating system), whereas others are proprietary systems developed specifically for the devices they manage (single-user, single-task operating system).

REAL-TIME OPERATING SYSTEMS

Do machines with built-in computers need an operating system? Machinery that is required to perform a repetitive series of specific tasks in an exact amount of time requires a **real-time operating system (RTOS)**. This type of operating system is a program with a specific purpose and must guarantee certain response times for particular computing tasks, or the machine's application is useless. For example, instruments such as those found in the scientific, defense, and aerospace industries that must perform regimented tasks or record precise results require real-time operating systems.

Real-time operating systems are also found in many types of robotic equipment. Television stations use robotic cameras with real-time operating systems that glide within a suspended cable system to record sports events from many angles. You also encounter real-time operating systems in devices you use in your everyday life, such as fuel-injection systems in car engines, video game consoles, and many home appliances (see Figure 5.2).

Real-time operating systems require minimal user interaction. The programs are written specifically to the needs of the devices and their functions. Therefore, there are no commercially available standard RTOS software programs.

SINGLE-USER OPERATING SYSTEMS

What type of operating system controls my personal computer? Because your computer, whether it's a desktop, laptop, or even a tablet PC, can handle only one person working on it at a time but can perform a variety of tasks simultaneously, it uses

a **single-user, multitask operating system**. Windows operating systems and the Macintosh operating system (Mac OS) are most commonly used as single-user multitask operating systems. (Note, however, that the newer versions, such as Windows XP, have networking capabilities so technically they also can be considered multiuser operating systems.) We will discuss the features of single-user, multitask operating systems in more detail in the next section of this chapter.

Usually, when you buy a desktop or laptop computer, its operating system software is already installed on the computer's hard disk. Sometimes you may need to install the OS yourself if you change or upgrade to a different version, or you might reinstall it in the case of a system problem.

Does the same kind of operating system also control my PDA? All computers on which one user is performing just one task at a time require a **single-user, single-task operating system**. PDAs currently can perform only one task at a time by a single user, so they require single-user, single-task operating system software such as Pocket PC or Palm OS.

Microsoft's Pocket PC is an application that includes both operating system software (Windows CE) and application components bundled specifically for PDAs (see Figure 5.3). Besides the address book, date book, memo pad, and to-do list that are standard with Windows CE, the bundled

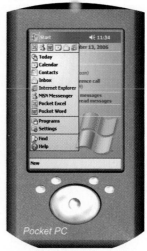

FIGURE 5.3

Although PDAs use a single-user, single-task operating system in which only one user can perform one task at a time, the operating system has a similar look to that of a traditional desktop operating system.

Pocket PC software also includes versions of Word, Excel, Outlook, and Internet Explorer that are designed specifically for PDAs. The latest version of Pocket PC, Windows Mobile 2003, comes with advanced wireless Internet connection capabilities.

Palm OS, on the other hand, is found in a number of devices but is strictly an operating system. If your PDA uses Palm OS as its operating system, you must purchase and install separately any additional software you want to run on your PDA.

Cell phones also use a single-user, single-task operating system that not only manages the functions of the phone but also provides other functionality, such as built-in phone directories, games, and calculators. Symbian is the leading OS software for mobile phones.

Are there any other single-user, single-task operating systems? **Microsoft Disk Operating System (MS-DOS)** is another example of a single-user, single-task operating system. DOS was the first widely installed operating system in personal computers. Compared to the operating systems we are familiar with today, DOS was a highly user "unfriendly" OS. To use it, you needed to type in specific commands. For example, to copy a file named "letter" from the hard drive to a floppy disk, you would type in the following command after the C prompt:

```
C:\>copy letter.txt A:
```

Although DOS is infrequently used today as a primary operating system, Information Technology (IT) professionals still use it to edit and repair system files and programs.

MULTIUSER OPERATING SYSTEMS

What kind of operating system do networks use? A **multiuser operating system** (also known as a **network operating system**) enables more than one user to access the computer system at one time by efficiently juggling all the requests from multiple users. Networks require a multiuser operating system because many users access the server computer at the same time and share resources such as printers. A network operating system is installed on the server and manages all user requests, ensuring they do not interfere with each other. For example, on a network on which users share a printer, the printer can produce only one document

at a time. The OS is therefore responsible for managing all the printer requests and making sure they are processed one at a time.

Examples of network operating systems include Linux, UNIX, Novell NetWare, and Windows Server 2003. Windows XP can be considered a network OS because it enables users to create a home network without needing to install a different operating system.

What other kinds of computers require a multiuser operating system? Large corporations with hundreds or thousands of employees often use powerful computers known as mainframes. These computers are responsible for storing, managing, and simultaneously processing data from all users. Mainframe operating systems fall into the multiuser category. Examples include UNIX and IBM's OS/2 and z/OS.

Supercomputers also use multiuser operating systems. Scientists and engineers use supercomputers to solve complex problems or to perform massive computations. Some supercomputers are single computers with multiple processors, whereas others consist of multiple computers that work together.

Desktop Operating Systems

As mentioned earlier, desktop computers (and laptops) use multitask operating systems, of which there are several available, including Windows, Linux, and Mac OS. The type of processor in the computer determines which operating system a particular desktop computer uses. The combination of operating system and processor is referred to as a computer's **platform**.

For example, Microsoft Windows operating systems are designed to coordinate with a series of processors from Intel Corporation and AMD (Advanced Micro Devices) that share the same or similar sets of instructions. However, until recently, Apple Macintosh operating systems worked primarily with processors from the Motorola Corporation and IBM designed specifically for Apple computers. These two operating systems (Windows and Mac OS), as well as application programs designed for those operating systems, are not interchangeable. If you attempt to load a Windows OS on a Mac (with a Motorola or IBM chip), for example, the Mac processor would *not* understand the operating system and will not function properly. This changed slightly in 2005 when Apple announced it would begin using Intel chips in their computers.

MICROSOFT WINDOWS

What is the most popular operating system for desktop computers?

Microsoft Windows is the market leader in operating system sales, maintaining an approximate 90 percent market share. Although Windows XP is the most recent version on the market, many computers still run earlier versions, such as Windows 95, Windows NT, Windows 98, Windows Millennium Edition (Me), and Windows 2000. Windows XP comes in a number of versions to suit different users, including Windows XP Home Edition, Windows XP Professional, Windows XP Tablet PC, and Windows XP Media Center Edition.

What is the difference between the various Windows operating systems?

Figure 5.4 presents a time line of the

FIGURE 5.4 Windows Time Line		
1985	Windows 1.0	Introduces, instead of the Disk Operating System (DOS) command line interface, a user environment with point-and-click commands with a mouse and includes modest multitasking capabilities and desktop applications.
1987	Windows 2.0	Includes better graphics capabilities and introduces keyboard shortcuts and the ability to overlap windows.
1990	Windows 3.0	Added programs to manage applications, files, and print jobs as well as improved icons.
1992	Windows 3.1	First widely used PC graphical user interface (GUI) operating system. Improved point-and-click mouse operations and multitasking capabilities.
1993	Windows NT 3.1	Fundamentally different operating system with increased security, power, performance, and multitasking scheduler.
1995	Windows 95	Provides major enhancements over Windows 3.1. This operating system runs faster and more efficiently, introduces Plug and Play capabilities, long filenames, short-cut right-click menus, and a cleaner desktop. Sells more than 1 million copies within 4 days.
1996	Windows NT 4.0	Has a similar feel to that of Windows 95 but with enhanced network support and security features.
1997	Windows CE	Released to compete with the Palm OS for Personal Digital Assistants (PDAs). It has the same look and features as Windows 95.
1998	Windows 98	This upgrade to Windows 95 includes additional file protection features and incorporates Internet Explorer 4.0, a customizable taskbar, and desktop features that let you customize backgrounds as well as live Web content such as a stock ticker or weather map.
2000	Windows 2000 Professional	This upgrade to Windows NT offers improvements to file security and Internet support.
2000	Windows Millennium Edition (ME)	This upgrade to Windows 95 and Windows 98 includes system backup and multimedia capabilities (such as Media Player).
2001	Windows XP Home and Professional	Offers a new multiuser desktop as well as improved digital media features and Internet capabilities.
2001	Windows XP Tablet PC	Designed specifically for new Tablet PC notebooks, this operating system incorporates a digital pen that enables users to write directly on the Tablet screen and perform mouse functions. It also includes built-in wireless technologies.
2002	Windows XP Media Center OS	Designed specifically for Media Center PCs, this operating system integrates digital entertainment (TV, movies, music, photos, and radio). For example, you can record live TV and radio programs, create your own DVDs, and edit and show photos.

evolution of Microsoft Windows. As you can see, with each new version, Microsoft made improvements. What was once only a single-user, single-task operating system is now a powerful multiuser operating system. Over time, Windows improvements have concentrated on increasing user functionality and friendliness, improving Internet capabilities, and enhancing file privacy and security.

MAC OS

How is Mac OS different from Windows?

Although Apple's **Mac OS** and the Windows operating systems are not compatible, they are very similar in terms of functionality. In 1984, Mac OS became the first operating system to incorporate the user-friendly point-and-click technology in a commercially affordable computer. Both operating systems now have similar window work areas on the desktop that house individual applications and support users working in more than one application at a time (see Figure 5.5).

Despite their similarities, there are many subtle and not-so-subtle differences that have created loyal fans of each product. Macs have long been recognized for their superior graphics display and processing capabilities. Users also attest to Mac's greater system reliability and better document recovery. Despite these advantages, there are fewer software applications available for the Mac platform and Mac systems tend to be a bit more expensive than Windows-based PCs.

The most recent version of the Mac operating system, Mac OS X, is based on the UNIX operating system. Mac OS X includes a new user interface and larger icons, among other features. For more information on Mac OS X, see the Technology in Focus feature "Computing Alternatives" on page 276.

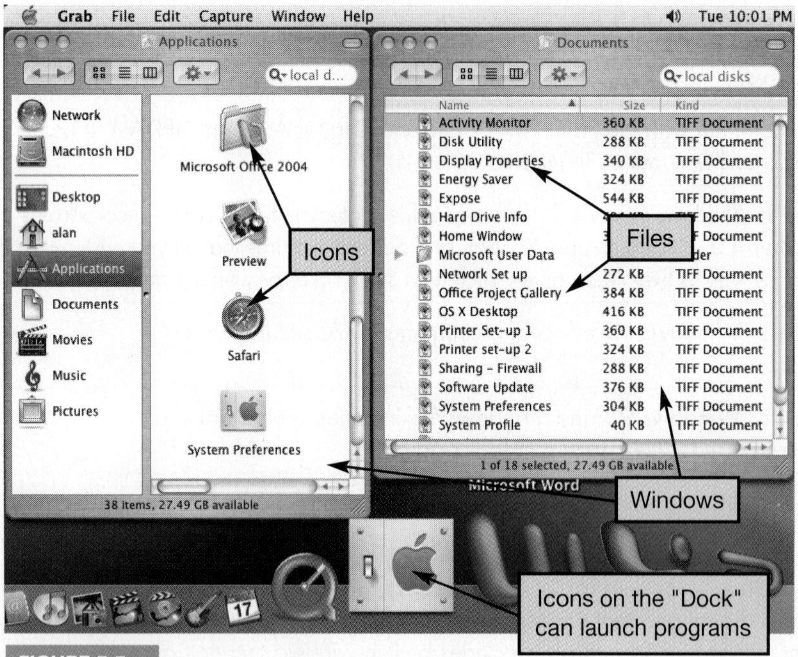

UNIX

What is UNIX?

UNIX is a multiuser, multitask operating system used primarily with mainframes as a network operating system, although it is also often found on PCs. Originally conceived in 1969 by Ken Thompson and Dennis Ritchie of AT&T's Bell Labs, the UNIX code was initially not proprietary—in other words, no company like Microsoft or Apple owned it. Rather, any programmer was allowed to use the code and modify it to meet his or her needs. Later, AT&T licensed the UNIX source code to the Santa Cruz Operation (SCO). UNIX is a brand that belongs to the company X/Open, but any vendor that meets testing requirements and pays a fee can use the UNIX name. Individual vendors then modify the UNIX code to run specifically on their hardware. HP/UX from Hewlett-Packard, Solaris from Sun, and AIX from IBM are some of the UNIX systems currently available in the marketplace.

LINUX

What is Linux?

Linux is an open-source operating system based on UNIX and designed for use on personal computers and as a network operating system. An **open-source program** is one that is freely available for developers to use or modify as they wish. Linux began in 1991 as a part-time project by a Finnish university student named Linus Torvalds, who wanted to create a free operating system to run on his home computer. He posted his operating system program code to the Web for others to use and modify. It has since been tweaked by scores of programmers as part of the Free Software Foundation GNU (or GNU's not UNIX) project.

FIGURE 5.5

The most recent version of the Mac operating system, Mac OS X, is based on the UNIX operating system. Although it is not compatible with Windows OS, Mac OS has very similar features to Windows.

Emerging Technologies: Open-Source Software—Why Isn't Everyone Using Linux?

Proprietary software, such as Microsoft Windows, is developed by corporations and sold for profit. This means that the *source code*, the actual lines of instructional code that make the program work, is not accessible to the general public. Without being able to access the source code, it's difficult to modify the software or see exactly how the program author constructed various parts of the system.

Restricting access to the source code protects companies from having their programming ideas stolen, and prevents customers from using modified versions of the software. This benefits the companies that create the software because their software code can't be pirated (or stolen). However, in the late 1980s, computer specialists became concerned over the fact that large software companies (such as Microsoft) were controlling a large portion of market share and driving out competitors. They also felt that proprietary software was too expensive and contained too many bugs (errors).

These people felt that software should be developed without a profit motive and distributed with its source code free for all to see. The theory was that if many computer specialists examine, improve, and change the source code, a more full-featured, bug-free product would result. Hence, the open-source movement was born.

Open-source software is freely distributed (no royalties accrue to the creators), contains the source code, and can in turn be redistributed freely to others. Most open-source products are created by teams of programmers and modified (updated) by hundreds of other programmers around the world. You can download the products for free off the Internet. Linux is probably the most widely recognized name in open-source software, but other products such as MySQL (a database program) and OpenOffice (a suite of productivity applications) are also gaining in popularity.

So, if an operating system such as Linux is free, why does Windows (which you must pay for) have such a huge market share? Corporations and individuals have grown accustomed to one thing that proprietary software makers can provide: technical support. It is almost impossible to provide technical support for open-source software because it can be freely modified, and there is no one specific developer to take responsibility for technical support (see Figure 5.6). Therefore, corporations have been reluctant to install open-source software extensively because of the cost of the internal staff of programmers that must support it.

Companies such as Red Hat have been combating this problem. Red Hat has been packaging and selling versions of Linux since 1994. The company provides a warranty and technical support for its version of Linux (which Red Hat programmers modified from the original source code). Packaging open source software in this manner has made using it much more attractive to businesses. Today, many Web servers are hosted on computers running Linux.

So, when will free versions of Linux (or another open-source operating system) be the dominant OS on home computers? The answer is maybe never. Most casual computer users won't feel comfortable without technical support; therefore, any open-source products for home use would probably need to be marketed the way Red Hat markets Linux. Also, many open-source products are not easy to maintain.

However, companies such as Linspire (**www.linspire.com**) are making easy-to-use visual interfaces that work with the Linux operating system. If one of these companies can develop an easy-to-use product and has the marketing clout to challenge Microsoft, you may see more open-source software deployed in the home computer market in the future.

FIGURE 5.6

Although free Linux software, provided by companies like Knoppix, is available, a lack of technical support scares many companies away from wide-scale adoption.

Today, Linux is gaining a reputation as a stable operating system that is not subject to crashes and failures. Because the code is open and available to anyone, Linux is quickly tweaked to meet virtually any new operating system need. For example, when Palm PDAs emerged, the Linux OS was promptly modified to run on this new device. Similarly, only a few weeks were necessary to get the Linux OS ready for the new Intel Xeon processor, a feat unheard of in proprietary operating system development. Linux is also gaining popularity among computer manufacturers, which have begun to ship it with some of their latest PCs.

Where can I buy Linux? You can download the open-source versions of Linux for free off the Internet. However, there are several versions of Linux that are more proprietary in nature. These versions come with support and other products not generally associated with the open-source Linux. Red Hat has been packaging and selling versions of Linux since 1994 and is probably the most well-known Linux distributor. Red Hat Enterprise Linux 4 is the current version on the market. Other Linux distributors include Mandrake, Debian GNU/Linux, and Gentoo Linux. For a full listing and explanation of all Linux distributors, visit **www.distrowatch.com**. For more information on Linux, see the Technology in Focus feature "Computing Alternatives" on page 276.

What the Operating System Does

As shown in Figure 5.7, the operating system is like a traffic cop that coordinates the flow of data and information through the computer system. In doing so, the OS performs several specific functions:

- It provides a way for the user to interact with the computer.

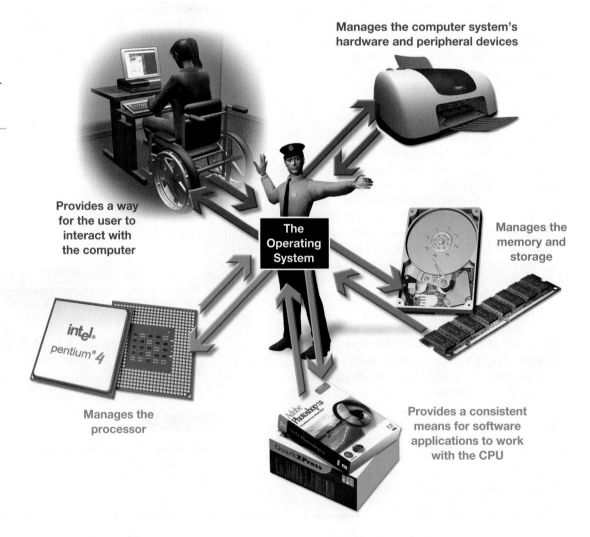

FIGURE 5.7

The operating system is the traffic cop of your computer, coordinating its many activities and devices.

Manages the computer system's hardware and peripheral devices

Provides a way for the user to interact with the computer

The Operating System

Manages the memory and storage

Manages the processor

Provides a consistent means for software applications to work with the CPU

- It manages the processor, or central processing unit (CPU).

- It manages the memory and storage.

- It manages the computer system's hardware and peripheral devices.

- It provides a consistent means for software applications to work with the CPU.

In this section, we look at each of these functions in detail.

THE USER INTERFACE

How does the operating system control how I interact with my computer? The operating system provides a **user interface** that enables you to interact with the computer. As noted earlier, the first personal computers had a DOS operating system with a command-driven interface, as shown in Figure 5.8a. A **command-driven interface** is one in which you enter commands to communicate with the computer system. The commands were not always easy to understand and as a result the interface proved to be too complicated for the average user. Therefore, PCs were used primarily in business and by professional computer operators.

The command-driven interface was later improved by incorporating a menu-driven interface, as shown in Figure 5.8b. A **menu-driven interface** is one in which you choose a command from menus displayed on the screen. Menu-driven interfaces eliminated the need to know every command because you could select most of the commonly used commands from a menu. However, they were still not easy enough for most people to use.

What kind of interface do operating systems use today? Most operating systems today, such as Mac OS and Microsoft Windows, use a **graphical user interface**, or **GUI** (pronounced "gooey"). Unlike the command- and menu-driven interfaces used earlier, GUIs display graphics and use the point-and-click technology of the mouse and cursor, making them much more user friendly. As illustrated in Figure 5.9, a GUI uses **windows** (rectangular boxes that contain programs displayed on the screen), **menus** (lists of commands that appear on the screen), and **icons** (pictures that represent an object such as a software application or a file

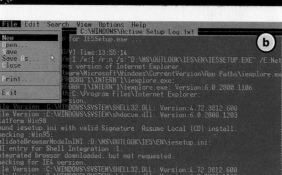

FIGURE 5.8

(a) Example of a command-driven interface. Such interfaces were not user-friendly.
(b) Menu-driven interfaces were a step toward today's user-friendly interfaces.

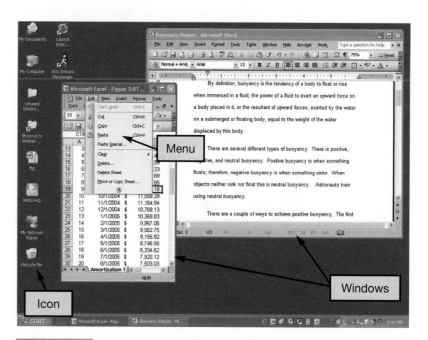

FIGURE 5.9

Today's operating systems include a graphical user interface (GUI). These user interfaces are much more user friendly than the DOS command-driven interfaces used previously.

or folder). Because users no longer have to enter commands to interact with the computer, GUIs are a big reason why desktop computers are now such popular tools.

Unlike Windows or Mac OS, Linux does not have a single, default GUI interface. Instead, users are free to choose among many commercially available or free interfaces, such as GNOME, KDE, and Motif, each of which provides a different look and feel. For example, GNOME (pronounced "gah-NOHM") actually allows you to select which desktop appearance (Windows or Mac) you'd like your system to display. This means that if you're using Linux for the first time, you don't have to learn a new interface: you just use the one you're most comfortable with already.

PROCESSOR MANAGEMENT

Why does the operating system need to manage the processor? When you use your computer, you are usually asking it to perform several tasks at once. For example, you might be printing a Word document, waiting for a file to download from the Internet, listening to a CD from your CD drive, and working on a PowerPoint presentation, all at the same time—or at least what *appears* to be at the same time. Although the processor is the powerful brains of the computer, processing all of its instructions and performing all of its calculations, it needs the operating system to arrange for the execution of all these activities in a systematic way to give the appearance that everything is happening simultaneously.

To do so, the operating system assigns a slice of its time to each activity requiring the processor's attention. The OS must then switch between different processes thousands of times a second to make it appear that everything is happening in a seamlessly fluid manner. Otherwise, you wouldn't be able to listen to a CD and print at the same time without experiencing delays in the process. When the operating system allows you to perform more than one task at a time, it is said to be **multitasking**.

How exactly does the operating system coordinate all the activities? When you type and print a document in Word, for example, many different devices in the computer system are involved, including your keyboard, mouse, and printer. Every keystroke, every mouse click, and each signal to the printer creates an action, or **event**, in the respective device (keyboard, mouse, or printer) to which the operating system responds.

Sometimes these events occur sequentially (such as when you type characters one at a time), but other events require two devices working simultaneously (such as the printer printing while you continue to type). Although it *looks* as though the keyboard and printer are working at the same time, in effect, the operating system switches back and forth between processes, controlling the timing of events the processor works on.

For example, assume you are typing and you want to print another document. When you tell your computer to print your document, the printer generates a unique signal called an **interrupt** that tells the operating system that it is in need of immediate attention. Every device has its own type of interrupt, which is associated with an *interrupt handler*, a special numerical code that prioritizes the requests. These requests are placed in the *interrupt table* in the computer's primary memory (or random access memory, RAM).

In our example, the operating system pauses the CPU from its typing activity when it receives the interrupt from the printer and puts a "memo" in a special location in RAM called a *stack*. The memo is a reminder of where the CPU was before it left off so that it can work on the printer request. The CPU then retrieves the printer request from the interrupt table and begins to process it. On completion of the printer request, the CPU goes back to the stack, retrieves the memo it placed about the keystroke activity, and returns to that task until it is interrupted again.

What happens if there is more than one document waiting to be printed? The operating system also coordinates multiple activities for peripheral devices such as printers. When the processor receives a request to send information to the printer, it first checks with the operating system to ensure that the printer is not already in use. If it is in use, the OS puts the request in another temporary storage area in RAM called the *buffer*. It will wait in the buffer until the *spooler*, a program that helps coordinate all print jobs currently being sent to the printer, indicates the printer is available. If more than one print job is waiting, a line, or *queue*, is formed so that the printer can process the requests in order.

MEMORY AND STORAGE MANAGEMENT

Why does the operating system have to manage the computer's memory?
As the operating system coordinates the activities of the processor, it uses RAM as a temporary storage area for instructions and data the processor needs. The processor then accesses these instructions and data from RAM when it is ready to process them. The OS is therefore responsible for coordinating the space allocations in RAM to ensure that there is enough space for all the waiting instructions and data. It then clears the items from RAM when the processor no longer needs them.

Can my system ever run out of RAM space?
RAM has limited capacity. The average computer system has anywhere from 128 megabytes (MB) to 2 gigabytes (GB) of memory in RAM. Although 2 GB of RAM may be sufficient if you're running several applications at the same time, those systems with 512 MB or less may be challenged by limited RAM resources.

What happens if my computer runs out of RAM?
When there isn't enough room in RAM for the operating system to store the required data and instructions, the operating system borrows room from the more spacious hard drive. This process of optimizing RAM storage by borrowing hard drive space is called **virtual memory**. As shown in Figure 5.10, when more RAM space is needed, the operating system swaps out from RAM the data or instructions that have not been recently used and moves them to a temporary storage area on the hard drive called the **swap file** (or **page file**). If the data and/or instructions in the swap file are needed later, the operating system swaps them back into active RAM and replaces them in the hard drive's swap file with less-active data or instructions. This process of swapping is known as **paging**.

Can I ever run out of virtual memory?
Only a portion of the hard drive is allocated to virtual memory. You can manually change this setting to increase the amount of hard drive space allocated, but eventually your computer system will become sluggish as it is forced to page more and more often. This condition of excessive paging is called **thrashing**. The solution to this problem is to increase the amount of RAM in your system so that you can avoid it having to send data and instructions to virtual memory. You'll learn how to monitor your RAM and virtual memory requirements in Chapter 6.

How does the operating system manage storage?
If it weren't for the operating system, the files and applications you save to the hard drive and other storage locations would be a complete mess. Fortunately, the OS has a file management system that keeps track of the name and location of each file you save and programs you install. We will talk more about file management later in the chapter.

HARDWARE AND PERIPHERAL DEVICE MANAGEMENT

How does the operating system manage the hardware and peripheral devices?
Each device attached to your computer comes with a special program called a **device driver** that facilitates the communication between the hardware device and the operating system. Because the

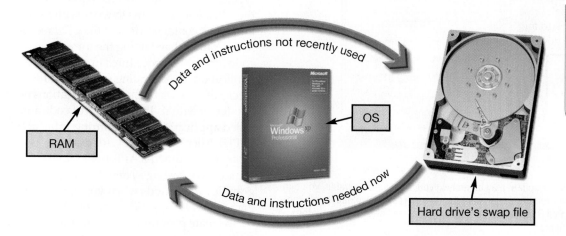

FIGURE 5.10

Virtual memory borrows excess storage capacity from the hard drive when there is not enough capacity in RAM.

RAM

Data and instructions not recently used

OS

Windows XP Professional

Data and instructions needed now

Hard drive's swap file

OS must be able to communicate with every device in the computer system, the device driver translates the specialized commands of the device to commands that the operating system can understand, and vice versa. Thus, devices will not function without the proper device driver, because the OS would not know how to communicate with them.

Do I always need a driver? Today, most devices come with the driver already preinstalled in Windows. The devices whose drivers are included in Windows are called **Plug and Play (PnP)**. However, Plug and Play is not a driver. Instead, it is a software and hardware standard that Microsoft created with the Windows 95 operating system. This standard is designed to facilitate the installation of a new piece of hardware in personal computers by including the driver the device needs to run in the OS. Because the OS includes this software, incorporating a new device into your computer system seems automatic. Plug and Play enables users to plug in their new device to a port on the system, turn on the system, and immediately play, or use, the device. The OS auto-matically recognizes the device and its driver without any further user manipulations to the system.

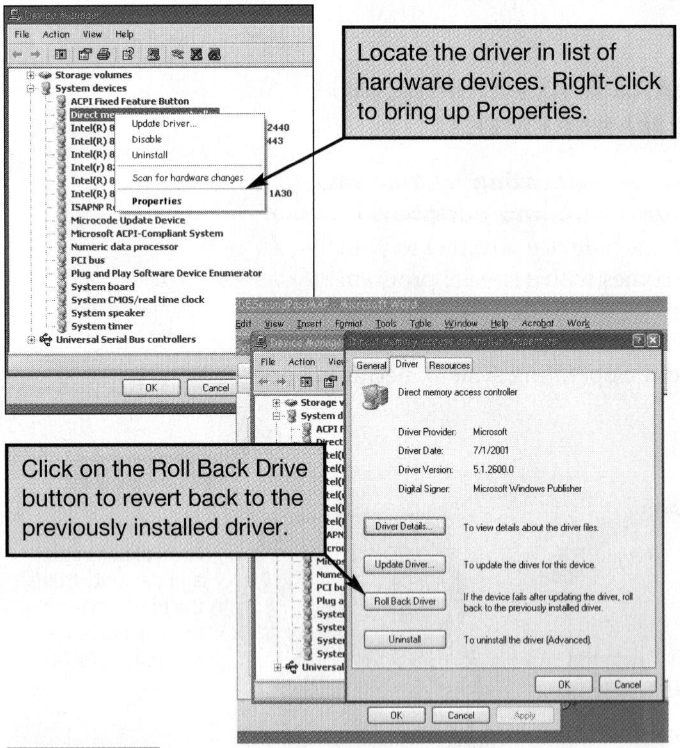

What happens if the device is not Plug and Play? Some devices, such as many types of printers, are not Plug and Play. Similarly, many older devices also may not be Plug and Play. When you install a non–Plug and Play device, you will be prompted to insert any media (such as CDs or floppy disks) that were provided with the device; these disks contain the necessary driver. If you obtain a non–Plug and Play device secondhand and did not receive the device driver, or if you are required to update the device driver, you can often download the necessary driver from the manufacturer's Web site. You can also check out Web sites such as **www.driverzone.com** or **www.driverguide.com** to locate drivers.

Can I damage my system by installing a device driver? Occasionally, when you install a driver, your system may become unstable (that is, programs may stop responding, certain actions may cause a crash, or the device or the entire system may stop working). Although this is not common, it can happen. Fortunately, Windows XP has a Roll Back Driver feature (accessible through the Control Panel) that reinstalls the old driver and remedies the problem (see Figure 5.11).

SOFTWARE APPLICATION COORDINATION

How does the operating system help software applications run on the computer? Software applications feed the CPU the instructions it needs to process data. These instructions take the form of computer code. Every software application, no matter what its type or manufacturer, needs to interact with the CPU. For programs to work with the CPU, they must contain code that the CPU recognizes. Rather than having the same blocks of code for similar procedures in each software application, the operating system includes the blocks of code that software applications need to interact with it. These blocks of code are called **application programming interfaces (APIs)**. Microsoft DirectX, for example, is a group of multimedia APIs built into the Windows operating system that improves graphics and sounds when you're playing games or watching video on your PC.

To create programs that can communicate with the operating system, software pro-

Locate the driver in list of hardware devices. Right-click to bring up Properties.

Click on the Roll Back Drive button to revert back to the previously installed driver.

FIGURE 5.11

If you think a recent driver update may be making your computer unstable, you can use the Roll Back Driver feature to get rid of the new driver and replace it with the last one that worked. Roll Back Driver permits only one level of rollback and does not work for printer drivers.

grammers need only *refer* to the API code blocks in their individual application programs, rather than including the entire code in the application itself. Not only do APIs avoid redundancies in software code, they also make it easier for software developers to respond to changes in the operating system.

Large software developers such as Microsoft have many software applications under their corporate umbrella and use the same APIs in all or most of their software applications. Because APIs coordinate with the operating system, all applications that have incorporated these APIs have common interfaces such as similar toolbars and menus. Therefore, the software applications have the same look to many of their features. An added benefit to this system is that applications sharing these same formats can also easily exchange data between different programs. As such, it's easy to create a chart in Microsoft Excel from data in Microsoft Access and incorporate the finished chart into a Microsoft Word document.

The Boot Process: Starting Your Computer

Although it only takes a minute or two, a lot of things happen very quickly between the time you turn on the computer and when it is ready for you to enter your first command. As you learned earlier, all data and instructions (including the operating system) are stored in RAM while your computer is on. When you turn your computer off, RAM is wiped clean of all its data (including the OS). So, how does the computer know what to do when you turn it on if there is nothing in RAM? It runs through a special process, called the **boot process** (or start-up process), to load the operating system into RAM.

What are the steps involved in the boot process? The boot process, illustrated in Figure 5.12, consists of four basic steps:

FIGURE 5.12

The Boot Process

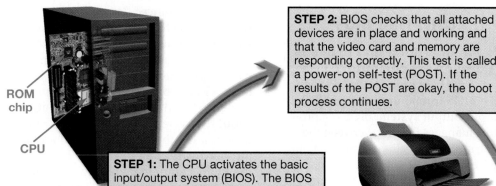

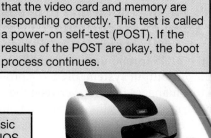

STEP 2: BIOS checks that all attached devices are in place and working and that the video card and memory are responding correctly. This test is called a power-on self-test (POST). If the results of the POST are okay, the boot process continues.

STEP 1: The CPU activates the basic input/output system (BIOS). The BIOS is located on a ROM chip. Data stored in ROM does not get erased when the computer is turned off.

ROM chip

CPU

STEP 3: BIOS first looks in the floppy disk drive for the system files. When it doesn't find the operating system in the floppy disk drive, it looks in the hard disk drive. It then loads the operating system from its permanent storage location on the hard disk to RAM.

STEP 4: The registry is checked for further configurations and customizations. If the entire system is checked out and loaded properly, the desktop appears on your screen. The computer system is now ready to accept your first command.

1. The basic input/output system (BIOS) is activated by powering on the CPU.
2. The BIOS checks that all attached devices are in place (called a power-on self-test, or POST).
3. The operating system is loaded into RAM.
4. Configuration and customization settings are checked.

As the computer goes through the boot process in Windows operating systems, indicator lights on the keyboard and disk drives will illuminate and the system will emit various beeps. If you have a version of Windows earlier than XP, text will scroll down the screen as well. When you boot up on a PC with Windows XP or a Mac, you won't hear any beeps or see any keyboard lights illuminate. Instead, a welcome screen will appear, indicating the progress of the start-up process. Once the boot process has completed these steps, it is ready to accept commands and data. Let's look at each of these steps in more detail.

STEP 1: ACTIVATING BIOS

What's the first thing that happens after I turn on my computer? In the first step of the boot process, the CPU activates the **BIOS** (pronounced "bye-OSE"), the **basic input/output system**. BIOS is a program that manages the data between the operating system and all the input and output devices attached to the system, hence its name. BIOS is also responsible for loading the OS from its permanent location on the hard drive to RAM.

BITS AND BYTES

How Did "Boot" Get Its Name?

The term *boot*, used to describe the process of starting a computer, gets its name from the term *bootstrap*. In the olden days, men used straps of leather, called bootstraps, to help them pull on their boots. The use of bootstraps in this way created the expression to "pull oneself up by the bootstraps." In computing terms, the *bootstrap loader* is a very small program that begins the process of loading a much larger and more powerful program that then controls the rest of the system.

BIOS itself is stored on a special read-only memory (ROM) chip on the motherboard. Unlike data stored in RAM, data stored in ROM is permanent and does not get erased when the power is turned off.

STEP 2: PERFORMING THE POWER-ON SELF-TEST

How does the computer determine whether the hardware is working properly? The first job BIOS performs is to ensure that essential peripheral devices are attached and operational. This process is called the **power-on self-test**, or **POST**. The POST consists of a test on the video card and video memory, a BIOS identification process (during which the BIOS version, manufacturer, and data are displayed on the monitor in Windows versions prior to XP), and a memory test to ensure memory chips are working properly.

The BIOS compares the results of the POST with the various hardware configurations that are permanently stored in CMOS (pronounced "see-moss"). CMOS, which stands for complementary metal-oxide semiconductor, is a special kind of memory that uses almost no power. A little battery provides enough power so its contents will not be lost after the computer is turned off. CMOS contains information about the system's memory, types of disk drives, and other essential input and output hardware components. If the results of the POST compare favorably to the hardware configurations stored in CMOS, the boot process continues. If new hardware has been installed, this will cause the POST to not agree with the hardware configurations in CMOS, and you will be alerted that new hardware has been detected.

STEP 3: LOADING THE OPERATING SYSTEM

How does the operating system get loaded into RAM? BIOS looks through the storage disks for the **system files**, the main files of the operating system. The first place it looks is the floppy disk drive. When it doesn't find the OS there, it looks in the hard disk drive. When it is located, the operating system loads from its permanent storage location on the hard drive to RAM.

Once the system files are loaded into RAM, the **kernel** (or **supervisor program**) is loaded. The kernel is the essential component of the operating system. It is responsible for managing the processor and all other components of the computer system. Because it stays in RAM the entire time your computer is powered on, the kernel is called *memory resident*. Other parts of the OS that are less critical stay on the hard drive and are copied over to RAM on an as-needed basis so that the entire RAM is not taken up. These programs are called *nonresident*. Once the kernel is loaded, the operating system takes over the control of the computer's functions.

STEP 4: CHECKING FURTHER CONFIGURATIONS AND CUSTOMIZATIONS

When are the other components and configurations of the system checked? CMOS checks the configuration of memory and essential peripherals in the beginning of the boot process. In this last phase of the boot process, the operating system checks the registry for the configuration of other system components. The **registry** contains all the different configurations (settings) used by the OS and by other applications. It contains the customized settings you put into place, such as mouse speed and the display settings for your monitor and desktop, as well as instructions as to which programs should be loaded first.

Why do I sometimes need to enter a password at the end of the boot process? In a networked environment, such as that found at most colleges, the operating system services many users. To determine whether a user is authorized to use the system (that is, whether a user is a paying student or college employee), authorized users are given a login name and password. The verification of your login name and password at the end of the boot process is called **authentication**. The authentication process blocks unauthorized users from entering the system.

You also may need to insert a password following the boot process to log in to your account on your home computer. The newest version of the Windows operating system, Windows XP, is a multiuser system. Even in a home environment, all users with access to a Windows XP computer (such as family members or roommates) can have their own user accounts. Users can set up a password to protect their account from being accessed by another user without permission. For more information on selecting a good password, see the Technology in Focus feature "Protecting Your Computer and Backing Up Your Data" on page 374.

How do I know if the boot process is successful? The entire boot process takes only a minute or two to complete. If the entire system is checked out and loaded properly, the process completes by displaying the desktop. The computer system is now ready to accept your first command.

HANDLING ERRORS IN THE BOOT PROCESS

What can go wrong during the boot process? During the boot process, if you come across a message like the following:

```
Non-system disk or disk error
Replace and strike any key when ready
```

check to see whether you've left a disk in the floppy disk drive. As explained earlier, when the BIOS is performing its system check, it first looks in the floppy drive for the operating system. With early computers, operating systems were not permanently stored on the hard drive but were instead loaded into the system from a floppy disk. (That's how DOS, or Disk Operating System, got its name.) If you have ever had a hard disk crash and needed to install the system repair disk, you understand why it's important that systems checked the floppy disk drive first. As floppy disk drives are phased out, this will not continue to be the case. Repair disks are now on CD and systems can be reconfigured to boot from a CD, if need be.

If BIOS doesn't find a floppy in the floppy drive, it proceeds to the hard drive. However, if it *does* find a floppy in the floppy drive, it will attempt to find the OS on that floppy. When it does not find the operating system software on the floppy, the boot process stops and displays the error message "Non-system disk or disk error." When this happens, simply remove the floppy disk and press any key to resume the boot process.

How can I tell if there are other errors during the boot process? During the boot process, if there is a problem with loading a device during the POST, an error message (generally on a blue background) appears on your screen.

Sometimes, however, the problem occurs before the video (display) card that controls your monitor has been activated, making a display message impossible. In those instances, you will hear a series of beeps. (These beeps are in place of the single beep you would hear if everything was loading properly.) Each device in your computer system is assigned a specific beep code. Because different BIOS manufacturers have different beep codes, you can identify the error by listening to the number of beeps and then comparing them to the beep codes listed in your computer's user manual or on the BIOS manufacturer's Web site.

Being able to identify an "error beep" during the boot process will facilitate conversations you may later have with a technical assistant to diagnose the problem.

What should I do if my keyboard or other device doesn't work after I boot my computer? Sometimes during the boot process, BIOS skips a device (such as a keyboard) or improperly identifies it. You won't hear any beeps or see any error messages when this happens. Your only indication that this sort of problem has occurred is that the device won't respond after the system has been booted. When that happens, you can generally resolve the problem by rebooting. If the problem persists, you may want to check the operating system's Web site for any patches (or software fixes) that may resolve the issue. If there are no patches or the problem persists, you may want to get technical assistance.

What is Safe mode? Sometimes Windows does not boot properly and you end up with a screen with the words *Safe Mode* in the corners, as shown in Figure 5.13. **Safe mode** is a special diagnostic mode designed for troubleshooting errors. When in Safe mode, only the essential devices of the system (such as the mouse, keyboard, and monitor) function. Even the regular graphics device driver will not be activated in Safe mode. Instead, the system runs in the most basic graphics mode, resulting in a neutral screen, elimi-

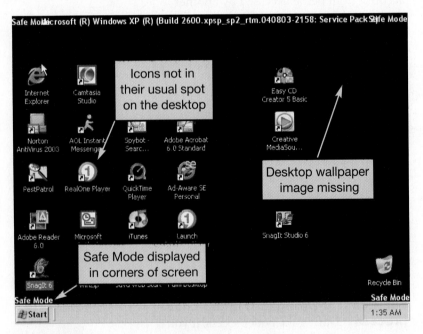

FIGURE 5.13

If your screen looks something like this, your computer has booted into Safe mode. This means that something did not function properly during the boot process. Safe mode provides you with enough functionality so that you can accomplish diagnostic testing.

nating any desktop images and nonessential icons.

What should I do if my operating system boots into Safe mode? If, after you boot, you end up in Safe mode, try rebooting the machine before doing anything else. If you still end up in Safe mode and if you have recently installed new software or a new hardware device, try uninstalling it. (Make sure you use the Add/Remove feature in Control Panel to remove the software.) If the problem then goes away after rebooting, you have determined the cause of the problem. You can then reinstall the device or software. If the problem does not go away, you should consult a technical support person for further diagnosis.

The Desktop and Windows Features

The **desktop** is the first interaction you have with the operating system and the first image you see on your monitor. As its name implies, your computer's desktop puts at your fingertips all of the elements necessary for a productive work session that are typically found on or near the top of a traditional desk, such as files and folders.

What are the main features of the desktop? The very nature of a desktop is that it enables you to customize it to meet your individual needs. As such, the desktop on your computer may be different from the desktop on your friend's computer. However, most desktops share common features, some of which are illustrated in Figure 5.14.

What are common features of a window? As noted earlier, one feature introduced by the graphical user interface is *windows* (with a lowercase *w*), the rectangular panes on your computer screen that display applications running on your system. Windows provide for a flexible,

FIGURE 5.14

The Windows desktop puts the most commonly used features of the operating system at your fingertips.

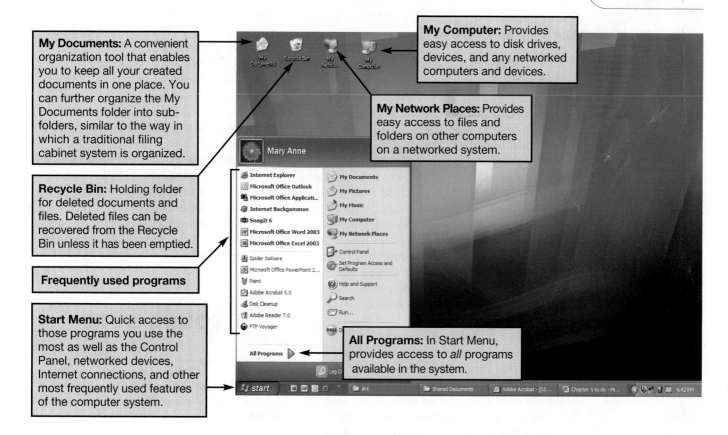

My Documents: A convenient organization tool that enables you to keep all your created documents in one place. You can further organize the My Documents folder into subfolders, similar to the way in which a traditional filing cabinet system is organized.

My Computer: Provides easy access to disk drives, devices, and any networked computers and devices.

My Network Places: Provides easy access to files and folders on other computers on a networked system.

Recycle Bin: Holding folder for deleted documents and files. Deleted files can be recovered from the Recycle Bin unless it has been emptied.

Frequently used programs

Start Menu: Quick access to those programs you use the most as well as the Control Panel, networked devices, Internet connections, and other most frequently used features of the computer system.

All Programs: In Start Menu, provides access to *all* programs available in the system.

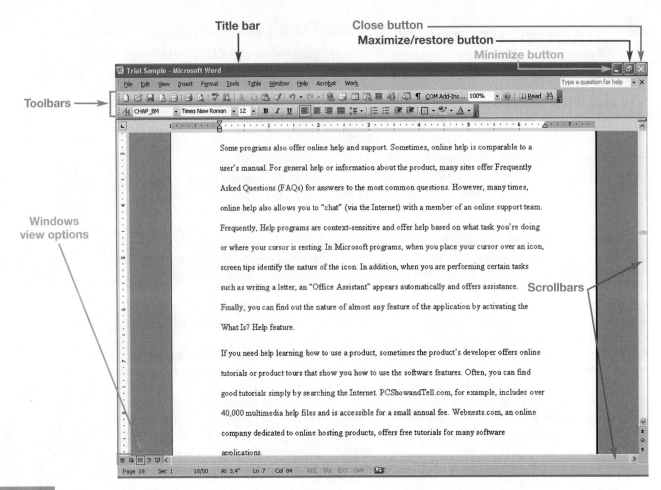

Title bar

Close button
Maximize/restore button
Minimize button

Toolbars

**Windows
view options**

Scrollbars

Some programs also offer online help and support. Sometimes, online help is comparable to a user's manual. For general help or information about the product, many sites offer Frequently Asked Questions (FAQs) for answers to the most common questions. However, many times, online help also allows you to "chat" (via the Internet) with a member of an online support team. Frequently, Help programs are context-sensitive and offer help based on what task you're doing or where your cursor is resting. In Microsoft programs, when you place your cursor over an icon, screen tips identify the nature of the icon. In addition, when you are performing certain tasks such as writing a letter, an "Office Assistant" appears automatically and offers assistance. Finally, you can find out the nature of almost any feature of the application by activating the What Is? Help feature.

If you need help learning how to use a product, sometimes the product's developer offers online tutorials or product tours that show you how to use the software features. Often, you can find good tutorials simply by searching the Internet. PCShowandTell.com, for example, includes over 40,000 multimedia help files and is accessible for a small annual fee. Webnests.com, an online company dedicated to online hosting products, offers free tutorials for many software applications.

FIGURE 5.15

Most windows in a graphical user interface share the same common elements.

user-friendly, multitasking environment. Figure 5.15 illustrates some of the features of windows, including **toolbars** (groups of icons collected together in a small box) and **scrollbars** (bars that appear at the side or bottom of the screen that control which part of the information is displayed on the screen). Using the Minimize, Maximize and Restore, and Close buttons, you can open, close, resize, and move windows anywhere on the desktop.

How can I see more than one window on my desktop at a time? You can easily arrange the windows on a desktop by tiling them, which means arranging separate windows so that they sit next to each other either horizontally or vertically. You also can arrange windows by cascading them so that they overlap one another, or you can simply resize two open windows so they appear on the screen at the same time.

Tiling windows makes accessing two or more active windows more convenient. For

example, as shown in Figure 5.16, you can input stock prices from a Web site into an Excel spreadsheet without clicking back and forth between the browser and Excel windows by tiling them horizontally. To untile the windows, or to bring a window back to its full size, click the Restore button in the top right corner of the window.

Can I move or resize the windows once they are tiled? Regardless of whether the windows are tiled, you can resize and move them around the desktop. You can reposition windows on the desktop by pointing to the title bar at the top of the window with your cursor and, when holding down the left mouse but-

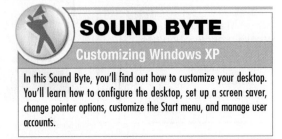

SOUND BYTE

Customizing Windows XP

In this Sound Byte, you'll find out how to customize your desktop. You'll learn how to configure the desktop, set up a screen saver, change pointer options, customize the Start menu, and manage user accounts.

FIGURE 5.16

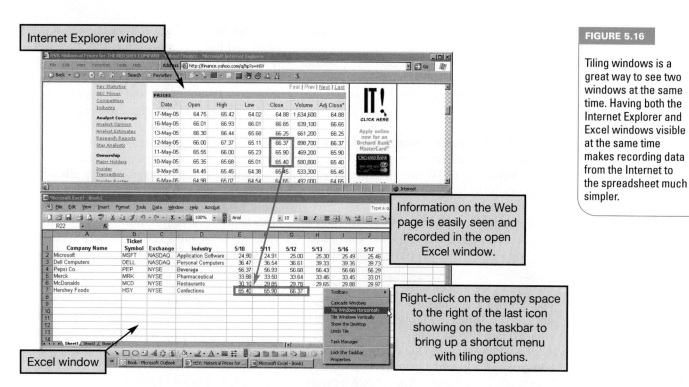

Internet Explorer window

Information on the Web page is easily seen and recorded in the open Excel window.

Right-click on the empty space to the right of the last icon showing on the taskbar to bring up a shortcut menu with tiling options.

Excel window

ton, drag them to a different location. To resize a window, place your cursor on any side or corner of a window until it changes to a double-headed arrow [↕]. You can then left-click and drag the window to the new desired size.

Organizing Your Computer: File Management

So far you have learned that the operating system is responsible for managing the processor, memory, storage, and devices, and that it provides a mechanism for applications and users to interact with the computer system. An additional function of an operating system is to enable **file management**, which entails providing organizational structure to the computer's contents. The OS allows you to organize the contents of your computer in a hierarchical structure of **directories** that includes *files, folders,* and *drives*. In this section, we discuss how you can use this hierarchical structure to create a more organized and efficient computer.

ORGANIZING YOUR FILES

What exactly is a file? Technically, a **file** is a collection of related pieces of information stored together for easy reference. A file in an operating system is a collection of program

instructions or data stored and treated as a single unit. Files can be generated from an application, such as a Word document or Excel spreadsheet. Additionally, files can represent an entire application, a Web page, a set of sounds, or an image. Files are stored on the hard drive, a flash drive, or another storage medium for permanent storage. As the number of files you save increases, it is important to keep them organized in **folders**, or collections of files.

How does the operating system organize files? Windows organizes the contents of the computer in a hierarchical structure with drives, folders, subfolders, and files. The hard drive, represented as the C drive, is where you permanently store most of your files. Other storage devices on your computer are also represented by letters. The A drive has traditionally been reserved for the floppy drive. Any additional drives (Zip, flash, CD, or DVD drives) installed on your computer are represented by other letters (D, E, F, or another letter designation).

How is the hard drive organized? The C drive, or hard drive, is like a large filing cabinet in which all files are stored. As such, the C drive is the top of the filing structure of the computer system and is referred to as the **root directory**. All other folders and files are organized within the root directory. There are areas in the root directory that the operating system has filled with folders holding special OS files. The programs within these files help run the computer and generally shouldn't be touched. The Windows operating system also creates other folders, such as My Documents and My Pictures, which are available for you to begin to store and organize your text and image files, respectively.

How can I easily locate and see the contents of my computer? If you use a Windows PC, **Windows Explorer** helps you manage your files and folders by showing the location and contents of every drive, folder, and file on your computer. You access Explorer by right-clicking the My Computer desktop icon or the Start button and selecting Explore from the shortcut menu. (If you use a Mac, the Finder is the program that enables you to manage your files and folders.) As illustrated in Figure 5.17, Explorer is divided into two sections.

The left pane shows the contents of your computer in a hierarchical tree structure. It displays all the drives of the system as well as other commonly accessed areas such as the Desktop and the My Documents folder. You can open the folders in the left pane to reveal their contents by clicking the plus (+) sign next to the folder name. Once you open

a folder, the plus sign changes to a minus (−) sign and the contents of that folder are displayed in the right pane of the Explorer window. You can choose to expand or collapse the view of the contents of a folder by clicking the plus or minus sign, respectively. If a folder does not have a plus or minus sign, there are no other folders contained within the folder, although it may contain files.

How should I organize my files? Creating folders is the key to organizing your files, because folders keep related documents together. Again, think of your computer as a big filing cabinet to which you can add many separate filing drawers, or subfolders. Those drawers, or subfolders, have the capacity to hold even more folders, which can hold other folders or individual files. For example, you can create one folder for your class work called Classes. Inside the Classes folder, you can create folders for each of your classes (such as Intro to Computers, Bio 101, and British Literature). Inside each of those folders, you can create subfolders for each class's assignments, completed homework, research, notes, and so on.

Grouping related files together in folders allows you to more easily identify and find

FIGURE 5.17

Windows Explorer lets you see the contents of your computer.

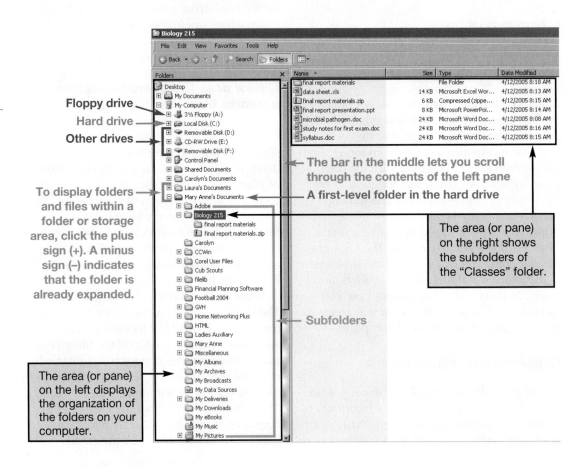

Floppy drive

Hard drive

Other drives

To display folders and files within a folder or storage area, click the plus sign (+). A minus sign (−) indicates that the folder is already expanded.

The bar in the middle lets you scroll through the contents of the left pane

A first-level folder in the hard drive

The area (or pane) on the right shows the subfolders of the "Classes" folder.

Subfolders

The area (or pane) on the left displays the organization of the folders on your computer.

files. Which would be easier, going to the Bio 101 folder to find a file or searching through the 143 individual files in My Documents hoping to find the right one? Grouping files in a folder also allows you to move them more efficiently, so you can quickly transfer critical files needing frequent backup to a CD, for instance.

VIEWING AND SORTING FILES AND FOLDERS

Are there different ways I can view and sort my files and folders?
In Windows XP, when you are in a folder, such as My Documents, you can use any of the viewing options located on the View menu to arrange and view your files and folders:

- **Tiles view** displays files and folders as icons in list form. Each icon includes the filename, the application associated with the file, and the file size. The display information is customizable. The Tiles view also displays picture dimensions, a handy feature for Web-page developers.

- **Icon view** also displays files and folders as icons in list form, but the icons are

smaller and include no other file information beside the filename. However, additional file information is displayed when you place your cursor over the file icon.

- **List view** is another display of even smaller icons and filenames. This is a good view if you have a lot of content in the folder and need to see most or all of it at once.

- **Thumbnails view**, illustrated in Figure 5.18, shows the contents of folders as small images. Thumbnails view is therefore the best view to use if your folder contains picture files. For those folders that contain collections of MP3 files, you can download the cover of the CD or an image of the artist to display on any folder to further identify that collection.

- **Details view** is the most interactive view. Files and folders are displayed in list form, and the additional file information is displayed in columns alongside the filename. You can sort and display the contents of the folder by any of the column headings, so you may sort the contents alphabetically by filename or type, or hierarchically by date last

SOUND BYTE

File Management

In this Sound Byte, you'll examine the features of file management and maintenance. You'll learn the various methods of creating folders, how to turn a jumble of unorganized files into an organized system of folders, and how to maintain your file system.

FIGURE 5.18

Thumbnails view is an especially good way to display folders containing picture files because some of the pictures in the folder are shown on the cover of the folder.

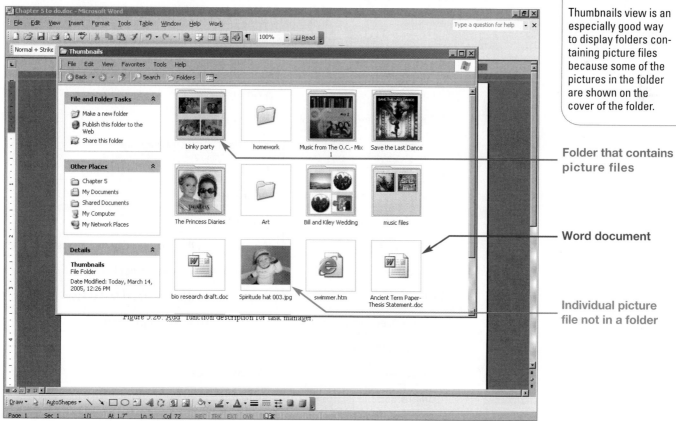

Folder that contains picture files

Word document

Individual picture file not in a folder

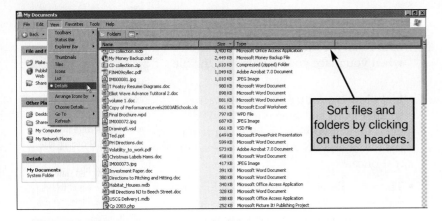

FIGURE 5.19

Details view enables you to sort and list your files in a variety of ways to further assist you in quickly finding the correct file.

modified or by file size (as shown in Figure 5.19).

What's the best way to search for a file? You've no doubt saved a file and forgotten where you saved it, or have downloaded a file from the Internet and were not sure where it was saved. What's the quickest way to find a file? Looking through every file stored on your computer could take hours, even with a well-organized file management system. Fortunately, Windows includes a Search feature, found on the Start menu, that searches through your hard drive or other storage device (CD, floppy, or flash memory) to locate files that match criteria you provide. Your search can be based on a part of the file-

name or just a word or phrase in the file. Advanced features let you narrow down your search by providing information about the type of file, which application was used to create the file, or even how long ago the file was saved. (Mac OS has a similar feature called Sherlock.)

NAMING FILES

Are there special rules I have to follow when I name files? Files have names just like people. The first part of a file, or the **filename**, is similar to our first names and is generally the name you assign to the file when you save it. For example, "bioreport" may be the name you assign a report you have completed for biology.

In a Windows application, following the filename and after the dot (.) comes an **extension**, or **file type**. Like our last name, this extension identifies what kind of family of files the file belongs to or which application should be used to read the file. For example, if the bioreport file is a Word document, it has a .doc extension and is named bioreport.doc. On the other hand, if bioreport is a document created in Works, it will have a .wks extension and be named bioreport.wks. Figure 5.20 lists the common file extensions and the types of documents they indicate.

FIGURE 5.20	**Filename Extensions**	
Extension	**Type of Document**	**Application that Uses the Extension**
.bmp	Bitmap image	Windows
.doc	Word processing document	Microsoft Word
.htm or .html	Web page	Hypertext Markup Language
.mdb	Database	Microsoft Access
.pdf	Portable Document Format	Adobe Acrobat
.ppt	PowerPoint presentation	Microsoft PowerPoint
.rtf	Text	Any program that can read text documents
.slr	Spreadsheet	Microsoft Works spreadsheet
.txt	Text	Any program that can read text documents
.wks	Word processing document	Microsoft Works word processing
.wpd	Word processing document	Corel WordPerfect
.xls	Spreadsheet	Microsoft Excel
.zip	Compressed file	WinZip

Do I need to know the extensions of all files to save them? As shown in Figure 5.21, when you save a file created in a Windows operating system, you do not need to add the extension to the filename; it is added automatically for you. Mac and Linux operating systems do not require file extensions. This is because the information as to the type of application the computer should use to open the file is stored inside the file itself. However, if you're using these operating systems and will be sending files to Windows users, you should add an extension to your filename so that they can more easily open your files.

Are there things I shouldn't do when naming my file? Each operating system has its own naming conventions, or rules, which are listed in Figure 5.22. Beyond those conventions, it's important that you name your files so that you can easily identify them. A filename like research.doc may be descriptive to you if you're only working on one research paper. However, if you create other research reports later and need to identify the contents of these files quickly, you'll soon wish you had been more descriptive. Giving your files more descriptive names, such as bioresearch.doc or, better yet, bio101research.doc, is a good idea.

Keep in mind, however, every file in the same folder or storage device (hard disk, floppy disk, CD, and so on) must be *uniquely* identified. Therefore, files may share the same filename (such as *bioreport*.doc or *bioreport*.xls), or they may share the same extension (bioreport.*xls* or budget.*xls*); however, no two files stored on the same device or folder can share *both* the same filename *and* the same extension.

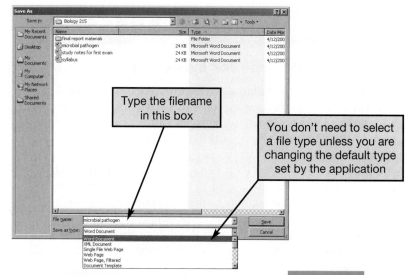

Type the filename in this box

You don't need to select a file type unless you are changing the default type set by the application

FIGURE 5.21

When you save a file in Windows, you type the filename in the Save As dialog box. The extension is added automatically, although you can change it if necessary.

How can I tell where my files are saved? When you save a file for the first time, you give the file a name and designate where you want to save it. For easy reference, the operating system includes default folders where files are saved unless you specify otherwise. In Windows, the default folders are "My Documents" for files, "My Downloads" for files downloaded from the Internet, "My Music" for audio files, and "My Pictures" for graphics files. Although you can create your own folders, these default folders are the beginning of a well-organized system.

You can tell the location of a file by its **file path**. The file path starts with the drive in which the file is located, and includes all folders, subfolders (if any), the filename, and extension. For example, if you were saving a picture of Emily Brontë for a term paper for an English Comp course, the file path might be

FIGURE 5.22 **File Naming Conventions**		
	MAC OS	**Windows**
FILE AND FOLDER NAME LENGTH	Up to 255 characters*	Up to 255 characters
CASE SENSITIVE?	Yes	No
FORBIDDEN CHARACTERS	The colon (:)	" / \ * ? < > | :
SPACES ALLOWED?	Yes	Yes
FILE EXTENSIONS NEEDED?	No	Yes
PATH SEPARATOR	:	\

*Note: Although Mac OS X supports filenames with up to 255 characters, many applications running on OS X still support only a maximum of 31-character filenames.

BITS AND BYTES

A File Type for Everyone

You are sending an e-mail to a diverse group of individuals. You are not sure what word processing software each of them uses, but you assume that there will be a mix between Word, WordPerfect, and even Writer. How can you be sure that everyone will be able to open the attachment regardless of the program installed on his or her computer? Save the file in Rich Text Format (.RTF) or Text (.txt) format. Both file formats can be read by any word processing program, although some formatting may be lost when saving as a Text (.txt) format. To save files as RTF or Text files, simply change the file type when saving your file. In Microsoft Word, for example, you can change the file type in the Save As dialog box shown in Figure 5.23.

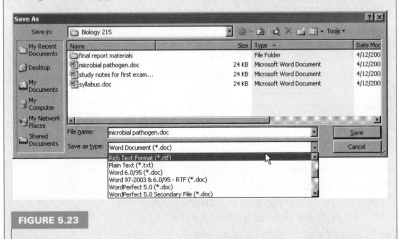

FIGURE 5.23

By changing a word processing file's type to RTF you can be sure that anyone can read your file, no matter which word processing program they are using.

ACTIVE HELPDESK

Organizing Your Computer: File Management

In this Active Helpdesk call, you'll play the role of a Helpdesk staffer, fielding calls about desktop and windows features and how the operating system helps keep the computer organized.

C:\My Documents\Spring 2005\English Comp\Term Paper\Illustrations\EBronte.jpg.

As shown in Figure 5.24, the C indicates the drive the file is stored on (in this case, the hard drive), and My Documents is the file's primary folder. Spring 2005, English Comp, Term Paper, and Illustrations are successive subfolders within the My Documents main folder. Last is the filename, EBronte, separated from the file extension (in this case, .jpg) by a period. Notice that in between the drive, primary folder, subfolders, and filename are backslash characters (\). These backslash characters, used by Windows and DOS, are referred to as **path separators**. Mac files use a colon (:) and UNIX and Linux files use the forward slash (/) as the path separator.

WORKING WITH FILES

How can I move and copy files? Once you've located your file with Windows Explorer, you can perform many other file management actions, such as opening, copying, moving, renaming, and deleting files. You open a file by clicking the file in its storage location. The operating system then determines which application needs to be loaded to open the requested file and opens the file within the correct application automatically. You can copy a file to another location using the Copy command. When you copy a file, a duplicate file is created and the original file remains in its original location. To move a file from one location to another, you use the Move command. When you move a file, the original file is deleted from its original location.

Where do deleted files go? One of the improvements made in Windows 95 is the **Recycle Bin**, a folder on the desktop, where files deleted *from the hard drive* reside until you permanently purge them from your system. Unfortunately, files deleted from other drives, such as the floppy drive, CD, flash drive, or network drive, do not go to the Recycle Bin but are deleted from the system immediately. (Mac systems have something similar to the Recycle Bin, called the Trash Can. To delete files on a Mac system, you simply drag the file to the Trash Can on the desktop. Then select Empty Trash from the Finder menu in OS X, or from the Special menu in earlier versions.)

Is it possible to retrieve a file that I've accidentally deleted? The benefit of the Recycle Bin is that you can restore the files you place there. To do so, open the Recycle Bin, locate the file, and select Restore. To delete your files from the Recycle Bin permanently, select Empty the Recycle Bin after clicking the desktop icon.

Utility Programs

You have learned that the operating system is the single most essential piece of software in your computer system because it coordinates all the system's activities and provides a means by which other software applications

FIGURE 5.24

Understanding File Paths

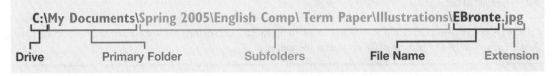

C:\My Documents\Spring 2005\English Comp\ Term Paper\Illustrations\EBronte.jpg

Drive   Primary Folder   Subfolders   File Name   Extension

BITS AND BYTES

Need to Recover a Deleted Recycle Bin File?

Once you empty the Recycle Bin, because you don't see the filename anymore, it looks as if the file has been erased from the hard drive. However, only the *reference* to the deleted file is deleted permanently, so the operating system has no easy way to find the file. The file data actually remains on the hard drive until otherwise written over. Should you delete a file from the Recycle Bin in error, you can immediately restore the deleted file by clicking the undo arrow on the toolbar. Programs such as RestoreIT! or Roxio's GoBack allow you to recover longer-term deleted files; however, the longer you wait to recover a deleted file, the chances of a full recovery decrease. That's because the probability that your file has been overwritten increases.

and users can interact with the system. However, there is another set of programs included in system software. Utility programs are small applications that perform special functions. Some utility programs help manage system resources (such as disk defragmenter utilities), others help make your time and work on the computer more pleasant (such as screen savers), and still others improve efficiency (such as file compression utilities).

Some of these utility programs are incorporated into the operating system. For example, Windows XP now has its own fire-wall and file compression utility. Other utility programs, such as antivirus and security programs, have become so large and require such frequent updating that they are sold as stand-alone off-the-shelf programs in stores or as Web-based services available for an annual fee. Sometimes utility programs are offered as software suites, bundled together with other useful maintenance and performance-boosting utilities. Still other utilities are offered as freeware or shareware programs and are available as downloads from the Web. Figure 5.25 illustrates some of the

FIGURE 5.25 **Utility Programs Available within Windows and as Stand-Alone Programs**		
Windows Utility Program	**Off-the-Shelf (Stand-Alone) Utility Program**	**Function**
File Management		
Add/Remove Programs	Aladdin Systems Easy Uninstall	Properly installs/uninstalls software
Windows Explorer File Compression	WinZip	Reduces file size
Windows System Maintenance and Diagnostics		
Backup	Norton Ghost	Backs up important information
Disk Cleanup	Ontrack System Suite	Removes unnecessary files from hard drive
Disk Defragmenter	Norton SystemWorks	Arranges files on hard drive in sequential order
Error-checking (previously ScanDisk)	Norton CleanSweep	Checks hard drive for unnecessary or damaged files
System Restore	FarStone RestoreIT!	Restores system to a previously established set point
Task Manager		Displays performance measures for processes; provides information on programs and processes running on computer
Task Scheduler		Schedules programs to run automatically at prescribed times

various types of utility programs available within the Windows operating system as well as those available as off-the-shelf programs in stores.

In this section, we explore many of the utility programs you'll find installed on a Windows operating system. Unless otherwise noted, you can find these utilities in the Control Panel or on the Start menu by selecting Programs, Accessories, and then System Tools. (We also take a brief look at some Mac utilities.) We will discuss antivirus and personal firewall utility programs in Chapter 7.

DISPLAY UTILITIES

How can I change the appearance of my desktop? The Display folder, found in the Control Panel, has all the features required to change the appearance of your desktop, providing different options for the desktop background, screen savers, windows colors, font sizes, and screen resolution. Although Windows has many different background themes and screen saver options available, there are hundreds of downloadable options available on the Web. Just search for backgrounds or screen savers on your favorite search engine to customize

your desktop. To access the background and screen saver options and all display utilities, choose Control Panel from the Start menu, then select the Display folder. (Note: If you have Windows XP and are showing the Categories view, the Display folder is in the Appearance and Themes category.)

Can I make the display on my LCD monitor clearer? If you use a laptop computer or have a flat-panel liquid crystal display (LCD) monitor, you may be interested in the Clear Type feature Windows XP offers. Turning this feature on smoothes the edges of screen fonts to make text easier to read. Note that Clear Type is not very effective with cathode-ray tube (CRT) monitors.

Do I really need to use a screen saver? Screen savers are animated images that appear on a computer monitor when no user activity has been sensed for a certain time. Originally, screen savers were used to prevent *burn-in*, the result of an image being burned into the phosphor inside the monitor's cathode-ray tube when the same image was left on the monitor for long periods of time. In the early CRT monitors, when the cursor was left blinking in the same spot for hours, burn-in was a concern. However, today's CRT display technology has changed; thus, burn-in is not probable. Screen savers are now used almost exclusively for decoration.

You can control how long your computer sits idle before the screen saver starts. For example, if you don't want people looking at what's on your screen when you leave your computer unexpectedly for a time, you may want to program your screen saver to run after only a minute or two of inactivity. However, if you find that you let your computer sit inactive for a while but need to look at the screen image (while you study or read a document or spreadsheet, for example), you may want to extend the period of inactivity a bit.

THE ADD OR REMOVE PROGRAMS UTILITY

What is the correct way to add new programs to the system? These days, when you install a new program to your system, the program automatically runs a wizard that walks you through the installation process. If a wizard does not initialize automatically, however, you should go to the Add or Remove Programs folder in the Control Panel. This prompts the operating system to look in the CD or floppy disk drive for the setup program of the new software and starts the installation wizard.

What is the correct way to remove unwanted programs from my system? Some people think that deleting a program from the Program Files folder on the C drive is the best way to remove a program from the system. However, most programs include support files such as a help file, dictionaries, and graphics files that are not located in the main program folder found in Program Files. Depending on the supporting file's function, support files can be scattered throughout various folders within the system. You would normally miss these files by just deleting the main program file from the system. By selecting the Add or Remove Programs icon in Control Panel, you not only delete the main program file, you also delete all supporting files as well.

FILE COMPRESSION UTILITIES

What is file compression? A file compression utility is a program that takes out redundancies in a file to reduce the file size. File compression is helpful because it makes a large file more compact, making it easier and faster to send over the Internet, upload to a Web page, or save onto a disk. As shown in Figure 5.26, Windows XP has built-in compression (or zip) file support. There are also several stand-alone freeware and shareware programs, such as WinZip (for Windows) and StuffIt (for Windows or Mac), that you can obtain to compress your files.

How does file compression work? Compression programs look for repeated patterns of letters and replace these patterns with a shorter placeholder. The repeated patterns and the associated placeholder are cataloged and stored temporarily in a separate file, called the dictionary. For example, in the following sentence, you can easily see the repeated patterns of letters:

> **The** rain in spain falls mainly on **the** plain.

Although in this example there are obvious repeated patterns (**ain** and **the**), in a large document, the repeated patterns may be more complex. The compression program's algorithm therefore runs through the file several times to determine the optimal repeated patterns to obtain the greatest compression.

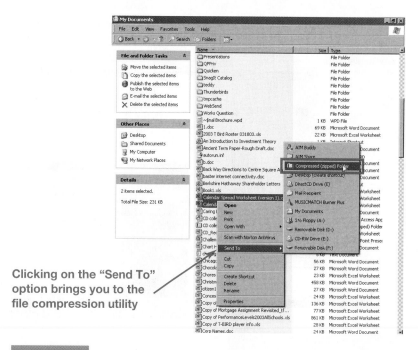

Clicking on the "Send To" option brings you to the file compression utility

FIGURE 5.26

File compression is now a built-in utility of the Windows operating system.

How effective are file compression programs? The effectiveness of file compression—that is, how much a file's size is reduced—depends on several factors, including the type and size of the individual file and the compression method used. Current compression programs can reduce text files by as much as 50 percent. However, some files, such as database files, already contain a form of compression and therefore do not compress further. Other file types, especially some graphics and audio formats, have gone through a compression process that reduces file size by permanently discarding "unnecessary" data. For example, image files such as Joint Photographic Experts Group (JPEG), Graphics Interchange Format (GIF), and Portable Network Graphics (PNG) files discard small variations in colors that the human eye may not pick up. Likewise, MP3 files permanently discard sounds that the human ear cannot hear.

How do I decompress a file I've compressed? When you want to restore the file to its original state, you need to decompress the file so that the pieces of file that the compression process temporarily removed are restored to the document.

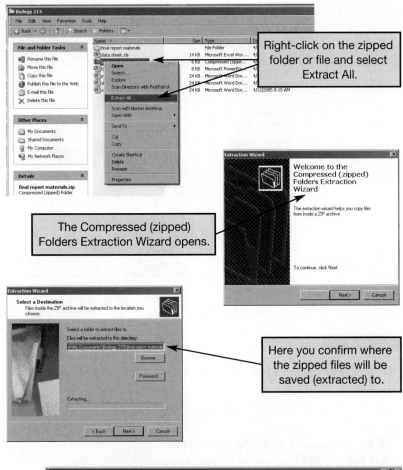

Right-click on the zipped folder or file and select Extract All.

The Compressed (zipped) Folders Extraction Wizard opens.

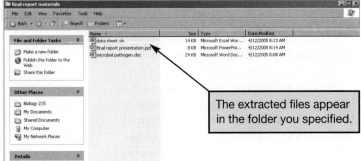

Here you confirm where the zipped files will be saved (extracted) to.

The extracted files appear in the folder you specified.

FIGURE 5.27

The Extraction Wizard in Windows XP makes unzipping compressed folders and files easy.

SOUND BYTE

File Compression

In this Sound Byte, you'll learn about the advantages of file compression and how to use Windows XP to compress and decompress files. If you own an earlier operating system, this Sound Byte will teach you how to find and install file compression shareware software programs.

Generally, the same program you used to compress the file has the capability to decompress the file as well (see Figure 5.27).

SYSTEM MAINTENANCE UTILITIES

Are there any utilities that make my system work faster? Disk Cleanup is a Windows utility that cleans unnecessary files from your hard drive. These include files that have accumulated in the Recycle Bin as well as temporary files, which are files created by Windows to store data temporarily when a program is running. Windows usually deletes these temporary files when you exit the program, but sometimes it forgets or doesn't have time if your system freezes up or incurs a problem preventing you from properly exiting a program. Disk Cleanup also removes temporary Internet files (Web pages stored on your hard drive for quick viewing) as well as offline Web pages (pages that are stored on your computer so you can view them without being connected to the Internet). If not deleted periodically, these unnecessary files can deter efficient operating performance.

How can I control which files Disk Cleanup deletes? When you run Disk Cleanup, the program scans your hard drive to determine which folders have files that can be deleted and calculates the amount of hard drive space that would be freed by doing so. You check off which type of files you would like to delete, as shown in Figure 5.28.

What else can I do if my system runs slowly? Over time, as you add and delete information to a file, the file pieces are saved in scattered locations on the hard disk. Locating all the pieces of the file takes extra time, making the operating system less efficient. **Disk defragmenter utilities** regroup related pieces of files together on the hard disk, allowing the OS to work more efficiently. You can find the Windows Disk Defragmenter utility under System Tools in the Accessories folder of the Start menu. On Macs, you can defrag your hard drive with Norton Utilities or Mac Tools. Depending on your usage, you should defrag your hard drive at least once a month.

How do I diagnose potential errors or damage on my storage devices? Error-checking, once known as ScanDisk, is a Windows utility that checks for lost files and fragments as well as physical errors on your hard drive. Lost files and fragments of files occur as you save, resave, move, delete, and copy files on your hard drive. Sometimes the system becomes confused, leaving references on the file allocation table to files that no longer exist or have been moved. Physical errors on the hard drive occur when the mechanism that reads the hard drive's data (which is stored as 1s or 0s) can no longer determine whether the area holds a 1 or a 0. These areas are called *bad sectors*. Sometimes Error-checking can recover the lost data, but more often, it deletes the files that are taking up space unnecessarily. Error-checking also makes a note of any bad sectors so the system will not use them again to store data.

Where can I find Error-checking? Windows XP has moved the Error-checking utility from System Tools (where it is located in previous versions of Windows when it was called ScanDisk) to Disk Properties. Right-click the disk you want to diagnose, select Properties, then select Tools.

Norton Disk Doctor is a stand-alone product included in Norton Utilities that performs the same check-and-repair routine. On Macs, you use the Disk First Aid utility to test and repair disks. You find this utility in the Utilities folder on your hard drive.

How can I check on a program that has stopped running? If a program on your system has stopped working, you can use the Windows **Task Manager utility** to check on the program or to exit the nonresponding program. Although you can access Task Manager from Control Panel, it is more easily accessible by pressing the Ctrl + Alt + Del keys on your keyboard at the same time, or by right-clicking an empty space on the taskbar at the bottom of your screen. The Applications tab of Task Manager lists all programs that you are using and indicates whether they are working properly (running) or have stopped improperly (not

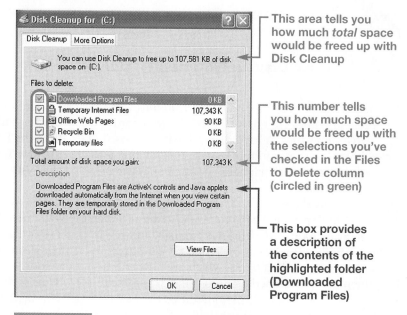

This area tells you how much *total* space would be freed up with Disk Cleanup

This number tells you how much space would be freed up with the selections you've checked in the Files to Delete column (circled in green)

This box provides a description of the contents of the highlighted folder (Downloaded Program Files)

FIGURE 5.28

Using Disk Cleanup will help free space on your hard drive.

responding). You can terminate programs that are not responding by clicking the End Task button in the dialog box.

SYSTEM RESTORE AND BACKUP UTILITIES

Is there an undo command for the system? Say you have just installed a new software program and your computer freezes. After rebooting the computer, when you try to start the application, the system freezes once again. You uninstall the new program, but your computer continues to freeze after rebooting. What can you do now?

Windows XP has a new utility called **System Restore** that lets you restore your system settings back to a specific date when everything was working properly. You can find System Restore under System Tools on the Accessories menu. If the computer was running just fine before you installed software or a new hardware device, you would restore your computer back to the settings before the software or hardware installation. System Restore does not affect your personal data files (such as Microsoft Word documents, browsing history, drawings, favorites, or e-mail), so you won't lose changes made to these files when you use System Restore.

SOUND BYTE

Hard Disk Anatomy Interactive

In this Sound Byte, you'll watch a series of animations that show various aspects of a hard drive, including the anatomy of a hard drive, how to read and write data to a hard drive, and the fragmenting/defragmenting of a hard drive.

How Disk Defragmenter Utilities Work

To understand how disk defragmenter utilities work, you must first understand the basics of how a hard disk drive stores files. A hard disk drive is composed of several platters, or round thin plates of metal, that are covered with a special magnetic coating that records the data. The platters are about 3.5 inches in diameter (approximately the width of a floppy disk) and are stacked onto a spindle. There are usually two or three platters in any hard disk drive, with data being stored on one or both sides. Data is recorded on hard disks in concentric circles, called *tracks*, which are further broken down into pie-shaped wedges called *sectors* (see Figure 5.29). The data is further identified by *clusters*, which are the smallest segments within the sectors.

When you want to save (or *write*) a file, the bits that make up your file are recorded onto one or more clusters of the drive. To keep track of which clusters hold which files, the drive also stores an index of all sector numbers in a table called the **File Allocation Table (FAT)**. To save a file, the computer will look in the FAT for clusters that are not already being used and will then record the file information on those clusters. When you open (or *read*) a file, the computer searches through the FAT for the clusters that hold the desired file and reads that file. Similarly, when you delete a computer file, you are actually not deleting the file itself, but rather the reference in the FAT to the file. This is why you are able to get the file back after the deletion, if necessary.

Windows XP offers a different file system than the FAT, called the **New Technology File System (NTFS)**. NTFS was developed with the Windows NT version and has been used in Windows 2000 and Windows XP. When you install Windows XP, you may choose whether to use FAT32 (FAT32 is the latest version of FAT and supports smaller cluster sizes than the original FAT) or NTFS as the file system, unless the manufacturer has already preinstalled NTFS.

Most system manufacturers are choosing to use the NTFS file system as a default system, but some have continued to preinstall FAT32. The benefits of NTFS over FAT32 are that NTFS supports hard drive capacities larger than 32 GB and file sizes larger than 4 GB. Most of today's hard drives have capacities that exceed 32 GB, and, with multimedia capabilities, it's not uncommon to see a file size greater than 4

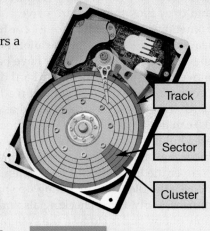

FIGURE 5.29

On a hard disk platter, data is recorded onto tracks, which are further broken down into sectors and clusters.

How does the computer remember its previous settings? Every time you start your computer, or when a new application or driver is installed, Windows XP automatically creates a snapshot of your entire system's settings. This snapshot is called a **restore point**. You also can create and name your own restore points at any time. Creating a restore point is a good idea before making changes to your computer such as installing hardware or software. If something goes wrong with the installation process, Windows XP can reset your system to the restore point. As shown in Figure 5.31, Windows includes a Restore Point Wizard that walks you through the process of setting restore points.

How can I protect my data in the event something goes awry with my system? When you use the Windows

Backup utility, you create a duplicate copy of all the data on your hard disk and copy it to another storage device, such as a CD or external hard drive. A backup copy protects your data in the event your hard disk fails or files are accidentally erased. Although you may not need to back up *every* file on your computer, you should back up the files that are most important to you and keep the backup copy in a safe location. Note that in Windows XP Home Edition, you must manually install the Backup utility from the ValueAdd folder on the CD-ROM. (For more information on backing up your files, see the Technology in Focus "Protecting Your Computer and Backing Up Your Data," on page 374.)

GB. Additionally, NTFS was designed to be more secure and more efficient and will ultimately nudge out FAT structure with subsequent operating system versions.

So, how does a disk become fragmented? When only part of an older file is deleted, the deleted section of the file creates a gap in the sector of the disk where the data was originally stored. In the same way, when new information is added to an older file, there may not be space to save the new information sequentially near where the file was originally saved. In that case, the system writes the added part of the file to the next available location on the disk, and a reference is made in the FAT or NTFS table as to the location of this file fragment. Over time, as files are saved, deleted, and modified, the bits of information for various files fall out of sequential order and the disk becomes fragmented.

Disk fragmentation is a problem because when a disk is fragmented, the operating system is not as efficient. It takes longer to locate a whole file because more of the disk must be searched for the various pieces, greatly slowing down the performance of your computer.

How can you make the files line up more efficiently on the disk? At this stage, the disk defragmenter utility enters the picture. The defragmenter tool takes the hard drive through a defragmentation process in which pieces of files that are scattered over the disk are placed together and arranged sequentially on the hard disk. Also, any unused portions of clusters that were too small

in which to save data before are grouped together, increasing the available storage space on the disk. Figure 5.30 shows before and after shots of a fragmented disk having gone through the defragmentation process.

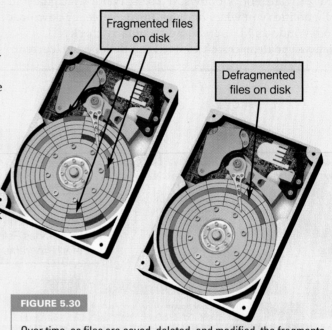

Fragmented files on disk

Defragmented files on disk

FIGURE 5.30

Over time, as files are saved, deleted, and modified, the fragments of information for various files fall out of sequential order on the hard disk and the disk becomes fragmented. Defragmenting the hard drive arranges file fragments so that they are located next to each other. This makes the hard drive run more efficiently.

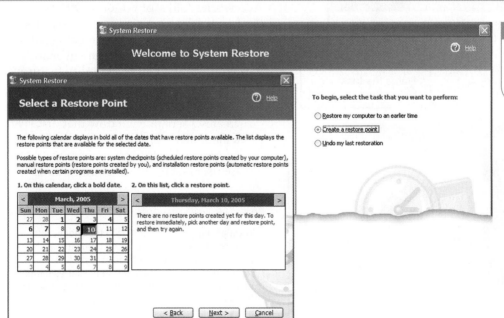

FIGURE 5.31

Setting a restore point is good practice before installing any hardware or software.

BITS AND BYTES

Need a System Software Update?

Bugs in software occur all the time. Software developers are constantly testing their products, even after releasing the software to the retail market, and users report errors they find. Windows Update is Microsoft's service for updating desktop operating system software. For Windows XP users, Windows Update automatically notifies you when updates are available for download. Non–Windows XP users should regularly check **windowsupdate.microsoft.com** to keep their system current.

THE TASK SCHEDULER UTILITY

How can I remember to perform all these maintenance procedures? To keep your computer system in top shape, it is important to routinely run some of the utilities described above. Depending on your usage, you may want to defrag your hard drive every month or so and clean out temporary Internet files once a week. However, many computer users forget to initiate these tasks. Luckily, the Windows **Task Scheduler utility**, shown in Figure 5.32, allows you to schedule tasks to run automatically at predetermined times, with no interaction necessary on your part.

ACCESSIBILITY UTILITIES

Are there utilities designed for users with special needs? Utility **Manager** is a utility found in the Accessories folder of Windows XP. Through the Utility Manager, you can magnify the screen image, have screen contents read to you, and display an on-screen keyboard (see Figure 5.33). The accessibility features include the following:

* The Magnifier is a display utility that creates a separate window that displays a magnified portion of your screen. This feature makes the screen more readable for users who have impaired vision.

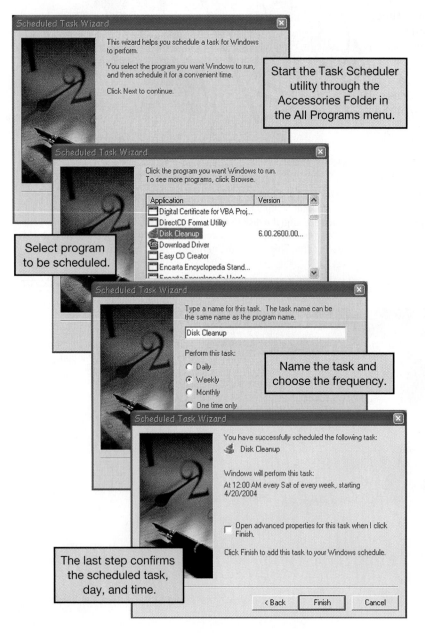

Start the Task Scheduler utility through the Accessories Folder in the All Programs menu.

Select program to be scheduled.

Name the task and choose the frequency.

The last step confirms the scheduled task, day, and time.

FIGURE 5.32

To keep your machine running in top shape, schedule a maintenance routine to run automatically at convenient times. Task Scheduler (listed as Scheduled Tasks), found in the Accessories folder on the All Programs menu, has a convenient wizard that guides you to select the program and assign the time you want it to run.

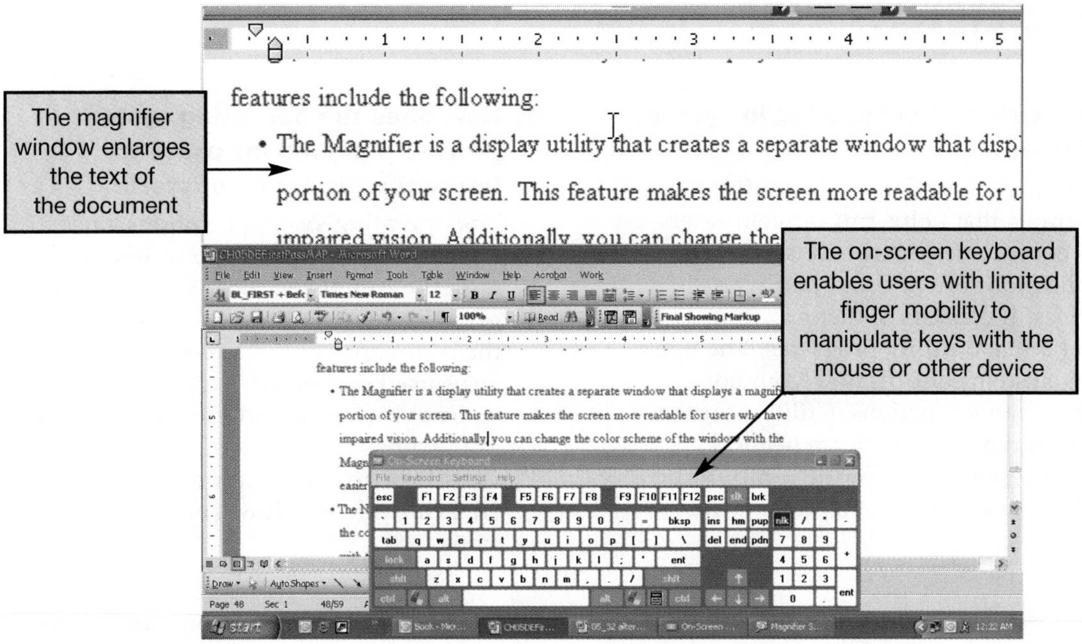

FIGURE 5.33

The magnifier window enlarges the text of the document

features include the following:

- The Magnifier is a display utility that creates a separate window that disp[lays a magnified] portion of your screen. This feature makes the screen more readable for u[sers who have] impaired vision. Additionally, you can change the...

The on-screen keyboard enables users with limited finger mobility to manipulate keys with the mouse or other device

Microsoft Windows includes some handy accessibility features, such as a magnifier and an on-screen keyboard, to help those with minor disabilities. These features are not meant to be sufficient for those users with severe disabilities. There are full-blown software applications to fill those needs.

Additionally, you can change the color scheme of the window with the Magnifier so that the screen colors are inverted. Some visually impaired individuals find it easier to see white text on a dark background.

- The Narrator utility is a very basic speech program that reads what is on-screen, whether it's the contents of a window, menu options, or text you have typed. The Narrator coordinates with text utilities, such as Notepad and WordPad, as well as Internet Explorer, but may not work correctly with other programs. For this reason, Narrator is not meant for individuals who must rely solely on a text-to-speech utility to operate the computer.

- The Onscreen Keyboard displays a keyboard on the screen. You type by clicking on or hovering over the keys with a pointing device (mouse or trackball) or joystick. This utility, which is similar to the Narrator, is not meant for everyday use for individuals with severe disabilities. A separate program with more functionality is better in those circumstances.

1. What software is included in system software?

System software is the set of software programs that helps run the computer and coordinates instructions between application software and hardware devices. It consists of the operating system (OS) and utility programs. The operating system controls how your computer system functions. Utility programs are programs that perform general housekeeping tasks for the computer, such as system maintenance and file compression.

2. What are the different kinds of operating systems?

Operating systems can be classified into four categories. Real-time OSs require no user intervention and are designed for systems with a specific purpose and response time (such as robotic machinery). Single-user, single-task OSs are designed for computers on which one user is performing one task at a time (such as PDAs). Single-user, multitask OSs are designed for computers on which one user is performing more than one task at a time (such as desktop computers). Multiuser OSs are designed for systems in which multiple users are working on more than one task at a time (such as networks).

3. What are the most common desktop operating systems?

Microsoft Windows is the most popular OS. It has evolved from being a single-user, single-task OS into a powerful multiuser operating system. Another popular OS is the Mac OS, which is designed to work on Apple Macs. Its most recent release, OS X, is based on the UNIX operating system. You'll find various versions of UNIX on the market, although it is most often used on networks. Linux is an open-source OS based on UNIX and designed primarily for use on personal computers.

4. How does the operating system provide a means for users to interact with the computer?

The operating system provides a user interface that enables you to interact with the computer. Most OSs today use a graphical user interface (GUI). Unlike the command- and menu-driven interfaces used earlier, GUIs display graphics and use the point-and-click technology of the mouse and cursor, making the OS more user-friendly. Common features of GUIs include windows, menus, and icons.

5. How does the operating system help manage the processor?

When you use your computer, you are usually asking it to perform several tasks at the same time. When the OS allows you to perform more than one task at a time, it is multitasking. To provide for seamless multitasking, the OS controls the timing of events the processor works on.

6. How does the operating system manage memory and storage?

As the OS coordinates the activities of the processor, it uses RAM as a temporary storage area for instructions and data the processor needs. The OS is therefore responsible for coordinating the space allocations in RAM to ensure that there is enough space for the waiting instructions and data. If there isn't sufficient space in RAM for all the data and instructions, the OS allocates the least necessary files to temporary storage on the hard drive called virtual memory. The OS manages storage by providing a file management system that keeps track of the names and locations of files and programs.

7. How does the operating system manage hardware and peripheral devices?

Programs called device drivers facilitate the communication between devices attached to the computer and the OS. Device drivers translate the specialized commands of devices to commands that the OS can understand, and vice versa, enabling the OS to communicate with every device in the computer system. Device drivers for common devices are included in the OS software, whereas other devices come with a device driver you have to install or download off the Web.

8. How does the operating system interact with application software?

All software applications need to interact with the CPU. For programs to work with the CPU, they must contain code the CPU recognizes. Rather than having the same blocks of code appear in each software application, the OS includes the blocks of code to which software applications refer. These blocks of code are called application programming interfaces (APIs).

9. How does the operating system help the computer start up?

When you start your computer, it runs through a special process, called the boot process. The boot process consists of four basic steps: (1) the basic input/output system (BIOS) is activated by powering on the CPU; (2) in the POST test, the BIOS checks that all attached devices are in place; (3) the operating system is loaded into RAM; and (4) configuration and customization settings are checked.

10. What are the main desktop and windows features?

The desktop is the first interaction you have with the OS and the first image you see on your monitor once the system has booted up. It provides you with access to your computer's files, folders, and commonly used tools and applications. Windows are the rectangular panes on your screen that display applications running on your system. Common features of windows include toolbars and scrollbars.

11. How does the operating system help me keep my computer organized?

The OS allows you to organize the contents of your computer in a hierarchical structure of directories that includes files, folders, and drives. Windows Explorer helps you manage your files and folders by showing the location and contents of every drive, folder, and file on your computer. Creating folders is the key to organizing files, because folders keep related documents together. Following naming conventions and using proper file extensions are also important aspects of file management.

12. What utility programs are included in system software and what do they do?

Some utility programs are incorporated into the OS; others are sold as stand-alone off-the-shelf programs. Common Windows utilities include those that enable you to adjust your display, add or remove programs, compress files, defrag your hard drive, clean unnecessary files off your system, check for lost files and errors, restore your system to an earlier setting, back up your files, schedule automatic tasks, and check on programs that have quit running.

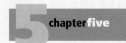

Key Terms

Buzz Words

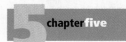

Word Bank

- defrag
- Error-checking
- files
- file compression
- file management
- folders

- Linux
- Mac OS
- platform
- sectors
- system software
- Task Manager

- Task Scheduler
- tracks
- utility programs
- Windows
- Windows Explorer
- Windows XP

Instructions: Fill in the blanks using the words from the Word Bank above.

Veena was looking into buying a new computer and was trying to decide what
(1) _____ to buy, a PC or a Mac. She had used PCs all her life, so she was more
familiar with the (2) _____ operating system. Still, she liked the way the
(3) _____ looked and was considering switching. Her brother didn't like either
operating system so used (4) _____ , a free operating system, instead.

After a little research, Veena decided to buy a PC. With it, she got the most recent version of
Windows, (5) _____ . She vowed that with this computer, she'd practice better
(6) _____ , because she often had a hard time finding files on her old computer.
To view all of the folders on her computer, she opened (7) _____ . She made sure
that she gave descriptive names to her (8) _____ and placed them in organized
(9) _____ .

Veena also decided that with her new computer, she'd pay more attention to the
(10) _____ , those little special-function programs that help with maintenance
and repairs. These special function programs, in addition to the OS, make up the
(11) _____ . Veena looked into some of the more frequently used utilities. She
thought it would be a good idea to (12) _____ her hard drive regularly so that
all the files lined up in contiguous (13) _____ and so that it was more efficient.
She also looked into (14) _____ utilities, which would help her reduce the size
of her files when she sent them to others over the Internet. Finally, she decided to use the
Windows (15) _____ utility to schedule tasks automatically so that she wouldn't
forget.

Becoming Computer Fluent

Using key terms from the chapter, write a letter to your computer-illiterate aunt explaining
the benefits of simple computer maintenance. First, explain any symptoms her computer
may be experiencing (such as a sluggish Internet connection), then include a set of steps she
can follow in setting up a regimen to remedy the problems. Make sure you explain some of
the system utilities described in this chapter, including, but not limited to, defrag, Disk
Cleanup, and Task Scheduler. Include any other utilities she might need and explain why
she should have them.

Self-Test

Instructions: Answer the multiple choice and true/false questions below for more practice with key terms and concepts from this chapter.

MULTIPLE CHOICE

1. PDAs use which category of operating system?
a. Single-user, single task
b. Multiuser, multitask
c. Single-user, multitask
d. Real-time

2. Which is something the operating system would not be expected to do?
a. Provide a means for the user to interact with the computer
b. Help the computer print and search the Web at the same time
c. Store data to the hard drive when there is insufficient volatile memory
d. The OS doesn't help with any of the above
e. The OS helps with all of the above

3. The combination of operating system and central processing unit is called the computer's
a. Platform
b. Structure
c. API
d. System unit

4. The process of optimizing RAM by borrowing space on the hard drive is called
a. Thrashing
b. Paging
c. Virtual memory
d. Cache

5. Plug and Play allows you to
a. Multitask by listening to a CD and surfing the Internet at the same time
b. Install gaming software without going through Add/Remove Programs
c. Install a hardware device without separately installing a driver
d. All of the above

6. The boot process happens in the following order
a. POST test, activate BIOS, check settings, load OS into RAM
b. Activate BIOS, POST test, load OS into RAM, check settings
c. Check settings, load OS into RAM, activate BIOS, POST test
d. Load OS into RAM, check settings, activate BIOS, POST test

7. When a computer is in Safe mode
a. Only the essential devices of the system function
b. The monitor will only display in basic graphics mode
c. All nonessential icons are eliminated from the desktop
d. All of the above

8. The program that is used on a Windows-based PC to manage your files and folders is called
a. Root directory
b. Windows Explorer
c. Finder
d. My Documents

9. Which Windows utility arranges files on the hard drive in sequential order?
a. System Restore
b. Disk Defragmenter
c. Windows Explorer
d. Disk Cleanup

10. Which utility do you use to check on a program that has stopped working?
a. Shut down
b. Task scheduler
c. Task manager
d. Disk Defragmenter

TRUE/FALSE

_____ 1. Before installing software or hardware, it's a good idea to create a restore point.

_____ 2. PDAs use a real-time operating system.

_____ 3. GUI is a command-driven user interface.

_____ 4. Every program that runs on Windows can also run on a MAC.

_____ 5. BIOS stands for Basic Input Operating System.

Making the Transition to... Next Semester

1. Organizing Files and Folders

It's the beginning of a new semester, and you promise yourself that you are going to keep all files related to your schoolwork more organized this semester. Develop a plan that outlines how you'll set up folders and subfolders for each subject. Identify at least three different folders for each class. If time and schedule permit, discuss your organization scheme with your instructor.

2. OS Compatibility Issues

Your school requires that you purchase a laptop to run on the school's system. The required machine runs on the Windows operating system. You have a reasonably new Apple computer at home.

a. Research the compatibility issues between the two computers.
b. How does a PDA running with Palm OS fit into the equation?
c. Can you synch the PDA with either or both machines?
d. Explore the application Virtual PC. What does it do? Would it be helpful in this situation?

3. Understanding Safe Mode

It is the night before the major term paper for your philosophy class is due. Your best friend comes screaming down the hall, begging for help. His only copy of his draft paper is on his desktop computer and it is suddenly booting up with the words *Safe Mode* in the corners of the screen. What would be the most useful questions to ask him? What steps would you take to debug the problem? If you cannot get the computer to come out of Safe mode, is there a way to retrieve the draft? How many times will you say, "Make backups!" that evening?

4. Software Requirements

This semester you have added six new applications to your laptop. You know which courses you will be taking next semester and realize they will require an additional eight major software applications. A friend who is in a similar position tells you she's not worried about putting that much software on her computer because she has a really big hard drive.

a. Is hard disk storage your only concern? Should it be your main concern or should you worry more about having sufficient RAM? How does your use of the programs impact your answer?
b. Does virtual memory management by your operating system allow you to ignore RAM requirements?

5. Connecting Peripherals

You decide to buy a new keyboard for next semester, a very fancy one that is wireless and that features integrated volume and CD player controls, and an integrated trackball. You also are planning to upgrade your printer. Do you have to worry about having the correct device drivers for these peripherals if:

a. You are using a Plug and Play operating system?
b. You have an older PC but are using the latest version of the Windows operating system?
c. You have an older PC and its original operating system, Windows 95?

Making the Transition to...
The Workplace

1. Organizing Files and Folders

You started a new job and are given a new computer. You never kept your files and folders organized on the computer you used when in college, but now you are determined to do a better job at keeping your files organized. You know you need folders for the several clients with whom you will be working. For each client, you'll need to have folders for billing information, client documents, and account information. In addition, you need folders for the MP3 files you will listen to when you're not working, as well as a folder for the digital pictures you'll take for personal and company reasons. Finally, you're working toward an advanced degree and will be taking business finance and introduction to marketing courses at night, so you'll need folders for all the homework assignments for both courses. Determine the file structure you would need to create to accommodate your needs. Start with the C drive and assume that My Documents, My Pictures, and My Music are the default folders for documents, pictures, and music files, respectively.

2. Using Mac Utility Programs

Your company has been having trouble with some of its Macintosh computers running inefficiently. Your boss asks you to research the utility programs your company could use on its Macs to make them run better. In particular, your boss would like you to find a disk defrag utility, a file compression utility, and a diagnostic utility you could run to check the hard drive for errors. Using the Internet, what utilities can you find? Will they run on all versions of the Mac OS?

3. Monitoring Activities with the OS

The company that you work for has just announced a new internal accounting structure. From now on, each department will be charged individually for the costs associated with computer usage, such as backup storage space, Internet usage, and so on.

   a. Research how the operating system may be set up to monitor such activity by department.
   b. What other activities do you think the operating system can be set up to monitor?

4. Choosing the Best OS

Your new boss is considering moving some of the department operations to UNIX-based computer systems. He asks you to research the advantages and disadvantages of moving to UNIX, Linux, or Mac OS X. How would these choices impact his department in the following areas?

   a. Budget for technical support for the systems
   b. Choice and budget for hardware for the systems
   c. Costs of implementation
   d. Possibility for future upgrades

Critical Thinking Questions

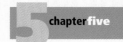

Instructions: Albert Einstein used "Gedanken experiments," or critical thinking questions, to develop his theory of relativity. Some ideas are best understood by experimenting with them in our own minds. The following critical thinking questions are designed to demand your full attention but require only a comfortable chair—no technology.

1. **Open-Source Pros and Cons**

   Open-source programming embraces a philosophy that states programmers should make their code available to everyone rather than keeping it proprietary. The operating system Linux has had much success as an open-source code. The chapter mentions some of the advantages of open-source code, such as quicker code updates in response to technological advances and changes.

   a. What are other advantages of open-source code?
   b. Can you think of disadvantages to open-source code?
   c. Why do you think that companies such as Microsoft maintain proprietary restrictions on their code?
   d. Are there disadvantages to maintaining proprietary code?

2. **The OS of the Future**

   Operating system interfaces have evolved from a text-based console format to the current graphical user interface. What direction do you think they will move toward next? How could operating systems be organized and used in a manner that is more responsive to humans and better suited to how we think? Are there alternatives to hierarchical file structures for storage? Can you think of ways in which operating systems could be able to adapt and customize themselves based on your usage?

3. **Which OS Would You Choose?**

   Suppose you are building a computer system from scratch and have complete discretion as to your choice of operating system. Which one would you install and why?

4. **The OS: With or Without Utilities?**

   Which environment do you think is better for consumers: to have companies develop smaller, more inexpensive operating systems and then allow competing companies to develop and market utility programs, or to have very large full-featured operating systems that include most utilities as part of the operating system itself? Do you think that including utility programs with the operating system makes the cost of the operating system higher?

Problem:

You have been hired to help set up the technology requirements for a small advertising company. The company is holding off buying anything until the decision has been made as to which platform the computers should run on. Obviously, one of the critical decisions is the operating system.

Task:

Recommend the appropriate operating system for the company.

Process:

1. Break up into three teams. Each team will represent one of the three primary operating systems today: Windows, Mac, and Linux.

2. As a team, research the pros and cons of your operating system. What features does it have that would benefit your company? What features does it not have that your company would need? Why (or why not) would your operating system be the appropriate choice? Why is your OS better (or worse) than either of the other two options?

3. Develop a presentation that states your position with regard to your operating system. Your presentation should have a recommendation, with facts to back it up.

4. As a class, decide which operating system would be the best choice for the company.

Conclusion:

Because the operating system is the critical piece of software in the computer system, the selection should not be taken lightly. The OS that is best for an advertising agency may not be best for an accounting firm. It is important to make sure you consider all aspects of the work environment and the type of work that is being done to ensure a good fit.

Multimedia

In addition to the review materials presented here, you'll find additional materials featured with the book's multimedia, including the *Technology in Action* Student Resource CD and the Companion Web site (**www.prenhall.com/techinaction**), which will help reinforce your understanding of the chapter content. These materials include the following:

ACTIVE HELPDESK

In Active Helpdesk calls, you'll assume the role of a Helpdesk operator taking calls about the concepts you've learned in this chapter. You'll apply what you've learned and receive feedback from a supervisor to review and reinforce those concepts. The Active Helpdesk calls for this chapter are listed here and can be found on your Student Resource CD:

- Managing Hardware and Peripheral Devices: The OS
- Starting the Computer: The Boot Process
- Organizing Your Computer: File Management
- Using Utility Programs

SOUND BYTES

Sound Bytes are dynamic multimedia tutorials that help demystify even the most complex topics. You'll view video clips and animations that illustrate computer concepts, and then apply what you've learned by reviewing with the Sound Byte Labs, which include quizzes and activities specifically tailored to each Sound Byte. The Sound Bytes for this chapter are listed here and can be found on your Student Resource CD and on the Companion Web site (**www.prenhall.com/techinaction**):

- Customizing Windows XP
- File Management
- File Compression
- Hard Disk Anatomy Interactive
- Letting Your Computer Clean Up After Itself

COMPANION WEB SITE

The *Technology in Action* Companion Web site includes a variety of additional materials to help you review and learn more about the topics in this chapter. The resources available at **www.prenhall.com/techinaction** include:

- **Online Study Guide.** Each chapter features an online true/false and multiple-choice quiz. You can take these quizzes, automatically check the results, and e-mail the results to your instructor.
- **Web Research Projects.** Each chapter features a number of Web research projects that ask you to search the Web for information on computer-related careers, milestones in computer history, important people and companies, emerging technologies, and the applications and implications of different technologies.

6

Understanding and Assessing Hardware:

Evaluating Your System

Objectives

After reading this chapter, you should be able to answer the following questions:

1. How can I determine whether I should upgrade my existing computer or buy a new one? **(pp. 236–238)**

2. What does the CPU do and how can I evaluate its performance? **(pp. 238–242)**

3. How does memory work in my computer and how can I evaluate how much memory I need? **(pp. 242–245)**

4. What are the computer's main storage devices and how can I evaluate whether they match my needs? **(pp. 245–252)**

5. What components affect the output of video on my computer and how can I evaluate whether they meet my needs? **(pp. 252–256)**

6. What components affect my computer's sound quality and how can I evaluate whether they meet my needs? **(pp. 256–257)**

7. What are the ports available on desktop computers and how can I determine what ports I need? **(pp. 258–261)**

8. How can I ensure the reliability of my system? **(pp. 262–264)**

ACTIVE HELPDESK

- Evaluating Your CPU and RAM **(p. 242)**
- Evaluating Your Storage Subsystem and Ports **(p. 261)**

To Upgrade or Not to Upgrade

After saving up for a computer, Natalie took the leap a few years ago and bought a new desktop PC. Now she is wondering what to do. Her friends with newer computers are burning CDs and DVDs, and they're able to hook their digital cameras right up to their computers and create multimedia. They seem to be able to do a hundred things at once without their computers slowing down at all.

Natalie's computer can't do any of these things—or at least she doesn't think it can. And lately it seems to take longer to open files and scroll through Web pages. Making matters worse, her computer freezes three or four times a day and takes a long time to reboot. Now she's wondering whether she should buy a new computer, but the thought of spending all that money again makes her think twice. As she looks at ads for new computers, she realizes she doesn't know what such things as "CPU" and "RAM" really are, or how they affect her system. Meanwhile, she's heard it's possible to upgrade her computer, but the task seems daunting. How will she know what she needs to do to upgrade, or whether it's even worth it?

How well is your computer meeting your needs? Are you unsure whether it's best to buy a new computer or upgrade your existing system? If you don't have a computer, do you fear purchasing one because computers are changing all the time? Do you know what all the terms in computer ads mean and how the different parts affect your computer's performance?

In this chapter, you'll learn how to evaluate your computer system to determine whether it is meeting your needs. You'll start by figuring out what you want your ideal computer to be able to do. You'll then learn about important components of your computer system (its CPU, memory, storage devices, audio and video devices, and ports) and how these components affect your system. Along the way, worksheets will help you conduct a system evaluation, and multimedia Sound Bytes will show you how to install various components in your system and how to increase its reliability. You'll also learn about the various utilities available to help speed up and clean up your system. If you don't have a computer, this chapter will provide you with important information you need about computer hardware to make an informed purchasing decision.

SOUND BYTES

- Questions to Ask Before You Buy a Computer **(p. 238)**
- Using Windows XP to Evaluate CPU Performance **(p. 240)**
- Memory Hierarchy Interactive **(p. 243)**
- Installing RAM **(p. 244)**
- Hard Disk Anatomy Interactive **(p. 246)**
- CD and DVD Reading and Writing Interactive **(p. 251)**
- Installing a CD-RW Drive **(p. 251)**
- Port Tour: How Do I Hook It Up? **(p. 260)**
- Letting Your Computer Clean Up After Itself **(p. 264)**

To Buy or to Upgrade: That Is the Question

There never seems to be a good time to buy a new computer. It seems that if you can just wait a year, computers will inevitably be faster and cost less. But is this actually true?

As it turns out, it is true. In fact, a rule of thumb often cited in the computer industry, called **Moore's Law**, describes the pace at which CPUs (the central processing unit)—the small chip that can be thought of as the "brains" of the computer—improve. This mathematical rule, named after Gordon Moore, the cofounder of the CPU chip manufacturer Intel, predicts that the number of transistors inside a CPU will increase so fast that CPU capacity will double every 18 months. (The number of transistors on a CPU chip helps determine how fast it can process data.)

As you can see in Figure 6.1, this rule of thumb has held true since 1965, when Moore first published his theory. Imagine if you could find a bank that would agree to treat your money this way. If you had put 10 cents in a savings account in 1965, you would have a balance of more than $3.3 million today!

In addition to the CPU becoming faster, other system components also improve dramatically. For example, the capacity of memory chips such as dynamic random access

FIGURE 6.1

Moore's Law predicts that CPUs will continue to get faster. The number of transistors on a CPU chip helps determine how fast it can process data. With the Intel Dual Core Itanium chip, more than a billion transistors can be fabricated into one chip.

Source: Adapted from the Moore's Law animated demo at **www.intel.com**.

FIGURE 6.2 The Growing Capacity of Memory Chips

Year	Capacity of Memory (Dram) Chip
1977	16 KB
1980	64 KB
1983	256 KB
1985	1,000 KB
1989	4,000 KB
1992	16,000 KB
1996	64,000 KB
2001	256,000 KB
2002	1,000,000 KB (1 GB)
2004	2,000,000 KB (2 GB)

Source: Adapted from David Patterson and John Hennesey, *Computer Architecture: A Quantitative Approach*, 3rd ed. (San Francisco, Calif.: Morgan Kaufmann, 2002), p. 22.

memory (DRAM)—the most common form of memory found on personal computers—increases about 60 percent every year, as shown in Figure 6.2. Meanwhile, hard disk

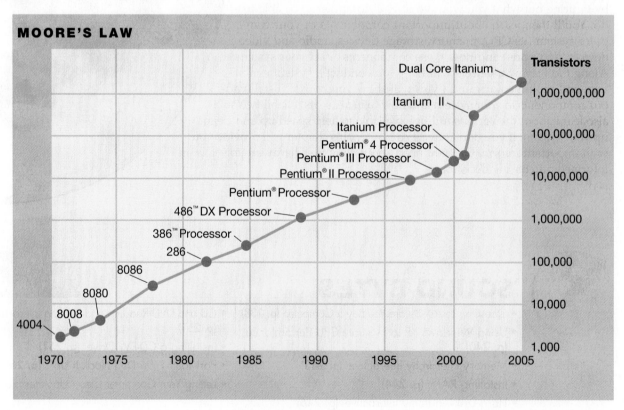

MOORE'S LAW

Transistors: 1,000,000,000 — Dual Core Itanium; 100,000,000 — Itanium II, Itanium Processor; 10,000,000 — Pentium 4 Processor, Pentium III Processor, Pentium II Processor; 1,000,000 — Pentium Processor, 486 DX Processor; 100,000 — 386 Processor, 286; 10,000 — 8086, 8080; 1,000 — 8008, 4004

Years: 1970, 1975, 1980, 1985, 1990, 1995, 2000, 2005

drives have been growing in storage capacity by about 50 percent each year.

So, with technology advancing so quickly, which is better: upgrading a current computer or buying a new one? Certainly, no one wants to buy a new computer every year just to keep up with technology. Even if money weren't a consideration, the time it would take to transfer all of your files and to reinstall and reconfigure your software would make buying a new computer every year terribly inefficient.

Of course, no one wants to keep doing costly upgrades that won't significantly extend the life of a system, either. So how can you determine if your system is suitable or needs upgrading? And how can you know which is the better option: upgrading or buying a new computer? In this chapter, you'll determine how to answer these questions by learning useful information about computer systems. The first step is figuring out what you want your computer to do for you.

What Is Your Ideal Computer?

As you decide whether you should upgrade or buy a new computer, it's important to know exactly what you want your ideal computer system to be able to do. Later, as you perform a system evaluation, you can compare your existing system to your ideal system. This will help you determine whether you should purchase hardware components to add to your system or buy a new system.

But what if I don't have a computer? Even if you're a new computer user, being able to understand and evaluate computer systems will make you a more informed buyer. What is a CPU and how does it affect your system? How much RAM do you need and what role does it play in your system? It's important that you're able to answer questions such as these before you buy a computer.

How do I know what my ideal system is? To determine your ideal system, consider what you want to be able to do with your computer. For example, do you want to be able to edit digital photos? Do you want to watch and record DVDs? Or are you just using your computer for word processing? The worksheet in Figure 6.3 lists a number of

FIGURE 6.3 What Should Your Ideal Computer System Be Able to Do?

Computer Uses	Do You Want Your System to Do This?	Can Your System Do This Now?
Entertainment Uses		
Access the Internet/Send E-Mail		
Play CDs and DVDs		
Record (Burn) CDs and DVDs		
Produce Digital Videos		
Record and Edit Digital Music		
Edit Digital Photos		
Play Graphics-Intensive Games		
Transfer Digital Photos (or Other Files) to Your Computer Using Flash Memory Cards		
Connect All Your Peripheral Devices to Your Computer at the Same Time		
Download Music from the Internet		
Other		
Educational Uses		
Perform Word Processing Tasks		
Use Other Educational Software		
Create CD or Zip Disk Backups of All Your Files		
Access Library and Newspaper Archives		
Create Multimedia Presentations		
Other		
Business Uses		
Create Spreadsheets		
Create Databases		
Work on Multiple Software Applications Quickly and Simultaneously		
Conduct Online Banking/Pay Bills Online		
Conduct Online Job Searches/Post Résumé		
"Synchronize" Your PDA and Desktop Computer		
Other		

ways in which you may want to use your computer. In the second column, place a check next to those computer uses that apply to you.

Next, look at the list of desired uses for your computer and determine whether your current system can perform these activities. If there are things you can't do, you may need to purchase additional hardware or a better computer. For example, if you want to play CDs, all you need is a CD-R drive. However, you need a CD-RW drive if you want to burn (record) CDs. Likewise, if you're going to edit digital video files or play games that include a lot of sounds and graphics, you may want to add more memory, buy a better set of speakers, and possibly invest in a new monitor. In this chapter, you'll learn about the hardware you may need to achieve your ideal system.

Note that you also may need new software and training to use new system components. Many computer users forget to consider the training they'll need when they upgrade their computer. Missing any one of these pieces might be the difference between your computer enriching your life or it becoming another source of stress.

How do I know if I need training? Although computers are becoming increasingly user-friendly, you still need to learn how to use them to your best advantage. Say you want to edit digital photos. You

know image-editing software exists, but how do you know if your computer's hardware can support the software? What will happen if you can't get it installed or don't know how to use it? If you have questions like these, you know you need training. Training shouldn't be an afterthought. Consider the time and effort involved in learning about what you want your computer to do before you buy hardware or software. If you don't, you may have a wonderful computer system but lack the skills necessary to take full advantage of it.

Assessing Your Hardware: Evaluating Your System

With a better picture of your ideal computer system in mind, you can make a more informed assessment of your current computer. To determine whether your computer system has the right hardware components to do what you ultimately want it to do, you need to conduct a **system evaluation**. To do so, you look at your computer's subsystems, what they do, and how they perform. These subsystems include the following:

- The CPU subsystem.
- The memory subsystem (your computer's random access memory, or RAM).
- The storage subsystem (your hard drive and other drives).
- The video subsystem (your video card and monitor).
- The audio subsystem (your sound card and speakers).
- Your computer's ports.

In the rest of this chapter, we examine each of these subsystems. At the end of each

BITS AND BYTES

Moving to a New Computer Doesn't Have to Be Painful

Ready to buy a new computer but dreading the prospect of transferring all your files and redoing all of your Windows settings? You could transfer all those files and settings manually, but Windows stores much information in the registry files, which can be tricky to update. So what do you do? PC migration software may be the thing for you. Applications such as Alohabob Pc Relocator (**www.alohabob.com**) and Desktop DNA (**http://ca.miramar.com**) are designed to make transitioning to a new computer easier. Walk-through wizards in the software take you through the otherwise arduous steps of transferring your files and settings to your new computer. Some migration programs can even move applications by uninstalling them from your computer and installing them on your new one. For the latest information on such utilities, search on migration software at **www.pcmag.com**. You'll be ready to upgrade painlessly in no time.

section, you'll find a small worksheet you can use to evaluate each subsystem on your computer. Note: This chapter discusses tools you can use to assess a Windows-based PC. For information on how to assess a Mac, refer to the Technology in Focus feature "Computing Alternatives" on page 276.

Evaluating the CPU Subsystem

As mentioned earlier, your computer's **central processing unit (CPU** or **processor)** is very important because it is the "brains" of the computer. The CPU processes instructions, performs calculations, manages the flow of information through a computer system, and is responsible for processing the data you input into information. The CPU, as shown in Figure 6.4, is located on the **motherboard**, the primary circuit board of the computer system. There are several types of processors on the market: Intel processors (such as the Pentium family) and AMD processors (such as the Athlon and Duron), both of which are used on PCs, and the PowerPC processors (such as the G5), which are used primarily in video gaming consoles.

How does the CPU work? The CPU is composed of two units: the **control unit** and the **arithmetic logic unit (ALU)**. The control unit coordinates the activities of all the other computer components. The ALU is responsible for performing all the arithmetic calculations (addition, subtraction, multiplication, and division). Additionally, the ALU makes logic and comparison decisions, such as comparing items to determine if one is greater than, less than, equal to, or not equal to another.

Every time the CPU performs a program instruction, it goes through the same series of steps: First, it fetches the required piece of data or instruction from RAM, the temporary storage location for all the data and instructions the computer needs while it is running. Next, it decodes the instruction into something the computer can understand. Once the CPU has decoded the instruction, it executes the instruction and stores the result to RAM before fetching the next instruction. This process is called a **machine cycle**. (We will discuss the machine cycle in more detail in Chapter 9.)

How is CPU speed measured? The computer goes through these machine cycles at a steady and constant pace. This pace, known as **clock speed**, is controlled by the system clock, which works like a metronome in music. The system clock keeps a steady beat, regulating the speed at which the processor goes through machine cycles. Processors work incredibly fast, going through millions or billions of machine cycles *each second*. Processor speed is measured in units of Hertz (Hz). Hertz means "machine cycles per second." Older machines run at speeds measured in **megahertz (MHz)**, or 1 million hertz, whereas more current systems run at speeds measured in **gigahertz (GHz)**, or 1 billion hertz. So a 3.8-GHz processor performs work at a rate of 3.8 billion machine cycles per second.

However, it's important to realize that CPU clock speed alone doesn't determine the performance of the CPU. We will discuss more of the factors that contribute to CPU performance in Chapter 9.

How can I tell how fast my CPU is? You can easily identify the speed of your current system's CPU. To do so, locate the My Computer icon on your desktop, right-click it, and select Properties. As shown in Figure 6.5, the General tab: System Properties dialog box shows you which CPU is installed in your system as well as its speed.

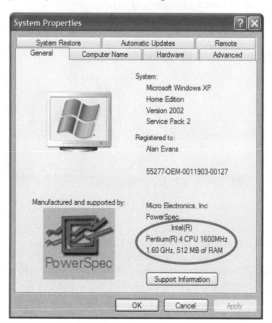

FIGURE 6.4

The CPU is a small chip that sits on the motherboard inside your system unit.

FIGURE 6.5

The General tab of the System Properties dialog box identifies which CPU you have as well as its speed. This computer contains an Intel Pentium 4 CPU running at 1.60 GHz.

How fast should my CPU be? At a minimum, your CPU should meet the requirements of your system's software and hardware. If your system is older and you are buying new software and peripheral devices, your CPU may not be able to handle the load.

For example, say your computer is three years old. For the past three years, you've been using it primarily for word processing and to surf the Internet. You recently purchased a digital camera. Now you want to edit your digital photos, but your system doesn't seem to be able to handle this. You check the system requirements on the photo-editing software you just installed and realize that the software runs best with a more powerful processor. In this case, if everything else in your system is running properly, a faster CPU would help improve the software's performance. Pentium III processors running at 700 MHz or higher and Pentium 4 processors running at any speed are good processors for the average user, enabling you to run most programs at a decent speed.

How can I tell whether my CPU is fast enough? The workload your CPU experiences varies considerably depending on what you're doing. Even though your CPU meets the minimum requirements

specified for a particular software application, if you're running other software (in addition to the operating system, which is always running), you'll need to check to see how well the CPU is handling the entire load. You can tell whether your CPU speed is limiting your system performance if you periodically watch how busy it is as you work on your computer. The percentage of time that your CPU is working is referred to as **CPU usage**.

A utility that can provide this kind of information is incredibly useful when considering whether you should upgrade and also when your performance suddenly seems to drop off for no apparent reason. In Windows XP, a program called Task Manager gives you easy access to all this data. If you have a machine running an older operating system such as Windows 98, you'll want to install a shareware utility (such as Task Info) to handle this kind of analysis. (Mac OS X has a utility similar to Task Manager called Activity Monitor.)

To view information on your CPU usage, right-click an open area of the System toolbar, select Task Manager, and click the Performance tab, shown in Figure 6.6. The CPU Usage graph records your CPU usage for the past several seconds. Of course, there will be periodic peaks of high CPU usage, but if you see that your CPU usage levels are greater than 90 percent during most of your work session, a new CPU would contribute a great deal to your system performance.

UPGRADING YOUR CPU

Is it expensive or difficult to upgrade a CPU? Replacement CPUs are expensive. In addition, although it is reasonably easy to install a CPU, it can be difficult to determine which CPU to install. Not all CPUs are interchangeable, and the replacement CPU must be compatible with the motherboard. Some people opt to upgrade the entire motherboard, but motherboards are a lot more difficult to install. As we discuss at the end of this chapter, if you plan on upgrading your computer in other ways in addition to upgrading the CPU, you may just want to consider buying a new computer.

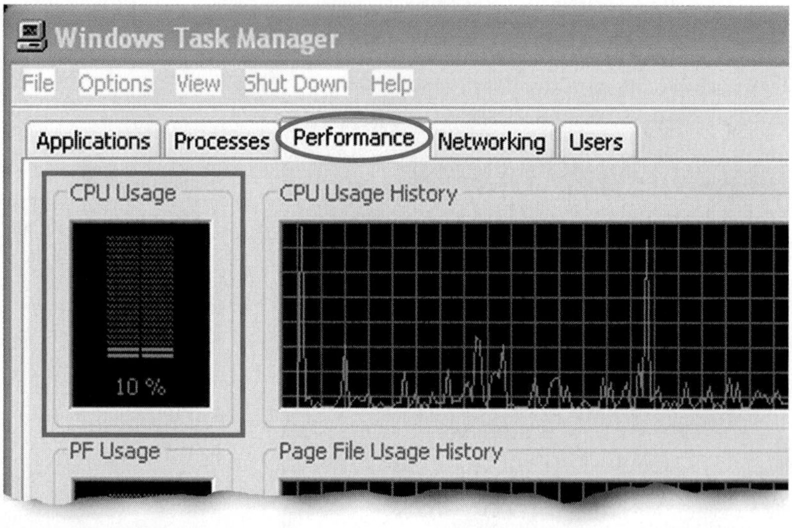

FIGURE 6.6

The Performance tab of the Windows Task Manager utility shows you how busy your CPU actually is when you're using your computer. In this case, current CPU usage level is at 10 percent. If CPU usage levels are above 90 percent for long periods of time, you may want to consider getting a faster, more powerful processor.

BITS AND BYTES

Feeling Hot Hot Hot

Heat isn't good for a computer system. However, computer chips, especially the CPU, produce heat, and if your system unit sits on the floor collecting dust, or has any vents blocked off, the temperature inside that case can climb very quickly. If the heat inside the system isn't dissipated, computer chips will have a shorter life. System cases are always designed with one internal fan, but if you're upgrading, you may want to consider a case that pays more attention to keeping your system cool. **www.highspeedpc.com** and **www.tigerdirect.com** are suppliers that offer cases featuring special venting designs and dual exhaust fans. You also can buy high-quality fans that sit directly on top of the CPU, dissipating heat directly off the chip. And if you want a more extreme solution, water cooling systems can replace the fans altogether (see Figure 6.7). The Corsair Hydrocool unit sits next to your computer and pumps coolant through hoses and past the CPU chip to remove heat more efficiently and quietly than airflow. Very cool indeed!

FIGURE 6.7

Like a radiator cools your car engine, running water past a CPU chip cools it off dramatically. The water picks up the heat and carries it away from the chip surface.

Are the fastest CPUs the best to use? If you decide to upgrade your CPU, consider buying one that is *not* the most recently released with the fastest speed but, rather, a slightly slower one of the same type. For example, if the Intel Pentium 4 family has just released a 3.4-GHz CPU, you will pay a premium to buy this newest processor. However, its release will drive down the prices on the earlier Pentium 4 chips running at speeds of 3.0 GHz, 2.8 GHz, and 2.6 GHz. Buying a slightly slower CPU and investing the savings in other system components (such as additional RAM) will often result in a better-performing system. The same is true if you're buying a new computer: often, you'll save money without losing a great deal of performance by buying a computer with a CPU slightly slower than the fastest one on the market.

What else do I need to consider if I want to upgrade my CPU? You first need to determine whether a new CPU is compatible with your system's motherboard. (**www.powerleap.com** has a great tool to walk you through CPU and motherboard compatibility.) Check your computer's manual for the make and model of the components on your motherboard.

In addition, because the CPU generates a lot of heat, a small cooling device called a *heat sink* sits directly on top of the CPU to absorb excess heat. If you upgrade your CPU, you need to make sure you purchase the correct heat sink for your processor (although often heat sinks come in a kit with the replacement CPU).

Be mindful that although replacing the CPU is not terribly difficult (as shown in Figure 6.8), it is important that you pick the right replacement part and process. It may be best to get the help of a professional should you decide to upgrade your CPU.

FIGURE 6.8

It can be fairly simple to replace a CPU: you line up the slots and drop it in. However, because it's important that you pick the right replacement part and process, many computer owners seek the help of professionals when upgrading their CPU.

Will replacing the CPU be enough to improve my computer's performance? You may think that if you have the fastest processor, you will have a system with the best performance. However, upgrading your CPU will affect only the *processing* portion of the system performance, not how quickly data can move to or from the CPU. Your system's overall performance depends on many other factors, including the amount of RAM installed as well as hard disk speed. Therefore, replacing or upgrading the CPU may not offer significant improvements to your system's performance if there is insufficient RAM or hard drive capacity.

FIGURE 6.9 Do You Need to Upgrade Your CPU?

	Current System	Upgrade Required?
CPU Speed (in MHz or GHz)		
CPU Usage at Appropriate Level?		

Evaluating RAM: The Memory Subsystem

Random access memory (RAM) is your computer's temporary storage space. Although we refer to RAM as a form of storage, RAM is really the computer's short-term memory. As such, it remembers everything that the computer needs to process the data into information, such as inputted data and software instructions, but only when the computer is on. This means that RAM is an example of **volatile storage**. When the power is off, the data stored in RAM is cleared out. This is why, in addition to RAM, systems always include **nonvolatile storage** devices for permanent storage of instructions and data when the computer is powered off. Hard disks provide the greatest nonvolatile storage capacity in the computer system.

Why not use a hard drive to store the data and instructions? It's about one million times faster for the CPU to retrieve a piece of data from RAM

than from a hard disk drive. The time it takes the CPU to retrieve data from RAM is measured in *nanoseconds* (billionths of seconds), whereas retrieving data from a fast hard drive takes an average of 10 *milliseconds* (or ms, thousandths of seconds). This difference is influential in designing a balanced computer system and can have a tremendous impact on system performance. Therefore, it's critical that your computer has more than enough RAM.

Where is RAM located? You can find RAM inside the system unit of your computer on the motherboard. **Memory modules** (or **memory cards**), the small circuit boards that hold a series of RAM chips, fit into special slots on the motherboard (see Figure 6.10). Most memory modules in today's systems are called dual inline memory modules (DIMMs).

Are there different types of RAM? To add to the confusion new computer users face, several different types of RAM are available. DRAM, static RAM (SRAM), synchronous DRAM (SDRAM), double data rate SDRAM (DDR SDRAM), and DDR2 RAM are all slightly different in how they function and in the speed at which memory can be accessed. Currently, DDR SDRAM is very common in the marketplace, although some high-performance systems offer the even faster DDR2 RAM. If you're purchasing a new system, you will see models offering all different kinds of RAM, such as SDRAM, DDR RAM, or DDR2 RAM. It's important to understand that although systems using the faster types of RAM will be more expensive, RAM has a significant impact on the overall performance of your computer.

If you're adding RAM to an older system, you must determine what type your system needs. Consult your user's manual or the manufacturer's Web site. In addition, many online RAM resellers (such as **www.crucial.com**) can help you determine the type of RAM your system needs based on the model number and brand of your computer. We will discuss the different kinds of RAM in more detail in Chapter 9.

How can I tell how much RAM I have installed in my computer? The amount of RAM that is actually sitting on memory modules in your computer is your computer's **physical memory**. The easiest way to see how much RAM you have is to look in the General tab of the System Properties dialog box. This is the same tab you looked in to determine your system's

CPU type and speed and is shown in Figure 6.5. RAM capacity is measured in megabytes (MB) or gigabytes (GB). The computer in Figure 6.5 has 512 MB of RAM installed.

More detailed information on physical memory is displayed in the Physical Memory table in the Performance tab of Windows Task Manager, shown in Figure 6.11. The Physical Memory table shows both the total amount of physical memory you have installed as well as the *available* physical memory you have at this moment. You can see this computer has approximately 524 MB (523,760 kilobytes, or KB) of total memory installed, and approximately 245 MB is available (which means 279 MB is being used). The amount of available memory will always be less than the amount of total memory because a certain portion of the physical memory is always tied up running the operating system.

How much memory does the operating system need to run? The memory that your operating system uses is referred to as **kernel memory**. This memory is listed in a separate Kernel Memory table in the Performance tab. In Figure 6.11, the Kernel Memory table tells you that approximately 46 MB (45,872 KB) of the total 524 MB of RAM is being used to run Windows XP.

As you know from Chapter 5, the operating system is the main software application that runs the computer. Without it, the computer would not work. At a minimum, the system needs enough RAM to run the operating system. Therefore, the amount of kernel memory that the system is using is the *absolute minimum* amount of RAM that your computer can run on. However, because you run additional applications, you need to have more RAM than the minimum.

How much RAM do I need? Because RAM is the temporary holding space for all the data and instructions that the computer uses while it's on, most computer users need quite a bit of RAM. In fact, it's not unusual to have 1 GB of RAM on a newer home system. The amount of RAM your system needs depends on how you use it. At a minimum, you need enough RAM to run the operating system (as explained earlier), plus whatever other software applications you're using, then a bit of additional RAM to hold the data you're inputting.

To determine how much RAM you need, list all the software applications you might be running at one time. Figure 6.12 shows an

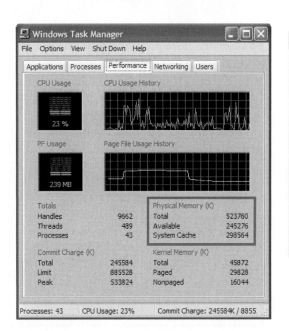

FIGURE 6.11

The Performance tab of the Windows Task Manager shows you how much physical memory is installed in your system, as well as how much is currently being used and how much is available. The computer shown here has approximately 245 MB of memory still available from a total of approximately 524 MB.

example of RAM requirements. In this example, if you are running your operating system, word processing and spreadsheet programs, a Web browser, a music player, and photo-editing software simultaneously, you would need a *minimum* of 460 MB RAM.

However, it's a good idea to have more than the minimum amount of RAM, so you can use more programs in the future. When upgrading RAM, the rule of thumb is to buy as much as you can afford but no more than your system will handle.

SOUND BYTES

Memory Hierarchy Interactive

In this Sound Byte, you'll learn about the different types of memory used in a computer system.

VIRTUAL MEMORY

Would adding more RAM improve my system performance? If your system is **memory bound**—that is, limited in how fast it can send data to the CPU

FIGURE 6.12 Sample RAM Requirements

Application	Minimum RAM Required
Windows XP	128 MB
MS Office Pro 2003	128 MB
Internet Explorer	12 MB
Windows Media Player	64 MB
Microsoft Picture It!	128 MB
Total RAM Required if Running All Programs Simultaneously	460 MB RAM

FIGURE 6.13

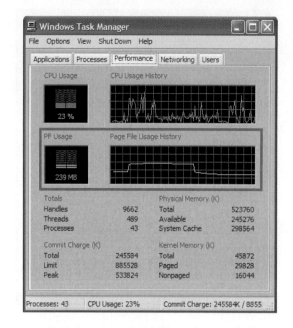

SOUND BYTE

Installing RAM

In this Sound Byte, you'll learn how to select the appropriate type of memory to purchase, how to order memory online, and how to install it yourself. As you'll discover, the procedure is a simple one and can add great performance benefits to your system.

the system to run more applications than can actually fit in your computer's RAM.

So far, this system of memory management sounds like a good idea, especially because hard drives are much cheaper than RAM per megabyte of storage. The drawback is speed. Remember that accessing data from the hard drive to send it to the CPU is more than one million times slower than accessing data from RAM. Another drawback is that some applications do not run well on virtual memory. So, using virtual memory is a method of last resort. If your system is running with a large page file (that is, if it is using a lot of virtual memory), adding more RAM will dramatically increase performance.

How do I determine how much virtual memory I'm using? As shown in Figure 6.13, the Performance tab of the Task Manager provides information about your computer's virtual memory (referred to as the *PF Usage*). By watching the information displayed in the PF Usage section, you can determine how much virtual memory is being used. If you consistently have a large page file in use (that is, more than 1.5 percent of the amount of RAM installed in your system) and very little physical memory available, adding more RAM will significantly improve your system performance.

ADDING RAM

Is there a limit to how much RAM I can add to my computer? Every computer is designed with a maximum limit on the amount of RAM it can support. Each

because there's not enough RAM installed—it will become sluggish, freeze more often, or just shut down during the day. If this is the case, adding more RAM to your system will have an immediate impact on performance.

How do I know whether my system is memory bound? You learned in Chapter 5 that if you don't have enough RAM to hold all of the programs you're currently trying to run, the operating system will begin to store the data that doesn't fit in RAM into a space on the hard disk called **virtual memory**. When it is using virtual memory, your operating system builds a file called the **page file** on the hard drive to allow processing to continue. This enables

FIGURE 6.14

computer is designed with a specific number of slots on the memory board in which the memory cards fit, and each slot may have a limit on the amount of RAM it can support. In addition, the operating system running on that machine may impose its own limit. (For example, Windows XP can support 4 GB of RAM.) To determine these limits, check your owner's manual or the manufacturer's Web site.

Once you know how much RAM your computer can support, you can determine the best configuration of memory cards to achieve the greatest amount of RAM. For example, say you have a total of four memory card slots: two are already filled with 128-MB RAM cards and the other two are empty. Maximum RAM allowed for your system is 512 MB. This means you can buy two more 128-MB RAM modules for the two empty slots, for a total of 512 MB (4 × 128 MB) of RAM. If all the memory card slots are already filled, you may be able to replace the old modules with greater-capacity RAM modules, depending on your maximum allowed RAM.

Is it hard to add RAM? Adding RAM to a computer is fairly easy (see Figure 6.14). RAM comes with installation instructions, which you should follow carefully. RAM is also relatively inexpensive compared with other system upgrade options. Still, the cost of RAM fluctuates in the marketplace as much as 400 percent over time, so if you're considering adding RAM, you should watch the prices of memory in online or print advertisements.

Evaluating the Storage Subsystem

As you've learned, there are two ways data is saved on your computer: temporary storage and permanent storage. RAM is a form of *temporary* (or *volatile*) *storage*—thus, anything residing in RAM is not permanently saved. Therefore, it's critical to have means to store data and software applications *permanently*.

Fortunately, several storage options exist within every computer system. Storage devices for a typical personal computer include the hard disk drive, floppy disk drive, Zip disk drive, USB flash drives, and CD and DVD drives. When you turn off

FIGURE 6.15 **Do You Need to Upgrade Your RAM?**

	Current System
Type of RAM Your System Is Using	
Maximum Amount of RAM You Need	
Amount of RAM in Your System Now	
Amount of RAM You Want to Add	
Number of Currently Empty Memory Module Slots	
Memory Module Size	
Total Amount of RAM You Can Add	

your computer, the data stored to these devices is saved. These devices are therefore referred to as *nonvolatile storage devices*. Of all the nonvolatile storage devices, the hard disk drive is used the most.

THE HARD DISK DRIVE

What makes the hard disk drive the most popular storage device? With storage capacities of up to 400 GB, **hard disk drives** (or just **hard drives**), shown in Figure 6.16, have the largest storage capacity of any storage device. The hard drive is also a much more economical device than floppy, Zip, or CD/DVD drives because it offers the most megabytes of storage per dollar.

Hard drive inside the system unit

FIGURE 6.16

Hard disk drives are the most popular storage device for personal computers. The hard disk drive is installed permanently inside the system unit.

DIG DEEPER

How a Hard Disk Drive Works

The thin metal platters that make up a hard drive are covered with a special magnetic coating that enables the data to be recorded onto one or both sides of the platter. Hard disk manufacturers prepare the disks to hold data through a process called low-level formatting. In this process, **tracks** (concentric circles) and **sectors** (pie-shaped wedges) are created in the magnetized surface of each platter, setting up a gridlike pattern used to identify file locations on the hard drive. A separate process, called high-level formatting, establishes the catalog that the computer uses to keep track of where each file is located on the hard drive. As you learned in Chapter 5, this catalog is called the **File Allocation Table (FAT)**.

Hard drive platters spin at a high rate of speed, some as fast as 15,000 revolutions per minute (rpm). Sitting between each platter are special "arms" that contain **read/write heads** (see Figure 6.17). The read/write heads move from the outer edge of the spinning platters to the center, up to 50 times per second, to retrieve (read) and record (write) the magnetic data to and from the hard disk. As noted earlier, the average total time it takes for the read/write head to locate the data on the platter and return it to the CPU for processing is the access time. A new hard drive should have an average access time of about 10 ms.

Access time is mostly the sum of two factors, seek time and latency. The time it takes for the read/write heads to move over the surface of the disk, between tracks, to the correct track is called the **seek time** (sometimes people incorrectly refer to this as access time). Once the read/write head locates the correct track, it may need to wait for the correct sector to spin to the read/write head. This waiting time is called **latency** (or rotational delay). The faster the platters spin (or the faster the rpm), the less time you'll have to wait for your data to be accessed. Currently, you can find new hard drives that spin between 5,400 and 7,200 rpm.

The read/write heads do not touch the platters of the hard drive; rather, they float above them on a thin cushion of air at a height of 0.5 microinches. As a matter of comparison, a human hair is 2,000 microinches thick and a particle of dust is larger than a human hair.

Second, the hard drive's **access time**, or the time it takes a storage device to locate its stored data and make it available for processing, is also the fastest of all permanent storage devices. Hard drive access times are measured in milliseconds, or thousandths of seconds. For large-capacity drives, access times of approximately 9.5 milliseconds—that's less than one-hundredth of a second—are not unusual. This is much faster than the access times of other popular storage devices, such as floppy and flash drives.

Another reason hard drives are popular is that they transfer data to other computer components (such as RAM) much faster than the other storage devices do. This speed of transfer is referred to as **data transfer rate** and depending on the manufacturer is expressed in either mega*bits* or mega*bytes* per second.

How is data stored on hard drives? As you learned in Chapter 5, a hard disk drive is composed of several coated **platters** (round, thin plates of metal) stacked onto a spindle. When data is saved to a hard disk, a pattern of magnetized spots is created on the iron oxide coating each platter. Each of these spots represents a 1, whereas the spaces not "spotted" represent a 0. These 0s and 1s are bits (or binary digits) and are the smallest pieces of data that computers can understand. When data stored on the hard disk is retrieved (or read), your computer translates these patterns of magnetized spots into the data you have saved.

How do I know how much capacity my hard drive has? Hard drive capacity is measured in MB or GB. To check how much total capacity your hard drive has, as well as how much is being used, simply double-click the My Computer icon, right-click the C drive icon, and select Properties from the shortcut menu. The Properties dia-

SOUND BYTE

Hard Disk Anatomy Interactive

In this Sound Byte, you'll learn about the internal construction of a hard drive and see how a hard drive reads and writes data. You'll also watch a disk being defragmented and learn how the defragmentation utility improves hard drive performance.

Therefore, it's critical to keep your hard disk drive free from all dust and dirt, as even the smallest particle could find its way between the read/write head and the disk platter, causing a **head crash**—a stoppage of the hard disk drive that often results in data loss.

Capacities for hard disk drives in personal computers exceed 400 GB. Increasing the amount of data stored in a hard disk drive is achieved by either adding more platters or by increasing the amount of data stored on each platter. How tightly the tracks are placed next to each other, how tightly spaced the sectors are, and how closely the bits of data are placed affect the measurement of the amount of data that can be stored in a specific area of a hard disk. Modern technology continues to increase the standards on all three levels, enabling massive quantities of data to be stored in small places.

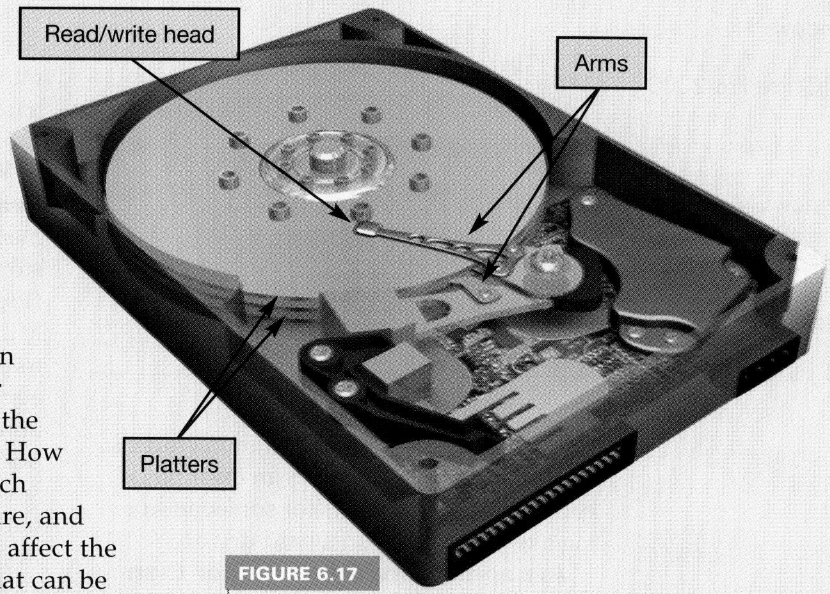

Read/write head

Arms

Platters

FIGURE 6.17

The hard drive is a stack of platters enclosed in a sealed case. Special arms fit in between each platter. The read/write heads at the end of each arm read from and save data to the platters.

log box displays a pie chart that indicates the total capacity of your hard drive as well as the capacity being used, as shown in Figure 6.18.

How do I know how much storage capacity I need? To determine the storage capacity your system needs, calculate the amount of storage capacity basic computer programs need to reside on your computer. Because the operating system is the most critical piece of software, your hard drive needs enough space to store that program. The demands on system requirements have grown with new versions of operating systems. Windows XP, the latest Microsoft operating system, requires a whopping 1.5 GB of hard drive capacity. Five years ago, such software wouldn't have fit on most hard drives.

In addition to having space for the operating system, you need enough space to store software applications you use, such as Microsoft Office, a Web browser, and games. It's always best to check the system requirements of any software program before you buy it to make sure your system can handle it. System requirements are found on the

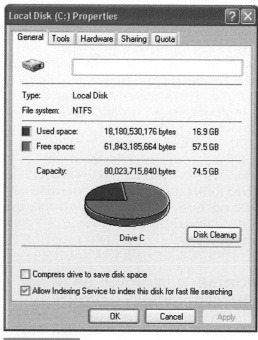

FIGURE 6.18

Using the pie chart in the General tab of the Properties dialog box, you can determine the capacity of your hard drive. This hard drive has 74.5 GB of space, with 57.5 GB of free space.

FIGURE 6.19 Sample Hard Drive Requirements

Application	Hard Disk Space Required
Windows XP	1.5 GB
MS Office Pro 2003	690 MB
Internet Explorer	75 MB
Windows Media Player	521 MB
Microsoft Picture It!	150 MB
Total Required	**2.94 GB**

software package or on the manufacturer's Web site. Figure 6.19 shows an example of hard drive requirements for someone storing a few programs on a hard drive.

Are some hard drives faster than others? There are several types of hard drives. Integrated Drive Electronics (IDE, also called parallel advanced technology attachment or PATA) is an older style that used wide cables to connect the hard drive to the motherboard. Serial advanced technology attachment (ATA) hard drives use much thinner cables and can transfer data more quickly than IDE drives. A slower drive is fine if you use your computer primarily for word processing, spreadsheets, e-mail, and the Internet. However, "power users," such as graphic designers and software developers, will benefit from the faster Serial ATA hard drive.

Another factor affecting a hard disk's speed is access time (or the speed with which it locates data for processing). As noted earlier, access time is measured in milliseconds (ms). The faster the access time the better, although often hard drives have similar access times.

PORTABLE STORAGE OPTIONS: THE FLOPPY AND BEYOND

If my hard drive is so powerful, why do I need other forms of storage? Despite all the advantages that the hard drive has as a storage device, one drawback is that data stored on it is not portable. To get data from one computer to another (assuming the computers aren't networked), you'll need a portable storage device, such as a floppy or flash drive. Equally important, you need alternate storage options to back up data on your hard drive in case it experiences a head crash or other system problems. Finally, despite the massive storage capacity of hard drives, you should remove infrequently used files from your hard drive to maintain optimal storage capacity.

What forms of portable storage are best? Several portable storage formats (or media) are popular, with varying ranges of storage capacity (see Figure 6.20). The **floppy disk**, with a storage capacity of 1.44 MB, holds the least amount of data but is the most inexpensive form of portable data storage. However, today's average user is generating much larger files because of the incorporation of multimedia. Floppy disks are too small to hold even one file that has been bulked up with multimedia. For this reason, floppy disks are becoming obsolete.

Zip disks, with storage capacities ranging from 100 MB to 750 MB, and CD-R, CD-RW, DVD-R, and DVD-RW discs, with storage capacities ranging from 700 MB to 9.4 GB, have become increasingly popular to store large files.

Flash memory cards are another form of portable storage. These tiny removable memory cards are often used in digital cameras, MP3 players, and PDAs. Some flash cards can hold as much as 4 GB of data. As the technology becomes more popular, capacities will continue to increase.

FIGURE 6.20 Portable Storage Capacities

Storage Media	Capacity
Floppy Disk	1.44 MB
Zip Disk	100 to 750 MB
CD	700 MB
DVD	9.4 GB
Flash Memory	16 MB to 4 GB (and up)
Portable Hard Drive	20 GB and up

Note: Capacities are accurate as of publication date but are expected to continue to increase.

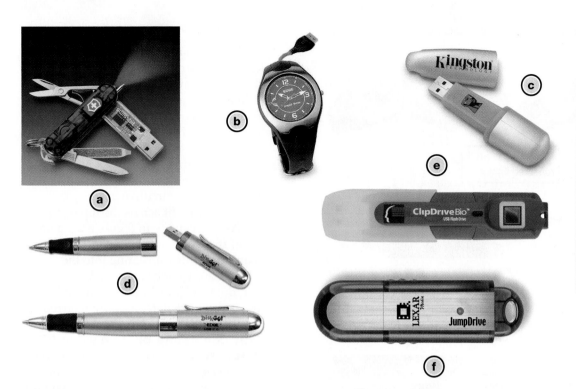

FIGURE 6.21

Flash drives, also known as thumb drives or jump drives, allow you to carry data in a variety of convenient packaging options. (a) Swiss Army knife with integrated flash drive, (b) watch with built-in flash drive, (c) typical flash drive, (d) pen with built-in flash drive, (e) flash drive with fingerprint recognition reader, (f) flash drive with keychain hook.

This same technology is also packaged as **flash drives** (sometimes called *thumb drives* or *jump drives*). Small enough to fit on a key chain, a flash drive can hold up to 4 GB of data and can be plugged into any USB port (see Figure 6.21). Windows XP instantly recognizes flash drives when they are plugged into a USB port and treats them as another hard drive on the system. For $20 you can carry 256 MB with you easily and have enough room to store a huge PowerPoint presentation, some pictures and videos, and even a bunch of MP3 songs.

Sometimes, for large amounts of portable storage, external hard drive devices are the best solution. Hard drives are now available in very small, light packages and can connect quickly to a USB 2.0 or FireWire port. Light devices you can carry in a pocket such as the Apple iPod are another option for portable storage and can hold 60 GB of data. Larger external hard drives, still small enough to carry in a handbag, can hold 400 GB or more of data. Connect them to a free USB port and they are recognized by the operating system as just another hard drive.

So there are a number of choices available to you for portable data storage. Consider the amount of data you want to routinely transport and then select the device that meets your needs at the lowest cost.

Floppy and Zip Disks

How is data stored on floppy and Zip disks? Inside the plastic cases of both floppy and Zip disks you'll find a round piece of plastic film. This film is covered with a magnetized coating of iron oxide. As is the case with hard drives, when data is saved to the disk, a pattern of magnetized spots is created on the iron oxide coating within established tracks and

BITS AND BYTES

Taking Care of Floppy and Zip Disks

The following guidelines will help you keep your floppy and Zip disks safe:

- Place disks in a protective case when carrying or mailing them.
- Keep disks away from devices that generate a magnetic field, such as speakers, televisions, and mobile phones.
- Use a felt-tip marker (not a pen or pencil) when labeling disks. Better yet, create a label and place it on the disk.
- Don't expose your disk to excessive heat or cold.
- Don't move the metal shutter that protects the disk. Dirt and dust that get into the disk can harm your data. If the metal shutter comes off the floppy, transfer the data immediately to the hard drive, because dust and dirt will corrupt the data on the exposed part of the floppy.

To read information stored on a disk, a laser inside the disk drive sends a beam of light through the spinning disk.

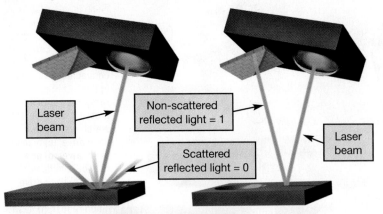

Laser beam

Non-scattered reflected light = 1

Scattered reflected light = 0

Laser beam

If the light reflected back is scattered in all directions (which happens when the laser hits a pit), the laser translates this into the binary digit 0

If non-scattered light is reflected back to the laser (which happens when the laser hits an area in which there is no pit), the laser translates this into the binary digit 1

Spinning CD

In this way, the laser reads the pits and non-pits as a series of bits (0s and 1s), which the computer can then process

FIGURE 6.22

Data is read from a CD using focused laser light.

CDs and DVDs

How is data saved onto a CD or DVD?

Like the hard drive and floppy and Zip disks, data is saved to CDs and DVDs within established tracks and sectors. However, unlike floppy and Zip disks, which store their data on a piece of magnetized film, CDs and DVDs store data as tiny pits that are burned into a disk by a high-speed laser. These pits are extremely small, less than 1 micron in diameter, so that nearly 1,500 pits fit across the top of a pinhead. As you can see in Figure 6.22, data is read off the CD by a laser beam, with the pits and non-pits translating into the 1s and 0s of the binary code computers understand. Because CDs and DVDs use a laser to read and write data, they are referred to as **optical media**.

Why can I store data on some CDs but not others? CD-ROMs are read-only optical disks, meaning you can't save any data onto them. To play a CD-ROM, you use a CD-ROM (or CD-R) drive. However, most computers today are equipped with special CD drives that allow you to save, or "burn," data onto specially designed CDs. **Compact Disc–Read/Writable (CD-RW) discs**, which use a CD-RW drive, can be written to hundreds of times. **Compact Disc–Recordable (CD-R) discs** can be written to once and can be used with either a CD-R drive or a CD-RW drive. If your computer isn't equipped with a CD-R or CD-RW drive, you can buy one at a reasonable cost, and they're quite simple to install.

What's the difference between CDs and DVDs? DVDs use the same optical technology to store data as CDs. The differ-

sectors. Each of these spots represents either a 0 or a 1, or a bit. When data stored on the disk is retrieved (read), your computer translates these patterns of magnetized spots into information. Because floppies and Zip disks use a magnetized film to store data, they are referred to as **magnetic media**.

BITS AND BYTES

Taking Care of CDs and DVDs

The following guidelines will help you keep your CDs and DVDs safe:

- Exercise care in handling your CDs and DVDs. Dirt or oil on CDs/DVDs can keep data from being read properly, whereas large scratches can interrupt data completely.

- To keep CDs/DVDs from warping, avoid placing them near heat sources and store them at room temperature.

- Clean CDs/DVDs by taking a bit of rubbing alcohol on a cotton ball and wiping them from the center to the edge of the disk in long swipes. Don't rub the CD/DVD in a circular motion, because you may cause more scratches.

- Use a felt-tip marker to label CDs/DVDs and write on the area provided for the label. Don't put stickers or labels on CDs/DVDs, unless they're specifically designed for that purpose.

ence is that a DVD's storage capacity is much greater than a CD's. To hold more data than CDs, DVDs have less space between tracks, as well as between bits. The size of pits on the DVD is also much smaller than those on a CD. Additionally, DVD audio and video quality is superior to that of a CD. Because of their versatile nature, DVDs are the standard technology for audio and video files as well as graphics and data files.

Are there discs that can hold even more data than DVDs? With the arrival of high-definition video, even the capacity of DVDs seems small. Blu-Ray (**www.blu-ray.com**) is one new emerging standard of data storage. A single layer Blu-Ray disc can hold 25 GB of data, while a double-layer disc can hold 50 GB, enough for four hours of high-definition video. The "blue" in the name refers to the fact that a blue laser, instead of a red laser, is used to write and read these discs. Experiments are also underway using fluorescent optical discs that can store data in as many as 100 different layers, for a final capacity of 450 GB!

Do I need a DVD-ROM drive *and* a CD-ROM drive? Although CDs and DVDs are based on the same technology, CD drives cannot read DVDs. If your system has only a CD drive, you need to add a DVD drive to view DVDs. However, because DVD drives can read CDs, if your system has a DVD drive, you do not need to add a CD drive to listen to CDs.

To record data to (burn) DVDs, you need recordable DVD discs and a read/write DVD drive. Unfortunately, technology experts have not agreed on a standard DVD format. Currently, there are two recognized formats, **DVD-R/RW** (pronounced "DVD dash") and **DVD+R/RW** (pronounced "DVD plus"). You can purchase a DVD-RW drive or a DVD+RW drive or even a "super drive" DVD-/+RW that can read and write both formats. Either the plus or dash format discs you write will be compatible in about 85 percent of all DVD players. (Web sites such as

www.customflix.com list the compatibility of various DVD players and the DVD plus and DVD dash formats.) However, you must make sure you purchase blank DVD discs that match the type of drive you own. Either type of DVD burner drive can burn CDs, however—the wars fought over the CD standard have been settled for several years now.

Are some CD and DVD drives faster than others? When you buy a CD or DVD drive, knowing the drive speed is important. Speeds are listed on the device's packaging. Record (write) speed is always listed first, rewrite speed is listed second (except for CD-R drives, which cannot rewrite data), and playback speed is listed last. For example, a CD-RW drive may have speeds of 48×12×48×, meaning that the device can record data at 48× speed, rewrite data at 12× speed, and play back data at 48× speed. For CDs, the × after each number represents the transfer of 150 KB of data per second. So, for example, a CD-RW drive with a 48×12×48× rating records data at 48 × 150 KB per second, or 7,200 KB per second.

DVD drives are much faster than CD drives. For example, a 1× DVD-ROM drive provides a data transfer rate of approximately 1.3 MB of data per second, which is roughly equivalent to a CD-ROM speed of 9×. CD and DVD drives are constantly getting faster. If you're in the market for a new CD-RW, you'll want to investigate the drive speeds on the market and make sure you get the fastest one you can.

BITS AND BYTES

Taking Care of Flash Drives

The following guidelines will help you keep your flash drives safe:

- A flash drive fits into a USB port only one way—do not force it if you feel resistance.

- When removing the drive, be sure any activity LED that may be on the drive is no longer lit. Then click the "Safely Remove Hardware" icon on the taskbar. Only remove the drive itself once the "Safe to Remove Drive" message appears. Pulling the drive out of the port earlier could corrupt your data.

- When not using the drive, keep the cap in place. Moisture and dust can damage the data stored on the drive.

UPGRADING YOUR STORAGE SUBSYSTEM

FIGURE 6.23

This external hard disk drive offers you extra storage and plugs into your computer through a FireWire port.

How can I upgrade my storage devices? There are several ways in which you can increase your storage capacity or add extra drives to your computer.

If you find your hard drive is running out of space, or you want a place to back up or move files to create more room on your hard drive, you have several options. You can replace the hard drive installed in your system unit with a bigger one. However, replacing your internal hard drive requires backing up your entire hard drive and reloading all the data onto your new hard drive. Instead, you may want to install an *additional* hard drive in your current system if you have an extra drive bay (the space reserved on the inside of your system unit for hard disk drives). In lieu of installing a bigger hard drive, you might just chose to use an external hard drive you can plug directly into a free USB 2.0 or FireWire port. Figure 6.23 shows an example of such an external hard drive.

You can also upgrade your storage subsystem by adding a new Zip drive or other drive to your system. If your computer did not come with an internal Zip, CD-RW, or DVD-RW drive, and if you have an open (unused) drive bay in your system, you can easily install a drive there. Most people upgrade to a CD-RW and DVD-RW not for more storage but because they want additional multimedia capabilities (such as the

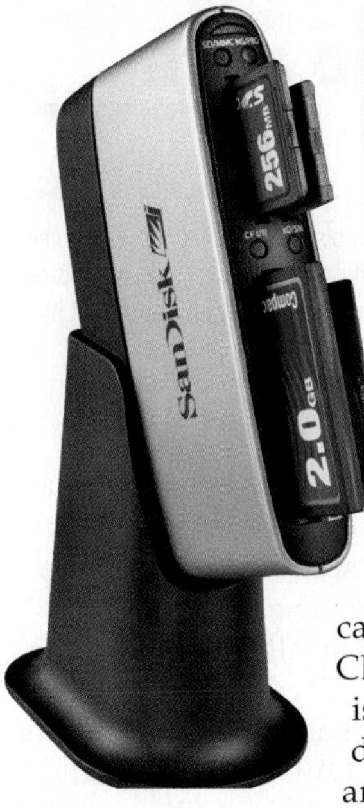

FIGURE 6.24

Flash card readers hook up to your computer through a USB port.

ability to burn CDs). If you don't have open bays in your system, you can still add Zip and CD/DVD drives. As is the case with hard drives, these drives are available as external units you attach to your computer through an open port.

What if I want to use flash memory? As flash memory becomes more popular, you may want your computer to be able to read flash memory cards. Although most desktop computers don't include internal **memory card readers**, you can purchase external memory card readers like the one shown in Figure 6.24 that connect to your system through an open USB port. Some flash memory comes in "sticks" that just plug directly into a USB port.

Evaluating the Video Subsystem

How video is displayed depends on two components: your video card and your monitor. It's important that your system have the correct monitor and video card to meet your needs. If you use your computer system to display files that have complex graphics, such as videos on DVD or from your camcorder, or even play graphics-rich games with a lot of fast action, you may want to consider upgrading your video subsystem.

VIDEO CARDS

What is a video card? A **video card** (or **video adapter**) is an expansion card that is installed inside your system unit to translate binary data into the images you view on your monitor. Today, almost all computers ship with a video card installed. Modern video cards, like the one shown in Figure 6.26, are

FIGURE 6.25 Do You Need to Upgrade Your Storage Subsystem?

	Current System	Upgrade Required?
Hard Disk Drive Capacity		
Floppy Disk Drive		
Zip Disk Drive		
CD-R/CD-RW Drive		
DVD-ROM Drive		
DVD-RW Drive		
Other Storage Devices Needed?		

Ethics: CD and DVD Technology: A Free Lunch—or at Least a Free Copy

Years ago, when the electronic photocopier made its debut, book publishers and others who distributed the printed word feared they would be put out of business. They were worried that people would no longer buy books and other printed matter if they could simply copy someone else's original. Years later, when the cassette player/recorder and VCR player/recorder arrived on the market, those who felt they would be negatively affected by these new technologies expressed similar reactions. Now, with the arrival of DVD-RW and CD-RW technology, which allows users to copy DVDs and CDs in a matter of minutes, the music and entertainment industries are up in arms.

Although copy machines and VCRs certainly didn't put an end to the industries they affected, some still say the music and entertainment industries will take a significant hit with CD-RW/DVD-RW technology. Already, CD and DVD sales are plummeting. Industry insiders are claiming that these new technologies are unethical, and they're pressing for increased federal legislation against such copying. And it's not just the CD-RW/DVD-RW technology that's causing problems—"copies" are not necessarily of the physical sort. Thanks to the Internet, *file transferring* copyrighted works—particularly music and films—is now commonplace. According to MusicUnited.org, more than 2.6 billion

files are downloaded illegally every month, and about one quarter of all Internet users worldwide have downloaded a movie from the Internet.

In a separate survey, the Recording Industry Association of America (RIAA), a trade organization that represents the interests of recording giants such as Sony, Capitol Records, and other major producers of musical entertainment, reported that 23 percent of music fans revealed they were buying less music because they could download it or copy a CD-ROM from a friend.

As you would expect, the music and entertainment industries want to be fairly compensated for their creative output. They blame the technology industry for the creation of means by which artists, studios, and the entertainment industry in general are being "robbed." Although the technology exists that readily allows consumers to transfer and copy music and videos, the artists who produce these works do not want to be taken advantage of. However, others claim that the technology industry should not bear the complete burden of protecting entertainment copyrights. The RIAA sums up the future of this debate nicely: "Goals for the new millennium are to work with [the recording] industry and others to enable technologies that open up new opportunities but at the same time to protect the rights of artists and copyright owners."

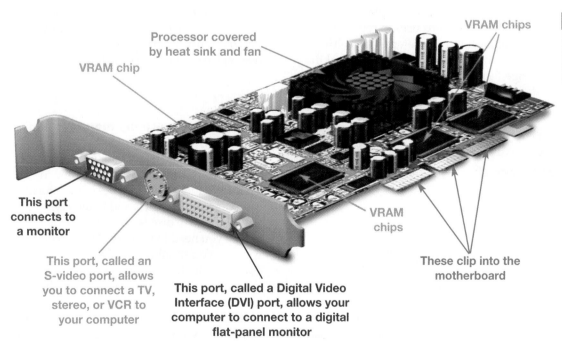

VRAM chip

Processor covered by heat sink and fan

VRAM chips

This port connects to a monitor

This port, called an S-video port, allows you to connect a TV, stereo, or VCR to your computer

This port, called a Digital Video Interface (DVI) port, allows your computer to connect to a digital flat-panel monitor

VRAM chips

These clip into the motherboard

FIGURE 6.26

Video cards have grown to be very specialized subsystems.

very sophisticated. They include ports allowing you to connect to different video equipment as well as their own RAM, called **video RAM (VRAM)**. Because displaying graphics demands a lot of the CPU, video cards also come with their own processors. Calls to the CPU for graphics processing are redirected to the processor on the video card, significantly speeding up graphics processing.

How can I tell how much VRAM my video card has? The Display Properties dialog box in Windows XP displays the *type* of video card in use on your computer. Unfortunately, it does not display the *amount* of VRAM that the card has. However, the documentation that came with your computer should contain specifications for the video card, including the amount of VRAM it has installed. If you can't find this documentation, check the Web site of your computer's manufacturer or the manufacturer of the video card.

How much VRAM does my video card need? The amount of VRAM your video card needs depends on what you want to display on your monitor. If you only work in Microsoft Word and conduct general Web searching, 16 MB is a realistic minimum. For the serious gamer, a 128-MB or 256-MB video card is essential, allowing games to generate smoother animations. Before purchasing new software, check the specifications to ensure your video card has enough VRAM to handle the load.

What else does the video card do? The video card also controls the number of colors your monitor can display. The number of bits the video card uses to represent each pixel on the monitor (referred to as **bit depth**) determines the color quality of the image displayed. The more bits, the better the color detail of the image. A 4-bit video

card displays 16 colors, the minimum number of colors your system works with (referred to as *Standard* VGA). Most video cards today are 24-bit cards, displaying over 16 million colors. This mode is called *true color mode* (see Figure 6.27).

The most recent generation of video cards can add some great features to your computer if you are a TV fan. Such cards as the ATI All-In-Wonder 9800 Pro can pop open a live TV window on your screen, including features such as picture-in-picture. Using this video card, you can record programs to your hard drive or pause live TV. The card even comes with a wireless remote control.

There are also video cards that allow you to import video. These models have a special video-in port that you can connect to a VHS tape player or an analog video camera. The video is then digitized into a file that is stored on your hard drive. Video editing software, often included with these video cards, enables you to edit, add effects or titles to your original clips, and produce polished versions of your favorite home movies. For more information on digital video editing, see the Technology in Focus feature "Digital Entertainment" on page 174.

So how do I know if I need a new video card? If your monitor takes a while to refresh when editing photos, surfing the Web, or playing a graphics-rich game, the video card could be short on memory. You also may want to upgrade if added features such as television viewing or importing analog video are important to you. Replacing a video card with one with more memory or bit depth is fairly simple: you simply insert the new video card in the correct expansion slot.

MONITORS

How do I evaluate my monitor? You've evaluated your video card to ensure the best display. However, if the monitor is no good, you're still out of luck. As you learned in Chapter 2, there are two types of monitors: cathode-ray tube (CRT) and liquid crystal display (LCD). We discussed in that chapter the factors you need to think about when deciding whether you should buy a CRT or an LCD. If you currently have a CRT monitor and believe the advantages of the LCD are worth the extra money, you may want to upgrade.

Another factor you need to consider in evaluating your monitor is its size. The most

FIGURE 6.27 Bit Depth and Color Quality

Bit Depth	Color Quality Description	Number of Colors Displayed
4-bit	Standard VGA	16
8-bit	256-Color Mode	256
16-bit	High Color	65,536
24-bit	True Color	16,777,216
32-bit	True Color	Over four billion

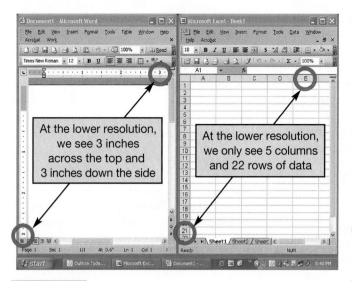

FIGURE 6.28

Here you see the screen display of a 15-inch flat-panel monitor with the resolution set to 800 × 600.

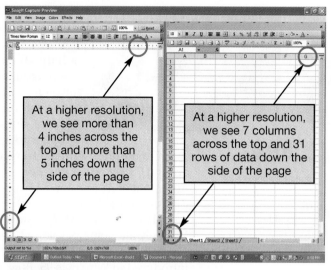

FIGURE 6.29

Here you see the same monitor and same screen display, but the screen resolution has been increased to 1,024 × 768. Notice you can see more of each application.

common monitor sizes are 15, 17, 19, and 21 inches. If your monitor is 15 inches or smaller, you may need to scroll horizontally and vertically to see an entire Web page, for example. Note that monitor size listed for CRT monitors is the diagonal measurement of the tube *before* it's placed in the screen case. The actual viewing size is smaller. LCD monitors are also measured diagonally, but the measurement is equal to the viewing size. Therefore, the viewable area of a 17-inch LCD is approximately equal to the viewable area of a 19-inch CRT. If you have a CRT monitor and want to increase the size of your monitor but can't afford giving up desktop space, you may want to consider buying the same size LCD monitor. If you can't afford to buy a larger screen but want to see more on the screen itself, you can try adjusting the resolution of your monitor.

How would changing my screen resolution help me see more on my screen? Most monitors can display different resolutions. Changing the screen resolution can make a difference in what is displayed. In Figure 6.28, the screen resolution on a 15-inch monitor is set to 800 × 600. Notice that it's difficult to see large portions of Word and Excel when they're both on-screen. In Figure 6.29, the screen resolution on the same monitor has been increased to 1,024 × 768. More of the Word and Excel screens are now visible, making it much easier to simultaneously view both documents. However,

although increasing the screen resolution allows more to be displayed on the monitor, it also makes the images on the screen smaller and perhaps more difficult to read.

How do I change my screen resolution? To change your screen resolution, right-click anywhere on the desktop to display the Display Properties dialog box. Next, left-click the Settings tab. The Screen Resolution section of this dialog box shows your current screen resolution. Left-click the slider bar and drag it to adjust the resolution. Finally, click the Apply button and the monitor resolution will reset itself.

What other features should I look for in a monitor? In Chapter 2, we discussed a number of factors that affect monitor quality, including *refresh rate* (the

FIGURE 6.30 Do You Need to Upgrade Your Video Subsystem?

	Current System	Upgrade Required?
Video Card VRAM		
Monitor Type (CRT or LCD)		
Monitor Size (Viewable Area)		
Monitor Refresh Rate		
Monitor Dot Pitch		

Speaker systems that include a subwoofer have a wider dynamic range that features more bass.

number of times per second the illumination of each pixel on the monitor is recharged) and *dot pitch* (the diagonal distance between pixels of the same color on the screen). For a clearer, brighter image, look for a monitor with a refresh rate of around 75 Hz and a low dot pitch (no more than 0.28 mm for a 17-inch screen or 0.31 mm for a 21-inch screen).

Is it easy to install a new monitor? Virtually all monitors sold today support the *Plug and Play* technology that Microsoft introduced in Windows 95. **Plug and Play**

means that once you've connected the new monitor to your computer and have booted up the system, Windows will automatically recognize the monitor and configure it to work with your system.

Evaluating the Audio Subsystem

Computers output sound by means of speakers and a sound card. For many users, the preinstalled speakers and sound card are adequate for the sounds produced by the computer itself—the beeps and so on that the computer makes. However, if you're listening to music, viewing DVDs, hooking into a household stereo system, or playing games with sophisticated sound tracks, you may want to upgrade your speakers or your sound card.

SPEAKERS

What kinds of computer speakers are available? Two types of speakers ship with most personal computers: amplified speakers (which use external power) or unamplified speakers (which use internal power). Amplified speakers are easy to identify: they come with a separate power transformer and must be plugged into an electrical outlet before they'll function. Unamplified speakers merely plug into the speaker jack on your sound card and require no extra outside power.

Which type of speaker is better? Amplified speakers generally produce better quality sound. However, they usually do not adequately reproduce the low-frequency bass sounds that make gaming and musical scores sound richer and fuller. For better bass sounds, consider purchasing a speaker system that includes a **subwoofer**, a special type of speaker designed to more faithfully reproduce low-frequency sounds (see Figure 6.31).

SOUND CARDS

What does the sound card do? Sound cards, like video cards, are expansion cards that attach to the motherboard inside your system unit. Like the video card that enables your computer to produce images on the monitor, sound cards enable the computer to produce sounds.

Front left speaker

Central speaker

Front right speaker

Subwoofer

Computer system

Side speaker L

Side speaker R

Rear left speaker

Rear right speaker

Dolby Digital 7.1 surround sound gives you better quality audio output.

Can I hook up a surround-sound system to my computer? Most computers ship with a basic sound card, most of which are **3D sound cards**. 3D sound is a technology that advances sound reproduction beyond traditional stereo sound (where the human ear perceives sounds as coming from the left or the right of the performance area). 3D sound is better at convincing the human ear that sound is omnidirectional, meaning you can't tell from which direction the sound is coming. This tends to produce a fuller, richer sound than stereo sound. However, 3D sound is not surround sound.

What is surround sound then? The current surround-sound standard is Dolby Digital 7.1. The 7.1 format takes digital sound from a medium (such as a DVD-ROM) and reproduces it in eight channels. Seven channels cover the listening field with placement to the left front, right front, and center of the audio stage, as well as the left rear and right rear, and then two extra side speakers are added, as shown in Figure 6.32. The eighth channel holds very low-frequency sound data and is sent to a subwoofer, which can be placed anywhere in the room. To set up surround sound on your computer, you need two things: a set of surround-sound speakers and a sound card that is Dolby 7.1 compatible. Dolby 6.1 and 5.1 are also still on the market and have six speakers plus subwoofer or five speakers plus subwoofer, respectively.

How can I tell if the sound card in my computer is Dolby 7.1 compatible? Unfortunately, the device manager in Windows XP does not show the model of sound card installed in your system. To identify your sound card, you'll need to once again consult the documentation that came with your computer or open your computer and search for a name and model number on the sound card. Manufacturers' Web sites usually provide specifications for the various models of sound cards.

I don't need surround sound on my computer. Why else might I need to buy an upgraded sound card? Most basic sound cards contain the following input and output jacks (or ports): microphone in, speaker out, line in, and a

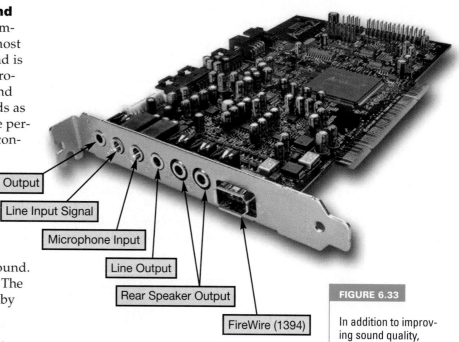

Analog/Digital Output

Line Input Signal

Microphone Input

Line Output

Rear Speaker Output

FireWire (1394)

FIGURE 6.33

In addition to improving sound quality, upgrading sound cards can provide additional jacks for your audio equipment.

gaming port. This allows you to hook up a set of stereo speakers, a microphone, and a joystick. However, what if you want to hook up a right and left speaker individually or attach other audio devices to your computer? To do so, you need more jacks, which are provided on upgraded sound cards like the one shown in Figure 6.33.

With an upgraded sound card, you can connect portable minidisc players, MP3 players, portable jukeboxes, headphones, and CD players to your computer. Musicians also create music on their computers by connecting special devices (such as keyboards) directly to sound card ports.

FIGURE 6.34 Do You Need to Upgrade Your Audio Subsystem?

	Current System	Upgrade Required?
Speakers (Amplified or Unamplified)		
3D Sound Card		
Dolby Digital 5.1, 6.1, or 7.1		
Sufficient Ports?		

Evaluating Port Connectivity

New computer devices are being introduced all the time, and the system you purchased last year may not support the hardware you're interested in today. A **port** is an interface through which external devices are connected to your computer. To evaluate your system's port connectivity, check the camera, camcorder, printer, scanner, and other devices you'd like to be able to connect to your computer and look for what type of port connection they require.

Does your system have the ports necessary to connect to all of these devices?

What types of ports are there? The most common types of ports include serial, parallel, universal serial bus (USB), FireWire, and Ethernet. Each type of port operates at a certain speed, measured in either kilobits per second (Kbps) or megabits per second (Mbps). Figure 6.35 lists the basic characteristics of these ports.

The **serial port** allows the transfer of data, one bit at a time, over a single wire at speeds of up to 56 Kbps. Typical devices that still connect to serial ports include external modems and PDA cradles. Traditional serial

---

FIGURE 6.35 Ports and Their Uses

Port Name	Port Shape	Connector Shape	Data Transfer Speed	Typical Devices Attached to Port
Legacy Technologies				
Serial	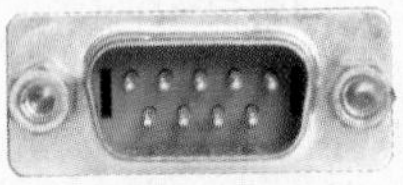	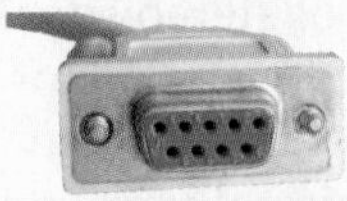	56 Kbps	Mice External modems
Parallel	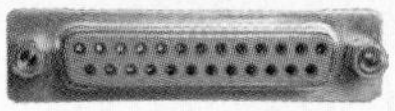	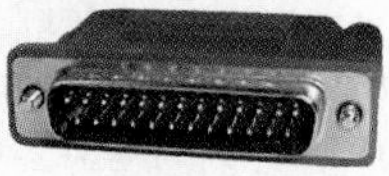	12 Mbps (12,000 Kbps)	Printers External Zip drives
USB 1.1			12 Mbps	Mice Keyboards External Zip drives Printers Scanners Game controllers
New Technologies				
USB 2.0		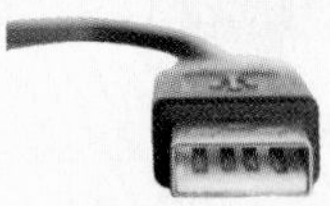	480 Mbps	Same as USB 1.1, but at faster transfer rates Also suitable for camcorders and digital cameras Maintains backward compatibility with USB 1.1
FireWire/FireWire 800			480 Mbps/ 800 Mbps	Digital video camcorders Digital cameras
Ethernet/Gigabit Ethernet			Up to 100 Mbps/ Up to 1,000 Mbps	Network connections Cable modems

---

ports are slowly being phased out by faster ports, such as the USB port.

A **parallel port** sends data between devices in *groups* of bits and is therefore much faster than a serial port. Parallel ports have traditionally been used to connect printers and scanners to computers. Today, most parallel ports achieve data transfer rates of 12 Mbps, much faster than the serial port. Despite this speed increase, parallel ports are becoming less popular now in favor of even higher speed ports.

The **universal serial bus (USB) port** is fast becoming the most common port on computers today. The original USB (version 1.1) port could transfer data at only 12 Mbps. However, in 2002, USB version 2 (USB 2.0) was released, increasing throughput to 480 Mbps. Printers, scanners, digital cameras, keyboards, mice and hard disk drives can all be connected to the computer using USB ports.

The **FireWire port** (previously called the **IEEE 1394 port**) is based on a standard developed by the Institute of Electrical and Electronics Engineers (IEEE). Until the introduction of USB 2.0, FireWire was the fastest port available, with a transfer rate of 400 Mbps. Today, it is most commonly used to connect digital video devices (such as digital cameras) or hard drives to the computer.

The **Ethernet port** (technically called an RJ-45 jack) is used to connect your computer to a local network or cable modem. Because one of the most common uses of RJ-45 jacks is for connecting Ethernet networks, it is often referred to simply as an Ethernet jack. Ethernet originally offered a transfer rate of 10 Mbps. Fast Ethernet (called 100Base-T), with a transfer rate of 100 Mbps, is the standard used in most personal computers today.

If you have a network that needs to transfer lots of large files such as video files, Gigabit Ethernet networking would be useful. Gigabit Ethernet can transfer at a rate up to 1,000 Mbps.

Are there any other kinds of ports? In addition to the more common ports, you may also need more specialized ports, such as IrDA, Bluetooth, and MIDI.

The **IrDA port** (shown in Figure 6.36) is based on a standard developed by the

Infrared Data Association for transmitting data. IrDA ports enable you to transmit data between two devices by using infrared light waves. IrDA ports have a maximum throughput of 4 Mbps and require that a line of sight be maintained between the two ports. Many printers, laptops, and PDAs include IrDA ports. If a printer and a laptop both have IrDA ports, the laptop can send a file to the printer without being physically connected to it.

Bluetooth technology uses radio waves to send data over short distances (see Figure 6.37). The maximum transfer rate of the original Bluetooth 1.0 is 1 Mbps. The newer standard Bluetooth 2.0 is three times faster, with a maximum transfer rate of 3 Mbps. Many laptops and PDAs include a small Bluetooth chip that allows them to transfer data wirelessly to any other device with a Bluetooth chip, such as a cell phone, PDA, or Bluetooth-enabled keyboard

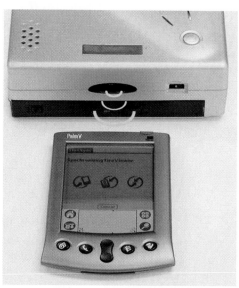

FIGURE 6.36

IrDA ports enable you to transmit data between devices without using wires.

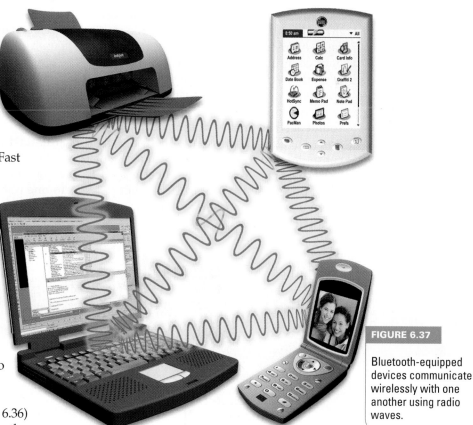

FIGURE 6.37

Bluetooth-equipped devices communicate wirelessly with one another using radio waves.

FIGURE 6.38

MIDI ports enable you to connect your computer to musical devices such as synthesizers.

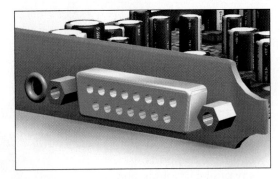

or mouse. The advantage of Bluetooth devices is that a clear line of sight isn't needed between the two devices, although the distance between the devices is limited to about 30 feet.

The other wireless transmission standards, WiFi and IrDA, differ slightly from Bluetooth. WiFi is designed to cover much longer distances and to allow much faster data transfer, up to 54 Mbps. Although WiFi is a great way to connect your laptop from the back porch to the PC in the upstairs bedroom, Bluetooth is a better solution for a short-distance connection, such as from a wireless keyboard to the system unit. IrDA uses infrared waves but, unlike Bluetooth, it requires that a line of sight exist between two devices to connect them.

A **MIDI port** (see Figure 6.38) is a port that allows you to connect electronic musical instruments (such as synthesizers) to your computer. Musical Instrument Digital Interface (MIDI) is a standard adopted by the music industry that provides for capturing specific data about a sound such as pitch, duration, and volume. That data is transferred between the computer and the MIDI device at a rate of 31.5 Kbps. In addition to synthesizers, MIDI ports also work with electronic drum machines and other electronically adapted instruments.

ADDING PORTS: EXPANSION CARDS AND HUBS

What if I don't have all the ports I need? New port standards are developed every few years, and special expansion cards are usually the only way to add the newest ports to an older computer or to expand the number of ports on your computer. For example, your computer may have only one USB port, but you may have several devices that connect to the computer with USB connectors. Just as sound cards and video cards provide ports for sound and video equipment to connect to the computer, there are also expansion cards that you can install in your system unit to provide you with additional ports (such as USB and FireWire). Like the other expansion cards, these cards clip into an open expansion slot on the motherboard. Figure 6.39 shows an example of such an expansion card.

What if there are no open slots on the motherboard for me to insert an expansion card? If there are no open slots on the motherboard and you still need extra ports, you can add an *expansion hub* (shown in Figure 6.40). An **expansion hub** is a device that connects to one port, such as a USB port, to provide four or eight new ports, similar to a multiplug extension cord you use with electrical appliances. You also can connect multiple USB devices through a single USB port by connecting the devices together in a *daisy chain*. In a daisy chain, you attach one device to another through its USB port, with the last device connecting to a USB port on the computer.

FIGURE 6.39

This expansion card provides your computer with additional ports.

USB

FireWire

If you don't have enough USB ports to support your USB devices, consider getting an expansion hub, which can add four or eight USB ports to your system.

Which devices benefit most from high-speed ports? Any device that requires the transfer of large amounts of data significantly benefits from using a high-speed port such as a FireWire or USB 2.0 port. For example, digital video cameras produce large files that need to be transferred to a computer. If your video camera has a FireWire port but your computer doesn't, investing in a FireWire expansion port would definitely be worth the cost (about $40) based on the time you'll save during downloads.

Is there a limit to the number of ports I can add? Using expansion hubs, you can expand your computer so that it can handle more USB and FireWire devices. For installation of other ports, you're limited by the number of open expansion slots in your computer. Most computer users won't need more than one or two FireWire ports and four USB ports, a number that you can easily achieve using expansion hubs and cards.

You also can add ports to an empty drive bay, giving you easy-to-reach new ports. The Koutech 10-in-1, shown in Figure 6.41, fits into a regular drive bay and adds front-panel access to two USB 2.0 ports, two FireWire ports, three audio jacks, and a 6-in-1 digital media card reader.

Which port should I use when I have a choice? Obviously, the fastest port is preferable but may not always be possible or cost effective. For example, most currently produced ink-jet printers offer the option of connecting by a parallel port or USB port. Because USB ports are faster, your printer will perform better if you connect it to a USB port. However, if you don't have an available USB port and you don't want to buy an expansion hub or card, you can connect the printer to a parallel port instead.

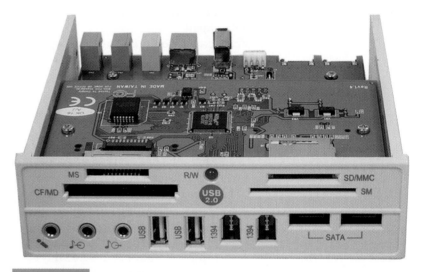

You also can use an empty drive bay to add additional ports and even a flash card reader to the front panel of the system unit.

ACTIVE HELPDESK

Evaluating Your Storage Subsystem and Ports

In this Active Helpdesk call, you'll play the role of a Helpdesk staffer, fielding calls about the computer's storage devices and ports.

FIGURE 6.42 Do You Need More Ports?	Current System	Upgrade Required?
Number of USB (1.1 or 2.0) Ports		
Number of FireWire Ports		
Number of Ethernet Ports		
IrDA Port Included?		
Bluetooth Included?		
MIDI Port Included?		

Evaluating System Reliability

Many computer users decide to buy a new system not necessarily because they need a faster CPU, more RAM, or a bigger hard drive, but because they are experiencing problems, such as slow performance, freezes, and crashes. Over time, your computer builds up excess files and becomes internally disorganized just from normal everyday use. This excess clutter and disorganization can lead to failing performance, or worse, system failure. Therefore, before you buy a new system because you think yours may be unreliable, make sure the problem is not one you can fix. Proper upkeep and maintenance also may postpone an expensive system upgrade or replacement.

What can I do to ensure my system performs reliably? There are several procedures you can follow to ensure your system performs reliably:

1. Clean out your Startup folder. Some programs install themselves into your Startup folder and are automatically run each time the computer reboots, whether you are using them or not. This unnecessary load causes extra stress on RAM. Check your Startup folder by clicking on Start, All Programs, and then click on the Startup folder and make sure all the programs listed are important to you. Right-click on any unnecessary program and select Delete to remove it from the Startup folder. Make sure you delete *only* programs you know for sure are unnecessary.

2. Clear out unnecessary files. Temporary Internet files can accumulate very quickly on your hard drive, taking up unnecessary space. Running the Disk Cleanup utility is a quick and easy way to ensure your temporary Internet files don't take up precious hard drive space. Likewise, you should delete any unnecessary files from your hard drive regularly, because they can make your hard drive run slower.

3. Run an antispyware program as well as an antiadware program. These often detect and remove different pests and should be used in addition to your regular antivirus package.

4. Run the Disk Defragmenter utility on your hard drive. When your hard drive becomes fragmented, its storage capacity is negatively impacted. When you defrag your hard drive, files are reorganized, making the hard drive work more efficiently. For more complete coverage of the Disk Defragmenter, refer to Chapter 5.

My system crashes often during the day. What can I do? Computer systems are complex. It's not unusual to have your system stop responding occasionally. If rebooting the computer doesn't help, you'll need to begin troubleshooting:

1. Make sure you have installed any new software or hardware properly. If you're using a PC, use the System Restore utility in Windows XP to "roll back" to a time when the system worked more reliably.

2. If you see an error code in Windows, visit the Microsoft Knowledge Base (**http://support.microsoft.com**), an online resource for resolving problems with Microsoft products. This may help you determine what the error code indicates and how you may be able to solve the problem.

3. Check that you have enough RAM. Often, systems with insufficient amounts of RAM crash.

Can my software affect my system reliability? Having the latest version of software products makes your system much more reliable. You should upgrade or update your operating system, browser software, and application software as often as new patches (or fixes) are reported for resolving errors. Sometimes these errors are performance-related; sometimes they're tied to maintaining better security for your system.

How do I know whether updates are available for my software? You can configure Windows XP so that it automatically checks for, downloads, and installs any available updates for itself and for Internet Explorer. In addition, products such as McAfee's Oil Change enable you to sort through numerous Web sites and quickly find the bug fixes for most application software.

Computers in Society: How to Donate Your Old Computer Safely

What happened to your last computer? If you threw it away hoping it would be safely recycled with your empty Coke cans, think again. Mercury in screens, cadmium in batteries and circuit boards, and flame retardant in plastic housing are all toxic, as are the four to eight pounds of lead in the cathode-ray tube of nearly every monitor. An alarming trend emerging is that discarded machines are beginning to create an e-waste crisis.

Instead of throwing your computer away, you may be able to donate it to a nonprofit organization. Some manufacturers such as Dell are now offering recycling programs and have formed alliances with nonprofit organizations to help distribute your old technology to those who need it.

If neither of these solutions work for you, you can take your computer to an authorized computer recycling center in your area (find a local one at **www.usedcomputer.com**). You may have to pay a small recycling fee, but it is worth it because you're helping protect the environment.

However, before donating or recycling a computer, make sure you carefully remove all data from your hard drive, or you may end up having your good deed turn bad, making you the victim of identity theft. What type of information is stored on a hard drive that could cause you troubles? Credit card numbers, bank information, social security numbers, tax records, passwords, and PIN numbers are just a few of the pieces of sensitive information that we casually record to our computer's hard drive.

Most people know that when they get rid of their computers, just deleting their files is not protection enough. But did you know that even if you reformat your hard drive, it's still not totally wiped clean? That's because when data is deleted from the hard drive—even through the reformatting process—only

the *link* to the data is removed. The data remains on the hard drive until it is written over by more data.

In early 2003, two MIT graduate students proved how much personal financial data is left on hard drives that are on the secondary sale market. They bought over 150 used hard drives from various sources. Although some of the hard drives were reformatted or damaged so the data was supposedly irrecoverable, the two students were able to retrieve medical records, financial information, pornography, personal e-mails, and over 5,000 credit card numbers!

What can you do to protect yourself without putting your hard disk drive through a metal shredder? The United States Department of Defense suggests a seven-layer overwrite for a "secure erase." That is, they suggest that you fill your hard drive *seven times over* with a random series of ones and zeros. Fortunately, several software programs are available that provide secure hard drive erasures, either of specific files on your hard drive or of the entire hard drive. Examples of these programs include Active@KillDisk, Eraser, CyberScrub, Wipe for Linux, and Shredit X for OS X.

Keep in mind that even these data erasure software programs can't provide the ultimate level in security. Computer forensic specialists or supercybercriminals can still manage to retrieve some data from your hard drive with the right tools. The ultimate level of protection is to destroy the hard drive altogether. Suggested methods include drilling holes in the hard drive, burning/melting the hard drive, or just taking an old-fashioned sledgehammer to it! Still, with a bit of common sense and some careful use of software, you can make your old computer a helpful gift instead of a source of pollution.

What if none of this helps? Is buying a new system my only option? If your system is still unreliable after these changes, you have two options:

1. Reinstall the operating system. To do so, you'll want to back up all of your data files before the installation and be prepared to reinstall your software after the installation. Make sure you have all of the original discs for the software installed on your system, along with the product keys, serial numbers, or other activation codes so that you can reinstall them.

2. Upgrade your operating system to the latest version. There are substantial increases in reliability with each major release of a new operating system. However, upgrading the operating sys-

tem may require hardware upgrades. Be sure to examine the *recommended* (not required) specifications of the new operating system.

Making the Final Decision

Now that you have evaluated your computer system, you need to shift to questions of *value*. How closely does your system come to meeting your needs? How much would it cost to upgrade the system you have to match what you'd ideally like your computer to do? How much would it cost to purchase a new system that meets these specifications?

To decide which option (upgrading or buying a new system) has better value for you, you need to price both scenarios. Figure 6.43 provides an upgrade worksheet you can use to evaluate both the upgrade path and the new purchase path. Be sure to consider what benefit you might obtain by having two systems, if you were to buy a new computer. Would you have a use for the older system? Would you donate it to a charitable organization? Would you be able to give it to a family member? Purchasing a new system is an important investment of your resources and you want to make a well-reasoned, well-supported decision.

FIGURE 6.43 **Upgrade vs. New Purchase Comparison Worksheet**

Needs	Hardware Upgrade Cost	Included on a New System?	Additional Expense for Item if It Is Not Included on a New System
CPU and Memory Subsystems			
CPU Upgrade			
RAM Upgrade			
Storage Subsystem			
Hard Disk Upgrade			
Zip Drive			
CD-R/CD-RW Drive			
DVD-ROM Drive			
DVD-RW Drive			
Flash Card Reader			
Other Storage Device			
Video and Audio Subsystems			
New Monitor			
Video Card Upgrade			
Speaker Upgrade			
Sound Card Upgrade			
Port Connectivity			
USB 1.1 or 2.0 Ports			
FireWire Port			
Ethernet Port			
IrDA Port			
Bluetooth Port			
MIDI Port			

1. How can I determine whether I should upgrade my existing computer or buy a new one?

To determine whether you need to upgrade or purchase a new system, you need to define your ideal system and what it can do. Then, you need to perform a system evaluation to assess the subsystems in your computer, including the CPU, memory, storage, video, audio, and ports. Last, you need to determine if it's economically practical to upgrade or whether buying a new computer would be best.

2. What does the CPU do and how can I evaluate its performance?

Your computer's CPU processes instructions, performs calculations, manages the flow of information through a computer system, and is responsible for processing into information the data you input. It is composed of two units: the arithmetic logic unit and the control unit. CPU speed is measured in megahertz or gigahertz, or millions or billions of machine cycles a second. A machine cycle is the process the CPU goes through to fetch, decode, execute, and store data. You can tell whether your CPU is limiting your system performance by watching how busy it is as you work on your computer. The percentage of time that your CPU is working is referred to as CPU usage, which you can determine by checking the Task Manager.

3. How does memory work in my computer and how can I evaluate how much memory I need?

RAM is your computer's short-term memory. It remembers everything that the computer needs to process data into information. However, it is an example of volatile storage. When the power is off, the data stored in RAM is cleared out. The amount of RAM sitting on memory modules in your computer is your computer's physical memory. The memory your OS uses is kernel memory. At a minimum, you need enough RAM to run the OS plus the software applications you're using, plus a bit more to hold the data you're inputting.

4. What are the computer's main storage devices and how can I evaluate whether they match my needs?

Storage devices for a typical computer system include a hard disk drive, floppy drive, Zip drive, and CD/DVD drives. When you turn off your computer, the data stored in these devices is saved. These devices are therefore referred to as nonvolatile storage devices. Hard drives have the largest storage capacity of any storage device and the fastest access time and data transfer rate of all nonvolatile storage options. Floppy disks have a storage capacity of 1.44 MB, Zip disks have capacities up to 750 MB, and CDs and DVDs have capacities from 700 MB to 9.4 GB. Portable flash drives allow easy transfer of 1 GB or more of data from machine to machine. To determine the storage capacity your system needs, calculate the amount of storage your software needs to reside on your computer. To add more storage, or to provide more functionality for your system, you can install additional drives, either internally or externally.

5. What components affect the output of video on my computer and how can I evaluate whether they are meeting my needs?

How video is displayed depends on two components: your video card and monitor. A video card translates binary data into the images you see. These cards include their own RAM (VRAM) as well as ports that allow you to connect to video equipment. The amount of VRAM you need depends on what you want to display on the monitor. If you only work in Microsoft Word and surf the Web, 16 MB is enough. More powerful cards allow you to play graphics-intense games and multimedia. Your moni-

tor's size, resolution, refresh rate, and dot pitch all affect how well the monitor performs. For a clearer, brighter image, buy a monitor with a high refresh rate and a low dot pitch.

6. What components affect the quality of sound on my computer and how can I evaluate whether they are meeting my needs?

Your computer's sound depends on your speakers and sound card. Two types of speakers ship with most computers: amplified speakers and unamplified speakers. If you're listening to music, viewing DVDs, or playing games, you may want to have speakers with a subwoofer. Sound cards enable the computer to produce sounds. Users upgrade their sound cards to provide for 3D sound, surround sound, as well as additional ports for audio equipment.

7. What are the ports available on desktop computers and how can I determine what ports I need?

A port is an interface through which external devices connect to the computer. Common ports include serial, parallel, universal serial bus (USB), FireWire, and

Ethernet, whereas specialized ports include IrDA, Bluetooth, and MIDI. To evaluate your port connectivity, check the devices you'd like to connect to your computer and look for what type of port they require. If your system doesn't have enough ports, you can add ports through expansion cards (which you install in your system unit) and expansion hubs (which connect to your system through a port).

8. How can I ensure the reliability of my system?

Many computer users decide to buy a new system because they are experiencing problems with their computer. However, before you buy a new system because you think yours may be unreliable, make sure the problem is not one you can fix. Make sure you have installed any new software or hardware properly, check that you have enough RAM, run system utilities such as Disk Defragmenter and Disk Cleanup, clean out your Startup folder, remove unnecessary files from your system, and keep your software updated with patches. If you continue to have troubles with your system, reinstall or upgrade your OS, and, of course, seek technical assistance.

Buzz Words

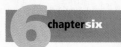

Word Bank

- access time
- Bluetooth
- CD-RW drive
- CPU
- expansion card
- expansion hub

- FireWire
- hard drive
- LCD
- monitor
- motherboard
- RAM

- sound card
- subwoofer
- system evaluation
- upgrading
- USB
- Zip drive

Instructions: Fill in the blanks using the words from the Word Bank above.

Joe already has a PC but just heard about a great deal on a new one. He decides to perform a(n) (1) _____ on his computer to see whether he should keep it or buy the new one. First, he right-clicks the My Computer icon to check his System Properties. By doing so, he can check what (2) _____ is in his computer. He sees he has a Pentium 4 processor running at 2.8 GHz. Next, he checks his internal memory, or (3) _____. He then turns to the Task Manager to evaluate his CPU and RAM usage to see if he needs to add more RAM should he keep his PC.

He continues to evaluate his system by checking out what components he has and what he'll need. He notes the storage capacity of the (4) _____ . Recently, he has been using a(n) (5) _____ to store files because his hard drive is nearing capacity. But the (6) _____ , or the amount of time it takes for the disk to find the right data, is so slow that the larger hard drive of a new computer is appealing. Joe also notes that he is unable to download large files from the Internet and save them onto a CD like his friends do. His current system does not have a(n) (7) _____ with which to burn CDs, but the new system would. The new system would also include speakers with a(n) (8) _____ to improve the sound. He also sees that it would include a(n) (9) _____ that would allow him to connect more of his audio equipment to his PC.

Joe's 15-inch (10) _____ doesn't fit well on his desktop, and having a(n) (11) _____ monitor would conserve space. He also knows that if he wants to attach more devices to his PC in the future, he'll need more (12) _____ ports, because his current system has only a few of these faster ports. He notes, however, that it may be just as cost effective to install a(n) (13) _____ in his system to give it more ports or to buy a(n) (14) _____ he could attach to his system unit to add more ports. Finally, Joe considers the cost of buying the new computer versus (15) _____ his current system. He realizes it's more economical right now to keep his current system.

Becoming Computer Fluent

Jen lives across the hall from you. She heard you worry last semester that your PC wasn't fast enough. Between the simulation program for math, the reports you did for English, and your programming class, your computer was running slowly and you were out of storage space. She's offered to help you upgrade your system but needs you to tell her what you want upgraded and why.

Instructions: Using the preceding scenario, write a letter to Jen using key terms from the chapter. Be sure your sentences are grammatically correct and technically meaningful.

Instructions: Answer the multiple choice and true/false questions below for more practice with key terms and concepts from this chapter.

MULTIPLE CHOICE

1. Processor speed is measured in which of the following?
   a. megabytes
   b. gigahertz
   c. gigabytes
   d. None of the above

2. Upgrading your system by replacing your CPU
   a. guarantees you better processing performance
   b. guarantees you better system performance
   c. guarantees that the hard drive access time will improve
   d. All of the above

3. Which is an example of volatile storage?
   a. ROM
   b. hard disk drive
   c. RAM
   d. flash drive

4. The amount of RAM that is actually sitting on memory modules in your computer is your computer's
   a. physical memory
   b. kernel memory
   c. page usage memory
   d. page file memory

5. The hard drive's access time is
   a. the fastest of all permanent storage devices
   b. measured in milliseconds
   c. the time it takes it to locate its stored data and make it available for processing
   d. All of the above

6. Zip disks are not examples of optical storage because
   a. they can hold megabytes of data
   b. they use magnetized film to record 1s and 0s
   c. they are not round and shiny
   d. they are thicker than floppy disks

7. Flash memory storage is available as
   a. Sony Memory Sticks
   b. compact flash cards
   c. flash or jump drives
   d. All of the above

8. VRAM, or the RAM on a video card, is
   a. always the same as the amount of RAM in the system
   b. always the same speed as the system RAM
   c. used for virtual memory if system RAM gets full
   d. used to ensure high-quality images

9. Which of the following is the fastest port?
   a. Parallel port
   b. FireWire port
   c. USB 2.0 port
   d. Ethernet port

10. To ensure your system runs reliably, you can
    a. run the disk defragmenter utility
    b. clean out your startup folder
    c. clear out unnecessary files on your hard drive
    d. All of the above

TRUE/FALSE

_____ 1. In a well-designed computer system, the CPU is always operating near 100 percent utilization.

_____ 2. If you try to run a set of programs that demand more memory than you have, space on the hard disk drive will be used to make up the difference.

_____ 3. The System Properties dialog box tells you what kind of CPU is installed but not how fast it can process data.

_____ 4. DVDs are unlike CDs and cannot be written to but instead provide read-only storage of data.

_____ 5. If you need more USB 2.0 ports, you can add an extension hub and have several new USB ports free to use.

Making the Transition to...
Next Semester

1. Evaluating Your System

A small worksheet follows the end of each section in this chapter to guide you as you evaluate your own system. These smaller worksheets have been combined into one complete worksheet that is on the book's companion Web site (**www.prenhall.com/techinaction**). Download the worksheet and fill it in based on the computer you are currently using when taking this class.

a. Research the costs of replacement parts for those components you feel should be upgraded.

b. Research the cost of a new system that would be roughly equivalent to your current computer *after* upgrades.

c. Determine whether it would be more cost effective to upgrade your computer or buy a new one.

2. Your Software Needs

What software do you need for the courses you're taking this semester? Will you need any different software for next semester? How many of these software applications do you run at one time? Examine the specs for those software packages. Prepare a table that lists the software applications you are currently using as well as any you may need to use in the future. For each, list the minimum RAM and hard disk space requirements. How does your system measure up against those requirements?

3. Campus Computer Use

What kinds of computers do students use in college and how do different people budget for their computer needs? To find an answer to these questions, interview several college students in different years of school. Ask them the following questions:

a. Did you need your own computing equipment or did you use your college's equipment when you first started school? Would you recommend I do the same?

b. Did you need to upgrade your computer *before* you came to college? How did you do this?

c. Was the computer you used in your first year of college able to handle your workload in later years?

d. If you used one computer, what upgrades did you need to perform?

e. If you had to buy a new computer, how much money did you budget and how much did you spend? What did you do with your old computer?

4. Buying Computers Online

Visit an online seller of computer systems and components (such as **www.coolcomputing.com**, **www.pricewatch.com**, **www.zdnet.com**, **www.tigerdirect.com**, or **www.campusdirect.com**) and answer the following questions:

a. What is the current cost of RAM?

b. How much additional RAM could you add to your system?

c. What are the prices of the most popular CPU upgrades?

d. How much would you need to spend to upgrade to a new operating system?

e. How would each of these help you in your work?

5. Comparing Monitor Specs

You have many different options regarding monitors. Using the Web, research several different monitors. Make sure you have both CRT and LCD monitors on your list. Compare specifications for all monitors, including screen size, size of viewable area, refresh rate, dot pitch, and cost. From your list, narrow down to the one monitor you would choose to add to your system tand explain why.

Making the Transition to...
The Workplace

1. Using Your Computer for Education and Business

As you move from an educational environment to a business environment, how you use your computer will inevitably change. Write a paragraph or two describing what your computer system is like now. Then write a paragraph or two describing what your ideal computer system would be like after you've graduated and have entered the workforce. What different components, if any, would your system need? Could you upgrade your current system to incorporate these new components, or would you need to buy a new system? Make sure you defend either position you take with information covered in this chapter. Fill out the worksheet similar to Figure 6.3 that is available on the book's companion Web site (**www.prenhall.com/techinaction**) to help you in your decision.

2. Assessing Memory Use

Your home office computer is running a bit sluggish, and you want to determine which application is the memory hog so you can either avoid using it or use it without any other programs running to preserve RAM. You've been told you can do this in the Processes tab in the Task Manager utility. On your computer, open the Task Manager utility and determine which application currently running is using the most memory. Can you tell how much it is using? Note that because the names of the programs have been shortened (for example, Microsoft Word is referred to as winword.exe), you may not immediately recognize the program names.

3. IT Support at Work

When you are evaluating potential employers, one consideration will be how well they support you as an employee and provide the environment you need to do productive work. What questions would you ask in an interview to determine what kind of Information Technology (IT) support you can expect in your new position?

4. Web Programming Software at Home

You are a Web programmer and you often work from home. You need to investigate whether your home computer would be able to run three programs you use most frequently at work: Adobe PhotoShop, Microsoft Visual Basic, and Microsoft Word. Use the Web to research RAM and hard disk requirements for these programs. Will your computer be able to handle the load?

5. Build an Ideal System

Imagine that a client tells you she wants a system that has at least 512 MB of RAM, the fastest processor on the market, and enough storage space to edit hours of video and music files. Price three systems that would meet the client's needs by visiting manufacturer Web sites such as **www.dell.com**, **www.gateway.com**, and **www.alienware.com**. Make a final selection and justify why this is the best solution.

Critical Thinking Questions

Instructions: Albert Einstein used "Gedanken experiments," or critical thinking questions, to develop his theory of relativity. Some ideas are best understood by experimenting with them in our own minds. The following critical thinking questions are designed to demand your full attention but require only a comfortable chair—no technology.

1. Your Ideal System

If you could buy any new system on the market, not worrying about the price, what would you buy? What kind of monitor would you have? How much RAM and CPU? Would you know how to use your ideal system?

2. Future Systems

Given current trends in technology, what kind of system can you imagine upgrading to or buying new in 10 years? Which components would change the most? Which components would need to stay the same, if any? What do you imagine the entire system would look like?

3. Portable Storage Solutions

Some newer computers do not include a floppy disk drive as standard. This is in response to many users requiring portable storage media to hold larger files that cannot fit on a floppy. What other solutions are possible? Are there reasons why floppy disks are still a viable means of portable storage?

4. Impacts of New Technology

We are constantly being bombarded with new technology. We hear of new tools and system improvements from our friends, relatives, and advertisements almost daily. This chapter talks about upgrading current systems so that we can take advantage of some of the newer technology. Some improvements we absolutely need (more RAM, perhaps), others we may just really want (such as an LCD monitor). What do you think are the societal, economic, and environmental impacts of our wanting to have the latest and greatest computers? Do you think the push toward faster and more powerful machines is a good thing?

5. New Technologies: Putting Industries at Risk?

The Trends in IT feature in this chapter discusses the impact DVD and CD technology has had on the music and entertainment industries. Can you think of other industries that might be at risk because of these new technologies?

6. Recycling Computers

Mercury in screens and switches, cadmium in batteries and circuit boards, and the four to eight pounds of lead in CRT monitors are all toxic. Discarded machines are beginning to create an e-waste crisis. Who do you think should assume the cost of recycling computers? The consumer, the government, the industry? What other options are there besides just throwing older computers away?

7. System Longevity

If you purchase a computer system for business purposes, the IRS allows you to depreciate its cost over three years. The IRS considers this a reasonable estimate of the useful lifetime of a computer system. What do you think most home users expect in terms of how long their computer systems should last? How does the purchase of a computer system compare with other major household appliances in terms of cost, value, benefit, life span, and upgrade potential?

Problem:

In a large organization, whether it is a company or a college, the IT department often has to install several different types of computing systems. There certainly would be advantages to having every computer be identical, but because different departments have different needs, and items are purchased at different times, it is typical for there to be significant differences between two computers in the same corporation.

Process:

Split your class into teams.

1. Select a department or computer lab on campus (or within your company, at the public library, and so on). Note: If you physically cannot go to the various labs, describe the type of components that would be needed by that particular department. (For example, if you choose the computer art department, you know you would need good graphics software. You also know you would need certain levels of RAM, and so forth, to accommodate that graphics software.)

2. Following the worksheet in Figure 6.3, analyze the computing needs of that particular department.

3. Using the System Evaluation worksheet (found on the book's companion Web site at **www.prenhall.com/techinaction**), develop a complete systems evaluation of the computers at the lab.

4. Consider possible upgrades in hardware, software, and peripherals that would make this lab better able to meet the needs of its users.

5. Write a report that summarizes your findings. If purchasing a new system is more economical, recommend which system the lab should buy.

Conclusion:

The pace of technological change can make computer science an uncomfortable field for some. For others, it is precisely the pace of change that is exciting. Being able to evaluate a computer system and match it to the current needs of its users is an important skill.

Multimedia

In addition to the review materials presented here, you'll find additional materials featured with the book's multimedia, including the *Technology in Action* Student Resource CD and the Companion Web site (**www.prenhall.com/techinaction**), which will help reinforce your understanding of the chapter content. These materials include the following:

ACTIVE HELPDESK

In Active Helpdesk calls, you'll assume the role of a Helpdesk operator taking calls about the concepts you've learned in this chapter. You'll apply what you've learned and receive feedback from a supervisor to review and reinforce those concepts. The Active Helpdesk calls for this chapter are listed here and can be found on your Student Resource CD:

- Evaluating Your CPU and RAM
- Evaluating Your Storage Subsystem and Ports

SOUND BYTES

Sound Bytes are dynamic multimedia tutorials that help demystify even the most complex topics. You'll view video clips and animations that illustrate computer concepts, and then apply what you've learned by reviewing with the Sound Byte Labs, which include quizzes and activities specifically tailored to each Sound Byte. The Sound Bytes for this chapter are listed here and can be found on your Student Resource CD and on the Companion Web site (**www.prenhall.com/techinaction**):

- Questions to Ask Before You Buy a Computer
- Using Windows XP to Evaluate CPU Performance
- Memory Hierarchy Interactive
- Installing RAM
- Hard Disk Anatomy Interactive
- CD and DVD Reading and Writing Interactive
- Installing a CD-RW Drive
- Port Tour: How Do I Hook It Up?
- Letting Your Computer Clean Up After Itself

COMPANION WEB SITE

The *Technology in Action* Companion Web site includes a variety of additional materials to help you review and learn more about the topics in this chapter. The resources available at **www.prenhall.com/techinaction** include:

- **Online Study Guide.** Each chapter features an online true/false and multiple-choice quiz. You can take these quizzes, automatically check the results, and e-mail the results to your instructor.
- **Web Research Projects.** Each chapter features a number of Web research projects that ask you to search the Web for information on computer-related careers, milestones in computer history, important people and companies, emerging technologies, and the applications and implications of different technologies.

Computing | Alternatives

You may think that there are just no viable alternatives to buying computers running Microsoft Windows and using Microsoft Office applications like Word and Excel. However, in this Technology in Focus feature, we explore software and hardware alternatives to Microsoft products that may provide you with cheaper and more flexible options. Let's get started by looking at alternatives to Microsoft Office products.

Application Software Alternatives

Commercial (proprietary) software is developed by corporations such as Microsoft to be sold for a profit. Opponents of proprietary software contend that software should be developed without profit motive and that the source code (the actual lines of instructional code that make the program work) should be made available so that others may modify or improve the software. **Open-source software** is freely distributed (no royalties accrue to the creators), contains the source code, and can in turn be distributed to others. Therefore, you can download open-source software for free from various Web sites, install it on as many computers as you wish, and redistribute it to anyone you wish (as long as you don't charge for distributing it). In this section, we look at some open-source software that you can download and use on your computer. For a list of open-source resources available on the Web, visit **www.sourceforge.net**.

PRODUCTIVITY SOFTWARE ALTERNATIVES: OPENOFFICE

As mentioned in Chapter 4, OpenOffice is a free suite of productivity software programs that provides similar functionality to Microsoft Office. Versions of OpenOffice are available for a variety of operating systems, including Windows, Linux, and Mac OS X. It currently offers support in over 45 languages, with more being added all the time by the development community. You can download the installation file you'll need to run OpenOffice at **www.openoffice.org.** The minimum system requirements for installing OpenOffice in a Windows environment are:

- A Pentium-compatible PC
- Microsoft Windows 98, NT, 2000, ME, or XP
- 128 MB of RAM
- 200 MB of hard disk space

The main components of OpenOffice are word processor (Writer), spreadsheet (Calc), and presentation (Impress) programs that provide similar functionality to the Word, Excel, and PowerPoint applications you're

familiar with in Microsoft Office. OpenOffice 2.0 now includes a program called Base that allows you to easily create and manipulate database tables.

The great thing about OpenOffice is that it allows you to open files created in Microsoft Office applications. Also, documents created with OpenOffice can be opened by other software programs. This means that if your friend uses Microsoft Office and you send her an OpenOffice file, she can still read it, and you can read all of her Microsoft Office files too. Although the individual applications in OpenOffice are not as full-featured as the ones in Microsoft Office, it is still a very powerful productivity software suite, and the price is right.

When you launch OpenOffice via the quickstart icon (see Figure 1), you are presented with a list of document types to chose from. Once you select the appropriate document type (such as spreadsheet, presentation, or text), the appropiate application will then open so you can begin work.

Writer

Writer, the OpenOffice word processing application, is very similar in look and feel to Microsoft Word. As is the case in Word, you can easily change text appearance in Writer by altering font type, style, alignment, and color. You can also easily insert graphics (pictures or clip art), tables, and hyperlinks into documents. Writer's Auto-Pilot feature provides

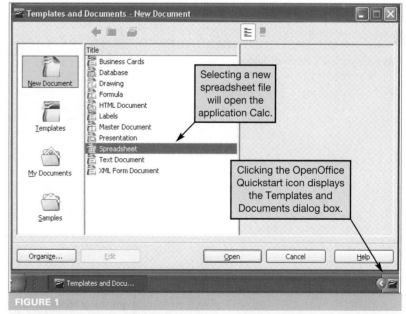

FIGURE 1

The Templates and Documents dialog box in OpenOffice 2.0 allows you to select the type of document you wish to start. The appropriate application will then open.

FIGURE 2

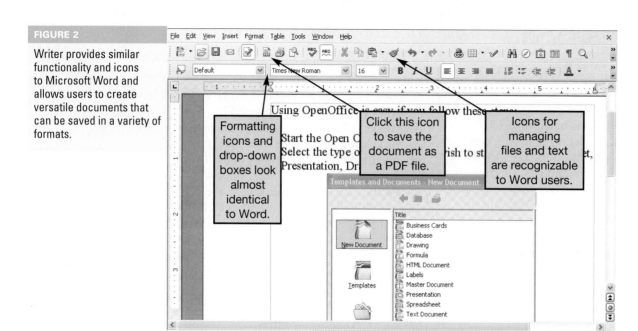

FIGURE 2
Writer provides similar functionality and icons to Microsoft Word and allows users to create versatile documents that can be saved in a variety of formats.

Formatting icons and drop-down boxes look almost identical to Word.

Click this icon to save the document as a PDF file.

Icons for managing files and text are recognizable to Word users.

you with a number of templates you can use to create standard documents such as faxes, memos, and letters. And using special tools in Writer you can also create bibliographic references, indexes, and a table of contents.

When saving a document in Writer, the default file format has an .swx extension. But by using the Save As command, you can save files in other formats, such as Word (.doc), Rich Text (.rtf), plain text (.txt), and HTML (.htm). The handy "Export Directly as PDF" icon in Writer allows you to save documents as PDF files (see Figure 2).

Calc

Opening a blank spreadsheet with Calc is just like starting one in Microsoft Excel. Once you open a spreadsheet, you enter text, numbers, and formulas into the appropriate cells. You can also apply a full range of formatting options (font size, color, style, and so on) to the cells, making it easy to create documents such as the monthly budget spreadsheet shown in Figure 3. Built-in formulas and functions simplify the job of creating spreadsheets, and as with Writer, a

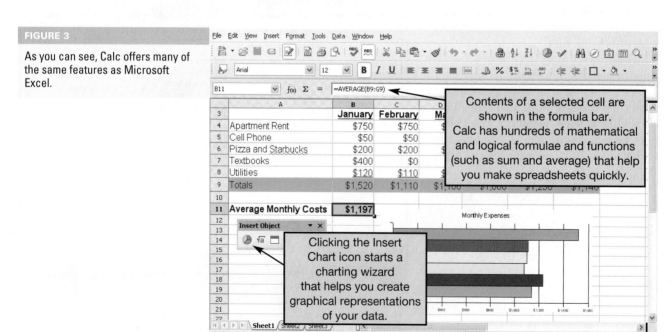

FIGURE 3

As you can see, Calc offers many of the same features as Microsoft Excel.

Contents of a selected cell are shown in the formula bar.
Calc has hundreds of mathematical and logical formulae and functions (such as sum and average) that help you make spreadsheets quickly.

Clicking the Insert Chart icon starts a charting wizard that helps you create graphical representations of your data.

special Auto-Pilot feature guides you through the wide range of functions available in Calc, providing suggestions as to which function to use.

When saving a document in OpenOffice Calc, the default file format has an .sxc extension. But, by using the Save As command, users can save files in other formats such as Excel (.xls). And the handy "Export Directly as PDF" icon is also available in Calc.

Impress

Starting Impress by selecting "Presentation" from OpenOffice's start-up interface presents you with a wizard that offers you the option of creating a blank presentation or building one from supplied templates. However, although Microsoft PowerPoint has a vast array of stunning templates, the templates supplied with the Impress are, well, less than impressive. Still, it is easy to construct attractive slides and save them as templates yourself. Or just Google the terms "OpenOffice Impress Templates" and you'll find a wide variety of templates for Impress that others have created that you can download for free.

DRAWING SOFTWARE ALTERNATIVES: DIA

Microsoft Visio is a popular program for creating flowcharts and diagrams. However, Visio is not cheap. OpenOffice includes a program called Draw that allows you to create simple graphs, charts, and diagrams. Another option is Dia, a free program that allows you to create Visio-like diagrams and charts (see Figure 4). You can download a Windows-compatible version of Dia from **www.gnome.org/projects/dia/** as well as tutorials to get you up and running.

DATABASES SOFTWARE ALTERNATIVES: MYSQL

OpenOffice 2.0 does contain a database product (with wizards) similar to Microsoft Access. However, if you're interested in getting your hands on a free high-end SQL database application, the most popular open-source alternative is MySQL (**www.mysql.com**). Sporting many of the features contained in SQL Server and Oracle 9i, MySQL is a powerful database program

you can use to develop serious database applications (see Figure 5). Although it is more difficult to learn and use than Microsoft Access, many books and online tutorials are available to help you get MySQL up and running.

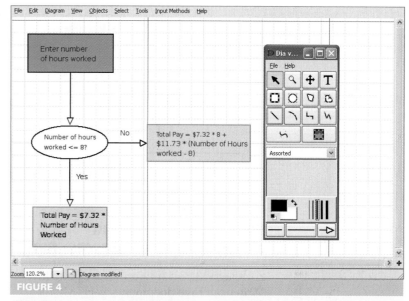

FIGURE 4

With Dia, you can create simple flowcharts such as this one that might be used by a computer programmer in developing algorithms. Although not as powerful as Visio, Dia is free.

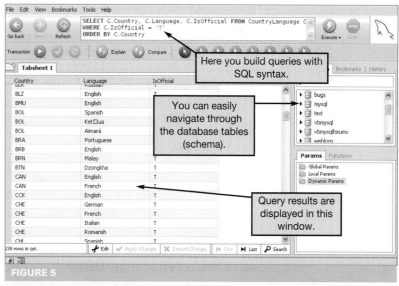

FIGURE 5

The two main components that you should download and install with MySQL are the Database Server and the Query Browser, shown here. You use the Database Server to create tables for your database and enter your data. The Query Browser provides a visual interface with the database to display the results of queries you create.

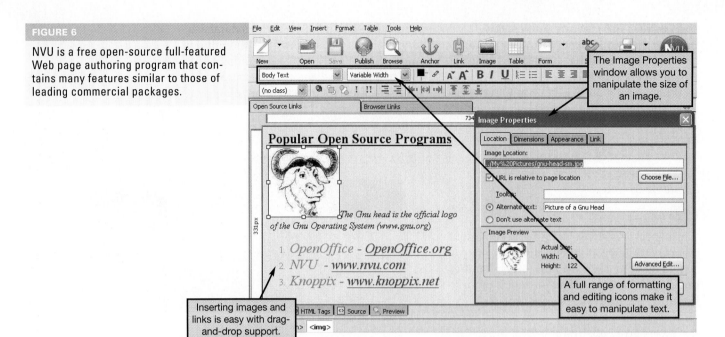

NVU is a free open-source full-featured Web page authoring program that contains many features similar to those of leading commercial packages.

WEB PAGE AUTHORING SOFTWARE ALTERNATIVES: NVU

Although Microsoft Word and OpenOffice Writer can save documents as HTML files, sometimes you need a more versatile tool for creating Web pages, especially for larger sites with many linked pages. Microsoft FrontPage and Macromedia Dreamweaver are popular commercial packages for building Web sites. But NVU (pronounced N-view and available at **www.nvu.com**) is a viable open-source alternative to these commercial packages (see Figure 6). And, like most open-source software, it's free. In addition to being available for the Windows operating systems, NVU also has versions that run on Mac OS X and Linux, among other OSs.

Another great thing about NVU is that you don't need to know HTML to generate a Web page: NVU generates the HTML code for you. However, you can reveal the HTML code with just a click of the mouse if you're knowledgeable with HTML and want to tweak it.

IMAGE-EDITING SOFTWARE ALTERNATIVES: THE GIMP

Need to create or edit some digital art but can't afford a high-end package like Adobe Photoshop or even a consumer package like Adobe Photoshop Elements? Download a free copy of The GIMP (short for GNU Image Manipulation Program) at

www.gimp.org and you'll find a set of tools almost as powerful as Photoshop. In addition, the GIMP is currently available for users running Windows, Mac OS X, Linux, or UNIX, and many good tutorials are deployed at **www.gimp.org/tutorials** to get you up to speed in no time.

Here are some handy things you can do with The GIMP in five minutes or less:

1. Crop or change the size of an image (see Figure 7).

2. Make a JPEG a smaller file size by changing the quality of the image.

3. Flip an image or rotate an image 90 degrees.

The GIMP also enables you to use more advanced skills, such as applying image filters, creating textures and gradients, drawing digital art, creating animated images through layer manipulation, and changing photos into a painting or sketch.

Operating System Alternatives

Installing open-source application software like OpenOffice on a Windows machine is simple. A bit more complex is changing your OS from Windows to an open-source OS such as Linux. But if you already own Windows and it's working for you, why would you want to switch to Linux?

Before Windows XP, many people felt Windows was not stable. Citing lockups and forced reboots, they were searching for an OS that would not crash as often. With Windows XP (especially with Service Pack 2 installed), Microsoft has done a great deal to address stability issues, and Windows is now less prone to lockups and crashes.

However, Windows is still plagued by security issues. A lot of spyware, computer viruses, and other hacker nuisances are designed to take advantage of security flaws in Windows. From a virus author's or hacker's perspective, because Windows is the most widely used OS, products that spread through Windows have the greatest chance of causing maximum annoyance. An open-source OS alternative such as Linux that is not as widely used might be less of a target for these annoyances.

Another reason to install an open-source OS is portability. Depending on which version of Linux you use (we'll discuss various options next), you may be able to take it with you on a CD and use it on almost any computer. This appeals to people who use a lot of

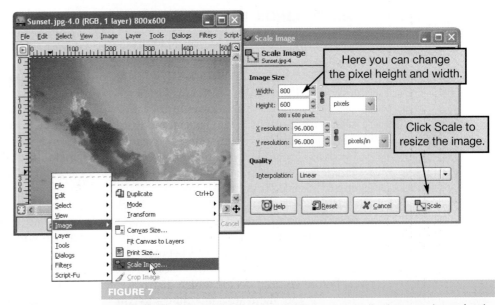

FIGURE 7

Using the Scale Image feature of The GIMP, you can easily change an image (such as this image of a sunset) to the exact pixel size you need in order to fit on a Web site, for example.

different computers (such as lab computers at school). Instead of getting used to a new configuration every time you're away from your home computer, wouldn't it be nice to have the same environment you're used to everywhere you go? In the next section, we explore the different varieties of Linux and how to install them on your computer.

Photo Management Software Alternatives: JAlbum

If you're like a lot of people, you have gigabytes of digital photos on your hard drive. But how can you easily organize photos for display on a Web site so you can share them with friends and family? An open-source option is JAlbum (available at **http://jalbum.net**), a program that allows you to create Web albums of your digital images easily using simple drag-and-drop tools. JAlbum is available for the Windows, Mac OS X, Linux, UNIX, and Solaris operating systems and supports 22 languages.

JAlbum provides significant advantages over some commercial photo management systems because it provides you with a high degree of control over the look and feel of the album you create. It also offers many precreated album styles if you don't have the time, energy, or artistic flair to create your own. You also can use JAlbum to create index and slide show pages, and the software will upload your album to the Internet. Best of all, your friends and family don't need any software other than a current Web browser to view your album. You can also choose to burn your albums onto a CD for sharing.

WHICH LINUX TO USE

Linux is available for download in various packages known as distributions, or "distros." Distros include the underlying Linux "kernel" (the code that provides Linux's basic functionality) and related programs. Distros also often contain special modifications or additional open-source software (such as OpenOffice). Think of distros as different makes and models of cars. So which distro is right for you?

A good place to start researching distros is **www.distrowatch.com.** This site tracks Linux distros and provides helpful tips for beginners in choosing one. Figure 8 lists some popular Linux distros and their home pages.

Before you can decide which distro is right for you, there are a few things to consider. The general overall requirements to run Linux are relatively modest:

- A 300-Mhz processor
- 128 MB of RAM
- 5 GB of hard drive space

However, just like any other software program, Linux will perform better with a faster processor and more memory. Also, depending on how much additional software is deployed in the distro you're using, you may need more hard drive space. Check the specific recommendations for the distro you're considering on the distro's Web site.

EXPERIMENTING WITH LINUX

Some distros of Linux (such as Knoppix and PCLinuxOS) are designed to be run from a CD. This alleviates your having to install files on the computer's hard drive. Therefore, you can boot up from a CD on an existing Windows PC and run Linux without disturbing the existing Windows installation. However, depending on the distro you use, you may not have full access to the files on your Windows hard drive.

Booting your existing computer from a CD-based version of Linux is a very low-risk way to experiment with Linux and see how well you like it. One such version of Linux is Knoppix, which you can download and burn onto a CD from **www.knoppix.com.** Knoppix uses a very Windows-like desktop. When you download Knoppix, you also get the Konqueror and Mozilla browsers as well as The GIMP, OpenOffice, and over 900 other software packages, including utilities and games. The minimum system requirements to run Knoppix are:

- An Intel-compatible CPU (i486 or later).

FIGURE 8 Popular Linux Distros and Their Home Pages

Distro	Home Page
Mandriva Linux (formerly Mandrakelinux)	**www.mandrivalinux.com**
Fedora Core (Red Hat)	**http://fedora.redhat.com**
SUSE LINUX (formerly SuSE Linux)	**www.suse.com**
Debian GNU/Linux	**www.debian.org**
Ubuntu Linux	**www.ubuntulinux.org**
Gentoo Linux	**www.gentoo.org**
Slackware Linux	**www.slackware.com**
KNOPPIX	**www.knoppix.com**
PCLinuxOS	**www.pclinuxonline.com/pclos**

- 20 MB of RAM for text mode, at least 96 MB for graphics mode (at least 128 MB of RAM is recommended to use the various office products).

- A bootable CD-ROM drive or a boot floppy and standard CD-ROM.

- A standard graphics card.

Figure 9 shows Knoppix in action after being booted up on a Pentium 4 PC with Windows currently installed. This computer is connected to the Internet via a high-speed connection as part of a home network. When the computer detected the Knoppix CD in the drive, it booted from it. As part of Knoppix's installation sequence, it automatically detects components of the computer (such as the network card) and configures Linux to recognize them. You'll have no trouble connecting to the Internet through Mozilla, and any files you create with OpenOffice you can save to a floppy or flash drive.

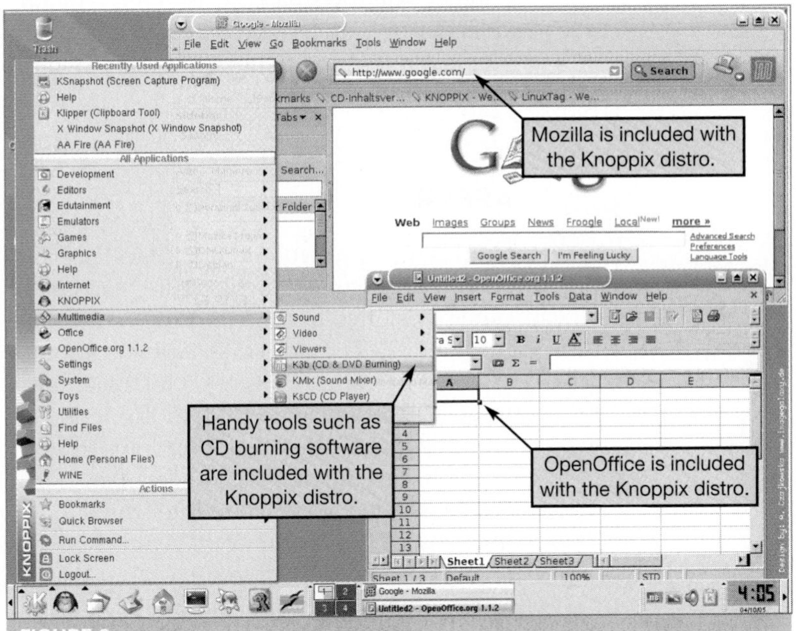

FIGURE 9

Here, the Linux distro Knoppix is running on a Pentium 4 computer. Notice how the user interface resembles the Windows desktop, including the trash container.

INSTALLING LINUX PERMANENTLY

If you want to install Linux permanently, Mandriva Linux (**www.mandrivalinux.com**) is a good choice, as it features one of the most fully automated installation procedures of all the Linux distros. Just follow the steps and you'll be guided through all the choices you need to make to configure your computer to use it. Beware though that when you install Mandriva you will overwrite your existing Windows files and reconfigure your hard drive. Thus, make sure you back up all your data files and read up on hard drive partitioning before installing Mandriva.

A wealth of application software is included with Mandriva, including:

- OpenOffice.

- Koffice (an office suite designed specifically for the desktop that Mandriva uses).

- Scribus (a desktop publishing program similar to Adobe Pagemaker).

- Karbon14 (a drawing program similar to Adobe Illustrator).

- Browsers (Mozilla, Konqueror, and Epiphany).

- Kontact (a program that combines e-mail, a calendar, an address book, and other features).

- GnuCash (a personal finance manager compatible with applications such as Quicken and Microsoft Money).

In addition to all this, Mandriva also includes security features. The OS divides security levels into five rankings, from "Very Low" to "Paranoid." Your choice depends on how you're using the system (select "Paranoid" if you're running business transactions through your computer). You also can set up a simple-to-configure firewall called Shorewall.

If you don't like Mandriva Linux after you've set it up, it doesn't cost you anything but your time, in which case you can head out to **www.distrowatch.com** and find another free Linux distro and install that. With the hundreds of distros available, you're sure to find one that fits your needs.

Hardware Alternatives

Tired of your Windows-based Intel PC? Old computer too slow for your current needs and not worth upgrading? If so, you may be in the market for some new hardware. But before you head off to the store to buy another Windows-based computer, why not consider two alternatives: (1) moving to an Apple platform or (2) building your own computer.

APPLES

Until 2005, Apple computers (Macs) used a completely different architecture than computers designed to run Windows (which use Intel and AMD processors). Apple computers used to feature PowerPC chips manufactured by Motorola and IBM; these chips required an OS other than Windows (the Mac OS, currently OS X). However, in 2005, Apple decided to switch to Intel chips in their computers. Fortunately, Apple had already designed OS X to run on Intel platforms. So moving to an Apple computer now is really all about using OS X. So why make the change?

Like earlier versions of Mac OS, OS X is based on the UNIX OS, which is very stable and reliable. Aside from being stable, security and safety are great reasons to switch to Mac OS X. OS X doesn't seem to suffer from the exploitation of security flaws as much as Windows does. This doesn't necessarily mean that the Mac OS is better constructed than Windows. It could just be that because Windows has a lead in market share, it is just a more attractive target for hackers. Regardless of the reason, you're probably somewhat less likely to be inconvenienced by viruses, hacking, and spyware if you're running Mac OS. Of course, you won't have any better protection from spam, phishing, or other Internet scams, so you still need to stay alert.

Some people are also switching to Macs because they love their iPods so much. Apple is leveraging the popularity of these digital devices by designing software for their computers to work seamlessly with them. And many Apple fans think Macs are more user-friendly and stylish than their PC competitors. Finally, some people change to Macs because many applications (especially for digital artists and graphic designers) deliver superior features on the Apple platform.

The best way to decide whether a Mac is right for you is to actually get your hands on one and take it for a test drive. Chances are someone you know has a Mac. If not, Apple has retail stores chock full of employees who are only too happy to let you test out the equipment. Be sure to check out the entry-level Macs in Figure 10.

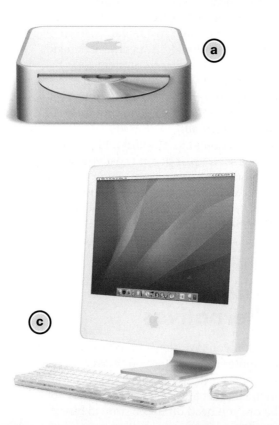

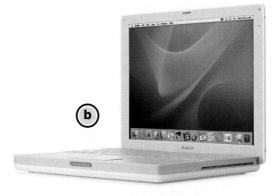

FIGURE 10

(a) At only 6.5" wide, 6.5" long, and 2" high, the Mac Mini is arguably one of the smallest system units ever made. Just add a monitor, keyboard, and mouse. This mini computer also has a mini price tag to go with it. (b) Apple's entry-level laptop computer, the iBook G4, weighs under five pounds and is about as big as a spiral-bound notebook when closed. (c) The iMac G5 line features sleek, space-saving desktop units sporting fast G5 processors.

The Mac Operating System: MacOS X

If you've been using Windows for a while, you shouldn't have any problem making the transition to Mac OS X. You'll notice immediately that the Mac OS uses the same desktop metaphors that Windows does, including icons for folders and a trash can (instead of a recycle bin) to delete documents. Screen real estate is managed using familiar-looking windows you're used to using on Windows.

When you start a Mac, a program called the Finder automatically starts. This program is like Windows Explorer and controls the desktop and the Finder windows with which you interact, as shown in Figure 11. It's always running when the Mac is on. At the top of the desktop is the menu bar. The options on the menu bar change according to which program is "active" at the moment (i.e., foremost on your screen). Notice the Apple icon in the upper left-hand corner: When you click this icon, a drop-down menu is displayed, from which you can select a number of options. The Dock is similar to the Taskbar in Windows and is a strip of icons that runs across the bottom of the desktop.

Each Finder window has an area on the left known as the Sidebar (see Figure 12). The Sidebar holds any folders you specify (even though the icons don't look like folders) to make navigation easier and faster. Navigating around a Finder window and copying or moving files works almost exactly the same way it does in Windows.

Configuring a Mac

In Windows, you make changes to settings and preferences through the Control Panel. In OS X, you use System Preferences, which is an option on the

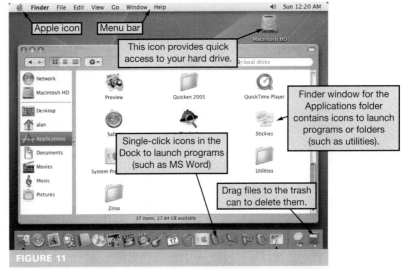

FIGURE 11

Here you see a typical desktop in Mac OS X with a Finder window open.

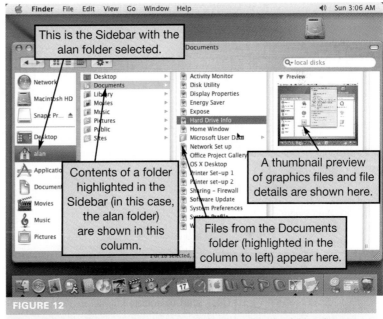

FIGURE 12

The Sidebar holds any folders you specify (such as the alan folder shown here). You can choose to view the contents of files and folders in three different views: icon view, list view, and column view.

New Software Is Necessary... Or Is It?

Switching to a new OS means buying new versions of your Windows-based software (such as Microsoft Office for Mac OS X). Or does it? Many open-source packages are also available for the Mac OS. If you really need to run your Windows-based software on your Mac, various software products such as Guest PC (**www.lismoresystems.com**) and iEmulator (**www.iemulator.com**) allow you to install Windows on your Mac and run Windows applications.

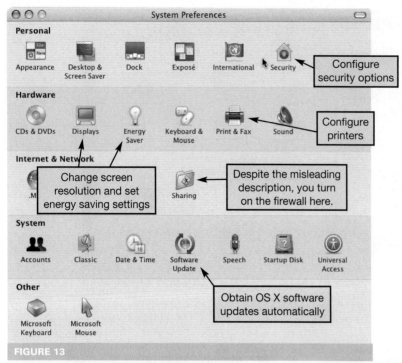

FIGURE 13

Much like the Control Panel in Windows, the System Preferences window allows you to customize and configure OS X.

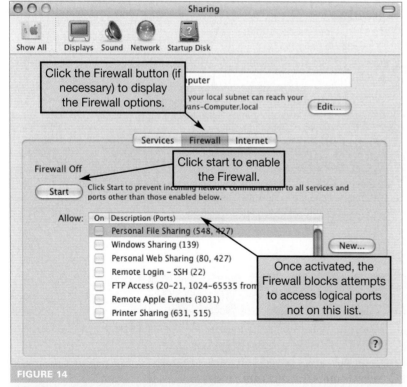

FIGURE 14

Macs have a firewall, but by default it is turned off. Make sure you turn on your Firewall before going out on to the Internet for the first time.

Apple menu. Selecting System Preferences from the Apple menu displays the window shown in Figure 13.

Protecting Your Mac

Although Macs tend to be attacked less often by viruses and other hacker nuisances, you can still be vulnerable if you don't take precautions. OS X comes with a firewall, but by default it is turned off. To configure it, click on the Sharing icon under the Internet and Network section of the System Preferences Window. When the Sharing Window opens, click on the Firewall button to display the Firewall configuration screen shown in Figure 14. Click the Start button to turn the firewall on. You should do this before going out on to the Internet for the first time.

In addition, hackers may be creating viruses and other nuisances to exploit security holes in OS X. Mac users should therefore keep their software up to date with the latest fixes and software patches by setting their system to check automatically for software updates on a periodic basis. On Macs, this feature is available through the System Preferences window by clicking the Software Update icon, as shown in Figure 15.

In addition to these precautions, there is antivirus software (such as Norton) available for OS X.

Utility Programs

Just like Windows, OS X contains a wide variety of utility programs to help users maintain and evaluate their Macs. In Macs, utility programs are located in a folder named Utilities within the Applications folder on the hard drive.

If you're a PC user, you know that to determine how a PC is performing, you use the Windows Task Manager utility. In Macs, this utility is called the Activity Monitor, shown in Figure 16. It shows what programs (processes) are currently running and how much memory they're using. The CPU, System Memory, Disk Activity, Disk Usage, and Network buttons indicate the activity in each of these crucial areas.

Like the Systems Properties box in Windows, the Mac OS System Profiler shown in Figure 17, displays all the hardware (and

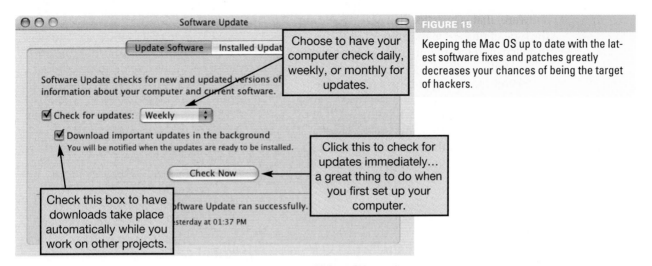

FIGURE 15

Keeping the Mac OS up to date with the latest software fixes and patches greatly decreases your chances of being the target of hackers.

Choose to have your computer check daily, weekly, or monthly for updates.

Click this to check for updates immediately... a great thing to do when you first set up your computer.

Check this box to have downloads take place automatically while you work on other projects.

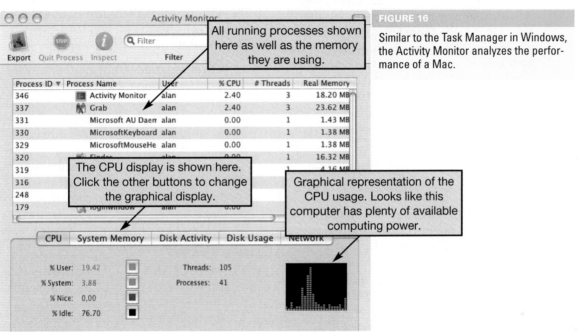

FIGURE 16

Similar to the Task Manager in Windows, the Activity Monitor analyzes the performance of a Mac.

All running processes shown here as well as the memory they are using.

The CPU display is shown here. Click the other buttons to change the graphical display.

Graphical representation of the CPU usage. Looks like this computer has plenty of available computing power.

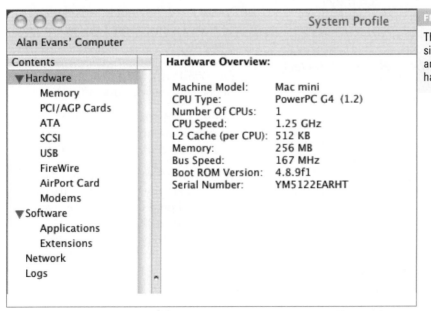

FIGURE 17

The System Profiler (found in the Utilities folder) is similar to the Systems Properties box in Windows and reveals a wealth of information about the hardware and software in your computer.

software) that is installed in a Mac, including the type of processor, the amount of RAM installed, and the amount of VRAM on the video card.

As you can see, operating a Mac is fairly simple, and is similar to the Windows environment. There are many books (such as the OS X books in the Peachpit Press Visual Quickstart Series) that will help you make a smooth transition to an Apple computer if you're interested.

DO IT YOURSELF!

The do-it-yourself craze has swept across America, so why not stop repainting the house and apply those DIY skills to building a computer? Of course, building a computer isn't for everyone, but for those who enjoy working with their hands and don't mind doing some up-front research, it can be a rewarding experience. The advantages and disadvantages of building your own computer are as follows:

Advantages	Disadvantages
You get exactly the configuration features you want	There is no technical support when things go wrong
You have the option of using higher-quality components than those that are used in mass-produced computers	You'll need to examine technical specifications (such as which CPU works with the motherboard you want), which may overwhelm the average computer user
You'll hopefully get a feeling of satisfaction from a job well done	You won't necessarily save money

Many Web sites can provide guidance for building your own computer; **www.buildyourowncomputer.net** and **www.pcmech.com/byopc** are two good places to start. Just Google "How to build your own computer" and you'll find plenty of online help and advice. To start, you need a list of parts. Here's what you'll typically need:

1. **A Case**: Make sure the case you buy is an ATX-style case, which accommodates the newest motherboards, and that it includes an adequate cooling fan. Also be sure there are enough drive bays in the case to handle the hard drive and any other peripheral drives (CD, DVD, etc.) you'll be installing.

2. **A Power Supply:** A power supply provides power to the computer. Many cases come with a power supply installed. Make sure to get a power supply with adequate wattage to handle the load.

3. **A Processor (CPU)**: Get the fastest one you can afford, as it will help greatly extend the life of your computer.

4. **A Motherboard**: Many motherboards come with sound, video, and network cards. These work fine for basic computing, but if you're building a PC for gaming, opt for a motherboard into which you can plug higher-end graphics and sound cards. Also make sure the motherboard you buy can accommodate the CPU you have chosen. And make sure the motherboard has PCI slots and a separate AGP slot for a high-end graphics card.

5. **RAM**: Check your motherboard specifications before buying RAM to ensure you buy the correct type and an amount that will fit into the available slots.

6. **Video Card**: Low-end cards with 32 or 64 MB of memory are fine for normal computer use, but for gaming or displaying high-end graphics or videos, get a card with 128 MB or more depending on your budget.

7. **Sound Card**: Make sure to get a PCI card that is Sound Blaster-compatible (the standard for sound cards).

8. **Removable Storage (Floppy, CD/DVD Drives)**: Floppy disks are pretty obsolete based on their low storage capacity, but they are a cheap option. A CD/DVD drive is a must for software installation.

9. **Hard Drive:** Price per MB has been rapidly coming down in recent years, so get a large-volume drive.

10. **Modem:** You need a modem only if you're connecting to the Internet via a dial-up connection.

11. **Network Card:** Network cards are sometimes integrated in the motherboard, so check before you buy one.

In addition to these components, you'll need a keyboard, mouse or other pointing device, monitor, and operating system software.

You can buy these components at national computer superstores such as CompUSA or at reputable Web sites such as **www.tigerdirect.com** or **www.newegg.com.** Once you have the components, it is almost as simple as bolting them into the case and connecting them properly together. Make sure you read all the installation instructions that come with your components before beginning installation. Don't forget to check the

Web sites of component manufacturers for handy how-to-videos and step-by-step installation guides. Then read through a complete installation tutorial such as the one found at **www.pcmech.com/byopc**, which provides an excellent overview of assembling a computer. Then grab your screwdriver and get started—you'll be up and running in no time.

So, as you can see, there are many options beyond a Windows-based computer running commercial software applications. We hope you spread your wings and try a few of them.

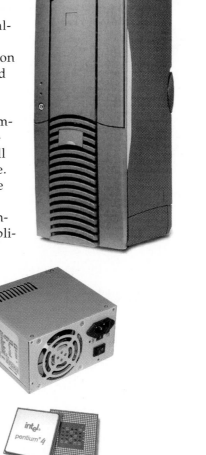

7

Networking and Security:

Connecting Computers and Keeping Them Safe from Hackers and Viruses

Objectives

After reading this chapter, you should be able to answer the following questions:

1. What is a network and what are the advantages of setting up one? **(p. 292)**

2. What is the difference between a client/server network and a peer-to-peer network? **(pp. 293–294)**

3. What are the main components of every network? **(pp. 294–296)**

4. What are the most common home networks? **(p. 296)**

5. What are wired Ethernet networks and how are they created? **(pp. 296–299)**

6. What are wireless Ethernet networks and how are they created? **(pp. 300–302)**

7. How are power-line and phoneline networks created and are they viable alternatives to Ethernet networks? **(pp. 302–308)**

8. How can hackers attack a network and what harm can they cause? **(pp. 309–313)**

9. What is a firewall and how does it keep my computer safe from hackers? **(pp. 314–317)**

10. Why are wireless networks more vulnerable than wired networks and what special precautions are required to ensure my wireless network is secure? **(pp. 317–318)**

11. From which types of viruses do I need to protect my computer? **(pp. 318–321)**

12. What can I do to protect my computer from viruses? **(pp. 321–323)**

ACTIVE HELPDESK

- Understanding Networking **(p. 303)**
- Understanding Firewalls **(p. 316)**

- Avoiding Computer Viruses **(p. 321)**

The Problems of Sharing

The Williams family is facing computer-sharing problems. Derrick and Vanessa realized that they both needed computers, and they bought their children, Stephanie and Jake, their own computers, too. Still, there is trouble in this "paradise."

Scarce Resources: Jake was using his computer to scan photos for a school Web site project. Just then, his sister Stephanie burst into his room and demanded to use his scanner because she didn't have one and needed to scan images for an art project. Jake wouldn't budge. The ensuing shouting match brought their mother Vanessa to the room. Because both projects were due the next day, Vanessa told Jake he would have to let Stephanie use the scanner at some point. In exchange, Stephanie would have to let Jake use her computer so he could print from the color printer attached to it. Neither was happy, but it was the best Vanessa could do.

Internet Logjam: Derrick frowned at his e-mail inbox. He was on vacation, but his boss had e-mailed him asking him to look over a marketing plan. Meanwhile, Vanessa needed to get online to confirm the family's reservations at Disney World. Because they had only one phone line, they constantly had to take turns getting online, and with Stephanie and Jake wanting to check their e-mail too, the phone line was almost always tied up.

Virus Attack: Later that night, Derrick booted up his computer to make some changes to the marketing plan. Right away, he noticed that many of his icons had disappeared from his desktop. As he launched Microsoft Word, a message flashed on the screen that read, "The Hacker of Death Was Here!" Suddenly, his screen went black. When he rebooted his computer, it was unable to recognize the hard drive. The next day, Derrick called the computer support technician at work and learned he had caught the "Death Squad" virus, which had erased the contents of his hard drive. Derrick mused that he should have bought an antivirus program instead of Mech Warrior 5.

If this scenario doesn't reflect the situation in your home, it may in the future. As the price of computers continues to drop, more families will have multiple home computers. To avoid inconvenience and the expense of redundant equipment, computers need to be able to communicate with each other and to share peripherals (such as scanners and printers) and resources (such as Internet connections). Thus, this chapter explores how you can network computers. In addition, you'll learn strategies for keeping unauthorized outsiders from prying into your computer when you're sharing resources with the outside world, as well as how to keep your computer safe from viruses.

SOUND BYTES

- Installing a Computer Network **(p. 296)**
- Installing a Personal Firewall **(p. 315)**
- Securing Wireless Networks **(p. 318)**
- Protecting Your Computer **(p. 322)**

Networking Fundamentals

Although you may not yet have a home network, you use and interact with networks all the time. In fact, every time you use the Internet you're interacting with the world's largest network. But what exactly *is* a network? A **computer network** is simply two or more computers that are connected together via software and hardware so they can communicate. Devices connected to a network are referred to as **nodes**. A node can be a computer, a peripheral (such as a printer), or a communications device (such as a modem). The main function for most networks is to facilitate information sharing, but networks provide other benefits as well.

What are the benefits of networks? One benefit of networks is that they allow users to share peripherals. For example, in Figure 7.1a, the computers are not networked; Computer 1 is connected to the printer, but Computer 2 is not. To print files from Computer 2, users have to transfer them using a floppy disk or another storage medium to Computer 1, or they have to disconnect the printer from Computer 1 and connect it to Computer 2. By networking Computer 1 and Computer 2, as shown in Figure 7.1b, both computers can print from the printer attached to Computer 1 without transferring files or moving the printer.

By networking computers, you can transfer files from one computer to another without using external storage media such as flash drives. And you can set up shared directories in Windows that allow the user of each computer on the network to store files that other computers on the network may need to access, as shown in Figure 7.2.

Can I use a network to share an Internet connection? If you install a device called a *router* to your network, you can share broadband Internet connections. Unfortunately, dial-up connections don't have sufficient bandwidth to support sharing an Internet connection. We'll discuss routers in detail later in the chapter.

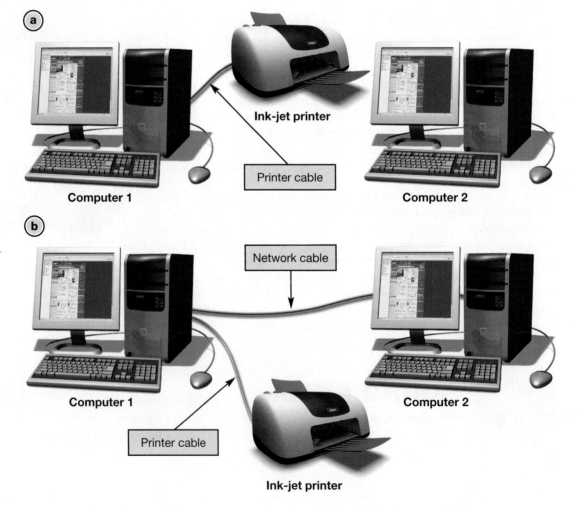

FIGURE 7.1

(a) Computer 1 and Computer 2 are not networked. Only Computer 1 can use the printer unless the printer is disconnected from Computer 1 and reconnected to Computer 2.
(b) Computer 1 and Computer 2 are networked. Both computers can use the printer without having to move it.

(a)

Ink-jet printer

Printer cable

Computer 1

Computer 2

(b)

Network cable

Computer 1

Computer 2

Printer cable

Ink-jet printer

Network Architectures

The term **network architecture** refers to the design of a network. Network architectures are classified according to the way in which they are controlled and the distance between their nodes.

DESCRIBING NETWORKS BASED ON NETWORK CONTROL

What do we mean by networks being "controlled"? There are two main ways a network can be controlled: locally or centrally. A *peer-to-peer network* is the most common example of a locally controlled network. The most common type of centrally controlled network is a *client/server network*.

What are peer-to-peer networks? In **peer-to-peer (P2P) networks**, each node connected to the network can communicate directly with every other node on the network, instead of having a separate device exercise central control over the entire network. Thus, all nodes on this type of network are in a sense *peers*. When printing, for example, a computer on a P2P network doesn't have to go through the computer that's connected to the printer. Instead, it can communicate directly with the printer. Figure 7.1b shows a very small peer-to-peer network.

Because they are simple to set up, P2P networks are the most common type of home network. We discuss different types of peer-to-peer networks that are popular in homes later in this chapter.

What are client/server networks? Very small schools and offices may have P2P networks. However, most networks that have 10 or more nodes are **client/server networks**. A client/server network contains two different types of computers: clients and servers. The **client** is the computer on which users accomplish specific tasks (such as construct spreadsheets) and make specific requests (such as that a file be printed). The **server** is the computer that provides information or resources to the client computers on the network. The server on a client/server network also provides central control for functions on the network (such as printing). Figure 7.3 illustrates a client/server network in action.

As you learned in Chapter 3, the Internet is an example of a client/server network. When

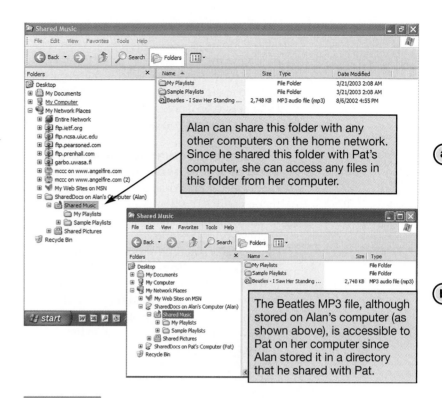

Alan can share this folder with any other computers on the home network. Since he shared this folder with Pat's computer, she can access any files in this folder from her computer.

(a)

The Beatles MP3 file, although stored on Alan's computer (as shown above), is accessible to Pat on her computer since Alan stored it in a directory that he shared with Pat.

(b)

FIGURE 7.2

This Windows XP network has two computers attached to it: (a) Alan and (b) Pat. Shared directories (the SharedDocs folders) have been set up so that Alan and Pat can share files. When Pat is working on her computer, she can easily access the files located in the shared directory on Alan's computer, such as the folder called Shared Music.

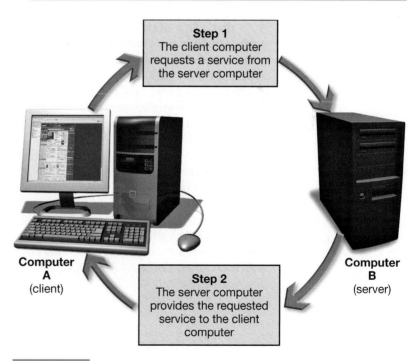

Step 1
The client computer requests a service from the server computer

Step 2
The server computer provides the requested service to the client computer

Computer A (client)

Computer B (server)

FIGURE 7.3

In a client/server network, a computer acts as a client, making requests for resources, or as a server, providing resources.

your computer is connected to the Internet, it is functioning as a *client computer*. When connecting to the Internet through an Internet service provider (ISP), your computer connects to a *server computer* maintained by the ISP. The server "serves up" resources to your computer so that you can interact with the Internet.

Are client/server networks ever used as home networks? Although client/server networks *can* be configured for home use, P2P networks are more often used in the home because they cost less than client/server networks and are easier to configure and maintain. To set up a client/server network in your home, you have to buy an extra computer to act as the server. (Although an existing computer could function as a server, its performance would be significantly degraded, making it impractical to use as both a client and a server.) In addition, you need training to install and maintain the special software client/server networks require. Finally, the major benefits a client/server network provides (such as centralized security and administration) are not necessary in most home networks.

DESCRIBING NETWORKS BASED ON DISTANCE

How does the distance between nodes define a network? The distance between nodes on a network is another way to describe a network. **Local area networks (LANs)** are networks in which the nodes are located within a small geographic area. A network in your home or a computer lab at school is an example of a LAN. **Wide area networks (WANs)** are made up of LANs connected over long distances. Say a school has two campuses (east and west) located in different towns. Connecting the LAN at the east campus to the LAN at the west campus (by telecommunications lines) would allow the users on the two LANs to communicate with each other. The two LANs would be described as a single WAN.

Network Components

To function, all networks include (a) a means of connecting the nodes on the network (by cables or wireless technology), (b) special devices that allow the nodes to communicate with each other and to send data, and (c) software that allows the network to run. We discuss each of these components, shown in Figure 7.4, next.

TRANSMISSION MEDIA

How are nodes on a network connected? All network nodes (computers and peripherals) are connected to each other and to the network by **transmission media**. A transmission medium establishes a communications channel between the nodes on a network and can take several forms:

1. Networks can use existing wiring (such as phone lines or power lines) to connect nodes.

2. Networks can use additional cable to connect nodes, such as twisted pair cable, coaxial cable, or fiber-optic cable. You have probably seen twisted pair and coaxial cable. Normal telephone wire is **twisted-pair cable** and is made up of copper wires that are twisted around each other and surrounded by a plastic jacket. If you have cable TV, the cable running into your TV or cable box is **coaxial cable**. Coaxial cable consists of a single copper wire surrounded by layers of plastic. **Fiber-optic cable** is made up of plastic or glass fibers that transmit data at very fast speeds.

3. Wireless networks use radio waves instead of wires or cable to connect nodes.

Different types of transmission media transmit data at different speeds. **Data transfer rate** (also called **bandwidth**) is the *maximum* speed at which data can be transmitted between two nodes on a network. **Throughput** is the *actual* speed of data transfer that is achieved and is usually less than the data transfer rate. Data transfer rate and throughput are usually measured in megabits per second (Mbps). A megabit, when applied to data transfer rates, represents one million bits. Twisted-pair cable, coaxial cable, and wireless media provide enough bandwidth for most home networks, whereas fiber-optic cable is sometimes used in client/server networks.

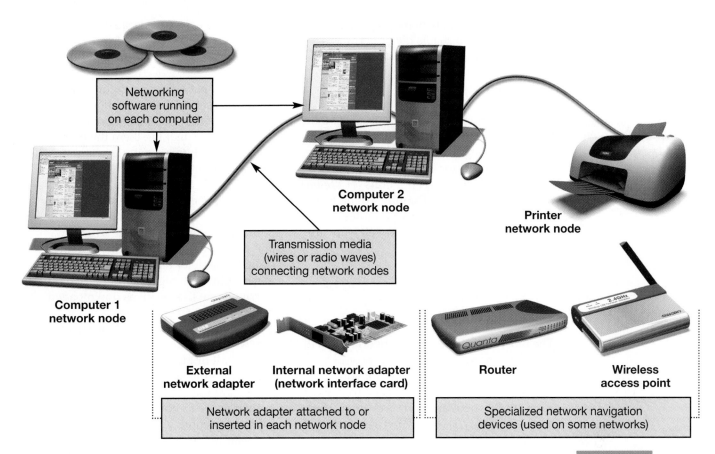

Networking software running on each computer

Computer 2 network node

Printer network node

Transmission media (wires or radio waves) connecting network nodes

Computer 1 network node

| External network adapter | Internal network adapter (network interface card) | Router | Wireless access point |

Network adapter attached to or inserted in each network node

Specialized network navigation devices (used on some networks)

FIGURE 7.4

Network Components

NETWORK ADAPTERS

How do the different nodes on the network communicate? Network **adapters** are devices connected to or installed in network nodes that enable the nodes to communicate with each other and to access the network. Some network adapters take the form of external devices that plug into an available USB port. Other network adapters are installed *inside* computers and peripherals as expansion cards. These adapters are referred to as **network interface cards (NICs)**. We discuss network adapters in more detail throughout the chapter.

NETWORK NAVIGATION DEVICES

How is data sent through a network? Data is sent over transmission media in bundles called **packets**. For computers to communicate, these packets of data must be able to flow between computers. **Network navigation devices** help to make this data flow possible. These devices, which are attached to the network, enable the transmission of data. In simple networks, navigation devices are built right into network adapters. More

sophisticated networks need specialized navigation devices.

The two most common specialized navigation devices are routers and switches. **Routers** transfer packets of data between two or more networks. For example, if a home network is connected to the Internet, a router is required to send data between the two networks (the home network and the Internet). **Switches** are the "traffic cops" of networks. They receive data packets and send them to the node for which they are intended *on the same network* (not between different networks). We discuss routers and switches in more detail later in the chapter.

NETWORKING SOFTWARE

What software do networks require? Home networks need operating system (OS) software that supports peer-to-peer networking. The most common versions of Windows used in the home (XP Home Edition, Millennium Edition, and Windows 2000 and 98) support P2P networking. You can connect computers running any of these OSs to the same network. You can also add computers that use the Windows 95 OS to the same

network, but you may need to install additional software to enable file or peripheral device sharing. The last several versions of the Mac OS (including OS X) also support P2P networking.

Client/server networks, on the other hand, are controlled by a central server that has specialized **network operating system (NOS)** software installed on it. This software handles requests for information, Internet access, and the use of peripherals for the rest of the network nodes. Examples of NOS software include Windows XP Professional, Windows Server 2003, and Novell Netware.

Types of Peer-to-Peer Networks

The most common type of network you will probably encounter is a peer-to-peer network, because this is the network you would set up in your home. Therefore, we'll focus on P2P networks in this chapter. There are four main types of P2P networks:

1. Wired Ethernet networks
2. Wireless Ethernet networks
3. Phoneline networks
4. Power-line networks

The major differences in these networks are the transmission media by which the nodes are connected. We will look at these networks and how each one is set up next.

WIRED ETHERNET NETWORKS

What are Ethernet networks?
Ethernet networks are so named because they use the Ethernet protocol as the means (or standard) by which the nodes on the network communicate. The Ethernet protocol was developed by the Institute of Electrical and Electronics Engineers (IEEE, pronounced I triple E). This nonprofit group develops many standard specifications for electronic data transmission that are adopted throughout the world. Each standard the IEEE develops is numbered, with 802.3 being the standard for wired Ethernet networks.

The Ethernet protocol makes Ethernet networks extremely efficient at moving data. However, to achieve this efficiency, the algorithms for moving data through an Ethernet

network are complex. Because of this complexity, Ethernet networks require additional devices (such as switches and routers).

Ethernet networks are slightly more complicated to set up than other home network options, but they're faster, more reliable, and less expensive, making them the most popular choice for home networks. Although 100-Mbps Ethernet networks are most commonly installed in homes, prices are falling quickly on one-gigabit-per-second (1 Gbps, or 1,000 Mbps) Ethernet components. In fact, home computers are starting to ship with one-gigabit Ethernet equipment preinstalled. The potential high throughput of gigabit Ethernet might be useful if you're moving large files (such as downloaded movies) around your home network.

How do I create an Ethernet network? An Ethernet network requires that you install or attach network adapters to each computer or peripheral you want to connect to the network. Because Ethernet networks are so common, most computers sold today come with Ethernet adapters preinstalled. As noted earlier, such internal network adapters are referred to as *network interface cards (NICs)*. Modern Ethernet NICs are usually 10/100-Mbps cards (see Figure 7.5a). This means they can handle the old 10-Mbps Ethernet data transfer rate as well as the newer 100-Mbps data transfer rate.

If your computer doesn't have a NIC, you can buy one and install it, or you can use a USB adapter, which you plug into any open USB port on the system unit (see Figure 7.5b). Although you can use USB versions in laptops, PC Card versions of Ethernet NICs are made especially for laptops (see Figure 7.5c). PC Cards are about the size of a credit card and fit into specially designed slots on a laptop.

How are nodes connected on wired Ethernet networks? The most popular transmission media option for wired Ethernet networks is **unshielded twisted-pair (UTP) cable**. UTP cable is composed of four pairs of wires that are twisted around each other to reduce electrical interference. You can buy UTP cable in varying lengths with RJ-45 connectors (Ethernet connectors) already attached. RJ-45 connectors resemble standard phone connectors (called RJ-11 connectors) but are slightly larger, as shown in Figure 7.6.

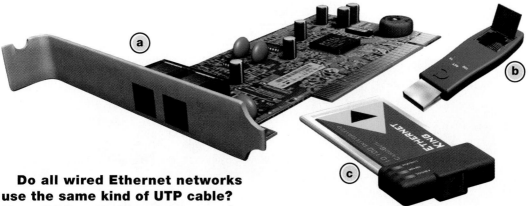

FIGURE 7.5

Ethernet network adapters come in a variety of versions, including (a) a 10/100 NIC, which is installed in an expansion slot inside the system unit; (b) a USB adapter, which you plug into an open USB port; and (c) a PC Card, which you slide into a specially designed slot on a laptop.

Do all wired Ethernet networks use the same kind of UTP cable? Figure 7.7 lists the three main types of UTP cable used in home wired Ethernet networks—Cat 5, Cat 5E, and Cat 6—and their data transfer rates. In general, it's better to install Cat 5E cable than Cat 5 because they're about the same price, and installing Cat 5E cable will enable you to take advantage of higher-bandwidth Ethernet systems when they become cost effective for home use. However, if you're planning on using a gigabit Ethernet network, use Cat 6 cable, which supports higher throughput.

Is UTP cable difficult to install? UTP cable is no more difficult to install than normal phone cable. You just need to take a few precautions: avoid putting sharp bends into the cable when running it around corners, because this can damage the copper wires inside and lead to breakage. Also, run the cable around the perimeter of the room (instead of under a rug, for example) to avoid damaging the wires from foot traffic.

How long can an Ethernet cable run be? Cable runs for Ethernet networks using UTP cable can't exceed 328 feet or else the signal starts to degrade. For cable runs over 328 feet, you can use **repeaters**, devices that are installed on long cable runs to amplify the signal. In effect, repeaters act as signal boosters. Repeaters can extend run lengths to 600 feet, but they can add up to $200 to the cost of a network. When possible, you should use continuous lengths of cable. Although you can splice two cables together with a connecting jack, this presents a source of failure for the cable, because connectors can loosen up in the connecting jack and moisture or dust can accumulate on the contacts. Usually, extending your wired network using wireless technology (discussed later in the chapter) is a better option than using repeaters or splicing cable.

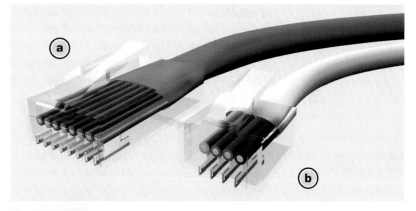

FIGURE 7.6

(a) An RJ-45 (Ethernet) connector, used on UTP cable, and (b) a typical RJ-11 connector, used on standard phone cord. Note the RJ-45 is larger and has contacts for eight wires (four pairs) instead of four wires. You must use UTP cable with RJ-45 connectors on an Ethernet network because phone cable will not work.

FIGURE 7.7 Data Transfer Rates for Popular Network Cable Types

UTP Cable Category	Data Transfer Rate
Category 5 (Cat 5)	Up to 100 Mbps
Category 5E (Cat 5E)	100 to 1,000 Mbps
Category 6 (Cat 6)	1,000 Mbps (1 Gbps) and higher

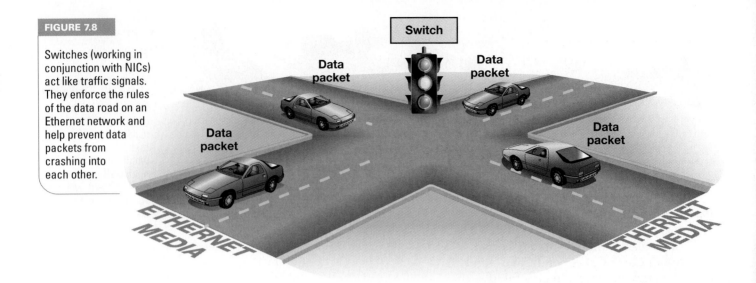

Switch

Data packet

Data packet

Data packet

Data packet

ETHERNET MEDIA

ETHERNET MEDIA

Ethernet Switches

How do Ethernet networks use switches?

Data is transmitted through the wires of an Ethernet network in packets. Imagine the data packets on an Ethernet network as cars on a road. If there were no traffic signals or rules of the road (such as driving on the right-hand side), we'd see a lot more collisions between vehicles, and people wouldn't get where they were going as readily (or at all). Data packets can also suffer collisions. If data packets collide, the data in them is damaged or lost. In either case, the network doesn't function efficiently.

As shown in Figure 7.8, a switch in an Ethernet network acts like a traffic signal by enforcing the rules of the data road on the transmission media. The switch keeps track of the data packets and, in conjunction with

network interface cards, helps the data packets find their destination without running into each other. This keeps the network running efficiently.

Switches are often referred to mistakenly as hubs. A *hub* is a network navigation device that merely retransmits a signal to all other nodes attached to it. Switches, on the other hand, are essentially "smart hubs," as they transmit data only to the node to which it should be sent. When Ethernet networks first came out, switches were much more expensive than hubs, so many home networks used hubs. However, today there is virtually no cost differential between hubs and switches. Therefore, most navigation devices sold for home networks are switches (even if they are mistakenly referred to as hubs).

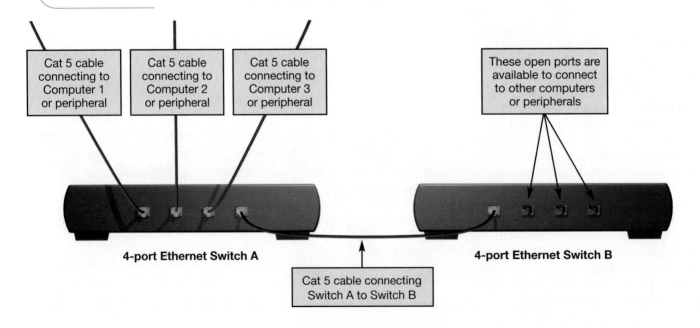

Cat 5 cable connecting to Computer 1 or peripheral

Cat 5 cable connecting to Computer 2 or peripheral

Cat 5 cable connecting to Computer 3 or peripheral

These open ports are available to connect to other computers or peripherals

4-port Ethernet Switch A

4-port Ethernet Switch B

Cat 5 cable connecting Switch A to Switch B

**How many computers and periph-
erals can be connected to a switch?**
Switches are differentiated by the number of
ports they have for connecting network
devices. Four- and eight-port switches are
often used in home networks. A four-port
switch can connect up to four devices to the
network, whereas an eight-port switch can
handle eight devices. Obviously, you should
buy a switch that has enough ports for all the
devices you want to connect to the network.
Many people buy switches with more ports
than they currently need so that they can
expand their network in the future.

A wonderful feature of switches is that
you can chain them together. Usually, one
port on a switch is designated for plugging
into a second switch. As shown in Figure
7.9, you can chain two four-port switches
together to provide connections for a total of
six devices. Most switches can be chained
together to provide hundreds of ports,
which would far exceed the needs of most
home networks.

Ethernet Routers
**How does data from an Ethernet net-
work get shared with the Internet or
another network?** As mentioned earlier,
routers are devices that transfer packets of
data between two or more networks. If a
home network is connected to the Internet,
you need a router to send data between the
home network and the Internet.

Because so many people are sharing
Internet access in home networks, manufacturers are making devices that combine
switches and routers and are specifically
designed to connect to DSL or cable modems.
These are often referred to as **DSL/cable
routers**. If you want your Ethernet network to
connect to the Internet through a DSL or cable
modem, obtaining a DSL/cable router is a
good idea. Although you could share an
Internet connection without one, a DSL/cable
router provides increased throughput and is
easier to configure than other methods. Figure
7.10 shows an example of an Ethernet network configured using a DSL/cable router.

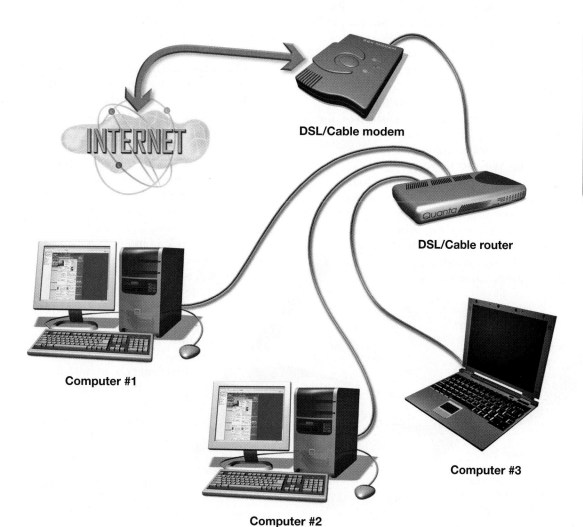

DSL/Cable modem

INTERNET

DSL/Cable router

Computer #1

Computer #2

Computer #3

FIGURE 7.10

This configuration
shows two desktop
computers and a lap-
top connected to a
DSL/cable router. This
configuration allows
all three computers to
share a broadband
Internet connection
easily.

BITS AND BYTES

One Brand Equals Fewer Headaches

Networking standards set by organizations such as the IEEE make it easier for manufacturers to produce devices that work with a variety of computers and peripherals. In theory, such standards should benefit consumers as well because equipment from different manufacturers should work together when placed on the same network. The reality, however, is that devices from different manufacturers—even if they follow the same standards—don't always work together perfectly. This is because manufacturers sometimes introduce proprietary hardware and software that deviate from the standards (such as in the case of Super G wireless). This means that an Ethernet NIC from Manufacturer A might not work with a DSL/cable router from Manufacturer B. The safe course of action is to use equipment manufactured by the same company.

WIRELESS ETHERNET NETWORKS

What is a wireless network? As its name implies, a **wireless network** uses radio waves instead of wires or cables as its transmission media. Just as it established the 802.3 standard for wired Ethernet networks, the IEEE has established standards for wireless Ethernet networks. Current wireless networks in the United States are based on the **802.11 standard**, established in 1997. The 802.11 standard is also known as **Wi-Fi** (short for Wireless Fidelity).

Three standards are currently defined under 802.11: 802.11a, 802.11b, and 802.11g. A fourth standard, 802.11n, is under development and is expected to be ratified in 2006 or 2007. The main difference between these standards is their maximum data transfer rate and the types of security that they support. For home networking, 802.11b and 802.11g are the standards most commonly used.

The 802.11b standard, which supports a maximum bandwidth of 11 Mbps, quickly became the accepted industry standard for home networks because of the low cost of implementation. However, the newer 802.11g standard, which supports a higher data transfer rate of 54 Mbps, is now the preferred standard for home use because it is much faster than 802.11b. Fortunately, 802.11g devices can be used together (that is, they have backward compatibility) with 802.11b devices.

Several manufacturers have also introduced products in a new Super G (also called Extreme G or Enhanced G) category, which can be confusing to buyers. These devices are still based on the 802.11g standard but use proprietary hardware and software tweaks to increase the maximum data transfer rate to a blistering 108 Mbps. Super G devices are designed to be backward-compatible with 802.11b and regular 802.11g devices. However, because Super G is not standards-based (i.e., it is not based on its own IEEE standard), Super G devices from one manufacturer might not work with those of another manufacturer.

What do I need to set up a wireless network? Just like other networks, each node on a wireless network requires a **wireless network adapter**. These adapters are available as NICs that are inserted into expansion slots on the computer (see Figure 7.11a) or as USB devices that plug into an open USB port (see Figure 7.11b).

Wireless network adapters differ from other network adapters in that they contain *transceivers*. A **transceiver** is a device that translates the electronic data that needs to be sent along the network into radio waves and then broadcasts these radio waves to other network nodes. Transceivers serve a dual function because they also receive the signals from other network nodes. As shown in Figure 7.11, wireless network adapters have antennas poking out of them, which are necessary for the transmission and reception of these radio waves.

FIGURE 7.11

Wireless network adapters have antennas poking out of them, which they use to communicate with the other devices in the network. Wireless network adapters are available as (a) NICs, which are inserted into an open expansion slot on the computer, or as (b) USB devices, which plug into an open USB port.

Do all nodes on the wireless network have to be computers? A node on a wireless network can also be a peripheral device such as a printer or scanner. The peripheral will need to be connected to a wireless network adapter so that other nodes on the network can communicate with it.

How do I share an Internet connection on a wireless network? Just as with wired Ethernet networks, wireless Ethernet networks require installation of a router to share an Internet connection. A **wireless router** (sometimes called a **gateway**) is a device that combines the capabilities of a wired router with the ability to receive wireless signals. Note that it is important that you do not mistakenly buy a wireless access point (which we discuss later) instead of a wireless router because a wireless access point does not perform the same function.

What types of problems can I run into when installing wireless networks? The maximum range of wireless devices is about 250 feet. However, as the distance between nodes increases, throughput decreases markedly. When the 802.11n standard is ratified, equipment that adheres to this standard should provide a greater bandwidth over longer distances.

Also, 802.11b and 802.11g devices work on a bandwidth of 2.4 GHz. This is the same bandwidth that many cordless phones use and therefore, your phone and wireless network may interfere with each other. The best solution is to buy a cordless phone that uses a bandwidth of 5.8 GHz.

Obstacles between wireless nodes also decrease throughput. Walls and large metal objects are the most common sources of interference with wireless signals. For example, placing a computer with a wireless network adapter next to a refrigerator may prevent the signals from reaching the rest of the network. And a node that has four walls between it and the Internet connection will most likely have lower than the maximum throughput. 802.11g devices have much better range than 802.11b devices and are less susceptible (but not immune to) interference.

What if a node on the network can't communicate with other nodes or with the router? Repositioning the node or the wireless network adapter within the same room (sometimes even just a few inches from the original position) can often

affect communication between the nodes. If this doesn't work, try moving the computers closer together or to other rooms in your house.

If these solutions don't work, you may need to add a wireless access point to your network, as shown in Figure 7.12. A **wireless access point** (WAP) is a device that attaches to a network and provides wireless nodes (such as a laptop with a wireless NIC installed) with a means of wirelessly connecting to the network. When you've got connection problems (say the laptop on your porch can't connect to the wireless router), often adding a WAP to the network will solve the problem. Essentially, you're extending the range of the wireless network by providing a second point to which nodes can connect to the network. The WAP must be connected to the network either directly to the switch on the router or to another node that is within range of the router.

FIGURE 7.12

Wireless access points help relay data between nodes on wireless networks.

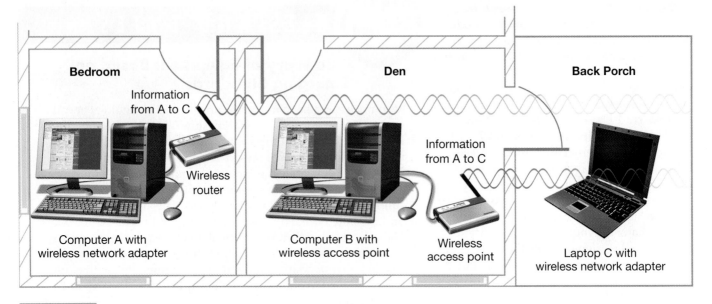

Bedroom
Information from A to C
Wireless router
Computer A with wireless network adapter

Den
Information from A to C
Computer B with wireless access point
Wireless access point

Back Porch
Laptop C with wireless network adapter

FIGURE 7.13

With a wireless access point installed on Computer B, data can travel from Laptop C (on the back porch) to the wireless router (in the bedroom).

For example, as you can see in Figure 7.13, Laptop C on the back porch and the wireless router (connected to Computer A in the bedroom) can't make contact. However, Laptop C can connect to Computer B in the den. By connecting a WAP to Computer B, all traffic from Laptop C is relayed to the wireless router through the WAP connected to Computer B.

Can I have wired and wireless nodes on one network? Many users want to create a network in which some computers (such as desktops) connect to the network with wires whereas other computers (such as laptops) connect to the network wirelessly. Most wireless DSL/cable routers allow you to connect wireless and wired nodes to the same network. This type of router contains both a WAP as well as ports

that allow you to connect wired nodes to the router. Figure 7.14 shows an example of a network with a wireless DSL/cable router attached to it. As you can see, the laptop maintains a wireless connection to the router whereas the other two computers are connected by wires. Using this type of router is a cost-effective way to have some wireless connections while still preserving the high-speed attributes of wired Ethernet where needed.

POWER-LINE NETWORKS

What are power-line networks?
Power-line networks use the existing electrical wiring in your home to connect the nodes in the network. Thus, in a power-line network, any electrical outlet provides a network connection. Power-line networks have a maximum data transfer rate of 14 Mbps. The HomePlug Power Line Alliance (**www.homeplug.org**) sets standards for home power-line networking.

How do I create a power-line network? To create a power-line network, you connect a *power-line network adapter* (similar to a network adapter in an Ethernet network) to each computer or peripheral that you're going to attach to the network. You can buy power-line network adapters in either USB or Ethernet versions. After you attach a network adapter to each node on the network, you plug the adapters into an electrical outlet. Most power-line network adapters will be automatically recognized by the Windows operating system.

BITS AND BYTES

Wireless Hot Spots

Public places (such as Starbucks) at which you can wirelessly connect to the Internet are known as "hot spots." Sometimes the service is free; other times there is a small charge. How can you tell? Just fire up your wireless-equipped laptop or PDA, start your browser, and try to access a Web site. If the service is not free, the store's "wireless gateway sentinel" software provides you with rates and an opportunity to pay for access. Either way, you are surfing in minutes while enjoying your latte. Going out of town and need to know where you can find a hot spot? Visit a site that offers hot spot directories, such as **www.wifinder.com** or **www.wi-fihotspotlist.com**.

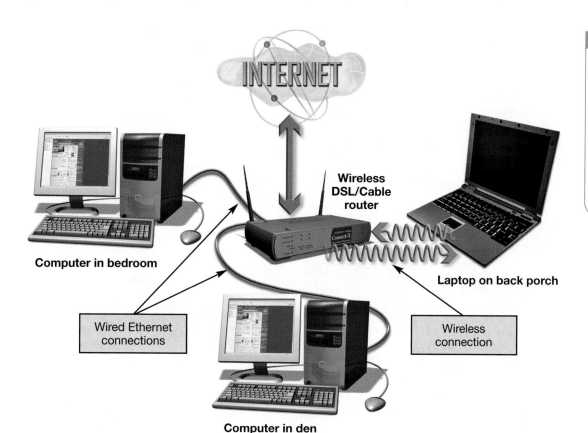

INTERNET

Wireless DSL/Cable router

Computer in bedroom

Laptop on back porch

Wired Ethernet connections

Wireless connection

Computer in den

FIGURE 7.14

Using a wireless DSL/cable router, the computers in the den and bedroom still maintain a high-speed wired Ethernet connection. However, the laptop can connect to the network wirelessly and be used in many areas of the home.

Why would I use a power-line network instead of an Ethernet network? Because of the low bandwidth of power-line networks and the lower costs of Ethernet networks, power-line networks are no longer very popular. However, if you're in a situation in which running new wires is not practical and you're experiencing too much interference to run a wireless network, you may want to consider installing a power-line network.

PHONELINE NETWORKS

What are phoneline networks?
Phoneline networks move data through the network using conventional phone lines rather than power lines. Thus, with a phoneline network, any phone jack in a house provides a network connection. Phoneline networks have a maximum data transfer rate of 10 Mbps. The Home Phone Line Networking Alliance (**www.homepna.org**) sets standards for home phoneline networking.

How do I create a phoneline network?
To create a phoneline network, you need to attach or install a *home phoneline network adapter* (also called an *HPNA adapter*) to

all computers and peripherals you want to attach to the network. You then attach the adapter to a phone jack on the wall with standard phone cord. To add computers or peripherals to the network, you attach a phoneline network adapter to the computer or peripheral you wish to add and plug it into another phone jack.

Why would I use a phoneline network instead of an Ethernet network?
Just as with power line networks, low bandwidth and the falling costs of Ethernet networks have made phoneline networks unpopular. However, if you have existing phone jacks in the right places, if running new wires is not practical, and if you're experiencing too much interference to run a wireless network, a phoneline network might work for you.

ACTIVE HELPDESK
Understanding Networking

In this Active Helpdesk call, you'll play the role of a Helpdesk staffer, fielding calls about home networks—their advantages, main components, and most common home networks—as well as about wireless networks and how they are created.

Choosing a Peer-to-Peer Network

If you're setting up a home network, the type of network you should choose depends on your particular needs. In general, consider the following factors in determining your network type:

- Whether you want wireless communications
- How fast you want your network connection to be
- Whether existing wiring is available
- How much money you can spend on your network

Figure 7.15 provides a flowchart that can help you decide which network to use in your home.

What if I want to use existing wiring for my home network? As noted earlier, you can use both phone lines

FIGURE 7.15

How to Choose a Home Network.

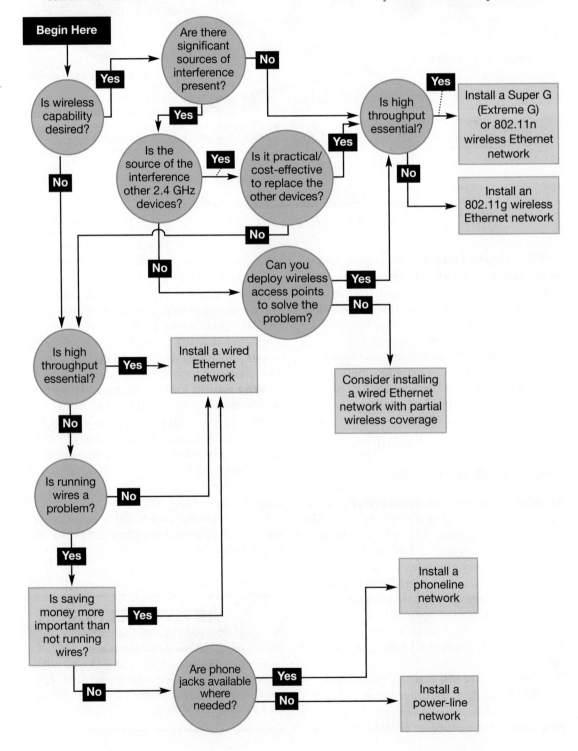

FIGURE 7.16 **Comparing the Major Types of Home Networks**

	Wired Ethernet	Wireless 802.11g	Wireless Enhanced G	Wireless 802.11n
Maximum data transfer rate (bandwidth)	100 Mbps to 1,000 Mbps (1 gigabit)	54 Mbps	108 Mbps	100 to 630 Mbps
Relative installation and equipment costs for networking two computers	$	$	$$	$$$

and power lines (electrical wiring) as media for a home network. For phoneline networks, you need a phone jack in each room where you want to connect a node to the network. Likewise, for power-line networks, you need an electrical outlet available in each room where you want to connect a node to the network. Because you have to plug most nodes (computers, printers, and so on) into an electrical outlet to operate them anyway, connecting a power-line network is usually convenient. However, these networks are more expensive and slower than wired or wireless Ethernet networks.

What are the pros and cons of wireless networks? Wireless networks free you from having to run wires in your home. In addition, you can use any flat surface as a workstation. However, wireless networks may not work effectively in every home. Therefore, you need to install and test the wireless network to figure out if it will work. To avoid unnecessary expenses, make sure you can return equipment for a refund if it doesn't work.

Which network provides the highest data transfer rate? Most routine home computing tasks (such as Web browsing and e-mailing), require minimal throughput (under 10 Mbps is sufficient). However, if high-speed data transmission is important to you (for example, if you play computer games or exchange large files), you may want a network with high throughput. With data transfer rates up to 1,000 Mbps, wired Ethernet networks are the fastest home networks. You may want to consider a

gigabit network if you engage in a lot of multiplayer gaming or transfer of video. Without high throughput, streaming video can appear choppy, games can respond slowly, and files can take a long time to transfer.

Do I need to consider the type of broadband connection I have? Whether you connect to the Internet by DSL, cable, or satellite makes no difference in terms of the type of network you select. The differences occur with your particular network's hardware and software requirements.

What cost factors do I need to consider in choosing a network? You may need to consider your budget when deciding what type of network to install. Figure 7.16 lists the approximate costs of installing the various types of peer-to-peer networks and their throughput.

Configuring Software for Your Home Network

Once you install the hardware for your network, you need to configure your operating system software for networking on your computers. In this section, you'll learn how to do just that using special Windows tools.

Is configuring software difficult? Windows XP makes configuring software relatively simple by providing the Network Setup Wizard, a portion of which is shown

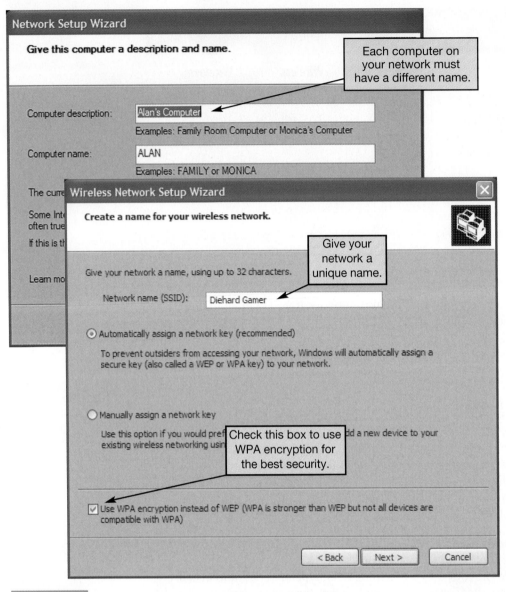

Network Setup Wizard

Give this computer a description and name.

Each computer on your network must have a different name.

Computer description: [Alan's Computer]

Examples: Family Room Computer or Monica's Computer

Computer name: [ALAN]

Examples: FAMILY or MONICA

The curre...

Some Int...

often true

If this is th...

Learn mo...

Wireless Network Setup Wizard

Create a name for your wireless network.

Give your network a name, using up to 32 characters.

Give your network a unique name.

Network name (SSID): [Diehard Gamer]

○ Automatically assign a network key (recommended)

To prevent outsiders from accessing your network, Windows will automatically assign a secure key (also called a WEP or WPA key) to your network.

○ Manually assign a network key

Use this option if you would pref... ...dd a new device to your existing wireless networking usin...

Check this box to use WPA encryption for the best security.

☑ Use WPA encryption instead of WEP (WPA is stronger than WEP but not all devices are compatible with WPA)

[< Back] [Next >] [Cancel]

FIGURE 7.17

(a) The Windows XP Network Setup Wizard helps you configure your software for your wired network. On this screen, you give the computer a unique name (on your network) so that the software can keep track of it. (b) The Windows Wireless Network Setup Wizard takes you step by step through configuring your wireless network.

in Figure 7.17a, for setting up wired networks. For wireless networks, Windows XP provides the Wireless Network Setup Wizard (see Figure 7.17b). As you learned in Chapter 4, a wizard is a utility program included with Microsoft software that you can use to help you accomplish a specific task. You can launch both of these wizards from the Control Panel. Prior to running these wizards, you should do the following:

1. Install network adapters on each node.
2. For a wired network, plug all the cables into the router, network adapters, and so on.
3. Turn on all computers and peripherals (printers, scanners, and so on).
4. Make sure your cable/DSL modem is connected to your router and that it is connected to the Internet.

Completing these steps enables the wizards to make decisions about how best to configure your network.

What if I don't have Windows XP on all my computers? Windows 98, 2000, and Millennium Edition (Me), the most common OSs found in the home other than Windows XP, all support P2P networking. Therefore, you can network these computers with other computers using Windows XP. If you have one computer with Windows XP but your other computers run on other versions of Windows, you should set up your Windows XP computer first. One step of the wizard gives you an option to create an installation disk (or copy the installation files onto a flash drive) that you can then use to set up non–Windows XP computers. Create the installation disk and then take the disk to your Windows 98 or Windows Me computers and follow the on-screen instructions.

What if I don't have Windows XP on *any* of my computers? Windows Me contains a similar wizard to Windows XP. (However, if you're mixing Windows XP and Windows Me computers, Microsoft recommends using the Windows XP wizard and an installation disk for the Windows Me computers.) If you're networking all Windows 98 machines, there is no wizard available, so you have to set up your computers manually. Various resources on the Internet can assist you in setting up Windows 98 networks. Not surprisingly, one of the best resources is the Microsoft Web site (**www.microsoft.com**).

Why does the wizard ask me to name my computer? Each computer on the network needs a unique name so that the network can identify it. This unique name ensures that the network knows which computer is requesting services and data so the data can be delivered to the correct computer.

FIGURE 7.18 **IP Addresses and Default Usernames/ Passwords for Major Router Manufacturers**

Manufacturer	IP Address	Default Username	Default Password
D-Link	http://192.168.0.1	Admin	No default password
Linksys	http://192.168.1.1	Admin	admin
Netgear	http://192.168.0.1	Admin	password
Microsoft	http://192.168.2.1	Admin	admin

Is that it? Assuming you installed and configured everything properly, your home network should be up and running and allowing you to share files, Internet connections, and peripherals. Most routers will work fine right out of the box. However, with some routers you may have to alter the configuration to connect to the Internet.

How do I set up my router so I can use it to connect to the Internet? You can access your router from Internet Explorer (or another Web browser) by entering the router's IP address. You can usually find your router's IP address in the documentation that came with the router. Figure 7.18 lists the IP

addresses of routers by several major manufacturers. You'll also need a username and password to log onto the router, both of which you'll also find in the documentation that came with the router.

Many routers feature their own wizard (which is different than the Windows Networking wizards) that takes you through unique configuration screens. A sample screen from a Netgear router is shown in Figure 7.19. If you're unsure of any information that needs to be entered to configure the router, call your ISP and ask for guidance.

In the next section, we explore how you can protect your computers and your network from intruders and hackers.

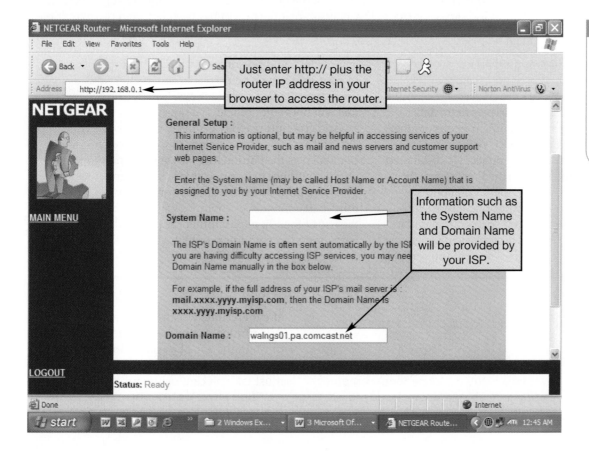

FIGURE 7.19

Although setups differ from router to router, basic information such as the domain name of your ISP is required to configure the router to work with your network.

Emerging Technologies: Grid Computing: Fighting Bioterrorism with Your Computer

Want to use your computer to help wage the war against bioterrorists? Finding more effective drugs to fight diseases such as smallpox doesn't require just laboratory research. Scientists also need huge amounts of computing power to analyze the data they amass in the lab. Strike a blow against terrorism and enlist your computer in the PatriotGrid, a network of computers working together to fight bioterrorism.

So, when does your computer have time to work on this project? Although you may use your computer many hours each day, even at peak times, your CPU rarely exceeds 20 percent of its maximum processing capability. Computers perform calculations in bursts. In between the bursts of activity (even between keystrokes), there are periods of inactivity, which amounts to wasted computing resources. This doesn't mean your computer is inefficient, it just means that the power of today's computers is so great that you can't fully use it. Turning these periods of inactivity into productive time periods is the aim of *grid computing*, a technology being used to provide huge increases in computational power for a reasonable price. Using specialized software, a company can create a computer grid that can effectively link millions of computers to perform complex calculations during lulls in their processing cycles.

To become involved in the PatriotGrid project, go to **www.grid.org** (sponsored by United Devices) and download the PatriotGrid software. This software uses your computer during idle times to run chemical analyses on agents that may be effective in fighting smallpox. When you're on the Internet, the software sends the results of its calculations back to the lab and retrieves more data to analyze. Your computer is now joining millions of other computers in the PatriotGrid project. Without the PatriotGrid, the smallpox analysis project was estimated to take 45 years to complete. With the PatriotGrid, the processing time is shortened to a matter of months.

Which companies use grid computing besides those fighting bioterrorism? Aircraft and spacecraft manufacturers need to perform complex design calculations, whereas pharmaceutical companies need to run complex

tests to determine how chemical compounds will react in the human body. By using grid software, these companies can link their employees' computers to take advantage of their computing power during periods of relative inactivity (especially at night). As opposed to leasing time on a supercomputer, using their employees' computers allows these companies to cut costs. Meanwhile, online games in which massive numbers of players play simultaneously require a lot of computing power. Companies such as Butterfly.net are creating grid computing programs to harness the power of multiple computers specifically to host large gaming networks.

Google also has jumped into the grid computing foray. A feature of the Google Toolbar called Google Computer is actually a grid computing feature that, when enabled, allows your computer to participate in grid computing projects. One such entity sponsored by Google Compute is Folding@home, a research project at Stanford University investigating the structure of proteins.

However, do your homework before joining any grid project. Although it hasn't happened yet, there is no telling when scam artists may use a fake grid project to gather sensitive information about you. Make sure to research the grid project and the company supporting it. Chances are if the project has been reported on in multiple legitimate media sources (*New York Times, Wired Magazine, PC Magazine*, etc.), it is a bona fide project and not a con game. You could potentially experience a small decrease in your computer's performance when the grid is using your computer for computations. But most of the time, this will not be noticeable.

Grid computing today is mostly confined to grids constructed at single organizations or to volunteer organizations such as the PatriotGrid. However, as network bandwidth continues to increase, third-party companies will construct grids and lease time to corporations. These third-party companies could very well pay consumers for the use of their home computers as part of these grids. Someday, your computer could pay for itself by working during its otherwise "off" hours.

Keeping Your Home Computer Safe

The media is full of stories about computer viruses damaging computers, and attacks on corporate Web sites have brought major corporations to a standstill. These are examples

of **cybercrime**, which is formally defined as any criminal action perpetrated primarily through the use of a computer. The existence of cybercrime means that computer users must take precautions to protect themselves. **Who perpetrates computer crimes?** **Cybercriminals** are individuals who use computers, networks, and the Internet to per-

BRINGING CIVILIZATION TO ITS KNEES...

FIGURE 7.20

Although not necessarily destroying civilization, hackers can cause problems for corporations and individuals alike.

petrate crime. Anyone with a computer and the wherewithal to arm themselves with the appropriate knowledge can be a cybercriminal. In the next sections, we discuss cybercriminals and the damage they can wreak on your computer. We also discuss methods for protecting your computer from attacks.

Computer Threats: Hackers

Although there is a great deal of dissention (especially among hackers themselves) as to what a hacker actually is, a **hacker** is defined as anyone who breaks into a computer system (whether an individual computer or a network) unlawfully.

Are there different kinds of hackers? Some hackers are offended by being labeled criminals and therefore attempt to divide hackers into classes. Many hackers who break into systems just for the challenge of it (and who don't wish to steal or wreak havoc on the systems) refer to themselves as **white-hat hackers**. They tout themselves as experts who are performing a needed service for society by helping companies realize the vulnerabilities that exist in their systems.

These white-hat hackers look down on those hackers who use their knowledge to destroy information or for illegal gain. White-hat hackers refer to these other hackers as **black-hat hackers**. The terms *white hat* and *black hat* are references to old Western movies in which the heroes wore white hats and the outlaws wore black hats. Irrespective of the opinions of the hackers, the laws in the United States (and in many foreign countries) consider any unauthorized access to computer systems a crime.

What about the teenage hackers who get caught every so often? Although some of these teenagers are brilliant hackers, the majority are amateurs without sophisticated computer skills. These amateur hackers are referred to as **script kiddies**. Script kiddies don't create programs used to hack into computer systems; instead, they use tools created by skilled hackers that enable unskilled novices to wreak the same havoc as professional hackers. Unfortunately, a search on any search engine will produce links to Web sites that feature hacking tools, complete with instructions, allowing anyone to become an amateur hacker.

Fortunately, because the users of these programs are amateurs, they're usually not proficient at covering their electronic tracks. Therefore, it's relatively easy for law enforcement officials to track them down and prosecute them. Still, script kiddies can cause a lot of disruption and damage to computers, networks, and Web sites before they're caught.

Why would a hacker be interested in breaking into my home computer? Some hackers just like to snoop. They enjoy the challenge of breaking into systems and seeing what information they can find. Other hackers are hobbyists seeking information about a particular topic wherever they can find it. Because many people keep proprietary business information on their home computers, hackers bent on industrial espionage may break into home computers. For other hackers, hacking is a way to pass time.

WHAT HACKERS STEAL

Could a hacker steal my credit card number? If you perform financial transactions online, such as banking or buying goods and services, you probably do so using a credit card. Credit card and bank account information can thus reside on your hard drive and may be detectable by a hacker. Even if this data is not stored on your computer, a hacker may be able to capture it when you're online by using a *packet sniffer*.

What's a packet sniffer? As you learned earlier, data travels through the Internet in small pieces called *packets*. The packets are identified with a string of numbers, in part to help identify on which computer they should end up. Once the packets reach their destination, they are reassembled into cohesive messages. A **packet sniffer** is a program that looks at (or sniffs) each packet as it travels on the Internet—not just those that are addressed to a particular computer, but *all* packets. Some packet sniffers are configured to capture all the packets into memory, whereas others capture only certain packets that contain specific content (such as credit card numbers).

What do hackers do with the information they "sniff"? Once a hacker has your credit card information, he or she can either use it to purchase items illegally or sell the number to someone who will. If hackers can gather enough information in conjunction with your credit card information, they may be able to commit **identity theft**. Identity theft is characterized by someone using personal information about you (such as your name, address, and social security number) to assume your identity for the purpose of defrauding others.

Although this sounds scary, you can protect yourself from packet sniffers by simply installing a firewall, which we discuss later in this chapter.

TROJAN HORSES

Is there anything else hackers can do if they break into my computer? Hackers often use individuals' computers as a staging area to do mischief. To perpetrate widespread computer attacks, for example, hackers need to control many computers at the same time. To this end, hackers often use Trojan horses to install other programs on computers. A **Trojan horse** is a program that appears to be something useful or desirable (like a game or a screen saver), but at the same time does something malicious in the background without your knowledge. The term *Trojan horse* derives from Greek mythology and refers to a wooden horse that the Greeks used to sneak into the city of Troy. By secreting soldiers in the belly of the horse, the Greeks were able to surprise the Trojans and conquer the city. Therefore, computer

BITS AND BYTES

Be Careful When Joining Social Networking Sites

Making contacts and meeting friends online has never been easier. Social networking services such as the well-established Friendster (**www.friendster.com**) and more recent entries such as Friendzy (**www.friendzy.com**) are signing up users at a rapid pace. These services have you list personal information about yourself (age, interests, hobbies, etc.) and encourage you to list connections to your friends. When your friends log on and view your profile, they can see themselves and long chains of other acquaintances. The idea is that your friends can see who else you know and get you to make appropriate introductions (or do it themselves).

Although the sites offer fairly tight protection of personal information (such as not revealing last names), you should think carefully about personal information that is visible on the site and be wary of disclosing additional information to people you meet online. Given the vast problems with identity theft, you should be wary of giving out your full name, address, social security number, and financial information. Also, be wary of accepting computer files from people you've met online because they could contain viruses or spyware. Just because you meet someone that is a friend of a friend of your second cousin in Wyoming doesn't mean that person isn't a hacker or a scam artist. So, enjoy meeting new people, but exercise the appropriate amount of caution that you would elsewhere on the Internet.

Computers in Society: Identity Theft: Is There More Than One You Out There?

You've no doubt heard of identity theft: a thief steals your name, address, social security number, and bank account and credit card information and runs up debts in your name. This leaves you holding the bag as you're hounded by creditors collecting on the fraudulent debts. It sounds horrible, and it is. Many victims of identity theft spend months trying to reestablish their credit.

Stories of identity theft abound in the media, such as the Long Island, New York, man accused of stealing over 30,000 identities, and should serve to make the public wary. However, many media pundits would have you believe that the only way your identity can be stolen is by a computer. This is simply not true. The U.S. Federal Trade Commission (**www.ftc.gov**) has identified the following as methods thieves use to obtain others' personal information:

1. Identity thieves steal purses and wallets, where people often keep unnecessary valuable personal information (such as their ATM PIN codes).
2. Identity thieves steal mail or look through trash for bank statements and credit card bills, which provide valuable personal information.
3. Identity thieves may pose as bank or credit card company representatives and trick people into revealing sensitive information over the phone.

Notice that none of these methods involve using a computer. Of course, you're at risk from online attacks, too. For example, you can give personal information to crooks by responding to bogus e-mail purportedly from your bank or ISP, a practice known as phishing. Once identity thieves have obtained your personal information, they can use it in a number of different ways:

Identity thieves can request a change of address for your credit card bill. By the time you realize that you aren't receiving your credit card statements, the thieves have rung up bogus charges on your account.

Identity thieves may open new credit card accounts in your name.

Identity thieves can open bank accounts in your name and write bad checks, ruining your credit rating. They can also counterfeit bank cards or checks for your legitimate accounts.

Although foolproof protection methods don't exist, the following precautions will help you minimize your risk:

1. Never reveal your password or PIN code to anyone or place it in an easy-to-find location.
2. Never reveal personal information unless you're sure that a legitimate reason exists for a business to know the information and you can confirm you're actually dealing with a legitimate representative. Banks and credit card companies usually request information by standard mail, not over the phone or online. If someone calls or e-mails asking you for personal information, decline and call the company where you opened your account.
3. Create hard-to-guess passwords for your accounts. Use a combination of letters and numbers and avoid using obvious passwords such as first or last names, birth dates, and so on.
4. When shopping online, be wary of unfamiliar merchants whom you can't contact through a mailing address or phone number or businesses whose prices are too good to be true. These can be an attempt to collect your personal information for use in fraudulent schemes.

Using common sense and keeping personal information in the hands of as few people as possible are the best defenses against identity theft. For additional tips on preventing identity theft or for procedures to follow if you are a victim, check out the U.S. federal government site on identity theft at **www.consumer.gov/idtheft**.

---

programs that contain a hidden "surprise" are referred to as Trojan horses.

What damage can Trojan horses do? Often, the malicious activity perpetrated by a Trojan horse program is the installation of **backdoor programs**, which allow hackers to take almost complete control of your computer without your knowledge. Using a backdoor program, hackers can access and delete all files on your computer, send e-mail, run programs, and do just about anything else you can do with your

computer. Computers that hackers control in this manner are referred to as **zombies**.

DENIAL OF SERVICE ATTACKS

What else can hackers do? Hackers can also launch an attack from your computer called a **denial of service (DoS) attack**. In a denial of service attack, legitimate users are denied access to a computer system because a hacker is repeatedly making requests of that computer system through a computer he or she has taken over as a zombie. Computers can handle only a certain number of requests for information at one time. When they are flooded with requests in a denial of service attack, they shut down and refuse to answer any requests for information, even if the requests are from legitimate users. Thus, the computer is so tied up responding to the bogus requests for information that authorized users can't gain access.

Launching a DoS attack on a computer system from one computer is easy to trace. Therefore, most savvy hackers use a **distributed denial of service (DDoS) attack**. DDoS attacks are automated attacks that are launched from more than one zombie at the same time. Figure 7.21 illustrates how a DDoS attack works. A hacker creates many zombies (sometimes hundreds or thousands) and coordinates them so they begin

sending bogus requests to the same computer at the same time. Administrators of the victim computer often have a great deal of difficulty stopping the attack because it comes from hundreds of computers.

DDoS attacks are a serious problem. In February 2000, many high-profile Web sites were subjected to DDoS attacks that succeeded in locking out authorized users. Yahoo! was the first victim on February 7. In subsequent days, eBay, Amazon, CNN, E*Trade, Excite, and Buy.com suffered similar interruptions in service. Business losses were estimated to be in the millions of dollars. This was the first example of a coordinated series of attacks; many other DDoS attacks have occurred since.

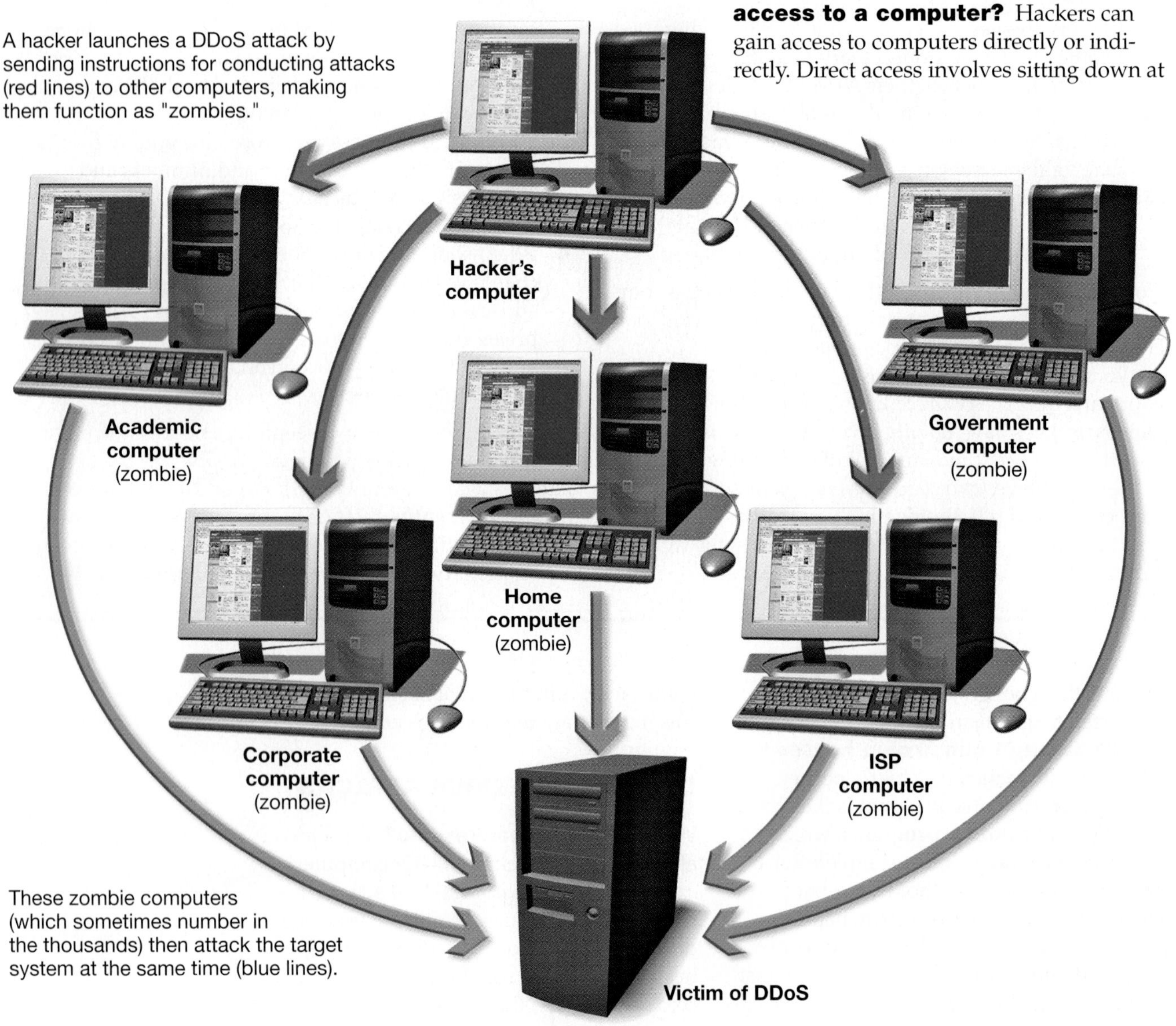

HOW HACKERS GAIN ACCESS

How exactly does a hacker gain access to a computer? Hackers can gain access to computers directly or indirectly. Direct access involves sitting down at

FIGURE 7.21

Zombies (sometimes hundreds or thousands of them) can be used to facilitate a distributed denial of service (DDoS) attack.

A hacker launches a DDoS attack by sending instructions for conducting attacks (red lines) to other computers, making them function as "zombies."

Hacker's computer

Academic computer (zombie)

Government computer (zombie)

Corporate computer (zombie)

Home computer (zombie)

ISP computer (zombie)

These zombie computers (which sometimes number in the thousands) then attack the target system at the same time (blue lines).

Victim of DDoS

a computer and installing hacking software. This rarely occurs in your home. However, to deter unauthorized use, you may want to lock the room that your computer is in or remove key components (such as the power cord) when strangers (repairmen and so on) are in your house and may be unobserved for periods of time.

The most likely method a hacker will take to access a computer is indirectly through its Internet connection. When connected to the Internet, your computer is potentially open to attack by hackers. Many people forget that their Internet connection is a two-way street. Not only can you access the Internet, but people on the Internet can access your computer as well.

Think of the computer as a house. Common sense tells you to lock your doors and windows when you aren't home to deter theft. Hooking your computer up to the Internet is like leaving the front door to your house wide open when you're not home. Anyone passing by can access your computer and poke around for valuables. Your computer obviously doesn't have doors and windows like a house; instead, it has logical ports.

What are logical ports? Logical **ports** are virtual (that is, *not* physical) communications gateways or paths that allow a computer to organize requests for information (such as Web page downloads, e-mail routing, and so on) from other networks or computers. Unlike physical ports (USB, FireWire, and so on), you can't see or touch a logical port. It is part of a computer's internal organization.

Logical ports are numbered and assigned to specific services. For instance, logical port 80 is designated for Hypertext Transfer Protocol (HTTP), the main communications protocol (or standard) for the Internet. Thus, all requests for information from your browser to the Web flow through logical port 80. E-mail messages sent by Simple Mail Transfer Protocol (SMTP), the protocol used for sending e-mail on the Internet, are routed through logical port 25. Open logical ports, like open windows in a home, invite intruders, as illustrated in Figure 7.22. Unless you take precautions to restrict access to your logical ports, other people on the Internet may be able to access your computer through them.

Fortunately, you can thwart most hacking problems by installing a firewall.

BITS AND BYTES

Terrorists Using the Internet?

Cyberterrorists are terrorists who use computers to accomplish their goals. Although there have been no major outbreaks of cyberterrorism yet, it is a concern of law enforcement agencies, ISPs, and major corporations. A cyberterrorist would attempt to disrupt the flow of information by attacking major networks, Web sites, or communications equipment. Bombing or otherwise disabling major ISPs could cripple network communications or the Internet. Disabling or corrupting the computer systems that control the New York Stock Exchange, for example, could undermine confidence in the financial markets, causing the economy to nosedive. Any action that would cause a disruption to the normal flow of information could potentially cause panic, which is the cyberterrorist's goal.

But the U.S. Government Office of Homeland Security has partnered with Dartmouth College's Institute for Security Technology Studies in an effort to head off potential threats. A project code named Livewire has been launched that simulates cyberattacks against large networks in both the public and private sectors. The results of these attacks are analyzed to assist in the development of a national cyber-response system.

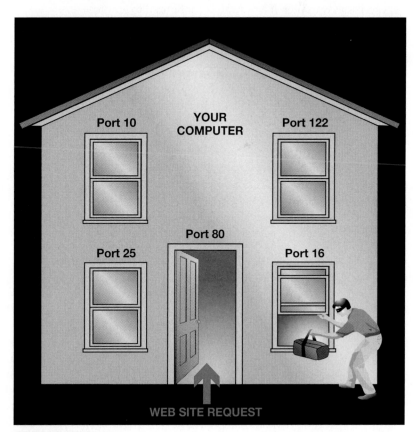

FIGURE 7.22

Open logical ports are an invitation to hackers.

Computer Safeguards: Firewalls

Firewalls are software programs or hardware devices designed to keep computers safe from hackers. Firewalls specifically designed for home networks are called **personal firewalls** and are made to be easy to install. By using a personal firewall, you can close off open logical ports to invaders and potentially make your computer invisible to other computers on the Internet.

DIG DEEPER

How Firewalls Work

Firewalls are designed to restrict access to a network and the computers on it. Firewalls protect you in two major ways: by blocking access to logical ports, and by keeping your computer's network address secure.

To block access to logical ports, firewalls examine data packets that your computer sends and receives. Data packets contain information such as the address of the sending and receiving computers and the logical port that the packet will use. Firewalls can be configured so that they filter out packets sent to specific logical ports (a process referred to as **packet filtering**). For example, File Transfer Protocol (FTP) programs are a typical way in which hackers access a computer. If a firewall is configured to ignore *all* incoming packets that request access to port 25 (the port designated for FTP traffic), no FTP requests will get through to your computer (a process referred to as **logical port blocking**). If port 25 were a window on your home, you would have effectively locked it so a burglar couldn't get in. If you need port 25 for a legitimate purpose, you could instruct the firewall to allow access to that port for a specified period of time or by a certain user.

For the Internet to share information seamlessly, data packets must have a way of getting to their correct location. Therefore, all computers connected to the Internet have a unique address. These addresses are called **Internet Protocol addresses** (**IP addresses** for short). As noted earlier, data packets contain the IP address of the computer to which they are being sent. Routing servers on the Internet make sure the packets get to the correct address. This is similar to the way addresses work on a conventional letter. A unique street address (such as 123 Main St., Anywhere, CA 99999) is placed on the envelope and the postal service routes it to its correct destination. Without such addressing, data packets, like letters, would not reach the intended recipients.

IP addresses are assigned when users log on to their Internet service provider (ISP) in a procedure known as **dynamic addressing**, illustrated in Figure 7.23. IP addresses are assigned out of a pool of available IP addresses licensed to the ISP. Because hackers use IP addresses to find victims and come back to their comput-

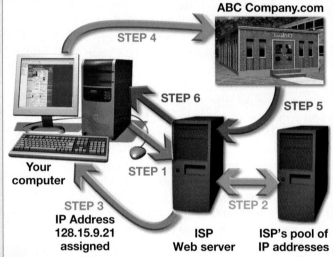

STEP 1: When you connect to your ISP, your computer requests an IP address.

STEP 2: The ISP's Web server consults its list of available IP addresses and selects one.

STEP 3: The selected IP address is communicated to your computer. The address remains in force for as long as you are connected to the ISP.

STEP 4: Once on the Internet, your Web browser requests access to ABC Company's Web site.

STEP 5: The ABC Company server consults an IP address listing and determines that the IP address of your computer is assigned to your ISP. It then forwards the requested information to the ISP's Web server.

STEP 6: The ISP's Web server knows to whom it assigned the IP address and therefore forwards the requested information on to your computer.

FIGURE 7.23

How Dynamic IP Addressing Works.

ers for more mischief, frequently switching IP addresses helps make users less vulnerable to attacks. However, because many broadband (cable and DSL) users leave their modems on for long periods of time (consecutive days or weeks), their IP addresses tend to change less frequently than those of dial-up users. Such **static addressing** (retaining the same IP address for a period of time) makes broadband users more vulnerable to hack-

Why are they called firewalls?

When houses were first being packed densely into cities (attached to each other with common walls), fire was a huge hazard because wood (the major construction component for houses) burns readily. An entire neighborhood could be lost in a single fire. Thus, builders started building common

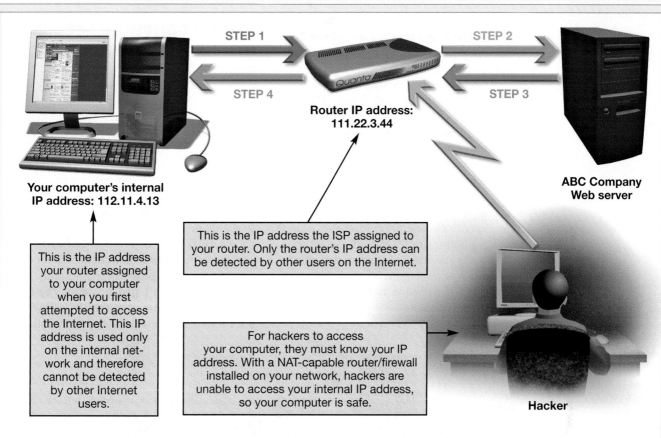

STEP 1

STEP 2

STEP 4

STEP 3

Router IP address: 111.22.3.44

Your computer's internal IP address: 112.11.4.13

ABC Company Web server

This is the IP address your router assigned to your computer when you first attempted to access the Internet. This IP address is used only on the internal network and therefore cannot be detected by other Internet users.

This is the IP address the ISP assigned to your router. Only the router's IP address can be detected by other users on the Internet.

For hackers to access your computer, they must know your IP address. With a NAT-capable router/firewall installed on your network, hackers are unable to access your internal IP address, so your computer is safe.

Hacker

STEP 1: Your computer's Web browser requests access to the ABC Company's Web site. This request travels through the router (which is configured as a firewall).

STEP 2: The router forwards your request to the ABC Company Web server. It directs the server to send the data back to the router IP address (111.22.3.44). The internal IP address of your computer (assigned by NAT) is not revealed to other computers outside your network.

STEP 3: The ABC Company Web server processes the request and sends the data back to the router IP address (111.22.3.44).

STEP 4: The router then passes the requested information on to the IP address of the computer that requested it (112.11.4.13).

FIGURE 7.24

Network Address Translation in Action.

ers because the hackers have a more permanent IP address with which to locate the computer. It also makes it easier for a hacker to go back to a computer repeatedly.

To combat the problems associated with static addressing, firewalls use a process called **Network Address Translation (NAT)** to assign internal IP addresses

on a network. These internal IP addresses are not shared with other devices that aren't part of the network, so the addresses are safe from hackers. Figure 7.24 shows how NAT works. You can use NAT in your home by purchasing a firewall with NAT capabilities. As noted earlier, many routers sold for home use are also configured as firewalls, and many feature NAT as well.

walls of nonflammable or slow-burning material to stop (or at least slow) the spread of fire. These came to be known as *firewalls*.

TYPES OF FIREWALLS

What kinds of firewalls are there? As noted earlier, firewalls can be configured using software or hardware devices. Although installing *either* a software or a hardware firewall on your home network is probably sufficient, you should consider installing both for maximum protection.

What software firewalls are there? The most popular software firewalls for the home include Norton Personal Firewall, McAfee Firewall, ZoneAlarm, and BlackICE PC Protection. (Windows XP, with Service Pack 2 installed, also includes a firewall that is simple but reliable.) These products are easy to set up and include options that allow the software to make security decisions for you based on the level of security you request. These programs also come with monitoring systems that alert you if your computer is under attack. The newest versions of these programs have "smart agents" that automatically stop attacks as they are detected by closing the appropriate logical ports or disallowing the suspicious activity.

What are hardware firewalls? You can also buy and configure hardware firewall devices. For example, when buying a router

for your network, make sure to buy one that also acts as a firewall. Manufacturers such as Linksys, D-Link, and Netgear make routers that double as firewalls. Just like software firewalls, the setup in hardware firewalls is designed for novices, and the default configuration is to keep unnecessary logical ports closed. Documentation accompanying the firewalls can assist more experienced users in adjusting the settings to allow access to specific ports if needed.

IS YOUR COMPUTER SECURE?

How can I tell if my computer is at risk? For peace of mind (and to ensure your firewall setup was successful), you can visit several Web sites that offer free services that test your computer's vulnerability. A popular site is Gibson Research (**www.grc.com**). The company's ShieldsUP and LeakTest programs are free and easy to run and can pinpoint security vulnerabilities in a system connected to the Internet. If you get a clean report from these programs, your system is probably not vulnerable to attack. Figure 7.25 shows the results screen from a ShieldsUP port probe test, which checks which logical ports in your computer are vulnerable.

What if I don't get a clean report from the testing program? If the testing program detects potential vulnerabilities

FIGURE 7.25

This screen shows results from a ShieldsUP port probe test. This test was run on a computer connected to the Internet with no firewall installed. Any ports that are reported as open (such as port 1025) by this test represent vulnerabilities that could be exploited by hackers. Installation of a hardware or software firewall should close any open ports.

143	IMAP	Closed	Your computer has responded that this port exists but is currently closed to connections.
389	LDAP	Closed	Your computer has responded that this port exists but is currently closed to connections.
443	HTTPS	Closed	Your computer has responded that this port exists but is currently closed to connections.
445	MSFT DS	Stealth	There is NO EVIDENCE WHATSOEVER that a port (or even any computer) exists at this IP address!
1002	ms-ils	Closed	Your computer has responded that this port exists but is currently closed to connections.
1024	DCOM	Closed	Your computer has responded that this port exists but is currently closed to connections.
1025	Host	OPEN!	One or more unspecified Distributed COM (DCOM) services are opened by Windows. The exact port(s) opened can change, since queries to port 135 are used to determine which services are operating where. As is the rule for all exposed Internet services, you should arrange to close this port to external access so that potential current and future security or privacy exploits can not succeed against your system.
1026	Host	Closed	Your computer has responded that this port exists but is currently closed to connections.
1027	Host	Closed	Your computer has responded that this port exists but is currently closed to connections.

Ports reported as closed or in stealth mode are safe from attack

Ports reported as open are subject to exploitation by hackers

and you don't have a firewall, you should install one as soon as possible. If the firewall is already configured and specific ports are shown as being vulnerable, consult your firewall documentation for instructions on how to close or restrict access to those ports.

Securing Wireless Networks

When running a wireless network, installing a firewall is a key precaution. But wireless networks present special vulnerabilities that wired networks do not. Therefore, there are additional specific steps you should take to keep your wireless network safe.

Why is a wireless network more vulnerable than a wired network? If you're keeping a wired network secure with a firewall, you're fairly safe from most hacker attacks. However, wireless networks, especially with 802.11g and 802.11n equipment, have wide ranges, including areas outside of your house. This makes it possible for a hacker to access your network without you even knowing it.

Why should I be worried about strangers using my wireless network? Some use of other people's wireless networks is unintentional. Houses are built close together. Apartments are clustered even closer together. Wireless signals can easily reach a neighbor's residence. Most wireless network adapters are set up to access the strongest wireless network signal detected. If your router is on the east side or your house and you and your laptop are on the west side, you may be getting a stronger signal from your neighbor's wireless network than from your own.

So why should you care if your neighbor is logged onto your network instead of his? Your neighbor probably isn't a hacker, but he might be using a lot of bandwidth—your bandwidth! If he's downloading a massive movie file while you're trying to do research for a term paper, he's probably slowing you down. Also, when some less than honest neighbors discover they can log onto your wireless network, they may cancel their own Internet service to save money by using yours.

In addition, since cyberattacks are traceable, criminals love to launch attacks (such as DDoS attacks) from public computers (such as in a library) so they can't be identified. If a criminal is sitting in his car outside your house and logging on to your wireless network, any cyberattacks he launches might be traced back to your IP address and you may find some law enforcement officials knocking on your door.

Won't a firewall protect me? Firewalls will protect you from a lot of cyberattacks. However, on a wireless network, because your packets of information are being broadcast through the airwaves, a savvy hacker can intercept and decode information from your transmissions that may allow him to bypass your firewall. Therefore, to secure a wireless network, you should take the following additional precautions:

1. **Change Your Network Name (SSID):** Each wireless network has its own name to identify it. Unless you change this name when you set up your router, the router uses a default network name (also known as the *service set identifier* or SSID) that all routers from that manufacturer use (such as "Wireless"). Hackers know the default names and access codes for routers. If you haven't changed the SSID, it's advertising the fact that you probably haven't changed any of the other default settings for your router either.

2. **Disable SSID Broadcast:** Most routers are set up to broadcast their SSID so other wireless devices can find them. If your router supports disabling SSID broadcasting, turn it off. This makes it more difficult for a hacker to detect your network.

3. **Change the Default Password on Your Router:** Hackers know the default passwords of most routers, and if they can access your router, they can probably break into your network. Change the password on your router to something hard to guess (use at least 8 characters with a combination of letters and numbers).

4. **Turn on Security Protocols:** Most routers ship with security protocols such as *Wired Equivalent Privacy (WEP)* or *Wi-Fi Protected Access (WPA)*. Both use *encryption* (a method of translating your data into code) to protect data in your wireless transmissions. WPA is a stronger protocol than WEP, so enable WPA if you have it; enable WEP if you don't. When you attempt to connect a

FIGURE 7.26

By running your router configuration wizard you can configure the security protocols available on your router and change the SSID, which helps protect your wireless network.

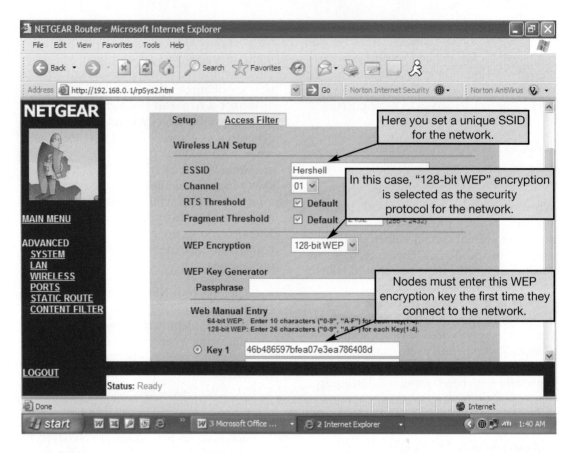

SOUND BYTE

Securing Wireless Networks

In this Sound Byte, you'll learn what "war drivers" are and why they could potentially be a threat to your wireless network. You'll also learn the simple steps to secure your wireless network against intruders.

node to a WEP- or WPA-enabled network for the first time, you're required to enter the encryption key. The encryption key (see Figure 7.26) is the code that computers on your network need to decrypt (decode) data transmissions. Without this key, it is very difficult (if not impossible) to decrypt the data transmissions from your network (see Figure 7.27). This prevents unauthorized access to your network as hackers won't know the correct key to use.

5. **Implement Media Access Control:** Each network adapter on your network has a unique number assigned to it by the manufacturer (like a serial number). This is called a Media Access Control address (or MAC address) and it is a number printed right on the network adapter. Many routers allow you to restrict access to the network to only certain MAC addresses. This helps ensure only authorized devices can connect to your network.

6. **Apply Firmware Upgrades:** Your router has read-only memory that has software written to it. This software is known as *firmware*. Periodically, as bugs are found in the firmware (which hackers might exploit), manufacturers issue patches, just as the makers of operating system software do. Periodically check the manufacturer's Web site and apply any necessary upgrades to your firmware.

Computer Threats: Computer Viruses

Keeping your computer safe entails keeping it safe from more than just hackers. You must also guard against computer viruses. A **computer virus** is a computer program that attaches itself to another computer program (known as the host program) and attempts to spread itself to other computers when files are exchanged. Viruses normally attempt to hide within the code of a host program to avoid detection.

What do computer viruses do? A computer virus's main purpose is to replicate itself and copy its code into as many other files as possible. Although virus replication can slow down networks, it is not usually the main threat. The majority of viruses have secondary objectives or side effects, ranging from displaying annoying messages on the computer screen to the destruction of files or the contents of entire hard drives. Because computer viruses do cause disruption to computer systems, including data destruction and information theft, virus creation is a form of cybercrime.

How does my computer catch a virus? If your computer is exposed to a file infected with a virus, the virus will try to copy itself and infect a file on your computer. If you never expose your computer to new files, it will not become infected. However, this would be the equivalent of a human being living in a bubble to avoid catching viruses from other people—quite unpractical, to say the least.

Sharing disks is a common source of virus infection, as is e-mail, although many people have misconceptions about how e-mail infection occurs. Just opening an e-mail message will not infect your computer with a virus. Downloading or running a file that is attached to the e-mail is how your computer becomes infected. Thus, be extremely wary of e-mail attachments, especially if you don't know the sender. Figure 7.28 shows how computer viruses are often passed from one computer to the next.

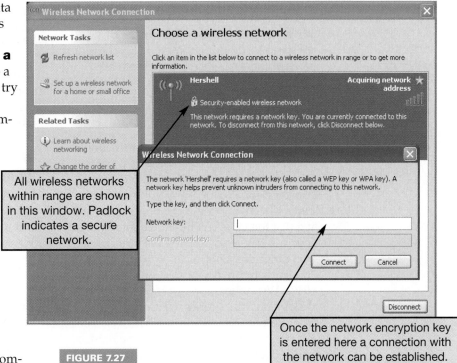

All wireless networks within range are shown in this window. Padlock indicates a secure network.

Once the network encryption key is entered here a connection with the network can be established.

FIGURE 7.27

The Windows wireless connection dialog box shows all wireless networks within range. Clicking on one allows you to connect to it. However, connecting to a security-enabled wireless network requires knowing the proper WEP or WPA network encryption key.

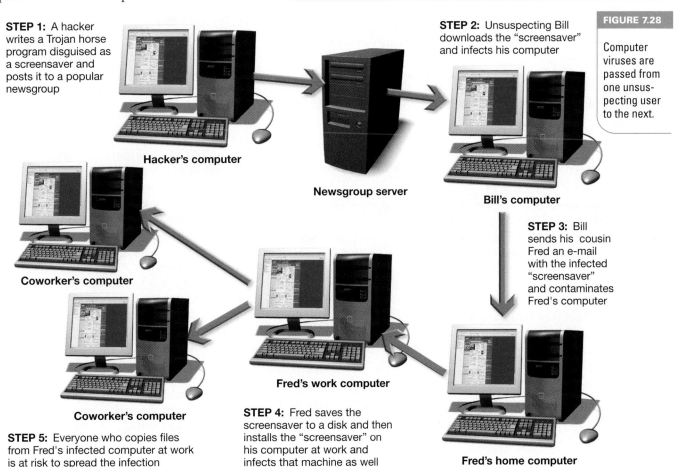

STEP 1: A hacker writes a Trojan horse program disguised as a screensaver and posts it to a popular newsgroup

STEP 2: Unsuspecting Bill downloads the "screensaver" and infects his computer

FIGURE 7.28

Computer viruses are passed from one unsuspecting user to the next.

Hacker's computer

Newsgroup server

Bill's computer

STEP 3: Bill sends his cousin Fred an e-mail with the infected "screensaver" and contaminates Fred's computer

Coworker's computer

Fred's work computer

STEP 4: Fred saves the screensaver to a disk and then installs the "screensaver" on his computer at work and infects that machine as well

Fred's home computer

Coworker's computer

STEP 5: Everyone who copies files from Fred's infected computer at work is at risk to spread the infection

TYPES OF VIRUSES

What are the different kinds of viruses? Although thousands of computer viruses and variants exist, they can be grouped into five broad categories based on their behavior and method of transmission.

Boot-Sector Viruses

What are boot-sector viruses? Boot-sector viruses replicate themselves into the Master Boot Record of a hard drive. The **Master Boot Record** is a program that executes whenever a computer boots up, ensuring that the virus will be loaded into memory immediately, even before some virus protection programs. Boot-sector viruses are often transmitted by a floppy disk left in a floppy drive. When the computer boots up with the disk in the drive, it tries to launch a Master Boot Record from the floppy, which is usually the trigger for the virus to infect the hard drive. Boot-sector viruses can be very destructive: they can erase your entire hard drive.

Logic Bombs and Time Bombs

What are logic bombs? Logic bombs are viruses that are triggered when certain logical conditions are met (such as opening a file, booting your computer or accessing certain programs). Time bombs are viruses that are triggered by the passage of time or on a certain date. The Michelangelo virus, first launched in 1992, is a famous time bomb that is set to trigger every year on March 6, Michelangelo's birthday. The effects of logic bombs and time bombs range from annoying messages being displayed on the screen to reformatting of the hard drive, causing complete data loss.

Worms

What are worms? Worms are slightly different from viruses in that they attempt to travel between systems through network connections to spread their infections. Viruses infect a host file and wait for that file to be executed on another computer to replicate. Worms can run independently of host file execution and are much more active in spreading themselves. The Sasser worm broke out in April 2004, infecting millions of individual computers and servers. This worm exploits a weakness in the Windows operating system and therefore antivirus software doesn't protect against this worm. However, having a firewall installed and applying software patches as they are issued can protect you from most worms.

Script and Macro Viruses

What are script and macro viruses? Some viruses are hidden on Web sites in the form of **scripts**. Scripts are lists of commands, actually mini programs, that are executed without your knowledge. Scripts are often used to perform useful, legitimate functions on Web sites, such as collecting name and address information from customers. However, some scripts are malicious. For example, say you receive an e-mail encouraging you to visit a Web site full of useful programs and information. Unbeknownst to you, clicking a link to display a video runs a script that infects your computer with a virus.

Macro viruses are attached to documents (such as Word and Excel documents) that use macros. A *macro* is a short series of commands that usually automates repetitive tasks. However, macro languages are now so sophisticated that viruses can be written with them. In March 1999, the Melissa virus became the first major macro virus to cause problems worldwide. It attached itself to a Word document. Anyone opening an infected document triggered the virus, which infected other Word documents on the victim's computer.

BITS AND BYTES

Virus Symptoms

If your computer is displaying any of the following symptoms, it may be infected with a virus:

1. Existing program icons or files suddenly disappear. Viruses often delete specific file types or programs.
2. Changes appear in your browser. If you fire up your browser and it takes you to an unusual home page (one you didn't set) or it has sprouted new toolbars, you may have a virus.
3. Odd messages or images are displayed on the screen or strange music or sounds play.
4. Data files become corrupted. Although there are many reasons why files become corrupt, a virus is one cause.
5. Programs don't work properly. This could be caused by either a corrupted file or a virus.

If you think you have a virus, boot up your computer with an antivirus software CD in your CD-ROM drive. This allows you to run the antivirus software before potential viruses load on the computer.

The Melissa virus was also the first practical example of an **e-mail virus**. E-mail viruses use the address book in the victim's e-mail system to distribute the virus. When executed, the Melissa virus sent itself to the first 50 people in the address book on the infected computer. This helped ensure that Melissa became one of the most widely distributed viruses ever released.

Trojan Horses

Are Trojan horses viruses? Trojan horses, although not technically viruses, behave similarly to viruses and are detected by most antivirus programs. Trojan horses do something unintended to the victim's computer (such as recording keystrokes to gather passwords) while pretending to do something else (such as acting as a screen saver). Once executed, they perform their malicious duties in the background, often invisible to the user. Trojan horses are generally deployed by hackers in attempts to control remote computers.

VIRUS CLASSIFICATIONS

How else are viruses classified? Viruses can also be classified by the methods they take to avoid detection by antivirus software:

- **Polymorphic viruses** change their own code (or periodically rewrite themselves) to avoid detection. Most polymorphic viruses infect one certain type of file (.exe files, for example).

- **Multipartite viruses** are designed to infect multiple file types in an effort to fool the antivirus software that is looking for them.
- **Stealth viruses** temporarily erase their code from the files where they reside and hide in the active memory of the computer. This helps them avoid detection if only the hard drive is being searched for viruses. Fortunately, antivirus software developers are aware of these tricks and have designed software to watch for them.

Computer Safeguards: Antivirus Software

Certain viruses merely present minor annoyances, such as randomly sending an ambulance graphic across the bottom of the screen, as is the case with the Red Cross virus. Other viruses can significantly slow down a computer or network or destroy key files or the contents of entire hard drives. The best defense against viruses is to install **antivirus software**, which is specifically designed to detect viruses and protect your computer and files from harm.

How often do I need to run antivirus software? You should run a virus check on your entire system at least once a week. By doing so, all files on your computer are checked for undetected viruses. Because these checks take time, you can configure the software to run these checks automatically when you aren't using your system, such as late at night (see Figure 7.29).

FIGURE 7.29

By setting up a schedule in the antivirus module of Norton Internet Security, complete virus scans can be set up to run automatically. This computer will be scanned every Friday at 8:00 P.M.

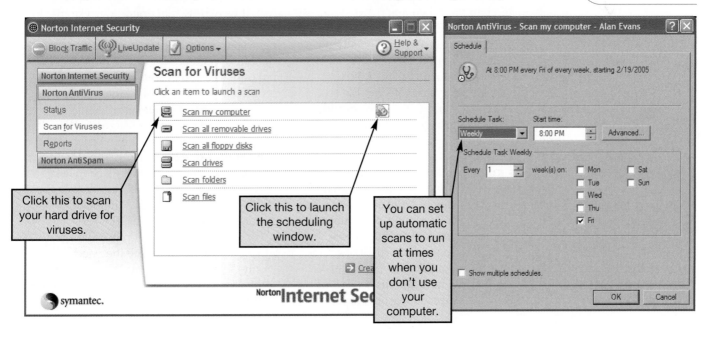

guise their virus code and hide the effects of a virus until just the right moment. This helps ensure the virus spreads faster and farther. Thus, your computer can still be attacked by a virus that your antivirus software doesn't recognize. To minimize this risk, you should keep your antivirus software up-to-date.

How do I make sure my antivirus software is up-to-date? Most antivirus programs have an automatic updates feature that downloads a list of upgrades you can install on your computer while you're online (see Figure 7.30). Automatic updates ensure your programs are up-to-date.

What should I do if I think my computer is infected with a virus? Boot up your computer with the antivirus CD that came with your antivirus software in your CD drive. This should prevent most virus programs from loading and will allow you to run the antivirus directly from the CD drive. If viruses are detected, you may want to research them further to determine whether your antivirus software will eradicate them completely or if you need to take additional manual steps to eliminate the virus. Most antivirus company Web sites (such as **www.symantec.com**) contain archives of information on viruses and provide step-by-step solutions for removing viruses.

FIGURE 7.30

Norton's LiveUpdate provides automatic updates on all virus and security products installed on the computer. It can be set to automatically update every time you connect to the Internet.

How does antivirus software work?

Most antivirus software looks for **virus signatures** in files. Signatures are portions of the virus code that are unique to a particular computer virus. Antivirus software scans files for these signatures and thereby identifies infected files and the type of virus that is infecting them.

The antivirus software scans files when they're opened or executed. If it detects a virus signature or suspicious activity (such as launching an unknown macro), it stops the execution of the file and virus and notifies you it has detected a virus. Usually it gives you the choice of deleting or repairing the infected file. Unfortunately, antivirus programs can't always fix infected files so that the files are usable again. You should keep backup copies of critical files so you can restore them in case a virus damages them irreparably.

Does antivirus software always stop viruses?

Antivirus software catches *known* viruses effectively. Unfortunately, new viruses are written all the time. To combat unknown viruses, modern antivirus programs search for suspicious virus-like activities as well as virus signatures. However, virus authors know how antivirus software works. They take special measures to dis-

OTHER SECURITY MEASURES

Is there anything else I should do to protect my system? Many viruses exploit weaknesses in operating systems. To combat these threats, make sure your operating system is up-to-date and contains the latest security patches (or fixes). Windows XP makes this easy by providing automatic updates. When you enable automatic updates, your computer searches for Windows updates on the Microsoft Web site every time it connects to the Internet.

How do I enable automatic updates? To enable automatic updates, click the Start button, select Control Panel, and double-click the System icon. Select the Automatic Updates tab, as shown in Figure 7.31.

For more information on how you can protect your computer, see the Special Feature with Technology in Focus feature "Protecting Your Computer and Backing Up Your Data" on page 374.

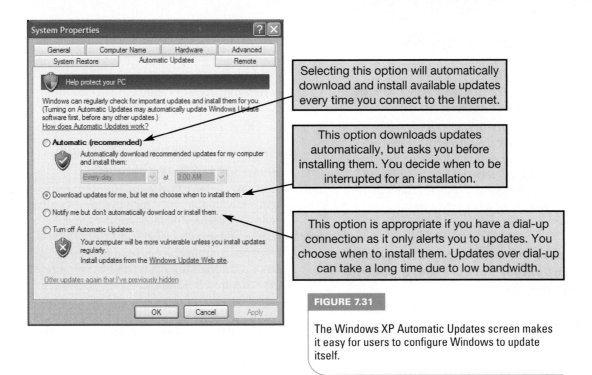

Selecting this option will automatically download and install available updates every time you connect to the Internet.

This option downloads updates automatically, but asks you before installing them. You decide when to be interrupted for an installation.

This option is appropriate if you have a dial-up connection as it only alerts you to updates. You choose when to install them. Updates over dial-up can take a long time due to low bandwidth.

FIGURE 7.31

The Windows XP Automatic Updates screen makes it easy for users to configure Windows to update itself.

TRENDS IN IT

Careers: Cybercops on the Beat: Computer Security Careers

With billions being spent on e-commerce initiatives every year, companies have a vested interest in keeping their Information Technology (IT) infrastructures humming along. The rise in terrorism has shifted the focus slightly from protecting just virtual assets and access to protecting physical assets and access points as well. The increased need for virtual and physical security measures means there should be a robust job market ahead for computer security experts.

What skill sets will be most in demand for security professionals? Obviously, strong technical skills with an emphasis on network engineering and data communications are essential. Security certifications certainly provide evidence of appropriate training and skills mastery. However, just as necessary are broad-based business experience and skills. IT security professionals need to understand the key issues of e-commerce and the core areas of their company's business (such as marketing, sales, and finance). Understanding how a business works is essential to pinpointing and correcting the security risks that could be detrimental to a company's bottom line. And because of the large number of attacks by hackers, security forensic skills and certifications are in high demand. Working closely with law enforcement officials is essential to rapidly solving and stopping cybercrime.

Another important attribute of security professionals is the ability to lead and motivate teams. Security experts need to work with diverse members of the business community, including customers, to forge relationships and understanding among diverse groups. Security professionals must conduct skillful negotiations to ensure that large project implementations are not unduly delayed by security initiatives, or pushed through with inadequate security precautions. Diplomacy is therefore a sought-after skill.

Look for more colleges and universities to roll out security-based degrees and certificate programs as the demand for security professionals increases. These programs will most likely be appropriate for experienced networking professionals who are ready to make the move into the IT security field. If you're just preparing for a career, consider a degree in network engineering, followed by network security training while you're working at your first job. This should ensure a smooth transition into the exciting world of cybersecurity.

1. What is a network and what are the advantages of setting up one?

A computer network is simply two or more computers that are connected together using software and hardware so they can communicate. Networks allow users to (1) share peripherals, (2) transfer files easily, and (3) share an Internet connection.

2. What is the difference between a client/server network and a peer-to-peer network?

In peer-to-peer networks, each node connected to the network can communicate directly with every other node instead of having a separate device exercise central control over the network. Peer-to-peer networks are the most common type of network installed in homes. Most networks that have 10 or more nodes are client/server networks. A client/server network contains two types of computers: a client computer on which users accomplish specific tasks, and a server computer that provides resources to the clients and central control for the network.

3. What are the main components of every network?

To function, all networks contain four components: (1) transmission media (cables or radio waves) to connect and establish communication between nodes; (2) network adapters that allow the nodes on the network to communicate; (3) network navigation devices (such as routers and hubs) that move data around the network; and (4) software that allows the network to run.

4. What are the most common home networks?

The two most common home networks are wired Ethernet and wireless Ethernet. Although waning in popularity, power-line and phoneline networks may still be an option in certain situations. The major difference in these networks is the trans-

mission media by which the nodes are connected.

5. What are wired Ethernet networks and how are they created?

Ethernet networks use the Ethernet protocol as the means by which the nodes on the network communicate. This protocol makes Ethernet networks efficient but also slightly complex. Because of this complexity, additional devices (switches or routers) are required in Ethernet networks. To create a wired Ethernet network, you connect or install network adapters or NICs to each network node. Network adapters connect via cables to a central network navigation device such as a switch or a router. Data flows through the navigation device to the nodes on the network.

6. What are wireless Ethernet networks and how are they created?

A wireless network uses radio waves instead of wires or cable as its transmission media. Current wireless protocols provide for networks with up to a maximum of 108 Mbps. To create a wireless network, you install or attach wireless network adapters to the nodes that will make up the network. If the nodes are unable to communicate because of distance, you can add a wireless access point to the network to help relay data between nodes. Wireless networks are susceptible to interference from other wireless devices such as phones.

7. How are power-line and phoneline networks created and are they viable alternatives to Ethernet networks?

Power-line networks use the electrical wiring in your home to connect the nodes in the network. Phoneline networks move data through the network using conventional phone lines. To create either of these networks, you connect special network adapters to each node on the network. These adapters are then plugged into either an electrical outlet or a phone jack, and data is transmitted through either the electrical wires or the phone cable. Power-line and phoneline networks have relatively low throughput and cost more than Ethernet networks.

8. How can hackers attack a network and what harm can they cause?

A hacker is defined as anyone who breaks into a computer system unlawfully. Hackers can use software to break into almost any computer connected to the Internet (unless proper precautions are taken). Once hackers gain access to a computer, they can (1) potentially steal personal or other important information; (2) damage and destroy data; or (3) use the computer to attack other computers.

9. What is a firewall and how does it keep my computer safe from hackers?

Firewalls are software programs or hardware devices designed to keep computers safe from hackers. By using a personal firewall, you can close off to invaders open logical ports and potentially make your computer invisible to other computers on the Internet.

10. Why are wireless networks more vulnerable than wired networks and what special precautions are required to ensure my wireless network is secure?

Wireless networks are even more susceptible to hacking than wired networks because the signals of most wireless networks extend beyond the walls of your home. Neighbors may unintentionally (or intentionally) connect to the Internet through your wireless connection and hackers may try to access it. To prevent unwanted instruction to your network, you should change the default password on your router (to make it tougher for hackers to gain access), use a hard to guess SSID (network name), turn off SSID broadcasting (harder for outsiders to detect your network), and enable security protocols such as WPA or WEP.

11. From which types of viruses do I need to protect my computer?

A computer virus is a program that attaches itself to another program and attempts to spread itself to other computers when files are exchanged. Computer viruses can be grouped into five categories: (1) boot-sector viruses, (2) logic bombs and time bombs, (3) worms, (4) scripts and macros, and (5) Trojan horses. Once run, they perform their malicious duties in the background, often invisible to the user.

12. What can I do to protect my computer from viruses?

The best defense against viruses is to install antivirus software. You should update the software on a regular basis and configure it to examine all e-mail attachments for viruses. You should periodically run a complete virus scan on your computer to ensure that no viruses have made it onto your hard drive.

Buzz Words

Word Bank

- antivirus software
- Cat 5E
- client/server
- cybercriminal
- firewall
- hacker(s)

- identity theft
- logical port(s)
- network adapter(s)
- network interface card(s)
- peer-to-peer (P2P)
- phone cable

- router
- throughput
- virus
- wired Ethernet
- wireless Ethernet
- zombie(s)

Instructions: Fill in the blanks using the words from the Word Bank above.

Cathi needed to network three computers for herself and her roommates (Sharon and Emily). She decided that a(n) (1) _____ network was the right type to install in their apartment because that was the most common type of home network. Because none of them were gamers or transferred large files, they didn't need high (2) _____ . Still, they decided to use the fastest type of home network, a(n) (3) _____ network, because it is reliable and easy to install. To connect the computers, they needed to buy (4) _____ cable. Because Sharon already had high-speed Internet access through the cable TV company, she needed to buy a(n) (5) _____ for the network to ensure all users could share the connection. Fortunately, all their computers already had (6) _____ installed, making it easy to connect the computers to the network.

Cathi's roommate Emily was skeptical of being hooked up to the Internet because she had been the victim of (7) _____ , which destroyed her credit rating. A(n) (8) _____ had obtained her credit card information by posing as an employee of her bank. Cathi assured Emily that the (9) _____ could be configured as a(n) (10) _____ to repel malicious (11) _____ . Turning off the unused (12) _____ would repel most attacks on their home network. With this protection, it was unlikely that a hacker would turn their PCs into (13) _____ to launch DDoS attacks. But after the scare with the Melissa (14) _____ , Cathi was careful to warn the others not to open files from untrusted sources. She also made sure they all installed (15) _____ on their PCs to protect them from viruses.

Becoming Computer Fluent

While attending college, you are working at the Snap-Tite company, a small manufacturer of specialty fasteners. Currently, they must copy files to floppy disks to transfer them between the four PCs the company owns. Only the company president has access to the Internet. The accounts payable clerk is the only one who has a printer and is constantly being interrupted by other employees when they want to print their files. Your boss heard that you were taking a computer course and asked you to create a solution.

Instructions: Using the preceding scenario, draft a networking plan for Snap-Tite using as many of the keywords from the chapter as you can. Be sure that the relatively computer-illiterate company president can understand the report.

Instructions: Answer the multiple choice and true/false questions below for more practice with key terms and concepts from this chapter.

MULTIPLE CHOICE

1. Which of the following is not a benefit of installing a home network?
   a. file sharing
   b. peripheral sharing
   c. bandwidth sharing
   d. Internet connection sharing

2. Which of the following is NOT a reason why client/server networks are generally not installed in homes?
   a. Servers are too difficult for most home users to set up.
   b. Client/server networks don't have as many security features as home networks.
   c. Client/server networks provide more security than is needed in a home network.
   d. Client/server networks are more expensive than peer-to-peer networks.

3. *All* networks contain the following elements except
   a. transmission media
   b. network adapters
   c. network software
   d. servers

4. Because of their complexity, Ethernet networks require network navigation devices. An example of such a device is a
   a. switch   b. packet mover
   c. Cat 5E   d. UPS

5. Wireless networks are popular because
   a. You don't need wires to install them.
   b. They are much less complicated to set up than wired Ethernet networks.
   c. They cost less than wired networks.
   d. all of the above

6. Power-line and phoneline networks are not very popular any longer mainly because
   a. They are expensive.

   b. They can't provide as much throughput as Ethernet networks.
   c. both A and B
   d. none of the above

7. When hackers use computers they have gained control over to launch an attack against a Web site that prevents legitimate users from accessing the site, this is called a
   a. Zombie Denial of Service Attack
   b. Worm Virus Attack
   c. Trojan Horse Attack
   d. Distributed Denial of Service Attack

8. Which of the following is NOT a benefit of firewalls?
   a. They make it harder for a hacker to locate specific computers on a network.
   b. They repeatedly change the IP address of the router.
   c. They close off unused logical ports.
   d. They filter out unwanted packets.

9. Wireless Ethernet networks are attractive to hackers because
   a. They are easier to penetrate than wired Ethernet networks because the 802.11 protocol has weak security rules.
   b. You can't install a firewall on a wireless Ethernet network.
   c. The signals from the network can travel beyond the walls of your home.
   d. They have greater bandwidth than wired networks, making it easier for hackers to conceal their activities.

10. Viruses that are often hidden in Microsoft Office documents are called
    a. worms   b. stealth viruses
    c. logic bombs   d. macro viruses

TRUE/FALSE

_____ 1. Wireless Ethernet networks provide the highest possible throughput for home networks.

_____ 2. Home networks require each computer on the network to be equipped with its own router.

_____ 3. A firewall will stop most hackers from accessing your network through your Internet connection.

_____ 4. Never downloading files from the Internet will ensure your computer is safe from viruses.

_____ 5. Wireless networks are subject to interference from large metal objects.

Making the Transition to... Next Semester

1. Dormitory Networking

Dave, Jerome, and Thomas were sitting in the common room of their campus suite staring at $80 piled up on the coffee table. Selling last semester's books back to the bookstore had been a good idea. As they waited for their other roommate Phil to come home, Dave said, "Wouldn't it be cool if we could network our laptops? Then we could play Ultra Super Robot Kill-fest in team mode!" Jerome pointed out it would be even more useful if they could all have access to Dave's laser printer because he owned the only one. "And Jerome's always bugging me to use my scanner when I'm trying to sleep," remarked Thomas. "And I can't believe the only high-speed Internet connection is out here in the lounge!" The three roommates ran down the hall and rapped on your door looking for some guidance. Consider how you would answer their questions:

a. Is $80 enough to set up a wired network for four laptops in four separate rooms? (Assume there are no phone jacks in the rooms.)

b. Can the roommates share a printer and a scanner if they set up a wired network?

c. How would they share the one high-speed Internet connection?

d. Phil just returned from the campus post office with a check from his aunt for $50. Do the roommates now have enough money to set up a wireless network to include their two friends across the hall?

To answer these questions, use the chapter text and the following resources: **www.coolcomputing.com, www.pricewatch.com, www.linksys.com, www.netgear.com, www.bestbuy.com,** *and* **www.tigerdirect.com**.

2. Grid Computing with SETI

In the Trends in IT feature, you learned about the PatriotGrid project in which computer users donate their computing power to help fight bioterrorism. Another grid computing project is being conducted by the Search for Extra Terrestrial Intelligence (SETI) Institute. The SETI@home project searches the heavens for radio waves indicating the presence of intelligent life in other solar systems. By installing free software, scientists use your computer during its otherwise idle periods to process data received by the SETI project.

a. Go to the SETI@home Web site (**http://setiathome.ssl.berkeley.edu**) and click the Learn about SETI@home link. Then download the software and install it.

b. Review the available information and write a short summary of how this program works.

c. Search the Web for other grid computing projects. What other projects did you find?

3. Identity Theft Awareness

Two students in your residence hall have recently been the victims of identity theft. You have been assigned to create a flyer telling students how they can protect themselves from identity theft in the residence hall. Using the information found in this chapter, materials you find on the U.S. federal government Web site on identity theft (**www.consumer.gov/idtheft**), as well as other Web resources, create a flyer that lists 5 to 10 ways in which students can avoid having their identities stolen.

Making the Transition to...
The Workplace

1. Antivirus Protection

Your employer recently installed high-speed Internet access at the office where you work. There are 50 workstations connected to the network and the Internet. Within a week, half the computers in the office were down because of a virus that was contracted by a screen saver. In addition, network personnel from a university in England contacted the company, claiming that your employer's computer systems were being used as part of a DDoS attack on their Web site.

a. Price out antivirus software on the Internet and determine the most cost-effective package for the company to implement on 50 workstations.

b. Write a "virus prevention" memo to all employees suggesting strategies for avoiding virus infections.

c. Draft a note to the CEO explaining how a firewall could prevent distributed denial of service attacks from being launched on the company network.

2. Public Wireless Access

Many corporations are using wireless technology to enhance or drive their businesses. Assume you are opening a local coffee shop in your town. Investigate the following:

a. Starbucks (**www.starbucks.com**) currently provides wireless access (for a fee) in many of its locations. Using **www.wifinder.com** or **www.wi-fihotspot.com**, find the closest Starbucks to your home that features wireless access. Will this store compete with your proposed store or is it too far away?

b. Contact or visit your local Starbucks and find out the cost of its wireless access. Research on the Internet and find out whether wireless access is profitable for Starbucks and whether it drives customers to their stores (many articles have been written about this).

c. As part of your business plan, write a paragraph or two explaining why you will (or will not) offer wireless connectivity at your coffee shop and whether it will be a pay service or a free service.

Can you find any free alternatives for wireless access within a 10-mile radius of your proposed store location? How will this affect your decision to offer wireless connectivity at your business?

3. Testing Your Computer

Visit Gibson Research at **www.grc.com** and run the company's ShieldsUP and LeakTest programs on your computer.

a. Did your computer get a clean report? If not, what potential vulnerabilities did the testing programs detect?

b. How could you protect yourself from the vulnerabilities these programs can detect?

Critical Thinking Questions

Instructions: Albert Einstein used "Gedanken experiments," or critical thinking questions, to develop his theory of relativity. Some ideas are best understood by experimenting with them in our own minds. The following critical thinking questions are designed to demand your full attention but only require a comfortable chair—no technology.

1. Home Networking: A Profession?

Many people will be installing computer networks in their homes over the next five years.

a. Would starting a home networking installation business be a good entry-level job for a college graduate? Could it be a good part-time job for a college student?

b. Assuming the home networking business failed, what other careers would the technicians be prepared to assume?

2. Upgrading Your Wireless

You have just spent $70 installing a new wireless network in your home. A new wireless standard of networking will be launched next month that is 10 times as fast as the wireless network you installed.

a. What types of applications would you need to be using heavily to make it worth upgrading to the new standard?

b. Can your next-door neighbor use his wireless-equipped notebook to surf off your Internet connection, thereby saving him the cost of purchasing a connection of his own? Is this ethical?

3. Ethical Hacking?

Hackers and virus authors cause millions of dollars worth of damage to PCs and networks annually. But hacking is a very controversial subject. Many hackers believe they are actually working for the "good of the people" or "exercising their freedom" when they engage in hacking activities. However, in most jurisdictions in the United States, hacking is punishable by stiff fines and jail terms.

a. Hackers often argue that hacking is for the good of all people because it points out flaws in computer systems. Do you agree with this? Why or why not?

b. What should the punishment be for convicted hackers and why?

c. Who should be held accountable at a corporation whose network security is breached by a hacker?

4. Keeping Networks Safe from Cyberterrorists

Many of us rely on networks every day, often without realizing it. Whether using the Internet, ordering a book from Amazon.com, or accessing your college e-mail from home, you are relying on networks to relay information. But what if terrorists destroyed key components of the Internet or other networks on which we depend?

a. What economic problems would result from DDoS attacks launched by terrorists on major e-commerce sites?

b. Research the precautions that the U.S. military and intelligence agencies (FBI, CIA) are taking to ensure that networks involving national defense remain secure from terrorist attacks? What else should they do?

5. Protection for Your Computer?

Do you have a firewall or antivirus software installed on your office computer? If not, why not? Have you ever been a victim of a hacker or a virus?

Problem:

Wireless technology is being adopted by leaps and bounds both in the home and in the workplace. Offering easy access free of physical tethers to networks seems to be a solution to many problems. However, wireless computing also has problems, ranging from poor reception to hijackers stealing your bandwidth.

Task:

Your campus has recently undertaken a wireless computing initiative. As part of the plan, your dorm has just been outfitted with wireless access points (base stations) to provide students with connectivity to the Internet and the college network. However, since the installation, students have reported poor connectivity in certain areas and extremely low bandwidth at other times. Your group has volunteered to research the potential problems and to suggest solutions to the college IT department.

Process:

Break the class into three teams. Each team will be responsible for investigating one of the following issues:

1. **Detecting Poor Connectivity:** Research methods that can be used to find areas of poor signal strength such as signal sniffing software (**www.netstumbler.com**) and handheld scanning devices such as WiFi Finder (**www.kensington.com.sg**). Investigate maximum distances between access points and network nodes (equipment manufacturers such as **www.netgear.com** and **www.linksys.com** provide guidelines) and make appropriate recommendations.

2. **Signal Boosters:** Research alternatives that can be used to increase signal strength in access points, antennas, and wireless cards. Signal boosters are available for access points. You can purchase or construct replacement antennas or antenna enhancements. Wi-Fi cards that offer higher power than conventional cards are now available.

3. **Security:** "War drivers" (people who cruise neighborhoods looking for open wireless networks from which to steal bandwidth) may be the cause of the bandwidth issues. Research appropriate measures to keep wireless network traffic secure from eavesdropping by hackers. In your investigation, look into the new Wi-Fi Protected Access (WPA) standard developed by the Wi-Fi Alliance. Check out the security section on the Wi-Fi Alliance Web site to start (**www.weca.net**).

Present your findings to your class and discuss possible causes and preventative measures for the problems encountered at your dorm. Provide your instructor with a report suitable for eventual presentation to the college IT department.

Conclusion:

As technology improves, wireless connectivity should eventually become the standard method of communication between networks and network devices. As with any other technology, security risks exist. Understanding those risks and how to mitigate them will allow you to participate in the design and deployment of network technology and provide peace of mind for your network users.

Multimedia

In addition to the review materials presented here, you'll find additional materials featured with the book's multimedia, including the *Technology in Action* Student Resource CD and the Companion Web site **(www.prenhall.com/techinaction)**, which will help reinforce your understanding of the chapter content. These materials include the following:

ACTIVE HELPDESK

In Active Helpdesk calls, you'll assume the role of a Helpdesk operator taking calls about the concepts you've learned in this chapter. You'll apply what you've learned and receive feedback from a supervisor to review and reinforce those concepts. The Active Helpdesk calls for this chapter are listed below and can be found on your Student Resource CD:

- Understanding Networking
- Understanding Firewalls
- Avoiding Computer Viruses

SOUND BYTES

Sound Bytes are dynamic multimedia tutorials that help demystify even the most complex topics. You'll view video clips and animations that illustrate computer concepts, and then apply what you've learned by reviewing with the Sound Byte Labs, which include quizzes and activities specifically tailored to each Sound Byte. The Sound Bytes for this chapter are listed here and can be found on your Student Resource CD and on the Companion Web site **(www.prenhall.com/techinaction):**

- Installing a Computer Network
- Installing a Personal Firewall
- Securing Wireless Networks
- Protecting Your Computer

COMPANION WEB SITE

The *Technology in Action* Companion Web site includes a variety of additional materials to help you review and learn more about the topics in this chapter. The resources available at **www.prenhall.com/techinaction** include:

- **Online Study Guide.** Each chapter features an online true/false and multiple-choice quiz. You can take these quizzes, automatically check the results, and e-mail the results to your instructor.

- **Web Research Projects.** Each chapter features a number of Web research projects that ask you to search the Web for information on computer-related careers, milestones in computer history, important people and companies, emerging technologies, and the applications and implications of different technologies.

chapter eight

Mobile Computing:

Keeping Your Data on Hand

Objectives

After reading this chapter, you should be able to answer the following questions:

1. What are the advantages and limitations of mobile computing? **(pp. 336–338)**

2. What are the various mobile computing devices? **(p. 338)**

3. What can pagers do and who uses them? **(pp. 338–339)**

4. How do cell phone components resemble a traditional computer and how do they work? **(pp. 339–343)**

5. What can I carry in an MP3 player and how does it store data? **(pp. 343–348)**

6. What can I use a PDA for and what internal components and features does it have? **(pp. 348–351)**

7. How can I synchronize my PDA with my desktop computer? **(pp. 351–354)**

8. What is a tablet PC and why would I want to use one? **(pp. 354–358)**

9. How powerful are laptops and how do they compare to desktop computers? **(pp. 359–363)**

ACTIVE HELPDESK

- Using MP3 Players **(p. 346)**
- Using PDAs **(p. 354)**

Using Mobile Computing Devices

Kendra wakes up at 5:00 A.M. to get an early start to what will be a long day. She's taking a business trip for her new job, and it's a long flight from Boston to LA. She's packed her cell phone, her laptop, and her personal digital assistant (PDA) and has updated her contact information for all her LA contacts. Despite her preparation, when she arrives at the airport, she finds her flight has been canceled. Trying not to get upset, she pulls out her PDA, accesses her wireless Internet account, and rebooks a ticket on a competing airline while fellow passengers are racing off to the ticket counter. With an e-mail to her business contacts in LA letting them know she'll be late, she smoothes the first wrinkle in her trip.

As Kendra waits for her new flight, she checks her work schedule on her PDA and e-mails a few clients. Because she'll be driving from the airport to the hotel on unfamiliar streets, she has purchased map software for her PDA that shows her the best route. She calls the rental car agency on her cell phone and tells them she'll be picking up the car later than planned, then checks out some LA restaurant reviews on the Internet. With an hour left before her plane takes off, she does some work on her laptop. She updates her expense report file, including the new flight information. Although canceled flights are never convenient, at least she's had a few hours to take care of some work before arriving in LA.

As this scenario indicates, mobile devices can offer you a great deal of convenience and can increase your productivity when you're away from the office. And going mobile is increasingly becoming the norm, as more people are buying cell phones and other mobile devices. In fact, more than 175 million Americans currently own cell phones, and that number is expected to rise in the next five years. In this chapter, we discuss the advantages and disadvantages of going mobile and look at the range of mobile computing devices you can choose from, discussing their components, features, and capabilities. Along the way, you'll learn how you can synchronize your mobile devices to make even better use of them. Whether you have already gone mobile or are still considering your options, this chapter will help you become a savvy consumer, taking full advantage of the world of mobile computing.

SOUND BYTES

- PDAs on the Road and at Home **(p. 352)**
- Connecting with Bluetooth **(p. 352)**
- Tablet and Laptop Tour **(p. 362)**

Mobile Computing: Is It Right for You?

Just 30 years ago, the idea of a powerful personal computer that could fit on a desktop was a dream. Today, you can carry computers around in your backpack, fit them in your pocket, and even incorporate them into your clothes. **Mobile computing devices**—portable electronic tools such as cell phones, personal digital assistants (PDAs), and laptops—are dramatically changing our day-to-day lives, allowing us to communicate with others, remain productive, and access a wide array of information no matter where we are.

Still, going mobile isn't for everyone. Although having instant access to your e-mail, schedule, and the Internet wherever you are during the day can be convenient and boost your productivity, there is a downside associated with mobile computing: Because mobile devices have been miniaturized, they're more expensive and less rugged than stationary desktop equipment. It's therefore important that you balance the advantages of going mobile with how well doing so fits your lifestyle.

How do I know whether mobile devices are right for me? Before you buy any mobile device, consider whether your needs match what mobile devices can offer. To do so, ask yourself these questions:

- **Do I need to communicate with others when I'm away from my desk?** Whether it means talking on the phone or checking your e-mail, if you need to communicate no matter where you are, mobile devices may be right for you.

- **Do I need to access my electronic information when I'm away from my desk?** If you need to access and make changes to electronic information (such as an Outlook schedule or Excel report) when you're out and about, mobile devices such as PDAs and laptops would be valuable tools. However, if it's as efficient for you to keep paper records when you're away from your computer and later enter that data into your computer, you may not need mobile devices.

- **Do I need to access the Internet when I'm away from my desk?** Mobile devices that are **Web-enabled**—that is, set up so that they can access the Internet through a wireless network—allow you to have constant access to the Internet wherever you are. Of course, you'll access the Internet at greater speeds and for less cost when you're at home or in the office. However, if you need quickly changing information when you're away from your desk, Web-enabled mobile devices may be right for you.

- **Are the convenience and productivity mobile devices offer important to me?** Mobile devices can provide you with a great deal of convenience and help you to be more productive. For example, a nursing student would have an easier time performing a diagnostic interview with a patient if the reference codes she needed were available in her PDA rather than in a huge stack of books. Likewise, students who take online classes with products such as Blackboard can download their course and carry it on a PDA so that they can work on their assignments anywhere, with or without Internet access.

- **Is the information I need to carry already in an electronic format?** Do you currently use personal information management (PIM) software such as Microsoft Outlook to store your daily schedule and contact list? Or are your schedule and contact list currently in paper form? Converting information to an electronic format and learning how to use mobile devices are hidden costs of going mobile.

MOBILE DEVICE LIMITATIONS

What are the limitations of mobile devices? In addition to the questions previously discussed, it's important that you consider whether your needs match the limitations mobile devices have:

- Battery life limits the usefulness of mobile devices.

- The screen is small on most devices (making the Internet experience very different).

- The speed of Internet connection available to mobile devices is currently very low.

The benefits of Internet connectivity are also dependent on the wireless Internet coverage in your area. For example, if you travel in rural areas, it may be impossible

CINGULAR NATION GSM
No Roaming or Long Distance Charges Nationwide

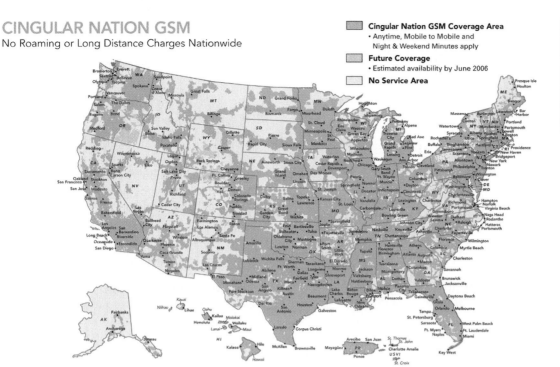

Cingular Nation GSM Coverage Area
- Anytime, Mobile to Mobile and Night & Weekend Minutes apply

Future Coverage
- Estimated availability by June 2006

No Service Area

FIGURE 8.1

This map shows Cingular's national network. Its wireless Internet coverage will most likely not cover all these areas.

to take advantage of wireless Internet connectivity. Figure 8.1 shows Cingular's network. Its wireless Internet coverage will most likely not cover all these areas.

As a student, you should consider how much of your campus is covered by wireless connectivity. Is your residence hall covered? Your classrooms? The library? Some schools create "wireless clouds" that enable you to be covered no matter where you are on campus. Other schools offer little coverage, making wireless connectivity to the Internet more difficult.

Finally, you must decide whether the extra cost of going mobile is worth the value and convenience. As mentioned earlier, mobile computing devices are more expensive and less rugged than desktop systems. Vibration, falls, dust, and liquids can all destroy your laptop, PDA, or cell phone. If the environment you live in or travel through is dusty or bumpy, for example, you should be prepared to spend money on additional warranty coverage or on repair and replacement costs. Finally, desktop systems always boast more expandability and better performance for the same cost when compared with mobile computers.

So, is mobile computing right for me? Figure 8.2 presents a checklist of the factors you need to consider when deciding

FIGURE 8.2 Are Mobile Devices Right for You?

Consideration	Yes	No
I need to be able to communicate with others when I'm away from my desk.		
I need to access my electronic information wherever I am.		
I need to access the Internet when I'm away from my desk.		
The added convenience and productivity mobile devices offer is important to me.		
The information I need to carry with me is already in an electronic format.		
My needs match the limitations of mobile devices (such as short battery life, small display screen on some devices, and low Internet connection speeds).		
Most of my living and travel locations are covered by wireless Internet access.		
It is worth the added expense for me to go mobile.		

whether to go mobile. Do your needs to communicate and access electronic information and the Internet when you're away from your desk make mobile devices a good investment?

Mobile Computing Devices

If you do decide to go mobile, there is a wide range of mobile computing devices on the market today:

- *Paging devices* provide you with limited communication capabilities but are inexpensive options if you want some of the features of mobile computing.
- *Cellular phones* feature traditional phone services such as call waiting and voice mail. Many now come with calendars, contact databases, text messaging, and e-mail capabilities.
- *MP3 players* allow you to carry music files and other digital files.
- *Personal digital assistants (PDAs)* are handheld devices that allow you to

carry much of the same digital information as desktop systems.
- *Tablet PCs* are larger and more powerful than PDAs and incorporate specialized handwriting-recognition software.
- *Laptop computers* are expensive and powerful tools for carrying electronic information.

Figure 8.3 lists the main features of these mobile devices. In the next sections, we look at each of these devices in detail.

Paging Devices

A **paging device** (or a **pager**) is a small wireless device that allows you to receive and sometimes send numeric (and sometimes text) messages on a small display screen. Pagers have very low power consumption, which means long battery lives, and are very compact. They're also the most inexpensive mobile computing device you can buy.

Are there different kinds of pagers? **Numeric pagers** display only numbers on their screens, telling you that you have received a page and providing you with the

FIGURE 8.3 Mobile Devices: Price, Size, Weight, and Capabilities

Device	Relative Price	Approximate Size	Approximate Weight	Standard Capabilities
Paging Device	$ (includes cost for the pager and a monthly plan)	2" × 2" × 0.5"	0.2 lbs.	Provides numeric and/or text messaging in one or two directions
Cell Phone	$$ (includes cost for the phone, a monthly plan, and Internet access)	5" × 2" × 0.5"	0.25 lbs.	Provides voice and e-mail connectivity
MP3 Player	$$–$$$	3" × 2" × 1"	0.25 lbs.	Provides storage of digital music files and other data
PDA	$$–$$$	5" × 3" × 1"	0.5 lbs.	Provides PIM capabilities, access to application software, and access to the Internet
Tablet PC	$$$$$	10" × 8" × 1"	3 lbs.	Provides PIM capabilities, access to application software, access to the Internet, and special handwriting- and speech-recognition capabilities
Laptop	$$$$–$$$$$	10" × 13" × 2"	5 to 8 lbs.	Provides all the capabilities of a desktop computer while also being portable

number you should call. Numeric pagers do not allow you to send a response. **Alphanumeric pagers** are much like numeric pagers, but they also can display text messages. Like numeric pagers, alphanumeric pagers do not allow you to send messages.

More useful are **two-way pagers**, which support both receiving and sending text messages. Two-way pagers have a small built-in keyboard so you can compose text messages, as shown in Figure 8.4. Advanced two-way pagers also include an address book that stores the phone numbers and e-mail addresses of your contacts. In addition, two-way pagers can notify you of e-mail and allow you to check it and send replies.

With all the new devices on the market, does anyone still use pagers? People who need to be reachable but want an inexpensive and lightweight device are the primary market for pagers. Some industries still use pagers to contact key staff on call, such as medical staff or critical computer technicians. Pagers cost less than a cell phone (they currently sell for about $35), and with monthly fees of around $10, they provide an inexpensive alternative to cell phones. However, as cell phones continue to drop in price and shrink in size, pagers will have a difficult time finding a market.

Cellular Phones

Cellular phones have evolved from their early days as large, clunky, boxlike devices to become compact, full-featured communication and information storage devices. Cell phones offer all of the features available on a traditional telephone system, including auto-redial, call timers, and voice-mail capabilities. Some cell phones also feature voice-activated dialing, which is important for hands-free operation. In addition, cell phones can offer Internet access, text messaging, personal information management (PIM) features, voice recording, and digital image and video capture.

CELL PHONE HARDWARE

Is a cell phone considered a computer? Cell phones are so advanced that they have the same components as a computer: a processor (central processing unit, or

CPU), memory, and input and output devices, as shown in Figure 8.5. A cell phone also requires software and has its own operating system (OS). One popular operating system for full-featured cell phones is the **Symbian OS**. Because many cell phones now handle e-mail, images, and even video, more complex operating systems such as Symbian are required to translate the user's commands into instructions for the processor.

FIGURE 8.4

The Motorola Talkabout T900 is an example of a two-way pager. It displays four large lines of text and supports preprogrammed replies and an address book.

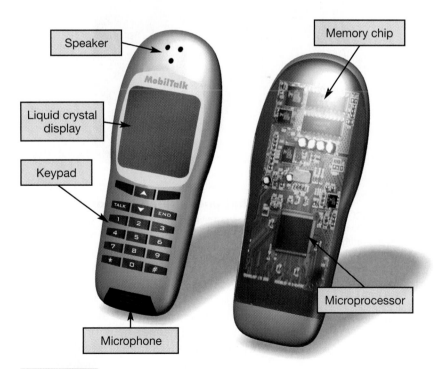

FIGURE 8.5

Inside your cell phone, you'll find some familiar components, including a microprocessor (CPU), a memory chip, input devices such as a microphone and a keypad, and output devices such as a display screen and a speaker.

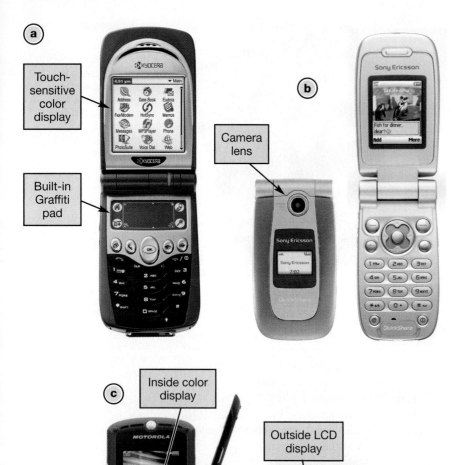

Touch-sensitive color display

Built-in Graffiti pad

Camera lens

Inside color display

Outside LCD display

FIGURE 8.6

(a) The Kyocera 7135 Smartphone includes a built-in Graffiti pad and touch-sensitive color screen. (b) The Sony Ericsson z500a can input both still photographs and video to your phone. With two color LCD displays, it offers picture caller-id support. (c) The Motorola's Moto RAZR V3 weighs less than 3.5 ounces and is smaller than 4" by 2" with an ultra-thin design.

What does the processor inside a cell phone do? Although the processor inside a cell phone is obviously not as fast or as high powered as a processor in a desktop computer, it is still responsible for a great number of tasks. The processor coordinates sending all of the data between the other electronic components inside the phone. It also runs the cell phone's operating system, which provides a user interface so that you can change phone settings, store information, play games, and so on.

What does the memory chip inside a cell phone do? The operating system and the information you save into your phone (such as phone numbers and addresses) need to be stored in memory. The operating system is stored in read-only memory (ROM) because the phone would be useless without that key piece of software. As you learned earlier in this text, there are two kinds of memory used in computers: *volatile memory*, which requires power to save data, and *nonvolatile memory*, which can store data even when the power is turned off. ROM is nonvolatile, or permanent, memory. This means that when you turn off your cell phone, the data that is stored in ROM (including the operating system) does not get lost.

Other phone data is stored in separate internal memory chips. Full-featured phones have as much as 16 megabytes (MB) of memory that you can use to store contact data, ring tones, images, and even small software applications such as currency converters or a world clock.

What input and output devices do cell phones use? The input devices for a cell phone are primarily the microphone, which converts your voice into electronic signals that the processor can understand, and a keypad, which is used for numeric or text entry. Some phones, such as the Kyocera 7135 Smartphone (shown in Figure 8.6a), feature the ubiquitous Palm Graffiti pad as well as touch-sensitive screens that allow you to input data. In addition, more and more cell phones include digital cameras. The Sony Ericsson z500a (shown in Figure 8.6b) offers a built-in camera that can input photographs or even capture live video to your phone.

Cell phone output devices include a speaker and a liquid crystal display (LCD) display. Higher-end models include full-color, high-resolution plasma displays. Such displays are becoming increasingly popular as more people are using their cell phones to send and receive the digital images included in multimedia text messages and e-mail. Certain cell phones, such as the Motorola Moto RAZR V3 shown in Figure 8.6c, include two displays: an outside LCD display you can see when the phone is folded and a separate color display inside.

Some phones also use display screens to offer picture caller-id. With picture caller-id, you store an image of a person in your phone contact list and then the image of that person automatically pops into view on the outside screen when he or she calls.

HOW CELL PHONES WORK

How do cell phones work? When you speak into a cell phone, the sound enters the microphone as a sound wave. Because analog sound waves need to be digitized (that is, converted into a sequence of 1s and 0s that the cell phone's processor can understand), an **analog-to-digital converter chip** converts your voice's sound waves into digital signals. Next, the digital data must be compressed, or squeezed, into the smallest possible space so that it will transmit more quickly to another phone. The processor cannot perform the mathematical operations required at this stage quickly enough, so a specialized chip, called the **digital signal processor**, is included in a cell phone to handle the compression work. Finally, the digital data is transmitted as a radio wave through the cellular network to the destination phone.

When you receive an incoming call, the digital signal processor *decompresses* the incoming message. An amplifier boosts the signal to make it loud enough, and it is then passed on to the speaker, from which you hear the sound.

What's "cellular" about a cell phone? A set of connected "cells" makes up a cellular network. Each cell is a geographic area centered on a **base transceiver station**, which is a large communications tower with antennas, amplifiers, and receivers/transmitters. When you place a call on a cell phone, a base station picks up the request for service. The station then passes the request on to a central location, called a **mobile switching center**. (The reverse process occurs when you receive an incoming call on a cell phone.) A telecommunications company builds its network by constructing a series of cells that overlap, in an attempt to guarantee that its cell phone customers have coverage no matter where they are.

As you move during your phone call, the mobile switching center monitors the strength of the signal between your cell phone and the closest base station. When the signal is no longer strong enough between your cell phone and the base station, the mobile switching center orders the next base station to take charge of your call. When your cell phone "drops out," it sometimes does so because the distance between base stations was too great to provide an adequate signal.

BITS AND BYTES

Are Cell Phones Bad for Your Health?

Cell phones work by sending electromagnetic waves into the air from an antenna. Depending on the phone's design—that is, whether there is a shield between the antenna and the user's head—up to 60 percent of the radiation emitted penetrates the area around the head. The amount of radiation a phone puts out is known as its Specific Absorption Rate (SAR). The Federal Communications Commission (FCC) limit for public exposure to cell phones is an SAR level of 1.6 watts per kilogram. So if you're concerned about the possible effects of radiation, buy a phone with as low an SAR as possible.

Still, it's not yet clear whether there are long-term health consequences of using cell phones because of the electromagnetic waves they emit. However, what is clear is that using a cell phone when driving is dangerous. Studies show that motorists are four to nine times more likely to crash when talking on a cell phone when driving, a risk similar to the effects of driving drunk. In many states, hands-free cell phone use is mandatory. For more information on laws in your state as well as links to sites with accident data, visit the Governors Highway Safety Association (GHSA) Web site at **http://www.statehighwaysafety.org/html/stateinfo/laws/index.html**.

CELL PHONE FEATURES: TEXT MESSAGING

What is text messaging? Short Message Service (SMS) (often just called **text messaging**) is a technology that allows you to send short text messages (up to 160 characters) over mobile networks. To send SMS messages from your cell phone, you simply use the numeric keypad or a presaved template and type in your message. You can send SMS messages to other mobile devices (such as cell phones or pagers) or to any e-mail address. You can also use SMS to send short text messages from your home computer to mobile devices, such as your friend's cell phone.

How does SMS work? SMS uses the cell phone network to transmit messages. When you send an SMS message, an SMS calling center receives the message and delivers it to the appropriate mobile device using something called "store-and-forward" technology. This technology allows users to send SMS messages to any other SMS device in the world.

Many SMS fans like text messaging because it can be cheaper than a phone call and it allows the receivers to read messages when it is convenient for them. In fact, in some countries, such as Japan, text messaging is more popular than voice messaging. However, entering text using your cell phone keypad can be time-consuming and hard on your thumbs. Frequent SMS users save typing time by using a number of abbreviations, some of which are shown in Figure 8.7.

Can I send and receive multimedia files over a cell phone? SMS technology allows you to send only text messages. However, an extension of SMS called **Multimedia Message Service (MMS)** allows you to send messages that include text, sound, images, and video clips to other phones or e-mail addresses. MMS messages actually arrive as a series of messages; you view the text and then the image and then the sound, and so on. You can then choose to save just one part of the message (such as the image), all of it, or none of it. MMS users can subscribe to financial, sports, and weather services that will "push" information to them, sending it automatically to their phones in MMS format.

CELL PHONE INTERNET CONNECTIVITY

How do I get Internet service for my phone? Just as you pay an Internet service provider (ISP) for Internet access for your desktop computer, connecting your cell phone to the Internet requires that you have a **wireless Internet service provider**. Phone companies that provide cell phone calling plans (such as T-Mobile, Verizon, and Cingular) usually double as wireless ISPs.

At what speed can my phone connect to the Internet? As noted earlier, accessing the Internet on a mobile device comes with limitations. For one, the connection is often slow. Although you may be able to connect to the Internet from your home PC at broadband speeds of 4,300 kilobits per second (Kbps) at home, your cell phone will probably connect at a much lower speed of just 15 Kbps.

There are some cell phones on the market that take advantage of a new technology called EDGE, short for Enhanced Data Rate for Global Evolution. EDGE brings data to mobile devices at much faster rates, up to 200 Kbps. Using an EDGE phone and a phone plan that allows data transfer, both uploading information (like e-mail messages that include photos) and downloading information (such as from a company intranet or the Internet) can take place much more quickly.

What is the Internet like on a phone? Because cell phones have a very limited amount of screen space and low screen resolution, the Internet experience is quite different. To make it possible for you to access the Internet, special **microbrowser** software runs on your cell phone. Figure 8.8 shows a typical microbrowser screen. Using a microbrowser, you can quickly purchase new ring tones or games for your phone.

FIGURE 8.7 Popular Text Messaging Abbreviations

AFAIK	As far as I know
B4N	Bye for now
BRB	Be right back
CUL	See you later
FBM	Fine by me
F2T	Free to talk
G2G	Got to go
HRU	How are you?
IDK	I don't know
JAS	Just a sec
LOL	Laughing out loud
QPSA	¿Qué pasa?
T+	Think positive
TTYL	Talk to you later
WUWH	Wish you were here
YBS	You'll be sorry

Web sites are beginning to create content specifically designed for wireless devices. This specially designed content, which is text-based and contains no graphics, is written in a format called **Wireless Markup Language (WML)**. Content is designed so that it fits the tiny display screens of cell phones and PDAs.

Can I keep my e-mail up to date using my cell phone? Because the screen size on cell phones is so small and navigating the Web was not customized for the small display screens on cell phones, checking e-mail by your cell phone can be frustrating. However, some devices, such as the Blackberrys handhelds, are small and portable and still work well with e-mail.

BlackBerrys incorporate special design features such as larger displays and integrated keyboards to make it easier to keep your inbox empty, even when you're away from your desk. They also use a special "push" technology to automatically deliver your e-mail to your phone so your e-mail finds you whether you're thinking about it or not.

Can I get a virus on my cell phone? Cell phone manufacturers and software engineers are bracing themselves for a wave of viruses targeted to cell phones.

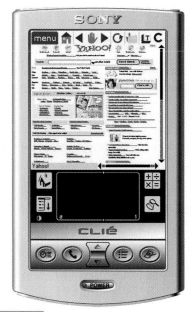

BITS AND BYTES

Don't Plug in Your Phone . . . Just Add Alcohol

Someday soon, instead of lugging a heavy power supply and searching for an electrical outlet to recharge your phone, you may just pour a few drops of alcohol into it. Researchers have developed a technology called a "biofuel cell" that could power mobile devices in the future using alcohol. A standard fuel cell (that is, a battery) derives its power from chemical reactions between its elements (such as zinc and manganese oxide). A biofuel cell would use biological molecules (in this case, alcohol enzymes) to generate power. The advantage is that the batteries are easily rechargeable—just add methanol! Toshiba is the first company to bring such fuel cells to market. Toshiba estimates their fuel cell can power an MP3 player for approximately 20 hours using just a few drops of methanol. So get ready to fuel up instead of recharge in the near future.

Most experts expect these viruses to be of the Trojan horse type (a virus that appears to be something else, such as a game). The potential of cell phone viruses ranges from the mildly annoying (features of your phone don't work) to the expensive (your phone is used without your knowledge to make expensive calls). How can you prevent cell phone viruses? There are no antivirus programs for cell phones yet, so the best precautions are commonsense ones. Don't download ring tones, games, or other software from unfamiliar Web sites, and check the phone manufacturer's Web site frequently to see whether your phone needs any software upgrades that could potentially patch security holes.

MP3 Players

MP3 is a format for efficiently storing music as digital files, or a series of bits. An **MP3 player** is a small portable device that enables you to carry your MP3 files around with you. Depending on the player, you can carry several hours of music or your entire CD collection in an incredibly small device. For example, the Apple iPod is 4 inches by 2.4 inches and can hold over 15,000 songs. The most compact players are the size of a cigarette lighter (although they hold far less music than the iPod). Figure 8.9 shows several popular models of MP3 players.

Are all music files named with .mp3 at the end? The letters at the end of a filename (the file extension) indicate how the data in the file is organized. MP3 is the name of just one type of file format used to store digital music, but many others, such as AAC and WMA, exist. All file formats compete on sound quality and compression, or how small the file can be and still store high-quality audio. If you buy a song from iTunes, for example, you receive an .AAC format file. AAC files can only be played on iPods but can be converted to the more widely seen MP3 or Windows Media Audio (WMA) formats. WMA files can be played on a wide variety of MP3 players.

FIGURE 8.9 Popular MP3 Players and Their Characteristics

	Approximate Number of MP3 Songs	Built-in Flash Memory	Hard Disk Drive Capacity	Connection to Computer	Other Features
Verge DEP 200 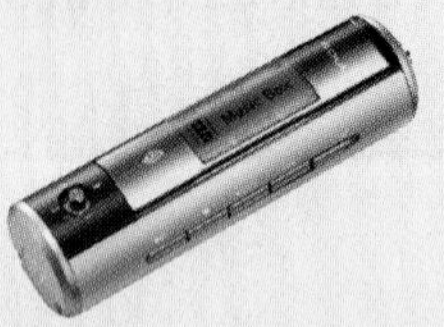	About 60 songs	256 MB	None	USB 1.0 port	Includes voice recorder, FM tuner, six backlit display colors, and six equalizer settings
Oregon Scientific MP120 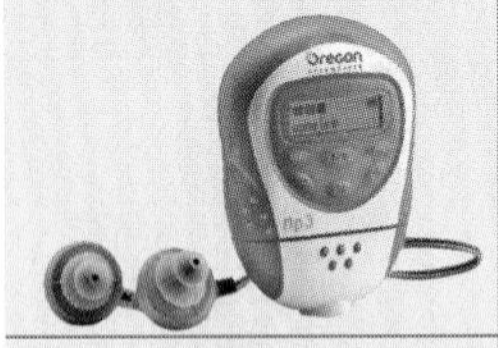	About 60 songs	256 MB	None	USB 2.0 port	Waterproof to a depth of 3 feet. Includes an equalizer, FM radio, and waterproof speaker buds
Apple iPod 	From 5,000 songs to 15,000 songs	None	20 GB to 60 GB	FireWire or USB 2.0 port	Newer versions include a calendar, contact database, and can store images, corporate logos, and live URLs. The Photo iPod can display photos or slide shows on a monitor or TV.
Apple iPod Mini 	From 1,000 songs on the 4-GB model to 1,500 songs on the 6-GB model	None	4 GB to 6 GB	FireWire or USB 2.0 port	Weighs only half what the largest iPod does and can be worn on armband
iRiver PMP-120 Media Player 	5,000 songs or up to 80 hours of video	No	20 GB	USB 2.0	3.5-inch color display and a built-in speaker on this audio/video viewer

MP3 HARDWARE

How do I know how much music an MP3 player can hold? The number of songs an MP3 player can hold depends on how much storage space it has. Some MP3 players use built-in **flash memory**, a type of nonvolatile memory, to store files. Other MP3 players use a hard disk drive and can store a much larger amount of music. Inexpensive players use flash memory (ranging from 64 MB, to 1 gigabyte [GB]), whereas expensive models use a built-in hard drive, which provides up to 60 GB of storage. Some of the MP3 players that use flash memory allow you to add storage capacity by purchasing removable flash memory cards.

Another factor that determines how much music a player can hold is the quality of the MP3 music files. The size of an MP3 file depends on the digital sampling of the song. The **sampling rate** is the number of times per second the music is measured and converted to a digital value. Sampling rates are measured in kilobits per second (Kbps). The same song could be sampled at 192 Kbps or 64 Kbps. The size of the song file will be three times larger if it is sampled at 192 Kbps instead of the lower sampling rate of 64 Kbps. The higher the sampling rate, the better quality the sound, but the larger the file size.

If you are "ripping," or converting, a song from a CD into a digital MP3 file, you can select the sampling rate yourself. You decide by considering what quality sound you want as well as how many songs you want to fit onto your MP3 player. For example, if your player has 64 MB of storage and you have ripped songs at 192 Kbps, you can fit about 45 minutes of music onto the player. The same 64 MB could store 133 minutes of music if it were sampled at 64 Kbps. Whenever you are near your computer, you can connect your player and download a different set of songs, but you are always limited by the amount of storage your player has.

MP3 FLASH MEMORY AND FILE TRANSFER

What if I want to store more music than what my MP3 player's memory allows? As noted earlier, some MP3 players allow you to add additional, removable flash memory cards. Flash memory cards are noiseless, very light, use very little power, and slide into a special slot in the player. If you've ever played a video game on PlayStation 2 or Nintendo and saved your progress to a memory card, you have used flash memory. Because flash memory is nonvolatile, when you store data on a flash memory card, you won't lose it when you turn off the player. In addition, flash memory can be erased and rewritten with new data.

What types of flash memory cards do MP3 players use? Several different types of flash cards are used with different models of MP3 players, as shown in Figure 8.10. One popular type is *Compact Flash* cards. These are about the size of a matchbook and can hold between 64 MB and 1 GB of data. They are very durable, so the data you store on them is safer than it would be on a floppy disk, for example. *Multimedia cards* and *SmartMedia* cards are about the same size as CompactFlash cards but are thinner and less rugged. A newer type of memory card called *Secure Digital* is faster and offers encryption capabilities so your data is secure even if you lose the card.

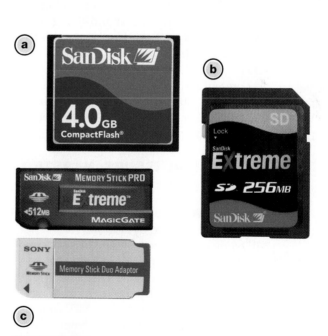

FIGURE 8.10

(a) CompactFlash memory cards offer rugged, portable storage. They can be dropped and exposed to hot and cold weather and still protect your data.
(b) Secure Digital cards are faster and offer security protection for your data.
(c) Memory Sticks are currently used only in Sony devices, but are becoming more widely accepted.

Sony devices use a special format of flash memory called the *Memory Stick*. These tiny rectangular "sticks"—measuring just 2 inches by less than 1 inch and weighing a fraction of an ounce—are currently used only in Sony devices but are becoming more widely accepted. Particular models of MP3 players can support only certain types of flash cards, so check your manual to be sure you buy compatible memory cards.

How do I transfer MP3 files to my MP3 player? All MP3 players come with software that enables you to transfer your MP3 files from your computer onto the player. As noted earlier, players that hold thousands of songs use internal hard drives to store music. For example, the Apple iPod is available with a 20-GB, 40-GB, or 60-GB hard drive (the iPod Mini has a 4-GB or 6-GB drive). To move that volume of data between your computer and MP3 player, you want a high-speed port. The iPod uses a FireWire port or the even faster USB 2.0 port, whereas some older MP3 players use the slower USB 1.0 port. Using a USB 2.0 port, you can transfer a complete CD to the iPod in less than 10 seconds.

Can MP3 players carry more than just music? MP3 players have become so popular that some manufacturers are redesigning their software and operating systems to support the transfer and storage of nonmusical data as well. The latest version of the iPod, the Photo iPod, sports a calendar and a contact database and can store images and present slide shows. Other high-end MP3 devices, such as the iRiver, shown in Figure 8.9, offer you the ability to transfer and store music, video, and image files.

ACTIVE HELPDESK

Using MP3 Players

In this Active Helpdesk call, you'll play the role of a helpdesk staffer, fielding calls about MP3 players, what they can carry and how they store data.

MP3 ETHICAL ISSUES: NAPSTER AND BEYOND

What was Napster all about? The initial MP3 craze was fueled by sites such as MP3.com, which stored its song files on a public server with the permission of the original artist or recording company. Therefore, you were not infringing on a copyright by downloading songs from sites such as MP3.com.

When originally introduced, Napster was a file-exchange site created to correct some of the annoyances found by users of MP3.com and similar sites. One such annoyance was the limited availability of popular music in MP3 format. With the MP3 sites, if you found a song you wanted to download, often the links to the sites the file was found

on no longer worked. Napster differed from MP3.com because songs or locations of songs were not stored in a central public server but instead were "borrowed" directly from other users' computers. This process of users transferring files between computers is referred to as **peer-to-peer (P2P) sharing**. Napster also provided a search engine dedicated to finding specific MP3 files. This direct search and sharing eliminated the inconvenience of searching links only to find them unavailable.

The problem with Napster was that it was so good at what it did. Napster's convenient and reliable mechanism to find and download popular songs in MP3 format became a huge success. The rapid acceptance and use of Napster—at one point, it had nearly 60 million users—led the music industry to sue the site for copyright infringement, and Napster was closed in June 2002. Napster has since reopened as a music site that sells music downloads and is sanctioned by the recording industry.

So now all music that is downloaded must be purchased? Although most music you download you need to pay for, artists are posting some songs for free. Business models are still evolving as artists and recording companies try to meet the audience's needs while at the same time protecting their own intellectual property rights. A number of different approaches exist. One is to deliver something called "tethered downloads" in which you pay for the music and own it but are subject to restrictions on its use. For example, Apple currently allows you to give songs you download to anyone on CD but only to five people as an electronic file. Other sites offer subscription services. For a monthly fee, Napster to Go allows you to download as many songs as you like to your MP3 player. These songs will only be usable, however, as long as you are paying the monthly subscription fee.

If the original Napster site was illegal, why are there still peer-to-peer (P2P) sharing sites? When Napster was going through its legal turmoil, other P2P Web sites were quick to take advantage of a huge opportunity. Napster was "easy" to shut down because it used a central index server that queried other Napster computers for requested songs. Current P2P Web sites (such as Gnutella and Kazaa) differ from Napster in that they do not limit themselves to sharing only MP3 files. More important, these sites don't have a central index server. Instead, they operate in a true P2P sharing environment in which computers connect directly to other computers.

The argument these P2P networks make to defend their legality is that they do not run a central server like the original Napster but only facilitate connections between users. Therefore, they have no control over what the users trade, and not all P2P file sharing is illegal. For example, it is perfectly legal to trade photos or movies you have created with other folks over a P2P site. Those against such file-sharing sites contend that the sites know their users are distribut-ing illegal files. Be aware that having illegal content on your computer, deliberately or by accident, is a criminal offense in many jurisdictions.

Will MP3 players eliminate radio stations? Radio stations have always had the advantages of early access to new music and the personalities and conversations they add to the listening experience. However, the Internet allows bands to release new songs to their fans immediately, without relying on radio airtime. This opens up new channels for bands to reach an audience and changes the amount of power radio stations have in the promotion of music.

TRENDS IN IT

Emerging Technologies: Why Carry Your Data When You Can Wear It?

By now, most of us expect to have Internet access in our wristwatches and radio transmitters in our coat buttons in the not-so-distant future. But how about having computers woven into your clothes?

The idea may not be so farfetched. Flexible synthetic "yarns" that can transmit electrical signals may soon be common components of cotton and polyester fabrics. Called *electrotextiles*, these textiles are already being woven into soldiers' vests to serve as radio antennas. Researchers see almost no limits to their possibilities and are working to make electrotextiles not only wearable but also washable, customizable, and even programmable. Experts predict that nearly every type of clothing will have some sort of electronic function in 10 years, ranging from Global Positioning Systems (GPSs) to medical sensors to fabrics that change colors and patterns at your command.

The new fibers are woven into fabric or sewn on in ribbon-like strips around the neck or sleeves of a garment. They are then connected to chips and batteries so that, for instance, blankets and clothing can adapt to body temperature and car seat fabric can tell a car's air bags to adjust their force to match the passenger's weight. Researchers at the Georgia Institute of Technology are already working on a T-shirt for fire-fighters that tracks the heart rate, body temperature, and other vital signs of the person wearing it and transmits this data to a wearable pager. Scientists at Germany's Infineon Technologies have made a proto-type of a hooded jacket that includes the electronic elements of an MP3 player in the pockets. The hood's drawstrings are used as the MP3 player's headphones, and controls are found on the sleeve. Researchers at France Telecom have created a display screen that is integrated into clothing. It can display information from a variety of sources, including the photos stored on the cell phone in your pocket (see Figure 8.11).

And just think: Once solar cells can be woven into fabric, you might be able to wear all your applications *and* your power source—in next year's hottest colors.

FIGURE 8.11

This jacket uses an optical fiber display system. You can display any image stored on your cell phone with these "communicating clothes."

Another development is podcasting, which allows users to download audio content and to then listen to those broadcasts on their MP3 players whenever they want. Podcasting is paving the way to enable anyone to create a radio show at home and to easily distribute it to an audience. Using inexpensive software like Propaganda (**www.makepropaganda.com**) and a microphone, you can record voiceovers, sequence songs, and "publish" your show to the Internet. Loyal fans can use podcasting software like ipodder (**www.ipodder.org**) to find their latest episode and automatically transfer it to their MP3 players.

Personal Digital Assistants (PDAs)

A **personal digital assistant (PDA)** is a small device that allows you to carry digital information. Often called *palm computers* or *handhelds*, PDAs are about the size of your hand and usually weigh less than 5 ounces. Although small, PDAs are quite powerful and can carry all sorts of information, from calendars to contact lists to specially designed personal productivity software programs (such as Excel and Word), to songs, photos, and games. And you can easily "synchronize" your PDA and your home computer so that the changes you make to your schedules and files on your PDA are made on your home or office computer files as well.

PDA HARDWARE

What hardware is inside a PDA? Like any computer, a PDA includes a processor (CPU), operating system software, storage capabilities, input and output devices, and ports. Because of their small size, PDAs (like cell phones) must use specially designed processors and operating system software. They store their operating system software in ROM and their data and application programs in random access memory (RAM).

What kinds of input devices do PDAs use? All PDAs feature touch-sensitive screens that allow you to enter data directly with a penlike device called a **stylus**. To make selections, you simply tap or write on the screen with the stylus. Other PDAs include integrated keyboards or support small, portable, folding keyboards. Figure 8.12 shows all of these input options.

With a touch screen and stylus, you can use either handwritten text or special notation systems to enter data into your PDA. One of the more popular notation systems is the **Graffiti** text system. As shown in Figure 8.13, with Graffiti, you must learn special strokes that represent each letter, such as an upside-down V for the letter A. Another popular system, **Microsoft Transcriber**, doesn't require special strokes and can recognize both printed and cursive writing with fairly decent accuracy. PDAs also support an on-screen keyboard so that you can use your stylus and "type" (tap out) messages.

FIGURE 8.12

To enter text, PDAs offer different options: (a) a text entry window that you use together with a stylus, (b) an integrated keyboard (shown here on a Sharp Zaurus SL-5500), and (c) a folding keyboard accessory.

What kinds of displays do PDAs have? PDAs come with LCD screens in a variety of resolutions. The more inexpensive models use 16 levels of gray (grayscale). For appointment schedules and to-do lists, this is fine. However, if you plan on using your PDA to display photos and play video clips, you should consider buying a PDA with a color display. High-end color displays are almost 4 inches and can have resolutions as high as 480 × 640.

How do I compare processors for PDAs? Popular PDA processors (CPUs) on the market today include the Motorola DragonBall, the Texas Instruments OMP, and the Intel XScale processor. When comparing PDA processors, one consideration to keep in mind is **processor speed**. Processor speed, which is measured in hertz (Hz), is the number of operations (or cycles) the processor completes each second. For example, the Dell Axim X50v PDA uses an Intel XScale processor running at 624 megahertz (MHz), or 624 million cycles per second. The Palm Zire uses a Texas Instruments OMP 311 ARM processor running at 126 MHz. Just as with computers, you should get the fastest processor your budget will allow.

If you're interested in running demanding software on your PDA, such as games and image-editing applications, getting a fast processor is important. For basic PDA functions such as a to-do list and a calendar, a slower processor works fine, but if you will be doing large sets of calculations in Excel workbooks, the speed difference between a fast processor and a slower one is very noticeable. The type of application software you plan on running should help you determine whether the additional processing power is worth the cost.

However, processor speed is not the only aspect of the processor that affects performance. The internal design of the processor, both in the software commands it speaks and its internal hardware, are other factors. To measure performance, PDA reviewers often run the same task on competing PDAs and then compare the time it takes to complete the task. This process is called **benchmarking** and gives a good indication of the unit's overall system performance. When comparing PDAs, look for benchmarks in magazines (such as *PC Magazine*) in addition to online reviews (such as those found at **www.wired.com**).

As well as having different speeds, each processor uses different amounts of power,

FIGURE 8.13

The Graffiti system uses special strokes to represent all the letters of the English alphabet.

affecting how long the PDA can run on a single battery. When comparing PDAs, look for the expected operating time on one battery charge.

PDA OPERATING SYSTEMS

How do I compare PDA operating systems? The two main operating system competitors on the PDA market today are the **Palm OS** from Palm and the **Pocket PC** system from Microsoft (also called Windows Mobile). Which operating system is better depends on your personal needs. Palm OS is found on PDAs made by Palm and Sony. Pocket PC is used by Compaq, Hewlett-Packard, and Toshiba on their PDA models. As you can see in Figure 8.14, both operating systems offer you graphical user interfaces.

FIGURE 8.14

The two most popular operating systems for PDAs are (a) Palm OS and (b) Pocket PC.

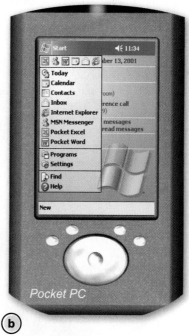

(a) (b)

Personal Digital Assistants (PDAs) **349**

FIGURE 8.15 Comparing PDA Operating Systems

PDA OS	Advantages	Disadvantages
Palm OS	• Requires less memory • Is easy to use • Is less expensive • Supports more third-party software applications	• Requires installation of separate Documents To Go software in order to support MS Word, Excel, and PowerPoint files • Requires installation of separate software to view video clips or listen to MP3 files
Pocket PC	• Supports specialized MS Office applications Word and Excel without installing additional software • Can play MP3 files and video clips without installing additional software	• Requires more memory • Is more expensive • Supports fewer third-party software applications

Palm OS is in some ways a better match to the PDA environment. It requires less memory, is easy to use, and focuses on supporting only the features most commonly used by PDA owners, such as a calendar, to-do list, and contact information. PDAs using the Palm OS can recognize and support Microsoft Word, Excel, and PowerPoint files, although this requires that you buy a software application named Documents To Go. Similarly, you can use the Palm OS to view movies or listen to MP3 files, but only with the purchase of separate application software.

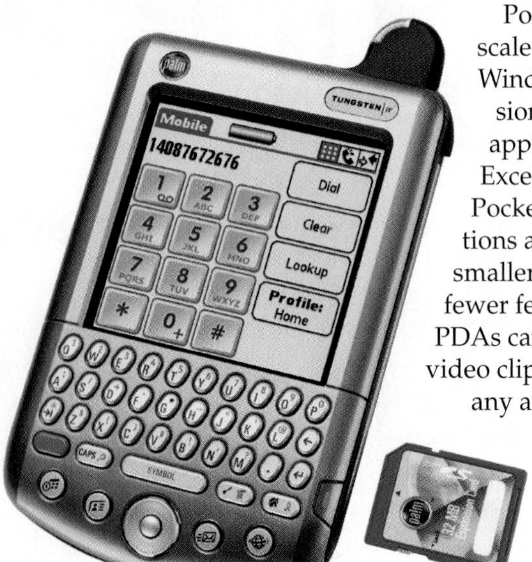

FIGURE 8.16

Different PDAs use different types of flash memory. However, all flash memory cards slide into a specialized slot on the side of the PDA.

Pocket PC is more of a scaled-down version of Windows. It supports versions of the Microsoft applications Word and Excel that can run on the Pocket PC. These applications are designed for the smaller PDA screen and have fewer features. Pocket PC PDAs can play MP3 files and video clips without installing any additional software. However, all of this comes at the cost of added memory requirements and added complexity. So, a Pocket PC PDA often ships with more base memory and is more expensive.

The PDA operating system affects you in another way. You may want to buy extra software for your PDA—a program to track your workouts at the gym or to provide driving directions, for example. Third-party companies, rather than the companies that built the PDAs, often develop software applications for PDAs. Because the Palm OS was the first PDA operating system on the market, much of the PDA software was originally designed for the Palm OS. Today, there are more than 13,000 software applications available for the Palm OS, and it still holds a dominant market share, outselling Pocket PC about 2 to 1. Although more software applications are now created for both operating systems, you should investigate exactly which applications you are interested in buying and make sure they're available for the operating system you're considering. Figure 8.15 lists the advantages and disadvantages of these operating systems.

PDA MEMORY AND STORAGE

What kinds of memory does a PDA use? In PDAs, ROM is used to hold the operating system as well as the most basic programs the PDA runs, such as the calendar, to-do list, and contact list. PDAs do not contain internal hard drives. Therefore, RAM holds additional applications and any data you load into the PDA. However, because RAM is volatile storage, and you do not want your data to disappear when you shut off your PDA, a small amount of power is taken from the battery to keep the data "alive" even when the PDA is off.

The main advantage of using RAM in this way is speed—RAM is incredibly fast compared with hard drives, so programs on a PDA load and run very quickly. The disadvantage is cost—RAM is expensive, so most PDAs have only 16 MB to 64 MB of RAM. In fact, applications for PDAs do not have all the functions that desktop versions include precisely because of their limited amount of RAM.

What if I need more memory on my PDA? Most PDAs cannot expand the amount of *internal* memory they contain. For memory needs beyond built-in RAM and ROM, PDAs use removable flash memory similar to that used in MP3 players. For

example, if you want your PDA to hold a large MP3 collection, you might not have enough built-in RAM. But you could add the MP3s to your PDA by copying them onto flash memory and sliding the flash card into a special slot on the PDA, as shown in Figure 8.16. Before buying a flash card, consult your PDA manual or manufacturer's Web site to make sure it's compatible with your PDA.

PDA FILE TRANSFER AND SYNCHRONIZATION

How do I transfer data from my PDA to my desktop? If you're transferring data from your PDA to another computer and it accepts the type of flash card you're using, you can simply pull the flash card out of your PDA and slip it into the flash card reader on your computer. If your desktop does not include a built-in card reader, you can connect an external memory card reader to your computer using a USB port.

You can also transfer your data from your PDA to a desktop computer by using a special device called a **cradle**. Most PDAs come with a cradle, which connects the PDA to the desktop using either a USB port or a serial port, as shown in Figure 8.18. You can also use the PDA cradle to synchronize your PDA with your computer.

How do I synchronize a PDA with a desktop computer? To be truly valuable as mobile computing devices, PDAs provide a means by which you can coordinate the changes you make to your to-do lists, schedules, and other files with the files on your home computer. This process of updating your data so the files on your PDA and computer are the same is called **synchronizing**. To synchronize your desktop and PDA, you simply place the PDA in its cradle (which is connected to the desktop computer using a USB or serial port) and touch a "hot sync" button. This begins the process of data transfer that updates both sets of files to the most current version.

Can I transfer files wirelessly from a PDA? Many PDAs include an infrared (IrDA) port that transmits data signals using infrared light waves. To transfer data between two PDAs, you can use the infrared port and "beam" data directly across. For example, if you missed a class, a fellow student could send you the assignment file by simply pointing her PDA at yours.

Compact Memory More Powerful Than Flash

Although flash memory is powerful, the highest-density memory option available is actually not flash memory but a 1-inch portable hard drive. The Hitachi Microdrive, shown in Figure 8.17, allows you to store 6 GB of data in a CompactFlash-size cartridge. Devices that support the Microdrive allow it to slide right into a CompactFlash slot. With so much storage, you can keep videos, photographs, and hours of music, all on your mobile device.

FIGURE 8.17

The 1-inch-square Hitachi microdrive can hold 6 GB of data for a PDA, digital camera, or other portable device.

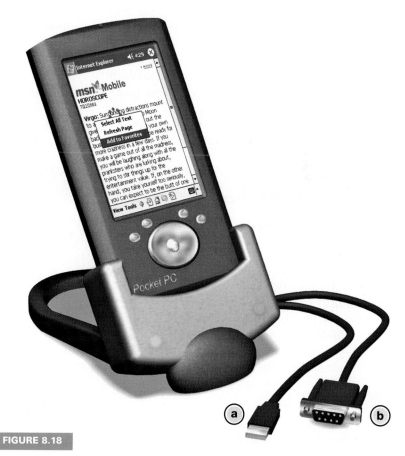

FIGURE 8.18

A cradle connects your PDA to your computer using either (a) a USB port or (b) a serial port.

Another type of wireless connection available for PDAs is **Bluetooth**. This technology uses radio waves to transmit data signals over short distances (up to about 30 feet). Many PDAs on the market today are Bluetooth-enabled, meaning they include a small Bluetooth chip that allows them to transfer data wirelessly to any other Bluetooth-enabled device. One benefit Bluetooth has over infrared is that direct line of sight does not have to be present between the two devices for them to communicate. You can also use Bluetooth to synchronize your PDA with your home computer or your Bluetooth cell phone. No cradle to connect, no buttons to push: the Bluetooth-enabled PDA and desktop or phone recognize each other and automatically begin the synchronization process.

PDA INTERNET CONNECTIVITY

How do PDAs connect to the Internet? As is the case with cell phones, connecting your PDA to the Internet requires that you have a wireless ISP, which costs an additional monthly fee. Once you're on the Internet, you can use your PDA to send and receive e-mail and use all the features you're familiar with from your desktop computer, including attachments, blind and carbon copies, and distribution lists.

However, you do not always need to be connected to the Internet to take advantage of its information resources. Web sites such as AvantGo (**www.avantgo.com**) allow you to

download the content of many different Web sites from your home computer to your PDA. Popular channels include CNN.com and RollingStone.com. You can then read this downloaded information any time you want without having to access the Internet. For static Web-based information, this is an ideal solution.

How are Web pages "communicated" to my PDA? Wireless Application Protocol (WAP) is the standard that dictates how handheld devices will access information on the Internet. WAP supports all the major PDA operating systems, including Palm OS and Pocket PC. As mentioned earlier, mobile devices such as cell phones and PDAs run software applications called *microbrowsers* that allow them to access the Internet.

As noted previously, Web sites are beginning to provide specialized sites for mobile device users. In addition, a new technology called **Web clipping** allows you to extract the information you are interested in from a Web site and format it so it is more useful on smaller PDA displays. This conserves both the resources of your PDA for displaying information and the demand you are making for bandwidth in communicating between your PDA and the Web server. Because most wireless plans for PDAs charge an extra fee based on the amount of data you transfer, Web clipping can save you money. A list of sites that support Web clipping can be found at **www.palmone.com**.

BITS AND BYTES

No Bluetooth? No Problem

Your computer doesn't have built-in Bluetooth? Devices are now available that enable you to add Bluetooth capabilities to almost any computer. One is the Linksys USB Bluetooth Adapter shown in Figure 8.19. When plugged into a computer's USB port, it adds wireless capability to your computer. The adapter comes with software that supports a wide range of Bluetooth services, including PDA synchronization, headset support, dial-up networking, network access, and file transfer.

FIGURE 8.19

Just plug a Bluetooth adapter into any USB port on your computer and install the Bluetooth manager software and you're ready to synchronize your PDA with your computer wirelessly.

PDA SOFTWARE AND ACCESSORIES

What PDA software is available? Most PDAs come with a standard collection of software such as a to-do list, contacts manager, and calendar. Software applications such as Word and Excel are also available for PDAs. Although these programs are not as full featured as their desktop counterparts, they can read and create files that can be transmitted to full-version applications on your home computer. In addition, a variety of games, tools, and reference applications are available for PDAs from numerous software companies. A good source to locate software applications for your PDA is **www.mobileplanet.com**. In addition, **www.download.com** includes a list of shareware and freeware applications for PDA platforms.

One application of interest is Colligo Networks' **BlueBoard**. This application allows you to use your PDA display as a drawing board and instantly connect it with up to four other PDAs. You can each be working on your own screen, updating and adding comments, and the changes you make are instantly seen by the other BlueBoard users on their screens (see Figure 8.20). The information is shared wirelessly using Bluetooth technology.

PDA OR CELL PHONE?

Do I need both a PDA and a cell phone? A number of devices are being released that attempt to combine a cell phone, an MP3 player, and a PDA into one unit. For example, the palmOne Treo 650 is a cell phone that has added PDA features (see Figure 8.21a). It also supports the use of flash memory and includes MP3 playing software so you can carry MP3 music with you. The BlackBerry 7100x (see Figure 8.21b) is a phone but is customized with features to make reading your e-mail simple, including a thumbwheel for easy scrolling and a bigger screen.

These kinds of mobile devices are called "smartphones" and represent a step toward the ideal of "convergence," being able to have a single compact device that features all of these capabilities. However, each is making some compromises: there are features available on the best cell phones and PDAs that are missing from the smartphones currently on the market. However, smartphones do strike a nice balance for people who need features from both phones and PDAs. Still, if your main need

FIGURE 8.20

The BlueBoard application allows up to four people to use their PDAs as a mutual brainstorming drawing board.

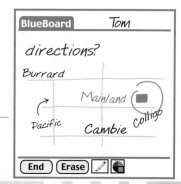

FIGURE 8.21

The palmOne Treo (a) and the BlackBerry 7100x (b) are part of the new generation of devices known as "smartphones." These devices combine the features of a cell phone and a PDA into a single handheld unit.

DIG DEEPER

The Power of GPS

Where in the world is Carmen San Diego? Or, more important, where in the world is the nearest gas station? Many people aren't whizzes at geography, but knowing your current location and the location of your destination can often come in handy. Luckily for those who are "directionally impaired," **Global Positioning System (GPS)** technology enables you to carry a powerful navigational aid in your pocket.

You've probably heard of GPS, but what is it exactly and how does it work? The Global Positioning System is a system of 21 satellites (plus three working spares), built and operated by the U.S. military, which constantly orbit the earth. GPS devices use an antenna to pick up the signals from these satellites and special software to transform those signals into latitude and longitude. Using the information obtained from the satellites, GPS devices can tell you what your geographical location is anywhere on the planet to within 10 feet (see Figure 8.22). Because they provide such detailed positioning information, GPS units are now used as navigational aids for aircraft, recreational boats, and automobiles, and they even come in handheld models for hikers.

Although this precise positioning information clearly redefines the fields of surveying and search and rescue operations, it has also changed other fields. Wildlife researchers now tag select animals and watch their migration patterns and how the population is distributed. Meanwhile, GPS was important to the two teams that created the Chunnel, the tunnel under the English Channel that connects England to France. One team worked from France toward England and the other from England toward France. They used GPS information along the way to make sure they were on target, and in 1990, the two sections joined to become

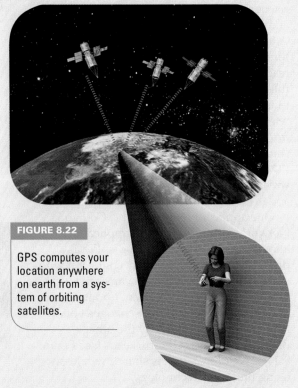

FIGURE 8.22

GPS computes your location anywhere on earth from a system of orbiting satellites.

the first physical link between England and the continent of Europe since the Ice Age.

GPS has made its way into several commercial products as well. Hertz rental cars offer in-car GPS assistance with the NeverLost system. The unit is mounted on the front dashboard and displays your location on a map that is updated in real time as you drive. Enter your destination and a voice warns you of lane changes and approaching turns. If you miss a turn, it automatically recalculates the required route and gives you

---

is voice communications and small size, get a cell phone. If your needs are more along the lines of keeping track of facts and figures or using Office application software programs, then you probably should opt for a PDA.

ACTIVE HELPDESK

Using PDAs

In this Active Helpdesk call, you'll play the role of a helpdesk staffer, fielding calls about PDAs — what you can use them for, what internal components and features they have, and how you can synchronize mobile devices with a desktop computer.

Tablet PCs

A **tablet PC** is a portable computer that is lightweight, features advanced handwriting recognition, and can be rotated into a clipboard style. Tablet PCs are available from a variety of manufacturers, come in a variety of designs, and are about the same size as a clipboard. Some weigh just three pounds with the removable keyboard attached, and just two pounds without it, making them very thin and light computing solutions.

Why are they called tablet PCs?
Tablet PCs are named such because the monitor can be used either in a traditional laptop

directions to get back on course. Flip to another screen and it shows you how far you have to drive to the next gas station, restaurant, or amusement park. Several car manufacturers such as Honda and Lexus are offering similar GPS navigation systems in their cars. And GPS navigation can be added to any vehicle using a PDA and a separate GPS accessory (see Figure 8.23).

You can purchase software maps for specific areas and get turn-by-turn driving directions from the PDA's speaker while your current location is displayed on the PDA screen.

However, having the ability to locate and track an object anywhere on earth does bring with it societal implications. The Federal Communications Commission (FCC) mandated that by the end of 2005, every cell phone must include a GPS chip. This enables the complete rollout of the Enhanced 911 (E911) program. E911 automatically provides dispatchers precision location information for any 911 call. It also means your cell phone records may include precise tracking information indicating where you are when you make a call.

GPS can be used in other ways as well. In 2003, a murder trial in the state of Washington used GPS data collected by police as evidence. William Jackson was suspected of a murder, although no body had been found. When he was a suspect for the murder, police placed a GPS monitoring device on his truck without his knowledge. The police then told Jackson that although they had not yet located the body of the victim, they would soon find the body. Soon afterward, Jackson drove to the site where he had buried the body to move it to a new location. Using GPS data, the police tracked his movements and gathered physical evidence of his involvement in the crime. He was later convicted and sentenced to 56 years

in prison based in part on the evidence. He appealed on the grounds that it was a violation of his rights to privacy to be tracked by the government in such a way. You can read the outcome of the appeal and the arguments made by both sides at **http://www.4law.co.il/Lea211.htm**.

What limits and supervision of the government needs to be in place to ensure the ethical use of GPS technologies? In what ways could the tracking information provided by GPS devices be used unethically? If GPS tracking information is recorded in your phone data, should the criteria for allowing government agencies to subpoena phone records be changed? Should users be allowed to turn off location information from their phones? Already, location records such as these were used in determining that the *New York Times* reporter Jayson Blair had been fabricating stories, resulting in his resignation. One rental car company, Acme Car Rental of New Haven, Connecticut, has used GPS records to fine customers for speeding violations. As a nation we now need to decide how we should balance the benefits and costs of using this new level of tracking information.

FIGURE 8.23

Garmin is one company that provides GPS accessories and navigation software for PDAs. A voice alerts you to upcoming turns and the unit automatically reroutes you if you happen to miss a turn anyway.

mode or in "tablet mode," much like an electronic clipboard, as shown in Figure 8.24. Tablet PCs also can be connected to a full-size keyboard and monitor.

When would a tablet PC be the best mobile solution? A tablet PC can be the ideal solution when you require a lightweight, portable computer with full desktop processing power.

FIGURE 8.24

A tablet PC can be held like a tablet (a) or rotated into traditional laptop mode (b).

Manufacturing sites, classrooms, and conference rooms are ideal settings for tablet PCs. They are very light and, with their handwriting-recognition capabilities, allow you to take notes silently with no distracting keystrokes.

TABLET PC HARDWARE

What hardware is inside a tablet PC? Like any computer, a tablet PC includes a processor (CPU), operating system software, storage capabilities, input and output devices, and ports. What makes the tablet PC unique, however, is the way in which you input data into it.

How do I input data to a tablet PC? The most innovative input technology on the tablet is its use of **digital ink**. Digital ink is an extension of the text-entry systems used on PDA devices. Supporting digital ink, the tablet PC's entire screen is pressure-sensitive and reacts to a **digital pen**, allowing you to easily draw images and enter text, as shown in Figure 8.25. Once you enter text with the pen using your own handwriting, it is automatically converted to type-written text. You can also select blocks of text and move them around to a different location on the page, or erase text using a scribble motion.

Using the tablet PC's digital pen and ink, you can also annotate (or mark up) existing documents, such as a Word document, by importing them into special tablet PC ink-enabled programs, such as One Note or Word 2003 or later. The original document is unchanged, but your digital ink annotations on the document are also saved. Using this feature, you can mark up an article and send it to a coworker, add notes to a meeting agenda, or draw a route on a map.

How seamless is the use of digital ink and pens? There are occasional mistakes in the handwriting recognition, so the experience is not exactly like using pen on paper. Still, being able to have your notes translated into text and being able to easily enter drawings and annotations are appealing features for many users. And if you prefer to use a keyboard, a software keyboard can appear on the screen and you can tap in text. Tablets also accept the Graffiti notation used in PDAs.

What are the storage and transfer options on tablets? Tablets are designed to be lightweight and to minimize the use of battery power, so they do not include a built-in DVD or CD drive. However, you can purchase external DVD/CD-RW (CD rewritable) drives so that you can transfer your files onto discs. Many tablets also include FireWire and USB 2.0 ports that enable you to attach high-speed peripherals such as external hard disk drives to your tablet PC. Some tablets offer flash memory slots as another option for storing and moving data, and some include built-in infrared ports that allow you to transfer data wirelessly at speeds up to 4.4 Mbps.

How can I quickly connect my tablet to my peripherals? A **docking station** is available for most tablet PC models. This piece of hardware allows you to connect printers, scanners, full-size monitors, mice, and other peripherals directly to the docking station (and therefore your tablet) very quickly. As shown in Figure 8.26, you simply slide your tablet into a docking station to connect it to all peripheral devices, rather than connecting all their cables individually.

What processors are used in tablet PCs? An important criterion for any portable tool like a tablet PC is low power consumption. The Intel Pentium M low-voltage processor is a popular choice, used in both the Gateway tablets and the Compaq TC100, and is specialized to use less power.

Consuming less power also means the battery can last much longer. Battery life is extended to almost a full workday on one charge, and batteries can be "bridged." This

FIGURE 8.25

You input data into a tablet PC by writing on the touch-sensitive screen with a digital pen. The tablet then uses handwriting recognition to convert your writing to type-written text.

FIGURE 8.26

A docking station makes it easy to connect your tablet to your desktop monitor and any other peripherals. Just slide the tablet in place and you're ready to go.

means the tablet can be put into standby mode, not shut down, while you install a new battery.

How much memory can fit in a tablet? The amount of RAM designed for a specific model will vary by manufacturer. Several models on the market now begin with 256 MB of RAM but can be expanded up to 2 GB. Hard drives are offered in a range of capacities up to 80 GB or more.

TABLET SOFTWARE

Do tablet PCs have a special operating system? Tablet PCs run the Windows XP Tablet PC operating system. This operating system is based on the Windows XP Professional operating system but is expanded to include features unique to tablets, such as handwriting recognition and digital ink annotation.

Can tablet PCs use the same software as desktop computers? Tablets can run any applications designed for Windows XP. All tablets include the Windows Journal application, which presents a legal pad-like interface you can use

for note taking. The notes you take can be sent as e-mail or converted into appointments or tasks in Outlook. A more full-featured note-taking application is Microsoft One Note. It allows you to easily incorporate audio recordings and clippings from Web sites and to mark material with searchable colored flags. Microsoft Office itself recognizes digital ink and you can add handwritten notes to any of the Office suite programs, including Word, Excel, Outlook, or PowerPoint.

TABLET OR PDA?

What benefits do tablet PCs have over PDAs and vice versa? Whereas tablet PCs have faster processors, a hard drive, and more RAM than PDAs, PDAs are smaller, lighter, and much cheaper. Thus, whether a tablet PC or a PDA is best for you depends on the needs you have for processing power and portability as well as your budget. Figure 8.27 compares tablet PCs and PDAs so you can find the one best suited to your particular needs.

FIGURE 8.27 Comparing PDAs and Tablet PCs

	Screen Size	CPU Speed	RAM	Hard Disk	Approximate Weight	Cost
PDA	3" to 4"	624 MHz	64 MB	None	5 oz.	$$–$$$
Tablet PC	12" to 14"	1.8 GHz	2 GB	80 GB	3 to 6 lbs.	$$$$$

BITS AND BYTES

Smart Displays

Want to be able to use your desktop computer in many different rooms of your house? "Smart displays," shown in Figure 8.28, are portable flat-screen monitors that allow you to access your regular desktop wirelessly from any room in your house, just like you can when you're sitting at your computer. These three-pound, touch-sensitive monitors can run for up to four hours on a single battery charge, and some come with wireless keyboards and desktop docking stations. They are already cheaper than tablet PCs, and as prices continue to drop, you'll see them appearing in more homes and offices.

FIGURE 8.28

Smart displays are flat-panel monitors that connect wirelessly to your desktop computer, allowing you to access your desktop from any room in your house.

TRENDS IN IT

Ubiquitous Networking: Wherever You Go, There You Are

Instead of having to move the files and programs you need onto mobile devices, how about having a network that "watches" your movements and moves the data so that it follows you? Researchers at the AT&T laboratories at Cambridge University are attempting to make this possible by creating a detection system that can track your location within a building, moving your files wherever you go. To take advantage of the network, users will carry a small device called a "bat," shown in Figure 8.29. This device will have a unique ID number and contain a radio transceiver and transmitter. A detection system (or central controller) installed in the building will keep track of the physical location of the bats and hence the people who carry them.

How does this system work? Suppose you go into a conference room that contains a computer and a phone. The controller is tracking the bat you have in your pocket, so it knows you entered the conference room and therefore routes all your phone calls to the phone in the conference room. It also sends your files and desktop settings to the computer in the conference room.

What if two people are in the conference room at the same time? The controller assigns available devices to the first person who enters the room.

However, using interactive buttons on your bat, you can indicate to the controller that you wish to take temporary possession of a device assigned to another person.

Ubiquitous networks such as this will force us to rethink our territorial approach to work and living spaces, as well as some of our ideas about privacy. In the future, because connectivity will follow us around, access to information may always be right where we are.

FIGURE 8.29

Bats are about the size of a pager device and therefore small enough to be carried comfortably. They allow the detection system to locate the bat owners wherever they roam in the facility.

Laptops

The most powerful mobile computing solution is a **laptop computer**, sometimes called a **notebook computer**. Laptops offer large displays and all of the computing power of a full desktop system (see Figure 8.30). Most laptops weigh more than tablets. This difference is important if you're carrying the unit all day, but not if you're going to be working on a desk where the laptop can rest.

LAPTOP HARDWARE

What hardware comes in a laptop?
Laptops can be equipped with DVD/CD-RW drives, large hard drives, and 2 GB or more of RAM. Although the size of a laptop might prohibit it from having all of the drives you're interested in, newer models feature **hot-swappable bays**. This means that when the laptop is running, you can remove a DVD drive and exchange it with a Zip disk drive, for example, allowing the laptop to be much more versatile. As we discussed in Chapter 2, input devices on laptops include keyboards with built-in mouse functionality. In terms of output devices, many laptops include large display screens measuring up to 17 inches diagonally.

What are popular CPUs for laptops?
CPUs available for laptops are usually a bit slower than the latest available CPU offered for desktop units. Whereas existing desktops can currently run a 3.4-GHz processor, most laptop CPUs run at speeds less than 2.4 GHz. You won't notice the difference if you're using word processing programs, but if you run many applications at the same time or use programs that make heavy demands on the CPU (such as video-editing software), the laptop's performance may seem sluggish compared with a desktop computer.

Many laptop systems use low-power processors such as the Intel Pentium M series, designed to consume less power and extend battery life. The Pentium M can be combined with two additional components, the Intel 855 chipset and the Intel PRO/Wireless network connection, in a package called the Intel Centrino. The Centrino is optimized to work in a highly mobile setting because it uses less power, is more stable, and provides integrated wireless capability.

LAPTOP OPERATING SYSTEMS AND PORTS

Are there special operating systems for laptops?
Laptops use the same operating systems that run on desktop systems. However, laptop operating systems do have some special settings, such as power management profiles. A power management profile contains recommended power-saving settings, such as turning off your hard drive after 15 minutes of no use, shutting down the display after 20 minutes of no movement, and switching the machine to standby or hibernation mode after a certain length of time.

Can laptops connect to other devices easily?
As you can see in Figure 8.31, laptops include a full set of ports,

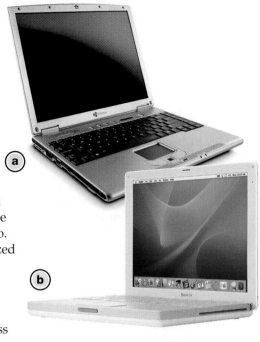

FIGURE 8.30

Laptop computers offer larger displays and more powerful processors than desktops could offer just a few years ago. Here you see (a) a PC laptop and (b) an Apple laptop.

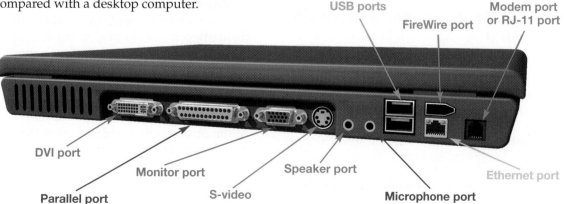

USB ports
FireWire port
Modem port or RJ-11 port

DVI port
Parallel port
Monitor port
S-video
Speaker port
Microphone port
Ethernet port

FIGURE 8.31

Laptops include many of the ports you're used to seeing on desktop computers.

including FireWire, USB 1.0 and 2.0, serial, parallel, infrared (IrDA); RJ-11 jacks for a modem connection; and Ethernet ports for wired networking connections. A newer version of FireWire, FireWire 800, is beginning to appear on laptop units as well. This port allows transfer speeds of twice the original FireWire connection, up to 800 Mbps. Video ports often include high-quality S-video connectors as well as digital DVI connectors, which allow a pure digital signal to run to a digital flat-panel monitor.

Often, the size limitations of laptops mean that they don't offer as many of each type of port as in a desktop system. Therefore, if you buy a laptop you should consider how you will use your machine and whether you will need an expansion hub. An expansion hub is a device that connects to a USB port, creating three or four USB ports from one. If you will be connecting a USB mouse, printer, and scanner to your laptop, you may be short one USB port, in which case a hub would come in handy.

How do laptops connect to wireless networks? Most laptops have integrated support for wireless connectivity. As we discussed in Chapter 7, the 802.11g Wi-Fi wireless standard is the standard used in most wireless networks and is a faster version of the earlier 802.11b Wi-Fi standard. The 802.11g standard allows wireless connections to operate at up to 54 Mbps instead of the 11 Mbps offered in the 802.11b standard. Often laptops will use a b/g card, which is compatible with either type of Wi-Fi network. Many laptops also offer built-in Bluetooth chips that allow you to connect to other Bluetooth-enabled devices.

BITS AND BYTES

More RAM Means Longer Battery Life for Your Laptop

Your laptop stores data both in RAM and on the hard disk drive. Increasing your RAM capacity makes your laptop perform more quickly because data can be read from RAM much faster than from a hard drive. Adding more RAM to your laptop will also make your battery last longer. This is because if the data needed is not in RAM, the hard drive must be powered up, requiring about 30 times as much battery power as simply reading directly from RAM.

LAPTOP BATTERIES AND ACCESSORIES

What types of batteries are there for laptops? Rechargeable batteries are lithium based (Li-ion batteries) or nickel-based (Ni-Cad). Lithium-based batteries are lighter than nickel-based batteries and do not show the "memory effect" that nickel-based batteries do. **Memory effect** means that the battery must be completely used up before it is recharged. If not, the battery won't hold as much charge as it originally did. Unless budget is a serious consideration, you should opt for the more expensive lithium batteries because low weight and lack of memory effect are significant advantages.

How long does a laptop battery last? The capacity of a battery is measured in ampere-hours (A-hrs). Ampere is a measure of current flow, so a battery rated at 5 A-hrs can provide 5 amps of current for an hour. Battery power depends on the device you're using and the work you're doing. A high-performance battery can operate a laptop for up to five hours if fully charged. However, using the laptop's DVD drive can consume a high-performance battery in as little as 90 minutes. Some laptop systems allow you to install two batteries at the same time, doubling the battery life but forcing you to purchase a second battery and have both fully charged.

Do I need to use my battery everywhere I go? Some environments support easy access to power for laptops. For example, you can use an AC/DC or DC/DC converter to enable a laptop to run in a car without using battery power. In addition, many airplanes offer laptop power connections at each seat, although to use such a connection you have to buy a power converter and adapter.

What if I need laptop computing power but in a smaller, lighter configuration? Just coming on the market are devices known as **subnotebook computers**, such as the oQo Model 01 shown in Figure 8.32. Subnotebooks pack major computing power into a tiny package and try to extend battery life as far as possible. Although currently more expensive than many conventional laptops, they may be just what you need if size is your biggest consideration.

What special purchases might a laptop require? Because a laptop is so easily stolen, purchasing a security lock is a wise investment. And as is the case with regular desktops, power surges can adversely affect laptops, so investing in a portable surge protector is also a good idea. (Be sure to read the Technology in Focus feature "Protecting Your Computer and Backing Up Your Data," page 374, for more information about protecting your laptop.)

If you frequently make presentations to large groups, adding a lightweight projector to your laptop might prove useful. Printers have also become travel-sized. Figure 8.33 shows some of these special laptop accessories.

LAPTOP OR DESKTOP?

How does a laptop compare to a desktop? Desktop systems are invariably a better value than laptops. Because of the laptop's small **footprint** (the amount of space on the desk it takes up), you pay more for each component. Each piece has had extra engineering time invested to make sure it fits in the smallest space. In addition, a desktop system offers you more expandability options. It's easier to add new ports and devices because of the amount of room available in the desktop computer's design.

FIGURE 8.32

The oQo is a Windows XP computer featuring a 1-GHz processor, a 20-GB hard drive, 256 MB of RAM, and integrated wireless as well as FireWire and USB ports. At only 4.9" by 3.4" and 14 ounces, it bridges the worlds of laptops and PDA devices.

Desktop systems are also more reliable. Because of the amount of vibration that a laptop experiences, as well as the added exposure to dust, water, and temperature fluctuations, laptops do not last as long as

(a)

(b)

FIGURE 8.33

(a) The Brother MPrint micro printer is equipped with Bluetooth and USB interfaces, so you can print with or without connecting cables. It fits in your jacket pocket and can print on plain paper, address labels, and even carbon paper. The Brother MPrint is compatible with Windows-based tablets and notebooks, Pocket PC–based PDAs, and Palm-based PDAs. (b) The InFocus LP 120 projector weighs about two pounds and can project to an auditorium or conference room.

desktop computers. Manufacturers offer extended warranty plans that cover accidental damage and unexpected drops, although at a price.

How long should I be able to keep my laptop? The answer to that question depends on how easy it is to upgrade your system. Take note of the maximum amount of memory you can install in your laptop. Internal hard disks are not easy to upgrade in a laptop, but if you have a FireWire or USB 2.0 port, you can add an external hard drive for more storage space. Most laptops are equipped with PC Card slots, which are slots on the side of the laptop that accept special credit card–sized devices called **PC Cards**, shown in Figure 8.34. PC Cards can add fax modems, network connections, wireless

adapters, USB 2.0 and FireWire ports, and other capabilities to your laptop.

You can also add a device that allows you to read flash memory cards, such as Compact Flash, Memory Sticks, and Secure Digital cards. As new types of ports and devices are introduced, many will be manufactured in PC Card formats so that you can make sure your laptop is not obsolete before its time.

TRENDS IN IT

Emerging Technologies: Nanotubes: The Next Big Thing Is Pretty Darn Small!

In the classic 1967 film *The Graduate*, Dustin Hoffman is a young man uncertain about which career he should embark on. At a cocktail party, an older gentleman provides him with some career advice, telling him, "I've got just one word for you . . . plastics!" This made sense at the time because plastics were coming on strong as a replacement for metal. If *The Graduate* were remade today, the advice would be, "I've got just one word for you . . . nanotubes!"

As you learned in Chapter 1, *nanoscience* involves the study of molecules and structures (called *nanostructures*) whose size ranges from 1 to 100 nanometers (or one-billionth of a meter). Using nanotechnology, scientists are hoping to one day build resources from the molecular level by manipulating individual atoms instead of using raw materials already found in nature (such as wood or iron ore). This would allow us to create microscopic computers, the ultimate in portable devices. Imagine nano-sized robotic computers swimming through your arteries clearing them of plaque. Consider carrying a supercomputer with you the size of a pencil eraser, or even better, having the power of your desktop computer implanted in your body as a nano-sized chip.

The possibilities of miniaturization are endless, but from what would the computer circuits for these devices be constructed? Carbon nanotubes are poised to be the building blocks of the future. You're familiar with carbon from pencils. The graphite core in a pencil is composed of sheets of carbon atoms laid out in a honeycomb pattern. Individual sheets of graphite are very strong, but don't bond well to other sheets. This makes them ideal for use in a pencil because, as you write, the graphite flakes off and leaves marks on the paper. Unfortunately, graphite doesn't conduct electricity very well. This, coupled with the lack of strong bonding principles, makes graphite unsuitable as a material to manufacture circuits.

In 1991, carbon nanotubes were discovered. Nanotubes are essentially a sheet of carbon atoms (much like graphite) laid out in a honeycomb pattern but rolled into a spherical tube, as shown in Figure 8.35. Arranging the carbon in a tube increases its strength astronomically. It is estimated that carbon nanotubes are 10 to 100 times stronger per unit of weight than steel. This should make them ideal for constructing many types of devices and building materials. Some day we may have earthquake-proof buildings constructed from nanotubes or virtually indestructible clothing woven from nanotube fibers.

But how does this help us build a computer? Aside from strength, the most interesting property of nan-

FIGURE 8.34

PC Cards add functionality to your laptop.

otubes is that they are good conductors of electricity. Nanotubes are actually classified as semimetal, meaning they can have properties that are a cross between semiconductors (such as silicon, which is used to create computer chips) and metals. In fact, depending on how a nanotube is constructed, it can change from a semiconductor to a metal along the length of the tube. These properties make it vastly superior to silicon for the construction of transistor pathways in computer chips, because it provides engineers with more versatility.

In addition, although the smallest silicon transistors that are likely to be produced in the future will be millions of atoms wide, scientists believe that transistors constructed of nanotubes would be only 100 to 1,000 atoms wide. This represents a quantum leap in miniaturization even surpassing the original invention of the transistor. Just imagine what can be done when nanotube transistors replace silicon transistors!

So, when can you buy that pencil eraser–sized computer? Not for quite a while. At this point, researchers can manufacture nanotubes only in extremely small quantities at a large cost. But the U.S. government and many multinational corporations are expected to pour billions of dollars into nanoscience research over the next five years. The ongoing research will hopefully lead to breakthroughs in manufacturing technology that will result in nano-scale computers within your lifetime.

FIGURE 8.35

Here is a highly magnified close-up of a carbon nanotube. Rolling the sheets of carbon atoms into a tube shape gives them incredible strength.

1. What are the advantages and limitations of mobile computing?

Mobile computing allows you to communicate with others, remain productive, and have access to your personal information and schedules, Internet-based information, and important software no matter where you are. However, because mobile devices have been miniaturized, they are more expensive and less rugged than desktop equipment. In addition, battery life limits the usefulness of mobile devices, the screen area is small on most devices, the speed of Internet connection is currently very low, and wireless Internet coverage is limited.

2. What are the various mobile computing devices?

There is a range of mobile computing devices on the market today, including paging devices (pagers), cell phones, MP3 players, personal digital assistants (PDAs), tablet PCs, and laptop (notebook) computers.

3. What can pagers do and who uses them?

A pager is a small wireless device that allows you to receive numeric (and sometimes text) messages on a small display screen. Two-way pagers support both receiving and sending messages. Pagers have long battery lives, are very compact, and are the most inexpensive mobile computing device. People who need to be reachable but want an inexpensive and lightweight device are the primary market for pagers.

4. How do cell phone components resemble a traditional computer and how do cell phones work?

Just like a computer system, cell phones include a processor (CPU), memory, input and output devices, software, and an operating system. When you speak into a cell phone, the sound enters as a sound wave. Analog sound waves need to be digitized, so an analog-to-digital converter chip converts these sound waves into digital signals. The digital information is then compressed (by a digital signal processor) so that it transmits more quickly to another phone. Finally, the digital information is transmitted as a radio wave through the cellular network to the destination phone.

5. What can I carry in an MP3 player and how does it store data?

An MP3 player is a device that enables you to carry MP3 files around with you. MP3 players store mainly digital music files, but some players also allow you to carry contact databases, images, and video and image files. The most inexpensive players use only flash memory to store data, whereas more expensive models use a built-in hard drive, which provides more storage.

6. What can I use a PDA for and what internal components and features does it have?

PDAs are powerful devices that can carry calendars, contact lists, personal productivity software programs, songs, photos, games, and more. Like any computer, a PDA includes a processor, operating sys-

tem software, input and output devices, and ports. All PDAs feature touch-sensitive screens that allow you to enter data with a stylus. You can use either handwritten text or special notation systems to enter data into a PDA. In terms of output devices, PDAs come with LCD screens in a variety of resolutions. The two main PDA operating systems are the Palm OS and the Pocket PC system. PDAs do not come with built-in hard drives, but for memory needs beyond their built-in RAM and ROM, PDAs use removable flash memory.

7. How can I synchronize my PDA with my desktop computer?

The process of updating your data so the files on your mobile device and desktop computer are the same is called synchronizing. To synchronize your desktop and PDA, you place the PDA in a cradle and touch a "hot sync" button. This begins the process of information transfer (or synchronization) that updates both sets of files to the most current version. Other options for synchronizing or transferring files include using IrDA ports and the Bluetooth wireless connectivity option.

8. What is a tablet PC and why would I want to use one?

A tablet PC is a portable computer that includes advanced handwriting and incorporates the use of digital ink. Tablet PCs are named such because the display monitor can be used either in a traditional laptop mode or in tablet mode. The most innovative input technology on the tablet PC is digital ink. Supporting digital ink, the tablet's screen is pressure-sensitive and reacts to a digital pen. A tablet PC can be the ideal solution when you require a lightweight, portable computer with full desktop processing power.

9. How powerful are laptops and how do they compare to desktop computers?

The most powerful mobile computing solution is a laptop (or notebook) computer. Laptops offer large displays and can be equipped with DVD/CD-RW drives, hard drives, and 2 GB or even more of RAM. Many models feature hot-swappable bays and a full set of ports. Still, desktop systems are more reliable and cost-effective than laptops. In addition, it is easier to upgrade and add new ports and devices to a desktop than to a laptop. And although powerful, CPUs for laptops are usually a bit slower than the latest CPU offered for desktop units. Still, many users feel the mobility laptops offer is worth the added expense.

Buzz Words

Word Bank

- Bluetooth
- cell phone
- cradle
- crib
- flash memory card
- GPS

- laptop
- microbrowser
- MMS
- mobile device
- MP3 player
- pager

- PDA
- processor
- SMS
- stylus
- synchronize
- tablet

Instructions: Fill in the blanks using the words from the Word Bank.

Kathleen's new job as a sales rep is going to mean a lot of travel. She'll need to start thinking about using (1) _____s to stay productive when she's out of the office. Because she needs voice communication and not just text exchange, she'll be selecting a(n) (2) _____ rather than a(n) (3) _____ . With her cell phone, she'll be able to exchange text messages with her coworkers using (4) _____ . When she accesses the Internet from her phone, she'll use (5) _____ software to check the latest stock prices.

Because she travels a lot and loves music, she has been considering buying a digital (6) _____ . However, she has instead decided to purchase a more expensive (7) _____ that includes MP3 capabilities. That way, she can use the device as more than just an MP3 player. She also invests in a removable (8) _____ on which she'll store her MP3 files. Because she's a hiker, she wants to use her PDA as a navigation device, so she may buy a(n) (9) _____ accessory to go with it.

To make sure she is getting the best device with the most powerful processor, Kathleen has been comparing benchmarks that measure (10) _____ . In addition, she wants to make sure she can (11) _____ her PDA with her desktop computer, so the files on both match. Thus, she bought a PDA that includes the wireless (12) _____ technology, as well as an external (13) _____ that connects her PDA to her PC through a USB port. Because she still needs to run powerful software packages when she's out of the office, she bought a(n) (14) _____ as well. It was a better choice than a full-sized (15) _____ because she carries it with her all day, taking notes while standing on the production floor.

Becoming Computer Fluent

You have a job as a sales rep at a large publishing company. Your boss is considering investing in some kind of mobile device with Internet access to help you perform your duties. However, first she requires a justification. What mobile device(s) would be best suited for your position? Would you need Internet access for it? Does it depend on which type of device you're using or your job responsibilities? What advantages would there be to the company? What hardware would be required?

Instructions: Using the preceding scenario, write a report using as many of the key words from the chapter as you can. Be sure the sentences are grammatically and technically correct.

Instructions: Answer the multiple choice and true/false questions below for more practice with key terms and concepts from this chapter.

MULTIPLE CHOICE

1. Mobile computing is a terrific help for
   a. professions that require a lot of travel
   b. work that requires intensive graphics
   c. work that is heavily computational
   d. all of the above

2. Currently, cell phones are designed without
   a. a microprocessor
   b. RAM
   c. an operating system
   d. a hard disk drive

3. Cell phones use ROM
   a. to store phone numbers
   b. to store their operating system
   c. both a and b
   d. cell phones have no ROM

4. The number of songs that can be stored on an MP3 player depends on
   a. the file format of the song
   b. the sampling rate used when the song was digitized
   c. the amount of memory on the player
   d. all of the above

5. Flash memory is
   a. available at up to 1 GB per card
   b. volatile and is erased when power is removed
   c. used in PDAs, MP3 players, and digital cameras
   d. all of the above

6. The device that would be best suited to quiet note-taking during a meeting is
   a. an MP3 player with attached voice recorder
   b. a PDA with a keyboard
   c. a tablet using a digital stylus
   d. a laptop

7. GPS stands for
   a. general purpose scanner
   b. global positioning system
   c. greater place sensor
   d. geo positioning system

8. The Intel Pentium M processor
   a. is identical to a Pentium IV
   b. is often used in mobile computing devices
   c. is used most commonly in PDAs
   d. is mainly used in high-performance computers such as tablets

9. Additional ports can be added to a laptop
   a. using a PC card or an external hub
   b. only if you have a FireWire port
   c. only if you have the Windows XP operating system
   d. if the battery is removable

10. Portable devices that can provide Internet access include
    a. tablets, laptops, PDAs, and cell phones
    b. iPods and cell phones
    c. pagers and GPS units
    d. any device with Bluetooth

TRUE/FALSE

_____ 1. Hard disk drives are only useful in desktops, laptops, and tablet PCs.

_____ 2. MP3 players with a built-in hard drive generally are able to carry more songs than those with flash memory.

_____ 3. A Bluetooth-enabled PDA can wirelessly exchange data with a Bluetooth-enabled cell phone.

_____ 4. MMS is short for Multimedia Message Service.

_____ 5. Wireless Internet access covers the entire United States.

Making the Transition to... Next Semester

1. Choosing Devices to Fit Your Needs

As a student, which devices discussed in this chapter would have the most immediate impact on the work you do each day? Which would provide the best value (that is, the most increase in productivity and organization per dollar spent)?

2. Choosing the Best Laptop

Compare the Apple PowerBook series of laptop computers with the Dell Inspiron XPS Gen 2 series. Consider price, performance, expandability, and portability. Explain which would be the better investment for your needs next semester.

3. Choosing the Best Cell Phone Plan

Major national cellular providers include Cingular, Verizon, T-Mobile, and Sprint. Visit their Web sites and compare the prices and features of their popular cellular plans for both minimal users and power users. Based on your research, which cell phone plan would be best for your needs?

4. Choosing the Best PDA

Visit the Electronics store at Amazon.com and locate the PDA section. Compare three different PDA models and list their price, input and output devices, operating systems, built-in memory, processor speed, and other special features.

a. Which of the three models you compared is the best value for your needs?

b. What special features does that PDA have? What accessories would you buy for your PDA to make it more useful?

c. Would you consider buying a used PDA? Why or why not?

d. Next, investigate PDA software on sites such as **www.download.com**. What software would you buy for a PDA and which operating system does that software require?

5. How Many MP3 Files Can You Fit?

Fill out the following table to determine how many minutes of MP3 files you could store depending on the sampling rate of the MP3 files. Use the following to help you fill in the table:

- Say you sample music at 192 kilobits per second. There are 8 bits in one byte, so 192 kilobits per second = 192/8 = 24 KB per second.

- There are 60 seconds in one minute, so the number of kilobytes per minute is equal to 24 KB per second times 60 seconds = 1,440 KB per minute.

- With 256 MB of space, which is 256,000 KB, there would be room for 256,000 KB divided by 1,440 KB per minute = approximately 177 minutes of songs that can be stored.

Sampling Rate, Kilobits Per Second	Number of Kilobytes (Kb) Per Second (Kb/Sec)	Number of Kilobytes Per Minute (Kb/minute)	Flash Card Memory	Minutes of Songs That Can Be Stored
192 Kbps	192/8 = 24 KBps	24 KBps* 60 seconds = 1,440 KB per minute	256 MB	256,000 KB/ 1,440 KB per minute = 177 minutes
128 Kbps			256 MB	
96 Kbps			256 MB	
64 Kbps			256 MB	

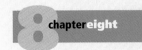

chapter**eight**

Making the Transition to...
The Workplace

1. Corporate Mobile Computing Needs

Imagine your company is boosting its sales force and looking to the future of mobile technology. Your boss has asked you to research the following issues surrounding mobile computing for the company:

a. Do mobile computing devices present increased security risks? What would happen if you left a flash memory card at a meeting and a competitor picked it up? Are there ways to protect your data on mobile devices?

b. Can viruses attack mobile devices? Is there any special software on the market to protect mobile devices from viruses?

c. Is there a role for mobile computing devices even if employees don't leave the building? Which devices would be important for a company to consider for use within corporate offices?

2. 3G Communications

The next generation of telecommunications (nicknamed "3G" for "third generation") allows the speed of cellular network transmissions to rise from 144 Kbps to 2 Mbps. How does that compare to dial-up and cable modem access for wired networks? What implications does it have on information access and e-commerce?

3. Mobile Speed Limits

Research the Internet and determine what speed limitations are expected to exist in the future with regards to mobile devices.

4. Too Much Mobile?

Imagine you are a manager of 18 employees, all of whom work in open air cubicles (i.e., there are no fixed walls or separate offices). As a manager, what concerns might you have about their personal cell phone usage? Do you think your employees would respond well to a "Quiet Zone," an area in which no personal cell phone usage is allowed? What about conduct during important meetings? Should employees be allowed to text message each other during the meeting? As a manager, are there concerns you might have if employees had a digital camera on their cell phones?

Critical Thinking Questions

Instructions: Albert Einstein used "Gedanken experiments," or critical thinking questions, to develop his theory of relativity. Some ideas are best understood by experimenting with them in our own minds. The following critical thinking questions are designed to demand your full attention but require only a comfortable chair—no technology.

1. **Mobile Devices and Society**

   Do you think we will ever become a completely wireless society? Will there always be a need for some land lines (physical wired connections)? How will broadband wireless communication infrastructure impact a city's social and economic development? Will there be more social interaction? Less? Will mobile computing promote increased understanding between people? More isolation?

2. **The Ultimate Mobile Devices**

   As devices become lighter and smaller, we are seeing a combining of multiple functions into one device.

   a. What would the ultimate convergent mobile device be for you? Is there a limit in weight, size, or complexity?

   b. America Online Instant Messenger (AIM) service is now available on many cellular phone systems. Would the ability to be alerted to IM buddies on your cell phone be useful to you? What would you be willing to pay for this feature?

3. **Protecting Intellectual Property**

   The recording industry, recording artists, and consumers find themselves in a complex discussion when the topic of peer-to-peer sharing systems is brought up.

   a. What solution would you propose to safeguard the business interests of the industry, the intellectual property rights of the musicians, and the freedoms of consumers?

   b. Have you ever downloaded music off the Web? If so, did you download the music from a legal site? Do you think illegal download sites should be allowed to exist?

4. **Privacy Concerns: Bats**

   Consider the implications of the bat tracking device we discussed in the Trends in IT feature. Would you agree to be "tracked" at work if it meant a more convenient way to use communication tools? What sorts of privacy risks do such devices pose?

5. **Privacy Concerns: GPS**

   Consider the following questions related to GPS security risks:

   a. Your employer asks you to carry a GPS-enabled cell phone. The GPS chip inside allows a private service (**www.ulocate.com**) to gather information on your last location, the path you took to get there, and your average speed from point to point. What are the privacy issues this presents? Would you agree to take the phone?

   b. Would you agree to insert a GPS-enabled tracking device into your pet? Your child? What legislation would be required if tracking data were available on you? Would you be willing to sell that information to marketing agencies? Should that data be available to the government if you were suspected of a crime?

6. **Wearable Computer Applications**

   What applications can you think of for the wearable computer technology discussed in the Trends in IT feature? What sorts of wearable computers do you think you would be likely to purchase?

7. **Nanotechnology Applications**

   The Trends in IT feature on nanotechnology describes a number of ways in which nano-sized computers may one day be used. What other applications for such powerful and tiny computers can you think of? Can you think of any security or privacy risks associated with such nano-sized computers?

Problem:

You have formed a consulting group that advises clients on how to move their businesses into the new mobile computing age.

Task:

Each team will be defined as an expert resource in one of the mobile devices presented in this chapter: cell phones, PDAs, tablet PCs, or laptops. For each of the scenarios described by a client, the group should assess how strong a fit their device is to that client's needs.

Process:

Divide the class into three or four teams and assign each group a different mobile device (cell phone, PDA, tablet PC, or laptop).

1. Research the current features and prices for the mobile device your team has been assigned.

2. Consider the following three clients:

   • An elementary classroom that wants to have students carry mobile devices to the nearby creek to do a science project on water quality.

   • A manufacturing plant that wants managers using a mobile device to be able to report back hourly on the production line's performance and problems.

   • A pharmaceutical company that wants to outfit its sales reps with the devices they need to be prepared to promote their products when they visit physicians.

   Discuss the advantages and disadvantages of your device for each of these clients. Consider value, reliability, computing needs, and communication needs as well as expandability for the future.

3. Prepare a final report for the group that considers the costs, availability, and unique features of the device that led you to recommend or not recommend it for each client.

4. Bring the research materials from the individual team meetings to class. Looking at the clients' needs, make final decisions as to which mobile device is best suited for each client.

Conclusion:

There are a number of mobile computing devices on the market today. Finding the best mobile device to use in any given situation depends on factors such as value, reliability, expandability, and the computing and communication needs of the client.

Multimedia

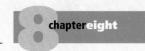

In addition to the review materials presented here, you'll find additional materials featured with the book's multimedia, including the *Technology in Action* Student Resource CD and the Companion Web site (**www.prenhall.com/techinaction**), which will help reinforce your understanding of the chapter content. These materials include the following:

ACTIVE HELPDESK

In Active Helpdesk calls, you'll assume the role of a Helpdesk operator taking calls about the concepts you've learned in this chapter. You'll apply what you've learned and receive feedback from a supervisor to review and reinforce those concepts. The Active Helpdesk calls for this chapter are listed here and can be found on your Student Resource CD:

- Using MP3 Players
- Using PDAs

SOUND BYTES

Sound Bytes are dynamic multimedia tutorials that help demystify even the most complex topics. You'll view video clips and animations that illustrate computer concepts, and then apply what you've learned by reviewing with the Sound Byte Labs, which include quizzes and activities specifically tailored to each Sound Byte. The Sound Bytes for this chapter are listed here and can be found on your Student Resource CD and on the Companion Web site (**www.prenhall.com/techinaction**):

- PDAs on the Road and at Home
- Connecting with Bluetooth
- Tablet and Laptop Tour

COMPANION WEB SITE

The *Technology in Action* Companion Web site includes a variety of additional materials to help you review and learn more about the topics in this chapter. The resources available at **www.prenhall.com/techinaction** include:

- **Online Study Guide.** Each chapter features an online true/false and multiple-choice quiz. You can take these quizzes, automatically check the results, and e-mail the results to your instructor.
- **Web Research Projects.** Each chapter features a number of Web research projects that ask you to search the Web for information on computer-related careers, milestones in computer history, important people and companies, emerging technologies, and the applications and implications of different technologies.

PROTECTING YOUR COMPUTER AND BACKING UP YOUR DATA

Just like any other valuable asset, computers and the data they contain require protection from damage, thieves, and unauthorized users. Although it's impossible to protect your computer and data completely, following the suggestions outlined in this Technology in Focus will provide you with peace of mind that you have done all you can to protect your computer from theft and keep it in working order.

PHYSICALLY PROTECTING YOUR COMPUTER

Your computer isn't useful to you if it is damaged. Therefore, it's essential to select and ensure a safe environment for your computer. This includes protecting it from environmental factors, power surges, and power outages.

Environmental Factors

There are a number of environmental factors you need to consider to protect your computer.

1 Sudden movements (such as a fall) can damage your computer or mobile device's internal components. Therefore, take special care in setting up your computer. Make sure that the computer sits on a flat, level surface, and carry your laptop in a padded case to protect it should you drop it. If you do drop your computer or laptop, have it professionally tested by a computer repair facility to uncover any hidden damage.

2 Electronic components do not like excessive heat. Unfortunately, computers generate a lot of heat. This is why they contain a fan to cool their internal components. Make sure that you place your computer so that the fan's input vents (usually found on the rear of the system unit) are unblocked so that air can flow inside.

3 Naturally, a fan drawing air into a computer also draws in dust and other particles, which can wreak havoc on your system. Therefore, keep the room in which your computer is located as clean as possible. Placing your computer in the workshop where you do woodworking and generate sawdust would obviously be a poor choice! Even in a clean room, the fan duct on your computer can become packed with dust, so vacuum it periodically to keep a clear airflow into your computer.

4 Because food crumbs and liquid can damage keyboards and other computer components, consume food and beverages away from your computer to avoid food-related damage.

Power Surges

Power surges occur when electrical current is supplied in excess of normal voltage (120 volts in the United States). Old or faulty wiring, downed power lines, malfunctions at electric company substations, and lightning strikes can all cause power surges. **Surge protectors** are devices that protect your computer against power surges (see Figure 1). To use a surge protector, you simply plug all your electrical devices into the outlets of the surge protector, which in turn plugs into the wall.

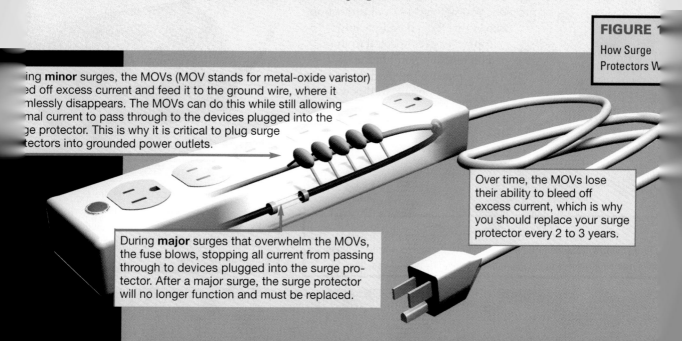

FIGURE 1

How Surge Protectors W...

...ing **minor** surges, the MOVs (MOV stands for metal-oxide varistor) ...ed off excess current and feed it to the ground wire, where it ...mlessly disappears. The MOVs can do this while still allowing ...mal current to pass through to the devices plugged into the ...ge protector. This is why it is critical to plug surge ...tectors into grounded power outlets.

During **major** surges that overwhelm the MOVs, the fuse blows, stopping all current from passing through to devices plugged into the surge protector. After a major surge, the surge protector will no longer function and must be replaced.

Over time, the MOVs lose their ability to bleed off excess current, which is why you should replace your surge protector every 2 to 3 years.

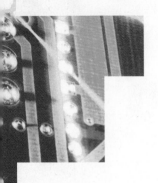

Surge protectors wear out over time (usually in less than five years), so buy a surge protector that includes indicator lights. Indicator lights illuminate when the surge protector is no longer functioning properly. Note that old surge protectors can still function as multiple-outlet power strips, delivering power to your equipment without protecting it. A power surge could ruin your computer and other devices if you don't protect them. Thus, at around $20, a surge protector is an excellent investment.

It's important to protect *all* your electronic devices, not just computers, from surges. Printers and other computer peripherals all require protection. However, it can be inconvenient to use individual surge protectors on everything. A more practical method is to install a **whole-house surge protector**, shown in Figure 2. Whole-house surge protectors function like other surge protectors but they protect *all* electrical devices in the house. Electricians usually install whole-house surge protectors, which cost $200 to $300 installed.

Data lines (transmission media), such as the coaxial cable or phone wires that attach to your modem, can also carry surges. Installing a **data line surge suppressor** for each data line connected to your computer through another device (such as a modem) provides you with additional protection (see Figure 3). A data line surge suppressor is connected to the data line at a point before it reaches the modem or other device. In this way, it intercepts surges on the data line before they reach sensitive equipment.

Surge protectors won't necessarily guard against all surges. Lightning strikes can generate such high amounts of voltage that they can overwhelm a surge protector. As tedious as it sounds, unplugging computers and peripherals during an electrical storm is the only way to achieve absolute protection.

Power Outages

Like power surges, power outages can wreak havoc on a system. Mission-critical computers such as Web servers are often protected by **uninterruptible power supplies (UPSs)**, shown in Figure 4. A UPS is a device that contains surge protection equipment and a large battery. When power is interrupted (such as during a blackout), the UPS continues to send power to the attached computer from its battery. Depending on the battery capacity, you have between about 20 minutes and 3 hours to save your work and shut down your computer properly.

SOUND BYTE
Surge Protectors

In this Sound Byte, you'll learn about the major features of surge protectors and how they work. You'll also learn about the key factors you need to consider before buying a surge protector, and you'll see how easy it is to install one.

FIGURE 2
A whole-house surge protector is usually installed at the breaker panel or near the electric meter. It protects all appliances in the home from electrical surges.

Surge protector

FIGURE 3
APC, a large manufacturer of surge protection devices, makes a wide range of data line surge suppressors to accommodate almost any type of data line.

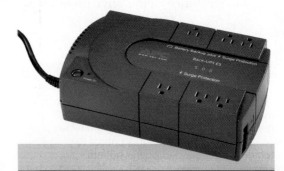

FIGURE 4
Although they look like a fat surge protector, UPS devices contain a large battery that kicks in during power outages. If your computer is plugged into such a device, you'll have time to save your work before losing power.

DETERRING THEFT

Because they are portable, laptops are easy targets for thieves. Common sense dictates that you don't leave your laptop unattended or in places where it can be easily stolen. Three additional approaches to deterring computer theft include alarming them, locking them down, or allowing the devices to tell you when they are stolen.

FIGURE 5

A laptop alarm sends out an ear-piercing sound if your laptop is moved before you deactivate the alarm.

Alarms

To prevent your laptop from being stolen, you can attach a motion alarm to it, shown in Figure 5. When you leave your laptop, you use a small device called a "key fob activator" to activate the alarm. If your laptop is moved while the alarm is activated, it emits a wailing 85-decibel sound. The fact that the alarm is visible acts as an additional theft deterrent, just like a "beware of dog" sign in a front yard.

Locks and Surrounds

Chaining a laptop to your work surface can be an effective way to prevent theft. As shown in Figure 6, a special locking mechanism is attached to the laptop (some laptops are even manufactured with locking ports), and a hardened steel cable is connected to the locking mechanism. The other end of the cable is looped around something large and heavy, such as a desk. The cable lock obviously requires that you use a key to free the laptop from its mooring.

Many people associate computer theft only with laptops or PDAs. But desktop computers are vulnerable to theft also, especially theft of internal components such as RAM. Cable locks are available that connect through special fasteners on the back of desktop computers, but components can still be stolen because these cables often don't prevent the system unit case from being opened. A more effective theft deterrent for desktops is a **surround** (or **cage**), shown in Figure 7. A surround is a metal box that encloses the system unit and makes it impossible to remove the case, while still allowing access to ports and devices such as CD players.

FIGURE 6

Cable locks are an effective deterrent to theft. New models have combination locks that alleviate keeping track of your keys.

FIGURE 7

Computer surrounds deter theft by making access to the internal components of the computer difficult while still allowing access to ports and drives.

Computers that "Phone Home"

You've probably heard of LoJack, the theft-tracking device used in cars. Car owners install a LoJack transmitter somewhere in their vehicle. Then, if the vehicle is stolen, police activate the transmitter and use its signal to locate the car. Similar systems now exist for computers. Tracking software, such as Computrace (**www.absolute.com**) and zTrace Gold (**www.ztrace.com**), enables the computer it is installed on to alert authorities as to its location if it is stolen.

To use this computer version of LoJack, you install the tracking software on your computer's hard drive. Once you install the software, it contacts a server at the software manufacturer's Web site each time you connect to the Internet. If your computer is stolen, you notify the software manufacturer, who then instructs your computer to transmit tracking information (such as an IP address) that will assist authorities in locating and retrieving the stolen computer.

The files and directories holding the software are not visible to thieves looking for such software. What if the thieves reformat the hard drive in an attempt to destroy all files on the computer? The tracking software is written in such a way that it detects a reformat and hides the software code in a safe place in memory or on the hard drive (some sectors of a hard drive are not rewritten during most formats). That way, it can reinstall itself after the reformatting is completed.

KEEPING PDAS AND CELL PHONES SAFE

PDAs and cell phones present their own unique hazards. Here are a couple of tips for keeping them secure.

Foiling PDA Data Theft

PDAs can be vulnerable to unauthorized access if they are left unattended or are stolen. **PDA bomb software** features data and password protection for your PDA in an attempt to combat this problem. If you have PDA bomb software, a thief who steals your PDA is forced to crack your password to gain access. When a thief launches a brute force attack (repetitive tries to guess a password) on the PDA, the software's bomb feature kicks in after a certain number of failed password attempts. The "bomb" erases all data contained on the PDA, thereby protecting your sensitive information. PDA Defense, found at **www.pdadefense.com**, is a popular example of PDA bomb software.

Preventing Bluetooth Attacks

Bluetooth is a transmission medium for exchanging data wirelessly over short distances. Many cell phones and PDAs are Bluetooth-enabled. Unfortunately, Bluetooth hardware and software is riddled with security holes, especially on cell phones. If you have a Bluetooth-enabled device, you are susceptible to two types of mischief:

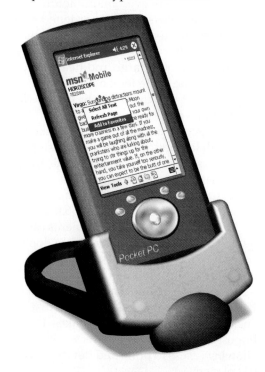

1 **Bluesnarfing:** Bluesnarfing involves exploiting a flaw in the Bluetooth access software for the purpose of accessing a Bluetooth device and stealing the information contained on it. Think how much valuable information is contained on your cell phone (names, contact information, meeting notes) that might be valuable to a business competitor. Unfortunately, Bluesnarfing is relatively easy (and cheap) to do, as there is a lot of Bluesnarfing software available on the Internet.

2 **Bluebugging:** Although much more difficult and expensive to execute, Bluebugging presents much more serious dangers. Bluebugging involves a hacker actually taking over control of a Bluetooth-enabled device so that he or she can do some or all of the following:

- Make phone calls
- Send, receive, or read SMS messages
- Establish Internet connections
- Write phonebook entries
- Set call forwarding

This is a real risk for Europeans, as Bluetooth and SMS are wildly popular there. Many Europeans use their cell phones to make micropayments (small purchases from merchants that eventually appear on their cell phone bill) by a process known as "reverse SMS." If a hacker Bluebugs your phone, they could potentially send payments to fake accounts they control using reverse SMS.

So how can you protect yourself from Bluetooth attacks? As vulnerabilities are discovered, cell phone and PDA manufacturers will issue software patches. You must ensure that you update the software in your phone (or PDA) just as you do for your computer operating system. Unfortunately, the only 100 percent foolproof way to protect your phone is to disable Bluetooth altogether.

PROTECTING YOUR COMPUTER FROM UNAUTHORIZED ACCESS

To protect yourself even further, you may want to restrict access to the sensitive data on your computer. Both software and hardware solutions exist to restrict others from accessing your computer, helping you keep its content safe.

Password Protection and Access Privileges

Windows XP has built-in password protection of files as well as the entire desktop. If your computer has been set up for multiple users with password protection, the Windows logon screen requires users to enter a password to gain access to the desktop. The computer can be set to default back to the Welcome screen after it is idle for a set period of time. This forces users to reenter a password to regain access to the computer. If someone attempts to log on to your computer without your password, that person won't be able to gain access.

Setting up a password also forces users to decide whether to share their files with other users. Figure 8 shows the dialog box

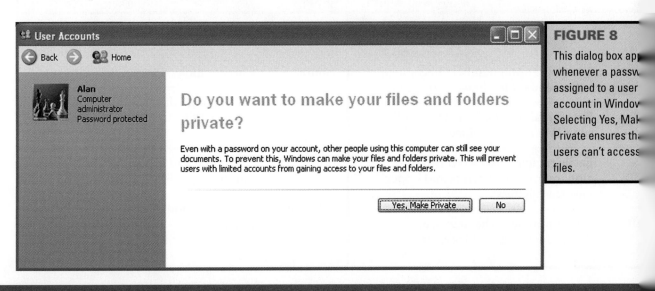

User Accounts

Back   Home

Alan
Computer administrator
Password protected

Do you want to make your files and folders private?

Even with a password on your account, other people using this computer can still see your documents. To prevent this, Windows can make your files and folders private. This will prevent users with limited accounts from gaining access to your files and folders.

Yes, Make Private   No

FIGURE 8

This dialog box ap[pears] whenever a passw[ord is] assigned to a user account in Window[s XP.] Selecting Yes, Mak[e] Private ensures th[at] users can't access [your] files.

ARE KLINGONESE PASSWORDS SAFE?

Many computer users are diehard science fiction fans. *Star Trek, Babylon 5,* and *Battlestar Galactica* have provided computer users with loads of planet names, alien races, alien vocabulary (Klingon words from the Star Trek series are very popular), and starship names to use as passwords. Unfortunately, hackers are on to this ploy. Recently developed hacking programs use dictionaries of "geek-speak" to attempt to break passwords. Although "Qapla" (Klingonese for "success" and also used as "goodbye") might seem like an unbreakable password, don't bet your data on it!

that appears in Windows XP asking you to make this choice when you set up a user account password. Files not shared remain safe from the prying eyes of other users unless they know your password.

Of course, password protection works only as well as your password does. Creating a secure password is therefore very important. To do so, follow the basic guidelines shown here:

- Your password should be five to eight characters long and contain both numbers and letters.

- Your password should not be a word found in the dictionary.

- Your password should not be easily associated with you (such as your birth date, the name of your pet, or your nickname).

- Secure passwords take the first letters of a group of unrelated words or words in a particular phrase. It is also good to insert special characters such as the ampersand sign (&) or dollar sign ($) in your password.

- You should never tell anyone your password or write it down in a place where others might see it.

- You should change your password if you think someone may know it.

Figure 9 shows some possible passwords and explains why they make good or bad candidates.

Managing Your Passwords

Good security practices suggest that you have different passwords for different Web sites that you access and that you change your passwords frequently. If you visit a lot of sites that require logon names and passwords, remembering them all can be tough. However, free password management software, such as AccountLogon **(www.accountlogon.com),** takes the worry out of forgetting passwords because it does the remembering for you.

To use the software, you enter into the password management program your logon

FIGURE 9
GOOD AND BAD PASSWORD CANDIDATES

GOOD PASSWORD	REASON	BAD PASSWORD	REASON
L8t2me	Uses letters and numbers to come up with memorable phrase "Late to me"	Jsmith	Combination of first initial, last name
IWALR	First initials of first line of Green Day song *I Walk a Lonely Road*	4smithkids	Even though this has alphanumeric combination, it is too descriptive of a family
P1zzA	Easily remembered word with mix of alphanumeric characters and upper-/lowercase letters	Brown5512	Last name and last four digits of phone number is easily decoded
S0da&IC	Mix of numbers, characters, and letters. Stands for "Soda and Ice Cream"	123Main	Your street address is an easily decoded password

name and password for every Web site you visit. You then navigate to the Web site and tell the software to associate the proper logon information with that particular site. After you have set up the software, one click (for example, on "Ebay Account," as shown in Figure 10) will take you to the eBay site and automatically log you in. With password management software like AccountLogon, you only need to remember one password (to access the password management program itself). Of course, when you change a password on a site, don't forget to update your password management software, too.

Keeping IM Sessions Safe

Virus attacks and other forms of malicious hacking are being perpetrated at an alarming rate via instant messenger (IM) programs such as AOL Instant Messenger and MSN Messenger. To keep your IM sessions safe, follow these precautions:

1 **Allow connections only from users on your Buddy List.** This prevents you from being annoyed by unknown parties. On the preferences screen for your IM program (as shown in Figure 11), select "Don't Allow" in the "For users not on my Buddy List" section.

2 **Disable potentially dangerous IM options such as file sharing, file transfer, and Direct IM (another file-sharing option)** (see Figure 11). Although these options are potentially useful for swapping files over IM, they are a common way of receiving malicious files, which can then infect your computer with viruses.

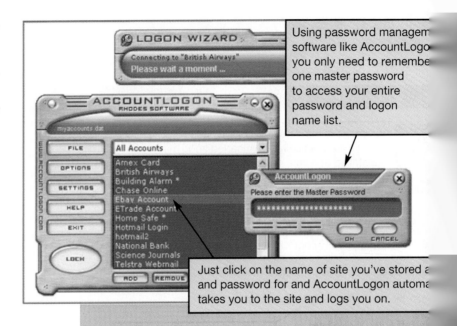

Using password managem[ent] software like AccountLogo[n] you only need to remembe[r] one master password to access your entire password and logon name list.

Just click on the name of site you've stored a[nd] and password for and AccountLogon automa[tically] takes you to the site and logs you on.

FIGURE 10

AccountLogon relieves you of the chore of having to remember logon names and passwords. Entering the one master password will enable you to log on to any site that you set up on your list.

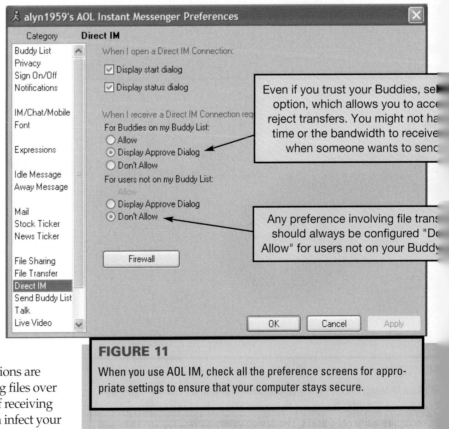

Even if you trust your Buddies, se[lect this] option, which allows you to acce[pt or] reject transfers. You might not ha[ve the] time or the bandwidth to receive [files] when someone wants to send [them.]

Any preference involving file trans[fer] should always be configured "D[on't] Allow" for users not on your Budd[y List.]

FIGURE 11

When you use AOL IM, check all the preference screens for appropriate settings to ensure that your computer stays secure.

Keeping Windows Up To Date

Software patches to close security holes in Windows (or other operating systems) are issued periodically. To be sure you are protected from spreading threats, make sure these patches are installed on your computer. This can be an automatic process with Windows XP Service Pack 2 (see Figure 12). From the Start menu in Windows, select Control Panel, then click on the Security Center icon to display the Security Center window. Under the topic "Manage Security Settings For," click Automatic Updates to display the dialog box shown in Figure 12. Pick the best option for your situation (the first two options are good for broadband connections; the third option is better for dial-up).

Biometric Authentication Devices

Biometric authentication devices are devices you can attach to your computer or PDA that read a unique personal characteristic, such as a fingerprint or the iris pattern in your eye, and convert that pattern to a digital code. When you use the device, your pattern is read and compared to the one stored on the computer. Only users having an exact fingerprint or iris pattern match are allowed to access the computer.

Because no two people have the same biometric characteristics (fingerprints and iris patterns are unique), these devices provide a high level of security. They also eliminate the human error that can occur in password protection. (You might forget your password, but you won't forget to bring your fingerprint to the computer!) Some newer PDAs feature built-in fingerprint readers, and Figure 13a shows a mouse that includes a fingerprint reader. Another useful device is the APC Biometric Password Manager (shown in Figure 13b), which after it identifies you by your fingerprint, provides logon information to password-protected Web sites you need to access. Other biometric devices include voice authentication and face pattern recognition systems, but these are usually too expensive for home use.

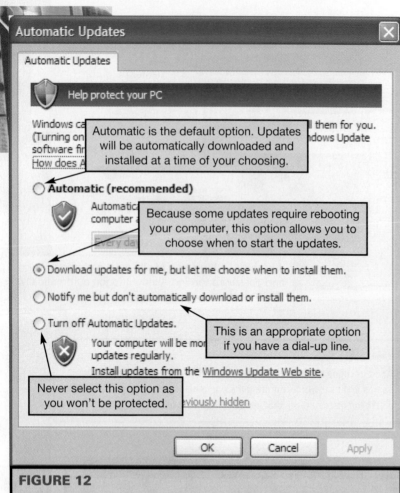

Automatic is the default option. Updates will be automatically downloaded and installed at a time of your choosing.

Because some updates require rebooting your computer, this option allows you to choose when to start the updates.

This is an appropriate option if you have a dial-up line.

Never select this option as you won't be protected.

FIGURE 12

Turning on the Automatic Updates feature of Windows XP is an essential part of protecting your computer.

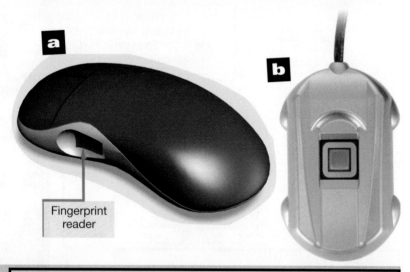

Fingerprint reader

FIGURE 13

(a) The BioLink U-Match Mouse is a two-button mouse that includes a digital fingerprint reader. (b) The APC Biometric Password Manager uses a fingerprint reader to recognize authorized users. The device stores all your logon names and passwords so you don't have to keep track of them. Up to 20 users can use the same device, making it perfect for shared computers.

Firewalls

As noted in Chapter 7, unauthorized access often occurs when your computer is connected to the Internet. You can best prevent such cases of unauthorized access by using either hardware or software **personal firewalls**. Hardware firewalls are often built into a router. Figure 14 lists popular software firewall programs. Setting up either a hardware or software firewall should adequately protect you from unauthorized access when connected to the Internet.

BACKING UP YOUR DATA

The data on your computer faces three major threats: unauthorized access, tampering, and destruction. As noted in Chapter 7, a hacker can gain access to your computer and steal or alter your data. However, a more likely scenario is that you will lose your data unintentionally. You may accidentally delete files; your hard drive may break down, resulting in complete data loss; a virus may destroy your original file; or a fire may destroy the room that houses your computer. Because many of these factors are beyond your control, you should have a strategy for backing up your files.

Making file **backups**—copies of files that you can use to replace the originals if they are lost or damaged—is important. When you back up your files, remember to store the copy in a different place than the original. Removable storage media such as external hard drives, Zip disks, DVDs, CDs, and flash drives are popular choices for backing up files because they hold a lot of data and can be easily transported.

Two types of files need backups—program files and data files:

- **Program files** are files you use to install software and usually come on CDs or DVDs. If any programs came preinstalled in your computer, you should still have received a CD or DVD that contains the original program. As long as you have the original media in a safe place, you shouldn't need to back up these files. However, if you have downloaded a program file from the Internet, you should copy the program onto a CD as a backup.

- **Data files** are files you create (such as spreadsheets, Word files, and so on), as well as contact lists, address books, e-mail archives, and your Favorites list from your browser.

SOUND BYTE
Securing Wireless Networks

In this Sound Byte, you'll learn what "war drivers" are and why they could potentially be a threat to your wireless network. You'll also learn simple steps to take to secure your wireless network against intruders.

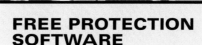

FREE PROTECTION SOFTWARE

If you want to protect your computer but don't want to buy software, you're not out of luck. You can download plenty of programs for free off the Internet. Many companies offer free versions of their software that either expire after a certain time or offer fewer features than commercial versions. In many cases, these free versions are sufficient for home use. One site for downloading free software is **www.download.com**. This should be your first stop when looking for free software you can use to protect your computer.

You should back up your data files frequently, depending on how much work you can afford to lose. You should always back up data files when you make changes to them, especially if those changes involve hours of work. It may not seem important to back up your history term paper file when you finish it, but do you really want to do all that work again if your computer crashes before you have a chance to turn in your paper?

PROTECTION FROM PHISHING SITES

As you learned in Chapter 3, phishing attacks are attempts to lure you to Web sites that look legitimate (such as banking sites) and then trick you into revealing information that can be used in identity thefts. But free tools such as the Cloudmark SafetyBar for Internet Explorer (**www.cloudmark.com**), shown in Figure 15, can help you identify suspicious sites. Once installed, the SafetyBar provides you with the site's safety rating based on reports from other Cloudmark users. You can also rate sites and help warn others of problems.

Another way to protect yourself is to never use your credit card number when you shop online. Although it sounds impossible, credit card providers such as Citibank are offering services like "Virtual Account Numbers" for their customers. Before purchasing a product online, you visit an online site, where you are assigned a new virtual account number each time you visit. This number is tied to your real credit card account but can only be used once. That means that if the number is stolen, it's no good to thieves because they can't use the virtual account number because you've already used it once.

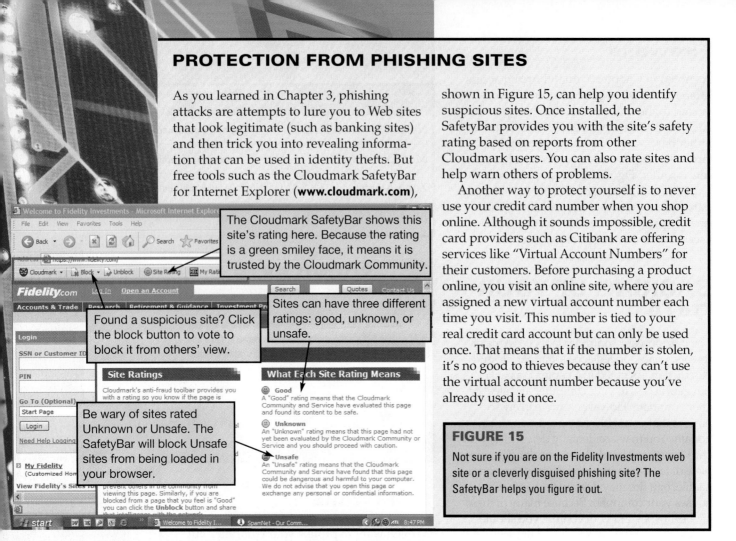

The Cloudmark SafetyBar shows this site's rating here. Because the rating is a green smiley face, it means it is trusted by the Cloudmark Community.

Found a suspicious site? Click the block button to vote to block it from others' view.

Sites can have three different ratings: good, unknown, or unsafe.

Be wary of sites rated Unknown or Unsafe. The SafetyBar will block Unsafe sites from being loaded in your browser.

FIGURE 15

Not sure if you are on the Fidelity Investments web site or a cleverly disguised phishing site? The SafetyBar helps you figure it out.

SHOULD YOU BACK UP YOUR FILES STORED ON THE SCHOOL NETWORK?

Most likely, if you're allowed to store files on your school's network, these files are backed up on a regular basis. However, you should check with your school's network administrators to determine how often they're backed up and how you would go about requesting files be restored from the backup media if they're damaged or deleted. But don't rely on these network backups to bail you out if your data files are lost or damaged. It may take days for the network administrators to get around to restoring your files. It is better to keep backups of your data files yourself (especially for homework and project files) so that you can immediately restore them.

To make backups easier, store all your data files in one folder on your hard drive. For example, you can create a folder on your hard drive called Data Files. You can then create subfolders (such as History Homework, Music Files, and so on) within the Data Files folder. If you store all your data files in one place, to back up your files, you simply copy the Data Files folder and all of its subfolders onto an alternate storage media. If you have a DVD/CD-RW drive in your computer, open Windows Explorer (as shown in Figure 16) and right-click the Data Files folder. You can then copy the contents of the folder to the appropriate media.

Backup Software

Many people forget to make backups and only learn when it's too late that they should have been performing a systematic backup routine. The good news is that **backup software**, such as Norton Ghost or BackUp MyPC (see Figure 17), allows you to schedule regular backups that occur automatically, with no intervention on your part. These products can back up individual files, folders, or an entire hard drive to another hard drive, such as an external drive connected to your computer by a USB port, or to a CD/DVD in the CD/DVD drive.

Backing up your entire hard drive greatly speeds up the recovery process should you experience a hard drive failure. With a backup of your entire hard drive, you won't need to reinstall all of the program software from the original CDs. Instead, you just replace the broken hard drive with the backup hard drive (or copy the contents of the backup drive to a new drive).

Online Backups

A final backup solution is to store backups of your files online. For a fee, companies such as NetMass (**www.systemrestore.com**) can provide you with such online storage. If you store a backup of your entire system on the Internet, you don't need to buy an additional hard drive for backups. This method also takes the worry out of keeping your backups in a safe place because they're always stored in an area far away from your computer (such as on the NetMass server). However, if you'd like to store your backups online, make sure you have high-speed Internet access such as cable or DSL; otherwise, your computer could be tied up as you transfer files.

ADDITIONAL RESOURCES

Hackers, spammers, and advertisers are constantly developing new methods for circumventing the protection that security software provides. Although the manufacturers of such software are constantly updating and improving security, you should keep abreast of new techniques being employed that could threaten your privacy and security. *SC Magazine* is a security magazine available in a free online version at **www.scmagazine.com**. Take a few minutes each month and scan the articles to make sure you have taken the appropriate protective measures on your computer to keep it safe and secure.

SOUND BYTE
Protecting Your Computer

In this Sound Byte, you'll learn how to use a variety of tools to protect your computer, including antivirus software and Windows utilities.

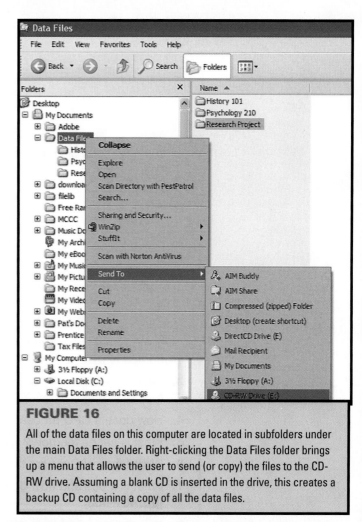

FIGURE 16

All of the data files on this computer are located in subfolders under the main Data Files folder. Right-clicking the Data Files folder brings up a menu that allows the user to send (or copy) the files to the CD-RW drive. Assuming a blank CD is inserted in the drive, this creates a backup CD containing a copy of all the data files.

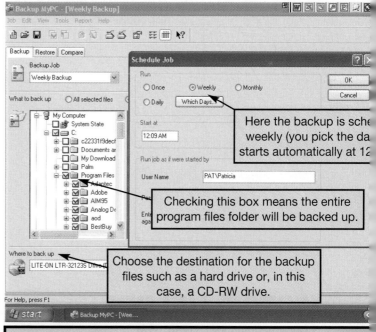

Here the backup is sche weekly (you pick the da starts automatically at 12

Checking this box means the entire program files folder will be backed up.

Choose the destination for the backup files such as a hard drive or, in this case, a CD-RW drive.

FIGURE 17

The software program BackUp MyPC from StompSoft Inc. features an easy-to interface for setting up automatic backups of individual folders or a complete drive. It is offered free for a limited 30-day trial and can be registered for a fee

Behind the Scenes:

A Closer Look at System Hardware

Objectives

After reading this chapter, you should be able to answer the following questions:

1. What is a switch and how does it work in a computer? **(pp. 388–389)**

2. What is the binary number system and what role does it play in a computer system? **(pp. 389–393)**

3. What is inside the CPU and how do these components operate? **(pp. 393–398)**

4. How does a CPU process data and instructions? **(pp. 395–398)**

5. What is cache memory? **(pp. 396–397)**

6. What types of RAM are there? **(pp. 399–401)**

7. What is a bus and how does it function in a computer system? **(pp. 401–403)**

8. How do manufacturers make CPUs so that they run faster? **(pp. 403–406)**

ACTIVE HELPDESK

- Understanding the CPU **(p. 398)**
- Understanding Types of RAM **(p. 402)**

Taking a Closer Look

Although twins, Jim and Joe are completely different in certain ways. Joe checks the oil in his car regularly, knows the air pressure in his tires, and can tell when the fan belt should be replaced. Jim, on the other hand, asks, "Oil level? What oil?" and drives from place to place relying on service departments to keep his car running. Although Jim's lack of maintenance hasn't resulted in any catastrophic problems, Joe warns his brother that by not learning a few things about cars, he'll end up paying more to keep up his car, if it even lasts that long.

Similarly, after taking a class in college, Joe has a strong but basic understanding of his computer and keeps his PC running well through periodic maintenance and upgrades. Not surprisingly, Jim is hands-off when it comes to his computer. He's happy to just turn it on and open the files he needs. He can't be bothered with all the acronyms: CPU, RAM, and all the rest. When there's a problem, Jim just calls his brother. He hates waiting and paying for technical service and is afraid he'll mess up his system if he tries to fix things himself. But after making another 2:00 A.M. call to Joe after his computer crashed, Joe told him, "Take a class or pay a technician!"

When it comes to your computer, are you most like Jim or Joe? Joe found out how easy it is to understand his computer and isn't dependent on anyone else to keep it running. But if you use a computer without understanding the hardware inside, you'll have to pay a technician to fix or upgrade it. Meanwhile, it won't be as efficient as if you were fine-tuning it yourself, and you may find yourself buying a new computer earlier than necessary.

There are other advantages to having a deeper understanding of computer hardware. If you're preparing for a career in programming, for example, understanding computer hardware will affect the speed and efficiency of the programs you design. In addition, if you're interested in computers, you're no doubt excited by advances you hear about. How do you evaluate the impact of a new type of memory or a new processor? A basic appreciation of how a computer system is built and designed is a good start.

In this chapter, we'll build on what you've learned about computer hardware in other chapters and go behind the scenes, looking at your system unit's components in more detail. First we examine how computers translate the commands you input into the digits they can understand: 1s and 0s. Next, we analyze the internal workings of the central processing unit (CPU) and memory. We then look at buses, the highways that transport data between the CPU, memory, and other devices connected to the computer. But first, let's look at the building blocks of computers: switches.

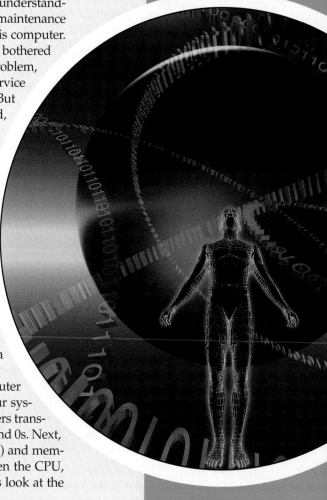

SOUND BYTES

- Binary Numbers Interactive **(p. 390)**
- Where Does Binary Show Up? **(p. 390)**
- Memory Hierarchy Interactive **(p. 400)**
- Computer Architecture **(p. 403)**

Digital Data: Switches and Bits

In earlier chapters, you learned that the **system unit** is the box that contains the central electronic components of the computer, including the central processing unit (CPU), memory, motherboard, and many other circuit boards that help the computer to function. But how exactly does the computer perform all of its tasks? How does it process the data you input? In this section, we discuss how the CPU performs its functions—adding, subtracting, moving data around the system, and so on—using nothing but a large number of on/off switches. In fact, as you'll learn, a computer system can be viewed as just an enormous collection of on/off switches.

ELECTRONIC SWITCHES

What are switches and what do they do? You learned earlier that, unlike humans, computers work exclusively with numbers (not words). To process data into information, computers need to work in a language they understand. This language, called **binary language**, consists of just two numbers: 0 and 1. Everything a computer does (such as process data or print a report) is broken down into a series of 0s and 1s.

Why do computers use 0s and 1s to process data? Because modern computers are electronic, digital machines, they understand only two states of existence: on and off. Computers represent these two possibilities, or states, using the numbers (or digits) 1 and 0. **Electronic switches**, are devices inside the computer that can be flipped between these two states: 1 or 0, on or off.

Although the notion of switches may seem complex, you use various forms of switches every day. For example, a button is a mechanical switch: pushed in, it could represent the value 1, whereas popped out, it could represent the value 0. Another switch you use each day is a water faucet. As shown in Figure 9.1, shutting it off so no water flows could represent the value 0, whereas turning it on could represent the value 1.

Because computers are built from a huge collection of switches, using buttons or water faucets obviously would limit the amount of data computers could store. It would also make computers very large and cause them to run at very slow speeds. Thus, the history of comput-

FIGURE 9.1

Water faucets can be used to represent binary switches. Turning the faucet on could represent the value 1, whereas shutting the faucet off so no water flows could represent the value 0.

ers is really a story about creating smaller and faster sets of electronic switches so that more data can be stored and manipulated quickly.

What were the first switches used in computers? The earliest generation of electronic computers used devices called **vacuum tubes** as switches, as shown in Figure 9.2a. Vacuum tubes act as computer switches by allowing or blocking the flow of electrical current. The problem with vacuum tubes is that they take up a lot of space. The first high-speed digital computer, the Electronic Numerical Integrator and Computer (ENIAC), was deployed in 1945 and used nearly 18,000 vacuum tubes as switches, which filled approximately 1,800 square feet of floor space. In addition to being very large, vacuum tubes produce a lot of heat. Thus, although they are still used as switches in some high-end audio equipment, vacuum tubes make for impractical switching devices in personal computers.

What do personal computers use as switching devices? Since the vacuum tubes of the ENIAC, two major revolutions have occurred in the design of switches, and consequently computers, to make them smaller and faster: the invention of the *transistor* and the fabrication of *integrated circuits*.

What are transistors? Transistors are electrical switches that are built out of layers of a special type of material called a **semiconductor**. A semiconductor is any material that can be controlled to either conduct electricity or act as an insulator (to not allow electricity to pass through). Silicon, which is found in common sand, is the semiconductor material used to make transistors.

By itself, silicon does not conduct electricity particularly well, but if specific chemicals are added in a controlled way to the silicon, it begins to behave like a switch. It allows electrical current to flow easily when a certain voltage is applied, and it prevents electrical current from flowing otherwise, thus behaving as an on/off switch. This kind of behavior is exactly what is needed to store digital information, the 1s and 0s in binary language.

Early transistors were built in separate units as small metal cans, each can acting as a single on/off switch, as shown in Figure 9.2b. These first transistors were much smaller than vacuum tubes, produced very little heat, and could be switched from on to off (allowing or blocking electrical current) very quickly. They also were less expensive than vacuum tubes.

However, it wasn't long before transistors reached their limits. Continuing advances in technology began to require more transistors than circuit boards at the time could reasonably handle. Something was needed to pack more transistor capacity into a smaller space. Thus, integrated circuits, the next technical revolution in switches, developed.

What are integrated circuits? **Integrated circuits** (or chips) are very small regions of semiconductor material, such as silicon, that support a huge number of transistors, as shown in Figure 9.2c. Along with all the many transistors, other components critical to a circuit board (such as resistors, capacitors, and diodes) are also located on the integrated circuit. Most integrated circuits are no more than a quarter inch in size.

Why are integrated circuits important? Because so many transistors can fit into such a small area, integrated circuits have enabled computer designers to create small yet powerful **microprocessors**, which are chips that contain a CPU. In 1971, the Intel 4004 was the first complete microprocessor to be located on a single integrated circuit chip, marking the beginning of true miniaturization of computers. The Intel 4004 contained slightly more than 2,300 transistors. Today more than 500 *million* transistors can be manufactured in a space as tiny as the nail of your pinky finger!

This incredible feat has fueled an industry like none other. In 1951, the Univac I computer was 10 feet high by 10 feet wide by 10 feet long (or 1,000 cubic feet) and cost $1 million. Thanks to advances in integrated circuits, the IBM PC released just 30 years later took up just 1 cubic foot of space, cost $3,000, and performed 155,000 times more quickly. (For more information about computer history, see the Technology in Focus feature "The History of the PC" on page 76.)

But how can computers store information in a set of on/off switches? So computers use on/off switches to perform their functions. But how can these simple switches be organized so that they enable us to use a computer to pay our bills online or write an essay? How could a set of switches describe a number or a word or give a computer the command to perform addition? Recall that to manipulate the on/off switches, the computer works in binary language, which uses only two digits, 0 and 1. Therefore, to understand how a computer works, we must first look at how the computer uses a special numbering system called the *binary number system* to represent all of its programs and data.

FIGURE 9.2

Electronic switches have become smaller and faster over time, from (a) vacuum tubes to (b) discrete single transistors to (c) integrated circuits that can hold more than 500 million transistors.

THE BINARY NUMBER SYSTEM

What is a number system? A **number system** is an organized plan for representing a number. Although you may not realize it, you are already familiar with one number system. The **base 10 number system**, also known as **decimal notation**, is the system you use to represent all of the numeric values you use each day. It's called "base 10" because it uses 10 digits, 0 through 9, to represent any value.

To represent a number in base 10, you break the number down into groups of ones, tens, hundreds, thousands, and so on. Each digit has a place value depending on where it shows up in the number. For example, using base 10, in the whole number 6,954, there are 6 sets of thousands, 9 sets of hundreds, 5 sets of tens, and 4 sets of ones. Working from right to left, each place in a number represents an increasing power of 10, as shown here:

$$6,954 = 6 * (1,000) + 9 * (100) + 5 * (10) + 4 * (1)$$
$$= 6 * 10^3 + 9 * 10^2 + 5 * 10^1 + 4 * 10^0$$

Note that in this equation, the final number 1 is represented as 10^0 because any number raised to the zero power is equal to 1.

Anthropologists theorize that humans developed a base 10 number system because we have 10 fingers. But computer systems, with their huge collections of on/off switches, are not well suited to thinking about numbers in groups of 10. Instead, computers describe a number as powers of 2 because each switch can be in one of two positions: on or off. This numbering system is referred to as the **binary number system**. It is the number system used by computers to represent all data.

How does the binary number system work? Because it only includes two digits (0 and 1), the binary number system is also referred to as the **base 2 number system**. However, even with just two digits, the binary number system can still represent all the same values that a base 10 number system can. Instead of breaking the number down into sets of ones, tens, hundreds, and thousands, as is done in base 10 notation, the binary number system describes a number as the sum of powers of 2. Binary numbers are used to represent *every* piece of data stored in a computer: all of the numbers, all of the letters, and all of the instructions that the computer uses to execute work.

Representing Numbers in the Binary Number System

How does the binary number system represent a whole number? As noted earlier, in the base 10 number system, a whole number is represented as the sum of ones, tens, hundreds, thousands—sums of powers of 10. The binary system works in the same way but describes a value as the sum of groups of 64s, 32s, 16s, 8s, 4s, 2s, and 1s, that is powers of 2: 1, 2, 4, 8, 16, 32, 64, and so on. Let's look at the number 67. In base 10, the number 67 would be 6 sets of tens and 7 sets of ones, as follows:

$$\text{Base 10: } 67 = 6 * 10^1 + 7 * 10^0$$

One way to figure out how 67 is represented in base 2 is to find the largest possible power of 2 that could be in the number 67. Two to the eighth is 256 and there are no groups of 256 in the number 67. Two to the seventh power is 128, but that is bigger than 67. Two to the sixth power is 64 and there is a group of 64 inside a group of 67. So,

67 has	1 group of	**64**	That leaves 3 and
3 has	0 groups of	**32**	
	0 groups of	**16**	
	0 groups of	**8**	
	0 groups of	**4**	
	1 group of	**2**	That leaves 1 and
1 has	1 group of	**1**	And now nothing is left

Therefore, the binary number for 67 is written as 1000011 in base 2:

You can also convert base 10 numbers to binary manually by repeatedly dividing the number by 2 and examining the remainder at each stage. An example will make this clearer. Let's convert the base 10 number 67 into binary:

$$
\begin{aligned}
\mathbf{67} \div 2 &= 33 \text{ remainder } \mathbf{1} \\
33 \div 2 &= 16 \text{ remainder } \mathbf{1} \\
16 \div 2 &= 8 \text{ remainder } \mathbf{0} \\
8 \div 2 &= 4 \text{ remainder } \mathbf{0} \\
4 \div 2 &= 2 \text{ remainder } \mathbf{0} \\
2 \div 2 &= 1 \text{ remainder } \mathbf{0} \\
1 \div 2 &= 0 \text{ remainder } \mathbf{1} \\
&1\ 0\ 0\ 0\ 0\ 1\ 1
\end{aligned}
$$

The binary number is then read from the bottom up. Therefore, 1000011 is the binary (base 2) equivalent of the base 10 number 67.

Is there a faster way to convert between base 10 and binary? Programmers and engineers who work with binary codes daily learn to convert between decimal and binary mentally. However, if you use binary notation less often, it is easier to use a calculator. Some calculators identify this operation with a button labeled DEC (for decimal) and one labeled BIN (for binary). In Windows, you can access a scientific calculator that supports base conversion between decimal (base 10) and binary (base 2) by choosing Start, Programs, Accessories, then choosing Calculator, then clicking the View menu to select the Scientific Calculator.

SOUND BYTE
Binary Numbers Interactive

This Sound Byte helps remove the mystery surrounding binary numbers. You'll learn about base conversion between decimal, binary, and hexadecimal interactively using colors, sounds, and images.

SOUND BYTE
Where Does Binary Show Up?

In this Sound Byte, you'll learn how to use tools that come with the Windows operating system to work with binary, decimal, and hexadecimal numbers. You'll also learn where you might see binary and hexadecimal values showing up as you use a computer.

$$
\begin{aligned}
\text{Base 2: } 67 &= 64 + 0 + 0 + 0 + 0 + 2 + 1 \\
&= (1 * 2^6) + (0 * 2^5) + (0 * 2^4) + (0 * 2^3) + (0 * 2^2) + (1 * 2^1) + (1 * 2^0) \\
&= (1000011) \text{ base 2}
\end{aligned}
$$

Advanced Binary and Hexadecimal Notations

You understand how the binary number system represents a positive number, but how can it represent a negative number? In the decimal (base 10) system, a negative value is represented with a special symbol, the minus sign (–). In the binary (base 2) system, one way to represent a negative value is to place an extra bit (or digit) in front of the binary number. This extra bit is referred to as a *sign bit*. The sign bit is set to 1 if the binary number has a negative value and is set to 0 if the binary number has a positive value. Therefore, using a sign bit, the base 10 number +13 is written as 01101 in binary, whereas the number –13 is written as 11101 in binary. This is referred to as *signed integer notation* and is one way to represent negative numbers in binary.

But how does the computer know that what it is looking at is a negative number and not just a longer binary number? The binary pattern 11101 can represent more than one number. If we know it is a binary number using a sign bit, we read the first bit (the sign bit) as 1 and therefore know that the number is a negative number. Following the sign bit are the digits that represent the value of the number itself. Because 1101 in binary (base 2) has the value 13 in base 10, the final interpretation of the bits 11101 would be –13.

But what if we were told in advance that 11101 is definitely a positive number? We would then read this number differently and compute $1 * 16 + 1 * 8 + 1 * 4 + 0 * 2 + 1 * 1$ and get the base 10 value of 29. The bits themselves are exactly the same. The only thing that has changed is our agreement on what the same five digits mean: the first time they represented a negative number, and the second time they represented a positive number.

The binary number system also can represent a decimal number. How can a string of 1s and 0s capture the information in a value like 99.368? Because every computer must store such numbers in the same way, the Institute of Electrical and Electronics Engineers (IEEE) has established a standard called the *floating-point standard* that describes how numbers with fractional parts should be represented in the binary number system.

Using a 32-bit system, an incredibly wide range of numbers can be represented. The method dictated by the standard works the same for any number with a decimal point, such as the number –0.75. The first digit, or bit (the sign bit), is used to indicate whether the number is positive or negative. The next eight bits store the *magnitude* of the number, indicating whether the number is in the hundreds or millions, for example. The standard says to use the next 23 bits to store the *value* of the number.

As you can imagine, some numbers in binary result in quite a long string of 0s and 1s. For example, the number 123,456 is a 17-digit sequence of 1s and 0s in binary code, 11110001001000000. When working with these long strings of 0s and 1s it is easy for a human to make a mistake. Thus, many computer scientists use **hexadecimal notation**, another commonly used number system, as a form of shorthand.

Hexadecimal notation is a base 16 number system, meaning it uses 16 digits to represent numbers instead of the 10 digits used in base 10 or the 2 digits used in base 2. The 16 digits it uses are the 10 numeric digits, 0 to 9, plus six extra symbols: A, B, C, D, E, F, with each of the letters, A through F, corresponding to a numeric value. So, A equals 10, B equals 11, and so on. Looking back at the number we started with: 123,456 is represented as 1E240 in hexadecimal notation. This is much easier for computer scientists to use than the long string of binary code. The scientific calculator in Windows XP (mentioned earlier) also can perform conversions to hexadecimal notation. (You can watch a video showing you how to perform conversions between bases using the Windows XP calculator in the Sound Byte "Where Does Binary Show Up?")

When will you ever use hexadecimal notation? Unless you write your own Web pages (where hexadecimal notation is used to represent colors), your only likely encounter with hexadecimal notation will be when you see an error code on your computer. Generally, the location of the error will be represented in hexadecimal notation.

Representing Letters and Symbols: ASCII and Unicode

How can the binary number system represent letters and punctuation symbols? We have just been converting numbers from base 10, which we understand, to base 2, or binary state that the computer understands. Similarly, we need a system that converts letters and other symbols that we understand to a binary state that the computer understands. To provide a consistent means for representing letters and other characters, there are codes that dictate how to represent characters in binary format. Older mainframe computers use Extended

Do I Ever See Binary Numbers on My Computer?

Internally, the computer "thinks" in binary numbers and stores all of your data and all the commands it is given in binary code. However, because computers interface with human users, who don't think in terms of binary code, messages and user interfaces are always presented in a style that is more comfortable to us. The only time most computer users ever encounter binary or hexadecimal code is when certain error messages appear, describing what the internal machine settings look like when an error occurred. Although confusing to most users, these strings of code can be useful to service technicians working to understand and correct computer problems. If you ever encounter such an error code, write down the complete error message so that you can better work with technicians to solve your problem.

Binary-Coded Decimal Interchange Code (EBCDIC, pronounced "Eb sih dik"). However, most of today's personal computers use the American National Standards Institute (ANSI) standard code, called the **American Standard Code for Information Interchange (ASCII code)**, to represent each letter or character as an 8-bit (or 1-byte) binary code.

As you know by now, binary digits correspond to the on and off states of your computer's switches. Each of these digits is called a **binary digit**, or **bit** for short. Eight binary digits (or bits) combine to create one **byte**. In the previous discussions, we have been converting base 10 numbers to a binary format. In such cases, the binary format has no standard length. For example, the binary format for the number 2 is two digits (10), whereas the binary format for the number 10 is four digits (1010). Although binary numbers can have more or less than 8 bits, each single alphabetic or special character is 1 byte (or 8 bits) of data and consists of a unique combination of a total of eight 0s and 1s. Eight bits is the standard length on which computers are built.

The ASCII code represents the 26 uppercase letters and 26 lowercase letters used in the English language, along with a number of punctuation symbols and other special characters, using 8 bits. Figure 9.3 shows a number of examples of ASCII code representation of letters and characters.

Can ASCII represent the alphabets of different languages? Because it represents letters and characters using only 8 bits, the ASCII code can assign only 256 (or 2^8) different codes for unique characters and letters. Although this is enough to represent English and many other characters found in the world's languages, ASCII code cannot represent *all* languages and symbols. Thus, a new encoding scheme, called **Unicode**, was created. By using 16 bits instead of the 8 bits used in ASCII, Unicode can represent more than 65,000 unique character symbols, enabling it to represent the alphabets of all modern languages and all historic languages and notational systems, including such languages as Tibetan, Tagalog, Japanese, and Canadian-Aboriginal syllabics. As we continue to become a more global society, it is anticipated that Unicode will replace ASCII as the standard character formatting code.

So *all* data inside the computer is stored as bits? Yes! As noted in the Dig Deeper feature, positive and negative numbers can be stored using signed integer notation, with the first bit (the *sign bit*) indicating the sign and the rest of the bits indicating the value of the number. Decimal numbers are stored according to the IEEE floating-point standard, whereas letters and symbols are stored according to the ASCII code or Unicode. All of these different number systems and codes exist so that computers can store different types of information in their on/off switches. No matter what kind of data you input in a computer—a color, a musical note, or a street address—that information will be stored as a string of

FIGURE 9.3 ASCII Standard Code for a Sample of Letters and Characters

ASCII Code	Represents This Symbol	ASCII Code	Represents This Symbol
01000001	A	01100001	a
01000010	B	01100010	b
01000011	C	01100011	c
01011010	Z	00100011	#
00100001	!	00100100	$
00100010	"	00100101	%

Note: For the full ASCII table see **http://www.lookuptables.com**

1s and 0s. The important lesson is that the *interpretation* of 1s and 0s is what matters. The same binary pattern could represent a positive number, a negative number, a fraction, or a letter.

How does the computer know which interpretation to use for the 1s and 0s? When your brain processes language, it takes sounds you hear and uses the rules of English along with other clues to build an interpretation of the sound as a word. If you are in New York City and hear someone shout, "Hey, Lori!" you expect someone is saying hello to a friend. If you are in London and hear the same sound— "Hey! Lorry!"—you jump out of the way because a truck is coming at you! You knew which interpretation to apply to the same sound because you had some other information—that you were in England.

Likewise, the CPU is designed to understand a specific language, a set of instructions. But certain instructions tell the CPU to expect a negative number next or to interpret the following bit pattern as a character. Because of this extra information, the CPU always knows which interpretation to use for a series of bits.

The CPU: Processing Digital Information

The **central processing unit** (**CPU** or **processor**), the "brains" of the computer, executes every instruction given to your computer. As you learned earlier, the entire CPU fits on a tiny chip, called the microprocessor, which contains all of the hardware responsible for processing information, including millions of transistors (the switches we discussed earlier).

The CPU is located in the system unit on the computer's **motherboard**, the main circuit board that connects all of the electronic components of the system: the CPU, memory, the expansion slots where you can insert expansion (or adapter) cards, and all of the electrical paths that connect these components together. Figure 9.4 shows a typical motherboard and the location of each of these components.

Looking at a CPU chip gives you very little information about how exactly it accomplishes its work. However, understanding more about how the CPU is designed and how it operates will give you greater insight

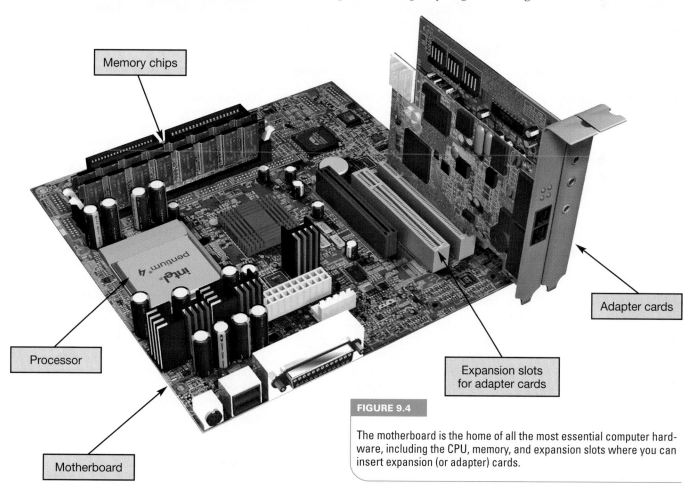

Memory chips

Processor

Motherboard

Adapter cards

Expansion slots for adapter cards

FIGURE 9.4

The motherboard is the home of all the most essential computer hardware, including the CPU, memory, and expansion slots where you can insert expansion (or adapter) cards.

FIGURE 9.5

(a) The Pentium 4 chip is used in many Windows-based PCs. (b) The Microsoft Xbox360 gaming console uses a custom PowerPC–based CPU to perform *1,000 billion* calculations per second.

into how computers work, what their limitations are, and what technological advances may be possible in the future.

What CPUs are used in desktop computers? Only a few major companies manufacture CPUs for desktop computers. Intel manufactures the Xeon, Celeron, and Pentium processors (including the Pentium II, III, and 4), shown in Figure 9.5a. Advanced Micro Devices (AMD) produces the AMD-K6, the Athlon XP, and the Athlon 64 FX processors. Both Intel and AMD chips are used in the majority of Windows-based PCs.

Apple computer systems (such as the iMac and the PowerBook series of laptops) have

used a different CPU design. The G4 and PowerPC G5 chip were used by Apple machines for over ten years. In 2005, Apple shook up the CPU playing field when it announced all of their systems would be redesigned to use Intel CPUs. However, versions of the PowerPC chip (shown in Figure 9.5b) will live on in several different video gaming system consoles such as the Nintendo GameCube and the Xbox 360.

As you learned in earlier chapters, the processor used on a computer also determines the operating system used. The combination of operating system and processor is referred to as a computer's *platform*.

What makes CPUs different from each other? The primary distinction between CPUs is processing power, which is determined by the number of transistors on each CPU. In addition, as you'll learn in the next section, other factors differentiate CPUs, but the greatest differentiators are how quickly the processor can work (called its *clock speed*) and the amount of immediate access memory the CPU has (called its *cache memory*). Figure 9.6

FIGURE 9.6 Processors on the Market Today

Processor	Manufacturer	Number of Transistors	Typical Clock Speed	Levels of Cache Storage	Notes
Athlon XP	AMD	54.3 million	2.2 GHz	2	AMD processor that competes against the Intel Pentium 4.
Athlon 64 FX	AMD	106 million	2.6 GHz	2	64-bit processor for heavy computation and demanding video gaming needs.
Centrino	Intel	77 million	2.1 GHz	2	Designed specifically for mobile computers; has built-in wireless local network capabilities.
Itanium 2	Intel	410 million	1.6 GHz	3	Seen in high-end server computers.
Pentium 4 Extreme Edition	Intel	169 million	3.7 GHz	3	The latest version of the Pentium chip. It uses dual cores and hyperthreading to process four tasks at once.
Pentium 4 Processor-M	Intel	55 million	2.6 GHz	2	The M is for mobile. This chip uses less power so it can run longer on a battery charge.
PowerPC G4	Motorola	57 million	1.3 GHz	3	The only processor that, until 2006, powered the Apple line of computers (iMacs, PowerBooks, and so on).
PowerPC G5	IBM	58 million	2.5 GHz	2	Powerful 64-bit processor for heavy computational needs.

shows the basic specifications of several of the major processors on the market today.

THE CPU MACHINE CYCLE

What exactly does the CPU do? Any program you run on your computer is actually a long series of binary code, 1s and 0s, describing a specific set of commands the CPU must perform. Each CPU is a bit different in the exact steps it follows to perform its tasks, but all CPUs must perform a series of similar general steps. These steps, referred to as a CPU **machine cycle** (or **processing cycle**), are shown in Figure 9.7 and are described here:

- **Fetch:** When any program begins to run, the 1s and 0s that make up the program's binary code must be "fetched" from their temporary storage location in random access memory (RAM) and moved to the CPU before they can be executed.

- **Decode:** Once the program's binary code is in the CPU, it is decoded into the commands the CPU understands.

- **Execute:** Next, the CPU actually performs the work described in the command. Specialized hardware on the CPU performs addition, subtraction, multiplication, division, and other mathematical and logical operations at incredible speeds.

- **Store:** The result is stored in **registers**, special memory storage areas built into the CPU, which are the most expensive, fastest memory in your computer. The CPU is then ready to fetch the next set of bits encoding the next instruction.

No matter what program you are running, be it an Internet browser or a word processing program, and no matter how many programs you are using at one time, the CPU performs these four steps over and over at incredibly high speeds. Shortly, we'll look at each stage in more detail so you can understand the complexity of the CPU's design, how to compare different CPUs on the market, and what enhancements to expect in CPU designs of the future. But first, let's examine a few other components of the CPU that help it perform its tasks.

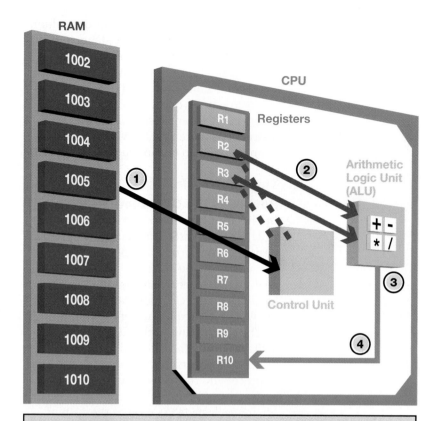

Step 1: FETCH: When a program begins to run, the program's binary code must be "fetched" from RAM and moved to the CPU's control unit before it can be executed.

Step 2: DECODE: Once the program's binary code is in the CPU, it is "decoded" into the commands the CPU understands. The control unit then tells the registers which data to feed to the arithmetic logic unit (ALU), the part of the CPU designed to perform mathematical operations.

Step 3: EXECUTE: The ALU performs the work described in the command.

Step 4: STORE: The result is stored in the registers. The CPU is then ready to fetch the next set of bits encoding the next instruction.

The System Clock

How does the CPU know when to begin the next stage in the machine cycle? To move from one stage of the machine cycle to the next, the motherboard contains a built-in **system clock**. This internal clock is actually a special crystal that shouts out "Next! . . . Next! . . . Next! . . ." over and over, thereby controlling when the CPU moves to the next stage of processing.

These "ticks" of the system clock, known as the **clock cycle**, set the pace by which the computer moves from process to process. The pace, known as **clock speed**, is measured in hertz (Hz), a unit of measure that describes how many times something happens per second. Today's system clocks are

FIGURE 9.7

The CPU Machine Cycle

measured in gigahertz (GHz), or one billion clock ticks per second. Therefore, in a 3-GHz system, there are three billion clock ticks each second. Computers with older processors would sometimes need one or more cycles to process one instruction. Today, however, CPUs are designed to handle more instructions more efficiently, therefore executing more than one instruction per cycle.

The Control Unit

How does the CPU know which stage in the machine cycle is next? The CPU, like any part of the computer system, is designed from a collection of switches. How can simple on/off switches "remember" the fetch-decode-execute-store sequence of the CPU machine cycle? How can they perform the work required in each of these stages?

The **control unit** of the CPU manages the switches inside the CPU. It is programmed by CPU designers to remember the sequence of processing stages for that CPU and how each switch in the CPU should be set, on or off, for each stage. As soon as the system clock shouts "Next!" the control unit moves each switch to its correct setting (on or off) and then performs the work of that stage.

Let's now look at each of the stages in the machine cycle in a bit more depth.

STAGE 1: THE FETCH STAGE

Where does the CPU find the necessary information? The data and program instructions the CPU needs are stored in different areas in the computer system. Data and program instructions move between these areas as needed or not needed by the CPU for processing. Programs (such as Microsoft Word) are permanently stored on the hard disk because the hard disk offers nonvolatile storage, meaning the programs remain stored there even when you turn the power off. However, when you launch a program (that is, when you double-click an icon to execute the program), the program, or sometimes only the essential parts of a program, is transferred from the hard disk into RAM.

The program moves to RAM because the CPU can access the data and program instructions stored in RAM more than one million times faster than if they are left on the hard drive. This is because RAM is much closer to the CPU than is the hard drive. As specific

instructions from the program are needed, they are moved from RAM into *registers* (the special storage areas located on the CPU itself), where they wait to be executed.

Why doesn't the CPU chip just contain enough memory to store an entire program? The CPU's storage area is not big enough to hold everything it needs to process at the same time. If enough memory were located on the CPU chip itself, an entire program could be copied to the CPU from RAM before it was executed. This certainly would add to the computer's speed and efficiency because there would not be any delay to stop and fetch instructions from RAM to the CPU. However, including so much memory on a CPU chip would make these chips very expensive. CPU design is so complex that there is only a limited amount of storage space available on the CPU itself.

Cache Memory

So, the CPU needs to fetch every instruction from RAM each time it goes through a cycle? Actually, there is another layer of storage that has even faster access than RAM, called **cache memory**. The word *cache* (pronounced "cash") is derived from the French word *cacher*, meaning "to hide." Cache memory consists of small blocks of memory located directly on and next to the CPU chip. These memory blocks are holding places for recently or frequently used instructions or data that the CPU needs the most. When these instructions or data are stored in cache memory, the CPU can more quickly retrieve them than if it had to access the instructions or data in RAM.

Taking data you think you'll be using soon and storing it nearby is a simple idea but a powerful one. This is a strategy that shows up other places in your computer system. For example, when you are browsing Web pages, images take a long time to download. Your browser software automatically stores images on your hard drive so that you don't have to wait to download them again if you want to go back and view a page you've already visited. Although this cache of files is not related to the cache storage space designed into the CPU chip, the idea is the same.

How does cache memory work? Modern CPU designs include a number of types of cache memory. If the next instruction to be fetched is not already located in a

CPU register, instead of looking directly to RAM to find it, the CPU first searches Level 1 cache. *Level 1 cache* is a block of memory that is built onto the CPU chip for the storage of data or commands that have just been used.

If the command is not located in Level 1 cache, the CPU searches Level 2 cache. Depending on the design of the CPU, *Level 2 cache* is located on the CPU chip but is slightly farther away from the CPU, or it's on a separate chip next to the CPU and therefore takes somewhat longer to access. Level 2 cache contains more storage area than does Level 1 cache. For the Intel Pentium 4 Extreme Edition, for example, the Level 1 cache is 28 kilobytes (KB) and the Level 2 cache is 1 megabyte (MB).

Only if the CPU doesn't find the next instruction to be fetched in either Level 1 or Level 2 cache will it make the long journey to RAM to access it, as shown in Figure 9.8.

Are there any other types of cache memory? The current direction of design in processors is toward larger and larger multilevel CPU cache structures. Therefore, some newer CPUs have an additional third level of cache memory storage, called *Level 3 cache*. On computers with Level 3 cache, the CPU checks this area for instructions and data after it looks in Level 1 and Level 2 cache, but before it makes the longer trip to RAM. The Level 3 cache holds between 2 megabytes (MB) and 4 MB of data. With 4 MB of Level 3 cache, there is almost enough storage for an entire program to be transferred to the CPU for its execution.

How do I use cache memory? As an end user of computer programs, you do nothing special to use cache memory. In fact, you will not even be able to notice that caching is being used—nothing special lights up on your system unit or keyboard. However, the advantage of having more cache memory is that you'll experience better performance because the CPU won't have to make the longer trip to RAM to get data and instructions as often. Unfortunately, because it is built into the CPU chip or motherboard, you can't upgrade cache: it is part of the original design of the computer system. Therefore, like RAM, it's important when buying a computer to consider buying the one, if everything else is equal, with the most cache memory.

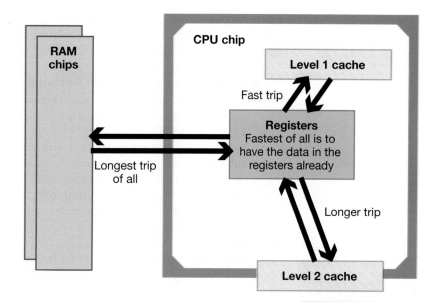

FIGURE 9.8

Modern CPUs have two or more levels of cache memory, which leads to faster CPU processing.

STAGE 2: THE DECODE STAGE

What happens during the decode stage? The main goal of the decode stage is for the CPU's control unit to translate (or decode) the program's instructions into commands the CPU can understand. A CPU can understand only a very small set of commands. The collection of commands a specific CPU can execute is called the **instruction set** for that system. Each CPU has its own unique instruction set. For example, the AMD Athlon 64 processor used in an Alienware Aurora gaming computer has a different instruction set than does the Intel Pentium 4 used in a Dell Inspiron laptop. The control unit interprets the code's bits according to the instruction set the CPU designers laid out for that

 BITS AND BYTES

Why Does Caching Work?

Did you know that 80 percent of the time your CPU spends processing it is working on the same 20 percent of code? Software monitoring programs have been built to test this conjecture for specific systems and it generally holds up well. This is the concept that cache memory exploits. It would be much too expensive to design a system with enough memory on the CPU to store an entire program. But if careful management of a cache of fast memory can make sure that the 20 percent of the program used the most often is already sitting in the cache (and is therefore closer to the CPU), the improvement in overall performance is great.

particular CPU. Based on this process of translation, the control unit then knows how to set up all the switches on the CPU so that the proper operation will occur.

What does the instruction set look like? Because humans are the ones to write the instructions initially, all of the commands in an instruction set are written in a language that is easier for humans to work with, called **assembly language**. However, because the CPU knows and recognizes only patterns of 0s and 1s, it cannot understand assembly language, so these human-readable instructions are translated into long strings of binary code. These long strings of binary code, called **machine language**, are used by the control unit to set up the hardware in the CPU for the rest of the operations it needs to perform. Machine language is a binary code for computer *instructions* much like the ASCII code is a binary code for letters and characters. Similar to each letter or character having its own unique combination of 0s and 1s assigned to it, a CPU has a table of codes consisting of combinations of 0s and 1s for each of its commands. If the CPU sees that pattern of bits arrive, it knows the work it must do. Figure 9.9 shows a few commands in both assembly language and machine language.

Many CPUs have similar commands in their instruction sets, including ADD (add), SUB (subtract), MUL (multiply), DIV (divide), MOVE (move data to RAM), STORE (move data to a CPU register), and EQU (check if equal). CPUs differ in the choice of additional assembly language commands selected for the instruction set.

Each CPU design team works to develop an instruction set that is both powerful and speedy.

STAGE 3: THE EXECUTE STAGE

Where are the calculations performed in the CPU? The **arithmetic logic unit (ALU)** is the part of the CPU designed to perform mathematical operations such as addition, subtraction, multiplication, and division and to test comparing values as greater than, less than, or equal to. For example, in performing its calculations, the ALU would decide whether the grade point average of 3.9 was greater than, less than, or equal to the grade point average of 3.5. The ALU also performs logical OR, AND, and NOT operations. For example, in determining whether a student can graduate, the computer would need to ascertain whether the student has taken all required courses AND obtained a passing grade in each of them. The ALU is specially designed to execute such calculations flawlessly and with incredible speed.

The ALU is fed data from the CPU's registers. The amount of data a CPU can process at a time is based in part on the amount of data each register can hold. The number of bits a computer can work with at a time is referred to as its **word size**. Therefore, a 64-bit processor can process more information faster than a 32-bit processor.

STAGE 4: THE STORE STAGE

What happens in the last stage of CPU processing? In the final stage, the result produced by the ALU is stored back in the registers. The instruction itself will explain which register should be used to store the answer. Now the entire instruction has completed. The next instruction will be fetched and the sequence fetch-decode-execute-store will begin again.

ACTIVE HELPDESK
Understanding the CPU

In this Active Helpdesk call, you'll play the role of a Helpdesk staffer, fielding calls about what is inside the CPU and how these components operate, as well as how a CPU processes data and instructions and how cache memory works.

FIGURE 9.9 Representations of Sample CPU Commands

Human Language for Command	CPU Command in Assembly Language (Language Used by Programmers)	CPU Command in Machine Language (Language Used in CPU's Instruction Set)
Add	ADD	1110 1010
Subtract	SUB	0001 0101
Multiply	MUL	1111 0000
Divide	DIV	0000 1111

TRENDS IN IT

Emerging Technologies: Printable Processors: The Ultimate in Flexibility

You know that the CPU is the "brains" of the computer. Without this important little chip, the computer couldn't process information. The innovations of the transistor and then the integrated circuit have shrunk the processor to a size so small that even a penlike instrument can house computer processing capabilities. Miniaturization has made technology very much a part of our lives.

Manufacturing tiny bits of electronic circuitry on silicon is a time-consuming and costly process. But imagine if making microprocessors were as easy as printing them out on your ink-jet printer. Or for larger projects, imagine printing out computer components on rolls similar to those that are fed through newspaper presses. Sound crazy? Not to Michael Sauvante and Jim Sheats, founders of Rolltronics Corporation. Their visions of what will one day be possible with computer technology make even the *Jetsons* seem old-fashioned.

According to Rolltronics, if computer processors could be printed out on common materials, such as flexible plastic or even paper, rather than manufactured on silicon, computers could be cheaper, smaller, and more completely incorporated into objects we use every day. In fact, the computer would be nearly invisible. You might, for example, download a processor from the Internet, then print this processor directly onto a plastic-type substance using your desktop printer. You could then incorporate these plastic-based processors into everything—even wallpaper that could change images or provide lighting for a room.

Printable processors might even have uses you would expect to see in a James Bond movie, such as wearable computers. Your jacket might have a processor with a built-in thermostat that "reads" your body temperature, and your sunglasses could include processors in the lenses that display visual information.

Sauvante and Sheats anticipate their technology will lead to other innovations, such as lightweight medical devices such as programmable heart and blood pressure monitors, food cans that could tell you when they are out of date, high-capacity memory devices, ultrathin batteries that are safe and inexpensive, and flexible information devices (like today's personal digital assistants) that could roll up and fit inside your purse or pocket. They also anticipate that printable processors will become extremely cheap, lowering the price as well as the size of most computing devices and helping to close the so-called digital divide.

Realistically, flexible processors are several years out from actual production. The use of flexible electronic technology, however, is already being seen in other applications. For example, the U.S. Display Consortium, a group of government, academic, and technological innovators, have agreed to combine their efforts to produce ultrathin, flexible displays. The intention is to integrate this technology in a wide variety of applications, military being at the top of the list. The new technology would enable the production of rollable maps and display-embedded uniforms. Anticipated commerce uses include improving on current automotive displays as well as other mobile displays for phones, tablet PCs, personal digital assistants (PDAs), and so on. Similar strides are being made in developing memory chips on plastic that are then printed using roll-to-roll technology.

Possibilities like these represent only the tip of the iceberg in terms of printable electronics. Another company, Plastic Logic, is also working on printing electronic circuitry onto plastic. In addition to the new and creative applications that plastic microprocessors would produce, Plastic Logic touts an added environmental benefit of printable processors. The technology to make them doesn't use toxic or environmentally damaging materials that are currently used in manufacturing silicon chips. So, in a few years, when the coat you're wearing senses that you're still cold and turns on a built-in heater, you may be able to thank the innovative processes of printable processors!

RAM: The Next Level of Temporary Storage

By now you are aware of **random access memory (RAM)** and the role it plays in your computer system. As you'll recall, RAM is volatile, meaning that when you turn off your computer, the data stored in RAM is erased. RAM is located as a set of chips on the system unit's motherboard and its capacity is measured in megabytes, with most modern systems containing from 512 MB to 1 GB of RAM. The type of memory chips your computer uses is tied to the type and speed of your CPU.

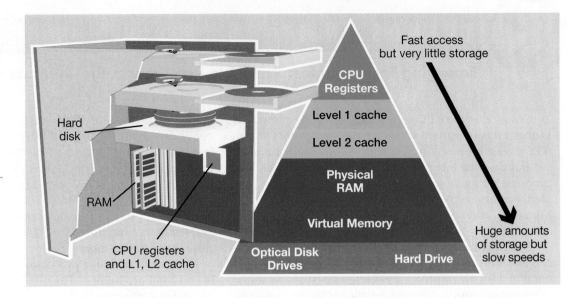

FIGURE 9.10

There are many different levels of memory in a computer system, ranging from the very small amounts in the CPU to the much slower but more plentiful storage of a hard disk drive.

Fast access but very little storage

CPU Registers

Level 1 cache

Level 2 cache

Physical RAM

Virtual Memory

Hard disk

RAM

CPU registers and L1, L2 cache

Optical Disk Drives

Hard Drive

Huge amounts of storage but slow speeds

Figure 9.10 shows a hierarchy of the different types of memory found in your computer system in addition to the more permanent storage devices. You've already read about the top two tiers: CPU registers and cache memory. The following section is about the various types of physical RAM in your system.

The time it takes the CPU to access RAM is very fast, which is why your computer uses RAM as a temporary storage location for data and instructions. The time it takes a device to locate data and instructions and make those data and instructions available to the CPU for processing is known as its **access time**. Recall that getting data and instructions from the hard disk drive to the CPU takes about 10 milliseconds (ms), or ten-thousandths of a second. The time it takes to get instructions from RAM to the CPU is expressed in nanoseconds (ns), or billionths of seconds. RAM is fast! However, although RAM always has faster access times than the hard drive, not all RAM is the same.

TYPES OF RAM

Why are there different types of RAM?
Like all other components of your computer, over time, improvements have been made to the design of RAM. Today, there are several kinds of RAM. Each type of RAM has a very different internal design, allowing some types to work at much faster speeds and to transfer data much more quickly than others.

Therefore, not all systems need the same type of RAM. Low-end computer systems may have one type of RAM, whereas more expensive computer systems that are designed for heavy multimedia use may

have another type. If you compare ads for computer systems, you'll see a number of different acronyms describing the various types of memory, including DRAM, SRAM, SDRAM, DDR SDRAM, and DDR2 RAM. Despite their differences in design, all of these forms of random access memory have the same purpose in a computer system: to store data and allow it to be quickly accessed by the CPU. Understanding the different types of RAM will make you a more knowledgeable consumer and will prepare you to evaluate future memory technologies.

What is the most basic type of RAM? The cheapest and most basic type of RAM is **dynamic RAM (DRAM)**. It is used in older systems or in systems in which cost is an important factor. DRAM offers access times on the order of 60 ns. This means that when the CPU requests a piece of information, it experiences a delay of 60 billionths of a second while the data is retrieved from DRAM.

How does DRAM work? In storing 1 bit of data inside DRAM, a transistor and a capacitor are used. As you learned earlier, a transistor is a switch that can be turned on (allowing electrical current to flow) or off (blocking current). A capacitor is an electronic device that is easily fabricated from silicon and that acts like a huge bathtub, or storage space, for the charged electrons coming from the transistors. To store a 1 (or an "on" bit), the transistor is turned to the "on" position and it fills the capacitor with charge. When a capacitor is full of charge, it will be read as a 1, whereas when the capacitor is empty, or without charge, it will be read as a 0.

Why is DRAM referred to as "dynamic" RAM? Like a leaky bathtub, capacitors leak charge all the time. If the

SOUND BYTE

Memory Hierarchy Interactive

There are so many different types of memory in a computer—cache, registers, RAM, the hard drive. This Sound Byte focuses on the differences in each of these types of memory and how they can be upgraded to improve performance.

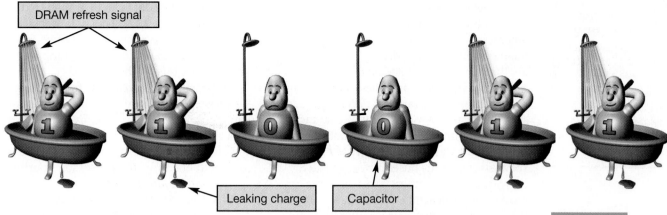

DRAM refresh signal

Leaking charge

Capacitor

FIGURE 9.11

The binary data 110011 is stored in DRAM using capacitors. However, like a bathtub with a leaky drain, these capacitors leak charge, so the DRAM must be refreshed (the bathtub refilled) with charge every clock cycle.

capacitor is just filled with charge once, it eventually loses all its charge. The data being stored in memory is read by looking at a specific capacitor for each bit. If the capacitor at that location is filled with enough charge to be called "on" (that is, if the "bathtub" has been filled with "water"), that bit is read as a 1. If that capacitor *should* be holding a 1 value, but has been sitting there for a while, it may have lost all its charge (that is, the charge may have leaked away over time). The bit would now be read as a 0 and the data stored there would be corrupted.

To make sure each capacitor holding a 1 value is filled with enough charge to be read as a 1 at any time, a refresh signal is applied. The refresh will flood current through the open transistors to refill the capacitors so they continue to store a valid 1. This is the dynamic factor in DRAM: the fact that capacitors leak charge and therefore must be recharged as they are used so the data they hold keeps its true value. This process is illustrated in Figure 9.11.

Are there different kinds of DRAM?
Yes. Not all DRAM is of the same design. A variety of types of DRAM are currently on the market, each with different performance levels and prices. For example, *synchronous DRAM (SDRAM)* is much faster than traditional DRAM. The current standard of DRAM in home systems is *double data rate synchronous DRAM (DDR SDRAM)*. DDR SDRAM is faster than regular SDRAM but not as fast as DDR2 SDRAM, which is the most recent entry on the market. The faster memory is often found on multimedia machines and on gaming systems where the speed is necessary to handle the demands of graphics and audio/video processing efficiently. Each of these types of DRAM increases the speed with which the CPU can access data but also increases the cost of the memory modules.

Is there a faster RAM than DRAM?
All of the refresh signals required to keep the data "fresh" in DRAM take time. A faster type of RAM is **static RAM (SRAM)**. In SRAM, more transistors are used to store a single bit, but no capacitor is needed. This eliminates the need for a refresh signal (thereby avoiding recharging), thus making SRAM much faster than DRAM. However, because it is more expensive than DRAM, it is used only in locations such as the CPU's cache, where the system demands the fastest possible storage.

What kind of memory should I buy for my system? You really do not have a choice in the type of RAM that comes with your system. As described earlier, the system manufacturer installs the specific type of RAM and it will vary depending on the system's performance requirements. As noted in Chapter 6, if you decide to purchase additional memory for your system you'll need to be sure to match the kind of RAM already installed. A system with SDRAM will not be compatible with RDRAM technology, for example.

Does ROM help the CPU work? As you've learned, **read-only memory (ROM)** is a set of memory chips located on the motherboard that stores data and instructions that cannot be changed or erased. ROM chips can be found on most digital devices and usually contain the start-up instructions the computer needs to boot up. ROM chips do not provide any other form of data storage.

Buses: The CPU's Data Highway

A **bus** is an electrical wire in the computer's circuitry—the highway that data (or bits) travels on between the computer's various

components. Computers have two different kinds of buses. **Local buses** are on the motherboard and run between the CPU and the main system memory. Most systems also have another type of bus, called an **expansion bus**, which expands the capabilities of your computer by allowing a range of different expansion cards (such as video cards and sound cards) to communicate with the motherboard.

Do buses affect a computer's performance? Some buses move data along more quickly than others, whereas some can move more data at one time. The rate of speed that data moves from one location to another, known as *bus clock speed*, affects the overall performance of the computer. Bus clock speed is measured in units of megahertz (MHz), or millions of clock cycles per second. The width of the bus (or the **bus width**) determines how many bits of data can be sent along a given bus at any one time. The wider the bus, the more data that can be sent at one time.

Bus width is measured in terms of bits, so a 32-bit bus can carry more data at one time than a 16-bit bus. Together, bus clock speed and bus width determine how quickly any

given amount of data can be transferred on a bus (see Figure 9.12). This data transfer rate (measured in units of megabytes per second) is calculated by multiplying the speed of the bus by the bus width.

The bus width also affects the processor's word size, or the number of bits a processor can manipulate at one time. Even if a processor can manipulate 64 bits at a time, if the bus width allows only 32 bits of data to be sent at one time, the processor's performance will be affected.

What kinds of expansion buses do I need to know about? As noted earlier, the motherboard contains expansion slots in which you insert expansion cards. These expansion cards enable you to connect peripheral devices (such as a monitor) to your computer. For the peripherals to be able to communicate (send and receive data) with your CPU, the motherboard includes expansion buses. The expansion buses provide the pathways that enable the CPU to communicate with the peripheral devices attached through the cards.

Expansion buses have evolved to provide faster transfer speeds and wider bit widths to deliver higher data transfer rates to the many peripheral devices you may connect to your computer. There are several types of expansion buses. Older computers include buses such as the **Industry Standard Architecture (ISA) bus** and the **Extended Industry Standard Architecture (EISA) bus** to connect devices such as the mouse, modem, and sound cards. These are being replaced by faster, more efficient connections.

In a modern computer system, you'll find **Peripheral Component Interconnect (PCI) buses**. PCI expansion buses connect directly to the CPU and support such devices as network cards and sound cards. They have been the standard bus for much of the past decade and continue to be redesigned to increase their performance.

On current systems, you'll also find **Accelerated**

FIGURE 9.12

Buses connect components in your computer so that data can move between them. The width of the bus (bus width) determines how many bits of data can be sent along a given bus at any one time. The wider the bus, the more data that can be sent at one time.

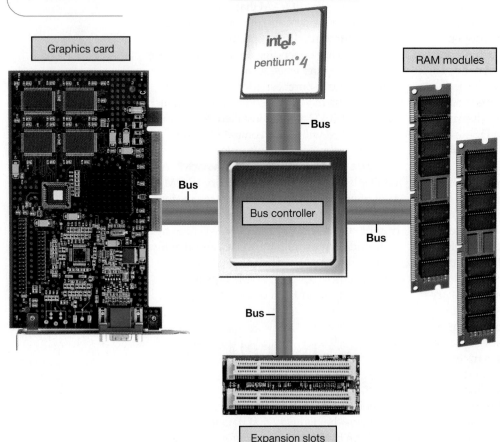

Graphics card

Microprocessor (CPU)

intel. pentium® 4

RAM modules

Bus

Bus

Bus controller

Bus

Bus

Expansion slots

FIGURE 9.13 **Bus Design Evolution**

Bus Architecture	Introduced	Bus Width	Bus Clock Speed	Data Transfer Rate	Notes
ISA (Industry Standard Architecture)	1982	8 or 16 bits	8 MHz	16 MB/sec	Increased performance from the original PC bus design
EISA (Extended Industry Standard Architecture)	Late 1980s	32 bits	8 MHz	32 MB/sec	Next evolution of ISA standard
PCI (Peripheral Component Interconnect)	Early 1990s	32 or 64 bits	33 to 133 MHz	133 to 1,024 MB/sec	Made popular with Windows 95 Long-lived with continued evolution
AGP (Accelerated Graphics Port)	1997	32 bits	66 to 533 MHz	266 to 2,133 MB/sec	Especially for 3-D graphics Uses pipelining to increase speed
PCI-Express	2004/5	1x = 8 bits; 16x = 128 bits	325 to 500 MHz	250 MB/sec for 1x; 4 GB/sec for 16x	Has better reliability and power management and can outperform AGP

Graphics Port (AGP) buses. The AGP bus design was specialized to help move three-dimensional graphics data quickly. It establishes a direct pathway between the graphics card and main memory so that data does not have to ride on the PCI bus, clogging up other system data being moved about.

Figure 9.13 lists the many bus architectures and their respective features.

Are there any newer buses being introduced? Newer versions of PCI and proposed new releases of AGP will keep these buses popular and allow them to accommodate the increasing user demands for information such as streaming video. Intel's proposal for a newer, revised version of AGP, named AGP 3.0, will allow the AGP bus to support data transfer at more than 2,100 MB per second (or 2.1 GB per second). The PCI bus has been extended with the introduction of PCI-Express, which can deliver data at 4.3 GB per second. This ultrafast bus design is currently seen in high-performance video cards and on some high-end home systems, such as the Alienware 7500.

The next generation of bus designs will include HyperTransport, an open specification that supports high-speed chip-to-chip communication, and Intel's proposed 3GIO (Third Generation I/O) standard. The first version of 3GIO that will be released will support data transfer rates at 0.5 GB per second but will later be scaled up to 8 GB per second. The HyperTransport bus will support data transfer rates up to 12.8 GB per second. These buses will provide a very different computer experience for users of high-performance graphics systems and peripherals because data will be able to move at speeds more than 12 times faster than what current desktop systems allow.

Making Computers Even Faster: Advanced CPU Designs

Knowing how to build a CPU that can run faster than the competition can make a company rich. However, building a faster CPU is not easy. When a company decides to design a faster processor, it must take into consideration the time it will take to design, manufacture, and test that processor. When the processor finally hits the market, it must be faster than the competition to even hope to make a profit. To create a CPU that will be released 36 months from now, it must be

SOUND BYTE

Computer Architecture

In this Sound Byte, you'll take animated tours that illustrate many of the hardware concepts introduced in this chapter. Along the way you'll learn about the machine cycle of the CPU, the movement of data between RAM and the CPU, and the hierarchy of the different types of memory in computer systems.

built to perform at least twice as fast as anything currently available.

In fact, as you learned in Chapter 6, Gordon Moore, the cofounder of processor manufacturer Intel, predicted more than 25 years ago that the number of transistors on a processor would double every 18 months. Known as Moore's Law, this prediction has been remarkably accurate—but only with tremendous engineering ingenuity. The first 8086 chip had only 29,000 transistors and ran at 5 MHz. Advances in the number of transistors on processors through the 1970s, 1980s, and 1990s continued to align with Moore's prediction.

However, there was a time near the turn of the 21st century when skeptics questioned how much longer Moore's Law would hold true. These skeptics were proved wrong with the continued growth in power of the microprocessor. Today's Pentium 4 Extreme Edition chip has 169 million transistors and runs at 3.6 GHz— nearly 300 times faster than its original counterpart. How much longer can Moore's prediction hold true? Only time will tell. One thing is for certain, though: CPU design is an area where companies can make great profits, but they risk great fortunes at the same time.

How can processors be designed so they are faster? There are many different ways processor manufacturers can increase CPU performance. One approach is to use a technique called *pipelining* to boost performance. Another approach is to design the CPU's instruction set so that it contains specialized, faster instructions for handling multimedia and graphics. In addition, some CPUs are now being designed so that they have two independent processing paths inside, allowing it to seem as if you are using more than one CPU at the same time. Some heavy computational problems are attacked by actually clustering together large numbers of computers working at the same time.

PIPELINING

Earlier in the chapter you learned that as an instruction is processed, the CPU runs through the four stages of processing in a sequential order: fetch, decode, execute, store. **Pipelining** is a technique that allows the CPU to work on more than one instruc-tion (or stage of processing) at a time, thereby boosting CPU performance.

For example, without pipelining, it may take four clock cycles to complete one instruction (one clock cycle for each of the four processing stages). However, with a four-stage pipeline, the computer can process four instructions *at the same time*. Like a car assembly line, instead of waiting for one car to go completely through each process of assembly, painting, and so on, you can have four cars going through the assembly line at the same time. When every component of the assembly line is done with its process, the cars all move on to the next stage.

Pipelined architectures allow several instructions to be processed at the same time. The computer allows several instructions to be processed at the same time. The ticks of the system clock (the clock cycle) indicate when all instructions move to the next process. The secret of pipelining is that the CPU is allowed to be fetching one instruction while it is simultaneously decoding another, executing a third, storing a fourth, and so on. Using pipelining, a four-stage processor can therefore potentially run up to four times faster because some instruction is finishing every clock cycle rather than waiting four cycles for each instruction to finish, as shown in Figure 9.14.

How many stages can a pipeline be? This depends entirely on design decisions. In this chapter we discussed a CPU that went through four stages in the execution of an instruction. The Intel Pentium 4 features a 20-stage pipeline and the PowerPC G4 processor uses a 13-stage pipeline. Thus, similar to an assembly line, in a 20-stage pipeline, there can be up to 20 different instructions being processed at any given time, making the processing of information much faster. However, because so many aspects of the CPU design interact, you cannot predict performance based solely on the number of stages in a pipeline.

Are there drawbacks to pipelining? There is a cost to pipelining a CPU. The CPU must be designed so that each stage (fetch, decode, execute, store) is independent. This means that each stage must be able to run at the same time as the other three stages are running. This requires more transistors and a more complicated hardware design. Despite this added cost, all processors on the market today feature some form of pipelined design.

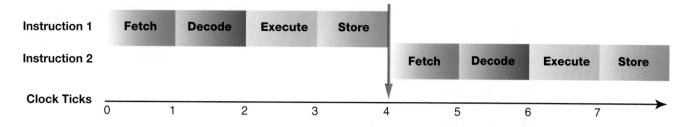

(a) Instruction Cycle, Non-Pipelined: At the end of four clock cycles, Instruction 1 has completed a cycle and Instruction 2 is about to be fetched from RAM.

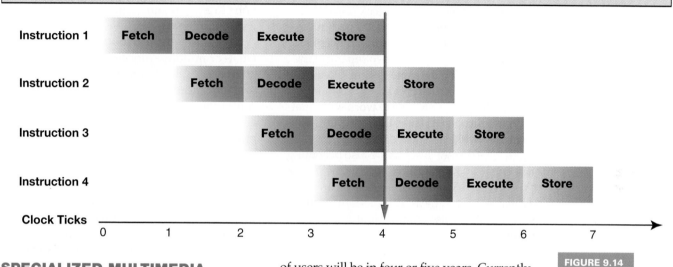

(b) Instruction Cycle, Pipelined: At the end of four clock cycles, Instruction 1 has completed a cycle, Instruction 2 has just finished executing, Instruction 3 has finished decoding, and Instruction 4 has been fetched from RAM.

FIGURE 9.14

The Effects of Pipelining

SPECIALIZED MULTIMEDIA INSTRUCTIONS

How are some processors designed to process multimedia more quickly than others? Each design team developing a new CPU tries to imagine what the greatest needs of users will be in four or five years. Currently, several processors on the market reflect this in the incorporation of specialized multimedia instructions into the basic instruction set. The hardware engineers have redesigned the chip so that there are new commands in the instruction set that are specially designed to

BITS AND BYTES

Does Your Computer Need More Power? Get It Some Help!

If one computer is powerful, two are twice as powerful, but only if you can get them to work together. A *computing cluster* is a group of computers connected by specialized clustering software which work together to solve complex equations. Most clusters work on something called the *load balancing principle*, which means that computational work is transferred from overloaded (busy) computers in the cluster to computers with more available computing resources. Computing

clusters, although not as fast as supercomputers, can perform computations faster than one computer working alone and are used for complex calculations such as weather forecasting and graphics rendering. You can even set up a computing cluster at home, as long as you have at least two computers. Using the Linux operating system and clustering software based on openMosix (**http://openmosix.sourceforge.net**) you can build your own computing cluster for free.

speed up the work needed for video and audio processing. For example, Intel has integrated the Streaming Single Instruction Multiple Data (SIMD) Extensions 2 set of commands into its Pentium 4 processor design, adding a special group of 144 commands to the base instruction set. These multimedia-specific instructions work to accelerate video, speech, and image processing in the CPU.

MULTIPLE PROCESSING EFFORTS

Can I have more than one CPU in my desktop computer? Although the vast majority of home and work desktop systems today use only one processor, it is becoming increasingly common to use dual processors. A **dual-processor** design has two separate CPU chips installed on the same system. Operating systems such as Windows XP Professional and Apple's Mac OS X are able to work with dual processors and automatically decide how to share the workload between them.

Dual-processor systems are also becoming less expensive. Computers such as the Apple Power Mac G5 with dual processors are now available for as little as $2,500. Many high-end server systems also employ dual processors. Often, these server systems can later be scaled so that they can accommodate four, six, or even eight processors. Some of the most powerful mainframes support up to 32 processors!

Meanwhile, Intel introduced a technology called **dual-core processing** in its Pentium 4 Extreme Edition chip. Chips with dual-core processing capabilities have two separate parallel processing paths inside them so they are almost as fast as having two separate CPUs. Combining this with another Intel approach called hyperthreading (or HT), the Extreme Edition Pentium 4 chip can run up to four tasks at one time. Dual-core processing is especially helpful now because antivirus software and other security programs are often running in the background as you use your system. A dual-core processor enables these multiple applications to execute much more quickly than with traditional CPUs.

When are dual processors used? Dual- or multiple-processor systems are often used when intensive computational problems need to be solved in such areas as computer simulations, video production, and graphics processing. Having two processors allows the work to be done *almost* twice as quickly, but not quite. It is not quite twice as fast because the system must do some extra work to decide which processor will work on which part of the problem and to recombine the results each CPU produces.

Could I have more than one machine working on a single task? Certain types of problems are well suited to a **parallel-processing** environment. In parallel processing, there is a large network of computers, with each computer working on a portion of the same problem simultaneously. To be a good candidate for parallel processing, a problem must be one that can be divided into a set of tasks that can be run simultaneously. If the next step of an algorithm can be started only after the results of the previous step have been computed, parallel processing will present no advantages.

A simple analogy of parallel processing is a laundromat. Instead of taking all day to do five loads of laundry with one machine, you can bring all your laundry to a laundromat, load it in five separate machines, and finish it all in approximately the same time it would have taken you to do just one load on a single machine. In real life, parallel processing is used for complex weather forecasting to run calculations over many different regions around the globe; in the airline industry to analyze customer information in an effort to forecast demand; and by the government in census data compilation.

BITS AND BYTES

Today's Supercomputers: The Fastest of the Fast

Supercomputers are the biggest and most powerful type of computer. Scientists and engineers use these computers to solve complex problems or to perform massive computations. Some supercomputers are single computers with multiple processors, whereas others consist of multiple computers that work together. The fastest supercomputer today is the IBM-developed Blue Gene/L, which is used for computing the safety of the nation's nuclear-weapons stockpile. It operates at over 135 teraflops (or 135 trillion operations per second). That's almost 135,000 times faster than the average personal computer! Of course, the Blue Gene does use over 65,000 separate processors at the same time. The supercomputer Columbia operates at 52 teraflops and supports NASA space exploration projects like the International Space Station. Its 10,000 processors can compute the impact of space shuttle damage on the craft's orbit in 24 hours, instead of the three months required by older systems.

Emerging Technologies: Computer Technology Changing the Face of Medicine

As you know by now, computers aren't just for gaming and spreadsheets any longer. Microprocessors, nanotechnology, and other technologies developed during the personal computing explosion of the last two decades are rapidly being adapted to the medical field. Aside from the surgical robotic techniques and patient simulators discussed in Chapter 1, you can look forward to the following medical advancements appearing within the next decade:

1. **Printer mechanisms delivering drugs**. Although drugs such as insulin are self-administered by patients, the current injection delivery method can be uncomfortable or difficult to handle, especially for young and elderly patients. Inhalation of insulin is viewed by many physicians as the answer (because most people do not find this unpleasant), but the difficulty is in developing an efficient aerosol delivery method. Aradigm, a California manufacturer, is developing an inhaler called AerX that uses the same technology as ink-jet printer nozzles to process liquid medication into an aerosol (required for appropriate absorption of the medication through the membranes in the lungs). For many, this may mean saying good-bye to syringes.

2. **An implantable chip that lets you forget to take your pills.** Many drugs must be delivered in precise doses on a regular basis to be effective in treating disease. Although you may be able to remember to take a pill three times a day, not everyone in America's aging population is capable of adhering to this schedule. Therefore, researchers are developing new technologies to deliver medication automatically without any patient intervention. One such promising technology is a dime-sized silicon wafer implant being developed by MicroCHIPS, a Massachusetts-based company. The implants, which are produced using the same methods used to produce silicon microchips for CPUs, contain hundreds of storage areas (called microwells) that store individual doses of medication. The chips are implanted beneath the skin in your abdominal area. Preprogrammed microprocessors on the chip tell the wafer when to administer the doses of medication. No human interaction needed!

3. **Less-invasive medical procedures.** If you need to have an endoscopy (an examination of your gastrointestinal tract), doctors today normally insert a rather large hose into your body that holds a camera. The Food and Drug Administration has approved a camera that uses small-scale (not yet nano-scale) computer technologies to shrink the camera down to the size of a small pill. A patient swallows the camera, which then beams images of the small intestine to a recording device worn on a belt. Now that's an easier pill to swallow.

4. **DNA computers monitoring your body functions.** Israeli scientists have devised a computer that runs on DNA molecules and enzymes as opposed to silicon chips. The computer, although having no practical applications just yet, is extremely fast—in fact, it can perform 330 trillion operations per second, approximately 100,000 times as fast as any personal computer on the market today. Also, where silicon chips are reaching their limit of miniaturization, DNA computers can be constructed using only a few molecules . . . you don't get much smaller than that! As shown in Figure 9.15, DNA computers are combinations of DNA and specially constructed enzymes. Within a single drop of this special fluid, chemical reactions are taking place in billions of DNA computers that generate data and perform rudimentary calculations.

DNA computers use chemical reactions caused by mixing enzymes and DNA molecules. The reactions are designed to provide data and the energy for any calculations needed. Because chemical reactions can be measured precisely and their outcomes predicted reliably, there is no need for conventional hardware and software. All information can be passed at the molecular level. Although DNA computing is in its infancy today, in the future, doctors envision devices constructed from DNA computers that will patrol our bodies and make repairs (such as clearing plaque from arteries) as soon as a problem is detected.

So, as you can see, computing technology can be used not only to improve the quality of your life, but will some day improve the quality of your health as well.

FIGURE 9.15

Here you see a representation of what it is like inside a DNA-based computer. The double-stranded DNA is combined with enzymes and together they become the CPU for this biological computing device.

1. What is a switch and how does it work in a computer?

Electronic switches are devices inside the computer that flip between two states: 1 or 0, on or off. Transistors are switches built out of layers of semiconductor. Integrated circuits (or chips) are very small regions of semiconductor material that support a huge number of transistors. Integrated circuits enable computer designers to fit millions of transistors into a very small area.

2. What is the binary number system and what role does it play in a computer system?

The binary number system uses only two digits, 0 and 1. It is used instead of the base 10 number system to manipulate the on/off switches that control the computer's actions. Even with just two digits, the binary number system can still represent all the same values that a base 10 number system can. To provide a consistent means for representing letters and other characters, codes dictate how to represent characters in binary format. The ASCII code uses 8 bits (0s and 1s) to represent 255 characters. Unicode uses 16 bits of data for each character and can represent more than 65,000 character symbols.

3. What is inside the CPU and how do these components operate?

The CPU executes every instruction given to your computer. CPUs are differentiated by their processing power (how many transistors are on the microprocessor chip), how quickly the processor can work (called clock speed), and the amount of immediate access memory the CPU has (called cache memory). The CPU consists of two primary units: the control unit controls the switches inside the CPU, and the arithmetic logic unit (ALU) performs logical and arithmetic calculations.

4. How does a CPU process data and instructions?

All CPUs must perform a series of similar general steps. These steps, referred to as a CPU machine cycle, include: fetch (loading program and data binary code into the CPU), decode (translating the binary code into commands the CPU can understand), execute (carrying out the commands), and store (placing the results in special memory storage areas, called registers, before the process starts again).

5. What is cache memory?

Cache memory consists of small blocks of memory located directly on and next to the

CPU chip that hold recently or frequently used instructions or data that the CPU needs the most. The CPU can more quickly retrieve data and instructions from cache than from RAM.

6. What types of RAM are there?

RAM is volatile storage, meaning that when you turn off your computer, the data stored there is erased. The cheapest and most basic type of RAM is DRAM (dynamic RAM). There are many types of RAM, including SDRAM, DDR RAM, and DDR2 DRAM). All of these forms of RAM store data that the CPU can access quickly.

7. What is a bus and how does it function in a computer system?

A bus is an electrical wire in the computer's circuitry through which data (or bits) travels between the computer's various components. Local buses are on the motherboard and run between the CPU and the main system memory. Expansion buses expand the capabilities of your computer by allowing a range of different expansion cards to connect to the motherboard. The width of the bus (or the bus width) determines how many bits of data can be sent along a given bus at any one time.

8. How do manufacturers make CPUs so that they run faster?

Pipelining is a technique that allows the CPU to work on more than one instruction (or stage of processing) at a time, thereby boosting CPU performance. A dual-processor design has two separate CPU chips installed on the same system. Dual-core or multiple-processor systems are often used when intensive computational problems need to be solved. In parallel processing, computers in a large network each work on a portion of the same problem at the same time.

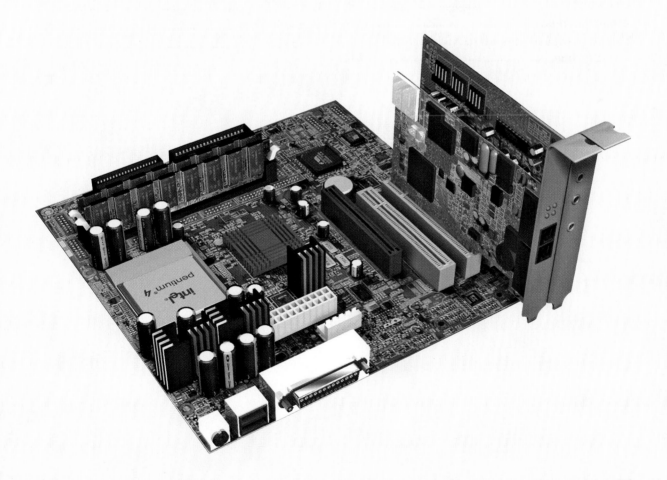

 **Key Terms**

Buzz Words

Word Bank

- AGP
- ALU
- ASCII
- binary
- bytes
- buses

- cache
- control unit
- decoded
- DRAM
- fetch
- instruction set

- Level 1 cache
- Level 2 cache
- Level 3 cache
- number system
- PCI
- registers

Instructions: Fill in the blanks using the words from the Word Bank.

Computers are based on a system of switches, which can be either on or off. The
(1) _____ number system, which has only two digits, models this well. A(n)
(2) _____ is a set of rules for the representation of numbers. Bits are organized
into groups of eight, or (3) _____ , so they are easier to work with. The
(4) _____ code organizes bytes in unique combinations of 0s and 1s to represent
characters, letters, and numerals.

The CPU organizes switches to execute the basic commands of the system. No matter what
command is being executed, the CPU steps through the same four processing stages. First it
needs to (5) _____ the instruction from RAM. Next the instruction is
(6) _____ , and the (7) _____ sets up all of the CPU hardware to perform that particular command. The actual execution takes place in the (8) _____ .
The result is then saved by storing it in the (9) _____ on the CPU. Another form
of memory the CPU uses is (10) _____ memory. (11) _____ is the
form of this type of memory located closest to the CPU. (12) _____ is located a
bit farther from the CPU.

RAM comes in several different types. (13) _____ must be refreshed each cycle
to keep the data it stores valid. The pathways connecting the CPU to memory are known as
(14) _____ . The speeds at which they can move data, or the data transfer rates,
vary. (15) _____ is a bus designed primarily to move three-dimensional graphics data quickly.

Becoming Computer Fluent

Your new boss is unsure what the differences between high-end systems are and would like
you to compile a report on two high-end systems, a G5 Macintosh and a Windows-based
PC. She has asked you to compare the price/performance ratio, the hardware features
including CPU design, and memory capacities.

Instructions: Using the preceding scenario, write a report using as many of the key
words from the chapter as you can. Be sure the sentences are grammatically correct and
technically meaningful.

Instructions: Answer the multiple choice and true/false questions below for more practice with key terms and concepts from this chapter.

MULTIPLE CHOICE

1. Electronic switches are
   a. devices inside the computer that can be flipped between two states: 1 or 0.
   b. always built out of layers of semiconductor.
   c. very small regions of semiconductor material that support many transistors.
   d. None of the above

2. Binary number notation is based on
   a. powers of 10.
   b. powers of 8.
   c. powers of 2.
   d. powers of 16.

3. The Unicode encoding system notation can represent
   a. only uppercase letters.
   b. only letters and symbols in English.
   c. most (but not all) of what the ASCII system can represent.
   d. the alphabets of all modern languages.

4. A CPU's clock speed
   a. is the only important factor in system performance.
   b. is measured in units of billions per second.
   c. depends on which time zone the machine is in.
   d. is a measure of the number of transistors on the chip.

5. The Fetch stage of the CPU cycle is used to
   a. gather data from the registers.
   b. execute an instruction in the ALU.
   c. pull data from the Level 1 cache.
   d. transfer data from RAM into the CPU's registers.

6. Dynamic RAM is called "dynamic" because
   a. it is faster than static RAM (SRAM).
   b. it must be refreshed to keep the data valid.
   c. it has a great personality.
   d. it changes its value every clock cycle.

7. A computer bus is characterized by
   a. its speed (data transfer rate).
   b. its width (how many bits move at one time).
   c. the standard it follows (such as ISA or AGP).
   d. All of the above

8. Pipelining is a technique that allows
   a. the CPU to be more efficient at handling multiple tasks at one time.
   b. data to be read more quickly by the CPU.
   c. RAM to be copied to the hard drive very quickly.
   d. cache memory to be ignored.

9. Computers can be designed to use
   a. more than one CPU in the same system.
   b. only one CPU but several different types of RAM.
   c. multiple CPUs, but only if each has its own hard drive.
   d. multiple CPUs, but only if each has its own operating system.

10. There is a "hierarchy" of memory in a computer system because
    a. there are large amounts of slow, cheap memory and smaller amounts of fast, expensive memory in the system.
    b. faster memory is more expensive so the system has less.
    c. there is a need for both volatile and nonvolatile storage.
    d. All of the above

TRUE/FALSE

_____ 1. Binary numbers use only two digits.

_____ 2. DDR RAM is standard in most new home desktop systems.

_____ 3. The system clock runs at different speeds depending on the workload.

_____ 4. CPU designers use pipelining to bring in data more quickly from RAM.

_____ 5. There are several different types of busses inside a computer system.

Making the Transition to...
Next Semester

1. Upgrading RAM

As your collegiate career continues, are you finding your computer needs to do more and more? Upgrading the RAM in your machine can greatly improve performance. What kind of RAM is installed in the computer you use for schoolwork (your own or the lab system you use)? How much would an upgrade to 512 MB of RAM cost for that type of RAM? An upgrade to 1 GB of RAM? Use the supplier Crucial Technology (**www.crucial.com**) to get information about the type of RAM in your system.

2. Lab Processors

It is always challenging for administrators to keep computer laboratories up-to-date. Investigate the type of processor installed in the computer systems you use in your lab. Visit the manufacturer's Web site to get detailed specifications about the design of that processor—how many levels of cache it has, how much total cache memory it has, its speed, and the number of pipeline stages in the CPU. How does that processor compare with the latest model available from the manufacturer?

3. Comparison Shopping for Systems

Do some comparison shopping. Pick three relatively comparable, moderately priced computer systems. Create a spreadsheet that outlines all the specific features of each machine. What kind of processor does each machine include? How fast is it? How many levels of cache and how much storage capacity does each cache level have? Look at the RAM: what kind and how much RAM does each machine have? What is the bus architecture of each machine?

4. Game Time

The next generation of video gaming consoles is appearing on the market and you want to reward yourself for having worked hard all semester. Consider the three main entries in the market: Microsoft's Xbox 360, Sony's Playstation 3, and Nintendo's Revolution. For each of these gaming consoles, find out what CPU is being used and what features it has that support high-end gaming. What overall processing power can the system achieve (measured in units of FLOPS or floating point operations per second)? What kind of graphics card is used? What kind of ports are included? How does the system handle Internet connectivity? Consider research sources like **www.wikipedia.com**, **www.gameinformer.com**, and the Sony, Microsoft, and Nintendo Web sites.

5. Which Processor?

Word gets out that you know a lot about CPUs, and you are suddenly the one everyone is coming to with questions. Some of your friends want to buy laptops, some want high-end video gaming systems, and some need inexpensive solutions. To prepare yourself to be the "CPU guru." look at the table in Figure 9.6 and find out what setting or application is most common for each processor. Use manufacturer Web sites as well as **www.pcmag.com** and **www.tomshardware.com** for information.

Making the Transition to...
The Workplace

1. Finding Your Network Adapter Address

Almost every business today uses networks to connect the computer systems they own. Each machine is assigned its own identifying number, called a network adapter address. This value is a long binary number that uniquely labels each adapter card in the business. On the networked machine, click Start, click Run, then type "command" in the Open text box of the Run dialog box. Then type "ipconfig" in the console window to find your own network adapter address. Is it presented in binary? hexadecimal? decimal? Why?

2. CPUs: The Next Generation

In an effort to stay technologically current, you have been asked to research the most recently released CPUs to determine whether it's worth buying new machines with the new CPUs or waiting for perhaps the next generation. Investigate the newest CPUs released by Intel, Motorola, and IBM. Compare these new CPUs with the current "best" CPUs. What technological advancements are present in the latest CPUs? From a cost perspective, does it make sense to replace the old systems with these new CPUs? What is the buzz on the next-generation CPUs? Would it be better to wait for these future CPUs to come out?

3. Using Pipelining

You work in a car assembly plant, so production lines are a familiar concept to your boss. However, he still doesn't understand the concept of pipelining and how it expedites a computer's processing cycle. Create a presentation for your boss that describes pipelining in enough detail so your boss will understand it. In doing so, compare it with the automobile assembly process.

4. Super Power

Your team at work is exploring a sophisticated stock price prediction model. But the algorithm requires a supercomputer or a computing cluster (multiple computers joined by software working together) to achieve maximum efficiency. Your boss is not interested in spending department funds on this but if you can find a way to explore this cheaply, using open source software that runs on Linux, he'll support it. Research low-cost cluster computing solutions (like Beowulf clusters) at sites such as **www.beowulf.org**, **http://openmosix.sourceforge.net**, and **http://bofh.be/clusterknoppix**. Would it be feasible to use existing Windows computers to run the cluster? Describe how to set up a small cluster and the benefits of doing so, including cost estimates for a 16-node cluster (using cheap PCs that can run Linux).

5. Error Handling Using Binary Numbers

At work you have been bothered by an error message that occasionally pops up from one of your programs. It displays the following message:

```
Error code Number 0011 1010 1111 0011 Please call tech support
help line.
```

Before you call in, take each group of four binary digits and write down the equivalent hexadecimal digit. You can do this by computing the base 10 equivalent of the four binary digits first, then figuring out the base 16 representation of that number.

Critical Thinking Questions

Instructions: Albert Einstein used "Gedanken experiments," or critical thinking questions, to develop his theory of relativity. Some ideas are best understood by experimenting with them in our own minds. The following critical thinking questions are designed to demand your full attention but require only a comfortable chair—no technology.

1. Processors of the Future

Consider the current limitations of the design of memory, how it is organized, and how a CPU operates. Think radically—what extreme ideas can you propose for the future of processor design? What do you think the limit of clock speed for a processor will be? How could a CPU communicate more quickly with memory? What could future cache designs look like?

2. Increasing Processor Speed

SIMD and 3DNow! (used by AMD in its processors) are two approaches to modifying the instruction set to speed up graphics operations. What do you think will be the next important type of processing users will expect from computers? How could you customize the commands the CPU understands so that processing occurs faster on the CPU you are designing?

3. The Impact of Registers

How would computer systems be different if we could place 1 GB of registers on a single CPU? How would that impact the design of video cards? Would it change the way RAM is used in the system?

4. The CPU Processing Cycle

The four stages of the CPU processing cycle are fetch, decode, execute, and store. Think of some real-world tasks you perform that could be described the same way. For each example, describe how it would be changed if it were pipelined. What additional resources would the pipelined task require?

5. Binary Style

Binary events, things that can be in one of only two positions, happen around you all the time. A common example is a light switch that is toggled on or off. How about a coin? It must always be either heads up or heads down. What other events or objects behave in a binary style?

6. Lots of Ways to Remember

Why does there need to be a memory hierarchy within a computer system, such as the one drawn in Figure 9.10? How would you design a system if it were very inexpensive to produce lots of CPU registers and very expensive to build hard disk drives? What if someone discovered a way to make hard disk drives a million times faster than they are today? How would you design a system then?

Problem:

For a system to be effective, it must be balanced—that is, the performance of each subsystem must be well matched so that there are no bottlenecks in the overall performance. In this exercise, teams will develop balanced hardware designs for specific systems within several different price ranges.

Task:

Each group will select one part of a computer—either the CPU, the memory, or the bus architecture. The group will be responsible for researching the available options and collecting information on both price and performance specifications. The group will write a report that recommends a specific product for each of three price ranges—entry level, mid-range, and high performance. Finally, the three groups will combine their reports so that the team has developed a specification for the entire system.

Process:

1. Divide into three groups: processor, memory, and bus design.
2. Consider the following three price ranges:
   - $500 to $1,000
   - $1,001 to $2,500
   - Unlimited

   For each price range, try to specify at least two components that would keep the system cost in range and would provide the best performance. Keep track of all performance information so you can later meet with the other groups and make sure each subsystem is well matched.

3. Bring the research materials from the group meetings to one final team meeting. Looking at the system level, make final decisions on the system design for each of the three price ranges. Each range is the sum of total cost that can be expended for hardware for the system unit (monitor and other peripherals not included). The system case, power supply, motherboard, RAM, video card, and storage must be included. Research vendors that supply parts to home developers, such as TigerDirect.com.

4. Produce a report that documents the decisions and trade-offs evaluated en route to your final selections.

Conclusion:

A performance increase in one subsystem contributes to the overall performance, but only in proportion to how often it is used. This affects system design and how limited financial resources can be spent to provide the most balanced, best-performing system.

Multimedia

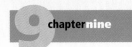

In addition to the review materials presented here, you'll find additional materials featured with the book's multimedia, including the *Technology in Action* Student Resource CD and the Companion Web site (**www.prenhall.com/techinaction**), which will help reinforce your understanding of the chapter content. These materials include the following:

ACTIVE HELPDESK

In Active Helpdesk calls, you'll assume the role of a Helpdesk operator taking calls about the concepts you've learned in this chapter. You'll apply what you've learned and receive feedback from a supervisor to review and reinforce those concepts. The Active Helpdesk calls for this chapter are listed here and can be found on your Student Resource CD:

- Understanding the CPU
- Understanding Types of RAM

SOUND BYTES

Sound Bytes are dynamic multimedia tutorials that help demystify even the most complex topics. You'll view video clips and animations that illustrate computer concepts, and then apply what you've learned by reviewing with the Sound Byte Labs, which include quizzes and activities specifically tailored to each Sound Byte. The Sound Bytes for this chapter are listed here and can be found on your Student Resource CD and on the Companion Web site (**www.prenhall.com/techinaction**):

- Binary Numbers Interactive
- Where Does Binary Show Up?
- Memory Hierarchy Interactive
- Computer Architecture

COMPANION WEB SITE

The *Technology in Action* Companion Web site includes a variety of additional materials to help you review and learn more about the topics in this chapter. The resources available at **www.prenhall.com/techinaction** include:

- **Online Study Guide.** Each chapter features an online true/false and multiple-choice quiz. You can take these quizzes, automatically check the results, and e-mail the results to your instructor.
- **Web Research Projects.** Each chapter features a number of Web research projects that ask you to search the Web for information on computer-related careers, milestones in computer history, important people and companies, emerging technologies, and the applications and implications of different technologies.

Behind the Scenes:

Software Programming

Objectives

After reading this chapter, you should be able to answer the following questions:

1. What is a system development life cycle and what are the phases in the cycle? **(p. 420–423)**

2. What is the life cycle of a program? **(p. 423)**

3. What role does a problem statement play in programming? **(pp. 424–425)**

4. How do programmers create algorithms? **(pp. 426–431)**

5. How do programmers move from algorithm to code and what categories of language might they code in? **(pp. 431–438)**

6. How does a programmer move from code in a programming language to the 1s and 0s the CPU can understand? **(pp. 438–439)**

7. How is a program tested? **(pp. 439–440)**

8. What steps are involved in completing the program? **(pp. 440–441)**

9. How do programmers select the right programming language for a specific task? **(pp. 441–442)**

10. What are the most popular programming languages for Windows and Web applications? **(pp. 441–450)**

ACTIVE HELPDESK

- Understanding Software Programming **(p. 440)**
- Selecting the Right Programming Language **(p. 442)**

Understanding Software Programming

Every day we face a wide array of tasks. Some tasks are complex and need a human touch, some require creative thought and higher-level organization. However, some tasks are routine, such as alphabetizing a huge collection of invoices. Tasks that are repetitive, work with electronic information, and follow a series of clear steps are candidates for computerization.

For many tasks, well-designed computer programs already exist. For example, if you want to write a research paper, Microsoft Word allows you to do just that. The program has already been designed to translate the tasks you want to accomplish into computer instructions. To do your work, you need only be familiar with the interface of Word; you do not have to create a program yourself.

However, for users who cannot find an existing software product to accomplish a task, programming is mandatory. Say a medical company comes up with a new smart bandage that is designed to transmit medical information about a wound directly to a diagnostic computer (these are under development). No software product on the market is designed to accumulate and relay information in this manner. Therefore, the company will need to deploy a team of software developers to generate the appropriate software for this bandage to function as designed.

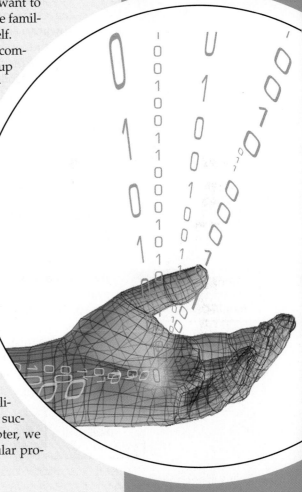

Even if you'll never create a program of your own, knowing the basics of computer programming is still helpful. For example, most modern software applications enable you to customize and automate various features using small custom-built "miniprograms" called *macros*. By creating macros, you can ask the computer to execute a complicated sequence of steps with a single command. Understanding how to program macros enables you to add custom commands to Word or Excel, for example, and automate frequently performed tasks, providing a huge boost to your productivity.

Understanding programming is therefore an important piece of working well with a computer system. If you plan to use only off-the-shelf software, having a basic knowledge of programming enables you to understand how application software is constructed and to add features that support your personal needs. If you plan to create custom applications from scratch, a detailed knowledge of programming is key to the successful completion of any project. Thus, in this behind-the-scenes chapter, we explore the stages of program development and survey the most popular programming languages.

SOUND BYTES

- Programming for End Users: Macros **(p. 423)**
- Looping Around the IDE **(p. 439)**

The Life Cycle of an Information System

Generally speaking, a *system* is a collection of pieces working together to achieve a common goal. Your body, for example, is a system of muscles, organs, and other components working together. The college you attend is a system with administrators, faculty, students, and maintenance personnel working together. An **information system** includes data, people, procedures, hardware, and software. You interact with information systems all the time whether you are at a grocery store, bank, or restaurant. In any of these instances, the parts of the system work together toward a similar goal. Because teams of individuals are required to develop such systems, an organized process (or set of steps) needs to be followed to ensure that development proceeds in an orderly fashion.

This set of steps is usually referred to as the *system development life cycle (SDLC)*. In this section, we provide you with an overview of systems development and show you how programming fits into the cycle.

SYSTEM DEVELOPMENT LIFE CYCLE

Why do you need a process to develop a system? If you have programming skills, you can sit down in a day, perhaps, to write a little program to balance your checkbook or to organize your CD collection. If you don't have such skills or the time or inclination to write a program, you can run out and buy one. However, one person does not develop in a day the programs you buy in a store. Those programs are generally far more complex than we would write ourselves, and they require many phases to make the product complete and saleable. Therefore, an entire team of people and a systematic approach are necessary. Because teams of individuals are required to develop systems, an organized process (or set of steps) needs to be followed to ensure that development proceeds in an orderly fashion. As noted earlier, this set of steps is usually referred to as the **system development life cycle (SDLC)**.

What steps constitute the SDLC? All of the six steps of the SDLC are shown in Figure 10.1. As the figure shows, this system is sometimes referred to as a "waterfall" system because each step is dependent on the previous step being completed first. A brief synopsis of each step follows.

1. **Problem/Opportunity Identification.** Corporations are always attempting to break into new markets, develop new sources of customers, or launch new products. For example, when the founders of eBay developed the idea of an online auction community, they needed a system that could serve customers and allow them to interact with each other. At other times, systems development is driven by a company's desire to serve its existing customers more efficiently or to respond to problems with a current system. For example, when traditional brick-and-mortar businesses want to launch e-commerce sites, they need to develop systems for customers to purchase products.

   Whether solving an existing problem or exploiting an opportunity, corporations usually generate more ideas for systems than they have the time and money to implement. Large corporations typically form a development steering committee to evaluate systems development proposals. The committee reviews ideas and decides which projects to take forward based on available resources (personnel and funding).

2. **Analysis.** In this phase, analysts explore in depth the problem to be solved and develop a *program specification*. The program specification is a clear statement of the goals and objectives of the project at hand. It is also at this stage that the first feasibility assessment is performed. The feasibility assessment determines

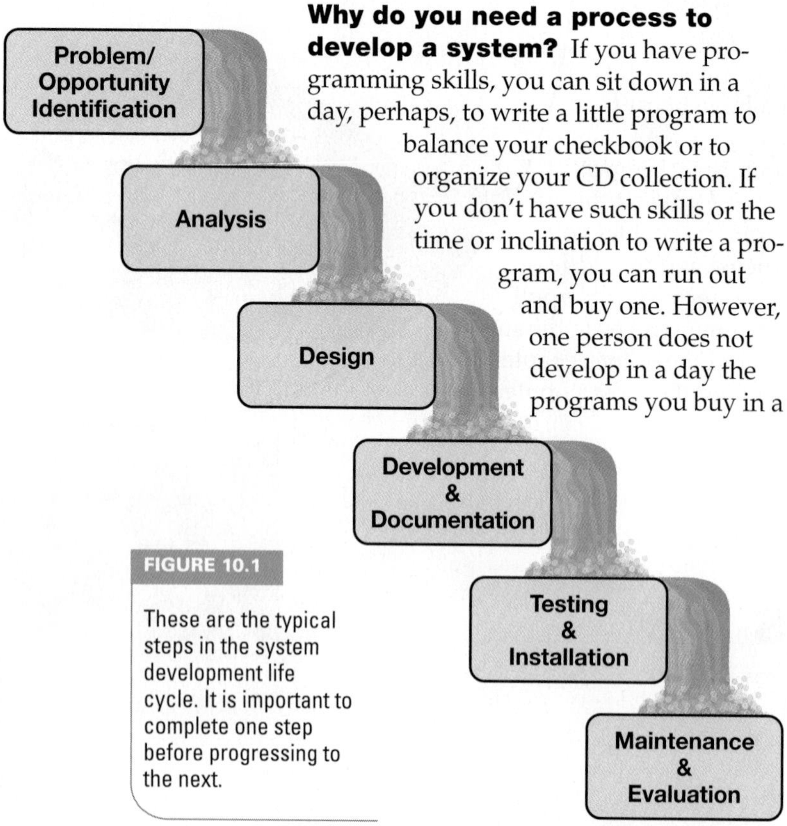

FIGURE 10.1

These are the typical steps in the system development life cycle. It is important to complete one step before progressing to the next.

Steps shown: Problem/Opportunity Identification → Analysis → Design → Development & Documentation → Testing & Installation → Maintenance & Evaluation

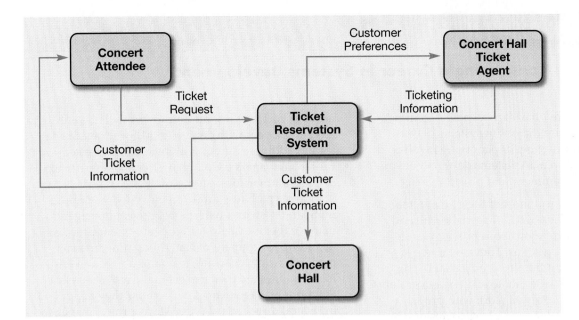

FIGURE 10.2

Data-flow diagrams trace the flow of data such as ticketing information. This is a top-level overview diagram. More detailed diagrams would be prepared for each piece of the system, showing specific pieces of information being tracked (such as customer name, payment information, and so on).

whether the project should go forward. You might have a great idea, but that doesn't mean that the company has the technical expertise or the financial or operational resources to develop it. Similarly, there may not be enough time to develop the product fully.

Assuming the project is feasible, the analysis team studies the current system (if there is one) and defines the user requirements of the proposed system. Finally, the analysts recommend a solution or plan of action, and the process moves to the design phase.

3. **Design.** Before a house is built, blueprints are developed so that the workers have a plan to follow. The design phase of the SDLC has the same objective: generating a detailed plan for programmers to follow. The current and proposed systems are documented using flowcharts and data-flow diagrams. Data-flow diagrams trace all data in an information system from the point at which data enters the system to its final resting place (storage or output). Figure 10.2 shows a high-level data-flow diagram illustrating the flow of concert ticket information.

The ultimate goal of the design phase with respect to software development is to design documents that programmers can follow in developing the actual system. It is also in this phase that the "make or buy" decision is made. Once the system plan is designed, a company evaluates existing software packages (off-the-

shelf software) to determine whether it needs to develop a new piece of software or buy something already on the market and adapt it to fit its own needs.

For instance, if you want to start an online auction site to compete with eBay, you might not have to build your own system. Numerous online auction software packages are for sale now that might meet your needs. If you cannot find an existing package that meets your needs, you would have to develop your own system. Or, perhaps, you

BITS AND BYTES

What Is Extreme Programming?

There are new models for software development emerging, some much different than the traditional SDLC. Extreme programming is one model becoming popular because it is able to adapt to changes in program specifications so quickly. In the extreme programming model, the customer is involved in the project very closely, right from the beginning. A representative for the customer may even come and work full time with the programming team. Programmers work in pairs with extensive review of their code. Testing is designed early and is run constantly throughout the development cycle. Another characteristic of extreme programming is the motto "Do the simplest thing that could possibly work." Extreme programmers have this motto because the simplest approach is easier to debug and change later if the demands on the program are revised. Extreme programmers work extremely hard but not in extremely complex ways!

Careers: Considering a Career in Systems Development?

Because large projects involve many people to complete them, many opportunities for jobs in systems development exist. Although a number of people are involved in the process, the key players in systems development are systems analysts, programmers, and project managers:

- **Systems analysts** spend most of their time in the beginning stages of the SDLC. They talk with end users to gather information about problems and existing information systems. They document systems and propose solutions to problems. Having good people skills is essential to success as a systems analyst. In addition, analysts work with programmers during the development phase to design appropriate programs to solve the problem at hand. Therefore, many organizations insist on hiring systems analysts with both a solid business background and prior programming experience (at least at a basic level). For entry-level jobs, a four-year degree is usually required. Many colleges and universities offer degrees in Management Information Systems (MIS) that include a mixture of systems development, programming, and business courses.

- **Programmers** participate in the SDLC, attending meetings to document user needs and working closely with systems analysts during the design phase. Programmers need excellent written communication skills because they often generate detailed systems documentation for end-user training purposes. Because programming languages are mathematically based, it is essential for programmers to have strong math skills and an ability to think logically. Programmers should also be proficient at more than one programming language. As you'll learn later, developers use different languages for different problems. Although Java, C++, and Visual Basic are popular languages today, programmers need to be prepared to learn new languages (such as C#) as well.

A four-year degree is usually required for entry-level programming positions. Computer science is the

major of choice, but some employers will hire entry-level employees with degrees in MIS with mathematics and additional programming courses as electives.

- **Project managers** usually have years of experience as programmers or systems analysts. This job is part of a career path upward from entry-level programming and systems analyst jobs. Project managers manage the overall systems development process, including assignment of staff, budgeting, management reporting, coaching team members, and ensuring deadlines are met. Project managers need excellent time-management skills because they are pulled in several directions at once. Many project managers obtain master's degrees to supplement their undergraduate degrees in computer science or MIS.

In addition to these people, the following are also involved in the systems development process:

- **Technical writers** provide documentation for the new system.
- **Network engineers** help the programmers and analysts design compatible systems, because many systems are required to run in certain environments (UNIX or Windows, for instance) and must work well in conjunction with other programs.
- **Database analysts and database administrators (DAs and DBAs)** design and implement database structures, because most systems interface with or populate one type of database or another.
- **Graphic designers and interface designers** create attractive and effective interface screens.

It is important to emphasize that all systems development careers are stressful. Deadlines are tight for development projects, especially if they involve getting a new product to market ahead of the competition. But if you enjoy challenges and can endure a fast-paced, dynamic environment, there should be plenty of opportunities in the decade ahead for good systems developers.

For more information on careers, see the Technology in Focus feature "Careers in IT" on page 586.

could *outsource*, or hire someone outside the corporation, to develop the program you need.

4. **Development and Documentation.** This is the phase during which actual programming takes place. This phase is also the first part of the program development life cycle (PDLC), described in detail in the rest of the chapter.

5. **Testing and Installation.** The next step in the SDLC is testing the program to ensure it works properly and installing the program so that it can be used.

6. **Maintenance and Evaluation.** Once the system is installed, its performance must be monitored to determine whether it is still meeting the needs of the end users. Bugs that were not detected in the test-

ing phase that the users discover subsequently must be corrected. Additional enhancements that users request are evaluated so that appropriate program modifications can be made.

The Life Cycle of a Program

Programming often begins with nothing more than a problem or a request: "We can't get our budget reports out on time" or "Can you tell me how many transfer students have applied to our college?" When problems or requests such as these arise, someone realizes computer programs could solve these problems more efficiently and reliably than the procedures they have in place.

As you just read, once the project has been deemed to be feasible and a plan is in place, the work of *programming* begins. **Programming** is the process of translating a task into a series of commands a computer will use to perform that task. It involves identifying which parts of a task a computer can perform, describing those tasks in a very specific and complete manner, and, finally, translating this description into the language spoken by the computer's central processing unit (CPU).

How do programmers tackle a programming project? Just as an information system has a development life cycle, each programming project follows a number of stages from conception to final deployment, sometimes referred to as the **program development life cycle (PDLC)**:

1. First, programmers must develop a complete description of the problem. The *problem statement* identifies the task to be computerized and describes how the software program will behave.

2. The problem statement is next translated into a set of specific, sequential steps that describe exactly what the computer program must do to complete the work. This is known as an *algorithm*. At this stage, the algorithm is written in natural language (the language the programmer speaks, such as English).

3. The algorithm is then translated into programming *code*, a language that is more friendly to humans than the 1s and 0s that the CPU speaks but that is still very structured. By coding the

FIGURE 10.3

Step 1
Describing the Problem
(The Problem Statement)

Step 2
Making a Plan
(Algorithm Development)

Step 3
Coding
(Speaking the Language of the Computer)

Step 4
Debugging
(Getting Rid of Errors)

Step 5
Finishing the Project
(Testing and Documentation)

The stages each programming project follows from conception to final deployment are collectively referred to as the program development life cycle (PDLC).

algorithm, programmers must think in terms of the operations that a CPU can perform.

4. The code then goes through a process of *debugging*, in which the programmers find and repair any errors in the code.

5. The software is then *tested*, both by the programming team and by the people who will use the program. The results of the entire project are *documented* for the users and the development team. Finally, users are *trained* so they can use the program efficiently.

Figure 10.3 illustrates the steps of a program's life cycle. Now that you have an overview of the process involved in developing a program, let's look at each step in more detail.

SOUND BYTE

Programming for End Users: Macros

In this Sound Byte, you'll be guided through the creation of a macro in the Microsoft Office suite. You'll learn how Office enables you to program with macros to customize and extend the capabilities it offers.

Describing the Problem: The Problem Statement

The **problem statement** is the starting point of programming work. It is a very clear description of what tasks the computer program must accomplish and how the program will execute these tasks and respond to unusual situations. Programmers develop problem statements so that they can better understand the goals of their programming efforts.

What kind of problems can computer programs solve? Not every problem is well suited to a computerized solution. The strengths of computing machines are that they are fast and work without error—unlike humans, computers don't introduce mistakes because they're tired or stressed. As mentioned earlier, tasks that are repetitive, work with electronic information, and follow a series of clear steps are candidates for computerization.

This might sound as if computers only help us with very dull and simplistic tasks. However, computer programs also can help solve sophisticated problems. For example, pharmaceutical companies design drugs using complex computer programs that model molecules. Using program simulations, chemists can "create" new drugs in the computer and quickly determine whether they will have the desired effects. Based on the program's data, chemists select the most promising choices and begin to test those compounds in the real laboratory. Not exactly simple stuff.

Still, computers cannot yet act with intuition or be spontaneously creative. They can attack very challenging problems, such as making weather predictions or playing chess, but only in a manner that takes advantage of what computers do best—making fast, reliable computations.

How do programmers create problem statements? Most computer users understand what jobs (or problems) they want to computerize, but not the details of the programming process. Therefore, the goal in creating a useful problem statement is to have programmers interact with users to describe three things relevant to creating a useful program:

1. The *input* that will be entered. This is the data users will have at the start of the job.

2. The *output* that the program will produce. This is the information users require at the end of the job.

3. The exact *processing* that converts these inputs to outputs. Programmers must determine how to transform the input into the correct output.

For example, say you want to compute how much money you'll earn working at a parking garage. Your salary is $7.32 per hour for an eight-hour shift, but if you work more than eight hours a day you earn $11.73 per hour for the overtime work. To determine how much money you make in any given day, you could multiply this out in your mind, write it out manually, use a calculator, or you could create a simple computer program to do the work for you. In this example, what are the three elements of the problem statement?

1. The *input*, the data that you know at the beginning of the problem, is the number of hours you worked.

2. The *output*, the information you need to have at the end of the problem, is your total pay for the day.

3. The *processing* is the set of steps that will take you from your input to an output. In this case, the computer program would check if you worked more than eight hours (that is, it would determine whether you worked any overtime). If you did not work overtime, the output is just $7.32 multiplied by the total number of hours you worked. If you did work overtime, the program would calculate your pay at $58.56 (eight hours at $7.32 per hour) for the regular part of your shift plus an additional $11.73 multiplied by the number of overtime hours you worked. This processing thereby transforms your input into your desired output.

How do programmers handle bad inputs? In the problem statement, programmers also must describe what the program should do if the input data is nonsense (users do make mistakes). This part of the problem statement is referred to as **error handling**. The problem statement also includes a **testing plan** that lists specific input numbers the program would typically expect the user to enter. It then lists the precise output values that a perfect program will return for those input values. Later, in a testing process, programmers use the input and output data values from the testing plan to determine whether the program they've created works in the way it should. (We talk about the testing process later in the chapter.)

Does the testing plan cover every possible use of the program? The testing plan cannot list *every* input that the program could ever encounter. Instead, programmers work with users to identify the *categories* of inputs that will be encountered, find a typical example of each input category, and specify what kind of output must be generated. In the preceding parking garage example, the error-handling process would describe what the program would do if you happened to enter –8 (or any other nonsense character) for the number of hours you worked. The error handling would specify whether the program would return a negative value, ask you to reenter the input, or yell at you and shut down (well, maybe not that last option). We could expect three categories of inputs in the parking garage example:

1. The user might enter a negative number for hours worked that day.

2. The user might enter a positive number equal to or less than 8.

3. The user might enter a positive number greater than 8.

The testing plan would describe how the error will be managed or how the output will be generated for each of these input categories.

Is there a standard format for a problem statement? Most companies (and instructors) have their own format for documenting a problem statement. However, all problem statements include the same basic components: the data that is expected to be provided (inputs), the information that is expected to be produced (outputs), the rules for transforming the input into output (processing), an explanation of how the program will respond if users enter data that doesn't make sense (error handling), and a testing plan. Figure 10.4 shows a sample problem statement for our parking garage example.

FIGURE 10.4 The Complete Problem Statement for the Parking Garage Example

Program Goal:	To compute the total pay for a fixed number of hours worked at a parking garage.
Inputs:	Number of Hours Worked.................... a positive number
Outputs:	Total Pay Earned............................. a positive number
Process:	The Total Pay Earned is computed as $7.32 per hour for the first eight hours worked each day. Any hours worked beyond the first eight are calculated at $11.73 per hour.
Error Handling:	The input Number of Hours Worked must be a positive real number. If it is a negative number or other non-acceptable character, the program will force the user to re-enter the information.

Testing Plan:	Input	Output	Notes
	8	8*7.32	Testing positive input
	3	3*7.32	Testing positive input
	12	8*7.32 + 4*11.73	Testing an overtime input
	–6	Error message/ask user to re-enter value	Handling error

Making a Plan: Algorithm Development

Once programmers understand exactly what the program must do and have finalized the problem statement, they can begin developing a detailed **algorithm**, a set of specific, sequential steps that describe in natural language exactly what the computer program must do to complete its task. Let's look at some ways in which programmers design and test algorithms.

Do algorithms appear only in programming? Although the term *algorithms* may sound like it would fall only under the domain of computing, you design and execute algorithms, or problem-solving procedures, constantly in your daily life. For example, say you are planning your morning. You know you need to (1) get gas for your car, (2) swing past the café and pick up a mocha latté, and (3) stop by the bookstore and buy the textbook before your 9:00 a.m. accounting lecture. In what order will you accomplish all these tasks? How do you decide? Should you try to minimize the distance you'll travel or the time you'll spend driving? What happens if you forget your credit card?

Figure 10.5 presents an algorithm you could develop to make decisions about how to accomplish these tasks. This algorithm lays out a specific plan that encapsulates all of the choices you need to make in the course of completing a particular task and shows the specific sequence in which these tasks will occur. At any point in the morning, you could gather your current information (that is, your inputs)—"I have $20 and my Visa card, but the ATM machine is down"—and the algorithm will tell you *unambiguously* what your next step should be.

What are the limitations of algorithms? The deterministic nature of an algorithm is what enables us to describe it completely on a simple piece of paper. It is a series of steps that is completely known—at each point we know *exactly* what step to take next. However, not all problems can be described as a fixed sequence of predetermined steps; some involve random and unpredictable events. For example, although the program that computes your parking garage take-home pay each day works flawlessly, programs that predict the weather are often wrong because many random events (inputs) can change the outcomes (outputs).

DEVELOPING AN ALGORITHM: DECISION MAKING AND DESIGN

How do programmers develop an algorithm? By now you understand that when programmers develop an algorithm they convert the problem statement into a list of steps (or actions) the program will take. For simple problems, this list is straightforward—the program completes this action first, this action second, this action third, and so on. However, only very simple algorithms execute the same series of actions every time they run.

More complex problems involve choices and therefore cannot follow a sequential list of steps to generate the correct output. Instead, the list of steps created for complex problems includes **decision points**, or points at which the program must choose from an array of different actions based on

FIGURE 10.5

An algorithm you might use to plan your morning would include a number of steps that encapsulate all of the decisions you might need to make and show the specific sequence in which these steps will occur.

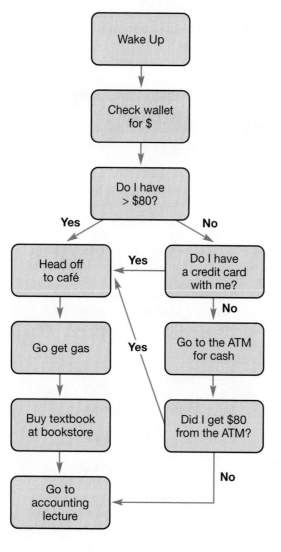

the value of its current inputs. Programmers therefore convert a problem into an algorithm by listing the sequence of actions that must be taken and recognizing the places where decisions must be made in this list.

So, in our parking garage example, if the number of hours you worked in a given day is eight or less, the program performs one simple calculation: it multiplies the number of hours worked by $7.32. However, if you worked more than eight hours in a day, the program takes a different path and performs a different calculation, shown in Figure 10.6.

What kinds of decision points are there? Two main types of decisions change the flow of an algorithm. One decision point that appears often in algorithms is a "fork in the road," or branch. Such decision points are called **binary decisions** because they can be answered in one of only two ways: as yes (true) or no (false). For example, the answer to the question, "Did you work at most eight hours today?" (Is number of hours worked ≤ 8 hours?), shown in Figure 10.6, is a binary decision because the answer can be only yes or no. The result of the decision determines which of the branch paths the algorithm will follow. If the answer is yes, the program will follow one sequence of steps; if the answer is no, it will follow a different path.

A second decision structure that often appears in algorithms is a repeating *loop*. In a **loop**, a question is asked and if the answer is yes, a set of actions is performed. Once the set of actions has been performed, the question is asked again (creating a loop). As long as the answer to the question is yes, the

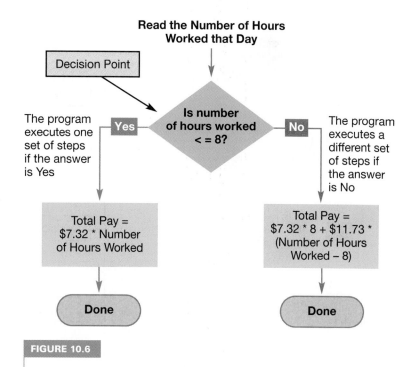

FIGURE 10.6

Decision points force the program to travel down one branch of the algorithm or another.

algorithm will continue to loop around and repeat the set of actions. When the answer to the question is no, the algorithm breaks free of the looping and moves on to the first step that follows the loop.

In our parking garage example, the algorithm would require a loop if you wanted to compute the total pay you earned in a full week of work rather than just in a single day. This is because for each day of the week, you would want to perform the same set of steps. Figure 10.7 shows how the idea

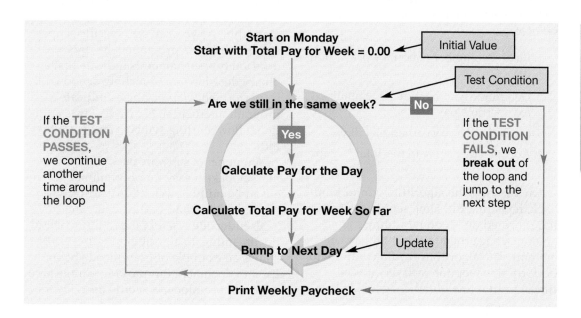

FIGURE 10.7

In this example of a loop, we stay in the loop until the test condition is no longer true. We then break free from the loop and move on to the next step in the algorithm outside of the loop.

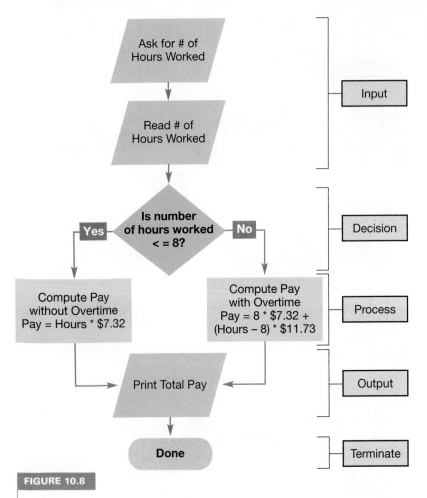

FIGURE 10.8

Programmers use flowcharts like this one to depict visually the flow of actions and decision points in their algorithms.

point the decision "Are we still in the same week?" becomes false. The program would stop and calculate the Total Pay for the entire week of work and print the weekly paycheck. As you can see, there are three important features to look for in a loop:

1. A beginning point (or **initial value**). In our example, the Total Pay for the week starts at an initial value of $0.00.

2. A set of actions that will be performed. In our example, the algorithm computes the daily pay each time it passes through the loop.

3. A check to see whether the loop is completed (or a **test condition**). In our example, the algorithm should run the loop seven times, no more and no less.

Note that almost every higher-level programming language supports both making binary yes/no decisions and handling repeating loops. **Control structures** is the general term used for keywords in a programming language that allow the programmer to control, or redirect, the flow of the program based on a decision.

How do programmers keep track of all these decision points and changes in flow in an algorithm? Programmers have a number of visual tools at their disposal to help them document the decision points and flow of their algorithm.

Flowcharts provide a visual representation of the patterns the algorithm comprises. Figure 10.8 presents an example of a flowchart used to depict the flow of an algorithm. As you can see, specific shape symbols indicate program behaviors and decision types. Diamonds indicate that a binary decision and branching action will be performed, and rectangles indicate a program instruction. Figure 10.9 lists additional flowcharting symbols and what they indicate.

A number of software packages on the market make it easy for programmers to create and modify flowcharts. Microsoft Visio is one popular flowcharting program.

Pseudocode is a text-based approach to documenting an algorithm. Figure 10.10 shows an example of pseudocode being used to document our parking garage algorithm. In pseudocode, words describe the

of looping would be useful in this part of our parking garage program. On Monday, the program would set the Total Pay to $0.00. It would then perform the following set of steps:

1. Read the number of hours worked that day.

2. Determine whether you have qualified for overtime pay.

3. Compute the pay earned that day.

4. Add that day's pay to the Total Pay for the week.

On Tuesday, the algorithm would loop back, repeating the same sequence of steps it performed on Monday, adding the amount you earned to the Total Pay amount. The algorithm would continue to perform this loop for each day (seven times) until it hits Monday again. At that

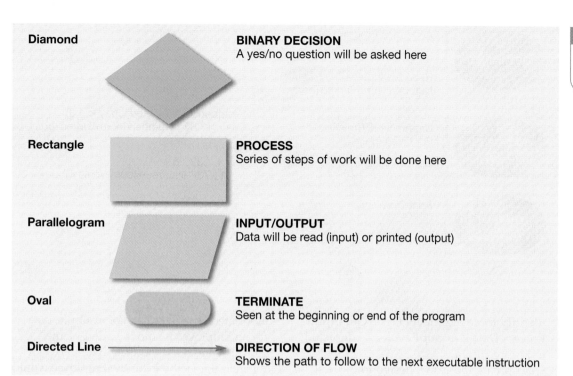

Diamond	**BINARY DECISION** A yes/no question will be asked here	
Rectangle	**PROCESS** Series of steps of work will be done here	
Parallelogram	**INPUT/OUTPUT** Data will be read (input) or printed (output)	
Oval	**TERMINATE** Seen at the beginning or end of the program	
Directed Line	**DIRECTION OF FLOW** Shows the path to follow to the next executable instruction	

FIGURE 10.9

Standard Symbols Used in Flowcharts

actions that the algorithm will take. Pseudocode is organized like an outline, with differing levels of indentation to indicate the flow of actions within the program. There is no standard set of vocabulary for pseudocode. Programmers use a combination of common words in their natural language and the special words they know are commands in the programming language they will be using.

How do programmers create algorithms for specific tasks? As we've discussed, it's difficult for human beings to force their problem-solving skills into the highly structured, detailed algorithms that computing machines require. Therefore, several different methodologies have been developed to support programmers, including *top-down design* and *object-oriented analysis*.

TOP-DOWN DESIGN

What is top-down design? **Top-down design** is a systematic approach in which a problem is broken down into a series of high-level tasks. In top-down design, programmers apply the same strategy repeatedly, breaking down each task into successively more detailed subtasks. They continue until they have a sequence of steps that are close to the types of commands allowed by the programming language they will use for coding. (Previous coding experience helps programmers know the appropriate level of detail to specify in the algorithm generated by top-down design.)

To understand more clearly how top-down design is used in programming, let's consider our parking garage example again. Initially, top-down design would

FIGURE 10.10

Pseudocode is a text-based approach programmers can use to document the flow of an algorithm. Looking at the algorithm in this outline format shows programmers both the actions and the information items that appear repeatedly in the algorithm. Note that the bold and underlining has been added for emphasis and is not part of the code.

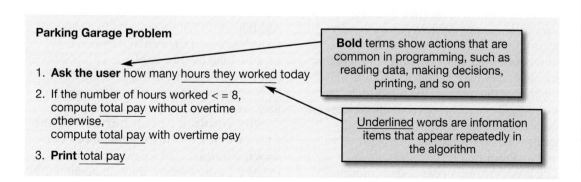

Parking Garage Problem

1. **Ask the user** how many hours they worked today
2. If the number of hours worked < = 8,
   compute total pay without overtime
   otherwise,
   compute total pay with overtime pay
3. **Print** total pay

Bold terms show actions that are common in programming, such as reading data, making decisions, printing, and so on

Underlined words are information items that appear repeatedly in the algorithm

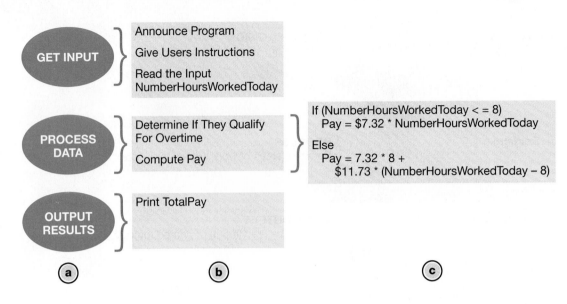

FIGURE 10.11

(a) In this figure, top-down design is applied to the highest level of task in our parking garage example. (b) Here, the tasks are further refined into subtasks. (c) Finally, the subtasks are refined into a sequence of instructions, or an algorithm.

GET INPUT
- Announce Program
- Give Users Instructions
- Read the Input NumberHoursWorkedToday

PROCESS DATA
- Determine If They Qualify For Overtime
- Compute Pay

If (NumberHoursWorkedToday < = 8)
    Pay = \$7.32 * NumberHoursWorkedToday
Else
    Pay = 7.32 * 8 +
        \$11.73 * (NumberHoursWorkedToday − 8)

OUTPUT RESULTS
- Print TotalPay

(a)　　(b)　　(c)

identify three high-level tasks: Get Input, Process Data, Output Results, as depicted in Figure 10.11a.

Applying top-down design to the first operation, Get Input, we'd produce the more detailed sequence of steps shown in Figure 10.11b: Announce Program, Give Users Instructions, Read the Input NumberHoursWorkedToday. When we try to refine each of these steps, we find that they are at the level of commands that most programming languages support (that is, they tell the computer to print and read statements). So, the operation Get Input has been converted to an algorithm.

Next, we move to the second high-level task, Process Data, and break it down into subtasks. In this case, we need to determine if overtime hours have been worked and compute the pay accordingly. We continue to apply top-down design on all tasks until we can no longer break tasks down into subtasks, as shown in Figure 10.11c.

OBJECT-ORIENTED ANALYSIS

What is object-oriented analysis? A very different approach to generating an algorithm is *object-oriented analysis*. With **object-oriented analysis**, programmers first identify all of the categories of inputs that are part of the problem the program is trying to solve. These categories are called **classes**. For example, the classes in our parking garage example might include a TimeCard and an Employee.

Classes are further defined by information (**data**) and actions (**methods** or **behaviors**)

associated with the class. For example, data for an Employee would include a Name, Address, and Social Security Number, whereas the methods for the Employee would be GoToWork(), LeaveWork(), or CollectPay(). Think of classes as nouns: persons, places, or things. Data describes classes, so it is characterized as an adjective, whereas methods are often characterized as verbs—the ways that the class acts and communicates with other classes. Figure 10.12 shows the data and methods the Employee class would contain.

In the object-oriented approach, programmers identify and define each class, as well as their data and methods. Programmers then determine how classes interact with each other. For example, when an Employee does GoToWork(), the Employee class must "talk" to the TimeCard and punch in for the day, setting the StartTime on the TimeCard.

Programmers may need to create several different examples of a class. Each of these is an **object**. In Figure 10.12, John Doe, Jane Doe, and Bill McGillicutty are each Employee objects, specific examples of the Employee class. Each object from a given class is described by the same pieces of data and has the same methods; for example, John, Jane, and Bill are all Employees and GoToWork, LeaveWork, and CollectPay. However, because John has one PayGrade (PayGrade 5) and Jane has another (PayGrade 10) and they all have different Social Security numbers, they are unique objects.

Why would a developer select the object-oriented approach over top-down design? Object-oriented analysis forces programmers to think in general terms about their problem, which tends to

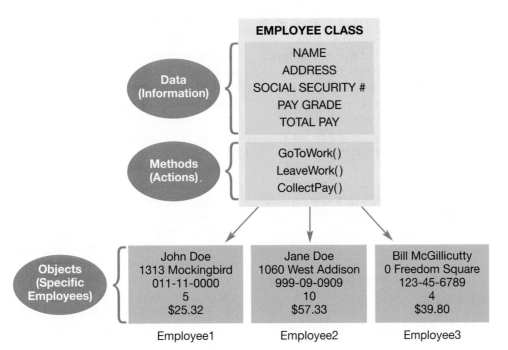

EMPLOYEE CLASS

Data (Information)
- NAME
- ADDRESS
- SOCIAL SECURITY #
- PAY GRADE
- TOTAL PAY

Methods (Actions)
- GoToWork( )
- LeaveWork( )
- CollectPay( )

Objects (Specific Employees)

| John Doe 1313 Mockingbird 011-11-0000 5 $25.32 | Jane Doe 1060 West Addison 999-09-0909 10 $57.33 | Bill McGillicutty 0 Freedom Square 123-45-6789 4 $39.80 |

Employee1 · Employee2 · Employee3

FIGURE 10.12

The Employee *class* includes the information (data) and actions (methods) that completely describe an Employee. It provides a blueprint for a programmer to build an Employee *object*. The objects are the actual employees, with real data.

lead to more general and reusable solutions. A very important aspect of object-oriented design is that it leads to **reusability**. Because object-oriented design generates a family of classes for each project, programmers can easily reuse existing classes from other projects, enabling them to produce new code quickly.

To take advantage of reuse, programmers must study the relationships between objects. Hierarchies of objects can be built quickly in object-oriented languages using the mechanism of *inheritance*. **Inheritance** means that a new class can automatically pick up all of the data and methods of an existing class, and then extend and customize those to fit its own specific needs.

The original class is called the **base class** and the new modified class is called the **derived class**. This is similar to making cookies. For example, you have a basic recipe for sugar cookies (base class: sugar cookies). However, in your family, some like chocolate-flavored sugar cookies (derived class: chocolate cookies) and some like almond-flavored sugar cookies (derived class: almond cookies). All the cookies share the same attributes with the basic sugar cookie. Instead of creating entirely new recipes for a chocolate cookie and an almond cookie, the two varieties inherit the basic sugar cookie recipe and then the recipe is customized to make chocolate- and almond-flavored cookies.

With the object-oriented approach, the majority of design time is spent in identifying the classes required to solve the problem, modeling them as data and methods, and thinking about what interactions they need to be able to have with each other. Constructing the algorithm becomes a process of enabling the objects to interact.

Coding: Speaking the Language of the Computer

Once programmers create an algorithm, they select the best programming language for the problem and then translate the algorithm into that language. Translating an algorithm into a programming language is the act of **coding**.

Although programming languages free programmers from having to think in binary (the 1s and 0s that computers understand), they force programmers to translate the ideas of the algorithm into a very precise format. Programming languages are very limited; they allow programmers to use only a few specific words and demand a very consistent structure.

How exactly do programmers move from algorithm to code? Once programmers have an algorithm, either in the form of a flowchart or as a series of pseudocode statements, they scan the algorithm and identify the key pieces of information it uses to make decisions. What steps are required in the calculation of new information? What is the exact sequence of the steps? Are there points where decisions have to be made? What kinds of decisions are made? Are there places where the same steps are repeated several times? Identifying the required information and the flow of how it will be changed by each step of the algorithm leads the programmer to begin converting the algorithm into computer code in a specific programming language.

CATEGORIES OF PROGRAMMING LANGUAGES

What exactly is a programming language? A programming language is a kind of "code" for the set of instructions the CPU knows how to perform. Computer programming languages use special words and strict rules to enable programmers to control the CPU without having to know all of its hardware details.

What kinds of programming languages are there? Programming languages are classified in several major groupings, sometimes referred to as generations. With each generation in language development, programmers have been relieved of more of the burden of keeping track of what the hardware requires. Programming is therefore becoming "easier" as languages continue to become more closely matched to how humans think about problems. Figure 10.13 shows small code samples of each generation of language.

What were the first programming languages? First-generation languages (1GLs) are the actual **machine languages** of a CPU, the sequence of bits—1s and 0s—that the CPU understands. Every CPU is designed with its own type of machine language, which CPU designers believe gives their CPU advantages in speed or ease of use over other processors.

Because machine language depends on the type of CPU, it is sometimes referred to as being *machine-dependent*. Although the first computer programmers had to be experts at machine language, it is very uncommon today for a programmer to program directly in machine language. However, no matter what programming language developers use, at some point it must be translated into machine language so that the computer can understand it.

How did designers make programming languages easier to use? Second-generation languages (2GLs) are also known as **assembly languages**. Although assembly languages are another low-level language like machine language, they are easier to work with than the sequence of 1s and 0s found in machine language. Assembly languages allow programmers to write their programs using a set of short, English-like commands that speak directly to the CPU and give the programmer very direct control of hardware resources.

Using a second-generation language, a programmer could use a command such as "ADD" to stand for addition or "R4" for the fourth register (or storage area) on the CPU. Thus, the assembly language statement "ADD R4, 5" would instruct the CPU to add five to the fourth memory storage location

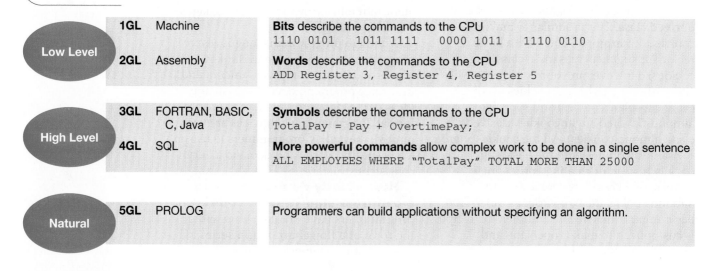

Low Level	1GL	Machine	**Bits** describe the commands to the CPU `1110 0101    1011 1111    0000 1011    1110 0110`
	2GL	Assembly	**Words** describe the commands to the CPU `ADD Register 3, Register 4, Register 5`
High Level	3GL	FORTRAN, BASIC, C, Java	**Symbols** describe the commands to the CPU `TotalPay = Pay + OvertimePay;`
	4GL	SQL	**More powerful commands** allow complex work to be done in a single sentence `ALL EMPLOYEES WHERE "TotalPay" TOTAL MORE THAN 25000`
Natural	5GL	PROLOG	Programmers can build applications without specifying an algorithm.

(register) on the CPU. In machine languages, the programmer would need to know that the bit pattern 1110 0000 1100 1101 tells the CPU to add five to the fourth register. As you can see, it's clear why second-generation languages were easier for programmers to work with than machine languages.

What kinds of languages do we use today? With **third-generation languages (3GLs)**, also called **high-level languages**, programmers are relieved of the burden of having to understand everything about the hardware of the computer to give it directions. 3GLs use symbols and commands to help programmers tell the computer what to do, making 3GL languages easier to read and remember. In addition, 3GLs allow programmers to name storage locations in memory with their own names so they are more meaningful to them. For example, a 3GL statement to add 5 to one of the storage locations of the CPU might read:

    TotalHoursWorked =
    TotalHoursWorked + 5

Most programming languages today are considered third generation. The list includes *BASIC, FORTRAN, COBOL, C, C++,* and *Java* to name only a few. We discuss these and other languages in more detail later in the chapter.

What languages use commands closer to our natural language? **Fourth-generation languages (4GLs)** work to continue this trend and make the commands that a programmer uses even closer to the natural language that we speak to each other. Many database query languages and report generators are 4GLs. Structured Query Language (SQL) is a database programming language that is an example of a 4GL. The following single SQL command would do a great deal of work, checking a huge table of data on the employees and building a new table showing all those employees who generated overtime by working more than eight hours in a day.

    SELECT ALL EMPLOYEES WHERE
    "TotalHours" TOTAL MORE THAN 8

But programmers always must work from algorithms, correct? **Fifth-generation languages (5GLs)** are considered the most "natural" of languages. With 5GLs, problems are presented as a series of facts or constraints instead of as a specific algorithm. The system of facts can then be queried, or asked questions. PRO-

LOG (PROgramming LOGic) is an example of a 5GL. A PROLOG program could be a list of family relationships and rules, like "Mike is Sally's brother. A brother and a sister have the same mother and father." After a huge collection of facts and rules has been collected, a user could ask for a list of all Mike's cousins, for example. PROLOG would find the answers by repeatedly applying the principles of logic instead of following a step-by-step algorithm that the programmer had provided.

Do programmers *have* to use a higher-level programming language to solve a problem with a computer? No, experienced programmers sometimes write a program directly in the CPU's assembly language. However, the main advantage of higher-level programming languages, such as C or Java, is that they allow programmers to think in terms of the problem they are solving rather than worrying about the internal design and specific instructions available for a given CPU. In addition, higher-level programming languages have the capability to produce a program easily that will run on both an Intel Pentium CPU and a Motorola G4 CPU. If programmers wrote directly in the assembly language for an Intel Pentium CPU, they would have to rewrite the program completely if they wanted it to run on an Apple Macintosh computer with a Motorola CPU. Thus, higher-level programming languages offer **portability**, the capability to move a completed solution easily from one type of computer to another.

CREATING CODE: WRITING THE PROGRAM

What happens first when writing a program? All of the inputs a program receives and all of the outputs the program produces need to be stored in the computer's memory, or RAM, while the program is running. Each input and each output item that the program will manipulate, also known as **variables**, will need to be announced early in the program so memory space can be set aside for them. A **variable declaration** tells the operating system that the program needs to allocate storage space in RAM. The following line of code is a variable declaration:

    int Day;

The Building Blocks of Programming Languages: Syntax, Keywords, Data Types, and Operators

Programming languages are evolving constantly. New languages emerge every year and existing languages change dramatically. Therefore, it would be very difficult and time consuming for programmers to learn every programming language. However, all languages have several common elements: rules of *syntax*, a set of *keywords*, a group of supported *data types*, and a set of allowed *operators*. By learning these four concepts, programmers can better approach any new language.

The transition from a well-designed algorithm to working code requires a clear understanding of the rules, or **syntax**, of the programming language being used. Syntax is an agreed-upon set of rules defining how a language must be structured. The English language has a syntax; it defines which symbols are words (for example, "poodle" is a word but "oodlep" is not) and in what order words and symbols (such as ; and ,) are allowed.

Likewise, all programming languages have a formal syntax that programmers must follow when creating code **statements**, sentences in a code. *Syntax errors* are violations of the strict, precise set of rules that define the language. Even misplacing a single comma or using a lowercase letter where a capital letter is required will generate a syntax error and make the program unusable.

Keywords are the set of specific words that have predefined meanings for a particular language. Keywords are used to translate the flow of the algorithm into the structured code of the programming language. For example, when the algorithm indicates that a binary decision must be made, the programmer translates that binary decision into the appropriate keyword from the language.

For example, in the programming language C++, the binary decision asking whether you worked enough hours to qualify for overtime pay would use the keywords **if else**. At this point in the code, the program can follow one of two paths: *if* you have indicated through your input that you have worked less than or equal to eight hours, it will take one path; if not (*else*), it will follow another. Figure 10.14 shows the binary decision in the algorithm and the lines of C++ code for this decision using the if else keywords.

Loops are translated from algorithm to code by using the appropriate keyword from the language as well. For example, in the programming language

Visual Basic, programmers use the keywords **For** and **Next** to implement a loop. After the keyword For, an input or output item is given a starting value. Then the statements in the body of the loop are executed. When the command Next is run, the program returns to the For statement and increments the value of the input or output item by 1. It then tests that the value is still inside the range given. If it is, the body of the loop is executed again. This continues until the value of the input or output item is outside the range listed. The loop is then ended and the statement that follows the loop is run. The following lines of Visual Basic code loop to sum the total pay for the entire week. In this statement the starting value of the input item Day is 1 and the program loops until Day equals 7:

```
For Day = 1 to 7
    TotalPay = TotalPay + Pay;
Next Day
```

Often, a quick overview of a language's keywords can reveal the unique focus of that language. For example, the language C++ includes the keywords "public," "private," and "protected," which indicate

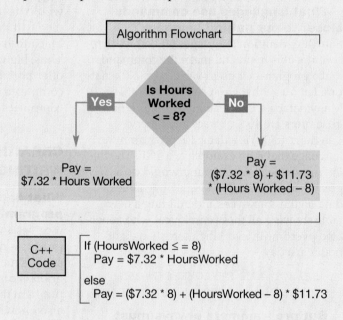

FIGURE 10.14

Here, the binary decision in the algorithm has been converted into C++ code.

that the language includes a mechanism for controlling security. Although people who are new to a language might not immediately understand how these keywords are used, examining the keywords of a language you are learning will often tell you what special features the language has and will help you ask important questions about it.

Each time programmers want to store data in their program, they must ask the operating system for storage space at a random access memory (RAM) location. **Data types** describe the *kind* of data that is being stored at the memory location. Each programming language has its own unique data types (although there is some degree of overlap among languages). For example, C++ includes data types representing integers, real numbers, characters, and Boolean (true/false) values. These C++ data types show up in code statements as *int* for integer, *float* for real numbers, *char* for characters, and *bool* for Boolean values.

Because it takes more room to store a real number such as 18,743.23 than it does to store the integer 1, programmers use data types in their code to indicate to the operating system how much memory it needs to allocate. Programmers must be familiar with all of the data types available in the language so that they can assign the most appropriate data type for each input and output value so as not to waste memory space.

Operators are the coding symbols that represent the fundamental actions of the language. Each programming language has its own set of operators. Many languages include common algebraic operators such as +,

−, *, / to represent the mathematical operations of addition, subtraction, multiplication, and division, respectively. The language called A Programmer's Language (APL) was specifically designed to solve mathematics problems. APL therefore includes the common mathematical operators, but it also includes the operators rho, sigma, and iota, each representing complex mathematical operations. Because it contains many unique operators, APL requires that programmers use a special keyboard when they input code, as shown in Figure 10.15.

Programming languages sometimes include other unique operators. For example, the C++ operator << is used to tell the computer to read data from the keyboard or from a file. The C++ operator && is used to tell the computer to check whether two statements are both true. "Is your weight greater than 120 AND less than 150?" is a question that requires the use of the && operator.

In the following C++ code, several operators are being used. The > operator checks whether the number of hours worked is larger than 0. The && operator checks that the number of hours worked is both positive AND less than or equal to 8 at the same time. If that happens, then the = operator sets the output Pay equal to the number of hours paid at $7.32 per hour:

```
if (Hours > 0 && Hours <= 8 )
    Pay = Hours * 7.32;
```

Knowing operators such as these, as well as the other common elements described earlier, helps programmers learn new programming languages.

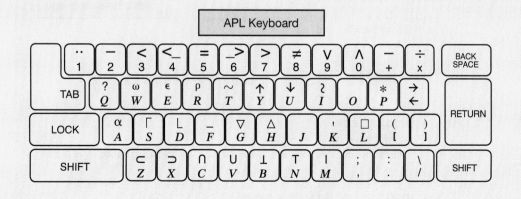

FIGURE 10.15

APL requires programmers to use a unique APL keyboard that includes the many specialized operators in the language.

This variable's name is Day. The "int" that precedes the Day variable indicates that this variable is always going to be an integer. This statement asks for enough RAM storage space to hold an integer. After the RAM space is found, it is reserved. As long as the program is running, these RAM cells will be saved for the Day variable; no other program can use that memory until the program ends. From that point on, when the program encounters the expression Day, it will access the memory cells it reserved as Day and find the integer stored there.

The following line of C++ code asks that a real number (represented by the keyword "float") be stored in RAM:

```
float TotalPay;
```

This line asks the operating system to find enough storage space for one real number.

Can programmers leave notes to themselves inside a program?
Programmers often insert **comments** (or **remarks**) into program code to explain the purpose of sections of code, to indicate the date they wrote the program, and to include other important information about the code so that fellow programmers can more easily understand and update it should the original programmer no longer be available. Comments are written into the code in plain English. Languages provide a special symbol

The green statements are **comments** that help programmers explain the code but are not C++ commands

The blue statements are C++ **keywords**, the set of special reserved words that define the language

The black statements are C++ **commands**, and must meet all the rules of that language

Step 1: Declare variables

Step 2: Create loop

Step 3: Collect input data

Step 4: Check for errors

Loop

Step 5: Process data

Step 6: Update variables

```cpp
#include <iostream>
using namespace std;

void
main()
{
    //Begin by asking for some variables to be stored in RAM

    float NumberHoursWorkedToday = 0.0;
    float Pay=0.0, TotalPay=0.0;
    int Day;

    //Set up a loop to ask the user how many hours they worked each day

    for( Day = 1; Day <= 7; Day++)
    {
        //Read the input data from the screen
        cout << " Enter the number of hours you worked on day " << Day << ": ";
        cin >> NumberHoursWorkedToday;

        //Check the input makes sense
        if ( NumberHoursWorkedToday < 0 )
        {
            //Wait a minute! We need to handle possible errors here.
            //Print a warning message to the user if they enter a negative value.

            cout << "You can't work negative hours! Try again :";
            cin >> NumberHoursWorkedToday;

        }

        if ( NumberHoursWorkedToday <= 8 )

            //Compute pay earned today at normal base rate
            Pay = NumberHoursWorkedToday * 7.32;

        else

            //Compute the pay earned using the overtime rule
            Pay = ( 8 * 7.32 ) * ( 11.73 * ( NumberHoursWorkedToday - 8) );

        // Update the total pay you have earned so far this week
        TotalPay = TotalPay + Pay;

    } // when we hit this brace, we bounce back up to the beginning of the loop

    //Now we're free from the loop! Let's print then go spend our paycheck!
    cout << " Your totalpay for this week comes to : " << TotalPay;

} // The program is done . |
```

or keyword to indicate that what follows is a comment, not part of the executable program. In C++, the symbol // at the beginning of a line indicates that the rest of the line is a comment. In Visual Basic, the keyword "REM," short for "REMark," does the same thing.

What would completed code for a program look like? Figure 10.16 presents a completed C++ program for our example parking garage problem. Each statement in a program is executed sequentially (that is, in order from the first statement to the last) unless the program encounters a keyword that changes the flow. In the figure, the program begins (Step 1) by declaring the variables needed to store the program's inputs and outputs in RAM. Next, the "for" keyword begins a looping pattern (Step 2). All of the steps between the very first bracket {and the last bracket} (shown in red for better identification) will be repeated seven times to gather the total pay for each day of the week.

The next section (Step 3) collects the input data from the user. The program then (Step 4) checks that the user entered a reasonable value (in this case, a positive number for hours worked) and, if needed, reads another input value. Now (Step 5) the program processes the data. If the user worked eight hours or less, he or she is paid at the rate of $7.32, whereas hours exceeding eight are paid at $11.73.

The final statement (Step 6) updates the value of the TotalPay variable. The last bracket } indicates the program has reached the end of

a loop. The program will repeat the loop to collect and process the information for the next day. When the seventh day of data has been processed, the Day variable will be bumped up to the next value, 8. The program then fails the test (Day <= 7 ?). At that point, the program exits the loop, prints out the results, and quits.

Are there ways in which programmers can make their code more useful for the future? One aspect of converting an algorithm into good code is the programmer's ability to design general code that can adapt easily to new settings. Sections of code that will be used repeatedly, with only slight modification, can be packaged together into reusable "containers" or components. These reusable components, depending on the language, are referred to as *functions, procedures, subroutines, modules,* or *packages.*

In our program, we could create a function that implements the overtime pay rule. As it stands in Figure 10.16, the code will work only in situations where the hourly pay is exactly $7.32 and the bonus pay is exactly $11.73. However, if we rewrote this part of the processing rules as a function, we could have code that would work for any base pay rate and any overtime rate. If the base pay rate or overtime rate changed, the function would use whichever values it was given as input to compute the output pay variable. Such a function, as shown in Figure 10.17, could be reused in many settings, without changing any of the code.

FIGURE 10.17

A function can be reused in many different settings.

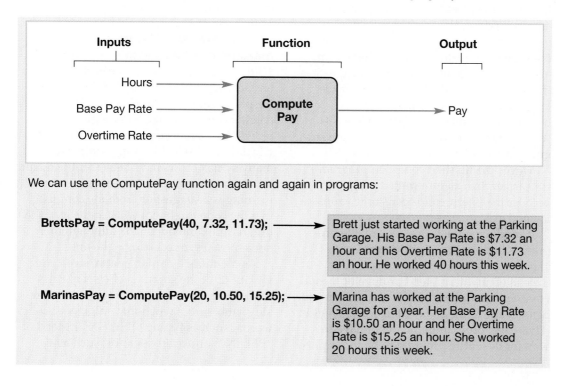

We can use the ComputePay function again and again in programs:

BrettsPay = ComputePay(40, 7.32, 11.73); ⟶ Brett just started working at the Parking Garage. His Base Pay Rate is $7.32 an hour and his Overtime Rate is $11.73 an hour. He worked 40 hours this week.

MarinasPay = ComputePay(20, 10.50, 15.25); ⟶ Marina has worked at the Parking Garage for a year. Her Base Pay Rate is $10.50 an hour and her Overtime Rate is $15.25 an hour. She worked 20 hours this week.

COMPILATION

How does a programmer move from code in a programming language to the 1s and 0s the CPU can understand? Compilation is the process by which code is converted into machine language, the language the CPU can understand. The **compiler** is the program that understands both the syntax of the programming language and the exact structure of the CPU and its machine language. It can "read" the **source code**—the instructions programmers have written in the higher-level language—and translate the source code directly into machine language—the binary patterns that will execute commands on the CPU.

Each programming language has its own compiler. In addition, separate versions of the compiler are required to compile code that will run on each different type of processor. One version of the compiler would create finished programs for a Motorola G4 processor and another version of the compiler would create programs for an Intel Pentium CPU.

At this stage, programmers finally have produced an **executable program**, the binary sequence that instructs the CPU to run their code. Executable programs cannot be read by human eyes because they are pure binary codes. They are stored as *.exe or *.com files on Windows systems.

Does every programming language have a compiler? Some programming languages do not have a compiler but use an *interpreter* instead. An **interpreter** translates the source code into an intermediate form, line by line. Each line is then executed as it is translated. The compilation process takes longer than the interpretation process because in compilation, *all* of the lines of source code are translated into machine language before any lines are executed. However, the finished compiled program runs faster than an interpreted program because the interpreter is constantly translating and executing as it goes.

If producing the fastest executable program is important, programmers would choose a language that uses a compiler instead of an interpreter. For developmental environments where a lot of changes are still being made to the code, interpreters have an advantage: programmers do not have to wait for the entire program to be recompiled each time they make a change. With interpreters, programmers can immediately see the results of their program changes as they are making them in the code.

CODING TOOLS: INTEGRATED DEVELOPMENT ENVIRONMENTS

Are there any tools that make the coding process easier? Modern programming is supported with a collection of tools to make the writing and testing of software easier. Compiler products feature an **integrated development environment (IDE)**, a developmental tool that helps programmers write, compile, and test their programs. As is the case with compilers, every language has its own specific IDE. Figure 10.18 shows the IDE for Microsoft Visual C++.

How does an IDE help programmers when they are typing in the code? The IDE includes tools that support programmers at every step of the coding process. **Code editing** is the step in which programmers actually type the code into the computer. IDEs include an **editor**, a special tool that helps programmers as they enter the code, highlighting keywords and alerting them to typos. Modern IDE editors also automatically indent the code correctly, aligning sections of code appropriately, and color-code comments to remind programmers that these lines will not be executed as code. In addition, IDEs provide help files that document and provide examples of the proper use of keywords and operators.

How does the IDE help programmers after code editing is finished? Editing is complete when the entire program has been keyed into the editor. At that time, the programmer clicks a button in the IDE and the compilation process begins. A pop-up window shows the compilation progress, which line is currently being compiled, how many syntax errors have been identified, and how many warnings have been generated. A warning is a suggestion from the compiler that the code might not work in the way the programmer intended it to, although there is not a formal syntax error on the line.

As mentioned earlier, **syntax errors** are violations of the strict, precise set of rules that define the language. Programmers create syntax errors when they misspell keywords (such as typing "BEEGIN" instead of "BEGIN") or use an operator (such as +)

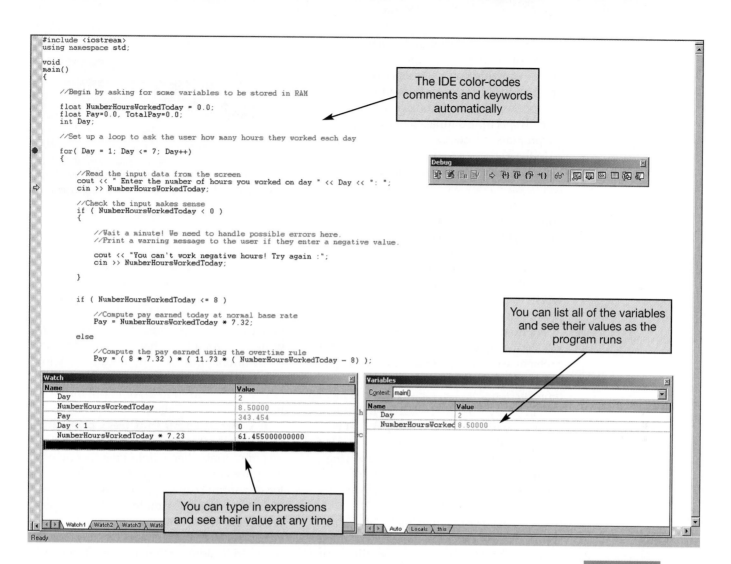

```
#include <iostream>
using namespace std;

void
main()
{
    //Begin by asking for some variables to be stored in RAM

    float NumberHoursWorkedToday = 0.0;
    float Pay=0.0, TotalPay=0.0;
    int Day;

    //Set up a loop to ask the user how many hours they worked each day

    for( Day = 1; Day <= 7; Day++)
    {
        //Read the input data from the screen
        cout << " Enter the number of hours you worked on day " << Day << ": ";
        cin >> NumberHoursWorkedToday;

        //Check the input makes sense
        if ( NumberHoursWorkedToday < 0 )
        {

            //Wait a minute! We need to handle possible errors here.
            //Print a warning message to the user if they enter a negative value.

            cout << "You can't work negative hours! Try again :";
            cin >> NumberHoursWorkedToday;

        }


        if ( NumberHoursWorkedToday <= 8 )

            //Compute pay earned today at normal base rate
            Pay = NumberHoursWorkedToday * 7.32;

        else

            //Compute the pay earned using the overtime rule
            Pay = ( 8 * 7.32 ) * ( 11.73 * ( NumberHoursWorkedToday - 8 ) );
```

The IDE color-codes comments and keywords automatically

Debug

You can list all of the variables and see their values as the program runs

Watch

Name	Value
Day	2
NumberHoursWorkedToday	8.50000
Pay	343.454
Day < 1	0
NumberHoursWorkedToday * 7.23	61.455000000000

Watch1 Watch2 Watch3 Watc

Ready

Variables

Context: main()

Name	Value
Day	2
NumberHoursWorked	8.50000

Auto Locals this

You can type in expressions and see their value at any time

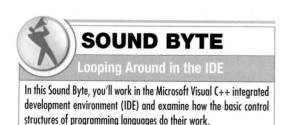
incorrectly (such as typing x = y ++ 2 instead of x = y + 2). Once compilation is finished, the IDE presents all of the syntax errors in one list on the screen. The programmer can then click any item in the list to see a detailed explanation of the type of error. By double-clicking an item in the list, the editor jumps to the line of code that contains the error, enabling the programmer to quickly repair syntax errors.

Debugging: Getting Rid of Errors

Once the program compiles without syntax errors, it has met all of the syntax rules of the language. However, this doesn't mean that the program behaves in a logical way or that it appropriately addresses the task the algorithm described. If programmers made errors in the strategy used in the algorithm or in how they translated the algorithm to code, problems will occur. The process of running the program over and over to find errors and to make sure the program behaves in the way it should is **debugging**.

How do programmers know whether there is anything wrong with their program? At this point in the process, the testing plan that was documented as part of the problem statement becomes very important to programmers. As

FIGURE 10.18

The IDE for Microsoft Visual C++ helps when the programmer is entering the code and when logical errors are found.

you'll recall from earlier in the chapter, the testing plan clearly lists input and output values, showing how the users expect the program to behave in each input situation. It is important that the testing plan contains enough specific examples that every part of the program is tested.

In the parking garage problem, we want to make sure the program calculates the correct pay for a day when you worked less than or equal to eight hours and a day when you worked more than eight hours. Each of these input values forces the program to make different decisions in its processing path, the sequence of steps that turns inputs into outputs. To be certain the program works as intended, programmers try every possible path.

For example, once we can successfully compile the example code for the parking garage problem, we can begin to use our testing plan. The testing plan indicates that an input of 3 for NumberHoursWorkedToday must produce an output of Pay = 3 * \$7.32 = \$21.96. In testing, we run the program and make sure that with an input value of 3, the output value is \$21.96. To check that the processing path involving overtime is correct, we input a value of 12 hours. That input must produce Pay = 8 * \$7.32 + (12 − 8) * \$11.73 = \$105.48.

A complete testing plan includes sample inputs that exercise all of the error handling required as well as all of the processing paths. Therefore, we would also want to check how the program behaves when NumberHoursWorkedToday is entered as −2.

If the testing plan reveals errors, why does the program compile? The compiler is itself a program. It cannot think through code or decide whether what the programmer wrote seems logical. It only can make sure the specific rules of the language are followed, that all of the keywords are spelled correctly, and that the operators being used are meaningful to that language.

For example, if in the parking garage problem we happened to type in the if statement as:

```
if (NumberHoursWorkedToday > 88)
    //Use the Overtime Pay rule
```

instead of

```
if (NumberHoursWorkedToday > 8)
    //Use the Overtime Pay rule
```

the compiler would not see a problem. It doesn't seem strange to the compiler that

you only get overtime after working 88 hours a day. These kinds of errors in the problem logic are only caught when the program executes and so are referred to as **runtime (or logic) errors**. Runtime errors can happen in many different ways. It is very easy for programmers to accidentally write code for a loop that loops one time too many or one time too few. It is also easy for programmers to forget to update a variable (an input or output item) or to put instructions in the wrong place.

Are there tools that help programmers find runtime errors? Most IDEs include a tool called a **debugger** that helps programmers dissect a program as it runs to locate runtime errors. The debugger pauses the program as it is running and allows programmers to examine the values of all the variables. The programmers can then run the program in slow motion, moving it forward just one line at a time. Stepping through the program enables programmers to see exactly the sequence of steps being executed and the outcome of each calculation in the code. They can then isolate the exact place in which a runtime error occurs, correct the error, and recompile the program.

Finishing the Project: Testing and Documentation

Once debugging has detected all of the runtime errors in the code, it is time for users to test the program. This process is called internal testing. In internal testing, a group within the software company uses the program in every way it can imagine—both as it was intended to be used and in ways only new users may think up. The internal testing group makes sure the program behaves as described in the original testing plan. Any differences in how the program responds are reported back to the programming team, which makes the final revisions and updates to the code.

The next round of testing is external testing. In this testing round, the intended users must work with the software to determine whether it matches their original vision.

What other testing does the code undergo? Before its commercial release, software is often provided at a reduced cost or no cost in **beta version** to certain test sites or to interested users. By providing users with a beta version of software, programmers can collect information about the remaining errors in the code and make a final round of revisions before officially releasing the program.

What happens if problems are found after beta testing? Often, users discover problems in the program after its commercial release. These problems are addressed with the publication of **software updates** or **service packs**. Users can download these software modules to repair errors identified in the program code. For example, the Windows XP operating system had a major revision released as Service Pack 2 that added many new security features and updates.

After testing, is the project finished? Once testing is completed, the work of **documentation** still exists. At this point, technical writers are responsible for creating internal documentation for the program, including describing the development and technical details, how the code works, and how the user interacts with the program. In addition, the technical publishing department produces all of the necessary user manuals that will be distributed to the program users. User training begins once the software is distributed. Software trainers work as instructors who take the software to the user community and teach them how to use it efficiently.

Programming Languages: Many Languages for Many Projects

In any programming endeavor, programmers want to create a solution that meets several competing objectives. They want the software to run quickly and reliably and to be simple to expand later when the demands on the system change. They also want it to be completed on time, for minimal cost, and to make the smallest possible requirements on system resources—the storage space required or the RAM utilized.

Because it will always be difficult to balance these conflicting goals, a wide variety of programming languages has been developed. Earlier in the chapter, you learned about the five main categories, or generations, of programming languages. In this section, we discuss the specific programming languages that are members of these different generations. Although programming languages often share many common characteristics, each language has specific traits that allow it to be the best fit for certain types of projects. The ability to understand enough about each language to match it to the appropriate style of problem is a very powerful skill for programmers to have.

What languages are popular in the market today? There are far too many languages for one person to become expert at them all, but understanding the range of languages and how they relate to one another is very useful. One quick way to determine which languages are popular is to examine the classified ads for programmers in the newspaper. At the moment, in-demand languages include C, C++, Java, and knowledge of Active Server Pages (ASP). In specific industries, certain languages tend to dominate the work. In the banking and insurance industries, for example, the programming language COBOL is still common, although it is not typically used in most other industries anymore.

How do I know which language to study first? A good introductory programming course will emphasize many skills and techniques that will carry over from one language to another. You should find a course that includes an emphasis on design, algorithm development, debugging techniques, and project management. All of these aspects of programming will help you in any language environment. **Pascal** is the only modern language that was specifically designed as a teaching language, but it is no longer often taught at the college level. Many colleges and universities have opted to begin students with Java or C++.

How does anyone learn so many languages? Professional programmers can work in a great number of different languages.

BITS AND BYTES

Many Languages on Display

At the site **www.99-bottles-of-beer.net**, you can find a simple program that displays the lyrics to the well-known song *99 Bottles of Beer on the Wall*. If you have ever sat through round after round of this song on a long school bus trip, you know it is very repetitive. That means the code to write this song can take advantage of looping statements. At this site, the program is presented in more than 800 different languages. Take a quick tour and see how much variety there is in programming!

They become proficient at learning new languages because they have become familiar with the basic components discussed in this chapter's Dig Deeper that are common to all languages: syntax, keywords, operators, and data types. The Bits and Bytes piece "Many Languages on Display" directs you to a site that displays an old song in over 800 different languages.

SELECTING THE RIGHT LANGUAGE

How do programmers know which language to select for a specific project? There are several considerations a programming team makes before selecting the language it will use for a specific project:

- **Space available**. Not all languages take up the same amount of space. Therefore, the target language should be well matched to the amount of space available for the final program. If the program will be embedded in a chip for use in a toaster, it is important the language chosen is very space efficient.

- **Speed required**. Similarly, some projects require a focus on speed rather than size. Some languages can execute faster than others. Therefore, some projects require the selection of a language that can produce code that executes in the fastest possible time. Although poorly written code will execute inefficiently in any language, it is still true that some languages produce faster code than others.

- **Organizational resources available**. Other considerations for managers are

the resources available in their group. Selecting a language that is easy to use and easy to maintain if there is a turnover in programmers is often an important consideration. Managers also may factor in the existing pool of talent available for the project. Having to train five programmers in a new language to tackle a project would have significant disadvantages over allowing them to work in a familiar language.

- **Type of target application**. Certain languages are customized to support a specific environment. Knowing which languages are most commonly used for which environments can be a helpful guide.

WINDOWS APPLICATIONS

What languages do programmers use if they want to build a Windows application? Software programs that run under the Windows operating system are very popular. These programs often have a number of common features—scroll bars, title bars, text boxes, buttons, and expanding/collapsing menus, to name a few. Several languages include customized controls that enable programmers to include these features in their programs easily. In these languages, programmers can simply use the mouse to lay out on the screen where the scroll bars and buttons will be in the application. The code needed to explain this to the computer is then written automatically when the programmer says the layout is complete. This is referred to as **visual programming**, and it helps programmers produce a final application much more quickly. In this section we'll discuss a few languages that are used to develop Windows applications and that take advantage of visual programming.

ACTIVE HELPDESK

Selecting the Right Programming Language

In this Active Helpdesk call, you'll play the role of a Helpdesk staffer, fielding calls about how programmers select the right programming language for a specific task and what the most popular Windows and Web applications are.

Visual Basic

What if programmers want to have a model of their program before it's fully developed? Earlier in the chapter, you read about how information systems are developed through the system development life cycle. Although the SDLC has been around for quite some time, it doesn't necessarily work for all environments and instances. Programmers often like to build a **prototype**, or small model, of their program at the beginning of a large project.

Although the entire project won't be finished for several months, it can be useful to have a simple shell of what the final program will look like to help with design. Prototyping is a form of **rapid application development (RAD)**, which is an alternative to the waterfall approach of systems development described at the beginning of the chapter. Instead of developing detailed system documents before the production of the system, developers create a prototype first and they generate system documents as they use and remodel the product.

Prototypes for Windows applications are often coded in **Microsoft Visual Basic (VB)**, which is a powerful programming language used to build a wide range of Windows applications. The strengths of VB include a simple, quick interface that is easy for a programmer to learn and use. It has grown from its roots in the language BASIC to become a sophisticated and full-featured object-oriented language. It is often used in the creation of graphical user interfaces for Windows.

The current version of Visual Basic is named VB.NET (pronounced "vee bee dot net"). VB.NET is very similar to VB version 6.0 if you are programming applications that do not interact with the Internet. However, for building software that will exchange information across the Internet with many computers or other Internet-aware devices, VB.NET is a much better development language (see Figure 10.19).

How does the Microsoft .NET Framework help programmers? The .NET environment is designed to enable Web sites to talk to each other easily. Too

FIGURE 10.19

Microsoft VB.NET supports visual programming by allowing the drag and drop of objects directly to build the application.

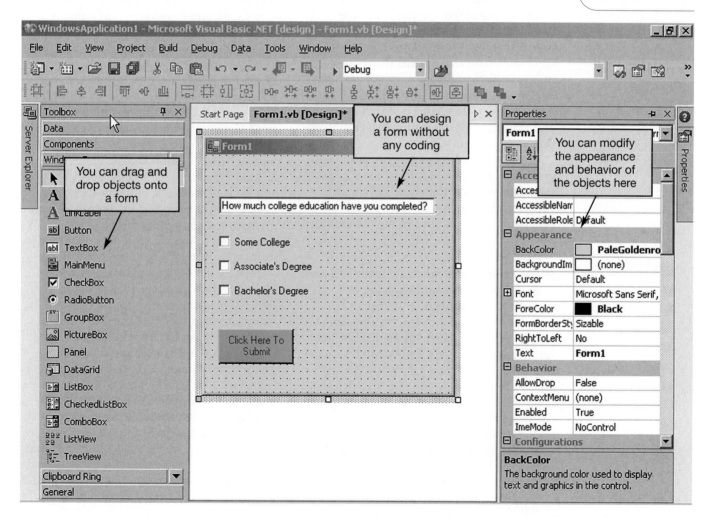

BITS AND BYTES

Cup of Java, Anyone?

The word *Java* is slang for coffee (a substance programmers use heavily to meet project deadlines), and there are many Java puns based on this slang. *JavaBeans*, for example, are tiny prewritten modules of code programmers can use to add functionality to their programs quickly. Java is also an island in Indonesia. One of the most popular sites for the exchange of ideas and code samples for Java programmers is **www.gamelan.com**. *Gamelan* is the Javanese word for an orchestra comprised mainly of instruments such as gongs, metal chimes, and xylophones. Computer programmers seem to love odd connections!

often, computer systems cannot exchange information. It might be because they have different operating systems or because they use different rules for the packaging of data. The .NET Framework introduces a standard way for software to interact through Web services. *Web services* are programs that a Web site uses to make information available to other Web sites. For example, your Web site could use the Google Web service to search for information or to check the spelling of a word. The Google Web service returns the requested information to your program in a standard package that you then decode. Instead of a human being submitting a search to Google and reading over the results, programs can now do that themselves.

The power of .NET and Web services will grow as more companies make some or all of their data available this way. The VB.NET programming tool has many supports for the programmer interested in using Web services.

C and C++

What languages do programmers use if the problem requires a lot of "number crunching"? A Windows application that demands raw processing power because there are difficult repetitive numerical calculations is most often a candidate for C or C++. Several companies sell C/C++ compilers equipped with a design environment that makes Windows programming as visual as with VB.

C, the predecessor of C++, was developed originally for system programmers. It was defined by Brian Kernighan and Dennis Ritchie of AT&T Bell Laboratories in 1978 as a

language that would make accessing the operating system easier. It provides higher-level programming language features (such as if statements and for loops) but still allows programmers to manipulate the system memory and CPU registers directly. This mix of high- and low-level access makes C very attractive to "power" programmers. Most modern operating systems (Windows XP, Mac OS X, and Linux) have been written in C.

C++ takes C to the next level. Bjarne Stroustrup, the developer of C++, used all of the same symbols and keywords as C, but extended the language with additional keywords, better security, and more support for the reuse of existing code through object-oriented design.

Neither C nor C++ was intended as a teaching language. The notation and compactness of the languages make them relatively difficult to master. They are in demand in industry, however, because C/C++ can produce fast-running code that uses a small amount of memory. Programmers often choose to learn C/C++ because their basic components (operators, data types, and keywords) are common to many other languages.

Java

What language do programmers use for applications that need to collect information from networked computers? Say a program that an insurance company runs each night needs to communicate with networked computers in many offices around the country, collect the policy changes and updates from that day's business, and update the company's main records. The programming team writing this program would want to use a language that already provides support for network communications.

Java would be a good choice. Sun Microsystems introduced Java in the early 1990s. It quickly became popular because its object-oriented model enables Java programmers to benefit from its large set of existing classes. For example, a Java programmer could begin to use the existing "network connection" class with very little attention to the details of how that code itself was implemented. Classes exist for many graphical objects and network objects. Microsoft has since released a language that competes with Java named C# (pronounced "sea sharp"). An attractive feature of Java is

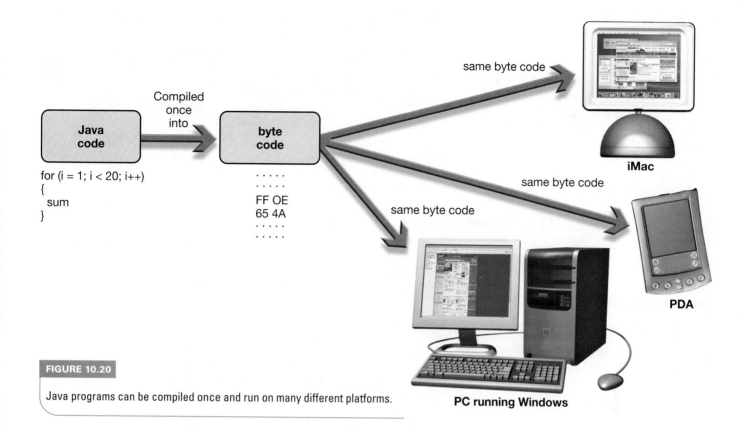

FIGURE 10.20

Java programs can be compiled once and run on many different platforms.

Labels within figure:

Java code

```
for (i = 1; i < 20; i++)
{
  sum
}
```

Compiled once into

byte code

```
. . . . .
. . . . .
FF OE
65 4A
. . . . .
. . . . .
```

same byte code

iMac

same byte code

PDA

same byte code

PC running Windows

---

that it is architecture neutral. This means that Java code needs to be compiled only once and it can run on many CPUs (see Figure 10.20). The Java program does not care what CPU, operating system, or user interface is running on the machine where it lands. This is possible because the target computer runs a Java Virtual Machine (VM), software that can explain to the Java program how to function on any specific system. There is a Java VM installed with Microsoft Internet Explorer, for example, which allows Internet Explorer to execute any **Java applets** (small Java-based programs) it encounters on the Internet. Although Java code does not perform as fast as C++, the

advantage of needing to compile only once before it can be distributed to any system is very important.

WEB APPLICATIONS: HTML/XHTML AND BEYOND

What is the most basic language for developing Web applications? A document that will be presented on the Web must be written using special symbols called *tags*. These markers control how a browser will display the text. Figure 10.21 shows several examples of these tags and their effect on the display of text. The tags are examples of

FIGURE 10.21 HTML/XHTML Tags and Displays

HTML/XHMTL TAG	SAMPLE HTML/XHTML CODE	DISPLAYED TEXT
Bold	\READ ME\	**READ ME**
Italics	\<i>italicized words\</i>	*italicized words*
Link (or anchor)	\<a href = "http://www.amazon.com"> Read more books!\</a>	<u>Read more books!</u>

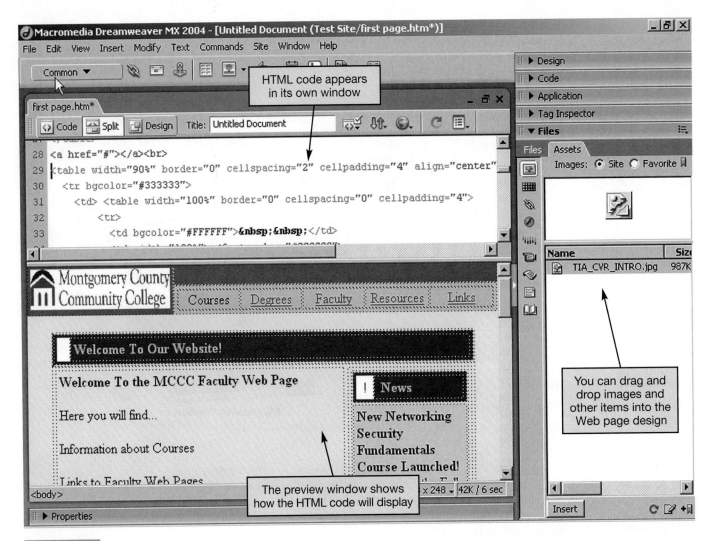

FIGURE 10.22

Macromedia Dreamweaver is a popular tool for creating Web pages.

HTML/XHTML, the Hypertext Markup Language/Extensible Hypertext Markup Language. Although HTML/XHTML knowledge is required to program for the Web, it is not itself a programming language. HTML/XHTML is just a series of tags that modify the display of text. HTML was the original standard defining these tags. XHTML is a newer standard that corrects some of the inconsistency problems found in HTML. For example, XHTML forces tags to always be used in pairs and makes sure that all tags are typed in lower case.

Many good HTML/XHTML tutorials are available on the Web at sites such as **www.learnthenet.com** and **www.webmonkey.com**. These sites include lists of the major HTML tags that can be used to create HTML documents.

Are there tools that help programmers write in HTML/XHTML? Several different programs are available to assist in the generation of HTML/XHTML. Macromedia Dreamweaver and Microsoft FrontPage present Web page designers with an interface that is similar to a word processor. Web designers can place text, images, and hyperlinks freely, and the corresponding HTML/XHTML tags are inserted automatically, as shown in Figure 10.22. For simple, static (nonchanging) Web pages, no programming is required.

JavaScript and VBScript

Which programming languages do programmers use to make complex Web pages? To make their Web pages more visually appealing and interactive, programmers include *JavaScript* code. **JavaScript** is a programming language often used to add interactivity to Web pages. JavaScript is not as full-featured as Java, but its syntax, keywords, data types, and operators are a subset of Java's. In

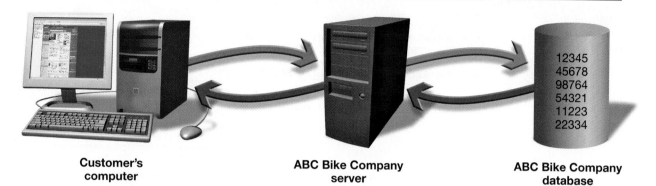

STEP 1: A customer clicks on an option to see all the red bikes on ABC Bike Company's Web page. The request travels to the ABC Bike Company's server.

STEP 2: The ABC Bike Company's server sends a request to its database computer to search for all red bikes.

STEP 3: The database computer returns a list of all red bikes.

Customer's computer

ABC Bike Company server

ABC Bike Company database

12345
45678
98764
54321
11223
22334

The ABC Bike Company's server uses an ASP program to write the HTML page displaying the red bike info. The page is sent to the customer, where it appears on his or her screen.

addition, JavaScript has a set of classes that represent the objects often used on Web pages: buttons, check boxes, and drop-down lists.

The JavaScript button class, for example, describes a button with a name and a type (whether it is a regular button or a Submit or Reset button). The language includes behaviors such as click() and can respond to user actions. For example, when a user moves his or her mouse over a button and pushes down to select it, the button "knows" the user is there and jumps in and performs a special action (such as playing a sound).

Often, programmers more familiar with Visual Basic than Java or C++ will use *VBScript* to introduce dynamic decision making into Web pages. **VBScript** is a subset of Visual Basic and is also used to introduce interactivity to a Web page.

ASP and JSP

How are interactive Web pages built?
To build Web sites with interactive capabilities, programmers use **Active Server Pages (ASP)** or **Java Server Pages (JSP)** to adapt the HTML/XHTML page to the user's selections. The ASP environment is used to translate the user's information into a request for information from the company's main computer, often using a database query language such as SQL. More ASP or JSP code controls the automatic writing of the custom HTML/XHTML page that is returned to the user's computer.

What does additional programming bring to my Web page? The most advanced Web pages interact with the user, collecting information and then customizing what they present based on the user's feedback. For example, as shown in Figure 10.23, an online store's page will collect a customer bicycle inquiry and then ask the company's main server for a list of red bicycles sold by the company. An ASP program then creates a

FIGURE 10.23

An online store is an example of the three-tier client/server type of Internet application.

BITS AND BYTES

How Does a Programmer Write Code for Everyday Appliances?

Programming code exists inside many of the appliances and devices in modern life. Washing machines make decisions on temperature and agitation time based on the types of stains in the laundry. Toasters include a microchip to decide when the toast is perfectly done. These are examples of embedded applications, very small software programs that are tucked away inside an appliance, automobile, or other device. The types of programs that are used in toasters or washing machines need to be very efficient and compact. They have no need for graphics systems or for networking. Embedded code is often written in C/C++ and then compiled into assembly language. Using assembly language, a programmer can fine-tune the use of registers and memory so that the final program is very efficient.

FIGURE 10.24

(a) An ASP program can write (b) HTML/XHTML code as its output. (c) The HTML/XHTML page it writes would show up in a browser.

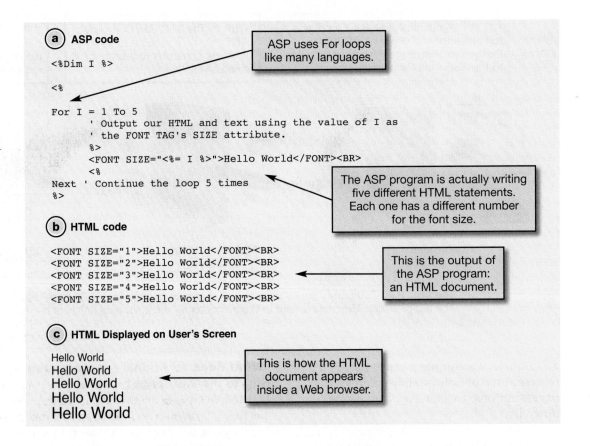

(a) ASP code

> *ASP uses For loops like many languages.*

```
<%Dim I %>

<%

For I = 1 To 5
    ' Output our HTML and text using the value of I as
    ' the FONT TAG's SIZE attribute.
    %>
    <FONT SIZE="<%= I %>">Hello World</FONT><BR>
    <%
Next ' Continue the loop 5 times
%>
```

> *The ASP program is actually writing five different HTML statements. Each one has a different number for the font size.*

(b) HTML code

```
<FONT SIZE="1">Hello World</FONT><BR>
<FONT SIZE="2">Hello World</FONT><BR>
<FONT SIZE="3">Hello World</FONT><BR>
<FONT SIZE="4">Hello World</FONT><BR>
<FONT SIZE="5">Hello World</FONT><BR>
```

> *This is the output of the ASP program: an HTML document.*

(c) HTML Displayed on User's Screen

Hello World
Hello World
Hello World
Hello World
Hello World

> *This is how the HTML document appears inside a Web browser.*

new HTML/XHTML page and delivers that to the user's browser, telling the customer what red bicycles (including details such as model and size) are currently sold by ABC.

Thus, ASP programs can have HTML/XHTML code as their output. They use what the user has told them from the list boxes, check boxes, and buttons on the page to make decisions. Based on those results, the ASP program decides what HTML/XHTML to write. A small example of ASP writing its own HTML/XHTML code is shown in Figure 10.24.

Flash and XML

What if a programmer wants to create a Web page that includes sophisticated animation? Many Web sites feature elaborate animations that interact with visitors. These sites include buttons and hyperlinks along with animation effects. These components can be designed with **Macromedia Flash**, a software product for developing Web-based multimedia. Flash includes its own programming language named ActionScript, which is very similar to JavaScript in its selection of keywords, operators, and classes.

Is HTML/XHTML the only markup language for the Web? When Web sites communicate with humans, HTML/XHTML works well because the formatting it controls is important. People respond immediately to the visual styling of textual information—its layout, color, size, and font design all help to transfer the message off the page to the reader. When computers want to communicate with each other, however, all of these qualities just interfere. **Extensible Markup Language (XML)** enables designers to define their own data-based tags, making it much easier for a Web site to transfer the key information on its page to another site.

Without XML, a Web site that wanted to look up current stock pricing information at another site would have to retrieve the HTML/XHTML page, then sort through the formatting information, and try to recognize which text on the page identified the data needed. With XML, groups can agree on standard systems of tags that represent important data elements. For example, the XML tag <stock> </stock> might delimit key stock quote information. Mathematicians have created a standardized set of XML tags

FIGURE 10.25 **Popular Programming Languages**

Programming Language	Features	Typical Setting
C/C++	Can create compact code that executes quickly Provides high- and low-level access	Industrial applications including banking and engineering
Flash ActionScript	Is similar in syntax to JavaScript but customized for the Flash animation environment	Used for control of Flash animations
Java	Is architecture neutral Is object-oriented	Used for creation of applets that can be delivered over the Web
JavaScript	Is similar in syntax to Java Has classes representing buttons, drop-down lists, and other Web page components	Creates code that lives on the client machine and supports interaction on Web pages
VBScript	Is similar in syntax to VB Has classes representing buttons, drop-down lists, and other Web page components	Creates code that lives on the client machine and adds interaction on Web pages
Visual Basic .NET	Is easy to learn and use Has drag-and-drop interface	Prototype development Design of graphical user interfaces
Web Technologies		
ASP/JSP	Set of rules and standards that allow Web sites to create their own HTML code based on user actions	Controls the automated writing of HTML pages
HTML/XHTML	Set of tags that control the display of text on a Web page	Controls layout and style of information presented on a Web page
XML	Allows users to define their own tags Facilitates exchange of information between Web sites	Used in the construction of Web services

for their work named MathML, whereas biometrics groups are developing an XML standard to describe and exchange biometric data such as DNA, fingerprints, and iris and face scans. We discuss both HTML/XHTML and XML in more detail in Chapter 13.

Figure 10.25 shows a table of popular programming languages as well as their features and the typical settings in which they are used.

THE NEXT GREAT LANGUAGE

What will be the next great language?
It is never easy to predict which language will become the next "great" language, but software experts predict that as software projects continue to grow in size, the amount of time for a completed project to compile will also grow. It is not uncommon for a large project to require 30 minutes or more to recompile. Interpreted languages, however, have virtually zero compile time because compilation occurs while the code is being edited. As projects get larger, this capability to be compiled instantaneously will become even more important. Thus, interpreted languages such as Python, Ruby, and Smalltalk could become more important in the coming years.

Will all languages someday converge to one? Certain characteristics of modern programming languages correspond well to how programmers actually think.

FIGURE 10.26 **ACM Special Interest Groups for Students**

Acronym	Name	Description
SIGACT	Algorithms and Computational Theory	Discusses the theoretical foundations of computer science, such as machine learning, graph theory, and distributed computation
SIGSOFT	Software Engineering	Discusses software safety mishaps and concerns to the public as well as software maintenance, design, and best practices
SIGWEB	Hypertext, Multimedia and Web	Discusses how to promote the best ideas about knowledge management and the use of multimedia on the Web and in independent environments
	Visit **www.acm.org/membership/student** for more details on joining the ACM.	

These traits support good programming practices and are therefore emerging as common features of most modern programming languages. The object-oriented paradigm is one example. Both Visual Basic and COBOL have moved toward a support of objects.

There will always be a variety of programming languages, however. Forcing a language to be so general that it can work for any task also forces it to include components that make it slower to compile, as well as produce larger final executables and require more memory to run. Having a variety of languages and mapping a problem to the best language create the most efficient software solutions.

So what do I do if I want to learn languages that will be relevant in the future? No absolute set of languages is best to learn and there is no one best sequence in which to learn them. The Association for Computing Machinery (ACM) encourages educators to teach a core set of mathematical and programming skills and concepts, but departments are free to offer a variety of languages.

Some geographical considerations come into play when selecting which programming language courses you should study. For example, in an area where a large number of pharmaceutical companies exist, there may be a demand for Massachusetts General Hospital Utility Multiprogramming System, or MUMPS. MUMPS is a language often used to build clinical databases, an important preoccupation of the pharmaceutical industry. Review the advertisements for programmers in area newspapers and investigate resources such as ComputerJobs (**www.computerjobs.com**) to identify languages in particular demand in your area. Also stay current on the direction of software engineering in general. Figure 10.26 lists some ACM special interest groups for students. Join the ones of interest to you and you will be up to date on the latest directions in the field of programming.

BITS AND BYTES

Some Software with that Lego?

Programming lessons can begin at a very early age. The Lego company conducts a programming competition each year using their Mindstorm series of Lego kits. These kits include gears, wheels, several motors, and a motorized programmable Lego "brick" that contains a microprocessor. Teams then use Robolab software (**www.robolabonline.com**) to develop programs and send them to the brick's microprocessor. The unit can be told to turn the motor on or off, to switch the direction of the wheel's rotation, or to turn on sensors to measure temperature or light levels. The Robolab software even allows beginning programmers to drag and drop elements such as "if" statements and loops. Together with an understanding of motors and a talent for logical thinking, teams design robots that can travel through mazes, cross bridges, and deliver packages—whatever tasks the Lego company has come up with for that year's tournament! For more information, see **www.firstlegoleague.org**.

Computers in Society: Alice: Making Programming Fun and Approachable

As you have seen from the examples presented in this chapter, writing lines of programming code requires careful attention to detail. A misplaced semicolon can stop an entire program from executing. Because of this, beginning students are often frustrated by their first programming experience and may give up on the idea of programming altogether. Lines and lines of text that make up programming code do nothing to appeal to visual learners. In addition, research has shown that young women especially find programming "boring" and "tedious" and have trouble seeing how the skill of programming has an impact on the real world.

In an attempt to address some of these problems, work begun by the University of Virginia Computer Science Department has been expanded upon by the Stage 3 Research Group at Carnegie Mellon University. The result is an open-source programming environment called Alice (available at **www.alice.org**). Alice allows beginning programming students to immediately create their own "worlds" where they can manipulate fun objects such as ice skaters, amusement park rides, and animals (such as bunnies and chickens). Little or no programming experience is required as the entire interface features drag-and-drop capabilities.

Want a skater to spin on the ice? As shown in Figure 10.27, just drag the skater from the object gallery onto your virtual world workspace. The skater object has pre-created methods (just like the methods associated with objects in object-oriented programming) that allow users to manipu-

late it . . . one of which is spinning. A few clicks of the mouse to select a parameter (such as how many times you want the skater to spin) and you're on your way to creating a virtual world. Alice is a very powerful environment. It is even possible to create interactive games (albeit not as sophisticated as console video games) with Alice.

So how is Alice being used? In primary education, Alice is being used to introduce young people to programming concepts in a friendly, fun environment. In secondary and collegiate education, Alice is used in two ways. First, it is used to introduce students who have never expressed an interest in computer programming to the basic concepts of programming. Second, it is used in beginning programming courses to teach students the basics of object-oriented programming prior to introducing them to an actual programming language. Studies conducted at universities where Alice is being used have shown that it increases retention of students in subsequent programming courses.

The creators of Alice have also observed a remarkable impact on young people—especially women—introduced to Alice. They often describe it as "fun" and "exciting," especially when working on creating worlds in student groups. Because they are creating a world full of animated objects (instead of trying to get a computer to print "Hello World" on the screen, a typical first programming assignment in computer science courses), it appears easier for them to relate programming tasks to some tangible goal (such as creating an ice-skating program). And instead of worrying about correct programming syntax, students can spend time exercising their creativity.

Not convinced . . . try it for yourself. Just go to **www.alice.org** and follow the download instructions. Alice can get you deeply immersed in powerful programming quickly and easily!

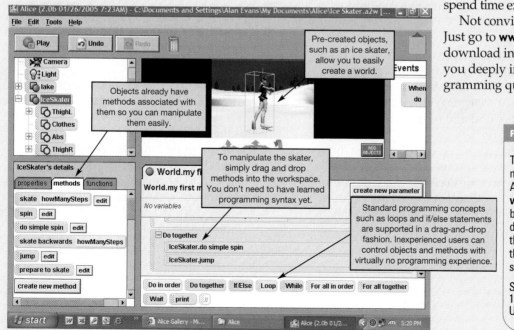

FIGURE 10.27

The open-source programming environment called Alice (available at **www.alice.org**) allows beginning programming students to immediately create their own "worlds" where they can manipulate objects such as ice skaters.

Source: Alice v2.0 © 1999–2005, Carnegie Mellon University. All rights reserved.

Summary

1. What is a system development life cycle and what are the phases in the cycle?

An information system includes data, people, procedures, hardware, and software. Teams of individuals are required to develop systems and an organized process (or set of steps) needs to be followed to ensure that development proceeds in an orderly fashion. This set of steps is usually referred to as the system development life cycle (SDLC). There are six steps in the SDLC. First, a problem or opportunity is identified. Next, the problem is analyzed and a program specification document is created to outline the project objectives. Next, a detailed plan for programmers to follow is designed using flowcharts and data-flow diagrams, from which the development and documentation of the program occurs. The program is then *tested* to ensure it works properly and *installed* so that it can be used. Maintenance and evaluation continues to ensure a working product is maintained.

2. What is the life cycle of a program?

Each programming project follows a number of stages from conception to final deployment. The *problem statement* identifies the task to be computerized and describes how the software program will behave. An *algorithm* specifies the sequential steps that describe what the program must do to complete the work and then is *translated* into very structured programming *code*. The code then goes through a process of *debugging*, in which the programmers find and repair any errors in the code, and further *testing*, both by the programming team and by the people who will use the program. The results of the entire project are *documented* for the users and the development team. Finally, users are *trained* so they can use the program efficiently.

3. What role does a problem statement play in programming?

The problem statement is a very clear description of what tasks the computer program must accomplish and how the program will execute these tasks and respond to unusual situations. It describes the *input* data that users will have at the start of the job, the *output* that the program will produce, and the exact *processing* that converts these inputs to outputs. In addition, potential errors and plans to address these errors are identified.

4. How do programmers create algorithms?

For simple problems, programmers create an algorithm by converting the problem statement into a list of steps (or actions) the program will take. For more complex problems, the programmer must identify where decision points occur in the list of steps. Some decisions are yes/no (binary), whereas others create a repeating action (loop). Algorithms are documented in the form of a flowchart or in pseudocode. Programmers either use a top-down or object-oriented analysis to produce the algorithm.

5. How do programmers move from algorithm to code and what categories of language might they code in?

Computer code uses special words and strict rules to enable programmers to control the CPU without having to know all of the hardware details of the CPU. Programming languages are classified in several major groupings, sometimes referred to as generations, with the first generation being machine language, the binary code of 1s and 0s that the computer understands. Assembly language is the next generation that uses short, English-like commands that speak directly to the CPU and gives the programmer very direct control of hardware resources. Each successive generation in language development relieves programmers of the burden of keeping track of what the hardware requires and becomes more closely matched to how humans think about problems.

6. How does a programmer move from code in a programming language to the 1s and 0s the CPU can understand?

Compilation is the process by which code is converted into machine language, the language the CPU can understand. The compiler is the program that understands both the syntax of the programming language and the exact structure of the CPU and its machine language. It can translate the instructions programmers have written in the higher-level language into machine language, the binary patterns that will execute commands on the CPU. Each programming language has its own compiler with separate versions that are required to compile code that will run on each different type of processor.

7. How is a program tested?

If programmers made errors in the algorithm or in translating the algorithm to code, problems will occur. Programmers debug the program by running it constantly to find errors and to make sure the program behaves in the way it should. Once debugging has detected all the code errors, users, both within the company and outside the company, test the program in every way they can imagine—both as it was intended to be used and in ways only new users may think up. Before its com-

mercial release, software is often provided at a reduced cost or no cost in beta version to certain test sites or to interested users for a last round of testing.

8. What steps are involved in completing the program?

Once testing is completed, technical writers create internal documentation for the program and the user manuals that will be distributed to users of the program. User training begins once the software is distributed to teach the user community how to use the software efficiently.

9. How do programmers select the right programming language for a specific task?

A programming team makes several considerations before selecting the language. Certain languages are best used with certain problems. The target language should be well matched to the amount of space available for the final program. Some projects require the selection of a language that can produce code that executes in the fastest possible time. Selecting a language with which the programmers are familiar is also helpful.

10. What are the most popular Windows and Web applications?

Visual Basic, C, C++, and Java are among those languages that enable programmers easily to include Windows control features such as scroll bars, title bars, text boxes, buttons, and expanding/collapsing menus. To develop Web applications, programmers use HTML/XHTML for basic Web design. For more complex Web designs, scripting programs such as JavaScript and VBScript are popular programs. Web page animations are done with ASP, JSP, Flash, and XML.

Buzz Words

Word Bank

- algorithm
- beta test
- C/C++
- classes
- compilation
- documentation

- embedded
- HTML/XHTML
- inheritance
- interpreter
- JavaScript
- machine language

- object-oriented
- problem statement
- testing plan
- top-down design
- Visual Basic
- XML

Instructions: Fill in the blanks using the words from the Word Bank.

Things are not running smoothly at the Whizgig factory. We need to keep track of how many Whizgigs are made every hour and how many are defective. We begin by calling in the programming team to work with users. Together they begin to build a software solution by creating a (1) _____ . All of the input and output information required is identified as well as the (2) _____ , which lists specific examples of what outputs the program will produce for certain inputs. The team then begins to design the (3) _____ by listing all the tasks and subtasks required to complete the job. This approach is called (4) _____ .

An alternative to this design method is the (5) _____ design, which develops the program based on objects. Objects that have similar attributes and behaviors can be grouped into (6) _____ . The benefit of using this type of design approach is that objects and classes can be reused in other programs. If necessary, new classes can be made by first "borrowing" the attributes of an existing class and then adding differentiating attributes. This concept is known as (7) _____ .

To select the best language for this problem, the team considers the resources at Whizgig. Although a lot of the programmers know the visual programming language of (8) _____ , the most important factors for this application will be how fast it runs, so the language (9) _____ is selected. Because Whizgig has no Web presence, the programmers will not be using (10) _____ . Once the program has been written in programming language, the (11) _____ translates it to (12) _____ or the binary code that the CPU understands. Now, the program is ready to be tested.

The (13) _____ looks for errors in the program code. Then the programmers put together the necessary (14) _____ that explains the program and how to use it. However, because this is a program that is to be used internally, the program does not need to be (15) _____ by a group of potential outside users.

Becoming Computer Fluent

Your new manager wants to design and deploy an Internet application to collect marketing information about potential customers. She wants to gather data and analyze it in one report, which can be shipped to the marketing department.

    Instructions: Write a memo to the manager describing what will have to be considered in the creation of this project. Write the letter using as many of the key terms from the chapter as you can.

Instructions: Answer the multiple choice and true/false questions below for more practice with key terms and concepts from this chapter.

MULTIPLE CHOICE

1. Which of the following is the first step in the SDLC?
   a. identifying the problem or opportunity
   b. developing a program specification
   c. testing the customer's facility
   d. building a testing plan

2. Algorithms document
   a. the programming languages to be used in the program.
   b. testing operations to be conducted by the program.
   c. the sequence of decisions and actions the program will take.
   d. documentation the program will include.
   e. All of the above

3. Programmers can document algorithms using
   a. flowcharts.
   b. pseudocode.
   c. Both a and b
   d. None of the above

4. First-generation languages
   a. are the same no matter which CPU the program is running on.
   b. are the actual machine languages of a CPU.
   c. All of the above
   d. None of the above

5. Object-oriented programming defines classes, which are a collection of
   a. data and methods.
   b. ideas and a testing plan.
   c. different programming languages.
   d. object variables.

6. Top-down software design
   a. requires that programmers do an object-oriented analysis first.
   b. begins at the most important part of the project.
   c. breaks the problem into a series of increasingly refined steps.
   d. never needs flowcharts.

7. A compiler translates
   a. English into a programming language.
   b. one programming language into another.
   c. an interpretation of the algorithm into a Web page.
   d. programming code into binary.

8. Debugging a program is not necessary if
   a. there is a testing plan.
   b. the program behaves correctly according to the testing plan.
   c. the program compiles.
   d. debugging is always needed

9. Which of the following is used in the design of Web applications?
   a. Cobol
   b. C/C++
   c. HTML/XHTML
   d. Windows XP

10. Which of the following languages is used if a problem requires a lot of number crunching?
   a. Cobol
   b. C/C++
   c. HTML/XHTML
   d. Windows XP

TRUE/FALSE

_____ 1. Given a large enough computer, every mathematical problem can be solved.

_____ 2. Programmers debug a program by running it constantly to find errors and to make sure the program behaves in the way it should.

_____ 3. The idea of inheritance makes object-oriented programming more reusable then code generated by top-down design.

_____ 4. Java is the ideal development language, which is why other programming languages are beginning to lose their importance.

_____ 5. Prototyping is a form of rapid application development (RAD), which enables programmers to build software that executes incredibly quickly.

Making the Transition to... Next Semester

1. **Core Programming Sequence**

   Research the core programming sequence at the college you are attending.

   a. How many courses are in the core sequence?
   b. How many languages does the sequence cover?
   c. How many object-oriented languages does your school offer?
   d. What is the Web-design sequence of courses?

2. **ACM Recommendations**

   How will you follow up an introductory programming class at your current school? Examine the recommendations from the Association for Computing Machinery (**www.computer.org/education/cc2001/steelman/cc2001/chapter7.htm**) and compare them with the course content at your school.

3. **Smalltalk**

   One of the original object-oriented programs is Smalltalk, developed by Xerox in its Palo Alto Research Center. Research Smalltalk on the Web and determine what programming situations would be best suited for Smalltalk.

4. **Beta Testing**

   Companies use beta testing to detect remaining problems in their programs before releasing the final version to the retail market. Go to **http://www.betanews.com** or to any other site that offers beta versions of your favorite software title. What programs would you be interested to beta test? Why do you think it would make sense to beta test a software program? What, if any, are the risks involved in beta testing a software program?

5. **Creating a Problem Statement**

   Create a problem statement for the process of registering for courses next semester. It should describe the inputs, outputs, and decision rules that need to be followed to register successfully for the correct courses.

6. **Code Reusability**

   This semester you wrote a program that plays a game of blackjack with the user. Next semester's course has an instructor who always assigns a more sophisticated version of this problem, for which you will need to develop much more complex logic in the blackjack strategy engine of your game. How could you design your code this semester so that it is the most reusable and helpful to you for next term? Discuss how the importance of reusability would impact your choice of language. How would the object-oriented design model be beneficial here?

Making the Transition to... The Workplace

1. Programming in the Workplace

If you work in a place that employs computer programmers, which languages do they work with?

a. Which IDEs do they use?

b. Why are these particular languages well matched to the goals of the department?

2. Using Macros

Check whether your office typically uses macros for automating common software tasks.

a. Do users share macros or simply develop them individually?

b. Are there other ways your office tries to automate routine tasks?

3. Choosing the Best Language

Using resources from the Web, determine which programming languages would be best to learn if you were going to program for the following industries:

a. Animated movies

b. Computer games

c. Database management

d. Robotics

4. Testing Software

Your company has a division that designs software to control the automatic transmission in a line of automobiles. How would you develop a testing plan for this software? What conditions would you need to examine to be sure you were minimizing the probability of software failure in the field?

5. The SDLC

This chapter presents the software development life cycle (SDLC) in six stages. In your new internship, you can pick the area of the company in which you'd like to spend your summer working. Which of those stages would involve work that is best suited to your personality and academic strengths? Which offers the most opportunity for growth within the company later? Which is the best match to your experience and skill set?

6. Go Extreme

The division you have joined in your company is considering using the extreme programming development cycle on one of its projects. Investigate resources such as **www.extremeprogramming.org** and **www.pairprogramming.com** to gather background information on extreme programming. What type of projects would be the best match to the extreme approach? What size project would benefit? What are the characteristics of the customer and the customer's needs that would make extreme programming a suitable approach? What would change in the development team if they moved away from the traditional SDLC?

Critical Thinking Questions

Instructions: Albert Einstein used "Gedanken experiments," or critical thinking questions, to develop his theory of relativity. Some ideas are best understood by experimenting with them in our own minds. The following critical thinking questions are designed to demand your full attention but require only a comfortable chair—no technology.

1. Using Data and Methods

Think about what classes would be important in modeling a Major League Baseball team. What data and methods would each class need? How are the classes related to each other?

2. Class Hierarchy

A common test for deciding the structure of a class hierarchy is the "is a" versus "has a" test. For example, a motorcycle "has a" sidecar, so Sidecar would be a data field of a Motorcycle object. However, a motorcycle "is a" kind of vehicle, so Motorcycle would be a subclass of the base class Vehicle. Use the "is-a has-a" tests to decide how a class structure could be created for computer peripherals. Work to separate the unique features into objects and to extract the most common features into higher-level classes.

3. Future Programming Languages

What do you think the computer programming language of the future should be able to do? How simple would it be? Would it use a graphical interface? Would it combine voice-recognition software with the coding process? Do you think computers will ever be able to create their own programs, or will humans always have to play a role in computer programming?

4. Programming Ethics

Some companies make their programmers sign agreements to prevent them from using code developed for one company with a new employer or competitor. When might this be an appropriate requirement? When might this not be necessary?

5. Debugging

You learned about how programs go through a testing process to rid the program of errors. However, some people are paid to create problems in the code. Why do you think this is necessary? What kinds of problems are these people trying to simulate?

6. Understanding Algorithms

Are there some problems whose solutions cannot be expressed as an algorithm? Are there problems that cannot be solved with a fixed algorithm but could be described with an algorithm that incorporates probability and chance?

Problem:

You and your team have just been selected to write a software program that tells a vending machine how to make proper change from the bills or coins the customer inserts. The program needs to deliver the smallest possible amount of coins for each transaction.

Task:

Divide the class into three teams: Algorithm Design, Coding, and Testing. The responsibilities of each team are outlined as follows.

Process:

1. The Algorithm Design team is required to develop two documents. The first document should present the problem as a top-down design sequence of steps. The second document should use object-oriented analysis to identify the key objects in the problem. Each object needs to be represented as data and behaviors. Inheritance relationships between objects should be noted as well. You can use flowcharts to document your results.

2. The Coding team needs to decide which programming language would be the most appropriate for the project. This program needs to be fast and take up only a small amount of memory. Make sure your team defends its position by finding information about the language you select on the Web.

3. The Testing team must create a testing plan for the program. What set of inputs would you test with to be sure the program is completely accurate? Develop a table listing combinations of inputs and correct outputs.

4. As a group, discuss how each team would communicate their results to the other teams. Once one team has completed its work, are the team members finished or do they need to interact with the other teams?

Conclusion:

Any modern programming project requires programming teams to produce an accurate and efficient solution to the problem. The interaction of the team members within the team as well as with the other teams is vital to successful programming.

Multimedia

In addition to the review materials presented here, you'll find additional materials featured with the book's multimedia, including the *Technology in Action* Student Resource CD and the Companion Web site (**www.prenhall.com/techinaction**), which will help reinforce your understanding of the chapter content. These materials include the following:

ACTIVE HELPDESK

In Active Helpdesk calls, you'll assume the role of a Helpdesk operator taking calls about the concepts you've learned in this chapter. You'll apply what you've learned and receive feedback from a supervisor to review and reinforce those concepts. The Active Helpdesk calls for this chapter are listed here and can be found on your Student Resource CD:

- Understanding Software Programming
- Selecting the Right Programming Language

SOUND BYTES

Sound Bytes are dynamic multimedia tutorials that help demystify even the most complex topics. You'll view video clips and animations that illustrate computer concepts, and then apply what you've learned by reviewing with the Sound Byte Labs, which include quizzes and activities specifically tailored to each Sound Byte. The Sound Bytes for this chapter are listed here and can be found on your Student Resource CD and on the Companion Web site (**www.prenhall.com/techinaction**):

- Programming for End Users: Macros
- Looping Around the IDE

COMPANION WEB SITE

The *Technology in Action* Companion Web site includes a variety of additional materials to help you review and learn more about the topics in this chapter. The resources available at **www.prenhall.com/techinaction** include:

- **Online Study Guide.** Each chapter features an online true/false and multiple-choice quiz. You can take these quizzes, automatically check the results, and e-mail the results to your instructor.
- **Web Research Projects.** Each chapter features a number of Web research projects that ask you to search the Web for information on computer-related careers, milestones in computer history, important people and companies, emerging technologies, and the applications and implications of different technologies.

Behind the Scenes:

Databases and Information Systems

Objectives

After reading this chapter, you should be able to answer the following questions:

1. What is a database and why is it beneficial to use databases? **(pp. 464–467)**

2. What components make up a database? **(pp. 467–470)**

3. What types of databases are there? **(pp. 470–471)**

4. What do database management systems do? **(pp. 471–480)**

5. How do relational databases organize and manipulate data? **(pp. 480–483)**

6. What are data warehouses and data marts and how are they used? **(pp. 483–486)**

7. What is an information system and what types of information systems are used in business? **(pp. 486–491)**

8. What is data mining and how does it work? **(pp. 491–493)**

ACTIVE HELPDESK

- Understanding Database Management Systems **(p. 472)**
- Using Databases **(p. 473)**
- Data Warehouses, Data Marts, and Information Systems **(p. 486)**

Using Databases

We're constantly being inundated with information. The rapid rise of the Internet and the widespread use of computers have only accelerated the flow of information into our lives. One way to manage this torrent of information effectively is to use databases. A *database* is an electronic collection of related data that is organized in such a way that people can access and derive useful information from it. Computerized databases enable us to regulate the relentless onslaught of information and organize it in a fashion that makes the information useful.

You come into contact with databases all the time. Whether you buy a ticket at the football stadium, purchase a book from Amazon.com, inquire by phone about your credit card balance, or sign up for cable television access, you're generating information that is stored in a database. Even something as simple as buying food at a fast-food restaurant involves interaction with a database. The cashier records the items in your order in a sales database just by keying them into the point-of-sale terminal.

In fact, the ability of modern businesses to thrive and grow depends on the quality and efficiency of their databases. Gaining an understanding of how databases work and the information systems that they support will assist you in understanding how any business you may work for captures and manages data. In addition, you'll gain an appreciation for the design issues surrounding the construction and deployment of databases, which may help you determine whether pursuing a career in database administration is right for you.

In this chapter we explore the basic building blocks from which databases are created. You'll see how a database is designed and walk through the process of creating a simple database. Along the way, we discuss important features of databases and the types of database programs organizations use. We also discuss the various types of information systems that use databases and explore modern data storage designs, such as data warehouses. Finally, we examine how data can be further analyzed (or "mined") to yield information beyond the original scope of the database design.

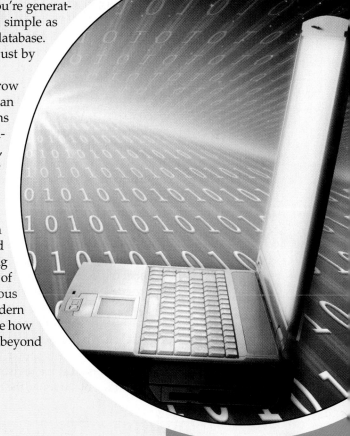

SOUND BYTES

- Creating an Access Database **(p. 475)**
- Improving an Access Database **(p. 482)**

Life Without Databases

Databases are electronic collections of related data that help us organize data so that we can more easily access and use it. By creating an organized structure for data, we hope to make data more meaningful and therefore more useful. In other words, we are attempting to turn data into *information*.

However, not every instance in which related data needs to be turned into organized information demands the complexity of a database. For simple tasks, *lists* are adequate. Often, word processing or spreadsheet software is used to create simple lists. A table you create in Microsoft Word can act as a list, as can a spreadsheet you create in Microsoft Excel.

Figure 11.1 shows a simple Books To Buy list you might create in Excel before beginning college. This list works well because it is simple and suited for just one purpose: to provide you with a list of the books you need to buy for a particular semester. If all information that needed to be tracked was as simple as the information in Figure 11.1, there would be no need for databases.

When is a list not appropriate? Any time *complex* information needs to be organized or more than one person needs to access it, a list no longer is efficient. For example, when you enrolled in college, you provided information about yourself to a number of people. This included your name, address, the classes you wished to take, and the meal plan you selected. Your school also tracks other information about you, such as the residence hall where you are housed. Consider the two lists shown in Figure 11.2. Figure 11.2a is a list the registrar's office uses to keep track of students, the classes they are taking, and the meal plan they selected. Figure 11.2b is a list the residence hall manager uses to track where students are housed.

What's the problem with having two lists? First, there is a great deal of duplicated data between the two lists in Figure 11.2. For example, each time William Wallace registers for a class, his name and address are entered. He needs to provide the same data to the residence hall manager when he receives his residence hall assignment. This **data redundancy**, although not a problem in the small lists in Figure 11.2, can be problematic when a college has 10,000 students. Imagine the wasted time in entering data multiple times, semester after semester, not to mention the increased likelihood of making a mistake.

Second, each time information in the list changes, multiple lists have to be updated. If Li Chan moves, his data will need to be updated in *all* the lists that contain his address. It would be easy to overlook one or more lists or even one or more rows in the same list. This would cause a state of **data inconsistency** to exist. It would not be possible to tell easily which data was correct. Also notice that Jennifer Evans's last record in Figure 11.2a contains a different street address from her other records. It's impossible to tell which address is correct, again resulting in a state of data inconsistency.

In addition, correct data can be entered into a list but in an inconsistent format. Look at students Jennifer Evans and Donald Lopez in Figure 11.2a. Both are registered for PSY 110, but two different course names have been entered (Intro to Psychology and Intro to Psych). Is this the same course? Which one is the correct name? Confusion arises when data is inconsistently entered. Establishing data consistency is therefore difficult to do with a list.

Aside from data redundancy and inconsistency, are there any other problems with using lists instead of databases? What if someone accidentally entered Jennifer Evans's enrollment data twice in the list shown in Figure 11.2a? Any reports (such as student bills) that are generated based on this list will be inaccurate because of the duplicate data that was introduced. For example, Jennifer would be sent two separate bills for her classes, resulting in confusion and potential headaches.

In Figure 11.2a, each student has selected one of the college's meal plans, and this data

	A	B	C	D
1	Books To Buy			
2				
3	Class	Title	Author	Bought
4	English Comp 1	The Prose Reader: Essays for Thinking, Reading, and Writing	Flachmann	Yes
5	Computer Programming 1	Java: How to Program	Deitel	Yes
6	Western Civilizations 1	The Western Heritage	Kagan, Ozment, Turner	
7	Intro to Psychology	Psychology	Wade	Yes
8	Inorganic Chemistry	Chemistry	McMurry, Fay	

FIGURE 11.1

A simple list created in Microsoft Excel (as a spreadsheet) or a table created in Microsoft Word is often sufficient to organize simple tasks.

	A	B	C	D	E	F	G	H	I	J	K
1	Class Registration List - Fall										
2											
3		Last	First					Class		# Of	Meal
4	SS #	Name	Name	Home Address	City	State	Zip Code	Code	Class Name	Credits	Plan #
5	234567891	Chan	Li	123 Main Street	Tuba City	NV	49874-7643	LAN 330	Japanese 1	3	2
6	234567891	Chan	Li	123 Main Street	Tuba City	NV	49874-7643	REL 216	Early Buddhism	3	2
7	234567891	Chan	Li	123 Main Street	Tuba City	NV	49874-7643	ENG 102	English Comp 2	3	2
8	456789123	Coyle	Diane	745 Station Drive	Springfield	MA	18755-5555				
9	123456789	Evans	Jennifer	123 Oak Street	Gotham City	PA	19999-8888	CIS 111	Programming	3	1
10	123456789	Evans	Jennifer	123 Oak Street	Gotham City	PA	19999-8888	ENG 101	English Comp 1	3	1
11	123456789	Evans	Jennifer	123 Oak Street	Gotham City	PA	19999-8888	HIS 103	Western Civ	3	1
12	123456789	Evans	Jennifer	123 Oak Street	Gotham City	PA	19999-8888	CHE 140	Chemistry	4	1
13	123456789	Evans	Jennifer	124 Oak Street	Gotham City	PA	19999-8888	PSY 110	Intro to Psychology	3	1
14	567891234	Lopez	Donald	3421 Lincoln Court	Spalding	ND	87564-2546	HIS 401	16th Century Europe	3	1
15	567891234	Lopez	Donald	3421 Lincoln Court	Spalding	ND	87564-2546	SOC 310	Interpersonal Relationships	3	1
16	567891234	Lopez	Donald	3421 Lincoln Court	Spalding	ND	87564-2546	PSY 110	Intro to Psych	3	1
17	345678912	Wallace	William	654 Front Street	Locust Glen	MI	67744-3584	HIS 204	Scottish History	3	3
18	345678912	Wallace	William	654 Front Street	Locust Glen	MI	67744-3584	PEH 125	Fencing 1	3	3
19	345678912	Wallace	William	654 Front Street	Locust Glen	MI	67744-3584	SOC 220	The Art of Negotiation	2	3

	A	B	C	D	E	F	G	H	I
1	Residence Hall Assignment List - Fall								
2								Residence	Room
3	SS #	Last Name	First Name	Home Address	City	State	Zip Code	Hall Name	Number
4	234567891	Chan	Li	123 Main Street	Tuba City	NV	49874-7643	Wilson Hall	218
5	456789123	Coyle	Diane	745 Station Drive	Springfield	MA	18755-5555	Montgomery Hall	231
6	123456789	Evans	Jennifer	123 Oak Street	Gotham City	PA	19999-8888	Montgomery Hall	312
7	567891234	Lopez	Donald	3421 Lincoln Court	Spalding	ND	87564-2546	Stone House	102
8	345678912	Wallace	William	654 Front Street	Locust Glen	MI	67744-3584	Forsman Quad	124

FIGURE 11.2

(a) This Class Registration List and (b) Residence Hall Assignment List are two lists a college may create to keep track of various student information.

must be entered into each row. What if someone enters a meal plan that doesn't exist on one of the rows pertaining to Donald Lopez? Not only is this wrong, but it can be confusing to anyone viewing the list. With a list, anything can be entered in a row or column, even if that information is incorrect.

In addition, information can be organized in many ways. Consider the Residence Hall Assignment List in Figure 11.2b. It is organized alphabetically by last name. This works well for the accounting clerk who needs to generate bills for student housing. But for the residence manager who wants to see which residence hall rooms are still vacant, it would be more useful to have the data organized by residence hall and room number. Reorganizing multiple lists in this way can be labor intensive.

A final problem with lists is how to handle incomplete data. In Figure 11.2a, Diane Coyle has enrolled in the college but has not yet selected a meal plan or registered for courses. Her known information has been entered, but just looking at her record you can't tell whether data relating to her course registrations and meal plans was available and just not entered, or is truly missing. In any event, it is one more source of confusion.

Can't I just exercise caution and set rules for updating lists? Carefully following the rules when you update a list like the ones shown in Figure 11.2 can address many of the problems mentioned, but there is still room for error. And it would not avoid the most pressing problems of lists: (1) the inability of the data to be shared and (2) data redundancy. Even if you could surmount all of these problems, you cannot easily change lists to accommodate the disparate needs of many users.

How can I solve the problems associated with lists? For single topics, a list is sufficient. But for any complex data that needs to be organized or shared, using a database is the most practical and efficient way to avoid the pitfalls associated with using lists.

Database Building Blocks

Almost any kind of data that needs organization and analysis can be put into a database. For example, America Online (AOL) maintains an online database accessible to the general public that enables you to find the e-mail address of listed AOL members. Publishers such as *Wired* magazine store subscribers' mailing addresses and payment information in a database. In this section, we explore the advantages of using databases as well as the terminology databases use to categorize data.

ADVANTAGES OF USING DATABASES

How do databases make our lives easier? Without databases, you could not store and retrieve large quantities of information easily. Consider airline reservation systems. Thousands of people fly across the United States on any given day. Without a database, it would be extremely difficult to keep track of such a large number of airline reservations. In addition, although you can look up information fairly quickly in a list, even very large electronic databases can provide the information you request in seconds.

Databases provide three main advantages: they enable information sharing, promote data integrity, and allow the flexible use of data.

How do databases make information sharing possible? Consider student records at a college. As noted earlier, without databases, financial aid, admissions, and student housing would all need their own student files. The information in these files might not match because each department would maintain its own records. If a change had to be made in a student's address, all three files (the financial aid file, the admissions file, and the student housing file) would have to be changed.

As shown in Figure 11.3, with a database, only one file is maintained, which reduces the possibility of errors when data is entered or updated. It also increases efficiency because there are no files to reconcile with each other. A database therefore provides for data centralization. There is no need for multiple lists. Each department that needs to use the student information accesses the same set of data.

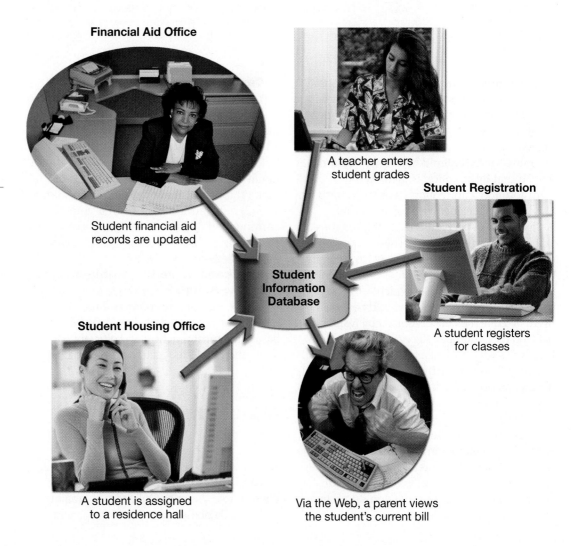

FIGURE 11.3

Using a database enables data to be centralized, requiring that only one copy of relevant data be maintained. All database users therefore access the same up-to-date information.

Financial Aid Office

Student financial aid records are updated

A teacher enters student grades

Student Registration

A student registers for classes

Student Housing Office

A student is assigned to a residence hall

Student Information Database

Via the Web, a parent views the student's current bill

How do databases promote data integrity? **Data integrity** means that the data contained in the database is accurate and reliable. Data centralization goes a long way toward ensuring data integrity. Instead of having to update multiple lists, your name and address information is maintained in only one place. If you move, your address has to be changed only once instead of on multiple lists.

How do databases provide flexibility? Another significant advantage of databases is that they are flexibly organized, enabling you to reorganize the information they contain in a variety of ways to suit the needs of the moment. Think back to the earlier example regarding lists. The registrar and housing manager need to see different information. With a list, you can organize information in only one way. If information is in a database, the registrar can easily view just the information she needs (such as the courses the student is taking), whereas the housing manager can easily view just the information he needs (such as the residence hall the student is assigned to).

Data flexibility can also make information dissemination tasks easier. Suppose your school wants to send out a mailing about a new course to all business majors. Having the contact information of students available in a database makes it easy to merge the data with Microsoft Word and create personalized letters and address labels. Obviously, this would be much faster than generating these items manually, and the results should contain fewer errors. Thus, databases can manage larger amounts of data and process that data more efficiently.

Are there any disadvantages associated with databases? Databases are more complex to construct and administer than lists. They also can be time-consuming and expensive to set up. Great care must be exercised in the design of databases to ensure they will function as intended. Although average individuals can design small databases, it is helpful to have an experienced **database administrator** (or **database designer**), an individual trained in the design and building of databases, assist with the construction of large databases. However, despite the increased complexity of databases, their advantages far outweigh the administrative disadvantages.

DATABASE TERMINOLOGY

How is data stored in a database?
Understanding how databases store information requires knowing the unique terminology developed to describe databases. As shown in Figure 11.4, databases have three main components: fields, records, and tables (or files).

Fields
What is a field? A category of information in a database is stored in a **field**. Fields are displayed in columns. The city where a

FIGURE 11.4

In a database, a category of information is stored in a field. A group of related fields is called a record, and a group of related records is called a table (or file).

Li Chan's contact information and class registration information constitute one record

The column City represents one field in this database

Class Code is a field name

SS #	Last Name	First Name	Home Address	City	State	Zip Code	Class Code	Class Name	# Of Credits	Meal Plan #
234567891	Chan	Li	123 Main Street	Tuba City	NV	49874-7643	ENG 102	English Comp 2	3	2
234567891	Chan	Li	123 Main Street	Tuba City	NV	49874-7643	REL 216	Early Buddhism	3	2
234567891	Chan	Li	123 Main Street	Tuba City	NV	49874-7643	LAN 330	Japanese 1	3	2
456789123	Coyle	Diane	745 Station Drive	Springfield	MA	18755-5555				
123456789	Evans	Jennifer	124 Oak Street	Gotham City	PA	19999-8888	PSY 110	Intro to Psychology	3	1
123456789	Evans	Jennifer	123 Oak Street	Gotham City	PA	19999-8888	CHE 140	Chemistry	4	1
123456789	Evans	Jennifer	123 Oak Street	Gotham City	PA	19999-8888	HIS 103	Western Civ	3	1
123456789	Evans	Jennifer	123 Oak Street	Gotham City	PA	19999-8888	ENG 101	English Comp 1	3	1
123456789	Evans	Jennifer	123 Oak Street	Gotham City	PA	19999-8888	CIS 111	Programming	3	1
567891234	Lopez	Donald	3421 Lincoln Court	Spalding	ND	87564-2546	PSY 110	Intro to Psych	3	1
567891234	Lopez	Donald	3421 Lincoln Court	Spalding	ND	87564-2546	SOC 310	Interpersonal Relation:	3	1
567891234	Lopez	Donald	3421 Lincoln Court	Spalding	ND	87564-2546	HIS 401	16th Century Europe	3	1
345678912	Wallace	William	654 Front Street	Locust Glen	MI	67744-3584	SOC 220	The Art of Negotiation	2	3
345678912	Wallace	William	654 Front Street	Locust Glen	MI	67744-3584	PEH 125	Fencing 1	3	3
345678912	Wallace	William	654 Front Street	Locust Glen	MI	67744-3584	HIS 204	Scottish History	3	3

FIGURE 11.5 Common Data Types and Examples of the Types of Information They Can Contain

Data Type	Used to Store	Example of Data Stored in the Field
Text	Alphabetic or alphanumeric data	Mary, CIS110
Numeric	Numbers	256, 1.347, $5600
Computational	Computational formulas	Credit hours × per-credit tuition charges
Date	Dates in standard date notation	4/15/2008
Memo	Long blocks of text	Four score and seven years ago our fathers brought forth on this continent, a new nation, conceived in Liberty, and dedicated to the proposition that all men are created equal.
Object	Multimedia files or entire documents	MP3 file, AVI file
Hyperlink	A hyperlink to a Web page on the Internet	**www.prenhall.com/techinaction**

student lives can be found in the City field in the Class Registration List shown in Figure 11.4. Each field is identified by a **field name**, which is a way of describing the field. Class Code is a field name in the Class Registration List database in Figure 11.4. In a database, fields have other characteristics to describe them (aside from the field name), such as field data types and field size.

What are data types? When fields are created in the database, the user assigns those fields a **data type** (or **field type**). The data type indicates what type of data can be stored in the field. Common data types are as follows and are listed in Figure 11.5:

- **Text fields** can hold any combination of alphanumeric data (letters or numbers) and are most often used to hold text. Although text fields can contain numbers (such as telephone numbers), they are stored as text and therefore cannot be used to store numbers that will be used in calculations.

- **Numeric fields** store numbers. Unlike in text fields, values in numeric fields can be used to perform calculations. For instance, the numbers stored in numeric fields can be used to calculate tuition owed.

- **Computational fields** (or **computed fields**) are numeric fields that store the

BITS AND BYTES

When a Number Isn't Really a Number

You might think that phone numbers should be defined as numeric data types. However, the data type you assign a phone number depends on what data needs to be stored *with* the phone number. If the phone number will be stored as a 10-digit number with no formatting (such as 3175553456), then a numeric field is appropriate. However, if you want to store the phone number so that it contains formatting to separate the area code, such as (317) 555-3456, the data type should be a text field because the parentheses and dash are text characters (and therefore can't be stored in a numeric field).

Numbers that will be used in a calculation must *always* be defined as numeric data types. For instance, the number of credits for a course is often used to compute a student's bill. If you stored this value as text, you couldn't multiply it by the cost per credit hour to generate a bill. However, text fields store data more efficiently than numeric fields so if size is a consideration, a text field might be more appropriate to store data. So, think carefully about what the data in fields will be used for before assigning a data type.

FIGURE 11.6

This Residence Hall Assignments database uses the social security number as the primary key. Social security numbers make ideal primary keys because even students with the same name won't have the same social security number.

Even though two students with the same name can exist, their social security numbers (primary keys) are unique

contents of a calculation, which is generated with a formula in the numeric field. This is similar to a formula computation in a spreadsheet cell.

- **Date fields** hold date data such as birthdays, due dates, and so on.
- **Memo fields** are text fields that are used to hold long pieces of text. For example, a paragraph describing your high school achievements would be stored in a memo field.
- **Object fields** hold objects such as pictures, video clips, or entire documents.
- **Hyperlink fields** store hyperlinks to Web pages.

What is meant by field size? Field **size** defines the maximum number of characters or numbers that a field can hold. If a numeric field has a size of 5, it can hold a number as high as 99999. As a rule, you should tailor the field size to the length of the data it will contain. If you define a field size of 50, space is reserved for 50 characters in that field, whether the characters are used or not. Therefore, if you know that a character field will have a maximum of two characters, defining the field size as 50 wastes space and makes the files unnecessarily larger.

Records and Tables

What are records and tables in databases? A group of related fields is called a **record**. A student's name, address, and class registration information is a record. A group of related records is called a **table** (or **file**). Tables usually are organized by a common subject. Figure 11.4 shows a table that contains records for all students registered for classes in the current semester.

PRIMARY KEYS

Can fields have the same values in the same table? Yes, they can. It is possible that two students will live in the same town or have the same last name. However, to keep records distinct, each record must have *one field* that has a value *unique* to that record. This unique field is called a **primary key** (or a **key field**). For example, as shown in Figure 11.6, in student records, the primary key might be the student ID or social security number. Establishing a primary key and ensuring that it is unique makes it impossible to duplicate records.

What makes a good primary key? We already have many numbers that follow us through our lives that make excellent primary keys. As noted earlier, our social security numbers are unique and are often selected as primary keys when data is captured about individuals. Driver license numbers are unique (within a particular state) as are the license plate numbers on our cars. State government agencies often use these numbers to track individuals and their transactions.

Primary keys don't have to be numbers that already represent something. For example, when you place an order with Amazon.com, your transaction gets a unique order number (most likely the next number in a sequence). This number is the Amazon database's primary key. You refer to this number when checking your order status, returning merchandise, and so on. It is essential to have a unique number for each order because, without one, it would be difficult to keep track of them.

Database Types

Many different types of electronic databases have been used since the invention of the computer. The three major types of databases currently in use are *relational*, *object-oriented*, and *object-relational* databases. Of these three, relational databases dominate the database market today.

RELATIONAL DATABASES

What is a relational database? A **relational database** organizes data in table format by logically grouping similar data into **relations** (or tables that contain related data). As we discussed earlier, each record in a database table is assigned a primary key to ensure that the record is unique. In relational databases, tables are logically linked to each other by including their primary keys in other tables with related information.

For example, at your college, a database about students would have a table with student contact information (name, address, phone number) and another table with class registration information (class number, meeting times). These two tables would be linked by a primary key such as student social security number. Data types common in relational databases are text, numeric, and date, although relational databases can possess other data types as well.

E. F. Codd first significantly defined the relational model in 1970. Since then, much research and development has been done on the relational database model, and the theories surrounding the model have been proved to be extremely reliable for storing and manipulating data.

OBJECT-ORIENTED DATABASES

What is an object-oriented database? An **object-oriented database** stores data in objects, not in tables. The models on which these databases are formed derive from the object-oriented programming paradigm, discussed in Chapter 10, which was catching on in the programming community in the late 1980s. Objects contain not only data, but *methods* for processing or manipulating that data.

For example, a Student object that contains data about the courses a student is taking might also store the instructions for generating a bill for the student based on his or her course load. Because object-oriented databases store the instructions for doing computations in the same place as the data, they can usually process requests for information faster than relational databases (which would only store the student information).

Also, whereas relational databases excel in the storage of **structured (analytical) data** (such as "Bill" or "345"), object-oriented database are more adept at handling unstructured data. **Unstructured data** includes nontraditional data such as audio clips (including MP3 files), video clips, pictures, and extremely large documents. Data of this type is known as a binary large object (BLOB) because it is actually encoded in binary form.

Object-oriented databases are based on complex models for manipulating data—much more complex than relational database models. Because many of these models have not been proven by decades of research (as has relational database theory), businesses do not yet view them as reliable. Therefore, most of the data businesses use today is stored in relational databases. For a business to use its data in an object-oriented database, it would need to undergo a costly conversion process. And although object-oriented databases provide faster access than relational databases, the speed differential is usually not significant enough to warrant the cost of conversion. For these reasons, object-oriented databases have not yet become commercially successful.

OBJECT-RELATIONAL DATABASES

What is an object-relational database? An **object-relational database** is a hybrid between a relational and an object-oriented database. It is based primarily on the relational database model, but it is better able to store and manipulate unstructured data such as audio and video clips.

Oracle Corporation, which made a popular relational database, changed the structure of its database to an object-relational database with the 1999 release of Oracle version 8i. This was primarily in response to customers who were using an Oracle database for applications deployed on the Web and needed better ways of storing image,

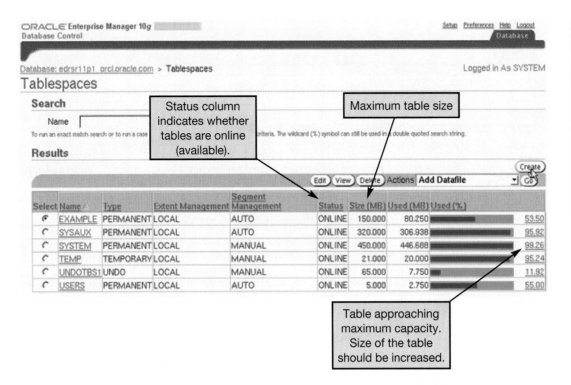

Status column indicates whether tables are online (available).

Maximum table size

Table approaching maximum capacity. Size of the table should be increased.

FIGURE 11.7

Oracle 10g is an extremely powerful database that is optimized for Web applications and management of audio and video files. The Tablespaces section of Enterprise Manager makes it easy to review data about tables in a glance.

audio, and video files. With object-relational databases, such as the current Oracle 10g (shown in Figure 11.7), businesses do not have to abandon the proven relational database model; rather, they can enhance it. As a result, object-relational databases have received greater acceptance than object-oriented databases.

Database Management Systems: Basic Operations

Databases are created and managed using a **database management system (DBMS)**. A DBMS is specially designed application software (such as Oracle or Microsoft Access) that interacts with the user, other applications, and the database to capture and analyze data. The four main operations of a DBMS are these:

- Creating databases and entering data
- Viewing (or browsing) and sorting (indexing) data
- Extracting (or querying) data
- Outputting data

In the next section, we look at each of these operations in detail.

CREATING DATABASES AND ENTERING DATA

How do I create a database with a DBMS? To create a database with a DBMS, you must first define the data to be captured. Therefore, you must create a description of the data. This description is contained in the database's files and is referred to as the **data dictionary** (or the **database schema**). The data dictionary defines the name, data type, and length of each field in the database. Describing the data helps to categorize and analyze it and to set parameters for entering valid data into the database (such as a nine-digit number in a social security number field).

How do I know what fields are needed in my database? Careful planning is required to identify each distinct piece of data you need to capture. Each field should describe a unique piece of data and should never combine two pieces of data.

For example, for student registration at a college, capturing the student's name, street address, city, state, and zip code is obviously important. But should a student's name be placed in one field or two? Because first and last names are separate pieces of data, you would want to create a separate field for each. For instance, suppose you wish to send a form letter to students addressing them by their first name (such as "Dear Susan"). If Susan's first and last name are in the same

FIGURE 11.8

(a) The Field Properties box is shown for the Student Information Table in an Access database. The Field Properties box represents the database's data dictionary. (b) The Student Information Table, ready for data input, results from setting up the data dictionary in Figure 11.8a. Notice that the default value for the State field is already filled in.

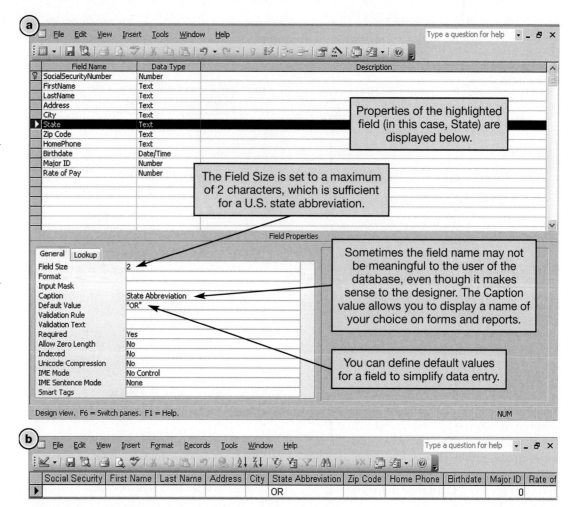

Properties of the highlighted field (in this case, State) are displayed below.

The Field Size is set to a maximum of 2 characters, which is sufficient for a U.S. state abbreviation.

Sometimes the field name may not be meaningful to the user of the database, even though it makes sense to the designer. The Caption value allows you to display a name of your choice on forms and reports.

You can define default values for a field to simplify data entry.

field in the database, it will be difficult to extract just her first name for the salutation.

What does a data dictionary look like and how do I create one? In Microsoft Access, the data dictionary is called the Field Properties box. Figure 11.8a shows the Field Properties box for a database table in Access. The first step in creating an entry in the data dictionary is creating a field name. Field names should be unique within a table. In the table in Figure 11.8a, the field name State is used to store the abbreviation for the state where the student lives.

Next, you must define a data type for each field. For the State field, you use a text data type because names are expressed using characters. Third, you should set a maximum field size (in this case, 2 characters) for the field. Data in the field can be shorter than the maximum but can never exceed it.

Finally, you can set **default values** for a field. These are the values the database will use for the field unless the user enters another value. Although not appropriate for

first names, because they vary widely, default values are useful for numbers that are frequently the same. For example, setting a default value for a Tuition Rate field will save users from having to enter it for each student.

You need to repeat these steps for each field in the table. When completed, the resulting Student Information Table, shown in Figure 11.8b, is ready for data entry.

The attributes (such as data type and field size) shown in Figure 11.8a and 11.8b, which are actually data describing other data, are called **metadata**. Metadata is an integral part of the data dictionary. You need to build the

ACTIVE HELPDESK

Understanding Database Management Systems

In this Active Helpdesk call, you'll play the role of a Helpdesk staffer, fielding calls about database management systems, what they do and how people can use them.

data dictionary for each table you will use in a database before you enter data into the database. However, this also has the benefit of forcing you to consider up front the data you need to capture and the metadata that describes it.

What happens if I forget to define a field in the data dictionary or if I want to add another one later? Databases are extremely flexible. You can add additional fields (or ones you forgot) as needed. However, don't forget that you will need to populate (enter data into) these new fields with the appropriate data. This could be difficult if you suddenly added a Birth Date field to a database that already contains records for 10,000 individuals. If you plan to use the Birth Date field to analyze the data, you need to have a plan for accumulating birth dates to ensure the completeness of the data.

INPUT FORMS

How do I get data into the database?

After you create a data dictionary for each table (or file) in the database and establish the fields you want the database to contain, you can begin creating individual records in the database. There's an old-fashioned way to get data into these records: you can key it directly into the database. However, today, a great deal of data already exists in some type of electronic format (such as a word processing document, spreadsheet, and so on). Fortunately, most databases can import data electronically from other application files, which can save an enormous amount of keying.

When importing data, most databases usually apply filters to the data to determine that it is in the correct format as defined by the data dictionary. Nonconforming data is flagged (either on-screen or in a report) so that you can modify the data to fit the database's format.

For small databases, or databases in which no electronic information is to be imported, you can create an input form to speed data entry. An **input form** provides a view of the data fields to be filled, with appropriate labels to assist database users in

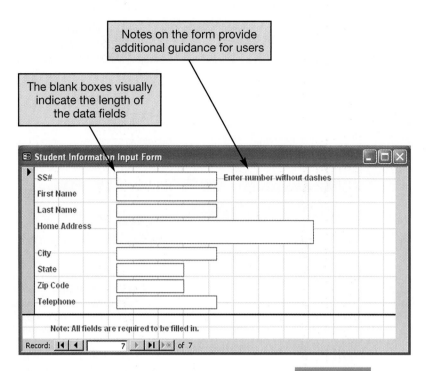

FIGURE 11.9

This input form is for entering data into the Student Information Table. Each field has a label indicating the data to be placed in the field (represented by the blank boxes). Notes can be added to the form as needed to guide the users.

populating the database. Figure 11.9 shows an example of an input form for the Student Information Table we created in Figure 11.8.

DATA VALIDATION

How can I ensure only valid data is entered into the database?
One feature of most DBMSs is the ability to perform data validation. **Validation** is the process of ensuring that data entered into the database is correct (or at least reasonable) and complete. When you registered for college, for example, the admissions clerk most likely asked you for your social security number. A social security number comprises nine digits formatted in the following fashion: 123-45-6789. **Validation rules** are set up in the student database to alert the user if clearly wrong entries, such as "Joh- nS-mith" or "2345," are entered in the Social Security field.

Validation rules are generally defined as part of the data dictionary. Violations of validation checks usually result in an error message being displayed on the screen so that the error can be addressed. Common types of validation checks include *range, completeness, consistency,* and *alphabetic* and *numeric checks.*

How does a range check work?
Range checks ensure that the data entered into the database falls within a certain range of numbers. For instance, rates of pay for student jobs usually fall within a certain

ACTIVE HELPDESK
Using Databases

In this Active Helpdesk call, you'll play the role of a Helpdesk staffer, fielding calls about databases, their benefits, components, and how relational databases organize and manipulate data.

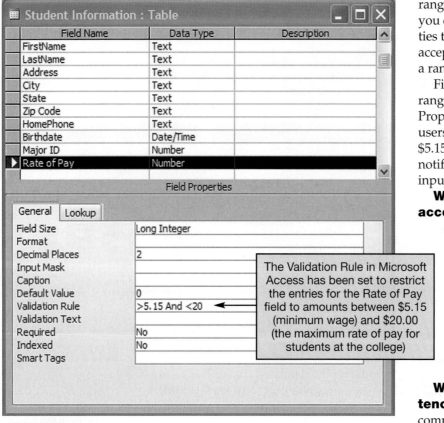

FIGURE 11.10

The Validation Rule in Microsoft Access has been set to restrict the entries for the Rate of Pay field to amounts between $5.15 (minimum wage) and $20.00 (the maximum rate of pay for students at the college)

FIGURE 11.10

Here, a validation rule is set to restrict rates of pay to a certain range.

range. Therefore, in a Student Pay database, you could set the **field constraints** (properties that must be satisfied for an entry to be accepted into the field) to restrict pay rates to a range you define.

Figure 11.10 shows how you set up a range check in a data dictionary (in the Field Properties box) for an Access database. If users tried to enter a rate of pay less than $5.15 or greater than $20, they would be notified of an invalid range error and the input would not be accepted.

What does a completeness check accomplish? If you have ever bought anything online, you have probably encountered error messages generated by completeness checks. In database systems, fields can be defined as "required," meaning data *must* be entered into them. A **completeness check**, such as the one shown in Figure 11.11, ensures that all fields defined as "required" have data entered into them.

What is the function of a consistency check? A **consistency check** compares the values of data in two or more fields to see if these values are reasonable. For example, your birth date and the date you enrolled in school are often in a college's database. It is not possible for you to have enrolled in college prior to having been born. Also, most college students are at least 16

FIGURE 11.11

A database completeness check, like this one shown for the Vermont Teddy Bear Company, ensures that all fields defined as "required" have data entered into them.

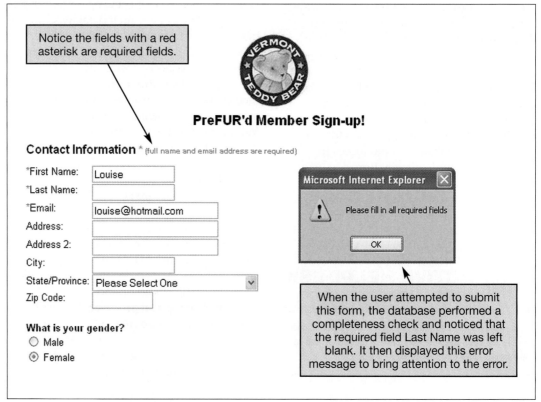

Notice the fields with a red asterisk are required fields.

When the user attempted to submit this form, the database performed a completeness check and noticed that the required field Last Name was left blank. It then displayed this error message to bring attention to the error.

years old. Therefore, a consistency check on these fields would ensure that your birth date is at least 16 or more years *before* the date you enrolled in college.

How are alphabetic and numeric checks used? You may want to restrict fields to only alphabetic or numerical data (such as for names and social security numbers). An **alphabetic check** confirms that only textual characters are entered in a field (such as "Gwen"). A **numeric check** confirms that only numbers are entered in the field. With these checks in place, St3v3 would not be accepted as a first name or a zip code. Figure 11.12 shows how you can set such checks and customize error messages in Access.

VIEWING AND SORTING DATA

How can I view the data in a database? Displaying the tables on-screen and **browsing** through the data (viewing records) is an option with most databases. In many instances you'll only want to view the data. For example, if you want to register for an additional course for the current semester, the admissions clerk would browse the Roster database to determine which courses you are already taking. Of course, browsing through a large database is time-consuming unless the records are in an order that makes your task easy.

How can I reorder records in a database? You can easily **sort** (or **index**) a database into the order that you need. Sorting a database merely involves organizing it in a new fashion. Figure 11.13a shows an Access data table in which the records were input in no particular order. By right-clicking the field name (in this case, Last Name) and selecting Sort Ascending, the database displays the records in alphabetical order by last name, as shown in Figure 11.13b.

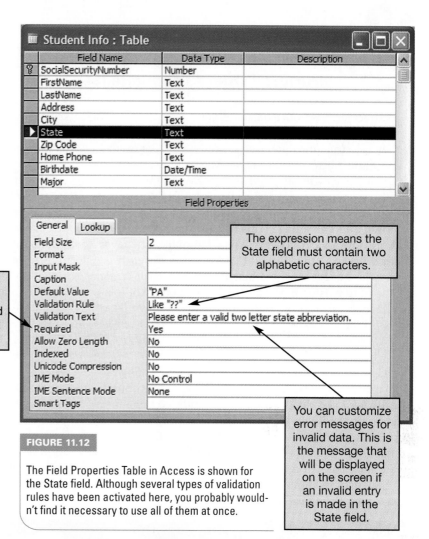

FIGURE 11.12

The Field Properties Table in Access is shown for the State field. Although several types of validation rules have been activated here, you probably wouldn't find it necessary to use all of them at once.

> This indicates that the State field is a required field and cannot be left blank.

> The expression means the State field must contain two alphabetic characters.

> You can customize error messages for invalid data. This is the message that will be displayed on the screen if an invalid entry is made in the State field.

> Sorting Options: Ascending (selected) or Descending.

FIGURE 11.13

(a) Shown is an unsorted table. Notice that the Last Name column (which we want to sort on) is selected (black). Selecting the highlighted sorting option (Ascending) produces the sorted output (b) with the records sorted in ascending alphabetical order of last name.

SOUND BYTE

Creating an Access Database

In this Sound Byte, you'll learn how to create an Access database to catalog a collection of CDs and DVDs. The Sound Byte will take you through a step-by-step process that will result in a fully functional small database.

Structured Query Language (SQL)

To extract records from a database, you use a query language. Almost all relational and object-relational databases today use structured query language, or SQL. For example, Oracle, Microsoft SQL Server, Microsoft Access, IBM DB2, and Sybase are all popular databases that use SQL.

When relational databases were first developed in the early 1970s, each DBMS software product contained its own query language. This meant that database administrators had to learn a new language whenever they worked with a different DBMS. Also, the early query languages were mathematically based and often difficult to master. E. F. Codd, called the father of relational databases, proposed a standardized query language when working at IBM in the mid-1970s.

The original language was called SEQUEL, short for structured English query language. The idea was to make queries easy by using English language–like sentence structure. Database software designers enthusiastically accepted the concept, and a modified version of the original SEQUEL language, named SQL, was developed. Oracle first introduced SQL in a commercial database product in 1979. It has been the de facto standard language for relational databases since then.

SQL uses relational algebra to extract data from databases. **Relational algebra** is the use of English-like expressions that have *variables* and *operations*, much like algebraic equations. Variables include table names, field names, or selection criteria for the data you wish to display. Operations include directions such as *select* (which enables you to pick variable names), *from* (which tells the database which table to use), and *where* (which enables you to specify selection criteria). The two most common queries used to extract data using relational algebra are *select queries* and *join queries*.

A **select query** displays a subset of data from a table based on the criteria you specify. A typical select query has the following format:

SELECT (Field Name 1, Field Name 2, . . .)

FROM (Table Name)

WHERE (Selection Criteria)

The first line of the query contains variables for the field names you want to display. The FROM statement enables you to specify the table name from which the data will be retrieved. The last line (the WHERE statement) is used only when you wish to specify which records need to be displayed (such as all students with a GPA greater than 3.2). If you wish to display all the rows (records) in the table, you do not use the WHERE statement.

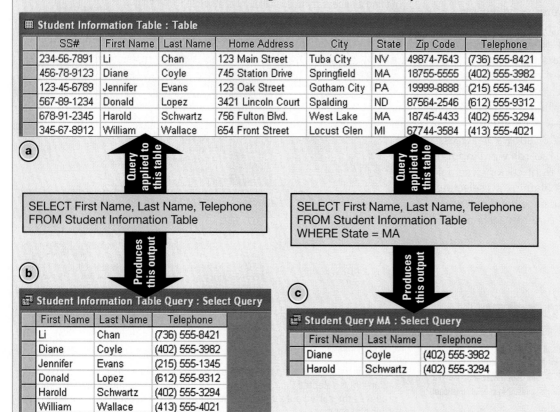

FIGURE 11.14

When the query on the left is applied to the Student Information Table (a), it restricts the output to only a phone list (b). The query on the right, which uses a WHERE statement, further restricts the phone list to only students from Massachusetts (c).

Suppose you want to create a telephone list from the Student Information Table, shown in Figure 11.14a, that includes all students. The SQL query you would send to the database would look like this:

SELECT (First Name, Last Name, Telephone)

FROM (Student Information Table)

Figure 11.14b shows the output from this query.

But what if you want a phone list only of students from Massachusetts? In that case, you would add a WHERE statement to the query as follows:

SELECT (First Name, Last Name, Telephone)

FROM (Student Information Table)

WHERE (State = MA)

This would restrict the output to students that live in Massachusetts, as shown in Figure 11.14c. Notice that the State field in the Student Information Table can be used by the query (in this case as a limiting criterion) but the contents of the State field are not required to be displayed in the query results. This explains why the output shown in Figure 11.14c doesn't show the State field.

When you want to extract data that is in two or more tables you use a **join query**. The query actually links (or joins) the two tables using the common field in both tables and extracts the relevant data from each. The format for a simple join query for two tables is as follows:

SELECT (Field Name 1, Field Name 2)

FROM (Table 1 Name, Table 2 Name)

WHERE (Table 1 Name.Common Field Name = Table 2 Name.Common Field Name)

AND (Selection Criteria)

Notice how similar this is to a select query, although the FROM statement must now contain two table names. Also, in a join query, the WHERE statement is split into two parts. In the first part (right after WHERE), the relation between the two tables is defined by identifying the common fields between the tables. The second part of the statement (after AND) is where the selection criteria are defined.

The AND means that both parts of the statement must be true for the query to produce results (that is, the two related fields must exist and the selection criteria must be valid). Figure 11.15 illustrates a join query for the Student Information Table and the Roster Master Table to produce a class roster for students.

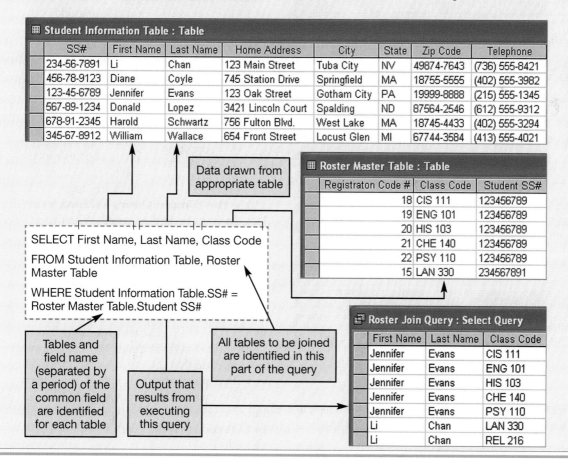

FIGURE 11.15

This join query will display a student roster for each student in the Student Information Table. Notice that the WHERE statement creates the join by defining the common fields (in this case SS# and Student SS#) in each table.

Student Information Table : Table

SS#	First Name	Last Name	Home Address	City	State	Zip Code	Telephone
234-56-7891	Li	Chan	123 Main Street	Tuba City	NV	49874-7643	(736) 555-8421
456-78-9123	Diane	Coyle	745 Station Drive	Springfield	MA	18755-5555	(402) 555-3982
123-45-6789	Jennifer	Evans	123 Oak Street	Gotham City	PA	19999-8888	(215) 555-1345
567-89-1234	Donald	Lopez	3421 Lincoln Court	Spalding	ND	87564-2546	(612) 555-9312
678-91-2345	Harold	Schwartz	756 Fulton Blvd.	West Lake	MA	18745-4433	(402) 555-3294
345-67-8912	William	Wallace	654 Front Street	Locust Glen	MI	67744-3584	(413) 555-4021

Data drawn from appropriate table

Roster Master Table : Table

Registraton Code #	Class Code	Student SS#
18	CIS 111	123456789
19	ENG 101	123456789
20	HIS 103	123456789
21	CHE 140	123456789
22	PSY 110	123456789
15	LAN 330	234567891

SELECT First Name, Last Name, Class Code

FROM Student Information Table, Roster Master Table

WHERE Student Information Table.SS# = Roster Master Table.Student SS#

Tables and field name (separated by a period) of the common field are identified for each table

Output that results from executing this query

All tables to be joined are identified in this part of the query

Roster Join Query : Select Query

First Name	Last Name	Class Code
Jennifer	Evans	CIS 111
Jennifer	Evans	ENG 101
Jennifer	Evans	HIS 103
Jennifer	Evans	CHE 140
Jennifer	Evans	PSY 110
Li	Chan	LAN 330
Li	Chan	REL 216

What if I want to find a particular piece of data in a database? Browsing records works for small databases, but if the amount of data you are managing is small, you probably would just maintain it in a list anyway. To find data in a large database quickly and efficiently, you need to be able to request only the data you are seeking. Therefore, database management systems let you "query" the data to enable you to find what you're looking for.

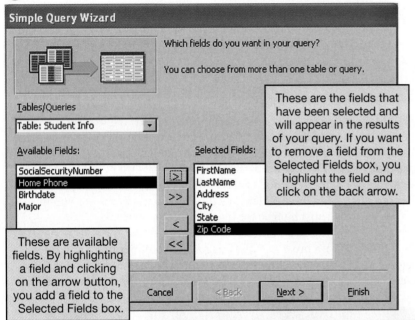

These are the fields that have been selected and will appear in the results of your query. If you want to remove a field from the Selected Fields box, you highlight the field and click on the back arrow.

These are available fields. By highlighting a field and clicking on the arrow button, you add a field to the Selected Fields box.

This is information produced as the result of your query.

FIGURE 11.16

(a) The Simple Query Wizard in Microsoft Access makes creating queries very easy. The wizard displays all fields available in your table so that you can select the ones you need to see. (b) In this example, name and address information are selected.

Student Info Query1 : Select Query

```
SELECT [Student Info].FirstName, [Student Info].LastName, [Student Info].Address, [Student Info].City, [Student Info].State, [Student Info].[Zip Code]
FROM [Student Info];
```

FIGURE 11.17

The SQL View window shows the SQL code that the wizard created for the query in Figure 11.16. Although it is a relatively simple SELECT statement, it is much easier to create with the wizard.

EXTRACTING OR QUERYING DATA

What is a query? A **query** is simply a question or inquiry. A **database query** is a question or inquiry you ask the database so that it provides you with the records you wish to view. When you query a database, you instruct it to search for a particular piece of data, such as a student's grade point average (GPA). Queries also enable you to have the database select and display records that match certain criteria, such as all of the students whose GPA is 3.2 or higher.

Is querying a database as simple as just asking the proper question? All modern DBMSs contain a **query language** that the software uses to retrieve and display records. A query language consists of its own vocabulary and sentence structure, which you use to frame the requests. Query languages are similar to full-blown programming languages but are usually much easier to learn. The most popular query language today is **structured query language**, or **SQL** (pronounced "sequel").

Do I have to learn a query language to develop queries for my database? Fortunately, modern database systems provide wizards to guide you through the process of creating queries. Figure 11.16 shows an example of an Access wizard being used to create a query. Not only does this speed up the process of creating queries, but also you don't have to learn a query language.

Did the Simple Query Wizard use SQL to create the query? When you use Access, you're actually using SQL commands without realizing it. The Simple Query Wizard takes the criteria you specify and creates the appropriate SQL commands behind the scenes.

However, you may want to create your own SQL queries in Access, modify existing queries at the SQL language level, or view the SQL code that the wizard created. To do so, with a query open, select SQL View from the View menu. This displays the SQL code that comprises the query. Figure 11.17 shows the SQL code that the query in Figure 11.16 created.

Computers in Society: Can a Database Catch a Criminal?

When you watch police dramas on TV, detectives often use fingerprints to catch criminals. But until recently, the process of identifying suspects by their fingerprints was time-consuming and ineffective in catching criminals who moved from state to state.

The use of fingerprints as a method of identification dates back to the beginning of the 20th century when the "Henry" method of fingerprint classification (still in use today) was developed in England. Fingerprints are unique to each individual and do not change during the course of a lifetime. Therefore, they are ideally suited for identification purposes in criminal investigations.

Originally, investigators collected fingerprints by placing ink on a person's fingertips and rolling his or her fingers on a piece of card stock. Fingerprint identification experts then manually compared new suspects' fingerprints with existing paper files of fingerprints. This was a time-consuming process, and the pool of potential suspects was limited to the fingerprints that the particular law enforcement agency had collected.

Lack of a large pool of fingerprints was less of a problem in the United States during the early 1900s because the population was not very mobile. However, in the 1930s, criminals became more mobile. The Federal Bureau of Investigation (FBI) thus undertook the maintenance of a large centralized manual database of fingerprint cards and photos of these cards and provided fingerprint identification services to local law enforcement agencies. However, identification was still performed manually, and many local law enforcement agencies had neither the manpower nor the money to submit their fingerprint records to the FBI. Although it still identified many criminals, the system was inefficient.

During the 1960s and 1970s, the FBI began researching methods for using computers to perform fingerprint identification. These early efforts led to the Integrated Automated Fingerprint Identification System (IAFIS). Thanks to the IAFIS, instead of using ink and card stock, new fingerprints are now digitally scanned directly into a computer. In addition, existing fingerprint cards can be scanned and captured in the database. The IAFIS made fingerprint searching and identification much quicker through the use of its computer searching algorithms.

In the late 1990s, the FBI released a software package called Remote Fingerprint Editing Software (RFES). The RFES package (shown in Figure 11.18) enables local law enforcement agencies to capture fingerprints electronically and perform searches in the IAFIS database. Law enforcement agencies use electronic readers to scan fingerprints lifted from crime scenes into the computer. The software then searches the IAFIS database for prints that match.

As more law enforcement agencies scan old fingerprint cards and post them to the IAFIS, the odds of finding a fingerprint match increases. In fact, criminal investigators are submitting fingerprints from old, unsolved cases to the IAFIS in attempts to find a match to fingerprints collected in cases where no suspects were found by conventional methods. In Pennsylvania in 2001, this approach resulted in the arrest and conviction of a suspect for a murder that had been unsolved for 14 years!

Developing an efficient, nationwide system of fingerprint identification would not be possible without the use of computerized databases. Databases enable the information to be stored, sorted, and retrieved quickly. Next time you're watching a police drama on television, don't forget that databases are working behind the scenes to identify the criminals.

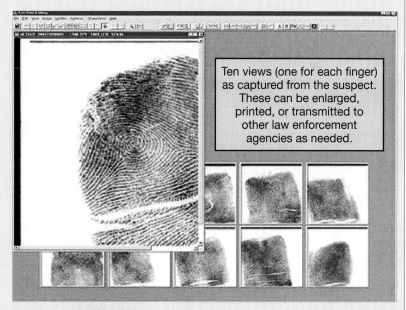

Ten views (one for each finger) as captured from the suspect. These can be enlarged, printed, or transmitted to other law enforcement agencies as needed.

FIGURE 11.18

Law enforcement agencies can use the FBI's Remote Fingerprint Editing Software (RFES) to search the IAFIS database, capture fingerprints from new suspects, or scan in information from existing fingerprint cards.

OUTPUTTING DATA

How do I get data out of a database?
The most common form of output for any database is a printed (or electronic) report. Businesses routinely summarize the data within their databases and compile **summary data reports**. For instance, your school prints a grade report for you at the end of a semester that shows the classes you took and the grades you received.

Database systems can also be used to **export** data to other applications. Exporting data involves putting it into an electronic file in a format that another application can understand. For example, the query shown in the wizard in Figure 11.16 may be used to generate a list of recipients for a form letter. In that case, the query output would be directed to a file that could be easily **imported** into Microsoft Word so that the data could be used in the Mail Merge tool to generate letters.

In the next section, we look at the operation of relational databases and explore how relationships are established among tables in these databases.

Relational Database Operations

As explained earlier, relational databases operate by organizing data into various tables based on logical groupings. For exam-

ple, all student address and contact information (phone numbers, e-mail addresses, and so on) would be grouped into one table. Because all of the data in a relational database is not stored in the same table, a methodology must be implemented to *link* data between tables.

In relational databases, the links between tables that define how the data is related are referred to as **relationships**. To establish a relationship between two tables, both tables must have a common field (or column). Common fields contain the same data (such as social security numbers), as shown in Figure 11.19.

NORMALIZATION OF DATA

How do I decide which tables I need and what data to put in them? You create database tables (or files) for two reasons: to hold unique data about a person or thing and to describe unique events or transactions. In databases, the goal is to reduce data redundancy by recording data only once. This process is called **normalization** of the data. Yet the tables must still work well enough together to enable you to retrieve the data when you need it. Tables should be grouped using logical data that can be identified uniquely.

Let's look at an example. In Figure 11.20, the Class Registration List contains a great deal of data related to individual students and their course registration. However, each table in a relational database should contain a *related group* of data on a *single topic*. There are two distinct topics in this list: student contact information and student registration information. Therefore, this list needs to be divided into two tables so the distinct data (contact data and registration data) can be categorized appropriately.

The Student Information Table shown in Figure 11.21 organizes all of the student contact information found in Figure 11.20 into a separate table. Notice that the information for each student needs to be shown only once instead of multiple times as in the list in Figure 11.20. The unique primary key for this table is the student's social security number. Student information might be needed in a variety of instances and by a variety of departments, but it needs to reside only in this one database table, which many departments of the school can share.

(a)

Student Information Table : Table

SS#	First Name	Last Name	Home Address	City	State	Zip Code	Telephone
234-56-7891	Li	Chan	123 Main Street	Tuba City	NV	49874-7643	(736) 555-8421
456-78-9123	Diane	Coyle	745 Station Drive	Springfield	MA	18755-5555	(402) 555-3982
123-45-6789	Jennifer	Evans	123 Oak Street	Gotham City	PA	19999-8888	(215) 555-1345
567-89-1234	Donald	Lopez	3421 Lincoln Court	Spalding	ND	87564-2546	(612) 555-9312
678-91-2345	Harold	Schwartz	756 Fulton Blvd.	West Lake	MA	18745-4433	(402) 555-3294
345-67-8912	William	Wallace	654 Front Street	Locust Glen	MI	67744-3584	(413) 555-4021

Common field in each table

Roster Master Table : Table

Registraton Code #	Class Code	Student SS#
15	LAN 330	234567891
16	REL 216	234567891
17	ENG 102	234567891
18	CIS 111	123456789
19	ENG 101	123456789
20	HIS 103	123456789
21	CHE 140	123456789
22	PSY 110	123456789
23	HIS 401	567891234
24	SOC 310	567891234
25	PSY 110	567891234
26	ENG 102	678912345
27	PSY 110	678912345
28	HIS 204	345678912
29	PEH 125	345678912
30	SOC 220	345678912

(b)

FIGURE 11.19

(a) The Student Information Table and the (b) Roster Master Table share the common field of student social security number. This allows a relationship to be established between the two tables.

FIGURE 11.20

	A	B	C	D	E	F	G	H	I	J
1	Class Registration - Fall									
2										
3	SS #	Last Name	First Name	Home Address	City	State	Zip Code	Class Code	Class Name	# of Credits
4	234567891	Chan	Li	123 Main Street	Tuba City	NV	49874-7643	LAN 330	Japanese 1	3
5	234567891	Chan	Li	123 Main Street	Tuba City	NV	49874-7643	REL 216	Early Buddhism	3
6	234567891	Chan	Li	123 Main Street	Tuba City	NV	49874-7643	ENG 102	English Comp 2	3
7	456789123	Coyle	Diane	745 Station Drive	Springfield	MA	18755-5555			
8	123456789	Evans	Jennifer	123 Oak Street	Gotham City	PA	19999-8888	CIS 111	Programming	3
9	123456789	Evans	Jennifer	123 Oak Street	Gotham City	PA	19999-8888	ENG 101	English Comp 1	3
10	123456789	Evans	Jennifer	123 Oak Street	Gotham City	PA	19999-8888	HIS 103	Western Civ	3
11	123456789	Evans	Jennifer	123 Oak Street	Gotham City	PA	19999-8888	CHE 140	Chemistry	4
12	123456789	Evans	Jennifer	124 Oak Street	Gotham City	PA	19999-8888	PSY 110	Intro to Psychology	3
13	567891234	Lopez	Donald	3421 Lincoln Court	Spalding	ND	87564-2546	HIS 401	16th Century Europe	3
14	567891234	Lopez	Donald	3421 Lincoln Court	Spalding	ND	87564-2546	SOC 310	Interpersonal Relationships	3
15	567891234	Lopez	Donald	3421 Lincoln Court	Spalding	ND	87564-2546	PSY 110	Intro to Psych	3
16	678912345	Schwartz	Harold	756 Fulton Blvd.	West Lake	MA	18745-4433	ENG 102	English Comp 2	3
17	678912345	Schwartz	Harold	756 Fulton Blvd.	West Lake	MA	18745-4433	PSY 110	Intro to Psych	3
18	345678912	Wallace	William	654 Front Street	Locust Glen	MI	67744-3584	HIS 204	Scottish History	3
19	345678912	Wallace	William	654 Front Street	Locust Glen	MI	67744-3584	PEH 125	Fencing 1	3
20	345678912	Wallace	William	654 Front Street	Locust Glen	MI	67744-3584	SOC 220	Negotiation	2

Data from unrelated topics is located in the Class Registration List. The column headings in blue are related to student contact data, whereas the column headings in red relate to course enrollment information. To construct a database, these topics should be contained in separate tables.

Next, we could put the registration data found in Figure 11.20 for each student in a separate table, as shown in Figure 11.22. There is no need to repeat student name and address data in this table. Instead, each student can be identified by his or her social security number. However, there are problems with this table. Each class name and class code has to be repeated for every student taking the course, and there is no unique field that can be used as a primary key for this table.

What can be done to fix the table in Figure 11.22? In Figure 11.22, we have identified more data that should be grouped logically into another separate table: class

Student Information Table : Table

SS#	First Name	Last Name	Home Address	City	State	Zip Code	Telephone
234-56-7891	Li	Chan	123 Main Street	Tuba City	NV	49874-7643	(736) 555-8421
456-78-9123	Diane	Coyle	745 Station Drive	Springfield	MA	18755-5555	(402) 555-3982
123-45-6789	Jennifer	Evans	123 Oak Street	Gotham City	PA	19999-8888	(215) 555-1345
567-89-1234	Donald	Lopez	3421 Lincoln Court	Spalding	ND	87564-2546	(612) 555-9312
678-91-2345	Harold	Schwartz	756 Fulton Blvd.	West Lake	MA	18745-4433	(402) 555-3294
345-67-8912	William	Wallace	654 Front Street	Locust Glen	MI	67744-3584	(413) 555-4021

FIGURE 11.21

Student contact data is grouped in the Student Information Table and needs to be entered only once for each student. The primary key for each record is a unique social security number.

Microsoft Access - [Class Registration List Fall : Table]

SS #	Class Code	Class Name	# Of Credits
123456789	PSY 110	Intro to Psychology	3
123456789	CIS 111	Programming	3
123456789	ENG 101	English Comp 1	3
123456789	HIS 103	Western Civ	3
123456789	CHE 140	Chemistry	4
234567891	LAN 330	Japanese 1	3
234567891	ENG 102	English Comp 2	3
234567891	REL 216	Early Buddhism	3
345678912	SOC 220	The Art of Negotiation	2
345678912	HIS 204	Scottish History	3
345678912	PEH 125	Fencing 1	3
567891234	PSY 110	Intro to Psychology	3
567891234	SOC 310	Interpersonal Relationships	3
567891234	HIS 401	16th Century Europe	3
678912345	ENG 102	English Comp 2	3
678912345	PSY 110	Intro to Psychology	3

Names and course numbers must be duplicated for each student taking the course.

Also, there is no unique field that can be used as a primary key. SS# cannot be used as the primary key since the same SS# will be entered on multiple records when a student enrolls in more than one course.

FIGURE 11.22

Although it contains related data (registration information), this table still contains a great deal of duplicate data and no usable primary key.

Relational Database Operations **481**

code and class name. Therefore, we should create another table for just this information. This will enable us to avoid repeating class names and codes. Figure 11.23 shows the Course Master Table. Note that the class code is unique for every course and acts as a primary key in this table.

To solve the other problems with the table in Figure 11.22, you need a way to uniquely identify each student registration for a specific course. This can be solved by creating a course registration number that will be unique and assigned by the database as records are entered. Figure 11.24 shows the resulting Roster Master Table.

How do I get the data in the tables to work together now that it is split up? The entire premise behind relational databases is that *relationships* are established among the tables to allow the data to be shared. As noted earlier, to establish a relationship between two tables, the tables must have a common field (column). This usually involves the primary keys of a table.

For instance, to track registrations by student in the Roster Master Table in Figure 11.24, the social security number of the student is the logical piece of data to use. The social security number is the primary key in the Student Information Table in Figure 11.21; however, in the Roster Master Table, the social security number is called a **foreign key**—the primary key of another table that is included for purposes of establishing relationships with that other table. Figure 11.25 shows the relationships that exist among the Course Master, Roster Master, and Student Information Tables. Relationships among tables can be established whenever you need them.

Because relationships are vital to the operation of the database, it is important to ensure that there are no inconsistencies in the data entered in the common fields of two tables. Each foreign key (Student SS# in the Roster Master Table in Figure 11.24) entered into a table must be a valid primary key from the related table (SS# from the Student Information Table in Figure 11.21).

For instance, if 392-13-5684 is not a valid social security number for any student listed in the Student Information Table, then it should not be entered into the Roster Master Table. Each entry in the Roster Master Table has to correspond to a student (linked by his or her SS#) in the Student Information Table. If this requirement is not applied to foreign keys, a relationship cannot be established between tables.

How do I ensure that a foreign key field contains a valid primary key from the related table? To apply this restraint, when defining a relationship in a database, you have the option of enforcing referential integrity for that relationship. **Referential integrity** means that for each value in the foreign key of one table, there is a corresponding value in the primary key of the related table.

FIGURE 11.23

Related information about courses (class code, class name, and the credits for the class) is grouped logically in one table. The unique class code is the primary key.

Course Master Table : Table

	Class Code	Class Name	Credits
+	CHE 140	Chemistry	4
+	CIS 111	Programming	3
+	ENG 101	English Comp 1	3
+	ENG 102	English Comp 2	3
+	HIS 103	Western Civ	3
+	HIS 204	Scottish History	3
+	HIS 401	16th Century Europe	3
+	LAN 330	Japanese 1	3
+	PEH 125	Fencing 1	3
+	PSY 110	Intro to Psychology	3
+	REL 216	Early Buddhism	3
+	SOC 220	The Art of Negotiation	2
+	SOC 310	Interpersonal Relations	3

FIGURE 11.24

The Roster Master Table shows only pertinent data related to a student's registration. Only three fields are needed: the registration code number (which is the unique primary key), the class code, and the student's social security number. This approach greatly minimizes duplicate data.

Roster Master Table : Table

	Registraton Code #	Class Code	Student SS#
	15	LAN 330	234567891
	16	REL 216	234567891
	17	ENG 102	234567891
	18	CIS 111	123456789
	19	ENG 101	123456789
	20	HIS 103	123456789
	21	CHE 140	123456789
	22	PSY 110	123456789
	23	HIS 401	567891234
	24	SOC 310	567891234
	25	PSY 110	567891234
	26	ENG 102	678912345
	27	PSY 110	678912345
	28	HIS 204	345678912
	29	PEH 125	345678912
	30	SOC 220	345678912

SOUND BYTE

Improving an Access Database

In this Sound Byte, you'll learn how to create input forms, queries, and reports to simplify maintenance of your CD and DVD database. You'll follow along step by step using Microsoft Access wizards to create and modify queries to suit your needs.

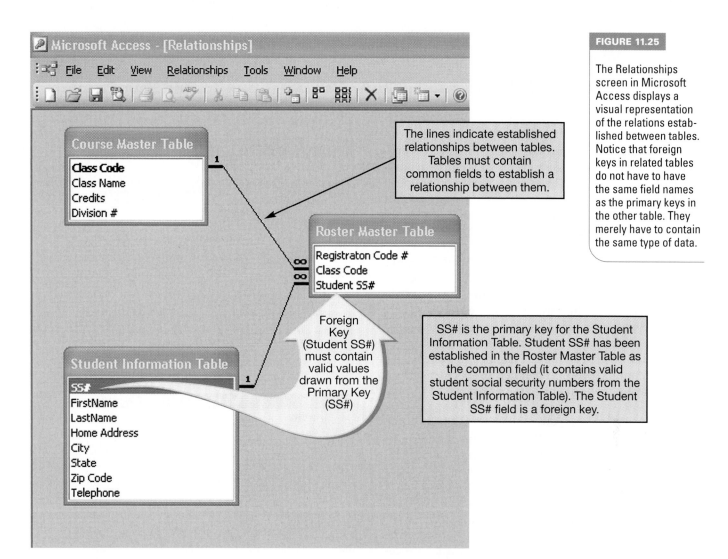

FIGURE 11.25

The Relationships screen in Microsoft Access displays a visual representation of the relations established between tables. Notice that foreign keys in related tables do not have to have the same field names as the primary keys in the other table. They merely have to contain the same type of data.

Within the figure:

Course Master Table
- **Class Code**
- Class Name
- Credits
- Division #

The lines indicate established relationships between tables. Tables must contain common fields to establish a relationship between them.

Roster Master Table
- Registraton Code #
- Class Code
- Student SS#

Foreign Key (Student SS#) must contain valid values drawn from the Primary Key (SS#)

SS# is the primary key for the Student Information Table. Student SS# has been established in the Roster Master Table as the common field (it contains valid student social security numbers from the Student Information Table). The Student SS# field is a foreign key.

Student Information Table
- **SS#**
- FirstName
- LastName
- Home Address
- City
- State
- Zip Code
- Telephone

For instance, if you attempt to enter a record in the Roster Master Table with a SS# of 156-78-4522 and referential integrity is being enforced, the database will check to ensure that a record with SS# 156-78-4522 exists in the Student Information Table. If the corresponding record does not exist, an error message will be displayed. Establishing referential integrity between two tables helps prevent inconsistent data from being entered.

All of the data that is collected in databases needs to be stored and managed. In the next section, we explore the types of systems where databases are typically used today.

Data Storage

At the simplest level, data is stored in a single database on a database server and you retrieve the data as needed. This works fine for small databases and when all of the data you are interested in is in a single database. But problems arise when the data you need is not all in one convenient spot. Large storage repositories called data warehouses and data marts help solve this problem.

DATA WAREHOUSES

What is a data warehouse? A **data warehouse** is a large-scale electronic repository of data that contains and organizes in one place all the data related to an organization. Individual databases contain a wealth of information, but each database's information usually pertains to one topic.

For instance, the order database at Amazon.com contains information about book orders, such as name, address, payment information, and book name. However, the order database does not contain information on inventory levels of books, nor does it list suppliers from which out-of-stock books can be obtained. Data warehouses, therefore, consolidate information from disparate sources to present an enterprise-wide view of business operations.

Computers in Society: Need Cash? Use Databases to Find Your Property

Did you ever lose a check before cashing it and forget to get it replaced (or figure you couldn't)? Did you ever relocate quickly and forget to get your security deposit back on your apartment? Did your grandmother open a bank account in your name and forget to tell you about it? These are all examples of unclaimed property. And thanks to the Internet and databases, it has never been easier to look for this "found money."

In most states, unclaimed property (bank accounts, security deposits on apartments, uncashed checks, and so on) is required by law to be turned over to the state treasury for safekeeping after a certain period of time. The state treasury is required to hold the property for a period of time (sometimes forever) to see if the rightful owner can make a claim. Until a few years ago, searching for your unclaimed property meant sifting through mountains of paper records at the state capitol.

But today, many states have unclaimed property databases deployed on the Web. Go to the official state Web site for the state where you think you may have unclaimed property and search on the terms "unclaimed property" or "abandoned property." California's site, located at **www.sco.ca.gov/col/ucp**, features a simple search box where you can enter your name to search for your pot of gold (see Figure 11.26). If you find an item that might be yours, follow the procedures set down by that state to make a claim and prove ownership.

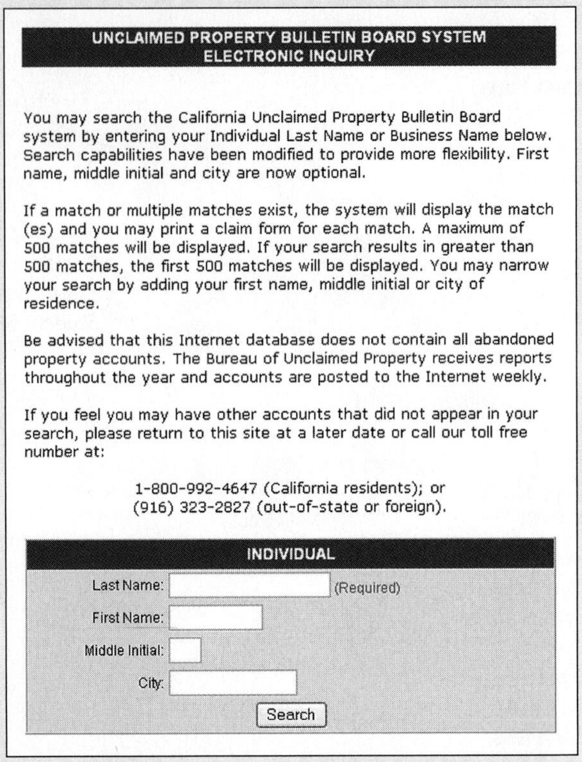

UNCLAIMED PROPERTY BULLETIN BOARD SYSTEM ELECTRONIC INQUIRY

You may search the California Unclaimed Property Bulletin Board system by entering your Individual Last Name or Business Name below. Search capabilities have been modified to provide more flexibility. First name, middle initial and city are now optional.

If a match or multiple matches exist, the system will display the match(es) and you may print a claim form for each match. A maximum of 500 matches will be displayed. If your search results in greater than 500 matches, the first 500 matches will be displayed. You may narrow your search by adding your first name, middle initial or city of residence.

Be advised that this Internet database does not contain all abandoned property accounts. The Bureau of Unclaimed Property receives reports throughout the year and accounts are posted to the Internet weekly.

If you feel you may have other accounts that did not appear in your search, please return to this site at a later date or call our toll free number at:

1-800-992-4647 (California residents); or
(916) 323-2827 (out-of-state or foreign).

INDIVIDUAL

Last Name: [   ] (Required)
First Name: [   ]
Middle Initial: [   ]
City: [   ]

[Search]

FIGURE 11.26

The state of California's unclaimed property Web site, at **www.sco.ca.gov/col/ucp**, might be just the place to find your missing funds.

Is data in a data warehouse organized the same way as in a normal database? Data in the data warehouse is organized by subject. Most databases focus on one specific operational aspect of business operations. For example, insurance companies sell many types of insurance, such as life, automobile, and homeowners' insurance. Different divisions of the insurance company are responsible for each type of insurance and track the policies they sell in different databases (one for automobile insurance policy sales and one for life insurance policy sales, for example), as shown in Figure 11.27.

These databases capture specific information about each type of policy. The Automobile Policy Sales database captures information about driving accident history, car model, and the age and gender of the drivers because this is pertinent to the pricing of car insurance policies. The Life Insurance Policy Sales database captures information about the age and gender of the policyholder and whether the insured smokes, but does not include details about cars or driving records.

However, total policies sold (and the resulting revenue generated) is critical to the management of the insurance company no matter what type of policy is involved. Therefore, an insurance company's data warehouse would have a subject called Policy Sales Subject (as shown in Figure 11.27) that would contain information about *all* policies sold throughout the company. The Policy Sales Subject is a database that contains information from the other databases the company maintains. However, all data in the Policy Sales Subject database is specifically related to policy sales.

From the Policy Sales Subject database, it is easy for managers to produce comprehensive reports such as the Total Policy Sales Report, as shown in Figure 11.27, which can contain information pertaining to all policy sales.

Are data warehouses much larger than conventional databases? Data warehouses, like conventional warehouses, are vast repositories of information. The data contained within them is not operational in nature, but rather archival. Data warehouse data is **time-variant data**, meaning it doesn't all pertain to one period in time.

The warehouse contains current values, such as amounts due from customers, as well as **historical data**. If you want to examine the buying habits of a certain type of customer, you need data about both current and prior purchases. Having time-variant data in the warehouse enables you to analyze the past, examine the present in light of historical data, and make projections about the future.

POPULATING DATA WAREHOUSES

How are data warehouses populated with data? Source data for data warehouses can come from three places:

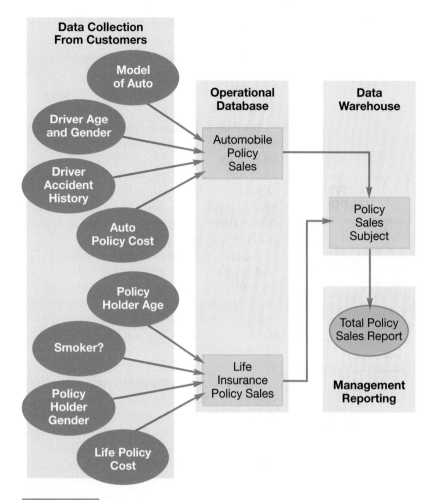

FIGURE 11.27

Data from individual databases is drawn together under appropriate subject headings in a data warehouse. Managers can then produce comprehensive reports that would be impossible to create from the individual databases.

BITS AND BYTES

Measuring Large Databases

Some databases take up only a few megabytes of space. However, businesses generate very large databases. It is widely accepted that the average business doubles the amount of data it accumulates every year. So, how big are a large corporation's databases? Many large databases are now measured in terabytes. A terabyte is 2^{40} bytes, or over 1 trillion bytes of data. If the bytes were typed pages of paper, a terabyte of pages would form a stack 51 miles high! What type of business generates such volumes of data? AT&T maintains a 26-terabyte data warehouse that holds two years of records relating to phone calls that traverse its network. Employees use the database to detect the fraudulent

use of calling cards, analyze calling volumes and patterns, and plan expansion and enhancements of the AT&T network.

But with data doubling every year, soon we'll be measuring databases in petabytes (that's 1,024 terabytes, or 2^{50} bytes). Now the stack of paper is about 52,000 miles high. And computer scientists are already prepared for even more data: an exabyte is a staggering 1,024 petabytes, or 2^{60} bytes. Large government scientific research projects already have databases spanning hundreds of terabytes. If databases double in size every year, it won't be long before there is a petabyte of data stored somewhere near you.

- Internal sources (such as company databases)
- External sources (suppliers, vendors, and so on)
- Customers or visitors to the company Web site

Internal data sources are obvious. Sales, billing, inventory, and customer databases all provide a wealth of information. However, internal information is not contained exclusively in databases. Spreadsheets and other ad hoc analysis tools may contain data that needs to be loaded into the warehouse.

External data sources include vendors and suppliers that often provide data regarding product specifications, shipment methods and dates, electronic billing information, and so on. In addition, a virtual wealth of customer (or potential customer) information is available by monitoring the clickstream of the company Web site.

What is a clickstream and why is it important? Companies can use software on their Web sites to capture information about each click that users make as they navigate through the site. This information is referred to as **clickstream data**. Monitoring the clickstream helps managers assess the effectiveness of a Web site. Using clickstream data-capture tools, a company can determine which pages users visit most often, how long users stay on each page, which sites directed users to the company site, and the user demographics. This data can provide valuable clues to what a company needs to improve on its site to stimulate sales.

DATA STAGING

Does all source data fit into the warehouse? No two source databases are the same. Therefore, although two databases might contain similar information (such as customer names and addresses), the format of the data is most likely different in each database. Therefore, source data must be "staged" before entering the data warehouse. **Data staging** consists of three steps:

1. Extraction of the data from source databases
2. Transformation (reformatting) of the data
3. Storage of the data in the warehouse

Many different software programs and procedures may have to be created to extract the data from varied sources and to reformat it for storage in the data warehouse. The nature and complexity of the source data determine the complexity of the data-staging process; it is different for every data warehouse.

Once the data is stored in the data warehouse, how can it be extracted and used? Managers can query the data warehouse in much the same way you query an Access database. However, because there is more data in the warehouse, significantly more flexible tools are needed to perform such queries. Online analytical processing (OLAP) software provides standardized tools for viewing and manipulating data in a data warehouse. The key feature of OLAP tools is that they enable flexible views of the data, which the software user can easily change.

DATA MARTS

Is finding the right data in a huge data warehouse difficult? Looking for the data you need in a data warehouse can be daunting when there are terabytes of data. Therefore, small slices of the data warehouse, called **data marts**, are often created. Whereas data warehouses have an enterprise-wide depth, the information in data marts pertains to a single department.

For instance, if you work in the sales department, you need accurate sales-related information at your fingertips—and you would not want to wade through customer service data, accounts payable data, and product shipping data to get it. Therefore, a data mart that contains information relevant only to the sales department can be created to make the task of finding this data easier. An overview of the data-warehousing process is illustrated in Figure 11.28.

Managing Data: Information Systems

Making intelligent decisions about developing new products, creating marketing strategies, and buying raw materials requires timely, accurate information. **Information systems** are software-based solutions used to gather and analyze information. A system that delivers up-to-the-minute sales data on books to the computer of Amazon.com's president is one example of an information system. Databases, data

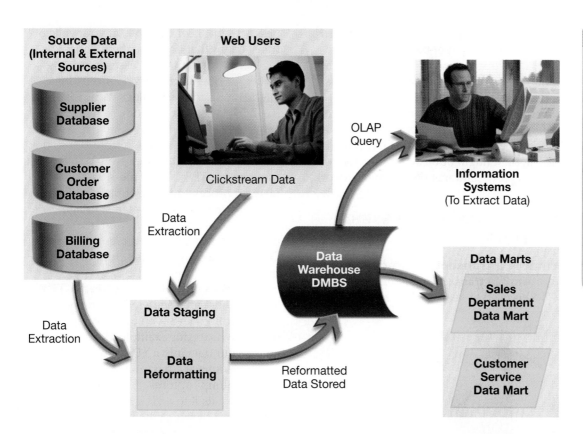

FIGURE 11.28

Shown here is an overview of the data warehouse process. Data staging is vital because different data must be extracted and then reformatted to fit the data structure defined in the data warehouse DBMS. Data can be extracted using powerful OLAP query tools or it can be stored in specialized data marts for use by specific employee groups.

marts, and data warehouses are integral parts of information systems because they store the information that makes information systems functional.

All information systems perform similar functions, including acquiring data, processing that data into information, storing the data, and providing the user with a number of output options with which to make the information meaningful and useful, as shown in Figure 11.29. Most information systems fall into one of four categories: office support systems, transaction processing systems, management information systems, and decision support systems. Each type of system almost always involves the use of one or more databases.

OFFICE SUPPORT SYSTEMS

What does an office support system accomplish? An **office support system (OSS)** is designed to assist employees in accomplishing their day-to-day tasks and to improve communications. Microsoft Office is an example of an OSS because it assists employees with routine tasks such as maintaining an employee phone list in Excel.

Modern OSSs include software tools with which you are probably familiar, including e-mail, word processing, spreadsheet, database,

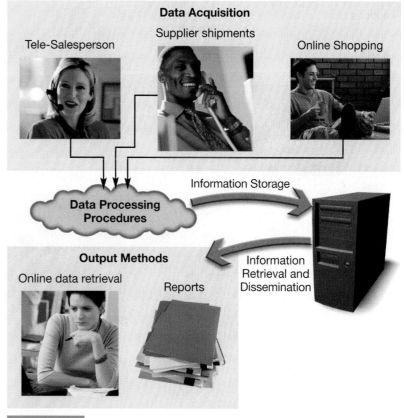

FIGURE 11.29

All information systems perform similar functions, including acquiring data, processing that data into information, storing the data, and providing the user with a number of output options with which to make the information meaningful and useful.

and presentation programs. OSSs had their roots in manual, paper-based systems that were developed before computers. After all, maintaining a company phone listing was necessary long before computers were invented. A paper listing of employee phone extensions typed by an administrative assistant is an example of an early OSS. A modern OSS system might publish this directory on the company's intranet (its internal network).

TRANSACTION PROCESSING SYSTEMS

What is a transaction processing system? A transaction processing system (TPS) is used to keep track of everyday busi-

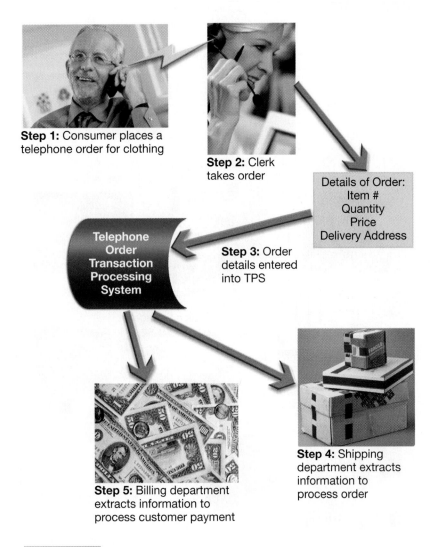

Step 1: Consumer places a telephone order for clothing

Step 2: Clerk takes order

Details of Order:
Item #
Quantity
Price
Delivery Address

Telephone Order Transaction Processing System

Step 3: Order details entered into TPS

Step 4: Shipping department extracts information to process order

Step 5: Billing department extracts information to process customer payment

FIGURE 11.30

Transaction processing systems (TPSs) help capture and track critical business information needed to complete business transactions successfully, such as the selling of merchandise over the telephone.

ness activities. For example, at your college, transactions that occur frequently include registering students for classes, accepting tuition payments, mailing course listings, and printing course catalogs. Your college has TPSs in place to track these types of activities.

When computers were introduced to the business world, they often were put to work first hosting TPSs. Computers were much faster at processing large chunks of data than previous manual systems. Imagine having clerks typing up tuition invoices for each student at a 10,000-student university. Obviously, a computer can print invoices much quicker from a database.

How do transactions enter a TPS? Transactions can be entered manually or electronically. When you call a company and order a sweater, for example, the call taker enters your data into a TPS. When you purchase gasoline at a pay-at-the-pump terminal, the pump captures your credit card data and transmits it to a TPS, which automatically records a sale (gallons of gasoline and dollar value). Transactions are either processed in batches or in real time. Various departments in an organization then access the TPSs to extract the information they need to process additional transactions, as shown in Figure 11.30.

What is batch processing? Batch processing means that transaction data is accumulated until a certain point is reached, then a number of transactions are processed all at once. Batch processing is appropriate for activities that are not time-sensitive, such as developing a mailing list to mail out the new course catalogs that students have requested. A mailing label could be printed for each person as he or she requests a catalog, but it is more efficient to batch the requests and process them all at once when the catalogs are ready to be addressed.

How does real-time processing work? For most activities, processing and recording transactions in a TPS occur in real time. Real-time processing means that the database is queried and updated while the transaction is taking place. For instance, when you register for classes, the registration clerk checks to make sure seats are still available for the classes you want and records your registration in the class immediately. This online transaction processing (OLTP) ensures that the data in the TPS is as up-to-date as possible.

MANAGEMENT INFORMATION SYSTEMS

What is a management information system?
A **management information system (MIS)** provides timely and accurate information that enables managers to make critical business decisions. MISs were a direct outgrowth of TPSs. Managers quickly realized that the data contained in TPSs was an extremely powerful tool only if the information could be organized and output in a useful form. Today's MISs are therefore often built in as a feature of TPSs.

What does an MIS provide that a TPS does not?
The original TPSs were usually designed to output detail reports. A **detail report** provides a list of the transactions that occurred during a certain time period. For example, during registration periods at your school, the registrar might receive a detail report that lists the students who registered for classes each day. Figure 11.31a shows an example of a detail report on daily enrollment.

Going beyond the detail reports provided by TPSs, MISs provide summary reports and exception reports. **Summary reports** provide a consolidated picture of detailed data. These reports usually include some calculation (totals) or visual displays of information (such as charts and graphs). Figure 11.31b shows an example of a summary report displaying total daily enrollment.

Exception reports show conditions that are unusual or that need attention by users of the system. The registrar at your college may get an exception report when all sections of a course are full, indicating that it may be time to schedule additional sections. Figure 11.31c shows an example of such an exception report.

DECISION SUPPORT SYSTEMS

What is a decision support system?
A **decision support system (DSS)** is designed to help managers develop solutions for specific problems. A DSS for a marketing department might provide statistical information on customer attributes (such as income levels, buying patterns, and so on) that would assist managers in making decisions regarding advertising strategy. Not only does a DSS use data from databases and

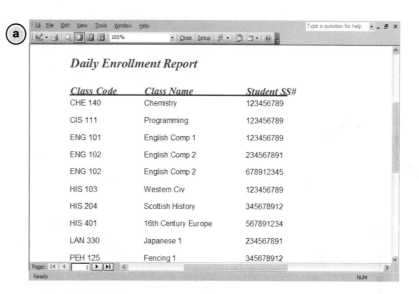

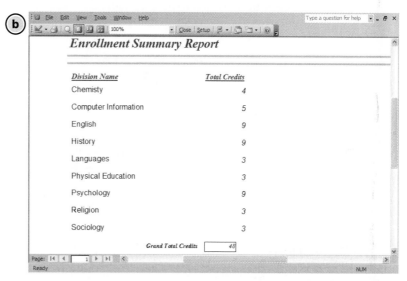

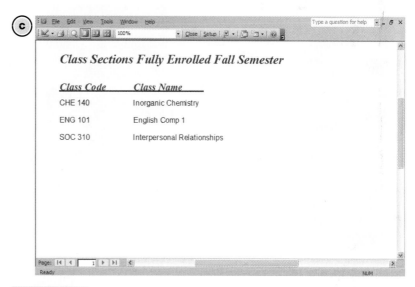

FIGURE 11.31

The three types of management information system reports are (a) detail report, (b) summary report, and (c) exception report.

data warehouses, it also enables users to add their own insights and experiences and apply them to the solution.

What does a decision support system look like? Database management systems, while playing an integral part of a DSS, are supplemented by additional software systems in a DSS. In a DSS, the user interface provides the means of interaction between the user and the system. An effective user interface must be easy to learn. The other major components of a DSS are internal and external data sources, model management systems, and knowledge-based systems. As shown in Figure 11.32, all of these systems work together to provide the user of the DSS with a broad base of information upon which to base decisions.

INTERNAL AND EXTERNAL DATA SOURCES

What are internal and external data sources for DSSs? Data can be fed into the DSS from a variety of sources. Internal data sources are maintained by the same company that operates the DSS. For example, internal TPSs can provide a wealth of statistical data about customers, ordering

patterns, inventory levels, and so on. External data sources include any source not owned by the company that owns the DSS, such as customer demographic data purchased from third parties, mailing lists, or statistics compiled by the federal government. Internal and external data sources provide a stream of data that is integrated into the DSS for analysis.

MODEL MANAGEMENT SYSTEMS

What function does a model management system perform? A **model management system** is software that assists in building management models in DSSs. A management model is an analysis tool that provides a view of a particular business situation (through the use of internal and external data) for the purposes of decision making. Models can be built to describe any business situation, such as the classroom space requirements for next semester or a listing of alternative satellite campus locations.

Internal models are developed inside the organization (such as a spreadsheet that shows current classroom utilization on a college campus). External models are pur-

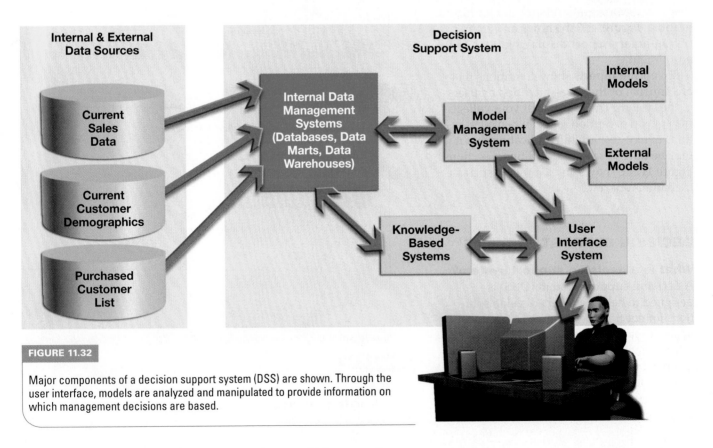

FIGURE 11.32

Major components of a decision support system (DSS) are shown. Through the user interface, models are analyzed and manipulated to provide information on which management decisions are based.

chased from third parties (such as statistics about student populations for two-year college students in the United States). Model management systems typically contain financial and statistical analysis tools used to analyze the data provided by models or to create additional models.

KNOWLEDGE-BASED SYSTEMS

What is a knowledge-based system and how is it used in DSSs? A **knowledge-based system** provides additional intelligence that supplements the user's own intellect and makes the DSS more effective. It can be an **expert system**, which tries to replicate the decision-making processes of human experts to solve specific problems. For example, an expert system might be designed to take the place of a physician in remote locations such as a scientific base on Antarctica. A physician expert system would ask the patient about symptoms just as a live physician would, and the system would make a diagnosis based on the algorithms programmed into it.

Another type of knowledge-based system is a **natural language processing (NLP) system**. NLP systems enable users to communicate with computer systems using a natural spoken or written language as opposed to using computer programming languages. Individuals with disabilities who cannot use a keyboard benefit greatly from NLP systems because they can just speak to the computer and have it understand what they are saying without using specific computer commands. Using an NLP system can simplify the user interface, making it much more efficient and user friendly. The speech-recognition feature of Microsoft Office 2003 is a type of NLP system.

All knowledge-based systems fall under the science of artificial intelligence. **Artificial intelligence (AI)** is the branch of computer science that deals with attempting to create computers that think like humans. To date, no computers have been constructed that can replicate the thinking patterns of a human brain. The failure to achieve artificial intelligence is primarily caused by the fact that scientists still do not fully understand how humans store and integrate knowledge and experiences to form human intelligence. But there is much research going on in the field of artificial and human intelligence that could lead to the development of truly intelligent machines within your lifetime.

How does a knowledge-based system help in the decision-making process? Databases and the models provided by model management systems tend to be very analytical and mathematical in nature. If we solely relied on databases and models to make decisions, the answers would be derived with a "yes or no" mentality, allowing no room for human thought. Fortunately, human users are involved in these types of systems, providing an opportunity to inject human judgment and experience into the decision-making process.

The knowledge-based system also provides an opportunity to introduce experience into the mix. Knowledge-based systems support the concept of fuzzy logic. Normal logic is very rigid: if "x" happens, then "y" will happen. **Fuzzy logic** enables the interjection of experiential learning into the equation by considering probabilities. Whereas an algorithm in a database has to be specific, an algorithm in a knowledge-based system could state that if "x" happens, 70 percent of the time "y" will happen.

For instance, managers at Amazon.com may find it extremely helpful if their DSSs informed them that 40 percent of customers who bought a certain book also bought the sequel. This could suggest that designing a discount program for sequels bought with the original book might spur sales. Fuzzy logic enables a system to be more flexible and to consider a wider range of possibilities than with conventional algorithmic thinking.

Data Mining

Just because you captured data in an organized fashion and stored it in a certain format that seems to make sense doesn't mean that an analysis of the data will automatically reveal everything you need to know. Trends can sometimes be hard to spot if the data is not organized or analyzed in a unique way. To make data work harder, companies employ data-mining techniques.

Data mining is the process by which great amounts of data are analyzed and investigated. The objective is to spot significant patterns or trends within the data that would otherwise not be obvious. For instance, through mining student enrollment data, a school may discover that 40

Emerging Technologies: Web Portal Enables Krispy Kreme to Manage Its Dough . . . Without Going Nuts!

Krispy Kreme didn't build its doughnut empire by managing information poorly. Now that the company operates more than 330 stores in the United States and is expanding internationally (it even has an outlet in the esteemed Harrods department store in London), effectively managing information is even more critical to making "dough." To combine all its information systems together and make them accessible to whomever needs them, Krispy Kreme created its own enterprise portal, as shown in Figure 11.33.

A *portal* is a Web site where many types of data services or applications can be accessed at one time. One of the best-known consumer portals is Yahoo!, which provides visitors with everything from telephone directory listings to games in a one-stop shop. But portal technology is not just for the consumer market. *Enterprise portals* integrate traditional back-office operations (such as supply ordering and deliveries) with services such as e-mail and employee training that front-line employees need to function. Today, many businesses are deploying enterprise portals based on technologies developed by Oracle, SAP, Open Text (Corechange), and IBM, to name a few.

Krispy Kreme's portal is called myKrispyKreme.com. One of the main reasons the company created the portal was to provide store managers and franchise owners

with an easy way to place orders. The company also hoped the portal would increase the speed of its order processing by transmitting all data electronically over the Web. Archaic methods such as faxing order sheets and manual data entry over modem-based systems have gone the way of the dinosaur. Since deploying the portal, Krispy Kreme ordering errors have decreased by almost 90 percent and distribution representatives (who are responsible for filling orders and having the materials distributed to the stores) can handle at least 10 additional stores each. Meanwhile, an inventory management system that is part of the portal provides store managers and corporate management with real-time views of inventory levels down to the specific doughnut type.

Other functions of the Krispy Kreme portal are to provide e-mail services, news updates, contest information, and employee training. Training videos are streamed over the Web to ensure that employees are consistently trained from outlet to outlet. And multilingual portions of the portal are in development to accommodate the planned expansion into markets such as Mexico, Japan, and South Korea. The portal and information management are now as critical to the company's success as the secret doughnut recipe developed almost 70 years ago!

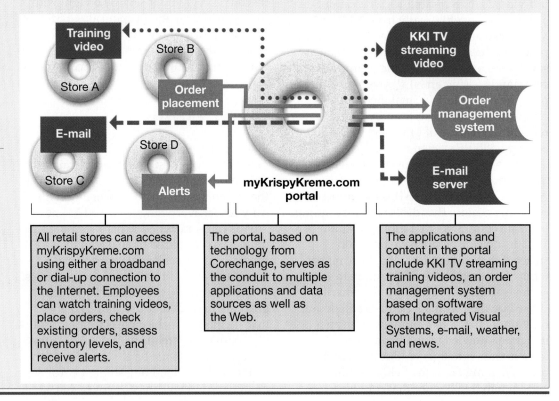

FIGURE 11.33

Doughnuts aren't the only thing hot at Krispy Kreme. The company's portal keeps information flowing between stores, corporate offices, and vendors.

All retail stores can access myKrispyKreme.com using either a broadband or dial-up connection to the Internet. Employees can watch training videos, place orders, check existing orders, assess inventory levels, and receive alerts.

The portal, based on technology from Corechange, serves as the conduit to multiple applications and data sources as well as the Web.

The applications and content in the portal include KKI TV streaming training videos, an order management system based on software from Integrated Visual Systems, e-mail, weather, and news.

percent of new nursing degree students are Hispanic.

Why do businesses mine their data? The main reason businesses mine data is to understand their customers better. If a company can better understand the types of customers who buy its products and what motivates them to do so, it can market effectively by concentrating its efforts on the populations that are most likely to buy.

How do businesses mine their data? Data mining enables managers to sift through data in a number of ways. Each method produces different information that managers can then base their decisions on. The following are five things managers do to make their data meaningful:

1. **Classification.** To analyze data, managers need to classify it. Therefore, before mining, managers define data classes that they think will be helpful in spotting trends. They then apply these class definitions to all unclassified data to prepare it for analysis. For example, "good credit risk" and "bad credit risk" are two data classes managers could establish to determine whether to grant mortgages to applicants. Managers would then identify factors (such as credit history and yearly income) they could use to classify applicants as "good" or "bad."

2. **Estimation.** When managers classify data, the record either fits the classification criteria or it doesn't. Estimation enables managers to assign a value, based on some criterion, to data. For example, assume a bank wants to send out credit card offers to people who are likely to be granted a credit card. The bank may run the customers' data through a program that assigns them a score based on where they live, their household income, and their average bank balance. This provides managers with an estimate of the most likely credit card prospects so that they can include them in the mailing.

3. **Affinity grouping or association rules.** When mining data, managers also can determine which data goes together. In other words, they can apply affinity grouping or association rules to the data. For example, suppose analysis of a sales database indicates that two items are bought together 70 percent of the time. Based on this data, managers might decide that these items should be pictured on the same page in the next mail-order catalog they send out.

4. **Clustering.** Clustering involves organizing data into similar subgroups, or clusters. It is different from classification in that there are no predefined classes. The data-mining software makes the decision about what to group together, and it is up to managers to determine whether the clusters are meaningful. For example, the data-mining software may identify clusters of customers with similar buying patterns. Further analysis of the clusters may reveal that certain socioeconomic groups have similar buying patterns.

5. **Description and visualization.** Often, the purpose of data mining is merely to describe data so managers can visualize it. Sometimes having a clear picture of what is going on with the data helps people to interpret it in new and different ways. For example, if based on large amounts of data we found out that left-handed males who live in suburban environments never take automotive technology courses, it would most likely spark a heated discussion about the reasons why. It would certainly provide plenty of opportunities for additional study on the part of psychologists, sociologists, and college administrators!

You may have noticed that products are frequently moved around in supermarkets. This is usually the result of data mining. With electronic scanning of bar codes, each customer's purchase is recorded in a database. By classifying the data and using cluster analysis, supermarket managers can determine which products people usually purchase with other products. The store then places these products close to each other so that shoppers can find them easily. For instance, if analysis shows that people often buy coffee with breakfast cereal, it would make sense to place these items in the same aisle.

1. What is a database and why is it beneficial to use databases?

Databases are electronic collections of related data that organize data so that it can be more easily accessed and manipulated. Properly designed databases cut down on data redundancy or duplicate data by ensuring relevant data is recorded in only one place. This also helps eliminate data inconsistency, which comes from having different data about the same transaction recorded in two different places. And when databases are used, multiple users can share and access information at the same time. Databases are used any time *complex* information needs to be organized or more than one person needs to access it. In these cases, lists (which are used to keep track of simple information) are no longer efficient.

2. What components make up a database?

A category of information in a database is stored in a field. Each field is identified by a field name, which is a way of describing the field. Fields are assigned a data type that indicates what type of data can be stored in the field. Common data types include text, numeric, computational, date, memo, object, and hyperlink. A group of related fields is called a record. A group of related records is called a table or file. To keep records distinct, each record must have one field that has a value unique to that record. This unique field is called a primary key (or a key field).

3. What types of databases are there?

The three major types of databases currently in use are relational, object-oriented, and object-relational databases. Relational databases are characterized by tables of data in which a common field is maintained in each of two tables and the information in the tables is linked by this field. Object-oriented databases contain not only data in their tables but also instructions about how that data is to be manipulated or processed. Object-relational databases are hybrid databases that contain characteristics of both relational and object-oriented databases.

4. What do database management systems do?

Database management systems (DBMSs) are specially designed application software (such as Oracle or Microsoft Access) that interact with the user, other applications, and the database itself to capture and analyze data. The main operations of a DBMS are creating databases, entering data, viewing (or browsing) data, sorting (indexing) data, extracting (or querying) data, and outputting data. To extract records from a database, you use a query language. Almost all relational databases today use structured query language, or SQL. However, most DBMSs include wizards that enable you to query the database without learning a query language. The most common form of output for any database is a printed report.

5. How do relational databases organize and manipulate data?

Relational databases operate by organizing data into various tables based on logical groupings. Because all of the data in a relational database is not stored in the same table, a methodology must be implemented to *link* data between tables. In relational databases, the links between tables that define how the data is related are referred to as relationships. To establish a relationship between two tables, both tables must have a common field (or column). Once linked, information can be drawn from multiple tables through the use of queries (for on-screen viewing of data) or report generators (used to produce printed reports).

6. What are data warehouses and data marts and how are they used?

A data warehouse is a large-scale electronic repository of data that attempts to contain and organize in one place all the relevant data related to an organization.

Data warehouses often contain information from multiple databases. Because it can be difficult to find information in a large data warehouse, small slices of the data warehouse, called data marts, are often created. The information in data marts pertains to a single department within the organization. Data warehouses and data marts consolidate information from a wide variety of sources to provide comprehensive pictures of operations or transactions within a business.

7. What is an information system and what types of information systems are used in business?

Information systems are software-based solutions that are used to gather and analyze information. Information systems fall into one of four categories. An office support system is designed to assist employees in accomplishing their day-to-day tasks and to improve communications. A transaction processing system is a system that is used to keep track of everyday business activities. A management information system provides timely and accurate information that enables managers to make critical business decisions. A decision support system is a system designed to help managers develop solutions for specific problems.

8. What is data mining and how does it work?

Data mining is the process by which large amounts of data are analyzed to spot otherwise hidden trends. Through processes such as classification, estimation, clustering, affinity grouping, and description, data is organized so that it provides meaningful information that can be used by managers to identify business trends.

Buzz Words

Word Bank

- data consistency
- data dictionary
- data mining
- data warehouse
- decision support system
- field
- join query
- memo field
- metadata
- numeric field
- object field
- primary key
- relational algebra
- select query
- SQL
- table
- text field
- transaction processing
- system

Instructions: Fill in the blanks using the words from the Word Bank.

When constructing a database (1) _____ , it is important to ensure each record is identified uniquely. A(n) (2) _____ should be established as a unique field to be included with each record. In a database, digits such as 1234 are normally stored in a(n) (3) _____ but could also be stored in a(n) (4) _____ if calculations do not need to be performed on the number. Extremely lengthy textual data is stored in a(n) (5) _____ , whereas video files are appropriately stored in a(n) (6) _____ . The (7) _____ fully describes each field in the database and its attributes. Data used to describe other data in this manner is referred to as (8) _____ .

Queries are used to prepare data for viewing or printing. A(n) (9) _____ displays requested information from one table. For displaying information from multiple tables, a(n) (10) _____ must be used. The most popular query language in use today is (11) _____ . Queries generated by this language make use of English-language statements driven by the mathematical principles of (12) _____ .

When individual databases are not sufficient to maintain all the data that needs to be tracked, a(n) (13) _____ should be installed. Databases are often key components of (14) _____ s, which record routine business activities. A(n) (15) _____ utilizes databases and other related systems to assist management with building business models and making critical decisions.

Becoming Computer Fluent

Everyone loves the jewelry you make and you've decided to start selling it. You have some customers already but plan to put your work in a few art shows and make some deals with area stores to feature it. Keeping track of all this information is going to be important but not your idea of fun, so you decide to hire a database consultant to design a database for this new business. Write a letter to the consultant describing what you expect from her. What kind of database do you wish to create? What kind of information do you need to be able to pull from it? How should that information be formatted? How do you imagine the business, and the database, growing?

Instructions: Answer the multiple choice and true/false questions below for more practice with key terms and concepts from this chapter.

MULTIPLE CHOICE

1. Two lists reflecting different data about the same person is an example of
  a. data redundancy.
  b. data inconsistency.
  c. data disparity.
  d. data duplication errors.

2. Which of the following is not an advantage of using a database versus lists?
  a. Information can be easily shared.
  b. Data integrity can be maintained.
  c. Data can be reorganized.
  d. Databases are easier to build and maintain than lists.

3. A category of information in a database is referred to as a
  a. primary key.
  b. record.
  c. field.
  d. data bit.

4. A group of related records is called a
  a. data mart.
  b. field.
  c. database.
  d. table.

5. A field that has a unique value for each record in a database is called the
  a. primary key.
  b. key field.
  c. data type.
  d. logical key.

6. The most common type of database in use today is the
  a. object-oriented database.
  b. object-relational database.
  c. relational database.
  d. structured database.

7. Which of the following is not one of the four main operations of a database management system?
  a. browsing data
  b. entering data
  c. querying data
  d. extrapolating data

8. Which of the following is not an example of a data validation procedure?
  a. range check
  b. reasonableness check
  c. completeness check
  d. consistency check

9. An electronic repository of data for an entire organization is known as a(n)
  a. data mart.
  b. office support system.
  c. data warehouse.
  d. management information system.

10. An electronic system used to record routine business events is known as a
  a. transaction processing system.
  b. decision support system.
  c. management information system.
  d. knowledge-based system.

TRUE/FALSE

_____ 1. A query is used to facilitate the entry of data into a database.

_____ 2. Completeness checks ensure that only data that falls within a certain range can be entered into the database.

_____ 3. Reducing data redundancy by recording data only once is called normalization.

_____ 4. A data mart is a smaller slice of a decision support system.

_____ 5. The main reason businesses use data mining is to understand their customers better.

Making the Transition to... Next Semester

1. Researching the Alumni Database

Many schools try to maintain contact with former students to keep them informed of new programs and courses being offered at the institution. Visit your school's alumni office and determine the following:

a. Is a separate database maintained for the purposes of communicating with alumni?

b. What type of database software is used?

c. What data is captured in this database?

d. How often is the data contained in the database verified with the alumni?

2. Developing an Alumni Database

If the alumni office doesn't maintain a separate database for the purposes of communicating with graduates, use the previous questions as a guideline for developing an alumni database design for your school.

3. Creating a Database

Imagine that you own 700 CDs and want to track them in a database. Determine the following:

a. What fields do you need in your database for categorizing and tracking your CDs? What would be a good primary key to use for this "CD" table?

b. What fields do you need for capturing information about your friends to whom you have loaned CDs? What would be the primary key of this "borrower" table?

c. What common field would you include in both tables to relate the "CD" table to the "borrower" table? Justify your answer.

4. Database Conversion

You've just volunteered to assist the director of a club at your school with a membership drive. The first order of business is to convert the existing paper membership records into an Access database. Consider the following issues:

a. What fields do you need in your "Membership" table for tracking valid members?

b. How would you distinguish active members in the "Membership" table from members who have not attended meetings in more than a year? Or would you put the inactive members into a separate table? Justify your answer.

c. After the Access database is constructed, what software would you suggest be used to generate appeal letters for the club's fund-raising campaign to benefit a local orphanage? How would you suggest the results of the fund-raising campaign be stored in the member database? A new table? Integrated into an existing table? Explain your answer sufficiently to convince the director of your decision.

Making the Transition to... The Workplace

1. Data Warehousing

You are a summer intern in the information services group of an office supply manufacturer. At the weekly staff meeting, the chief information officer (CIO) indicates that the president is requesting information about sales of all lines of goods for the past 10 years. Unfortunately, data more than three years old is not maintained in the current sales database and has been archived to tape. A volunteer is needed (and everyone looks to you) to extract the data from the tapes and prepare the needed reports.

As you are spending your 16th evening extracting the data, the CIO mentions that manufacturing, shipping, and accounts receivable may need their own reports that include different data but span the same time period as your current assignment. The CIO assures you that most of the information is available on tape, but if not, it can be located in the mountains of paper stored in the old warehouse. You know that this tedious work could be avoided by the introduction of a data-warehousing system!

a. Prepare a data-warehousing plan for the CIO. Describe briefly the benefits of data warehousing and provide an overview of the process.

b. For sales, manufacturing, shipping, and accounts receivable data, suggest the types of information that should be captured in the d̶_____

2. Creating a Database

You have a part-time job in the information technology (IT) department at your school. The school's fund-raising foundation has been manually maintaining detailed records of donors and fund-raising activities. The school's president has recently asked the CIO to computerize the foundation's records. The CIO has asked for your help in designing the tables for the donor database. The following information is captured in the manual records:

- Donor name, address, and phone number.
- Amount of donation
- Name of fund-raising campaign (Student Scholarship Fund, New Technology Center Building Fund, Bell Tower Fund, etc.)

a. What specific fields should be set up for the electronic database? Make sure to suggest fields that should be included but are currently not in the manual system.

b. Assume three tables are set up: Donor Contact Information, Campaign (which includes the names of all the specific fund-raising campaigns), and Donation (which tracks individual donations by donor). What is an appropriate primary key to use for the Donor Contact Information table? (Note that social security numbers are not currently captured.)

c. Do you think it would be feasible to collect social security numbers of current donors to use as primary keys?

d. For the Donation table, what should be used as a primary key? How will two donations by the same donor be differentiated?

Critical Thinking Questions

Instructions: Albert Einstein used "Gedanken experiments," or critical thinking questions, to develop his theory of relativity. Some ideas are best understood by experimenting with them in our own minds. The following critical thinking questions are designed to demand your full attention but require only a comfortable chair—no technology.

1. Database Ethics

Internet databases abound with personal information about you. You probably provided some of this information, but it may have been sold to other companies. Other information about you may have been obtained without your knowledge while you surfed Web sites. Consider the following:

a. Is it ethical for a company to sell personal information (such as household income) that you voluntarily gave to it?

b. Is gathering information about people's surfing and buying habits by tracking their clicks through a Web site an invasion of privacy?

c. Should Web sites be legally required to inform users that they are tracking surfing habits? Why or why not?

2. IRS Database

The Internal Revenue Service (IRS) maintains large databases about taxpayers that include a wealth of information on personal income that can be easily sorted by geographic location. This information would be of great value to marketing professionals for targeting marketing programs to consumers. Currently, the IRS is prohibited from selling this information to third parties. However, the IRS (and other government agencies) are under increasing pressure to find ways to increase revenue or decrease expenses.

a. Do you favor a change in the laws that would permit the IRS to sell names and addresses with household income information to third parties? Why or why not?

b. Would it be acceptable for the IRS to sell income information to marketing firms if it did not include personal information (such as names and addresses) but only included income statistics for certain geographic areas? How is this better (or worse) than selling personal information?

c. How would you feel about the IRS marketing financial products (such as tax software) directly to consumers? Would this be a conflict of interest with the IRS's main mission (the collection of tax revenue and enforcement of tax compliance)?

3. The Total Information Awareness Program

After the terrorist attacks on September 11, 2001, some U.S. citizens began demanding more scrutiny of foreign nationals and people wishing to emigrate to the United States. In response to these concerns, the Department of Defense launched the Total Information Awareness (TIA) Program. The program was created to develop data-mining techniques to probe massive federal databases as well as commercial and private employment, medical, and financial databases. The objective was to spot trends that would identify people who were threats to national security. Initially, the public did not complain, but as more stories surfaced about the program, citizens began to resent this invasion of privacy.

a. Research the TIA program and determine its current status. Is the program still around or has it been terminated? If the program has been discontinued, has another replaced it?

b. Do you think the government should institute a program like TIA?

c. Which is more important to you: safeguarding your privacy or protecting the United States from terrorists? Why?

Problem:

Many schools use student data information systems that were installed more than 10 years ago. When preparing to transition to a newer system, additional information is often identified that needs to be captured in the new system that was not recorded in the old system (such as e-mail addresses). Also, in preparation for transferring legacy data to a new system, the data often needs to be "groomed." Grooming data means verifying the data accuracy, ensuring data consistency, and correcting problems.

Task:

Your class has volunteered to assist the IT department with the transition to a new student information system. Customers (students) often provide unique perspectives and should always be consulted (when possible) during the design and implementation of new systems. The school administration feels your input into the design process will enhance the usability of the new system.

Process:

Divide the class into small groups.

1. Your group should examine your school's current student information system (from a user perspective). Identify the data that is being captured from students (when enrolling or registering for courses). Compile a list of suggestions for data that does not need to be captured (but currently is captured) and for additional data that should be gathered (but is not currently). Determine the extent to which student services can be accessed over the Internet and suggest services that require Internet accessibility but are not currently offered.

2. Present your group's findings to the class. Compare your suggestions to those of other groups. Be sure to address the needs of all groups of students (residents, commuters, and online students).

3. Prepare a list of recommendations for improvements to the current student information system for the director of student affairs. Clearly indicate how the proposed changes will benefit both students and the school employees who are interacting with the system.

Conclusion:

Colleges and universities are competing for students more fiercely than ever before. Those institutions that listen to their students and find innovative ways to serve their needs will have a distinct advantage in attracting and retaining students. Listening to customers is a basic principle of business that educational institutions should not overlook.

Multimedia

In addition to the review materials presented here, you'll find additional materials featured with the book's multimedia, including the *Technology in Action* Student Resource CD and the Companion Web site (**www.prenhall.com/techinaction**), which will help reinforce your understanding of the chapter content. These materials include the following:

ACTIVE HELPDESK

In Active Helpdesk calls, you'll assume the role of a Helpdesk operator taking calls about the concepts you've learned in this chapter. You'll apply what you've learned and receive feedback from a supervisor to review and reinforce those concepts. The Active Helpdesk calls for this chapter are listed here and can be found on your Student Resource CD:

- Understanding Database Management Systems
- Using Databases
- Data Warehouses, Data Marts, and Information Systems

SOUND BYTES

Sound Bytes are dynamic multimedia tutorials that help demystify even the most complex topics. You'll view video clips and animations that illustrate computer concepts, and then apply what you've learned by reviewing with the Sound Byte Labs, which include quizzes and activities specifically tailored to each Sound Byte. The Sound Bytes for this chapter are listed here and can be found on your Student Resource CD and on the Companion Web site (**www.prenhall.com/techinaction**):

- Creating an Access Database
- Improving an Access Database

COMPANION WEB SITE

The *Technology in Action* Companion Web site includes a variety of additional materials to help you review and learn more about the topics in this chapter. The resources available at **www.prenhall.com/techinaction** include:

- **Online Study Guide.** Each chapter features an online true/false and multiple-choice quiz. You can take these quizzes, automatically check the results, and e-mail the results to your instructor.
- **Web Research Projects.** Each chapter features a number of Web research projects that ask you to search the Web for information on computer-related careers, milestones in computer history, important people and companies, emerging technologies, and the applications and implications of different technologies.

12

Behind the Scenes:

Networking and Security

Objectives

After reading this chapter, you should be able to answer the following questions:

1. What are the advantages of a business network? **(p. 506)**

2. How does a client/server network differ from a peer-to-peer network? **(pp. 506–508)**

3. What are the different classifications of client/server networks? **(pp. 508–510)**

4. What components are needed to construct a client/server network? **(pp. 510–511)**

5. What do the various types of servers do? **(pp. 511–513)**

6. What are the various network topologies (layouts) and why is network topology important in planning a network? **(pp. 513–518)**

7. What types of transmission media are used in client/server networks? **(pp. 518–522)**

8. What software needs to be running on computers attached to a client/server network and how does this software control network communications? **(pp. 522–525)**

9. How do network adapters enable computers to participate in a client/server network? **(pp. 525–527)**

10. What devices assist in moving data around a client/server network? **(pp. 527–530)**

11. What measures are employed to keep large networks secure? **(pp. 530–535)**

ACTIVE HELPDESK

- Selecting a Network Topology and Cable **(p. 508)**
- Using Servers **(p. 512)**
- Selecting Network Navigation Devices **(p. 528)**

Understanding How Networks Work

Computer networks are everywhere. In fact, the Internet is a large (actually, the largest) network of networks. Most people interact with other, smaller computer networks on a daily basis, whether they are aware of it or not. Even something as simple as buying gas involves interacting with a network. The "pay-at-the-pump" convenience of purchasing gas with a credit card is made possible because the gas pump is part of a network. When you swipe your card at the pump, the pump connects to the network at the oil company that owns the gas station. That network connects with the network at your credit card company and checks to ensure you're not over your credit limit. Assuming you have sufficient credit, the oil company network sends an authorization back to the pump to enable you to buy gas.

When your transaction is complete, the pump sends the purchase information to the corporate network. The amount of gas you purchased is then recorded in an inventory control database and is used to help determine when a gas delivery needs to be made to the gas station. Without networks, you couldn't buy gas conveniently at the pump because there would be no way to check your credit. Also, without the corporate network tracking gas purchases, your neighborhood station might run out of gas more frequently. As you can see, networks assist in making your life easier.

Why is understanding networks and their capabilities important? For one, it will help you interact with the information technology professionals responsible for configuring and maintaining the networks where you work or go to school. Additionally, a fundamental grasp of network principles can help you decide whether you want to pursue additional coursework or even a career in networking. Finally, it can enhance your productivity by keeping you connected with today's fast-moving world.

This chapter builds on the information you learned about networks in Chapter 7 and takes you behind the scenes of networking principles. We look at how client/server networks work and examine exactly how these networks are designed and built. Along the way, we discuss the various kinds of servers used in such networks as well as the layout and equipment used to create them. Finally, we discuss how large networks are kept secure.

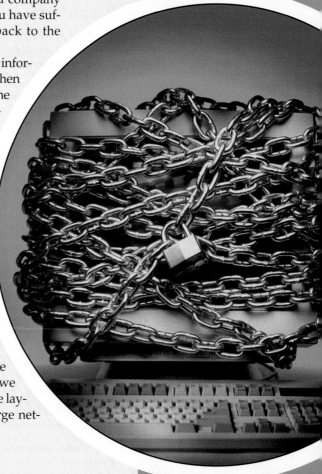

SOUND BYTES

- Network Topology and Navigation Devices **(p. 514)**
- What's My IP Address? (and Other Interesting Facts About Networks) **(p. 527)**
- A Day in the Life of a Network Technician **(p. 530)**

Networking Advantages

As you learned in Chapter 7, a **network** is a group of two or more computers (or nodes) that are configured to share information and resources such as printers, files, and databases. Essentially, a network enables computers and other devices to communicate with each other. But why do we network computers? As discussed in Chapter 7, home networks enable users to share peripherals (such as printers), transfer files simply, and share Internet connections. Large business networks provide similar and additional advantages over individual stand-alone computers:

- **Networks increase productivity.** Computers are powerful stand-alone resources. However, to increase productivity, people need to be able to share data and peripherals with coworkers and communicate with them efficiently. Without a network, only one person at a time can access information because it would reside on a single computer. Information sharing is therefore the largest benefit a company gains by installing a network.

- **Networks enable expensive resources to be shared.** Networks enable people to share peripherals such as printers, eliminating the need for duplicate devices. You probably have a printer hooked up to your home computer. Think about how often it sits idle. Compound that by having an office of 20 employees, each with his or her own printer. Having 20 printers sitting idle 90 percent of the time is a tremendous waste of money. Installing a network enables two printers (working most of the time) to serve all 20 employees, generating cost savings.

- **Networks enable software sharing.** Installing a new version of software on everyone's desktop in a company with 1,000 employees can be time-consuming. However, if the computers are networked, all employees can access the same copy of a program from the server. Although companies must still purchase a software license for each employee, with a network they avoid having to install the program on every desktop. This also saves space on individual desktops, because the software doesn't reside on every computer.

- **Networks facilitate Internet connectivity.** Most employees need to connect to the Internet to perform their jobs. Providing each employee's computer with its own dedicated connection to the Internet (using a modem) is costly. Through a network, large groups of employees can share one Internet connection, reducing Internet connectivity expenses.

Are there disadvantages to businesses using networks? Because business networks are often complex, additional personnel are usually required to maintain them. These people, called **network administrators**, have training in computer and peripheral maintenance and repair, networking design, and the installation of networking software. In addition, networks require additional equipment and software to operate. However, most companies feel the cost savings of peripheral sharing and the ability to have employees access information simultaneously outweigh the costs associated with network administrators and equipment.

Aside from very small networks (such as peer-to-peer networks, which are typically used in homes and small businesses), the majority of computer networks are based on the client/server model of computing.

Client/Server Networks

As you've learned, a **server** is a computer that both stores and shares resources on a network, whereas a **client** is a computer that requests those resources. A **client/server network** (also called a **server-based network**) contains servers as well as client computers. The inclusion of servers is what differentiates a client/server network from a typical peer-to-peer (P2P) network. (As you'll recall, each node connected to the P2P network can communicate directly with every other node on the network, instead of having a separate device exercise control over the network.) Figure 12.1 illustrates the client/server relationship.

The main advantage of a client/server relationship is that it makes data flow more efficiently than in peer-to-peer networks. Servers can respond to requests from a large number of clients at the same time. Also, servers are configured to perform specific tasks (such as handling e-mail or database requests) efficiently.

For instance, say you are hungry and go to a fast-food restaurant. As the customer ordering food, you are the *client* making a request. The cook, in the role of the *server*, responds to the request and prepares the meal. Certainly, you could go to the restaurant and cook your own meal, but this would hardly be efficient. You would be floundering around in the kitchen with other customers trying to cook their meals. By assigning specialized tasks to a fast-food cook (the server), many customers (clients) can be served efficiently at the same time. This is how servers work. One server can provide services efficiently to a large number of clients at one time.

Does my home network have a server? As you'll recall from Chapter 7, peer-to-peer networks, which are typically set up in homes or very small businesses, do not require servers. In these networks, computers act as both clients and servers when appropriate.

Why don't businesses use peer-to-peer networks? P2P networks become difficult to administer when they are expanded beyond 10 users. Each individual computer may require updating for changes to the network, which is not efficient. Also, security can't be implemented centrally on a P2P network but instead must be handled by each individual user. As noted earlier, client/server networks contain at least one server that provides shared resources and

services (including security) to the client computers that request them.

In addition, client/server networks move data more efficiently than P2P networks, making them appropriate for large numbers of users. For example, Figure 12.2 shows a

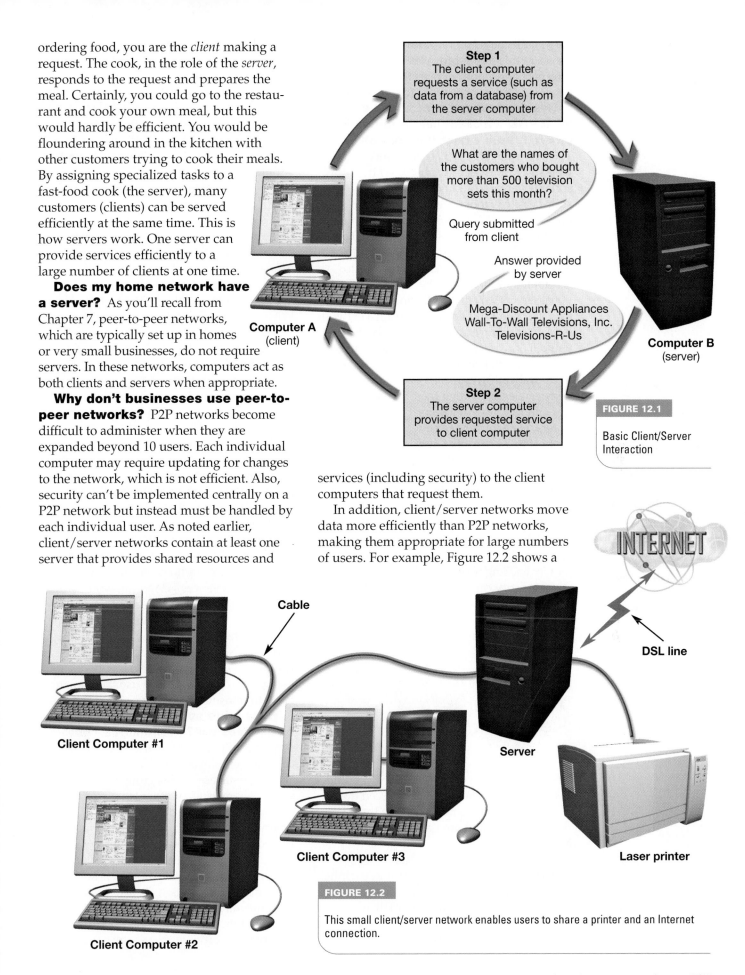

Step 1
The client computer requests a service (such as data from a database) from the server computer

What are the names of the customers who bought more than 500 television sets this month?

Query submitted from client

Answer provided by server

Mega-Discount Appliances Wall-To-Wall Televisions, Inc. Televisions-R-Us

Computer A
(client)

Computer B
(server)

Step 2
The server computer provides requested service to client computer

FIGURE 12.1

Basic Client/Server Interaction

Cable

INTERNET

DSL line

Client Computer #1

Client Computer #3

Server

Laser printer

Client Computer #2

FIGURE 12.2

This small client/server network enables users to share a printer and an Internet connection.

very small client/server arrangement. The server in this figure provides printing and Internet connection services for all of the client computers connected to the network.

Besides having a centralized server, what makes a client/server network different from a peer-to-peer network? The main difference is that client/server networks have increased scalability. With a **scalable network**, additional users can be added easily without affecting the performance of the other network nodes (computers or peripherals). Because servers handle the bulk of tasks performed on the network (printing, Internet access, and so on), it is easy to accommodate more users by installing additional servers to help with the increased workload. Installing additional servers on a network is relatively simple and can usually be done without disrupting services for existing users.

In addition, peer-to-peer networks are **decentralized**. This means that users are responsible for creating their own data backups and for providing security for their computers. In client/server networks, all clients connect to a server that performs tasks for them. Therefore, client/server networks are said to be **centralized**. Many tasks that individual users must handle on a P2P network can be handled centrally at the server.

For instance, data files are normally stored on the server. Therefore, backups for all users on a network can be performed by merely backing up all the files on the server. Also, security can be exercised over the server instead of on each user's computer; this way, the server, rather than the individual user, coordinates file security.

ACTIVE HELPDESK

Selecting a Network Topology and Cable

In this Active Helpdesk call, you'll play the role of a Helpdesk staffer, fielding calls about how a client/server network differs from a peer-to-peer network, the different classifications of client/server networks, various network topologies, and the types of transmission media used in client/server networks.

Classifications of Client/Server Networks: LANs, WANs, and MANs

Networks are generally classified according to their size and the distance between the physical parts of the network. The three main classifications are LANs, WANs, and MANs.

Local area networks (LANs) are generally small groups of computers and peripherals linked together over a relatively small geographic area. The computer lab at your school or the network on the floor of the office where you work is probably a LAN.

For large companies that operate at diverse geographic locations, a LAN is not sufficient for meeting their computing needs. **Wide area networks (WANs)** comprise large numbers of users or separate LANs that are miles apart and linked together. A large college campus would have a WAN that spans all of its lecture halls, residence halls, and administrative offices.

Likewise, corporations often use WANs to connect two or more geographically diverse branches. For example, Nike has manufacturing plants and administrative offices all over the globe. The LAN at each Nike office is connected to other Nike LANs, forming a global Nike WAN. Figure 12.3 shows an example of what part of the Nike WAN might look like.

The Internet is the largest WAN in existence, comprising hundreds of thousands of internetworked computers around the world.

Sometimes government organizations or civic groups establish WANs to link users in a specific geographic area (such as within a city or county). These special type of WANs are known as **metropolitan area networks (MANs)**.

What sort of network connects personal digital assistants (PDAs) and cell phones? Personal area networks (PANs) are used to connect wireless devices (such as Bluetooth-enabled devices) in close proximity to each other. (Bluetooth technology uses radio waves to transmit data over short distances.) PANs are wireless and operate in the personal operating space of an individual, which is generally defined to be within 30 feet (or 10 meters) of your body. Today, PANs free you from having wires running to and from the devices you're using. One day, PANs may use the human body to transmit and receive signals.

What other sort of networks do businesses use? An **intranet** is a private corporate network that is used exclusively by company employees to facilitate information sharing, database access, group scheduling, videoconferencing, or other employee collaboration. Intranets are deployed using Transmission Control Protocol/Internet Protocol (TCP/IP) networks (which we discuss in Chapter 13) and generally include links to the Internet. The intranet is not accessible to nonemployees; a firewall protects it from the Internet.

One of the main uses of intranets is groupware, software that enables users to

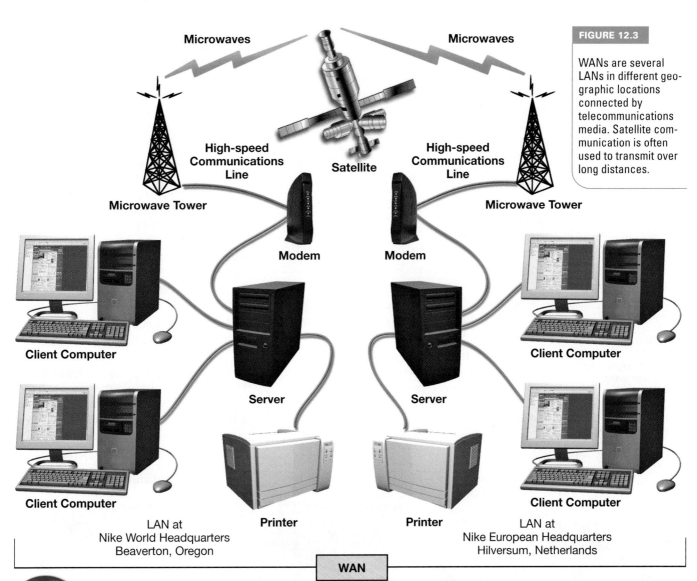

FIGURE 12.3

WANs are several LANs in different geographic locations connected by telecommunications media. Satellite communication is often used to transmit over long distances.

Microwaves

Microwaves

High-speed Communications Line

Satellite

High-speed Communications Line

Microwave Tower

Microwave Tower

Modem

Modem

Client Computer

Client Computer

Server

Server

Client Computer

Client Computer

Printer

Printer

LAN at
Nike World Headquarters
Beaverton, Oregon

LAN at
Nike European Headquarters
Hilversum, Netherlands

WAN

BITS AND BYTES

Traffic Nirvana Thanks to MANs!

How are metropolitan area networks (MANs) used? Singapore has found a great way: to collect traffic information and to smooth traffic congestion. All 92 miles of Singapore's freeways are "smart" highways, meaning they are wired with sensors or video cameras to collect information on traffic flow. This information is transmitted to a central location using a MAN for processing. Tollbooths that collect tolls electronically from sensors placed on cars are also wired into the MAN. Intelligent traffic lights are part of the system and control the flow of traffic, and lighted signs provide drivers with accurate predictions of destination arrival times.

The San Diego Traffic Management Center (TMC) also uses a MAN to analyze traffic patterns. Real-time information is gathered from a variety of sources

such as electronic sensors in the roadways, video cameras, phone calls from motorists, and traffic reporters. The system is used to make a variety of decisions such as setting up detours, dispatching road repair crews, alerting motorists to problems using changeable road signs, and the closure of highways because of disasters (such as earthquakes). The general public can view traffic maps created by the TMC on the Web at **www.dot.ca.gov/sdtraffic**.

So, when will all this happen on a roadway near you? Currently, only 5 percent of U.S. highways are "smart" (most of them in California) and able to collect real-time data on traffic. Unfortunately, federal funds are not available to make the rest of them "smart" any time soon.

share and collaborate on documents. Software such as Lotus Notes, a type of groupware, facilitates sharing of employee information and brainstorming to solve problems. Most groupware programs also support messaging and group calendaring.

Constructing Client/Server Networks

In Chapter 7, we discussed the main components of peer-to-peer networks. Client/server networks share many of the same components of P2P networks as well as some components specific to client/server networks:

- **Server.** Unlike peer-to-peer networks, client/server networks contain at least one computer that functions solely as a server.
- **Network topology.** Because client/server networks are more complex than peer-to-peer networks, the layout and structure of the network, which is called the *network topology*, must be carefully planned.

- **Transmission media.** Data needs a way to flow between clients and servers on networks. Therefore, an appropriate type of *transmission media* (cable or wireless communications technology) is needed based on the network topology. Client/server networks use a wider variety of cable types than do simpler P2P networks.
- **Network operating system (NOS) software.** All client/server networks require *network operating system (NOS) software*, which is specialized software that is installed on servers and client computers that enables the network to function. Most modern operating systems (such as Windows XP and OS X) include the software needed for computers to function as clients on a network.
- **Network adapters.** As is the case with peer-to-peer networks, *network adapters* (or *network interface cards*) must be attached or installed to each device on the network. These adapters enable the computer (or peripheral) to communicate with the network using a common data communication language, or *protocol*.

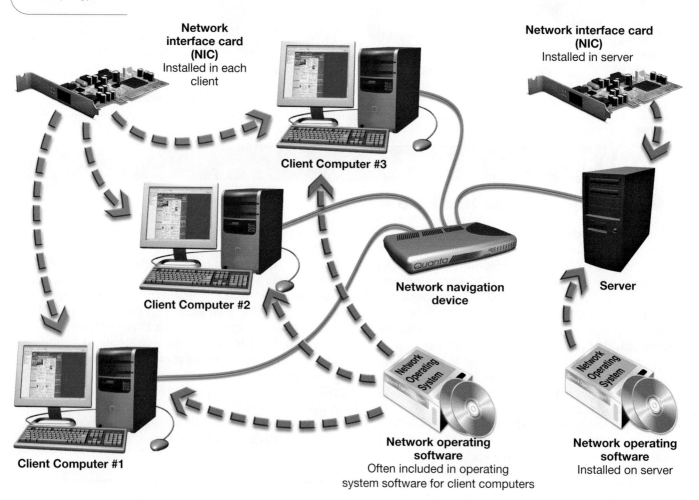

Network interface card (NIC)
Installed in each client

Client Computer #3

Network interface card (NIC)
Installed in server

Client Computer #2

Network navigation device

Server

Client Computer #1

Network operating software
Often included in operating system software for client computers

Network operating software
Installed on server

- **Network navigation devices.** Because of the complexity of a client/server network, specialized *network navigation devices* (such as *routers*, *hubs*, and *switches*) are needed to move data signals around the network.

Figure 12.4 shows the components of a simple client/server network. In the following sections, we explore each component in more detail.

Servers

Servers are the workhorses of the client/server network. They serve many different network users and assist them with accomplishing a variety of tasks. The number and types of servers on a client/server network depend on the network's size and workload. Small networks (such as the one pictured in Figure 12.2) would have just one server to handle all server functions such as file storage, delivery of applications to the clients, printing, and so on.

As more users are added to a network, dedicated servers are also added to take the load off of the main server. **Dedicated servers** are used to fulfill one specific func-tion (such as handling e-mail). When dedicated servers are deployed, the main server then becomes merely an authentication server and/or a file server.

What are authentication and file servers? Authentication servers keep track of who is logging on to the network and which services on the network are available to each user. Authentication servers also act as overseers for the network. They manage and coordinate the services provided by any other dedicated servers located on the network. **File servers** store and manage files for network users. On the network at your workplace or school, you may be provided with space on a file server to store files you create.

What functions do dedicated servers handle? Any task that is repetitive or demands a lot of time of the server's processor (CPU) is a good candidate to relegate to a dedicated server. Common types of dedicated servers are print servers, application servers, database servers, e-mail servers, communications servers, and Web servers. Servers are connected to a client/server network so that all client computers that need to use their services can access them, as shown in Figure 12.5.

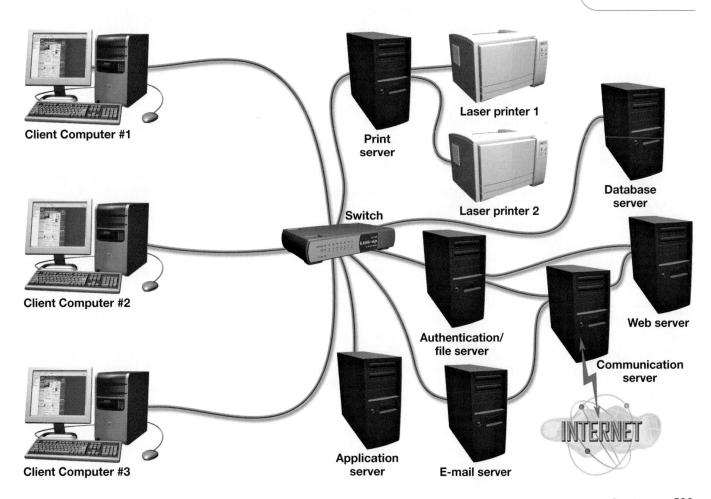

Client Computer #1

Client Computer #2

Client Computer #3

Print server

Laser printer 1

Laser printer 2

Switch

Database server

Web server

Authentication/ file server

Communication server

Application server

E-mail server

INTERNET

PRINT SERVERS

How does a print server function?
Printing is a function that takes a large chunk of central processing unit (CPU) time and that most people do quite often. Setting up a **print server** to manage all client-requested printing jobs for all printers on the network helps enable client computers to complete more productive work than printing. When you tell your computer to print a document, it passes off the task to the print server. This frees the CPU on your computer to do other jobs.

When the print server receives a printing request (or job) from a client computer, it puts the job into a print queue on the print server. A print queue is a software holding area for printing jobs. Normally, each printer on a network has its own uniquely named print queue. Jobs receive a number when entering the queue and are sent to the printer in the order in which they are received. Print queues thus function like the "take a number" machines at a supermarket deli. They keep disputes from breaking out over which job is served next by the printer. Another useful aspect of print servers is that they can prioritize print jobs. Different users and types of print jobs can be assigned different priorities, and higher-priority jobs are printed first. For instance, in a company where documents are printed on demand for clients, you would want these print jobs to take precedence over an employee printing routine correspondence.

APPLICATION SERVERS

What function does an application server perform? In many networks, all users run the same application software (such as Microsoft Office) on their computers. In a network of thousands of personal computers, installing application software on each individual computer is time consuming. An **application server** therefore acts as a repository for application software.

When a client computer connects to the network and requests an application, the application server delivers the software to the client computer. Because the software does not reside on the client computer itself, this eases the task of installation and upgrading: the application needs to be installed or upgraded only on the application server, not on each network client.

DATABASE SERVERS

What does a database server do? Just like its name implies, a **database server** provides client computers with access to information stored in a database. Often, many people need to access databases at the same time. For example, airline ticketing clerks can serve multiple people at the same time because they all have access to the ticket reservation database. This is achieved by storing the database on a database server, which each clerk's computer can access through the network. If the database were not on a network but instead on a stand-alone computer, only one clerk could use it at a time, making the ticketing system very inefficient.

E-MAIL SERVERS

When is an e-mail server necessary?
The volume of e-mail on a large corporate network could quickly overwhelm a server that was attempting to handle other functions as well. Therefore, the sole function of an **e-mail server** attached to the network is to process and deliver incoming and outgoing e-mail. On a network with an e-mail server, when you send an e-mail from your computer, it goes to the e-mail server, which then handles the routing and delivery of your message. The e-mail server functions much like a postal carrier, who picks up your mail and sees that it finds its way to the correct destination.

COMMUNICATIONS SERVERS

What types of communications does a communications server handle? A **communications server** handles all communications between the network and other networks, including managing Internet connectivity. All requests for information from the Internet and all messages being sent through the Internet pass through the communications server. Because Internet traffic is substantial at most organizations, the communications server has a heavy workload.

Often, the communications server is the only device on the network connected to the Internet. E-mail servers, Web servers, and other devices needing to communicate with the Internet usually route all their traffic through the communications server. Providing a single point of contact with the outside world makes it easier to secure the network from hackers.

ACTIVE HELPDESK

Using Servers

In this Active Helpdesk call, you'll play the role of a Helpdesk staffer, fielding calls about various types of servers and client/server software.

WEB SERVERS

What function does a Web server perform? A **Web server** is used to host a Web site available through the Internet. Web servers run specialized software, such as Apache (open-source server software) or Microsoft Internet Information Server, that enables them to host Web pages. Not every large network has a Web server. Many companies use an Internet service provider (ISP) to host their corporate Web sites instead.

Network Topologies

Just as buildings have different floor plans depending on their uses, networks have different blueprints delineating their layout. **Network topology** refers to the physical or logical arrangement of computers, transmission media (cable), and other network components. Because networks have different uses, not all networks will have the same topology.

In this section, we explore the most common network topologies (bus, ring, and star) and discuss when each topology is used. As you'll see, the type of network topology used is important because it can affect the network's performance and scalability. Knowing how the basic topologies work and the strengths and weaknesses of each will help you understand

BITS AND BYTES

Too Much Data? Here Comes the SAN

Databases can become so large that conventional database servers can't handle the information flowing in and out of them. A *storage area network (SAN)* is specifically designed to store and disseminate large amounts of data to client computers or servers. SANs are made up of several *network attached storage (NAS)* devices, which are specialized devices attached to a network whose sole function is to store and disseminate data. Picture a computer with nothing but hard drives in it and you have a pretty good idea of what a NAS device looks like. NAS devices are the filing cabinets of the new millennium and exist merely to store the huge amounts of data network users generate. Although they behave like dedicated servers, NAS devices have their own operating systems and file storage algorithms. Because they don't perform any network services other than storage and retrieval, they can do so quickly and efficiently. Any large database that will be searched by many users simultaneously, such as Amazon or eBay, is a good candidate for a SAN.

why particular network topologies were chosen on the networks you use.

BUS TOPOLOGY

What does a bus topology look like? In a **bus (or linear bus) topology**, all computers are connected in sequence on a single cable, as shown in Figure 12.6. This topology

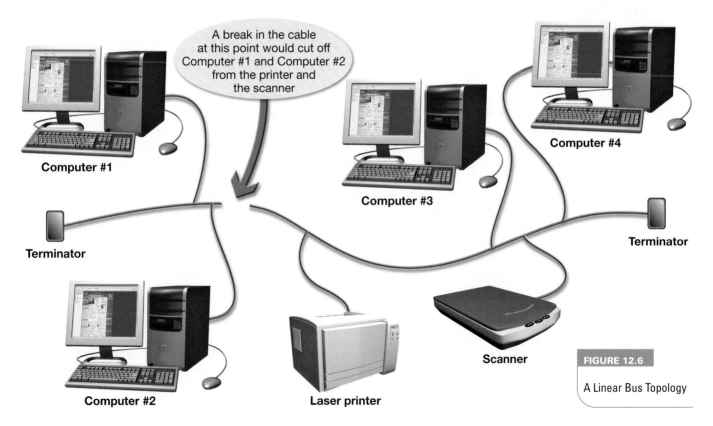

A break in the cable at this point would cut off Computer #1 and Computer #2 from the printer and the scanner

Computer #1

Terminator

Computer #2

Laser printer

Computer #3

Scanner

Computer #4

Terminator

FIGURE 12.6

A Linear Bus Topology

is deployed most often in peer-to-peer networks (not client/server networks). Each computer on the bus network can communicate with every other computer on the network directly. A limitation of bus networks is that data collisions can occur very easily if two computers transmit data at the same time because a bus network is essentially composed of one main communication medium (single cable).

Think of a data collision as having a group of three people (e.g., Diane, Janet, and Lee) sitting in a room having a conversation. For the conversation to be effective, only one person can speak at a time; otherwise, they would not be able to hear and understand each other. Therefore, if Diane is speaking, Janet and Lee must wait until she finishes before presenting their ideas, and so on.

Because two signals transmitted at the same time on a bus network may cause a data collision, an **access method** has to be established to control which computer is allowed to use the transmission media at a certain time. Computers on a bus network behave the same way as a group of people having a conversation. The computers "listen" to the network data traffic on the media. When no other computer is transmitting data (that is, when "conversation" stops), the computer knows it is allowed to transmit data on the media. This means of taking turns "talking" avoids **data collisions**, which happen when two computers send data at the same time and the sets of data collide somewhere in the media. When data collides, it is often lost or irreparably damaged.

How does data get from point to point on a bus network? When it is safe to send data (that is, when no other computers are transmitting data), the sending computer broadcasts the data onto the media. The data is broadcast throughout the network to *all* devices connected to the network. The data is broken into small segments called **packets**. Each packet contains the address of the computer or peripheral device to which it is being sent. Each computer or device connected to the network listens for data that contains its address. When it "hears" data addressed to it, it takes the data off the media and processes it.

For example, say your computer needs to print something on the printer attached to the network. Your computer "listens" to the network to ensure no other nodes are trans-

mitting. It then sends the print job out onto the network. When the printer "hears" a job addressed to it (the print job your computer just sent), it pulls the data off the network and executes the job.

The devices (nodes) attached to a bus network do nothing to move data along the network. This makes a bus network a **passive topology**. The data merely travels the entire length of the medium and is received by all network devices. The ends of the cable in a bus network are capped off by terminators (as shown in Figure 12.6). A **terminator** is a device that absorbs the signal so it is not reflected back onto parts of the network that have already received it.

What are the advantages and disadvantages of bus networks? The simplicity and low cost of configuring a bus network are the major reasons why this topology is deployed most often in P2P networks. The major disadvantage is that if there is a break in the cable, the bus network is effectively disrupted, because some computers are cut off from others on the network.

Also, because transmission signals degrade as the distance of the cable increases, a bus network is difficult to expand to a large number of users. And because only one computer can communicate at a time, adding a large number of nodes to a bus network limits performance and causes delays in sending data. Therefore, you rarely see a bus network deployed except in very small networks that are not expected to grow.

RING TOPOLOGY

What does a ring topology look like? Not surprisingly, given its name, the computers and peripherals in a **ring** (or **loop**) **topology** are laid out in a circle, as shown in Figure 12.7. Data flows around the circle from device to device in one direction only. Because data is passed using a special data packet called a **token**, this type of topology is commonly referred to as a **token-ring topology**.

How is a token used to move data around a ring? A token is passed from computer to computer around the ring until it is grabbed by a computer that needs to transmit data. The computer holds onto the token until it is done transmitting data. Only one computer on the ring can "hold" the token at a time, and usually only one token exists on each ring.

SOUND BYTE

Network Topology and Navigation Devices

In this Sound Byte, you'll learn about common network topologies, the types of networks they are used with, and various network navigation devices.

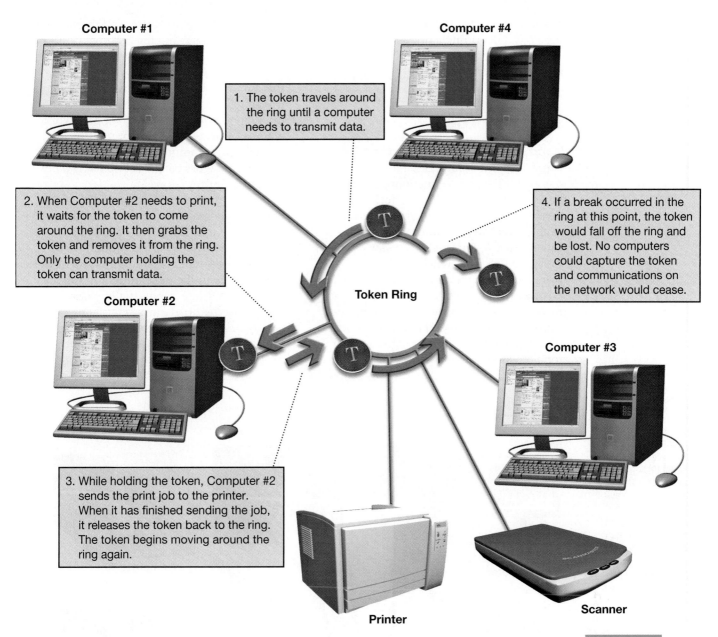

Computer #1

Computer #4

1. The token travels around the ring until a computer needs to transmit data.

2. When Computer #2 needs to print, it waits for the token to come around the ring. It then grabs the token and removes it from the ring. Only the computer holding the token can transmit data.

4. If a break occurred in the ring at this point, the token would fall off the ring and be lost. No computers could capture the token and communications on the network would cease.

Token Ring

Computer #2

Computer #3

3. While holding the token, Computer #2 sends the print job to the printer. When it has finished sending the job, it releases the token back to the ring. The token begins moving around the ring again.

Printer

Scanner

FIGURE 12.7

A Token-Ring Topology

If a computer (or node) has data to send, it waits for the token to be passed to it. It then takes the token out of circulation and sends data to its destination. When the receiving node receives a complete transmission of the data, it sends an acknowledgment to the sending node. The sending node then generates a new token and starts it going around the ring again. This **token method** is the access method that ring networks use to avoid data collisions.

A ring topology is an **active topology** because each node on the network is responsible for retransmitting the token or the data to the next node on the ring. Large ring networks have the capability to use multiple tokens, which help move more data faster.

Is a ring topology better than a bus topology? A ring topology provides a fairer allocation of network resources than does a bus topology. By using a token, a ring network enables all nodes on the network to have an equal chance to send data. One "chatty" node cannot as easily monopolize the network bandwidth because after sending a batch of data, it must pass the token on.

In addition, the ring topology's performance remains acceptable even with large numbers of users. However, if one computer fails on a ring network, it can bring the entire network to a halt because that computer is unavailable to retransmit tokens and data. Problems in the ring can also be hard for network administrators to find. It's easier to expand a ring topology than a bus topology, but adding a node to a ring does cause the ring to cease to function while the node is installed.

STAR TOPOLOGY

What is the layout for a star topology?
A **star topology** is the most widely deployed client/server network layout in businesses today because it offers the most flexibility. In a star topology, the nodes connect to a central communications device called a *switch*, thus forming a star, as shown in Figure 12.8. The switch receives a signal from the sending node and retransmits it to all other nodes on the network. The network nodes examine data and only pick up the transmissions addressed to them. Because the switch retransmits data signals, a star topology is an active topology. (We discuss switches in more detail later in this chapter.)

Many star networks use the Ethernet protocol. Networks using the Ethernet protocol are by far the most common type of network in use today. Although many students think that Ethernet is a type of network topology, it is actually a communications protocol. A topology is a physical design of a network, whereas a **protocol** is a set of rules for exchanging communication. Therefore, an Ethernet network can be set up using a bus, ring, or a star topology.

For example, assume that your class has to send a message to the class next door. You decide to arrange your class in a straight line from your classroom to the other classroom. Each student will whisper the message to the next student in the line until the message is eventually passed to a student in the other classroom. The arrangement of the students in a straight line is your topology. The passing of the message from student to student using the English language is your protocol.

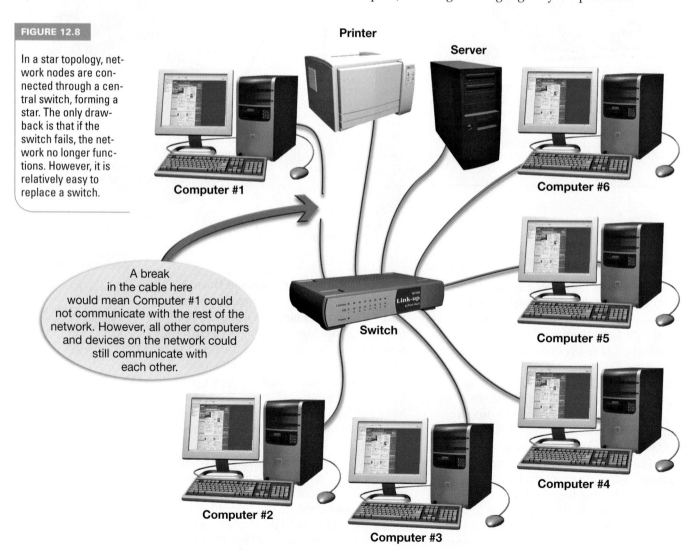

FIGURE 12.8

In a star topology, network nodes are connected through a central switch, forming a star. The only drawback is that if the switch fails, the network no longer functions. However, it is relatively easy to replace a switch.

A break in the cable here would mean Computer #1 could not communicate with the rest of the network. However, all other computers and devices on the network could still communicate with each other.

Printer

Server

Computer #1

Computer #6

Switch

Computer #5

Computer #2

Computer #4

Computer #3

How do computers on a star net-work avoid data collisions? Because most star networks are Ethernet networks, they use the method used on all Ethernet networks to avoid data collisions: **CSMA/CD** (short for Carrier Sense Multiple Access with Collision Detection). With CSMA/CD, a node connected to the network listens (that is, has carrier sense) to determine that no other nodes are currently transmitting data signals. If the node doesn't hear any other signals, it assumes it is safe to transmit data. All devices on the network have the same right (that is, they have multiple access) to transmit data when they deem it safe. It is therefore possible for two devices to begin transmitting data signals at the same time. If this happens, the two signals collide.

What happens when the signals collide? As shown in Figure 12.9, when signals collide, a node on the network detects the collision. It then sends a special signal called a **jam signal** to all network nodes, alerting them that

a collision has occurred. The nodes then stop transmitting and wait a random amount of time before retransmitting their data signals. The wait time needs to be random; otherwise, both nodes would start transmitting at the same time and another collision would occur.

What are the advantages and disadvantages of a star topology? Because of the complexity of the layout of star networks, they require more cable and are often more expensive than bus or ring networks. However, star topologies are generally considered to be superior to a ring topology because if one computer fails it doesn't affect the rest of the network. This is extremely important in a large network, in which one disabled computer affecting the operations of several hundred other computers would be totally unacceptable.

It is also easy to add nodes to star networks, and performance remains acceptable even with large numbers of users. In addition,

FIGURE 12.9

Avoiding Data Collisions on an Ethernet Network

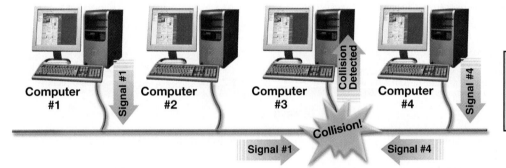

Step 1: Computer #1 and Computer #4 begin transmitting data signals at the same time. A data collision occurs, which is detected by Computer #3.

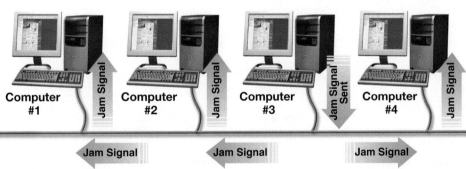

Step 2: Computer #3 sends a jam signal to all nodes on the network, informing them that a collision has occurred.

Step 3: Computer #1 and Computer #4 wait random amounts of time, then send their signals again. Since the signals are resent at different times, a second collision should not occur.

14 nanoseconds later   18 nanoseconds later

the centralization of communications (through a switch) makes troubleshooting and repairs on star networks easier for network technicians. Technicians can usually pinpoint a communications problem just by examining the switch, as opposed to searching for a particular length of cable that broke in a ring network.

COMPARING TOPOLOGIES

So which topology is the best one?
Figure 12.10 lists the advantages and disadvantages of bus, ring, and star topologies. In all but the smallest networks, star topologies are the most common. Because networks are constantly adding new users, the ability to add new users simply (that is, by installing a new switch) without affecting users already on the network is the deciding factor. The networks you'll encounter at school and in the workplace will almost certainly be laid out in a star topology. However, bus topologies are still the most common layout for simple home networks, and ring topologies are popular when fair allocation of network access is a major requirement of the network.

Can topologies be combined within a single network? Because each topology has its own unique advantages, topologies are often combined to construct business networks. Combining multiple topologies into one network is known as constructing a **hybrid topology**. For instance, fair allocation of resources may be critical for reservation clerks at an airline (requiring a token ring network), whereas a purchasing department's network may require a star topology. One disadvantage of hybrid topologies is that hardware changes must usually be made to switch a node from one topology to another.

Transmission Media

When constructing a house, a variety of building material is available, depending on the needs of the builder. Similarly, when building a network, network engineers can use different types of media. **Transmission media**, whether it is cable or wireless communications technology, comprise the routes data takes to flow between devices on the network. Without transmission media, network devices would be unable to communicate.

FIGURE 12.10 Advantages and Disadvantages of Bus, Ring, and Star Topologies

Topology	Advantages	Disadvantages
Bus	Uses a minimal amount of cabling Easy, reliable, and inexpensive to install	Breaks in the cable can disable the network Large numbers of users will greatly decrease performance because of high volumes of data traffic
Ring	Allocates access to the network fairly Performance remains acceptable even with large numbers of users	Adding or removing nodes disables the network Failure of one computer can bring down the entire network Problems in data transmission can sometimes be difficult to find
Star	Failure of one computer does not affect other computers on the network Centralized design simplifies troubleshooting and repairs Easy to add additional computers or network segments as needed (high scalability) Performance remains acceptable even with large numbers of users	Requires more cable and is often more expensive than a bus or ring topology The switch is a central point of failure. If it fails, all computers connected to that switch are affected.

WIRED TRANSMISSION MEDIA

What types of cable are commonly used for networks?

In Chapter 7, you learned that most home networks use either twisted pair cable (phone wire or Ethernet) or electrical wires as transmission media. For business networks, the three main cable types that are used today are twisted pair, coaxial, and fiber optic. Although each type is different, they share many common factors that need to be considered when choosing a cable type:

- **Maximum run length.** Each type of cable has a maximum run length over which signals sent across it can be "heard" by devices connected to it. Therefore, when designing a network, network engineers must accurately measure the distances between devices to ensure that appropriate cable is selected.

- **Bandwidth.** As you learned in earlier chapters, **bandwidth** is the amount of data that can be transmitted across a transmission medium in a certain amount of time. Each cable is different and is rated by the maximum bandwidth it can support. Bandwidth is measured in bits per second, which represents how many bits of data can be transmitted along the cable each second.

- **Bend radius (flexibility).** When installing cable, it is often necessary to bend the cable around corners, surfaces, and so on. The bend radius of the cable defines how many degrees a cable can be bent in a one-foot segment before it is damaged. If many corners need to be navigated when installing a network, network engineers use cabling with a high bend radius.

- **Cable cost.** The cost per foot of different types and grades of cable varies widely. Cable selection may have to be made on the basis of cost if adequate funds are not available for the optimal type of cabling.

- **Installation costs.** Certain cable (such as twisted pair, which is used in home networks) is easy and inexpensive to install. Fiber-optic cable requires special training and equipment to install, which increases the installation costs.

- **Susceptibility to interference.** Signals traveling down a cable are subject to two types of interference. Electromagnetic interference (EMI), caused by the cable being exposed to strong electromagnetic fields, can distort or degrade signals on the cable. Fluorescent lights and machinery with motors or transformers are the most common sources of EMI emissions. Cable signals also can be disrupted by radio frequency interference (RFI), which is usually caused by broadcast sources (television and radio signals) being located near the network. Cable types are rated as to how well they resist interference.

- **Signal transmission methods.** Coaxial cable and twisted pair cable both send electrical impulses down conductive material to transmit data signals. Fiber-optic cable transmits data signals as pulses of light.

In the sections that follow, we discuss the characteristics of each of the three major types of cable. We also discuss the use of wireless media as an alternative to cable.

Twisted Pair Cable

What does twisted pair cable look like?

Twisted pair cable should be familiar to you because the telephone cable (or wire) in your home is one type of twisted pair cable. Twisted pair cable consists of pairs of copper wires twisted around each other and covered by a protective jacket (or sheath). The twists are important because they cause the magnetic fields that form around the copper wires to intermingle, which makes them less susceptible to outside interference. It also reduces the amount of crosstalk interference, or the tendency of signals on one wire to interfere with signals on a wire next to it.

If the twisted pair cable contains a layer of foil shielding to reduce interference, it is known as **shielded twisted pair (STP) cable**. If it does not contain a layer of foil shielding, it is known as **unshielded twisted pair (UTP) cable**, which is more susceptible to interference. Figure 12.11 shows illustrations of both

FIGURE 12.11

Anatomy of (a) unshielded twisted pair (UTP) cable and (b) shielded twisted pair (STP) cable.

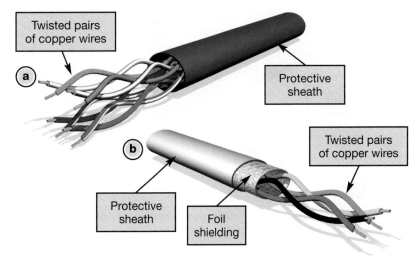

Twisted pairs of copper wires

Protective sheath

Protective sheath

Foil shielding

Twisted pairs of copper wires

types of twisted pair cable. Because of its lower price, UTP is more widely used, unless significant sources of interference must be overcome (such as in a production environment where machines create magnetic fields). However, there are different standard categories of UTP cable from which to choose.

What types of UTP cable are available? The two most common types of UTP cable in use today are Category 5E (Cat 5E) and Category 6 (Cat 6). Cat 6 cable can handle a bandwidth of 1 gigabit per second (Gbps), whereas Cat 5E can handle a bandwidth of just 200 megabits per second (Mbps).

Unless severe budget constraints are in place, network engineers usually install the highest-bandwidth cable possible because reinstalling cable later (and the subsequent tearing up of walls and ceilings) can be very expensive. Therefore, since the fall of 2002, when the standard for Cat 6 cable was approved, new cable runs in businesses have been made with Cat 6 cable. Home networks that use twisted pair cable generally use Cat 5E cable because it's less expensive.

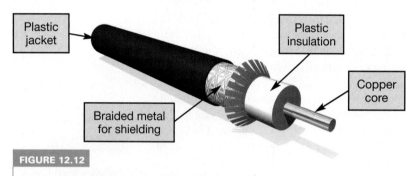

Plastic jacket

Braided metal for shielding

Plastic insulation

Copper core

FIGURE 12.12

Coaxial cable consists of four main components: the core, an insulated covering, a braided metal shielding, and a plastic jacket.

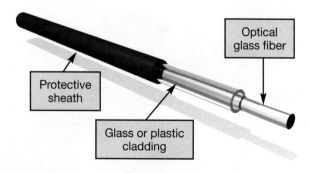

Protective sheath

Glass or plastic cladding

Optical glass fiber

FIGURE 12.13

Fiber-optic cable is made up of a glass (or plastic) fiber (or a bundle of fibers), a glass or plastic cladding, and a protective sheath.

Coaxial Cable

What does coaxial cable look like?
Coaxial cable should be familiar to you if you have cable television, because most cable television installers use coaxial cable. Coaxial cable (as shown in Figure 12.12) consists of four main components:

1. The core (usually copper) is in the very center and is used for transmitting the signal.

2. A solid layer of nonconductive insulating material (usually a hard, thick plastic) surrounds the core.

3. A layer of braided metal comes next to reduce interference with signals traveling in the core.

4. Finally, an external jacket of lightweight plastic covers the internal cable components to protect them from damage.

Although coaxial cable used to be the most widely used cable in business networks, advances in twisted pair cable shielding and transmission speeds, as well as twisted pair's lower cost, have reduced the popularity of coaxial cable.

Are there different types of coaxial cable? The two main coaxial cable types are ThinNet and ThickNet. ThinNet is the cable used by the cable TV company to wire your home and is usually covered by a black plastic jacket. ThickNet, usually distinguished by a yellow jacket, is similar to ThinNet, only it is more rigid and better shielded to protect against interference. ThickNet, because it is better shielded, is used in industrial settings where there is a lot of electrical interference. ThinNet is used in homes because it is cheaper and because most houses do not have significant sources of interference (such as industrial machinery).

Fiber-Optic Cable

What does fiber-optic cable look like?
As shown in Figure 12.13, **fiber-optic cable** is composed of a glass (or plastic) fiber (or a bundle of fibers) that comprises the core of the cable (where the data is transmitted). Cladding, a protective layer made of glass or plastic, is wrapped around the core to protect it. Finally, for additional protection, an outer jacket (sheath) is added, often made of durable materials such as Kevlar (the substance used to make bullet-proof vests). Data transmissions can pass through fiber-optic cable in only one

direction. Therefore, usually at least two cores are located in each fiber-optic cable to enable transmission of data in both directions.

How does fiber-optic cable differ from twisted pair and coaxial cable? As noted earlier, the main difference between fiber-optic cable and other types of cable is the method of signal transmission. Twisted pair and coaxial cable use copper wire to conduct electrical impulses. In a fiber-optic cable, electrical data signals from network devices (client computers, peripherals, and so on) are converted to light pulses before they are transmitted. Because EMI and RFI do not affect light waves, fiber-optic cable is virtually immune to interference.

WIRELESS MEDIA OPTIONS

What wireless media options are there? Although the word *wireless* implies no wires, in businesses, **wireless media** are usually add-ons to extend or improve access to a wired network. In the corporate environment, wireless access is often provided to give employees a wider range to their working area. For instance, if conference rooms offer wireless access, employees can bring their laptops to meetings and gain access to the network during the meeting. However, when they go back to their offices, they may connect to the regular wired network through a wired connection. So, today's corporate networks are often a combination of wired and wireless media.

As you learned in earlier chapters, wireless devices must use the same communications standard to communicate with each other. Wireless networks in the United States are currently based on the **802.11 standard**, also known as **Wi-Fi** (short for Wireless Fidelity), established by the Institute of Electrical and Electronics Engineers (IEEE). Wireless devices attached to networks using the 802.11 standard communicate with each other using radio waves.

The 802.11 standard is actually divided into a number of separate standards. The 802.11b standard was in widespread use both in business and in homes in the late 1990s and early 2000s because manufacturers using the 802.11b standard produced the first cost-effective wireless devices. However, 802.11b devices have largely been replaced with faster technology.

With a maximum throughput of 54 Mbps, the 802.11a and 802.11g standards are now widely deployed in corporate and personal networks. 802.11g devices include Super G (also called Extreme G or Enhanced G) devices, which use proprietary algorithms and hardware to increase maximum throughput to 108 Mbps. However, 802.11g devices will soon be replaced by 802.11n devices. The 802.11n standard will support much higher throughput and greatly increased range (most likely by using multiple antennas to send and receive signals), which will make it very popular for providing wireless coverage over entire offices. Expect to see 802.11n devices hit the market in late 2006 or 2007.

COMPARING TRANSMISSION MEDIA

So which medium is best for client/server networks? Network engineers specialize in the design and deployment of networks and are responsible for selecting network topology and media types. Their decision as to which transmission medium the network will use is based on the topology selected, the length of the cable

BITS AND BYTES

A Network on the Move!

When you think of cutting-edge technology, do you think of city buses? If you visited Portsmouth, England, you would. Portsmouth is a small city that gets over 6.5 million tourists each year. Because the city is always full of people, 320 buses are deployed in it, each one equipped with a very sophisticated wireless network, including an onboard computer and wireless network card. And each bus stop is equipped with an Internet terminal that enables patrons to check e-mail, buy bus tickets, and check exactly where the bus they are waiting for is located and when it will arrive. The network keeps track of the exact location of all the network nodes (the computers on the buses) by sending test signals (pings) to them and measuring the time communications take to travel back and forth. The network doesn't use 802.11 technology; instead, it uses a competing standard developed for the military called QDMA (quad-division multiple access). The main advantage of QDMA is that it can network devices moving as fast at 250 miles an hour without losing the link. However, there are plans to add 802.11-compatible wireless access points at bus kiosks and on the buses to allow riders to use their own computers, PDAs, and cell phones to surf the net.

FIGURE 12.14 Comparison of Characteristics of Major Cable Types

Cable Characteristics	Twisted Pair (Cat 6)	Coaxial (ThinNet)	Coaxial (ThickNet)	Fiber Optic
Maximum Run Length	328 feet (100 m)	607 feet (185 m)	1,640 feet (500 m)	Up to 62 miles (100 km)
Bandwidth	1,000 Mbps	10 Mbps	10 Mbps	100 Mbps to 2 Gbps
Bend Radius (Flexibility)	No limit	360 degrees/foot	30 degrees/foot	30 degrees/foot
Cable Cost	Very low	Low	Moderate	High
Installation Cost	Very low	Low	Slightly higher than ThinNet	Most expensive because of installation training required
Susceptibility to Interference	High	Low	Very low	None (not susceptible to EMI and RFI)

runs needed, the amount of interference present, and the need for wireless connectivity.

Figure 12.14 compares the attributes of the major cable types. Most large networks have a mix of media. For example, coaxial cable may be appropriate for the portion of the network that traverses the factory floor where interference from magnetic fields is significant. However, unshielded twisted pair cable may work fine in the general office area. And wireless media may be required in conference rooms and other areas where employees are likely to connect their laptops or where it is impractical or expensive to run cable.

Network Operating Systems

Merely connecting computers and peripherals with media does not create a client/server network. Special software, known as a **network operating system (NOS)**, needs to be installed on each client computer and server connected to the network to provide the services necessary for them to communicate. Many modern operating systems (such as Windows XP and Mac OS X) include NOS client software as part of the basic installation. However, if your operating system does not include NOS client software, it must be installed on each client. The NOS provides a set of common rules (a protocol) that controls communication between devices on the network. The major

NOSs on the market today include Windows Server 2003, UNIX, and Novell NetWare.

Do peer-to-peer networks need special NOS software? The software that P2P networks require is built into the Windows and Macintosh operating systems. Therefore, there is no need to purchase specialized NOS software.

How does NOS software differ from operating system software? Operating system (OS) software is designed to facilitate communication between the software and hardware components of your computer. NOS software is specifically designed to provide server services, network communications, management of network peripherals, and storage. To provide network communications, the client computer must run a small part of the NOS in addition to the OS. Windows XP is an OS and is installed on home computers. As noted above, because it also has some NOS functionality, client computers (in a client/server network) that have Windows XP installed as the OS do not need an additional NOS. Windows Server 2003 is an NOS that is deployed on servers in a client/server network.

How does the NOS control network communications? Each NOS has its own proprietary communications language, file management structure, and device management structure. The NOS also sets and controls the protocols (rules) for all devices wishing to communicate on the network. Many different proprietary networking protocols exist, such as Novell's Internetwork Packet Exchange (IPX), Microsoft's NetBIOS

TRENDS IN IT

Emerging Technologies: Virtual Network Computing Is Here and It's Free

Have you ever been in someone else's office or dorm room on another floor of your building and needed to access something on your computer? Virtual Network Computing (VNC) enables you to access the information on your computer when you are away from it!

The AT&T Laboratories, located at Cambridge University, have developed a free software program that enables you to access your computer from another computer. VNC consists of two software parts: a "server" and a "viewer." To use VNC, you run the software server program on your desktop computer before you leave it. This makes your computer accessible from other computers running the appropriate viewer software.

You then install and run the viewer software (which fits on a floppy disk) on the computer from which you wish to control your desktop computer. The good news is that the software works on virtually any platform (although the free version of the software is available

only for the Windows and Linux operating systems). This means that your desktop computer can be running Windows, for instance, but you can access it remotely from a Linux machine. The only requirement is that a TCP/IP connection (the normal Internet connection used on most computers) must exist between the two machines.

Once you take control of your desktop computer from the remote computer, everything you do (opening and saving files, and so on) is reflected on your desktop computer. When you return to your desk, your computer will reflect all the changes you made to it at the remote computer. This can be a tremendous timesaver if you are frequently away from your desk and need to access your computer. Figure 12.15 shows a Windows XP desktop being accessed remotely from another Windows computer.

For more information on Virtual Network Computing, visit **www.realvnc.com**.

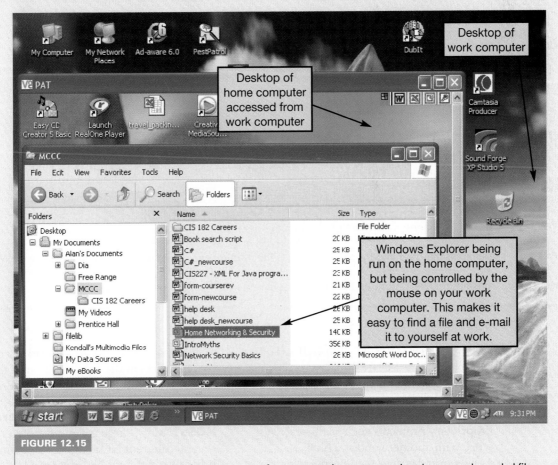

FIGURE 12.15

Using VNC, it is easy to access your home computer from your work computer and retrieve a much-needed file.

The OSI Model: Defining Protocol Standards

The Institute of Electrical and Electronics Engineers (IEEE) has taken the lead in establishing recognized worldwide networking protocols, including a standard of communications called the Open Systems Interconnection (OSI) reference model. The OSI model, which was quickly adopted as a standard throughout the computing world, provides the protocol guidelines for all modern networks. All modern NOS protocols are designed to interact in accordance with the standards set out by the OSI model.

The OSI model divides communications tasks into seven distinct processes called *layers*. Each layer of an OSI network has a specific function. Figure 12.16 shows the layers of the OSI model and their functions. Each layer knows how to communicate with the layer above and below it.

This layering approach makes communications more efficient because specialized pieces of the NOS perform specific tasks. It is akin to assembly line manufacturing. Producing thousands of cars per day would be difficult if one person had to build a car on his or her own. By splitting up the work of assembling a car into specialized tasks (such as installing the engine, bolting on the bumpers, and so on), people who are exceptionally good at certain tasks can be assigned to do them and achieve higher efficiency. This is how the OSI layers work. By handling specialized tasks and communicating only with the layers above and below them, the layering approach makes communications more efficient.

Let's look at how each OSI layer functions by following an e-mail you create and send to your friend.

FIGURE 12.16 The Layers of the OSI Model and Their Functions

Layer Name	Layer Function
Application Layer	Handles all interfaces between the application software and the network Translates user information into a format the presentation layer can understand
Presentation Layer	Reformats data so that the session layer can understand it Compresses and encrypts data
Session Layer	Sets up a virtual (not physical) connection between the sending and receiving devices Manages communications sessions
Transport Layer	Creates packets Handles packet acknowledgment
Network Layer	Determines where to send the packets on the network
Data Link Layer	Assembles the data into frames, addresses them, and sends them to the physical layer for delivery
Physical Layer	Transmits (delivers) data on the network so it can reach its intended address

Extended User Interface (NetBEUI), and the Apple File Protocol (AFP). These protocols were developed for a specific vendor's operating system. For example, IPX was developed for networks running the Novell NOS. Proprietary protocols such as these do not work with another vendor's NOS.

However, because the Internet uses an open protocol (called TCP/IP) for communications, many corporate networks use TCP/IP as their standard networking protocol regardless of the manufacturer of their NOS. All modern NOSs support TCP/IP. (We discuss TCP/IP in more detail in Chapter 13.)

Can a network use two different NOSs? Many large corporate networks use several different NOSs at the same time. This is because different NOSs provide different features, some of which are more useful in certain situations than others. For instance,

Application Layer

- The *application layer* handles all interaction between the application software and the network. It translates the data from the application into a format that the presentation layer can understand. For example, when you send an e-mail, the application layer takes the e-mail message you created in Microsoft Outlook, translates it into a format your network can understand, and passes it to the presentation layer.

Presentation Layer

- The *presentation layer* reformats the data so that the session layer can understand it. It also handles data encryption (changing the data into a format that makes it harder to intercept and read the message) and compression if required. In our e-mail example, the presentation layer notices that you selected an encryption option for the e-mail message and encrypts the data before sending it to the session layer.

Session Layer

- The *session layer* sets up a virtual (not physical) connection between the sending and receiving devices. It then manages the communication between the two. In our e-mail example, the session layer would set up the parameters for the communications session between your computer and the Internet service provider (ISP) where your friend has her e-mail account. The session layer then tracks the transmission of the e-mail until it is satisfied that all the data in the e-mail was received at your friend's ISP.

Transport Layer

- The *transport layer* breaks the data up into packets and sequences them appropriately. It also handles acknowledgment of packets (that is, it determines whether the packets were received at their destination) and decides whether packets need to be sent again. In our e-mail example, the transport layer breaks your e-mail message up into packets and sends them to the network layer, making sure that all the packets reach their destination.

Network Layer

- The *network layer* determines where to send the packets on the network and the best way to route them there. In our e-mail example, the network layer examines the address on the packets (the address of your friend's ISP) and determines how to route the packets so they get to your ISP and can ultimately get to the receiving computer.

Data Link Layer

- The *data link layer* is responsible for assembling the data packets into *frames* (a type of data packet that holds more data), addressing the frames, and delivering them to the physical layer so they can be sent on their way. It is the equivalent of a postal worker who reads the address on a piece of mail and makes sure it gets sent to the proper recipient. In our e-mail example, the data link layer assembles the e-mail data packets into frames, which are addressed with appropriate routing information received from the network layer.

Physical Layer

- The *physical layer* takes care of delivering the data. It converts the data into a signal and transmits it out onto the network so it can reach its intended address. In our e-mail example, the physical layer sends the data out over the Internet to its ultimate destination (your friend's ISP).

By following standardized protocols set forth by the OSI model, NOS software can communicate happily with the computers and peripherals attached to the network as well as with other networks.

---

although the employees of a corporation may be using a Microsoft Windows environment for their desktops and e-mail, the file servers and print servers may be running a Novell NOS.

Because NOSs use different internal software languages to communicate, they can't communicate directly with each other. However, if both NOSs are using the same protocol (such as TCP/IP), they can pass information between the networks and it can be interpreted by the other network.

Network Adapters

As we noted in Chapter 7, client computers and peripherals need an interface to connect with and communicate on the network. **Network adapters** are devices that perform specific tasks to enable computers to communicate on a network. Certain network adapters are installed *inside* computers and peripherals as expansion cards. These adapters are referred to as *network interface cards (NICs)*.

Although you could use network adapters that plug into universal serial bus (USB) ports on a client/server network, most network adapters are NICs. That's because external devices are more susceptible to damage.

What do network adapters do? Network adapters perform three critical functions:

1. **They generate high-powered signals to enable network transmissions.** Digital signals generated inside the computer are fairly low-powered and would not travel well on network media (cable or wireless technology) without network adapters. Network adapters convert the signals from inside the computer to higher-powered signals that have no trouble traversing the network media.

2. **They are responsible for breaking the data down into packets and preparing them for transmission across the network.** They also are responsible for receiving incoming data packets and, in accordance with networking protocols (rules), reconstructing them, as shown in Figure 12.17.

3. **They act as gatekeepers for information flowing to and from the client computer.** Much like a security guard

in a gated community, network adapters are responsible for permitting or denying access to the client computer and controlling the flow of visitors (data).

Are there different types of network adapters? Although there are different types of network adapters, almost without exception, Ethernet (either wired or wireless) is the standard communications protocol used on most current networks. Therefore, the adapter cards shipping with computers today are always Ethernet compliant. The majority of Ethernet adapters provide connection ports that accept RJ-45 (Ethernet) connector plugs for connection to twisted pair cable. However, adapters are available that provide other types of connectors for direct connections to other types of network media (such as fiber-optic cables).

Do wireless networks require network adapters? Most corporate networks are not entirely wireless, but they do provide wireless connectivity to some computers. Computers that connect to the network using wireless access need special network adapter cards called **wireless network interface cards (wireless NICs)** installed in the system unit. Unlike wired NICs, wireless NICs don't connect to the network with cables. Instead, the network must be fitted with devices called **wireless access points** that provide wireless devices a sending and receiving connection point to the network.

Figure 12.18 shows an example of a typical corporate network with a wireless access point. The access point is connected to the wired network through a conventional

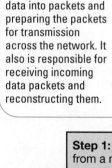

FIGURE 12.17

A network interface card (NIC) is responsible for breaking down data into packets and preparing the packets for transmission across the network. It also is responsible for receiving incoming data packets and reconstructing them.

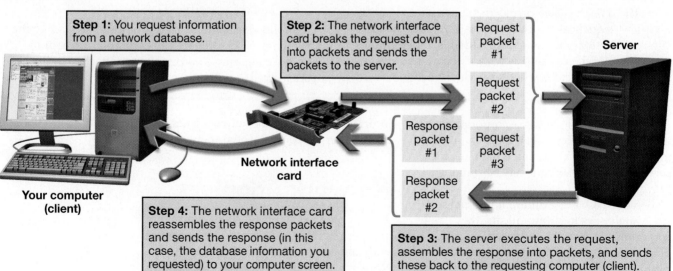

Step 1: You request information from a network database.

Step 2: The network interface card breaks the request down into packets and sends the packets to the server.

Request packet #1

Request packet #2

Response packet #1

Request packet #3

Response packet #2

Server

Your computer (client)

Network interface card

Step 4: The network interface card reassembles the response packets and sends the response (in this case, the database information you requested) to your computer screen.

Step 3: The server executes the request, assembles the response into packets, and sends these back to the requesting computer (client).

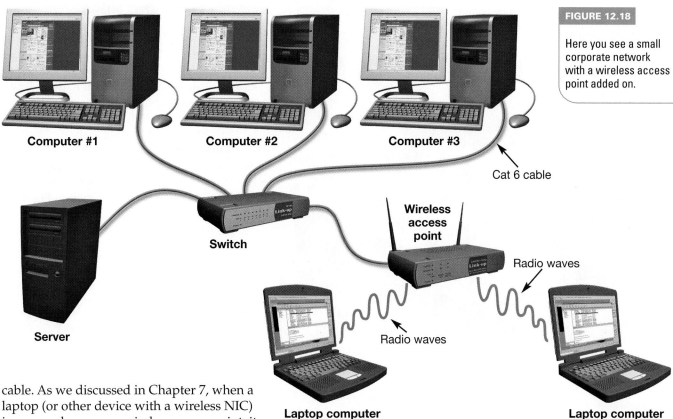

FIGURE 12.18

Here you see a small corporate network with a wireless access point added on.

Computer #1

Computer #2

Computer #3

Cat 6 cable

Switch

Server

Wireless access point

Radio waves

Radio waves

Laptop computer with wireless NIC

Laptop computer with wireless NIC

cable. As we discussed in Chapter 7, when a laptop (or other device with a wireless NIC) is powered on near a wireless access point, it establishes a connection with the access point using radio waves. Many computers can communicate with the network through a single wireless access point.

Do network adapters require software? Because the network adapter is responsible for communications between the client computer and the network, it needs to speak the same language as the network's special operating system software. Therefore, special communications software called a *device driver* is installed on all client computers in the client/server network. **Device drivers** enable the network adapter to communicate with the server's operating system and with the operating system of the computer in which the adapter is installed.

Network Navigation Devices

Earlier in this chapter, you learned that to flow through the network, data is broken into small segments called *packets*. Data packets are like postal letters. They don't get to their destinations without some help. In this section, we explore the various conventions and devices that help speed data packets on their way through the network.

MAC ADDRESSES

How do data packets know where to go on the network? Each network adapter has a physical address similar to a serial number on an appliance. This is called a **Media Access Control (MAC) address** and it is made up of six two-digit numbers such as 01:40:87:44:79:A5. The first three numbers (in this case, 01:40:87) specify the manufacturer of the network adapter, whereas the second set of numbers (in this case, 44:79:A5) comprise a unique address. Because all MAC addresses must be unique, the IEEE runs a committee that is responsible for allocating blocks of numbers to network adapter manufacturers.

Are MAC addresses the same as IP addresses? MAC addresses and Internet Protocol (IP) addresses are not the same thing. A MAC address is used for identification purposes *internally* on a network, similar to giving people different names to differentiate them. An IP address is the address *external* entities use to communicate with your network and is similar to your home street address. Think of it this way: the postal carrier delivers a package (data packet) to your dorm building based on its street address (IP address). The dorm's mail clerk

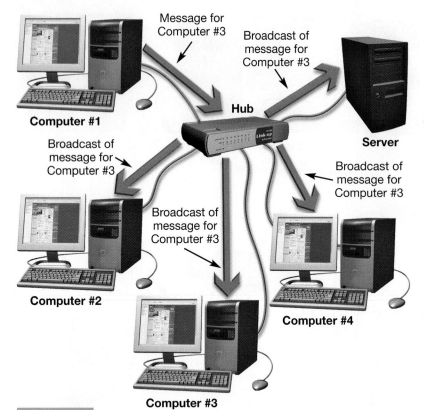

Message for Computer #3

Broadcast of message for Computer #3

Computer #1

Hub

Server

Broadcast of message for Computer #3

Broadcast of message for Computer #3

Broadcast of message for Computer #3

Computer #2

Computer #4

Computer #3

delivers the package to your room because it has your name on it (MAC address) and not that of your neighbor. Both pieces of information are necessary to ensure that the package (or data) reaches its destination.

How does a data packet get a MAC address? As mentioned in the Dig Deeper feature, **frames** are containers that can hold multiple data packets. This is similar to placing several letters going to the same postal address in a big envelope. When the data packets are being assembled into frames, the NOS software assigns the appropriate MAC address to the frame. The NOS keeps track of all devices and their addresses on the network. Much like a letter placed into the postal service, the frame is delivered to the MAC address that the NOS assigned to the frame.

What delivers the frames to the correct device on the network? In a small bus network, frames just bounce along the wire until the correct client computer notices the frame is addressed to it and pulls the signal off the wire. This is inefficient in a larger network. Therefore, many types of devices have been developed to deliver data to its destination efficiently. These devices are designed to amplify signals, route signals, and exchange data with other networks.

REPEATERS AND HUBS

What types of devices amplify signals on a single network? **Repeaters** are relatively simple devices whose sole function is to amplify a signal and retransmit it. Repeaters are used to extend cable runs beyond the maximum run length (over which a signal would degrade and be unreadable).

As you learned in Chapter 7, **hubs** are devices that also transmit signals. In addition, they have multiple ports to which devices are connected. As shown in Figure 12.19, the hub receives the signal from a device, reconstructs it, and transmits it to all other ports on the hub.

SWITCHES AND BRIDGES

Which devices are used to route signals through a single network? Switches and bridges are used to send data on a specific route through the network. A **switch** can be viewed as a "smart" hub. It makes decisions, based on the MAC address of the data, as to where the data is to be sent. Therefore, only the intended recipient of the data receives the signal as opposed to a hub, which sends out data to all devices connected to it. This improves network efficiency by helping ensure that devices receive data intended only for them.

Switches are generally not needed on small networks (such as home networks) because there is not a large amount of data traffic, making increasing efficiency unnecessary. Figure 12.20 shows a switch being used to rebroadcast a message.

As a corporate network grows in size, performance can decline as many devices compete for transmission time on the network media. To solve this problem, a network can be broken into multiple segments known as *collision domains*. **Bridges** are devices that are used to send data between these different collision domains. A bridge sends data between collision domains depending on where the recipient device is located, as indicated in Figure 12.21. Most home networks contain only one segment and therefore do not require bridges.

ROUTERS

What device is designed to move data to another network? Whereas repeaters, hubs, switches, and bridges perform their functions within a *single network*,

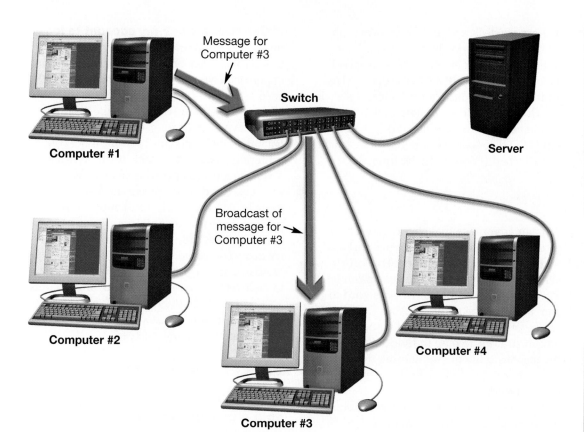

Message for
Computer #3

Switch

Server

Computer #1

Broadcast of
message for
Computer #3

Computer #2

Computer #4

Computer #3

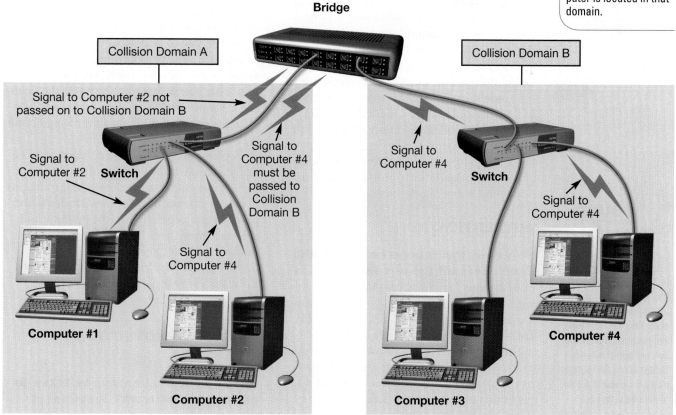

Bridge

Collision Domain A

Collision Domain B

Signal to Computer #2 not
passed on to Collision Domain B

Signal to
Computer #2   **Switch**

Signal to
Computer #4
must be
passed to
Collision
Domain B

Signal to
Computer #4   **Switch**

Signal to
Computer #4

Signal to
Computer #4

Computer #1

Signal to
Computer #4

Computer #2

Computer #3

Computer #4

routers are designed to send information *between two networks*. To accomplish this, routers must look at higher-level network addresses (such as IP addresses), not MAC addresses. When the router notices data with an address that does not belong to a device on the network from which it originated, it sends the data to another network to which it is attached (or out onto the Internet).

Network Security

A major advantage that client/server networks have over peer-to-peer networks is that they contain a higher level of security. With client/server networks, users can be forced to use a user ID and a password to gain access to the network. Also, the security can be centrally administered by network administrators, freeing individual users of the responsibility of maintaining their own data security (as they must do on a peer-to-peer network).

In this section, we explore the challenges network administrators face to keep a client/server network secure. We use a college network as our example, but note that the same principles apply to all client/server networks.

Who does a college network need to be secure from? A college network, like any network, is vulnerable to unauthorized users and manipulation or misuse of the data contained on it. The person who sat next to you last semester in English class who failed may be interested in changing his grade to an A. Hackers may be interested in the financial and personal information (such as social security numbers and credit card numbers) stored in college financial office databases on the network. Thus, one of the network administrator's key functions is keeping the network data secure.

AUTHENTICATION

How does the college keep unauthorized users off the network? As mentioned earlier, to gain access to a typical college client/server network, you have to enter a user ID and a password. This is a process known as **authentication**. By correctly inputting your ID and password, you prove to the network who you are and that you have authorized access (because the ID was generated by the network administrator when you became a student).

Can hackers use my account to log on to the network? If a hacker knows your user ID and password, he or she can log on and impersonate you. Sometimes network user IDs are easy to figure out because they have a certain pattern (such as your last name and first initial of your first name). Because of this potential vulnerability, network administrators often configure accounts to disable themselves after several logon attempts with invalid passwords have been tried. This prevents hackers from using brute force attacks to attempt to crack passwords. **Brute force attacks** are delivered by specialized hacking software that attempts to try many combinations of letters, numbers, words, or pieces of your user ID in an attempt to discover your password. If network accounts aren't set to disable themselves after a small number of incorrect passwords is tried, these attacks may eventually succeed.

ACCESS PRIVILEGES

How can I gain access to everything on the college network? The simple answer is you can't! When your account was set up, certain access privileges were granted to indicate which systems you are allowed to use. For example, your access privileges probably include the ability to access the Internet. You also might have access privileges to view your transcript and grades online, depending on the sophistication of your college network. However, you definitely were not granted access to the grade reporting system, which would enable you to change your grades. Likewise, you do not have access to the financial systems; otherwise, you might be able to change your account, indicating that your bill was paid when it had not been.

Because network access accounts are centrally administered on the authentication server, it is easy for the network administrator to set up accounts for new students and grant them access only to the systems and software they need. The centralized nature of the creation of access accounts and the ability to restrict access to certain areas of the client/server network make it more secure than a peer-to-peer network.

PHYSICAL PROTECTION MEASURES

Are any physical measures taken to protect the network? Restricting physical access to servers and other sensitive

SOUND BYTE

A Day in the Life of a Network Technician

In this Sound Byte, you'll learn firsthand about the exciting, fast-paced job of a computer technician. Interviews with actual network technicians and tours of networking facilities will provide you with a deeper appreciation for the complexities of the job.

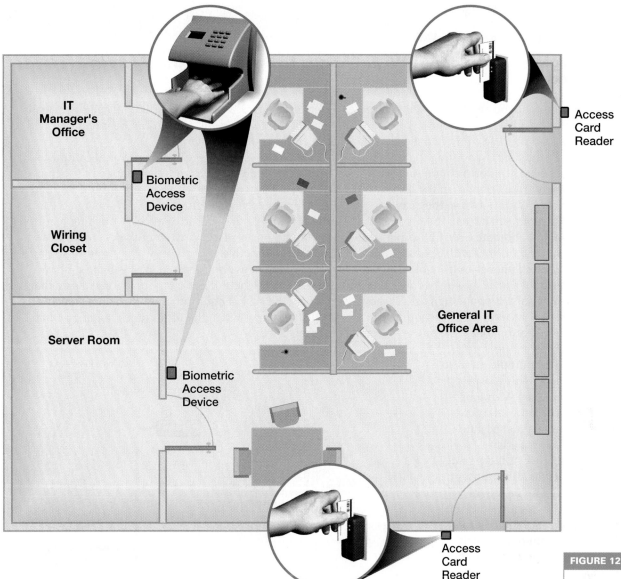

IT Manager's Office

Wiring Closet

Server Room

Biometric Access Device

Biometric Access Device

General IT Office Area

Access Card Reader

Access Card Reader

equipment is critical to protecting the network. Where are the servers that power your college network? They are most likely behind locked doors to which only authorized personnel have access. Do you see any routers or hubs lying about in computer labs? Of course you don't. These devices are securely tucked away in ceilings, walls, or closets, safe from anyone who might tamper with them in an attempt to sabotage the network or breach its security.

As shown in Figure 12.22, access to sensitive areas must be controlled. Many different devices can be used to control access. **Magnetic card readers** are relatively cheap devices that read information from a magnetic strip on the back of a credit card–like access card (such as your student ID card). The card reader, which can control the lock on a door, is programmed to admit only authorized personnel to the area. Card readers are easily programmed by adding authorized ID card numbers, social security numbers, and so on.

Biometric access devices are becoming more popular, although they still remain cost prohibitive to many organizations, especially colleges. Biometric devices use some unique characteristic of human biology to identify authorized users. Some devices read fingerprints or palm prints when you place your hand on a scanning pad. Other devices shine a beam of laser light into your eye and read the unique patterns of your retina to identify you. Facial recognition systems store unique characteristics of an individual's face for later comparison and identification. All of these devices are preprogrammed when authorized individuals use them for the first

Emerging Technologies: Wi-Fi Phones Keep Doctors and Nurses Connected

Have you ever noticed that you can't make cell phone calls when you're in a hospital? Cell phone signals can interfere with sensitive electronic equipment such as heart monitors and IV monitors, rendering them ineffective. Unfortunately, this means doctors and nurses can't communicate quickly with cell phones in the hospital either. However, using a Wi-Fi network, they can.

A number of U.S. hospitals, such as Mission Community Hospital in Panorama City, California, are providing their nurses and doctors with SpectralLink NetLink Wi-Fi-enabled cell phones that enable communications over the hospital's 802.11g wireless network (instead of by conventional cell phone signals). These phones cause no interference with medical equipment, and, unlike conventional cell phones, the phones offer a special feature that allows users to broadcast a message to multiple phones throughout the hospital. This is especially useful for emergency situations (like a "code blue" cardiac arrest alert) when various personnel must be gathered quickly to deal with a crisis.

How does this all work? Unlike traditional cell phone calls that flow through a telephone company's switching or microwave system, Wi-Fi-enabled cell phones route calls through the Internet either to land lines or out to other cell phones (see Figure 12.23), avoiding the

interference associated with traditional cell phone calls. In addition, the NetLink system can be integrated with conventional phone systems.

Any business or college with a physical campus could potentially benefit from the connectivity achieved by such a network. And with concerns about responding to emergencies growing since 9/11, being able to alert an entire organization at once by pushing a button and talking makes this type of network communications very attractive. Of course, it does require all participants in the network to have a Wi-Fi-enabled phone. Time will tell whether more organizations decide that it is worth the cost of equipping key personnel (such as security guards) when the time comes to replace their existing phones.

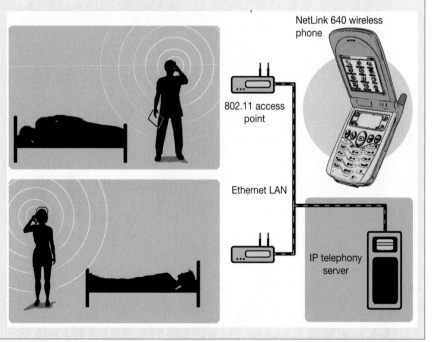

FIGURE 12.23

Keeping connected, especially in emergencies, is safe and easy when doctors and nurses can use special Wi-Fi-enabled cell phones to communicate.

---

time and then their fingerprints, face patterns, or retinal patterns are scanned and stored in a database.

Financial institutions and retail stores are considering using such devices to attempt to eliminate the growing fraud problem from theft and counterfeiting of credit and debit cards. If fingerprint authorization were required at Wal-Mart to make a purchase, no thief who stole your wallet and attempted to use your credit card would be successful.

However, biometric devices currently on the market don't always function as intended.

Facial recognition and retinal systems can sometimes be fooled using pictures or videos of an authorized user. Fingerprint readers have been reported as being thwarted by an unauthorized person breathing on the sensor, which makes the previous user's fingerprint visible (fingers leave an oily residue behind when you touch a surface). Next-generation systems are being designed so they can't be fooled as easily. Future retinal readers will check to see whether the person blinks or if their eyes contract when a bright light is shone on them. Because bodies conduct electrical current, future fingerprint

Configure a Firewall Before Going Online

As more virulent worms are released, you can be susceptible to virus infection from the very first time you connect your computer to the Internet. You may wish to use a product like Norton Internet Security that contains, among other things, a firewall application. However, the Windows firewall included with Windows XP (Service Pack 2) provides very adequate protection from the majority of hacking problems. When you use the Connection Wizard to create a new Internet connection or you enter the Security Center from the Control Panel, you have the opportunity to enable the Windows firewall. To check to ensure your computer has the Windows firewall enabled, double click the Security Center icon on the control panel. Then left-click the Windows Firewall link at the bottom of the security center dialog box to display the Windows Firewall dialog box shown in Figure 12.24. Make sure the first option is selected to turn the firewall on.

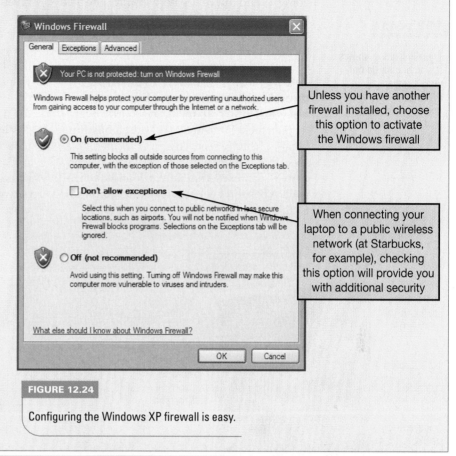

FIGURE 12.24

Configuring the Windows XP firewall is easy.

readers may ensure that they sense electrical current when a finger touches the reader. Suffice it to say, these devices have a ways to go until they are foolproof.

FIREWALLS

Is the college Internet connection vulnerable to hackers? Just like a home network, when a college network is connected to the Internet, this creates an attractive nuisance. A college network will most likely have a high-bandwidth connection to the Internet that will attract hackers. Just like in a home network, a well-defended college network includes a firewall. Firewalls can be composed of software or hardware, and many sophisticated firewalls include both. Routers are often equipped to act as hardware firewalls.

Does the firewall on my college network work the same way as a personal firewall installed on a home network? Although the firewall at your school may contain a few extra security options, making it even harder to breach than a personal firewall, the school's firewall works on the same basic principles as a home network. At a minimum, most firewalls work as packet screeners. **Packet screening** involves examining incoming data packets to ensure they originated from or are authorized by valid users on the internal network. The router is the device that performs the packet screening. Unauthorized or suspect packets are discarded by the firewall before reaching the network.

Packet screening also can be configured for outgoing data to ensure that requests for information to the Internet are from legitimate users. This helps detect Trojan horse programs that may have been installed by hackers. As you learned in Chapter 7, Trojan horses masquerade as harmless programs but have a more sinister purpose. They often try to disguise where they are sending data from by using bogus IP addresses on the packets the programs send instead of an authorized IP address belonging to the network.

If packet screening is working, packets going in and out of the network are checked to ensure they are either from or addressed to a legitimate IP address on the network. If the addresses are not valid addresses for the network, the firewall discards them.

What other security measures does the firewall on a client/server network use? To increase security even further, most large networks add a **bastion host**—a heavily secured server located on a special perimeter network between the company's secure internal network and the firewall. A bastion host gets its name from the fortified towers (called *bastions*), located along the outer walls of medieval castles, which were specifically designed to defend the castles against attackers.

To external computers, the bastion host gives the appearance of being the internal network server. Hackers can waste a lot of time and energy attacking the bastion host. However, even if a hacker breaches the bastion host server, the internal network is not vulnerable because the bastion host is not on the internal network. And during the time the hackers spend trying to penetrate the bastion host, network administrators can detect and thwart their attacks.

Bastion hosts are often configured as **proxy servers**. A proxy server acts as a go-between for computers on the internal network and the external network (the

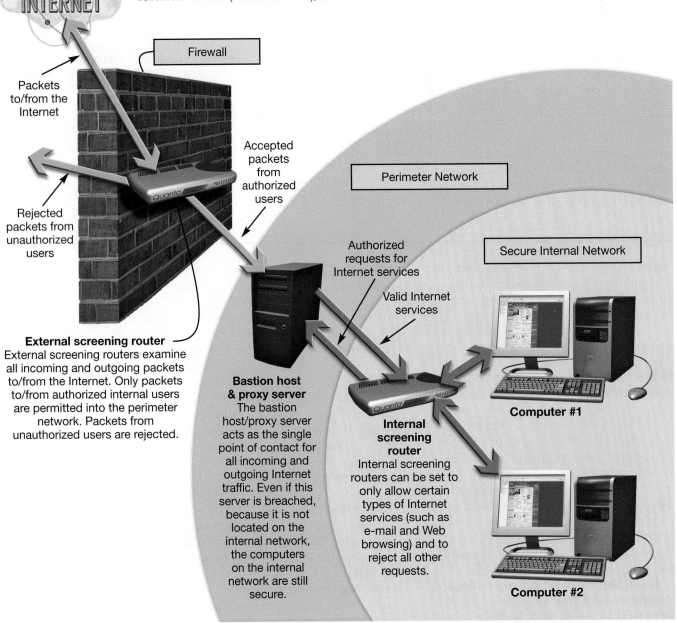

INTERNET

Firewall

Packets to/from the Internet

Accepted packets from authorized users

Perimeter Network

Rejected packets from unauthorized users

Secure Internal Network

Authorized requests for Internet services

Valid Internet services

External screening router
External screening routers examine all incoming and outgoing packets to/from the Internet. Only packets to/from authorized internal users are permitted into the perimeter network. Packets from unauthorized users are rejected.

Bastion host & proxy server
The bastion host/proxy server acts as the single point of contact for all incoming and outgoing Internet traffic. Even if this server is breached, because it is not located on the internal network, the computers on the internal network are still secure.

Internal screening router
Internal screening routers can be set to only allow certain types of Internet services (such as e-mail and Web browsing) and to reject all other requests.

Computer #1

Computer #2

Computers in Society: What's Shakin'? California Maintains a Reliable Network to Respond to Earthquake Emergencies

Californians often worry about earthquakes and when "the big one" will strike. We all hope that another major earthquake, like the 9.0 boomer that hit the Indian Ocean in 2004, will never take place. However, given the fault lines that run under California, most seismologists agree that another large earthquake is inevitable. Getting emergency response crews where they are most needed after an earthquake can have a critical impact on saving lives.

Many separate agencies and monitoring stations have been recording information on earthquakes for decades, but efforts to coordinate data collection and analysis were lacking. In 2002, the California Integrated Seismic Network (CISN) was formed. The founding partners include the California Geological Survey, the Seismological Laboratory of Caltech, U.S. Geological Survey (USGS) sites at Menlo Park and Pasadena, and the Berkeley Seismological Laboratory. CISN's mission is to maintain a statewide network of computers to supply scientists and emergency response teams with up-to-date quake information, even if the Internet goes down. The USGS hosts the main server but various backup servers are maintained at different locations in case a quake or other natural disaster disables the main server.

Within minutes of an earthquake (greater than magnitude 3.5), CISN generates a ShakeMap (see Figure 12.26). Through color coding, these maps show the areas most affected by the quake. Emergency response teams, state and local police, and the National Guard can use the ShakeMaps to determine how to deploy labor and resources to assist victims of a quake.

In addition to ShakeMaps, CISN maintains an archive of seismological data and ground motion records for all earthquakes recorded in California. This data is available through the Internet to scientists and the general public for the purpose of conducting further research into the causes and behaviors of earthquakes.

Computer networks and the Internet make achieving the CISN's mission possible. Without a robust network, it would be impossible to accumulate and disseminate quickly the data needed to respond to these natural disasters.

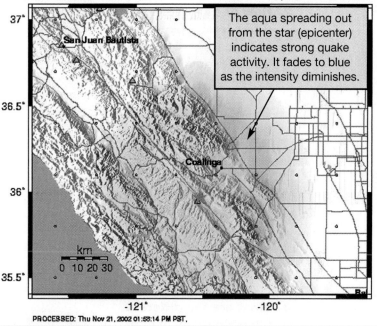

USGS/UCB/CDMG Rapid Instrumental Intensity Map for event: 40138111
Tue Nov 12, 2002 06:48:25 AM PST M 4.2 N35.97 W120.52 Depth: 8.4km ID:40138111

The aqua spreading out from the star (epicenter) indicates strong quake activity. It fades to blue as the intensity diminishes.

PROCESSED: Thu Nov 21, 2002 01:53:14 PM PST.

FIGURE 12.26

This color-coded ShakeMap was generated by the California Integrated Seismic Network (CISN).

Internet). All requests from the internal network for Internet services are directed through the proxy server. Likewise, all incoming requests from the Internet must pass through the proxy server. It is much easier for network administrators to maintain adequate security on one server than it is to ensure security is maintained on hundreds or thousands of computers in a college network. Figure 12.25 shows a network secured by a firewall, a bastion host, and a screening router.

1. What are the advantages of a business network?

A network enables employees to communicate with each other more easily even over large distances. Networks also enable expensive resources, such as printers, to be shared, saving the cost of providing these resources to individual employees. Software can be deployed from a network server, thereby reducing the costs of installation on each user's computer. And networks enable employees to share an Internet connection, avoiding the cost of providing each employee with a dedicated Internet connection.

2. How does a client/server network differ from a peer-to-peer network?

A client/server network requires that at least one server be attached to the network. The server coordinates functions such as data transmission and printing. In a peer-to-peer network, each node connected to the network can communicate directly with every other node on the network, instead of having a separate device exercise control over the network. Data flows more efficiently in client/server networks than in peer-to-peer networks. In addition, client/server networks have increased scalability, meaning users can be added to the network easily.

3. What are the different classifications of client/server networks?

Local area networks (LANs) are small groups of computers (as few as two) and peripherals linked together over a small geographic area. A group of computers on the floor of the office where you work is most likely a LAN. Wide area networks (WANs) are comprised of large numbers of users or of separate LANs that are miles apart and linked together. Corporations often use WANs to connect two or more branches (such as an office in California and one in Ohio). Sometimes government organizations or civic groups establish WANs to link users in a specific geo-

graphic area (such as within a city or county). These special WANs are known as metropolitan area networks (MANs).

4. What components are needed to construct a client/server network?

Client/server networks have many of the same components of peer-to-peer networks as well as some components specific to client/server networks, including servers, a network topology, transmission media, network operating system (NOS) software, network adapters, and network navigation devices.

5. What do the various types of servers do?

Dedicated servers are used on large networks to increase efficiency. Authentication servers control access to the network and ensure that only authorized users can log on. File servers provide storage and management of user files. Print servers manage and control all printing jobs initiated on a network. Application servers provide access to application software (such as Microsoft Office). Database servers store database files and provide access to users who need the information in the databases. E-mail servers control all incoming and outgoing e-mail traffic. Communications servers are used to control the flow of information from the internal network to outside networks (such as the Internet). Web servers are used to host a Web site.

6. What are the various network topologies (layouts) and why is network topology important in planning a network?

In a bus topology, all nodes are connected to a single linear cable. Ring topologies are comprised of nodes arranged roughly in a circle in which the data flows from node to node in a specific order. In a star topology, nodes are connected to a central communication device (a switch) and branch out like points of a star. A hybrid topology is a blending of other types of topologies in one network. Each topology has its own advantages and disadvantages. Topology selection mainly depends on two factors: (1) the network budget and (2) the specific needs of network users (speed, fair allocation of resources, and so on).

7. What types of transmission media are used in client/server networks?

In addition to wireless media, three main cable types are used: twisted pair cable, coaxial cable, and fiber-optic cable. Twisted pair cable consists of four pairs of wires twisted around each other to reduce interference. Coaxial cable is the same type of cable used by your cable TV company to run a signal into your house. It provides better shielding from interference than twisted pair cable but is more expensive. Fiber-optic cable uses glass or plastic bundles of fiber to send signals using light waves. It provides the largest bandwidth, but is expensive and difficult to install. Wireless media utilizes radio waves to send data between nodes on a network.

8. What software needs to be running on computers attached to a client/server network and how does this software control network communications?

Network operating system (NOS) software needs to be installed on each computer and server connected to a client/server network to provide the services necessary for the devices to communicate. The NOS provides a set of common rules (called a protocol) that controls communication between devices on the network.

9. How do network adapters enable computers to participate in a client/server network?

Network adapters provide three critical functions: (1) They take low-power data signals generated by the computer and convert them into higher-powered signals that can traverse network media easily. (2) They break the data generated by the computer into packets and package them for transmission across the network media. (3) They act as gatekeepers to control the flow of data to and from the computer. Without a network adapter, a computer could not communicate on a network.

10. What devices assist in moving data around a client/server network?

Repeaters are used to amplify signals on a network ensuring signals are received even at the end of a long cable run. Hubs receive and retransmit signals to all devices attached to them. Switches are "smart" hubs in that they can read the address of data packets and retransmit a signal to its destination instead of to every device connected to the switch. Routers are used to route data between two different networks such as between a corporate network and the Internet.

11. What measures are employed to keep large networks secure?

Access to most networks requires authentication procedures (such as entering a user ID and password) to ensure that only authorized users access the network. The system administrator defines access privileges for users so that they can access only specific files. Network equipment is physically secured behind locked doors, which are often protected by biometric access devices. Biometric devices, such as fingerprint and palm readers, use unique physical characteristics of individuals for identification purposes. Firewalls are also employed to keep hackers from attacking networks through Internet connections. Packet screeners review traffic going to and from the network to ascertain whether it was generated by a legitimate user.

Buzz Words

Word Bank

- administrator
- application server
- bastion host
- bridges
- bus
- database server
- fiber-optic
- frames
- LAN
- packet screener
- PAN
- repeater
- routers
- scalable
- star
- switch
- twisted pair
- WAN

Instructions: Fill in the blanks using the words from the Word Bank.

As a network (1) _____ , Susan's first task was to configure her company's new network. Because the company had branch offices in three different states, she knew it would be necessary to configure the network as a(n) (2) _____ . However, to handle all the wireless devices the sales representatives carried, provisions for roving (3) _____ s throughout the building would need to be made. Software would need to be shared among 50 employees, so a robust (4) _____ would be a necessity. And because the company was experiencing rapid growth, the network would have to be highly (5) _____ , which would require the selection of a (6) _____ topology as opposed to a(n) (7) _____ topology, which would only work for a small network.

Powerful electrical fields on the factory floor would make using (8) _____ cabling an absolute necessity in the manufacturing plant, whereas (9) _____ cabling would be sufficient for the office areas. Because the company had experienced hacking on its old network, Susan insisted that a(n) (10) _____ be installed to further bolster the network defenses. Combined with a(n) (11) _____ installed in the firewall, she felt they would be adequately protected from wily hackers.

(12) _____ would be necessary to shift (13) _____ between collision domains on the network. For the farthest reaches of the building, (14) _____ s would need to be installed to amplify the network data signals. If a star topology was to be used, several (15) _____ s would need to be deployed to handle all 50 network users.

Becoming Computer Fluent

Chemco Brothers, Inc., a manufacturer of specialty chemicals, has decided that to increase the accuracy of its production records, the network used for management and clerical workers should extend onto the manufacturing floor. Although most employees do not travel more than a few feet from their main work areas during their shift, the three supervisors roam the entire plant and need access to computers wherever they go.

Instructions: Draft a memo (with supporting diagrams, if necessary) detailing how to deploy 15 computers (12 for workers, 3 for supervisors) in the factory areas. Justify the network topology you select, explain your choice of transmission media, and indicate the device(s) needed to connect the computers to the existing network.

Self-Test

Instructions: Answer the multiple choice and true/false questions below for more practice with key terms and concepts from this chapter.

MULTIPLE CHOICE

1. Which of the following is an advantage of installing a network in a business?

  a. increased productivity

  b. facilitation of Internet connectivity

  c. sharing of peripherals

  d. All of the above

2. What is the major difference between a client/server network and a peer-to-peer network?

  a. Client/server networks are cheaper to install.

  b. Client/server networks contain dedicated servers.

  c. Peer-to-peer networks are more scalable.

  d. Security is much easier to implement on a peer-to-peer network.

3. If a corporate network connects three offices in different geographic areas, the network would be classified as a

  a. WAN   b. MAN

  c. PAN   d. LAN

4. Which of the following elements is not necessary in all client/server networks?

  a. server

  b. NOS software

  c. transmission media

  d. repeaters

5. To efficiently manage Internet communications, a corporate network would include

  a. an Internet server.

  b. an e-mail server.

  c. a communications server.

  d. an application server.

6. Which type of network topology is most common today?

  a. ring   b. star

  c. bus   d. token

7. When would fiber-optic cable most likely be required in a corporate network?

  a. when cost is more important than speed

  b. when there is absolutely no electrical or magnetic interference present

  c. when there is a low budget for installation costs

  d. when speed is more important than cost

8. NOS software is

  a. absolutely essential for running a client/server network.

  b. only needed on the servers in a client/server network.

  c. not included with most operating system software.

  d. only needed when configuring a network in a star topology.

9. Network adapters are

  a. only found in servers.

  b. only found in client computers.

  c. necessary in both client computers and servers.

  d. necessary only in networks using the bus topology.

10. Providing adequate security on a corporate network involves all of these issues except

  a. physical security.

  b. authentication.

  c. access control.

  d. transit rejection.

TRUE/FALSE

_____ 1. Switches are used to route data between two or more networks.

_____ 2. Two different types of network operating software can be deployed on the same network.

_____ 3. Coaxial cable is less susceptible to interference than twisted pair cable.

_____ 4. Peer-to-peer networks are more scalable than client/server networks.

_____ 5. An application server is used to control access to a client/server network.

Making the Transition to...
Next Semester

chapter twelve

1. Internet Usage Policy

Schools face many potential liability issues when they connect students to the Internet. Your school most likely has a written policy (perhaps posted on the school's Web site) on appropriate usage of the network and the Internet by students. Other issues network usage policies typically address include guidelines on student file storage, antivirus protection, and backups. Obtain a copy of your school's policy (or speak with the appropriate IT personnel) and answer the following questions:

a. What types of sites are students not permitted to access?

b. Are there restrictions in effect on usage of peer-to-peer file-sharing sites? What are those restrictions?

c. How much storage space is provided for student files (if any)?

d. How often are student files backed up (if ever)? Are these incremental backups (only new files or files that have changed are backed up) or full backups (all files are backed up)?

e. Are files deleted after each semester?

f. Are all computers on campus protected by antivirus software? How often is the software updated?

2. Wireless Connections at School

Wireless networks are growing in popularity as more and more students are bringing laptops and other portable devices onto campus. Investigate the following:

a. Does your school offer wireless connectivity to students? If so, what areas of the campus are currently covered by wireless access?

b. What technologies are being deployed for connectivity (802.11b, 802.11a, or 802.11g)? If 802.11b currently is deployed, is there a plan to upgrade to a faster standard in the future?

c. Is access to the wireless network restricted (i.e., is authentication required to log on)? If not, is this under consideration to prevent poaching of bandwidth by neighbors and visitors?

3. Internet Security Measures at School

Visit your IT services department and investigate the current security measures in place for the following:

a. **Firewall protection of the Internet connection.** What hardware/software is installed? Have there been any recent hacking attempts? If so, were they successful?

b. **Antivirus protection.** Is antivirus software installed on all computers deployed on campus? If so, what package is being used and how often is it updated? What measures (if any) are in place to prevent users who bring their own computers onto campus (such as laptops connected wirelessly) and connect to the network from infecting the network with a virus?

541

1. Security Issues at Work

You are interning in the IT department of a start-up biotechnology research firm. The proprietary scientific research that the employees generate is very valuable. One morning, the president calls a general staff meeting and announces that his daughter found a summary of the latest molecules that the company was investigating on a Web site. Because this is extremely sensitive information, it could damage the company if the information fell into competitors' hands. The president alluded to his suspicions that an employee was deliberately leaking information. After the meeting, an employee suggested to you that maybe a hacker had planted a "keylogger" on the network to capture information. You aren't too sure what a keylogger is and you know that the company president will have no idea.

a. Using the Internet, research keyloggers and their properties. Prepare a one-page memo for senior executives explaining why a keylogger could be responsible for the problem noted at the staff meeting.

b. Write a second memo suggesting products that the company could install to detect keylogging software in the future. If possible, provide cost estimates for installation on 30 computers. Possible resources are **www.symantec.com** and **www.pestpatrol.com**.

2. Client/Server Networks

The owner of the company for which you work announces that the company will be hiring another 25 workers over the next six months. Currently, your peer-to-peer network is adequately handling the needs of the 10 employees who now work at the company. However, you know that adding 25 more employees to the network would overload it.

a. Write a memo explaining why a switch to a client/server network would be appropriate. Be sure to explain which topology you think would be best to install.

b. In the memo, estimate the costs of constructing a 35-person client/server network, including the costs of one server, cabling, workstations for the 25 new employees, and switches. Use resources such as **www.dell.com** and **www.compaq.com** for designing and pricing network components.

3. Antivirus Solutions at Work

Recently, the company you work for had its network brought to a halt by an employee that inadvertently infected the server after opening an e-mail attachment containing a worm. Your boss has charged you with the task of locating a cost-effective antivirus solution to protect the corporate network. Complete the following tasks:

a. Compare the costs of installing antivirus products from the two industry leaders, McAfee (**www.mcafee.com**) and Norton (**www.norton.com**) on each of the 20 computers and the one server in your corporate network.

b. Write a draft memo to employees explaining the types of e-mail messages and attachments they should avoid opening and passing on to others. Make sure to include warnings about Phishing, attachments containing viruses, and hoaxes.

Critical Thinking Questions

Instructions: Albert Einstein used "Gedanken experiments," or critical thinking questions, to develop his theory of relativity. Some ideas are best understood by experimenting with them in our own minds. The following critical thinking questions are designed to demand your full attention but require only a comfortable chair—no technology.

1. Internet Risks at School

Internet access is deemed essential to enable students to research projects and papers adequately. But granting that access potentially invites people to engage in dangerous or unacceptable behaviors.

a. Do you think your school should restrict access to certain Internet sites (such as peer-to-peer file-sharing services) to prevent students from violating laws by illegally sharing copyrighted material?

b. Plagiarism is thought to be spreading because of the easy exchange of information on the Internet. What should the penalty be for a student who plagiarizes material from a Web site and why? Should a student who plagiarizes have his or her Internet access privileges revoked? Why or why not?

2. Ethical Hackers?

Some hackers argue that hacking should not be a crime because they are performing a service to the companies that they are hacking by pointing out weaknesses in network security.

a. Do you think hackers should be punished for gaining unapproved access to computer systems?

b. Are there any instances in which hacking is a "necessary evil" and the law enforcement officials should just look the other way?

c. Is it unethical for software companies not to share with users known security risks in their software?

3. Acceptable Use Internet Policies

Many companies are drafting acceptable use policies for computers and Internet access to inform employees of the approved uses for corporate computing assets. Consider these areas of a potential company policy:

a. Should employees be allowed to use their computers and Internet access for personal use (such as checking noncompany e-mail, shopping online, or playing games)? If so, how much time per day is reasonable for employees to spend on personal tasks? Should employees be permitted to use their computers for personal tasks only during personal time (such as breaks and lunch hours)?

b. Should employee computer and Internet usage be monitored to ensure compliance with the personal use policies? What should the penalties be for violating these policies?

c. Many corporations block access to Internet Web sites that would enable employees to participate in potentially illegal activities (such as downloading music, gambling, or viewing pornography). Should corporations have the right to block users from Web sites when they are at work? Why or why not?

4. Network Layout Designs

Assume you are designing the network layout for an insurance company. Which employees would you suggest be provided with laptop computers? In which areas of the office would you provide wireless network access? Would you provide all employees with Internet access? If not, who would you exclude?

Team Time Wireless Network Access on Campus

Problem:

As wireless devices become more prevalent, increased demands for wireless access will be placed on networks. Although many schools already deploy adequate wireless access, there is room for improvement of coverage in numerous areas.

Task:

The network manager at your school has requested that you assist in developing a plan for deploying/expanding wireless coverage for the campus. Your group has been selected to assist with the research. Before presenting your findings to the network manager, your group needs to fine-tune its recommendations.

Process:

Divide the class into small teams.

1. Explore the areas of your campus where students congregate to socialize or engage in research. Determine if these areas are covered by wireless Internet access (this may require interviewing your school's network manager). For areas of the school that are covered by wireless technology (such as the library), test the signal strength of the connection by attempting to connect to the Internet in various locations.

2. Present your findings to your class. Lead a discussion with the other students and solicit feedback as to their experiences with wireless connectivity on the campus. In which other areas of the campus do you feel wireless technology should be deployed?

3. Prepare a report for the network manager of your suggestions for improvements/upgrades to the wireless network on your campus. If possible, address options for wireless connectivity when students are off campus for field trips, seminars, and so on.

Conclusion:

Being tied down to a wired computer terminal just doesn't cut it in the 21st century. Although wireless technology can be difficult and expensive to deploy in some instances, today's students will continue to demand the portable connections that they need to function effectively. Some day, your children may visit the Smithsonian Institution to view wired computers and see what hardships Mom and Dad had to endure in the "good old days."

Multimedia

In addition to the review materials presented here, you'll find additional materials featured with the book's multimedia, including the *Technology in Action* Student Resource CD and the Companion Web site (**www.prenhall.com/techinaction**), which will help reinforce your understanding of the chapter content. These materials include the following:

ACTIVE HELPDESK

In Active Helpdesk calls, you'll assume the role of a Helpdesk operator taking calls about the concepts you've learned in this chapter. You'll apply what you've learned and receive feedback from a supervisor to review and reinforce those concepts. The Active Helpdesk calls for this chapter are listed here and can be found on your Student Resource CD:

- Selecting a Network Topology and Cable
- Using Servers
- Selecting Network Navigation Devices

SOUND BYTES

Sound Bytes are dynamic multimedia tutorials that help demystify even the most complex topics. You'll view video clips and animations that illustrate computer concepts, and then apply what you've learned by reviewing with the Sound Byte Labs, which include quizzes and activities specifically tailored to each Sound Byte. The Sound Bytes for this chapter are listed here and can be found on your Student Resource CD and on the Companion Web site (**www.prenhall.com/techinaction**):

- Network Topology and Navigation Devices
- What's My IP Address? (and Other Interesting Facts About Networks)
- A Day in the Life of a Network Technician

COMPANION WEB SITE

The *Technology in Action* Companion Web site includes a variety of additional materials to help you review and learn more about the topics in this chapter. The resources available at **www.prenhall.com/techinaction** include:

- **Online Study Guide.** Each chapter features an online true/false and multiple-choice quiz. You can take these quizzes, automatically check the results, and e-mail the results to your instructor.
- **Web Research Projects.** Each chapter features a number of Web research projects that ask you to search the Web for information on computer-related careers, milestones in computer history, important people and companies, emerging technologies, and the applications and implications of different technologies.

Behind the Scenes:

The Internet: How It Works

Objectives

After reading this chapter,
you should be able to
answer the following
questions:

1. Who manages and pays for the Internet? **(p. 548)**

2. How do the Internet's networking components interact? **(pp. 548–552)**

3. What data transmissions and protocols does the Internet use? **(pp. 553–555)**

4. Why are IP addresses and domain names important for Internet communications? **(pp. 555–560)**

5. What are FTP and Telnet and how do I use them? **(pp. 560–561)**

6. What are HTML and XML used for? **(pp. 561–566)**

7. How do e-mail and instant messaging work and how are messages kept secure? **(pp. 566–573)**

ACTIVE HELPDESK

- Understanding IP Addresses, Domain Names, and Protocols **(p. 557)**
- Keeping E-mail Secure **(p. 572)**

Knowing How the Internet Works

At this point, you know what the Internet is, and you've certainly used some of its features, such as the Web and e-mail. So why do you need to know how the Internet works? Most people can drive a car without knowing how an internal combustion engine is designed and built. However, a more thorough understanding of auto mechanics is useful when you're making decisions about buying a car or when you need to fix it when it breaks down. Similarly, understanding the mechanics behind the Internet can assist you in a number of ways.

In the business world, even if you aren't making a career out of information technology (IT), you'll be interacting with coworkers in IT departments on a regular basis. Communicating with IT employees is much easier if you speak a common language. For example, when the IT manager tells you that the sales system you just proposed won't be feasible because the "router" can't handle the volume of outgoing requests, it would be helpful for you to understand what a router is and does.

Gaining a thorough understanding of the Internet and its capabilities also can help you determine whether you want to pursue additional coursework in Web development and networking. Creating and maintaining Web sites and the equipment that enables Internet connectivity takes many people with different talents. If you understand the jobs of the various individuals who support the infrastructure and services provided by the Internet, you'll be better able to assess whether an Internet-related career is right for you.

This chapter builds on what you learned in Chapter 3 and takes you behind the scenes of the Internet. We look at who manages the Internet and discuss in detail how the Internet works and the various standards it follows. Along the way, we go behind the scenes of some Internet communication features, such as e-mail and instant messaging services, and discuss just how safe these features are and what you can do to make your communications even more secure. Finally, we'll look at how the Internet will be changing in the future so you'll be poised to take advantage of new technologies as they emerge.

SOUND BYTES

- Constructing a Simple Web Page **(p. 563)**
- The Best Utilities for Your Computer **(p. 566)**

The Management of the Internet

You learned about the history of the Internet in Chapter 3. But to keep the Internet functioning at peak efficiency, it must be governed and regulated.

Who owns the Internet? Although the U.S. government funded the development of the technologies that spawned the Internet, no one really owns it. The individual local networks that constitute the Internet are all owned by different individuals, universities, government agencies, and private companies. Government entities, such as the National Science Foundation (NSF) and NASA, and many large, privately held companies all own pieces of the communications infrastructure (the high-speed data lines that transport data between networks) that makes the Internet work.

Does anyone manage the Internet? Although no single entity owns all of the individual networks that participate in the Internet, the Internet would grind to a halt without some sort of organization. Therefore, a number of nonprofit organizations and user groups, each with a specialized purpose, are responsible for management. Figure 13.1 shows the major organizations that play a role in the governance and development of the Internet.

Many of the functions handled by these nonprofit groups were previously handled by U.S. government contractors because the Internet developed out of a U.S. government military project. However, because the Internet now serves the global community, not just the United States, passing off responsibilities to organizations with global memberships is helping to speed along the internationalization of the Internet. Through close collaboration of the organizations listed in Figure 13.1 (and a few others), the Internet's vast collection of users and networks is managed.

Who pays for the Internet? You do! The U.S. government pays for a large portion of the Internet infrastructure as well as funds research and development for new technologies. The primary source of these funds is your tax dollars. Originally, U.S. taxpayers footed the entire bill for the Internet, but as the Internet grew and organizations were formed to manage it, businesses, universities, and other countries began paying for Internet infrastructure and development.

Internet Networking

Despite being the largest network on earth, the Internet's response to our requests for information seems almost magical at times. By simply entering a URL in your browser, you can summon up information that is

FIGURE 13.1 Major Organizations That Play a Role in Internet Governance and Development

Organization's Name	Organization's Purpose	Web Address
Internet Society (ISOC)	Professional membership society comprising more than 20,100 organizations and individuals. Provides leadership for the orderly growth and development of the Internet.	www.isoc.org
Internet Engineering Task Force (IETF)	A subgroup of ISOC made up of individuals and organizations that research new technologies for the Internet to improve capabilities or to keep the infrastructure functioning smoothly.	www.ietf.org
Internet Architecture Board (IAB)	Technical advisory group to IETF. Provides direction for the maintenance and development of the protocols that are used on the Internet.	www.iab.org
Internet Corporation for Assigned Names and Numbers (ICANN)	Organization responsible for management of the Internet's Domain Name System and the allocation of IP addresses.	www.icann.org
World Wide Web Consortium (W3C)	Consortium whose 350 member organizations set standards and develop protocols for the Web.	www.w3.org

stored on servers half a world away. But there is no magic involved, just a series of communication transactions that enable the Internet to function as a global network. In this section, we explore the various networks that make up the Internet and examine the workings of Internet data communications.

Is the Internet officially considered a network? Although the Internet can connect individual computers to each other, the Internet is really a network of networks. The word *internet* (with a lowercase *i*, not to be confused with the Internet with an uppercase *I*) was originally used to describe a connection between two or more networks. The word eventually became capitalized (Internet) and associated with the worldwide network of computer systems that grew explosively in the 1990s. The Internet does behave like a network in that it follows a set of communications protocols and is used for transferring data between computers. A *protocol* is simply a set of rules for communicating. All computers connected to the Internet need to

use common protocols so they can understand one another.

CONNECTING INTERNET SERVICE PROVIDERS

How are computers connected to the Internet? As you learned in Chapter 3, to connect individual computers or networks to the Internet, home users and businesses use Internet service providers (ISPs). As shown in Figure 13.2, ISPs are classified in a hierarchy that consists of three tiers: Tier 1, Tier 2, and Tier 3.

At the heart of the Internet are **Tier 1 ISPs**, located in the green zone in Figure 13.2. Tier 1 ISPs route a large percentage of the traffic on the Internet and have extremely high-speed connections with other ISPs, sometimes in the 2.5 to 10 gigabits per second (Gbps) range. As you learned in Chapter 3, the high-speed communications lines that Tier 1 ISPs use are referred to as

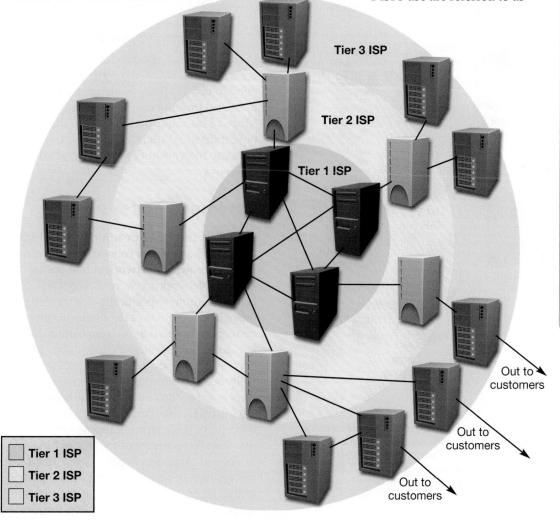

Internet

Tier 3 ISP

Tier 2 ISP

Tier 1 ISP

Out to customers

Out to customers

Out to customers

☐ Tier 1 ISP
☐ Tier 2 ISP
☐ Tier 3 ISP

FIGURE 13.2

Tier 1 ISPs make up the Internet backbone, responsible for moving large amounts of data rapidly. Tier 2 ISPs are regional providers that serve a large number of local (Tier 3) ISPs and provide connectivity to the Tier 1 ISPs. Tier 3 ISPs provide Internet access to homes or small- to medium-sized businesses. These ISPs normally cover a local geographical area. All Tier 3 ISPs need to be connected to a Tier 2 ISP, and all Tier 2 ISPs need to be connected to a Tier 1 ISP.

the *Internet backbone*. There are dozens of Tier 1 ISPs, each of which is required to be directly connected to *all other* Tier 1 ISPs. For example, AT&T and Sprint have subsidiaries that are Tier 1 ISPs. Tier 1 ISPs are also normally connected to a large number of Tier 2 ISPs and span international borders.

Tier 2 ISPs, located in the yellow zone in Figure 13.2, usually have a regional or national focus. Large companies and universities often connect directly to a Tier 2 ISP. To enable their customers to reach any possible point on the *global* Internet, Tier 2 ISPs must route at least a portion of their traffic through the global Tier 1 ISPs. Information flow between Tier 1 ISPs and the Tier 2 ISPs occurs using high-speed data lines, although these lines usually have less bandwidth than the lines connecting Tier 1 ISPs to each other.

The thousands of Tier 3 ISPs, located in the blue zone in Figure 13.2, provide Internet access to homes or small- to medium-sized businesses. These ISPs normally cover a local area. All Tier 3 ISPs need to be connected to at least one Tier 2 ISP. The ISP you're using at your home is most likely a Tier 3 ISP.

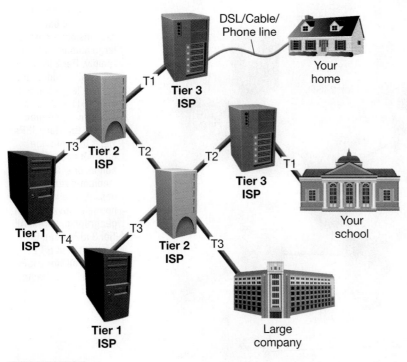

FIGURE 13.3

The bandwidth of the connections between ISPs and end users depends on the amount of data traffic required. Whereas your home wouldn't require a T line, the volume of Internet traffic at your school probably requires that it use at least a T-1 line to move data to the school's ISP. Large companies usually need T-2 or T-3 lines running to their ISPs. Because Tier 1 ISPs are moving a great deal of data, they need the bandwidth of T-4 lines.

T LINES

Are the data lines connecting ISPs faster than DSL or cable connections? Most high-speed communications between ISPs are achieved using *T lines*. T lines are high-speed fiber-optic communications lines that are designed to provide much higher throughput than conventional voice (telephone) and data (DSL) lines. T lines come in a variety of speeds:

- A **T-1 line** can support 24 simultaneous voice or data channels and achieve a maximum throughput of 1.544 megabits per second (Mbps). Businesses or Tier 3 ISPs often use T-1 lines to connect to the Internet because of the large volume of Internet traffic they experience. If a business's bandwidth requirements grow, it can upgrade to higher-capacity T lines.

- **T-2 lines** are composed of four T-1 lines and deliver a throughput of approximately 6.3 Mbps.

- **T-3 lines**, often used by Tier 2 ISPs and very large businesses, are a bundle of 28 T-1 lines. T-3 lines deliver a whopping 44.736 Mbps of bandwidth.

Still, this isn't enough for Tier 1 ISPs to communicate with each other. They usually need to use **T-4 lines**, which contain 168 T-1 lines and provide an astounding 274.176 Mbps of throughput. Figure 13.3 illustrates how individual users, organizations, and ISPs use the various T lines to send and receive data.

NETWORK ACCESS POINTS

How are the ISPs connected to each other? The points of connection between ISPs are known as **network access points (NAPs)**. Network access points contain groups of routers specifically designed to move large amounts of data quickly between networks. As you'll recall from earlier chapters, **routers** are devices that send data packets between networks. Because the Internet is really a large collection of connected networks, routers are needed to move data throughout the Internet. Large backbone providers or third-party telecommunications companies maintain these groups of routers, or NAPs.

As you can see in Figure 13.4, a Tier 1 ISP can connect to many network access points. In this figure, a Tier 1 ISP connects to a network access point in Denver, London, and

FIGURE 13.4

Network access points, essentially large collections of routing equipment, provide a central point of connection where many Tier 2 ISPs can connect to a Tier 1 ISP.

Tier 1 ISP

Tier 2 ISP CO

T-3 Line

Tier 2 ISP FL

T-3 Line

T-3 Line

Routers

Network access point (NAP) Denver, Colorado

Tier 2 ISP CO

Routers

Network access point (NAP) Miami, Florida

Tier 2 ISP FL

Tier 2 ISP CO

Tier 2 ISP FL

Tier 2 ISP UK

Routers

Tier 2 ISP UK

Network access point (NAP) London, England

Tier 2 ISP UK

Miami. This provides many points where Tier 2 ISPs can connect to a Tier 1 ISP. Many ISPs can connect through the same network access point. Tier 2 ISPs pay for third-party high-speed leased communications lines (such as T-1s and T-3s) to connect their networks to the Tier 1's network access points.

Tier 2 ISPs are charged for access to the Tier 1 ISPs based on the amount of bandwidth connecting the two. Bandwidth

charges are like tolls on the highway. The higher the volume of vehicles, the more tolls are paid. To reduce bandwidth charges from the high-speed ISPs, Tier 2 ISPs often connect directly to each other if there is a high volume of traffic passing between them (see Figure 13.5). For example, say it costs $1 for each message sent by a Tier 2 ISP through a Tier 1 ISP. Assume two Tier 2 ISPs send 100 messages to each other a month. If they can

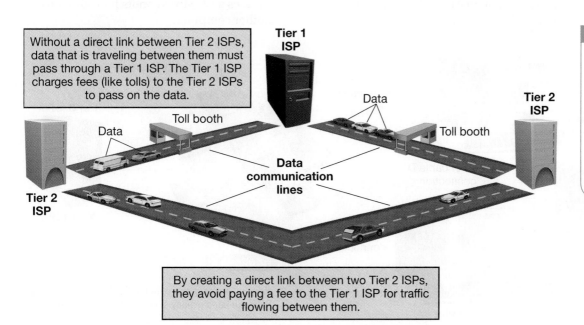

Without a direct link between Tier 2 ISPs, data that is traveling between them must pass through a Tier 1 ISP. The Tier 1 ISP charges fees (like tolls) to the Tier 2 ISPs to pass on the data.

Tier 1 ISP

Data

Toll booth

Data

Tier 2 ISP

Toll booth

Tier 2 ISP

Data communication lines

By creating a direct link between two Tier 2 ISPs, they avoid paying a fee to the Tier 1 ISP for traffic flowing between them.

FIGURE 13.5

Just like cars traveling a toll road, sending data between Tier 2 ISPs and Tier 1 ISPs costs money. To reduce costs, some Tier 2 ISPs build their own data communications highways to reduce data charges.

establish a direct connection between them (say for $50 a month), they don't have to send their messages through the Tier 1 ISP and they save $100 a month (less the $50 for the direct connection).

POINTS OF PRESENCE

How do individuals connect to an ISP? Whether dialing up through a conventional modem or connecting through high-speed access (such as cable or DSL), individual Internet users enter an ISP through a **point of presence (POP)**, which is basically a bank of modems (shown in Figure 13.6) through which many users can connect to an ISP simultaneously. ISPs maintain multiple POPs throughout the geographic area they serve.

THE NETWORK MODEL OF THE INTERNET

What type of network model does the Internet use? The majority of Internet communications follows the **client/server model** of network communications, which we defined in earlier chapters as client computers requesting services and servers providing (serving up) those services to the clients. In the case of the Internet, the *clients* are devices such as computers, cell phones, and PDAs using browsers (or other interfaces) that request services (Web pages and so on). There are various types of *servers* deployed on the networks that make up the Internet from which clients can request services:

- **Web servers** are computers running specialized operating systems that enable them to host Web pages (and other information) and provide requested Web pages to clients.
- **Commerce servers** host software that enables users to purchase goods and services over the Web. These servers generally use special security protocols to protect sensitive information (such as credit card numbers) from being intercepted.
- **File servers** are deployed to provide remote storage space or to act as a repository for files that users can download. For example, Yahoo! provides a file storage option for its users called Yahoo! Briefcase. Storing files in your personal "briefcase" (file folder) enables you to access these files from anywhere you can access the Web with a browser. When you use the briefcase feature of Yahoo!, you're storing files remotely on a file server.

Do all Internet connections take place in a client/server mode? Certain services on the Internet operate in a peer-to-peer mode, as depicted in Figure 13.7. For example, Kazaa is a popular file-sharing service through which Internet users can exchange files. Kazaa and other file-sharing services require the user's computer to act as *both* a client *and* a server. When requesting files from another user, the computer behaves like a client. It switches to server mode when it in turn provides a file stored on its hard drive to another computer.

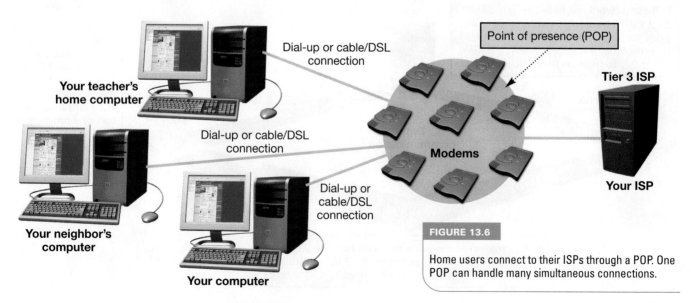

Dial-up or cable/DSL connection

Your teacher's home computer

Dial-up or cable/DSL connection

Your neighbor's computer

Dial-up or cable/DSL connection

Your computer

Point of presence (POP)

Modems

Tier 3 ISP

Your ISP

FIGURE 13.6

Home users connect to their ISPs through a POP. One POP can handle many simultaneous connections.

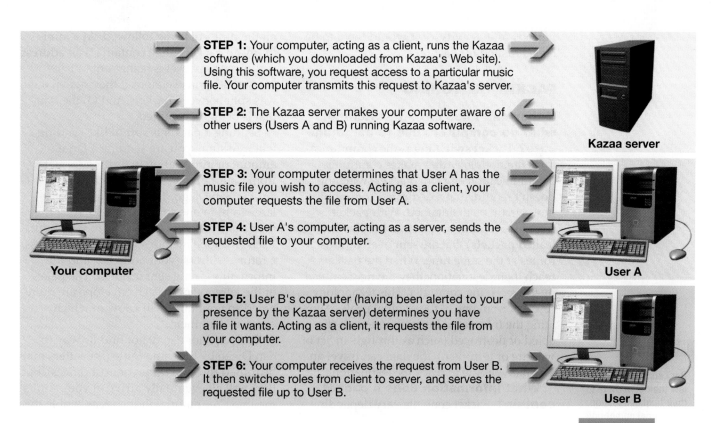

STEP 1: Your computer, acting as a client, runs the Kazaa software (which you downloaded from Kazaa's Web site). Using this software, you request access to a particular music file. Your computer transmits this request to Kazaa's server.

STEP 2: The Kazaa server makes your computer aware of other users (Users A and B) running Kazaa software.

Kazaa server

STEP 3: Your computer determines that User A has the music file you wish to access. Acting as a client, your computer requests the file from User A.

STEP 4: User A's computer, acting as a server, sends the requested file to your computer.

Your computer

User A

STEP 5: User B's computer (having been alerted to your presence by the Kazaa server) determines you have a file it wants. Acting as a client, it requests the file from your computer.

STEP 6: Your computer receives the request from User B. It then switches roles from client to server, and serves the requested file up to User B.

User B

FIGURE 13.7

File-Sharing Services in Action

Data Transmission and Protocols

Just like any other network, the Internet follows standard protocols to send information between computers. A **computer protocol** is a set of rules for accomplishing electronic information exchange. If the Internet is the information superhighway, then protocols are the rules of the road.

To accomplish the early goals of the Internet, protocols needed to be written and agreed upon by users. The protocols needed to be **open systems**, meaning their designs would be made public for access by any interested party. This was in direct opposition to the **proprietary systems**, or private systems, that were the norm at the time.

As we mentioned in earlier chapters, when common communication protocols (rules) are followed, networks can communicate even if they have different topologies, transmission media, or operating systems. The idea of an open-system protocol is that anyone can use it on their computer system and be able to communicate with any other computer using the same protocol. The three biggest Internet tasks (e-mail, Web surfing, and file transfer) are all being done the same way on any system that is following accepted Internet protocols.

Were there problems developing an open-system Internet protocol?

Agreeing on common standards was relatively easy. However, the tough part was developing a new method of communication because the current technology, *circuit switching*, was not efficient for computer communication. Circuit switching has been used since the early days of the telephone for establishing communication. In **circuit switching**, a dedicated connection is formed between two points (two people on telephones) and the connection remains active for the duration of the transmission. This method of communication is extremely important when communications must be received in the order in which they are sent (such as in telephone conversations).

When applied to computers, however, circuit switching is inefficient. Computer processing and communication take place in bursts. As a computer processor performs the operations necessary to complete a task, it transmits data in a group (or burst). The processor then begins working on its next task and ceases to communicate with output devices or other networks until it is ready to transmit data in the next burst. Circuit switching is inefficient for computers because the circuit either would have to remain open (and therefore unavailable to any other system) with long periods of inactivity, or it would have to be reestablished for each burst.

PACKET SWITCHING

If they can't use circuit switching, what do computers use to communicate? Packet switching is the communications methodology that makes computer communication efficient. Packet switching doesn't require that a dedicated communications circuit be maintained. With packet switching, data is broken into smaller chunks (called **packets**) that are sent over various routes at the same time. When the packets reach their destination, they are reassembled by the receiving computer. This technology resulted from one of the original goals of creating the Internet: if Internet nodes are disabled or destroyed (such as through an act of warfare or terrorism), the data can travel an alternative route to reach its destination.

What information does a packet contain? Packet contents vary depending on the protocol being followed. At a minimum, all packets must contain (1) an address to which the packet is being sent, (2) reassembling instructions if the original data was split between packets, and (3) the data that is being transmitted.

Sending a packet is sort of like sending a letter. Assume you are sending a large amount of information in written format from your home in Philadelphia to your aunt in San Diego. The information is too large to fit in one small envelope, so you mail three different envelopes to your aunt. Each envelope includes your aunt's address, a return address (your address), and the information being sent inside it. The pages of the letters sent in each envelope are numbered so your aunt will know in which order to read them.

Each envelope may not find its way to San Diego by the same route (the letters may be routed through different post offices), but they will all eventually arrive in your aunt's mailbox. Your aunt will then reassemble the

FIGURE 13.8

Packets can each follow their own route to their final destination. Sequential numbering of packets ensures they are reassembled in the correct order at their destination.

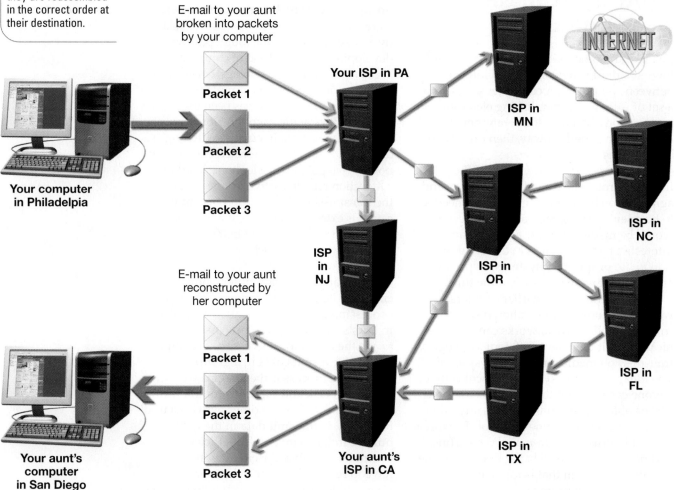

message (put the pages of the letters in order) and read it. The process of sending a message through the Internet works in much the same way. This is illustrated in Figure 13.8, which traces an e-mail message sent from a computer in Philadelphia to a computer in San Diego.

Why do packets take different routes and how do they decide which route to use? The routers that connect ISPs with each other monitor traffic and decide on the most efficient route for packets to take to their destination. The router works the same as a police officer during a traffic jam. When routes are clogged with traffic, police officers are deployed in areas of congestion to direct you to an alternate route to get to your destination.

TCP/IP

What protocol does the Internet use for transmitting data? Although many protocols are available on the Internet, the main suite of protocols used is **TCP/IP**. The suite is named after the original two protocols that were developed for the Internet: the **Transmission Control Protocol (TCP)** and the **Internet Protocol (IP)**. Although most people think that the TCP/IP suite consists of only two protocols, it actually comprises many interrelated protocols, the most important of which are listed in Figure 13.9.

Which particular protocol actually sends the information? The Internet

Protocol (IP) is responsible for sending the information from one computer to another. The IP is like a postal worker who takes a letter (a packet of information) that was mailed (created by the sending computer) and sends it on to another post office, which in turn routes it to the addressee (receiving computer). The postal worker never knows whether the recipient actually receives the letter. The only thing the postal worker knows is that the letter was handed off to an appropriate post office that will assist in completing the delivery of the letter.

IP Addresses and Domain Names

As you learned in Chapter 3, each computer, server, or device (router, etc.) connected to the Internet is required to have a unique number identifying it, called an **IP address**. IP addresses fulfill the same function as street addresses. For example, to get directions to John Doe's house in Walla Walla, Washington, you have to know his address. John might live at 123 Main Street, which is not a unique address (many towns have a Main Street). But 123 Main Street, Walla Walla, WA 99362 is a unique address.

What helps make it unique? The numeric zip code provides unique identification for a specific geographic area. The

FIGURE 13.9 The Main Protocols Contained in the TCP/IP Protocol Suite

Protocol Name	Main Protocol Function
Internet Protocol (IP)	Sends data between computers on the Internet
Transmission Control Protocol (TCP)	Prepares data for transmission and provides for error checking and resending lost data
User Datagram Protocol (UDP)	Prepares data for transmission—no resending capabilities
File Transfer Protocol (FTP)	Enables files to be downloaded to a computer or uploaded to other computers
Telnet	Enables logging in to a remote computer and working on it as if sitting in front of it
Hypertext Transfer Protocol (HTTP) and Secure HTTP (S-HTTP)	Transfers Hypertext Markup Language (HTML) data from servers to browsers
Simple Mail Transfer Protocol (SMTP)	Used for transmission of e-mail messages across the Internet

Internet Corporation for Assigned Names and Numbers (ICANN) is responsible for allocating IP addresses to network administrators, just like the U.S. Postal Service is responsible for assigning zip codes to geographic areas.

What does an IP address look like?
A typical IP address is expressed as follows:

197.24.72.157

An IP address expressed like this is called a **dotted decimal number**. However, computers work with binary numbers. The same IP address in binary form is as follows:

11000101.00011000.01001000.10011101

The four numbers in the dotted decimal notation are each referred to as an **octet**. This name derives from the fact that each number would have eight positions when shown in binary form. Because there are 32 positions available for IP address values (four octets with eight positions each), IP addresses are considered 32-bit numbers. A position is either filled by a 1 or a 0, resulting in 256 (2^8) possible values for each octet. Values start at 0 (not 1); therefore, each octet can have a value from 0 to 255. The entire 32-bit address can represent 4,294,967,296 values (or 2^{32}), which is quite a few Internet addresses!

Will we ever run out of IP addresses? When the original IP addressing scheme, **Internet Protocol version 4 (IPv4)**, was created, no one foresaw the explosive growth of the Internet in the 1990s. (Of course, the Internet wasn't yet the exciting visual medium that it is today.) Therefore, four billion values for an address field seemed like enough to last forever. However, as the Internet grew rapidly, it quickly became apparent that we were going to run out of IP addresses.

What is being done to make sure we have enough IP addresses in the future? Internet Protocol version 6 (IPv6) is a proposed IP addressing scheme (developed by the Internet Engineering Task Force) that makes IP addresses longer, thereby providing more available IP addresses. It uses eight groups of 16-bit numbers, referred to as *hexadecimal notation* (or *hex* for short), which you learned about in Chapter 9. An IPv6 address would have the following format:

0000:0000:0000:0000:0000:0000:0000:0000

Hex addressing provides a much larger field size that will enable a much larger number of IP addresses (approximately 340 followed by 36 zeros). This should be a virtually unlimited supply.

Is IPv6 being used today? IPv6 has been slow to catch on. The complexities involved with adopting IPv6 include designing a new TCP/IP protocol. Not many vendors have rolled out IPv6 protocols yet. The good news is that IPv6 will be backward compatible with IPv4, so there will be no need to change current IPv4 systems.

How does my computer get an IP address? You learned in Chapter 7 that IP addresses are either assigned *statically* or *dynamically*. **Static addressing** means that the IP address for a computer never changes and is most likely assigned manually by a network administrator. **Dynamic addressing**, in which your computer is assigned an address from an available pool of IP addresses, is more common. A connection to an ISP could use either method. If your ISP uses static addressing, you were assigned an IP address when you applied for your service and had to configure your computer manually to use that address. More often, though, your ISP assigns your computer a temporary (dynamic) IP address.

BITS AND BYTES

What's Your IP Address?

Curious as to what your IP address is? In Windows XP, start the command prompt (located under Accessories). At the c:>, type ipconfig and hit Enter. A screen similar to Figure 13.10 will be displayed that shows, among other things, the IP address your PC is currently using.

```
C:\>ipconfig

Windows IP Configuration

Ethernet adapter Network Bridge (Network Bridge):

        Connection-specific DNS Suffix  . : walngs01.pa.comcast.net
        IP Address. . . . . . . . . . . . : 192.168.0.3
        Subnet Mask . . . . . . . . . . . : 255.255.255.0
        Default Gateway . . . . . . . . . : 192.168.0.1

C:\>
```

FIGURE 13.10

Running ipconfig at the command prompt reveals your computer's IP address.

How exactly are dynamic addresses assigned? Dynamic addressing is normally handled by the **Dynamic Host Configuration Protocol (DHCP)**, which belongs to the TCP/IP protocol suite. DHCP takes a pool of IP addresses and shares them with hosts on the network on an as-needed basis. ISPs don't need to maintain a pool of IP addresses for *all* of their subscribers because not everyone is logged on to the Internet at one time. Thus, when a user logs on to an ISP's server, the DHCP server assigns that user an IP address for the duration of the session. Similarly, when you log on to your computer at work in the morning, DHCP assigns your computer an IP address. These temporary IP addresses may or may not be the same from session to session.

What are the benefits of dynamic addressing? Although having a static address would seem to be convenient, dynamic addressing provides for better security measures to keep hackers out of computer systems. Imagine how hard it would be for burglars to find your home if you changed your address every day!

DOMAIN NAMES

I've been on the Internet, so why have I never seen IP addresses? Computers are fantastic at relating to IP addresses and other numbers. However, humans remember names better than they remember strings of numbers. (Would you rather call your friend 1236231 or Maria?) As the Web was being formed, a naming system needed to be developed to enable people to work with names instead of numbers. Hence, *domain names* were born. As you learned in Chapter 3, a **domain name** is simply a name that takes the place of an IP address, making it easier for people to remember it. You've most likely visited **www.yahoo.com**. Yahoo.com is a domain name. The server

where Yahoo!'s main Web site is deployed has an IP address (such as 123.45.67.89), but it's much easier for you to remember to tell your browser to go to Yahoo.com than it is to type in the nine-digit IP address.

How are domains organized? Domains are organized by level. As you'll recall from Chapter 3, the portion of the domain name farthest to the right (after the dot) is the top-level domain (TLD). The TLDs are standardized pools established by ICANN (such as .com and .org). (Refer back to Figure 3.10 in Chapter 3 for a list of the TLDs that are currently approved and in use.) Within the top-level domains are many **second-level domains**. In the .com domain, there are popular sites such as Amazon.com, Google.com, and Microsoft.com. Each of the second-level domains needs to be unique within that particular domain, but not necessarily unique to all top-level domains. For example, Mycoolsite.com and Mycoolsite.org could be registered as separate domain names.

Who controls domain name registration? ICANN assigns companies or groups to manage domain name registration. Because names can't be duplicated within a top-level domain, one company is assigned to oversee each TLD and maintain a listing of all registered domains. For instance, Network Solutions oversees the .com domain and provides a database that lists all the registered domains and their contact information. You can look up any .com domain at **www.networksolutions.com/en_US/whois/index.jhtml** to see if it is registered and who owns it. Country-specific domains are controlled by groups in those countries. You can find a complete list on the Internet Assigned Numbers Authority Web site at **www.iana.org**.

DNS SERVERS

How does my computer know the IP address of another computer? Say you want to get to Yahoo.com. To do so, you type the URL **www.yahoo.com** into your browser. However, the URL is not important to your computer; only the IP address of the computer hosting the Yahoo! site is. When you enter the URL in your browser, your computer must convert the URL to an IP address. To do this, your computer consults a database maintained on a **DNS server**, which functions like a phone book for the Internet.

Making the Connection: Connection-Oriented Versus Connectionless Protocols

The Internet Protocol is responsible only for *sending* packets on their way. The packets are created by either the TCP or the **User Datagram Protocol (UDP)**. You don't decide whether to use TCP or UDP. The choice of protocol was made for you by the developers of the computer programs you are using or by the other protocols (such as those listed in Figure 13.9) that will interact with your data packet.

As explained earlier, data transmission between computers is very efficient if connections do not need to be established (as in circuit switching). However, there are benefits to maintaining a connection, such as less data loss. The difference between TCP and UDP is that TCP is a *connection-oriented protocol*, whereas UDP is a *connectionless protocol*.

A **connection-oriented protocol** requires two computers to exchange control packets, which set up the parameters

of the data exchange session, prior to sending packets that contain data. This process is referred to as **handshaking**. TCP uses a process called a **three-way handshake** to establish a connection, as shown in Figure 13.11a. Perhaps you need to report sales figures to your home office. You phone the sales manager and tell him or her that you are ready to report your figures. The sales manager then prepares to receive the information by getting a pencil and a piece of paper. By confirming he or she is ready and by your beginning to report the figures, a three-way (three-step) handshaking process is completed.

Your computer does the same thing when it wishes to send an e-mail through your ISP, as shown in Figure 13.11b. It establishes a connection to the ISP and announces it has e-mail to send. The ISP server responds that it is ready to receive. Your computer then

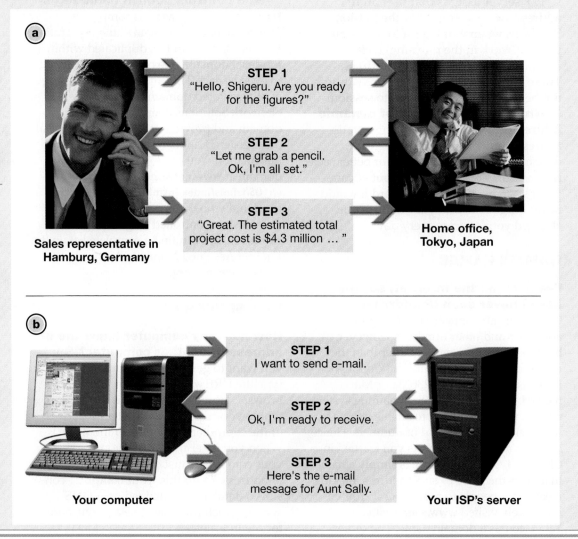

FIGURE 13.11

(a) Colleagues in Hamburg and Tokyo are establishing communication using a three-way handshake.
(b) Here, two computers are establishing communication the same way.

a

STEP 1
"Hello, Shigeru. Are you ready for the figures?"

STEP 2
"Let me grab a pencil. Ok, I'm all set."

STEP 3
"Great. The estimated total project cost is $4.3 million … "

Sales representative in Hamburg, Germany

Home office, Tokyo, Japan

b

STEP 1
I want to send e-mail.

STEP 2
Ok, I'm ready to receive.

STEP 3
Here's the e-mail message for Aunt Sally.

Your computer

Your ISP's server

acknowledges the ready state of the server and begins to transmit the e-mail.

A **connectionless protocol** does not require any type of connection to be established or maintained between two computers that are exchanging information. Just like mailing a letter, the data packets are sent without notifying the receiving computer or receiving any acknowledgment that the data was received. UDP is the Internet's connectionless protocol.

Besides establishing a connection, TCP provides for reliable data transfer. Reliable data transfer means that the application that uses TCP can rely on this protocol to deliver all the data packets to the receiver free from errors and in the correct order. TCP achieves reliable data transfer by using acknowledgments and providing for the retransmission of data, as shown in Figure 13.12.

Assuming two systems, X and Y, have established a connection, when Y receives a packet from X, it sends a **positive acknowledgment (ACK)** when it receives a data packet that it can read. If X does not receive an ACK in an appropriate period of time, it resends the packet. If the packet is unreadable (damaged in transit), Y sends a **negative acknowledgment (NACK)** to X, indicating the packet was not received in understandable form. X will then retransmit that packet. Acknowledgments assure that the receiver has gotten a complete set of data packets. If a packet is unable to get through after being resent several times, the user is generally presented with an error message indicating the communications were unsuccessful.

You may wonder why you wouldn't always want to use a protocol that provides for reliable data transfer. On the Internet, speed is often more important

than accuracy. For certain applications (such as e-mail), it's very important that your message be delivered completely and accurately. For streaming multimedia, it's not always important to have every frame delivered accurately because most streaming media formats provide for error correcting caused by data loss. It is, however, extremely important for streaming media to be delivered at a high rate of speed; otherwise, playback quality can be affected. Therefore, a protocol such as TCP using handshakes and acknowledgments would probably not be appropriate when viewing a movie trailer over the Internet.

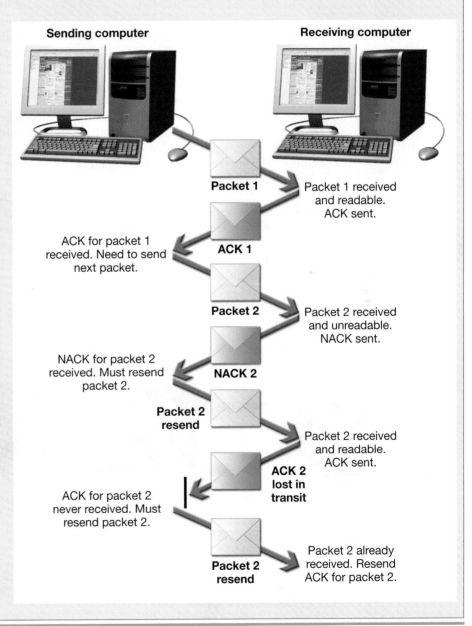

Sending computer   Receiving computer

Packet 1 — Packet 1 received and readable. ACK sent.

ACK for packet 1 received. Need to send next packet. — ACK 1

Packet 2 — Packet 2 received and unreadable. NACK sent.

NACK for packet 2 received. Must resend packet 2. — NACK 2

Packet 2 resend — Packet 2 received and readable. ACK sent.

ACK 2 lost in transit

ACK for packet 2 never received. Must resend packet 2.

Packet 2 resend — Packet 2 already received. Resend ACK for packet 2.

FIGURE 13.12

Packet Acknowledgment in Action

What Is an Internet Cache?

Your Internet cache is a section of your hard drive that stores information that you may need again for surfing (such as IP addresses, frequently accessed Web pages, and so on). However, caching of domain name addresses also takes place in DNS servers. This helps speed up Internet access time because the DNS server doesn't have to query master DNS servers constantly for TLDs. However, caches do have limited storage space, so entries are held in the cache only for a fixed period of time and then are deleted. The time component associated with cache retention is known as the Time To Live (TTL). Without caches, surfing the Internet would take a lot longer.

FIGURE 13.13

DNS Servers in Action

Your ISP's Web server has a default DNS server (one that is convenient to contact) that it goes to when it needs to translate a URL to an IP address (illustrated in Figure 13.13). Your ISP or network administrator defines the default DNS server. If the default DNS server does not have an entry for the domain name you requested, it queries another DNS server (perhaps maintained by a Tier 2 or Tier 1 ISP).

If all else fails, it contacts one of the many *root DNS servers* maintained throughout the Internet. The **root DNS servers** know the location of all the DNS servers that contain the master listings for an entire TLD. Your default DNS receives the infor-

mation from the master DNS (say, for the .com domain), then stores that information in its cache for future use and communicates the appropriate IP address to your computer.

Other Protocols: FTP and Telnet

The TCP/IP protocol suite contains numerous protocols, although some of them are not used very often. Other commonly used protocols on the Internet are the *File Transfer Protocol (FTP)* and *Telnet*.

How does FTP work? The **File Transfer Protocol (FTP)** enables users to share files that reside on local computers with remote computers. If you're attempting to download files using FTP to your local computer, the FTP client program (most likely a Web browser) first establishes a TCP session with the remote computer. FTP provides for authentication and password protection, so you may be required to log in to an FTP site with a username and password.

Can I upload files with FTP? Most FTP sites allow you to upload files. To do so, you either need a browser that handles FTP transfer (current versions of Internet Explorer and Firefox do), or you need to obtain an FTP client application. Many FTP client programs are available as freeware or shareware. Searching on the term "FTP" on

STEP 1: Your browser requests information from ABC.com

STEP 2: Your ISP doesn't know the IP address of ABC.com, so it requests the address from its default DNS server

STEP 3: The default DNS server doesn't know the IP address of ABC.com either, so it queries the root server of the .com domain

Your computer

Your ISP's Web server

Your ISP's default DNS server

Root server for .com domain

STEP 7: Your computer then routes its request to ABC.com and stores the IP address in cache for later use

STEP 6: Your ISP's Web server also stores the correct IP address for ABC.com for future reference and passes it on to your computer

STEP 5: The default DNS server stores the correct IP address for ABC.com for future reference and passes it on to your ISP's Web server

STEP 4: The root server provides the default DNS server with the appropriate IP address of ABC.com

www.download.com will produce a list of programs to choose from. FTP Voyager is a popular FTP shareware program you can try for free and later pay for if you want to continue using it.

What is Telnet? Telnet is both a protocol for connecting to a remote computer and a TCP/IP service that runs on a remote computer to make it accessible to other computers. At colleges, students sometimes use Telnet to connect to mainframe computers or servers from their personal computers. The Telnet client application (which runs on your personal computer) connects to the Telnet server application (running on a remote computer). Telnet enables you to take control of a remote computer (the server) with your computer (the client) and manipulate files and data on the server as if you were sitting in front of that server.

How do I use Telnet? To establish a Telnet session, you need to know the domain name or IP address of the computer to be connected to using Telnet. In addition, logon information (ID and password) is generally required. You can start Telnet in Windows by clicking the Start button in the taskbar, selecting the Run command, entering "telnet" in the dialog box that opens, and clicking the OK button. This will then display the window shown in Figure 13.14. Typing ?/ at the command prompt displays the available Telnet commands. To connect to a remote computer, type "open" and the host name (or IP address) of the remote computer and follow the logon instructions (which vary from system to system).

HTTP, HTML, and Beyond

Although most people think that the Internet and the Web are the same thing, the World Wide Web (WWW or the Web) is a grouping of protocols and software that *resides* on the Internet (which is a collection of linked networks). The Web provides an engaging interface for exchanging graphics, video, animations, and other multimedia on the Internet.

Did the same people who invented the Internet invent the Web? The Web was invented many years after the original Internet. In 1989, Tim Berners-Lee, a physicist at the European Organization for Nuclear Research (CERN), wanted a method for linking his research documents together so that other researchers could access them. In conjunction with Robert Cailliau, Berners-Lee developed the basic architecture of the Web and created the first Web browser. The original browser could handle only text and was usable only on computers running the NeXT operating system (a commercially unsuccessful OS), which limited its usage. So, Berners-Lee put out a call to the Internet community to assist with development of browsers for other platforms.

In 1993, the National Center for Supercomputing Applications (NCSA) released the Mosaic browser for use on the Macintosh and Windows operating systems. Mosaic could display graphics as well as text. As the popularity of this browser grew, Marc Andreessen, the leader of the Mosaic

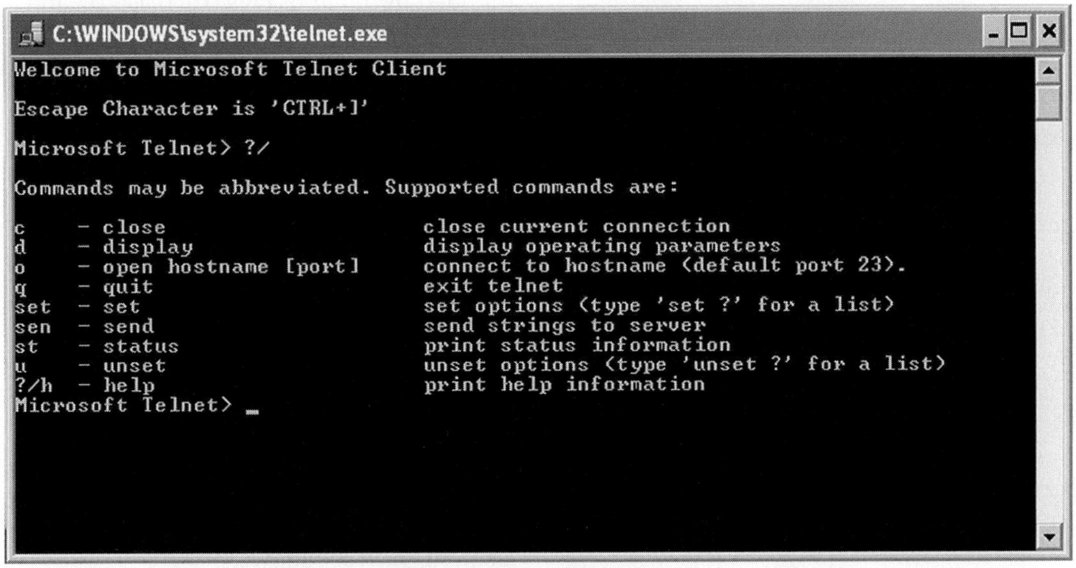

```
C:\WINDOWS\system32\telnet.exe

Welcome to Microsoft Telnet Client

Escape Character is 'CTRL+]'

Microsoft Telnet> ?/

Commands may be abbreviated. Supported commands are:

c    - close              close current connection
d    - display            display operating parameters
o    - open hostname [port] connect to hostname (default port 23).
q    - quit               exit telnet
set  - set                set options (type 'set ?' for a list)
sen  - send               send strings to server
st   - status             print status information
u    - unset              unset options (type 'unset ?' for a list)
?/h  - help               print help information
Microsoft Telnet> _
```

FIGURE 13.14

This Telnet command window shows the commands it has available.

development team, formed a company called Mosaic Communications (later renamed Netscape Communications) with Jim Clark. Within six months, many of the developers from the original Mosaic project at the NCSA were working for this new company. The Netscape browser (version 1.0) was released by the company in December 1994. This new browser featured improvements in usability over Mosaic and quickly became the dominant Web browser. The launch of Netscape heralded the beginning of the Web's monumental growth.

HTTP AND SSL

Which Internet protocol does a browser use to send requests? The **Hypertext Transfer Protocol (HTTP)** was created especially for the transfer of hypertext documents across the Internet. **Hypertext** documents are documents in which text is linked to other documents or media (such as video clips, pictures, and so on). Clicking a specific piece of text (called a *hyperlink*) that has been linked elsewhere takes you to the linked file.

When the browser sends a request, does it do anything to make the information secure? Commerce servers use security protocols to protect sen-

sitive information from being intercepted by hackers. One common protocol is the **Secure Sockets Layer (SSL)**, which provides for the encryption of data transmitted using TCP/IP protocols such as HTTP. All major Web browsers support SSL.

There are at least two indications you are using SSL. When on a site using SSL, your browser displays a padlock icon in the status bar at the bottom of the browser. Also, when a URL begins with https:// instead of http://, that Web site is requiring information to be sent using SSL encryption. On a Web site that is using SSL, you can be secure in the knowledge that the information you are sending (such as your credit card number) is encrypted and would be extremely difficult (if not impossible) for unauthorized users to decode.

HTML/XHTML

How are Web pages formatted? A Web page is merely a text document that is formatted using the **Hypertext Markup Language (HTML)**. The current version of HTML is called the **Extensible Hypertext Markup Language (XHTML)**. XHTML has much more stringent rules than HTML regarding tagging (for instance, all elements require an end tag). XHTML is the development environment of choice for Web developers today, although many people still refer to Web site formatting as HTML tagging.

HTML/XHTML are not programming languages; rather, they are sets of rules for marking up blocks of text so that a browser knows how to display them. Blocks of text in HTML/XHTML documents are surrounded by a pair of **tags** (such as <b> and </b> to indicate bolding). These tags and the text between them are referred to as **elements**. The elements are interpreted by the browser and appropriate effects are applied to the text. The following is an element from an HTML/XHTML document:

```
<i> This should be italicized.</i>
```

The browser would display this element as:

This should be italicized.

The first tag <i> tells the browser that the text following it should be italicized. The end </i> tag indicates that the browser should cease applying italics to the text. Note that tags can be combined in a single element, such as follows:

```
<b><i>This should be bolded
and italicized.</b></i>
```

The browser would display this element as:

This should be bolded and italicized.

Obviously, the <b> tag indicates bolding.

Tags for creating hyperlinks appear as follows:

```
<a href = http://www.pren-
hall.com/> Prentice Hall
Publishing</a>
```

(<a href = http://www.prenhall.com/>) defines the link's destination. The </a> tag indicates the end of the hyperlink element. The text in between the two tags (Prentice Hall Publishing) is the link label. The link label is the text (or image) that is displayed on the Web page as clickable text for the hyperlink.

Can I see the HTML/XHTML coding of a Web page? HTML/XHTML documents are merely text documents with tags applied to them. If you want to look at the HTML/XHTML coding behind your favorite Web page, just right-click anywhere on the page (or select View Source from your browser menu) and a dialog box will appear. Select the View Source option and the HTML/XHTML code for that page will be displayed as shown in Figure 13.15. For more on how to build Web pages, see the Sound Byte "Constructing a Simple Web Page."

SOUND BYTE
Constructing a Simple Web Page

Creating simple Web pages using Microsoft Word is relatively easy. In this Sound Byte, you'll learn the basics of Web page creation by setting up a Web site featuring a student résumé.

THE COMMON GATEWAY INTERFACE

Can you use HTML/XHTML to do everything you need to do on a Web page? Because HTML/XHTML was originally designed to link text documents, HTML/XHTML by itself can't do all the amazing things we expect modern Web pages to do. As we mentioned earlier, HTML/XHTML are not programming languages; rather, they are sets of tags for determining how text is displayed and where elements are placed. Fortunately, the limitations of HTML/XHTML were recognized early and the *Common Gateway Interface (CGI)* was developed.

Most browser requests merely result in a file being displayed in your browser (such as the eBay.com main Web page). Displaying a file is fine if you're just going to be reading text. However, to make a Web site interactive, you may need to run a software

FIGURE 13.15

Displaying the source code in a browser opens a Notepad window containing the HTML text document.

program to perform a certain action (such as gathering a name and address and adding it to a database). The **Common Gateway Interface (CGI)** provides a methodology by which your browser can request that a program file be executed (or run) instead of just being delivered to the browser. This enables functionality beyond the simple displaying of information.

CGI files can be created in almost any programming language, and the programs created are often referred to as **CGI scripts**. Common languages that are used to create CGI scripts are PERL, C, and C++ . Because programming languages are very powerful, almost any task can be accomplished by writing a CGI script. You have probably encountered CGI scripts on Web pages without realizing it. Have you ever left an entry in a guest book on a Web page? Have you used a search engine to create a customized results page based on keywords you entered? Have you filled out a form to be added to a mailing list? All of these tasks are commonly done using CGI scripts.

How do CGI programs get executed? On most Web servers, a directory called **cgi-bin** is created by the network administrator who configures the Web server. All CGI scripts are placed into this directory. The Web server knows that all files in this directory are not to be merely read and sent, but also need to be run. Because these programs are run on the Web server as opposed to running inside your browser, they are referred to as **server-side** programs.

For instance, a button on a Web site may say "Click Here to Join Mailing List" (see Step 1 in Figure 13.16). Clicking this button may call a script file (perhaps called mailinglist.pl) from the cgi-bin directory on the Web server hosting the site (Step 2). This file generates a form that is sent to your browser, which includes fields for a name and e-mail address and a button that says "Submit" (Step 3). After filling in the fields and clicking the Submit button, the mailinglist.pl program sends the information back to the server. The server then records the information in a database (Step 4).

CLIENT-SIDE APPLICATIONS

Aside from CGI scripts, are there other ways to make a Web site interactive? Sometimes running programs on the server is not optimal. Server-side program execution can require many communication sessions between the client and the server to achieve the goal. Often it is more efficient to run programs on your computer (the client). Therefore, *client-side applications* were created. A **client-side application** is a computer program that runs on the client and requires no interaction with a Web server. Client-side applications are fast and efficient because they run at your desktop

FIGURE 13.16

Information Flow When a CGI Program Is Run

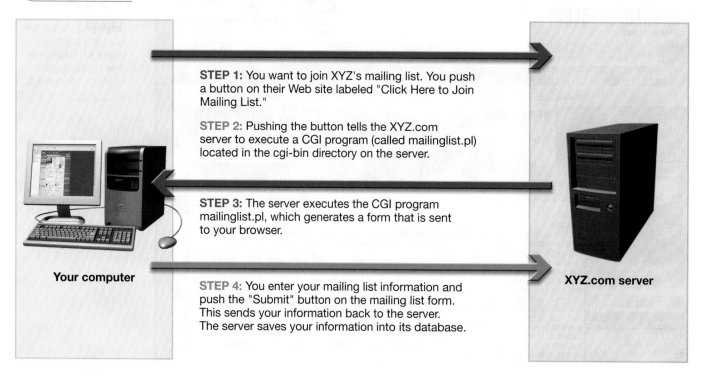

STEP 1: You want to join XYZ's mailing list. You push a button on their Web site labeled "Click Here to Join Mailing List."

STEP 2: Pushing the button tells the XYZ.com server to execute a CGI program (called mailinglist.pl) located in the cgi-bin directory on the server.

STEP 3: The server executes the CGI program mailinglist.pl, which generates a form that is sent to your browser.

Your computer

STEP 4: You enter your mailing list information and push the "Submit" button on the mailing list form. This sends your information back to the server. The server saves your information into its database.

XYZ.com server

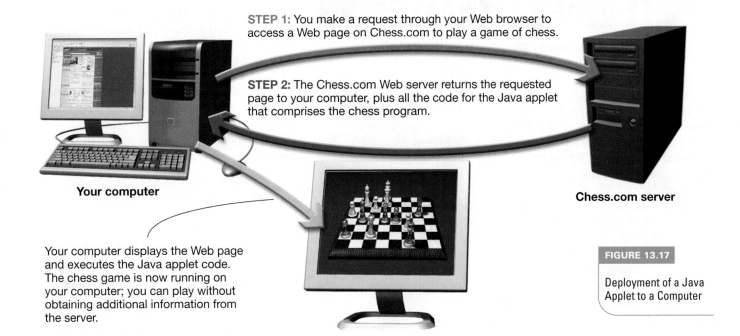

STEP 1: You make a request through your Web browser to access a Web page on Chess.com to play a game of chess.

STEP 2: The Chess.com Web server returns the requested page to your computer, plus all the code for the Java applet that comprises the chess program.

Your computer

Your computer displays the Web page and executes the Java applet code. The chess game is now running on your computer; you can play without obtaining additional information from the server.

Chess.com server

FIGURE 13.17

Deployment of a Java Applet to a Computer

and don't depend on sending signals back and forth to the Web server.

Two main types of client-side methods exist. The first involves embedding programming language code directly within the HTML/XHTML code of a Web page using an **HTML/XHTML embedded scripting language**. The most popular embedded language is **JavaScript**, which was developed through the joint efforts of Netscape and Sun Microsystems. It is often confused with the Java programming language because of the similarity in the name. Although they share some common elements, the two languages function very differently.

Pure HTML/XHTML documents don't respond to user input. However, through the use of JavaScript, HTML/XHTML documents can be made responsive to mouse clicks and typing. When JavaScript code is embedded in an HTML/XHMTL document, it is downloaded with the HTML/XHTML page to the browser. All actions dictated by the embedded JavaScript commands are executed on the client computer (the one with the browser). Without JavaScript, Web pages would be pretty lifeless.

The second type of client-side application is an **applet**, a small program that resides on a server. When requested, a compiled version of the program is downloaded to the client computer and run there. The Java language is the most common language used to create applets for use in browsers. The

applets can be requested from the server when a Web page is loaded, and they will be run once they're downloaded to the client computer.

Although there can be some delay in functionality while waiting for the Java applet to download to the client, once the applet arrives, it can execute all its functions without further communication with the server. Games are often sent to your browser as applets. In Figure 13.17, your browser makes contact with the game site (Chess.com) and makes your request to play a game of chess (Step 1). The Web server returns the Java applet (Step 2) that contains all the code to run the game on your computer. Your computer executes the applet code and the game runs on your computer.

XML

Can I create my own HTML/XHTML tags to fit my special needs? For HTML/XHTML, you're required to use the standard predefined tags that constitute the HTML/XHTML standard. This works fairly well for displaying information on Web pages, but is less optimal if two Web pages need to exchange information. Information exchange has become much more common with the rise of business-to-business (B2B) electronic commerce. B2B transactions involve two businesses selling products and services

BITS AND BYTES

Are Old Web Pages Really Gone Forever?

Have you ever tried to find a site you've visited on the Web, only to find it no longer exists? Or have you ever discovered that information you want to access has been removed from a site? Is the information lost forever? Groups such as the Internet Archive (**www.archive.org**) are trying to prevent the loss of information on the Internet as a result of Web site updates or the discontinuance of a site. Since 1996, the Internet Archive has been collecting information from the Web and preserving it. Their "Wayback Machine" allows you to visit archived versions of Web sites from prior time periods. Want to see how Yahoo! has changed since 1996? Just type the URL into the Wayback Machine engine and you'll see links to various snapshots of Yahoo! at various points in time. So next time you try to access a site that is no longer there, check the Wayback Machine and all may not be lost.

to each other without a retail customer involved. Because HTML/XHTML was not designed for information exchange, *Extensible Markup Language (XML)* was created.

How is XML different from HTML/XHTML? Extensible Markup **Language (XML)** is a set of tools you can use to create your own markup language. In a sense, it is a more flexible version of HTML/XHTML. Instead of being locked into standard tags and formats for data, users can build their own markup languages to accommodate particular data formats and needs.

For example, three pieces of typical information that need to be captured for an e-commerce transaction are credit card number, price, and zip code. In HTML/XHTML, the paragraph tags (<p> and </p>) are used to define text and numeric elements. Almost anything can fall between these tags and be treated as a paragraph. So, in our example, the HTML/XHTML code would appear as follows:

```
<p>1234567890123456</p>
(credit card number)
<p>12.95</p> (price)
<p>19422</p> (zip code)
```

The browser will interpret this data as separate paragraphs. But the paragraph tags tell us nothing about the data contained within them. Without the labels added (not part of the HTML/XHTML code), we may not real-

ize what data was contained within. Also, <p> tags don't provide any methodology for data validation. Credit card numbers are usually 16 numbers long. But any length of data could be inserted between <p> and </p> tags. How would we know if the credit card number was a valid length? The answer lies in creating tags that are specific to the task at hand, and that actually describe the data contained within them. Here's how our data might look in XML:

```
<credit card num-
ber>1234567890123456</credit
card number>
<price>12.95</price>
<zip code>19422</zip code>
```

We have created the tags we need for data capture. Our XML specification provides a tag called "credit card number" that is used exclusively for credit card data. As well as defining how the browser will display information tagged as <credit card number>, you also can require that the tagged data be numeric and 16 numbers long. With XML, you can achieve the data validation necessary for ensuring data is exchanged accurately between applications.

Communications Over the Internet

A new communications revolution was started when Internet use began to explode in the mid-1990s. The volume of Internet e-mail is growing exponentially every month (unfortunately, over 80 percent of it is spam), instant messaging is a major method of communication, and the popularity of Internet telephony is also on the rise. In the following sections, we explore all of these communications media in more detail and show you how to keep your information exchanges efficient and secure.

Careers: If You Build It, Will They Come?
Web Development and Design Careers

Although Web development careers span a vast array of job functions, many students endeavoring to pursue these opportunities insist on seeking information on becoming a Webmaster. However, in the modern Internet economy, Webmasters are quickly becoming a thing of the past.

As the term implies, *Webmaster* originally meant the person who was solely responsible for the Web site at a company. In 1994, you might have been a Webmaster because you were the only person in the company who knew HTML code. At that time, Web sites were static and changed little from day to day. In the 21st century, Web sites are large, dynamic, and key to many companies' business strategies. Users are demanding and expect fresh content and new services to be offered frequently. Therefore, most modern business Web sites cannot be supported by just one person.

Teams that support today's Web sites are usually organized into four areas:

1. *Web server administrators* are specialized versions of network administrators. Their primary responsibility is to install and maintain the Web servers that host a company's Web pages. Web server administrators have specialized training in products such as Apache and Microsoft IIS Web servers as well as general networking training.
2. *Content creators* generate the words and images on the Web. Journalists, writers, and editors prepare an enormous amount of Web content, while video producers, graphic artists, and animators create Web-based multimedia. Content creators have a thorough understanding of their own fields as well as HTML/XHTML and JavaScript. They also need to be familiar with capabilities and limitations of modern Web development tools so that they know what the Web publishers can accomplish.
3. *Web publishers* build Web pages to deploy the material content creators develop. They wield the Web tools (such as Macromedia's Dreamweaver and Microsoft's FrontPage) that develop the Web pages and create links to databases (using products such as Oracle and SQL Server) to keep information flowing between users and the Web page. They must possess a solid understanding of client- and server-side Web languages (HTML/XHTML, XML, Java, JavaScript, ASP, and PERL) and development environments such as the Microsoft .NET Framework.
4. The *customer interaction team* provides feedback to a Web site's customers. Answering e-mail, sending requested information, funneling questions to appropriate personnel (technical support, sales, and so on), and providing suggestions to Web publishers for site improvements are major job responsibilities. Extensive customer service training is essential to work effectively in this area.

As you can see, there are many opportunities to be part of a modern Web development team, and not all of these jobs require extensive programming capabilities. They do all require hard work, imagination, and attention to detail. The Web is only as useful as you make it! We talk more about Web-related IT careers in the Technology in Focus "Careers in IT" on page 586.

E-MAIL

Who invented e-mail? In 1971, Ray Tomlinson, a computer engineer who worked on the development of the ARPANET (the precursor to the Internet) for the U.S. government, created e-mail. E-mail grew from a simple program that Tomlinson wrote to enable computer users to leave text messages for each other on a single machine. The logical extension of this was sending text messages between machines on the Internet. Tomlinson created the convention of using the @ sign to distinguish between the mailbox name and the destination computer. E-mail became the most popular application on ARPANET, and by 1973, it accounted for 75 percent of all data traffic.

How does e-mail travel the Internet? Just like other kinds of data that flow along the Internet, e-mail has its own protocol. The **Simple Mail Transfer Protocol (SMTP)** is responsible for sending e-mail along the Internet to its destination. As in most other Internet applications, e-mail is a client/server application. Two primary kinds of e-mail client software are in use today. Although client-based e-mail software, such as Microsoft Outlook, America Online (AOL), and Eudora, continues to be very popular, Web-based e-mail software, in use on sites such as Yahoo! and Hotmail, also has grown in popularity.

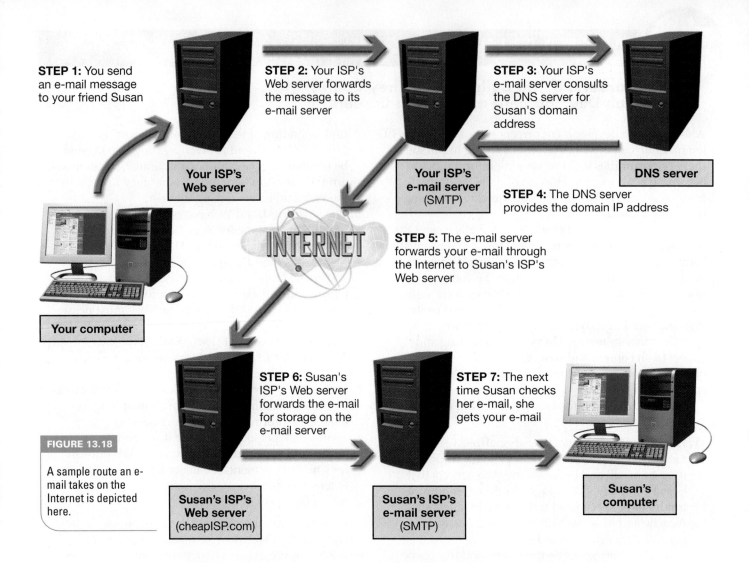

STEP 1: You send an e-mail message to your friend Susan

Your computer

STEP 2: Your ISP's Web server forwards the message to its e-mail server

Your ISP's Web server

STEP 3: Your ISP's e-mail server consults the DNS server for Susan's domain address

Your ISP's e-mail server (SMTP)

DNS server

STEP 4: The DNS server provides the domain IP address

STEP 5: The e-mail server forwards your e-mail through the Internet to Susan's ISP's Web server

INTERNET

STEP 6: Susan's ISP's Web server forwards the e-mail for storage on the e-mail server

Susan's ISP's Web server (cheapISP.com)

STEP 7: The next time Susan checks her e-mail, she gets your e-mail

Susan's ISP's e-mail server (SMTP)

Susan's computer

FIGURE 13.18

A sample route an e-mail takes on the Internet is depicted here.

Client-based software is installed on your computer and all functions are supported and run from your computer. Web-based software is launched from a Web site; the programs and features are stored on the Web and are accessible anywhere you have access to an Internet connection. No matter which type of client software you use, your mail will pass through **e-mail servers**—specialized servers whose sole function is to store, process, and send e-mail—on the way to its destination.

Where are e-mail servers located? If your ISP provides you with an e-mail account, it runs an e-mail server that uses SMTP. For example, as shown in Figure 13.18, say you are sending an e-mail message to your friend Susan. Susan uses Cheapisp.com as her ISP. Therefore, your e-mail to her is addressed to Susan@cheapisp.com. When you send the e-mail message, your ISP's Web server receives it and passes it to your ISP's e-mail server.

The e-mail server reads the domain name (cheapisp.com) and communicates with a DNS server to determine the location of Cheapisp.com. Once the address is located, the e-mail message is forwarded to Cheapisp.com through the Internet and arrives at a mail server maintained by Susan's ISP. The e-mail is then stored on Susan's ISP's e-mail server. The next time Susan logs on to her ISP and checks her mail, she will receive your message.

If e-mail was designed for text messages, why are we able to send files as attachments? SMTP was designed to handle text messages. When the need arose to send files by using e-mail (in the early 1970s), a program had to be created to convert binary files to text. The text that represented the file was appended to the end of the e-mail message. When the e-mail arrived at its destination, the recipient had to run another program to translate the text back into a binary file. Uuencode and uudecode were the two most popular programs used for encoding and decoding binary files.

Computers in Society: Have You Ever Used an Extranet or a Virtual Private Network?

As mentioned in Chapter 12, *intranets* are private corporate networks that are used exclusively by employees of the company to facilitate information sharing, database access, group scheduling, videoconferencing, or other employee collaboration. Sometimes, though, restricting access only to employees doesn't meet the company's needs. In these cases, an *extranet* is employed.

Extranets are pieces of intranets that only certain corporations or individuals can access. The owner of the extranet decides who will be permitted to access it. Customers and suppliers are typical entities that would benefit from accessing information on an extranet. Extranets are useful for enabling electronic data interchange (EDI). EDI provides for the exchanging of large amounts of business data (such as orders for merchandise) in a standardized electronic format. Other uses of extranets include providing access to catalogs and inventory databases and sharing information of use to partners or industry trade groups.

Because of security concerns, intranets and extranets often use *virtual private networks* to keep information secure. A **virtual private network (VPN)** uses the public Internet communications infrastructure to build a secure, private network between various locations. Although wide area networks (WANs) can be set up using private leased communications lines, these lines are expensive and tend to increase in price as the distance between points increases. VPNs use special security technologies and protocols that enhance security, enabling data to traverse the Internet as securely as if it were on a private leased line. Installing and configuring a VPN requires special hardware such as VPN-optimized routers and firewalls. In addition, VPN software must be installed on users' PCs.

The main technology for achieving a VPN is called *tunneling*. Data packets are placed inside new data packets. The format of the new data packets is encrypted and only understood by the sending and receiving hardware, known as *tunnel interfaces*. The hardware is optimized to seek efficient routes of transmission through the Internet. This provides a high level of security and makes information much more difficult to intercept and decrypt.

Imagine you have to deliver a message to a branch office. You could have one of your employees drive to the other office and deliver the message. But suppose he has to go through a bad neighborhood or has never been to the office before? The messenger could be waylaid by a carjacker or could become hopelessly lost. Using a VPN (as shown in Figure 13.19) is the equivalent of hiring a limousine and an armed guard to drive your employee through a private tunnel directly to the destination. Of course, a VPN avoids the enormous cost associated with this method!

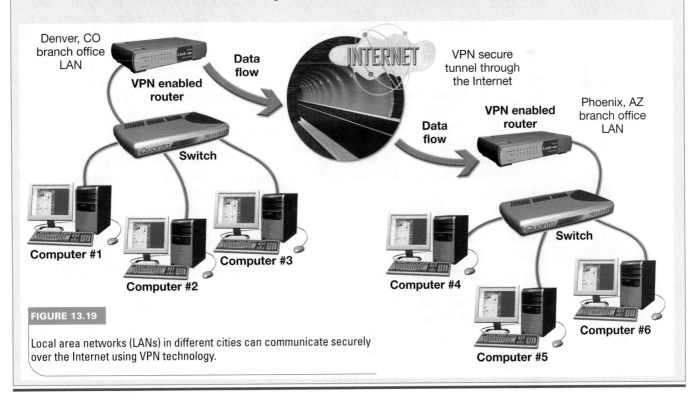

FIGURE 13.19

Local area networks (LANs) in different cities can communicate securely over the Internet using VPN technology.

BITS AND BYTES

Using the Internet to Make Phone Calls

Many conventional telephone service providers (and cable TV companies) use *Internet telephony*, also called *Voice over IP (VoIP)*, to transmit conventional long-distance phone calls. VoIP consists of transmitting phone calls over the same data lines and networks that make up the Internet. In fact, you've probably used such a connection without even knowing it when making a long-distance call. So why do phone companies use VoIP? As mentioned earlier, conventional phone calls use a process called circuit switching in which a connection between two phones is established and maintained during the entire call. The bandwidth is dedicated to that call even if there are gaps in the conversation. With VoIP, calls use the same packet-switching technology as other messages traveling the Internet. Therefore, bandwidth is not dedicated to a single phone call, so more messages can be sent over the same bandwidth. Using less bandwidth per call means the telephone provider can send more calls over the same network and thereby increase billings.

Want to make Internet phone calls for free? Skype (**www.skype.com**) is a free service that allows you to make calls from one computer to another computer (although there is a charge to call landlines or cell phones). Aside from the Skype software, all you need is a microphone and speakers and you're ready to go. The calls are encrypted for privacy.

This was fine in the early days of the Internet when users were mostly computer scientists. However, when the Internet started to become popular in the early 1990s, it became apparent that a simpler methodology was needed for sending and receiving files. The **Multipurpose Internet Mail Extensions (MIME)** specification was introduced in 1991 to simplify attachments to e-mail messages. All e-mail client software now uses this protocol for attaching files.

E-mail is still being sent in text, but the e-mail client using the MIME protocol now handles the encoding and decoding for the users. For instance, in Yahoo! mail, on the Attach Files screen you merely browse to the file you want to attach (located somewhere on your hard drive), select the file, and click the Attach Files button. Unbeknownst to you, the Yahoo! e-mail client encodes the file for transmission.

E-MAIL SECURITY: ENCRYPTION AND SPECIALIZED SOFTWARE

If e-mail is sent in regular text, can other people read my mail? E-mail is very susceptible to being read by unintended parties because it's sent in plain text. Also, copies of your e-mail message may exist (temporarily or permanently) on numerous servers as it makes its way through the Internet. Two options exist for protecting your sensitive e-mail messages: *encryption* and *secure data transmission software*.

How do I encrypt my e-mail? **Encryption** refers to the process of coding your e-mail so that only the person with the key to the code (the intended recipient) can decode (or decipher) and read the message. Secret codes for messages can be traced almost to the dawn of written language. The military and government espionage agents are big users of codes and ciphers. The trick is making the coding system easy enough to use so that everyone who needs to communicate with you can.

There are two basic types of encryption: *private-key* and *public-key*. In **private-key encryption**, only the two parties involved in sending the message have the code. This could be a simple shift code where letters of the alphabet are shifted to a new position (see Figure 13.20). For example, in a two-position right-shift code, the letter *a* becomes *c*, *b* becomes *d*, and so on. Or it could be a more complex substitution code (*a* = *h*, *b* = *r*, *c* = *g*, etc.). The main problem with private-key encryption is key security. If someone steals a copy of the code, the code is broken.

In **public-key encryption**, two keys, known as a **key pair**, are created. You use one key for coding and the other for decoding. The key for coding is generally distributed as a **public key**. You can place this key on your Web site, for instance. Anyone wishing to send you a message codes it using your public key.

When you receive the message, you use your **private key** to decode it. You are the only one who ever possesses the private key and therefore it is very secure. The keys are generated in such a way that they can work only with each other. The private key is generated first. The public key is then generated by running the public key through a complex mathematical formula. The computations are so complex that they are considered unbreakable. Both keys are necessary to decode a message; if one key is lost, the other key cannot be used by itself.

What type of encryption is used on the Internet? Public-key encryption is the most commonly used encryption on the Internet. Tried-and-true public-key packages, such as **Pretty Good Privacy (PGP)**, are available for download at sites such as **www.download.com**, and you can usually use them free of charge (although there are now commercial versions of PGP). After obtaining the PGP software, you can generate key pairs to provide a

A = C	N = P
B = D	O = Q
C = E	P = R
D = F	Q = S
E = G	R = T
F = H	S = U
G = I	T = V
H = J	U = W
I = K	V = X
J = L	W = Y
K = M	X = Z
L = N	Y = A
M = O	Z = B

The word **C O M P U T E R** using the two-position code at the left now becomes:

E Q O R W V G T

This is difficult to interpret without the code key at the left.

FIGURE 13.20

A Sample Code Using a Two-Position Right Shift

private key for you and a public key for the rest of the world.

What does a key look like? A key is a binary number (a string of 1s and 0s). Keys vary in length depending on how secure they need to be. A 10-bit key has 10 positions and might look like this:

1001101011

BITS AND BYTES

Random Numbers: The Lifeblood of Encryption

E-mail encryption, SSL encryption, and just about anything we do to achieve privacy on the Internet requires random numbers. Encryption is accomplished using *random number sequences*, which are sequences of numbers in which no patterns can be recognized. Even for an e-commerce transaction (say, buying a book from Amazon.com) that uses SSL encryption to encode your credit card number, up to 368 bits of random data might be needed. Only 128 bits are needed for the encryption key, but other random data is needed to create authentication codes and to prevent replay attacks. *Replay attacks* are when hackers attempt to copy packets traveling across the Internet and extract data from them (such as encryption codes) to reuse (replay) them to gain access to networks or transac-

tions. So, where do all these random numbers come from?

Generating true random sequences is more difficult than it sounds. But in 1996, Landon Noll and two colleagues came up with a system called LavaRnd that used lava lights (you read that right) to generate random numbers. The lamps have since been replaced with another random source: a webcam with the lens cap still on. The webcam emits "thermal noise," which is then digitized and run through a mathematical algorithm that generates the number set and strips out any sections that are predictable. This service is open source, unpatented, and license free, so anyone can set up a server and generate much-needed random numbers. For more information, check out **www.lavarnd.org**.

Longer keys are more secure because they have more possible values. A 10-bit key provides 1,024 different possible keys, whereas a 40-bit key allows for 1,099,511,627,776 possible values. The key and the message are run through a complex algorithm in the encryption program (such as PGP) that converts the message into unrecognizable code. Each key will turn the message into a different code.

Is my private key really secure? Because of the complexity of the algorithms used to generate key pairs, it is impossible to deduce the private key from the public key. However, that doesn't mean your coded message can't be cracked. A brute force attack, as you learned in Chapter 12, occurs when hackers try every possible key combination to decode a message. This type of attack can enable hackers to deduce the key and decode the message.

What is considered a safe key then? In the early 1990s, 40-bit keys were thought to be totally resistant to brute force attacks and were the norm for encryption. But in 1995, a French programmer used a unique algorithm of his own and 120 workstations simultaneously to attempt to break a 40-bit key. He succeeded in just eight days. Since then, 128-bit keys have become the standard. Even using supercomputers, no one has yet to crack a 128-bit key. It is believed that even with the most powerful computers in use today, it would take hundreds of billions of years to crack a 128-bit key.

How else can I protect my e-mail? Using encryption doesn't always solve the other problems associated with e-mail. Messages leave a trail as they travel over the Internet, and copies of messages can exist on servers for long periods of time. In addition, immediate reading of sensitive documents is often essential, but encryption software doesn't provide a means for confirming your messages have been delivered. To combat these issues, companies such as Securus Systems Ltd. (**www.safemessage.com**) have developed secure data transmission software (called SafeMessage) that works outside of the conventional SMTP mail servers.

How is SafeMessage software used? Both parties wishing to send secure messages install the SafeMessage software. When messages are to be sent, a secure point-to-point connection is established between the sender and the recipient's e-mail boxes. Proprietary protocols with encryption, not SMTP, are used to send the messages. Additional options are provided such as delivery confirmation, message shredding (destruction of messages on command), and the ability to have messages erase themselves after a set period of time. Although not free, this type of software is catching on in the business community where fear of industrial espionage is high.

INSTANT MESSAGING

What do I need to run instant messaging? Instant messaging (IM) is another client/server application that can run on a PC or Mac. AOL Instant Messenger (AIM), ICQ, Yahoo! Messenger, and MSN Messenger are the top four instant messaging applications in use today. No matter which one you choose, you need to run the appropriate client software on your computer.

How does instant messaging work? The client software running on your computer makes a connection with the chat server using your Internet connection as shown in Figure 13.21. Once contact is established, you can log in to the server with your name and password (the first time you can sign up for a free account). The client software provides the server with connection information (such as the IP address) for your computer. The server then consults the list of contacts ("Buddies" or friends) that you have previously established in your account and checks to see if any of your contacts are online. If any are, the server sends a mes-

ACTIVE HELPDESK
Keeping E-Mail Secure

In this Active Helpdesk call, you'll play the role of a Helpdesk staffer, fielding calls about how e-mail and instant messaging work and how messages are kept secure.

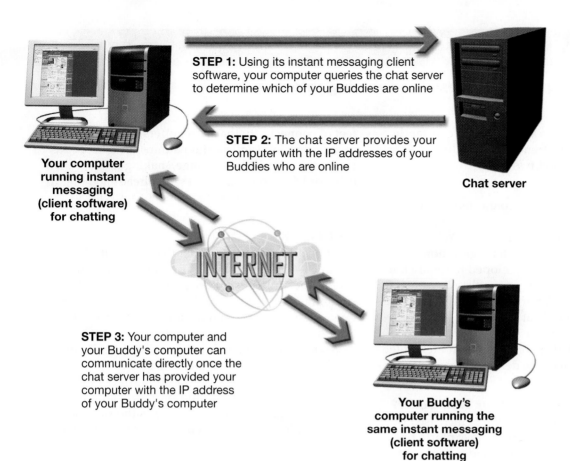

FIGURE 13.21

How an Instant Messaging Program Works

STEP 1: Using its instant messaging client software, your computer queries the chat server to determine which of your Buddies are online

STEP 2: The chat server provides your computer with the IP addresses of your Buddies who are online

Your computer running instant messaging (client software) for chatting

Chat server

STEP 3: Your computer and your Buddy's computer can communicate directly once the chat server has provided your computer with the IP address of your Buddy's computer

Your Buddy's computer running the same instant messaging (client software) for chatting

sage back to your client providing the necessary connection information (the IP addresses) for your friends. You can now click your friends' names to establish a chat session with them.

Because both your computer and your friend's computer have the connection information (the IP addresses) for each other, the server isn't involved in the chat session. Chatting takes place directly between the two computers over the Internet.

Can I communicate with my friend who uses ICQ if I use AOL Instant Messenger? Each instant messaging service uses its own proprietary software and

file format. Therefore, instant messaging services aren't compatible with each other. Fortunately, because the services are free, you can belong to several at the same time, enabling you to communicate with all of your friends even if they don't use your favorite IM program.

Is sending an instant message secure? Most instant messaging services do not use a high level of encryption for their messages, if they bother to use encryption at all. Therefore, it is not a good idea to send sensitive information using instant messaging because it is susceptible to interception and possible misuse by hackers.

Emerging Technologies: The Evolving Internet

The Internet and the ways you use it are constantly evolving. Here are some trends and products you can expect to see over the next two years:

Fiber-Optics, Anyone?

In the 1990s, most home users connected to the Internet with a dial-up modem. Today, DSL, cable, and satellite provide faster connections. Yet consumers are demanding even faster connections, and new technologies are being developed to satisfy the need. Fiber-optic technology, currently available only to corporate and urban America, is slowly making its way to the suburbs and rural areas. This technology not only enables the transmission of data at close to the speed of light but also provides an uninterrupted data pathway that makes the delivery of communications more reliable.

Or Would You Prefer to Use Your Wall Outlet?

There is more on the horizon than just increased fiber-optic reach. Numerous companies are exploring a technology that sends data, voice, and video signals over normal electric power lines. That's right, someday, you may be able to connect to the Internet through your normal wall outlet. Called *power-line connectivity*, this technology is being tested in Europe, Australia, and in a few U.S. cities. With a power-line Internet connection, you could one day transfer exobits of data—that's 1 with 18 zeros after it—per second through power lines. Now that's *fast*.

Why Not WiMAX?

With the rise in portable computing devices, people want Internet access wherever they go. An up-and-coming wireless alternative to standard Wi-Fi connections is WiMAX. Instead of the 300 feet of connectivity that Wi-Fi offers, WiMAX has a range of up to 31 miles, and its transmission speeds run in the 5- to 10-Mbps range, making it faster than cable or DSL. Some U.S. cities are already looking to create citywide wireless networks using WiMAX one day.

Or Blimps?

Most people are unaware that the high altitude of satellites—currently used to provide wireless Internet access—actually poses barriers to high-speed data communications. One solution currently being developed is deploying communications platforms at lower altitudes by using airships, or blimps. The company Sanswire has developed the Stratellite (see Figure 13.22), a 245-foot-long unmanned airship that is designed to sail 13 miles above the surface of the Earth. One such airship could provide communications coverage for an area as large as the state of Texas. Aside from wireless Internet access, this tech-

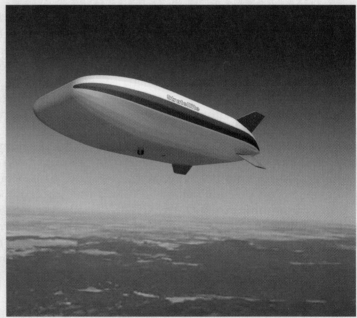

FIGURE 13.22

Airships such as the Sanswire Stratellite will help break down barriers to high-speed wireless access.

nology could also serve as an alternative to satellites for cellular telephony.

Looking for a Hotspot?

Computing devices will continue to get smaller in the future, so hotspots—places where users can connect to the Internet wirelessly—will continue to abound. If you're looking for a hotspot, portable wireless network detectors, such as the WiFi Finder from Kensington, make it easy to detect wireless networks wherever you are. And if you know where you'll be in advance, you can use the SmartView feature of Yahoo!'s map site (see Figure 13.23) to locate hotspots.

No hotspot where you want one? With devices such as the Linksys WRV54G Wireless-G VPN Broadband router, you can turn any high-speed Internet connection into a wireless hotspot . . . even the connection in your home. In apartment buildings, enterprising individuals are setting up hotspots to allow tenants from different apartments to share a single Internet connection (and thereby cut costs).

Want a Safer Internet?

More research is needed to anticipate and defend against future cyberterror attacks. To this end, the National Science Foundation (NSF) has issued a $5.46 million grant to the University of California, Berkley, and the University of Southern California's Information Sciences Institute in Cyber Defense Technology Experimental Research (DETER) Network. The money will be used to construct a cybersecurity testbed that will simulate the real Internet. All types of cyberattacks (from

worms to denial of service attacks) will be launched on the testbed's infrastructure. The testbed will provide researchers with a tool to learn how to better detect and deter cyberattacks that could potentially cripple the Internet.

A Laptop for $100?

The Internet is a fantastic tool but only if you can access it. The MIT media lab, in conjunction with partners such as Google, AMD, and News Corp., are undertaking an ambitious project to develop a $100 laptop computer. This would provide underprivileged children with access to electronic textbooks and other learning aids—and eventually the Internet. Achieving the $100 price point is possible if the computers are ordered in quantities of at least one million units. It is anticipated that governments would initially order the computers to put in the hands of school children. Such a laptop may be in production as early as 2007.

Look for these and other Internet-related technologies coming soon to computers near you.

FIGURE 13.23

By selecting the Show Hotspots option on any Yahoo! map, SmartView technology provides you with a list of hotspots where you can go to connect to the Internet.

1. Who manages and pays for the Internet?

Management of the Internet is carried out by a number of nonprofit organizations and user groups such as the Internet Society (ISOC), the Internet Engineering Task Force (IETF), the Internet Architecture Board (IAB), the Internet Corporation for Assigned Names and Numbers (ICANN), and the World Wide Web Consortium. Each group has different responsibilities and tasks. Currently, the U.S. government (and subsequently the U.S. taxpayers) funds a majority of the Internet costs.

2. How do the Internet's networking components interact?

Individual computers or networks connect to the Internet using Internet service providers (ISPs). These providers are ranked in tiers according to the volume of traffic they carry and the speed at which they transfer data. The connections between Tier 1 ISPs are extremely high speed and are known collectively as the Internet backbone. Tier 1 ISPs are connected to Tier 2 ISPs, which are in turn connected to Tier 3 ISPs. Individuals or corporations connect to Tier 2 or Tier 3 ISPs, which have regional or local focus, respectively. ISPs are connected by T lines of various speeds depending upon the amount of data flowing between them. The points of connection between ISPs are known as network access points (NAPs).

3. What data transmissions and protocols does the Internet use?

Data is transmitted along the Internet using packet switching. Data is broken up into discrete units known as packets, which can take independent routes to the destination before being reassembled. Although many protocols are available on the Internet, the main suite of protocols used to move information over the Internet is TCP/IP. The suite is named after the original two protocols that were developed for the Internet: the Transmission Control Protocol (TCP) and the Internet Protocol (IP). Whereas TCP is responsible for preparing data for transmission, IP actually sends data between computers on the Internet.

4. Why are IP addresses and domain names important for Internet communications?

An IP address is a unique number assigned to all computers connected to the Internet. The IP address is necessary so that packets of data can be sent to a particular location (computer) on the Internet. A domain name is merely a name that stands for a certain IP address and makes it easier for people to remember it. MyWebPage.com is a domain name and is much easier to remember than the IP address 124.53.111.14. DNS servers act as the phone books of the Internet. They enable your computer to find out the IP address of a domain by looking up its corresponding domain name (which you typed into your browser).

5. What are FTP and Telnet and how do I use them?

The File Transfer Protocol (FTP) enables users to share files that reside on local computers with remote computers. Current versions of browsers enable you to connect to FTP sites on the Internet and drag and drop files to download or upload them to FTP sites. Telnet is both a protocol for connecting to a remote computer and a TCP/IP service that would run on a remote computer to make it accessible to other computers. The Telnet client application (which is run on your personal computer) connects to the Telnet server application (running on a remote computer). Telnet enables you to take control of a remote computer (the server) with your computer (the client) and manipulate files and data on the server as if you were sitting in front of that server.

6. What are HTML and XML used for?

The Hypertext Markup Language (HTML) is a set of rules for marking up blocks of text so that a browser knows how to display them. Most Web pages are generated with at least some HTML code. Blocks of text in HTML documents are surrounded by a pair of tags (such as <b> and </b> to indicate bolding). These tags and the text between them are referred to as elements. By examining the elements, your browser determines how to display them on your computer screen. Because HTML was not designed for information exchange, Extensible Markup Language (XML) was created. Instead of being locked into standard tags and formats for data, XML enables users to create their own markup languages to accommodate particular data formats and needs. XML is used extensively in e-commerce for exchanging data between corporations.

7. How do e-mail and instant messaging work and how are messages kept secure?

Simple Mail Transfer Protocol (SMTP) is the protocol responsible for sending e-mail over the Internet. As in most other Internet applications, e-mail is a client/server application. E-mail passes through e-mail servers whose function is to store, process, and send e-mail to its ultimate destination. ISPs and portals such as Yahoo! maintain e-mail servers to provide e-mail functionality to their customers. Your ISP's e-mail server uses DNS servers to locate the IP addresses for the recipients of the e-mail you send. Encryption software, such as Pretty Good Privacy (PGP), is used to code messages so they can be decoded only by the authorized recipients.

Buzz Words

Word Bank

- applet
- backbone
- DNS
- circuit switching
- FTP
- HTTP

- ICANN
- IP address
- packet switching
- PGP
- point of presence
- public key encryption

- SMTP
- SSL
- T-1
- TCP/IP
- Tier 3
- XML

Instructions: Fill in the blanks using the words from the Word Bank.

As a network administrator, Patricia knows that she can count on the organization (1) _____ to ensure that she has an appropriate range of IP addresses for her worksite. Her high-speed connection to her company's (2) _____ ISP was vital to providing the connectivity her employees need to get their jobs done. Recently, the company moved up from a DSL connection to a(n) (3) _____ line because of the high volume of Internet traffic they were generating. Hopefully, Patricia thinks, the government will continue to fund projects to continue research to improve the Internet (4) _____ , the main highway to the Internet, and other vital technologies. But Patricia has indulged in enough daydreaming. It is time to ensure that the Internet connection to the bank of modems, or (5) _____ provided by the Tier 3 ISP her company is using, is fully functional before the majority of the employees arrive for work. Because the company sends a tremendous amount of e-mail, old-fashioned (6) _____ technology would never have sufficed for sending messages. Fortunately, the Internet employs (7) _____ to enable messages to be sent over widely varying routes. Of course, she knows that the main suite of protocols that controls Internet data traffic is called (8) _____ .

After ensuring all is functional, Patricia begins to assist the Web development team with Web page creation. To provide robust interaction with company databases, (9) _____ is being used to code Web pages for the corporate Web site instead of HTML. Unsure of her instructions, she e-mails the director of Web development for clarification, knowing that the (10) _____ protocol will ensure the e-mail is delivered to the director at the company's U.K. office. Requiring secure communications, she encrypts the e-mail using a(n) (11) _____ algorithm, knowing that the director can retrieve Patricia's key from her personal Web site.

After reading the response to her e-mail, she quickly writes a Java (12) _____ to produce an interactive form to collect customer names and addresses. Using the (13) _____ protocol, Patricia posts her completed Web page to the corporate site. Of course, users will view the completed Web page using the (14) _____ protocol. And because the Web page contains potentially sensitive information, Patricia makes sure the (15) _____ protocol is in use to provide added security for the data. Just another exciting day in the life of a network administrator!

Becoming Computer Fluent

While attending college, you are working at MultiPharm, Inc., which is a small manufacturer of specialty steel products. The new CEO has charged your supervisor with bringing the company into the 21st century by connecting it to the Internet and developing a company Web site. Your supervisor has asked you to help draft a memo to the CEO, laying out the benefits of having an Internet presence.

Instructions: Draft a memo for your boss detailing the benefits of connecting the company to the Internet. Make sure to suggest which types of Internet connections would be appropriate and which type of ISP would be needed. While trying to use as many of the keywords from the chapter as you can, ensure that the report can be presented to computer-illiterate managers.

Instructions: Answer the multiple choice and true/false questions below for more practice with key terms and concepts from this chapter.

MULTIPLE CHOICE

1. Who is responsible for managing the Internet?
   a. ISPs
   b. the United States government
   c. all of the users of the Internet
   d. a group of nonprofit organizations

2. The Internet backbone connects
   a. Tier 3 ISPs to Tier 2 ISPs.
   b. Tier 1 ISPs to other Tier 1 ISPs.
   c. Tier 2 ISPs to Tier 1 ISPs.
   d. Tier 3 ISPs to other Tier 3 ISPs.

3. ISPs are connected to each other through
   a. DNS servers.
   b. points of presence (POPs).
   c. network access points (NAPs).
   d. IPv6 networks.

4. All of the following are common servers found on the Internet except
   a. Web servers.
   b. commerce servers.
   c. file servers.
   d. application servers.

5. Packet switching
   a. does not require a dedicated connection to be maintained.
   b. keeps all data together when being transmitted so none of it is lost.
   c. requires a dedicated connection to be maintained.
   d. can only be used to send data that does not exceed 2,056 KB.

6. The main suite of protocols used on the Internet is called
   a. FTP.   b. TCP/IP.
   c. XHMTL.   d. Telnet.

7. Files are uploaded to the Internet mainly by using which of these protocols?
   a. TCP/IP   b. DNS
   c. SMTP   d. FTP

8. E-mail is sent across the Internet using which of the following protocols?
   a. SMTP   b. TCP/IP
   c. MIME   d. PGP

9. Which type of encryption is most commonly used on the Internet?
   a. private key encryption
   b. TCP/IP encryption
   c. public key encryption
   d. SSL encryption

10. Instant messaging services (such as AOL IM)
   a. can easily communicate with any other message service because they all use TCP/IP to send their messages.
   b. should not be used to send sensitive messages because most don't use encryption.
   c. are required by ICANN to use a high level of encryption when sending messages.
   d. should only be used on home networks as their operation will interfere with normal client/server network operations.

TRUE/FALSE

_____ 1. The Internet is a network of networks.

_____ 2. Individual users connect to the Internet via banks of modems known as network access points.

_____ 3. Packet switching is more practical than circuit switching because a constant connection is maintained that speeds the flow of data.

_____ 4. DNS servers are used by other web servers to locate IP addresses of Web sites.

_____ 5. Messages sent through instant messaging services on the Internet are secure because most IM services use PGP encryption.

Making the Transition to... Next Semester

1. Creating a Web Site: Issues

Your American History instructor has asked your group to design a Web site on the Battle of Gettysburg. The site will include textual and graphical information on the battle as well as an interactive quiz. Users will be encouraged to post college term papers on the site as a resource for other students. The following issues need to be addressed for your portion of the project:

a. In which domain should you register the site? Why do you think this is appropriate?

b. What is a catchy name for the Web site? Is this name already registered? Be sure to check in the appropriate domain and make sure it isn't already registered and provide proof that it isn't.

c. How would you ensure that people can find the site once it's on the Web?

d. What Internet protocols will users need to access the site?

e. What software will be required to access the site?

2. Creating a Web Site: Issues 2

As president of your school's Future Business Leaders of America club, you would like to build a mailing list for your quarterly newsletter. You also would like to ensure that the newsletter is available on the college's Web site. When you visit the college Web developer, she asks you to provide the following information:

a. What data do you want to require all online subscribers to provide?

b. What optional data would you like to request that subscribers provide?

c. Will an e-mail address be provided to potential subscribers if they wish to make inquiries? If so, who will be reviewing and responding to these e-mails? What time frame will you guarantee for an answer to e-mails?

3. Creating a Web Site: Issues 3

You have been asked to create a Web page to promote a campus club of which you are a member. Investigate the following:

a. Most schools will provide Web pages for sanctioned clubs on their Web server. Does your school place any content restrictions on club Web sites? How much storage space is provided for club Web pages? Can club Web pages gather data from prospective members (such as contact information) for storage in a database?

b. Assume your club is unsanctioned and your school will not provide space for a Web page. Using Web sites such as **www.ispfinder.com** and **www.findanisp.com**, find three ISPs where you could potentially host the Web site and prepare a chart comparing the following for each ISP:

- Cost per month for hosting
- Amount of disk storage space provided
- Number and type of e-mail accounts provided
- Data throughput (transfer) allowed per month
- Level of technical support provided

c. Which ISP will you recommend to your club and why?

4. Searching for Employment on the Web

With tuition costs rising, you feel it would be appropriate to find a part-time job next semester. Visit some popular employment sites such as **www.monster.com** and **www.careerbuilder.com** and complete the following tasks:

a. Search for a part-time job or internship opportunity in your field of study. Provide a listing of opportunities you think would be appropriate for you.

b. Search for full-time jobs for which you might apply when you graduate. What are the average starting salaries? Do the starting salaries vary by geographic location or are they reasonably similar?

Making the Transition to... The Workplace

1. Web Site Security Issues

Your employer, a distributor of specialty stereo equipment, offers high-speed Internet access at the office where you work. Thirty-five workstations are connected to the Internet, which employees use to send e-mail and conduct research. Recently, company trade secrets (traced to an employee e-mail) were printed in the local press. The company president has enlisted your help in determining preventative measures to avoid such security breaches in the future. Draft a memo that includes the following:

a. An employee e-mail policy that requires the use of encryption technologies.

b. Other suggested uses for the Internet access that would benefit the employees.

2. Posting a Résumé Online

The director of your college placement office has suggested that you prepare a résumé that can be posted on the new college graduate employment site that the university is developing. It must be in HTML format and include a picture of yourself. Consider the following:

a. What software would you use to develop the résumé?

b. Would straight HTML be sufficient or would you need to use JavaScript to display the picture?

c. Aside from your college's Web site, find at least three other Web sites where you could post your résumé so employers could see it.

3. "Googling"

At your company, someone was just fired because sensitive information related to a company product was associated with their name on the Internet. Discretion being the better part of valor, you decide to do a search for your name on the Web (in a search engine such as **www.google.com**) just to see what is out there. Prepare a report on what you found by exploring the following:

a. Did you find any accurate information about yourself (such as your homepage, résumé, etc.)? Any erroneous information that you need to correct?

b. Did you find Web sites or information about other people with the same name as you? Could any of that information be damaging to your reputation if someone thought the other person was you? Provide examples.

c. Is there information that you found about yourself or others that you think should never be available on the Internet? What types of information should not be available online about individuals?

Critical Thinking Questions

Instructions: Albert Einstein used "Gedanken experiments," or critical thinking questions, to develop his theory of relativity. Some ideas are best understood by experimenting with them in our own minds. The following critical thinking questions are designed to demand your full attention but require only a comfortable chair—no technology.

1. Domain Names

Domain names often spark fierce controversy between competing companies. Legal wrangling over the rights to attractive names such as Buynow.com and Lowprices.com can generate large fees for attorneys. Meanwhile, some famous individuals have had to fight for the right to own domains based on their own names.

a. Should everyone be entitled to a Web site in a certain domain (say, .com) that contains their own name? How would you handle disputes by people who have the exact same name (say, two people named John Smith)?

b. Is it ethical to register a domain name (say, Coke.net) just for the purpose of selling it to the organization that may benefit from it the most (such as the Coca-Cola Company)?

c. Aside from the domains currently approved (such as .com and .org), what domain names do you think would have commercial appeal? For which types of Web sites would these domains be used?

2. Network Security

Ensuring that computer-based information is secure is a key objective of many companies today.

a. How would you prepare for a job as a network security specialist?

b. Aside from computer-based security measures, what physical precautions should be taken to enhance computer data security?

3. Encryption

Encryption programs built on 128-bit encryption algorithms are currently considered unbreakable.

a. Because strong encryption programs using 128-bit encryption or better are considered unbreakable, the U.S. government places restrictions on exports of these encryption products. The government is also considering a requirement that all encryption products should have a "back door" code that would enable government agencies (such as the CIA and FBI) to read encrypted messages. Do you think this should be implemented? Why or why not?

b. Assuming you figure out how to break 128-bit encryption, should you post that information on the Internet for anyone to use? Why or why not?

Problem:

As Web usage increases exponentially, demands are constantly placed on the Internet's infrastructure. Development groups, such as the Internet2 consortium, are designed to foster the innovation of new technologies to improve delivery of Internet services. In this Team Time, you'll research up-and-coming technologies and consider their impact on the Internet.

Task:

Your group has just received an invitation to speak at a technology conference being held at your school. Your topic is cutting-edge Internet technologies. You will be given 20 minutes at the conference to deliver a presentation to a group of approximately 250 students and educators, all interested in (but not necessarily familiar with) technology.

Process:

Break the class into small teams of three or four students. Each team should prepare a report as follows:

STEP 1. Explore sites such as **www.howstuffworks.com**, **www.internet2.edu**, and **www.wired.com** to investigate new technologies. Prepare a list of current innovations that are being developed.

STEP 2. Briefly present your group's findings to the class for debate and discussion. Are any ideas a replacement for the Internet as opposed to an extension of its capabilities? Your objective is to determine which topic would be of most interest to your class for a presentation.

STEP 3. Develop a PowerPoint presentation on the most popular topic. If the technology you chose seems very futuristic or unbelievable, make sure you convey to the class why this will be achievable in the next 50 years.

Conclusion:

Don't be afraid to envision communications media that go beyond the current confines of the Internet. Great inventors, such as Edison, Gates, and Cerf, forced themselves to think outside the box instead of being trapped by current technology and engineering limitations. Encourage your friends to daydream about the future of data communications . . . the next communications revolution may start with you!

Multimedia

In addition to the review materials presented here, you'll find additional materials featured with the book's multimedia, including the *Technology in Action* Student Resource CD and the Companion Web site (**www.prenhall.com/techinaction**), which will help reinforce your understanding of the chapter content. These materials include the following:

ACTIVE HELPDESK

In Active Helpdesk calls, you'll assume the role of a Helpdesk operator taking calls about the concepts you've learned in this chapter. You'll apply what you've learned and receive feedback from a supervisor to review and reinforce those concepts. The Active Helpdesk calls for this chapter are listed here and can be found on your Student Resource CD:

- Understanding IP Addresses, Domain Names, and Protocols
- Keeping E-Mail Secure

SOUND BYTES

Sound Bytes are dynamic multimedia tutorials that help demystify even the most complex topics. You'll view video clips and animations that illustrate computer concepts, and then apply what you've learned by reviewing with the Sound Byte Labs, which include quizzes and activities specifically tailored to each Sound Byte. The Sound Bytes for this chapter are listed here and can be found on your Student Resource CD and on the Companion Web site (**www.prenhall.com/techinaction**):

- Constructing a Simple Web Page
- The Best Utilities for Your Computer

COMPANION WEB SITE

The *Technology in Action* Companion Web site includes a variety of additional materials to help you review and learn more about the topics in this chapter. The resources available at **www.prenhall.com/techinaction** include:

- **Online Study Guide.** Each chapter features an online true/false and multiple-choice quiz. You can take these quizzes, automatically check the results, and e-mail the results to your instructor.
- **Web Research Projects.** Each chapter features a number of Web research projects that ask you to search the Web for information on computer-related careers, milestones in computer history, important people and companies, emerging technologies, and the applications and implications of different technologies.

TECHNOLOGY IN FOCUS

Careers in IT

It's hard to imagine an occupation in which computers are not used in some fashion. Even such previously low-tech industries as junkyards and fast food use computers for inventory management and commodity ordering. In this Technology in Focus feature, we explore various information technology (IT) career paths open to you.

What to Consider First: Job Outlook

If you want to investigate a career with computers, the first question you probably have is: "Will I be able to get a job?" With all the media hoopla surrounding the loss of IT jobs to other countries in the last several years, many people think the boom in computer-related jobs is over. However, current projections of the U.S. Department of Labor's Bureau of Labor Statistics show that 5 out of the top 20 fastest-growing occupations (through 2012) are still in a computer field, as shown in Figure 1.

Percent change in employment in occupations projected to grow fastest, 2002–2012

Medical assistants
Network systems and data communications analysts
Physician assistants
Social and human service assistants
Home health aides
Medical records and health information technicians
Physical therapist aides
Computer software engineers, applications
Computer software engineers, systems software
Physical therapist assistants
Fitness trainers and aerobics instructors
Database administrators
Veterinary technologists and technicians
Hazardous materials removal workers
Dental hygienists
Occupational therapist aides
Dental assistants
Personal and home care aides
Self-enrichment education teachers
Computer systems analysts

Percent change — 0, 10, 20, 30, 40, 50, 60

Source:
Bureau of Labor Statistics

Figure 1

The Bureau of Labor Statistics is projecting huge growth in five different computer occupations, as highlighted in this chart.

Despite this forecast, recent surveys by the Computer Research Association indicate a 38 percent *drop* in declared computer science majors since 2000. Because of declining enrollment, shortages of computing professionals in the United States are projected over the next 5 to 10 years. So in terms of job outlook, this is a perfect time to consider an IT career.

Regardless of whether you choose to pursue a career in IT, you should visit the Bureau of Labor Statistics site at **www.bls.gov**. One of the site's most useful features is the *Occupational Outlook Handbook*. Aside from projecting job growth in a career field, it describes typical tasks that workers perform, the amount of training and education needed, and salary estimates.

Setting the Record Straight: Common Myths About IT Careers

Many people have misconceptions about pursuing a career in IT that scare them away from considering a career in computing or convince them to pursue a computing career for the wrong reasons. Do you have any of the following misconceptions?

COMMON MYTHS ABOUT IT CAREERS

Myth #1: *Getting a computer science degree means you're going to be rich.* Computer-related careers often offer high salaries, but choosing a computer career isn't a guarantee you'll get a high-paying job. Just as in other professions, you'll need years of training and on-the-job experience to earn a high salary.

Myth #2: *All the jobs are going offshore.* Although many programming jobs have been lost to international competition over the past few years, most networking, systems analyst, database analyst, and creative jobs (such as digital media creation and game development) have stayed in the United States. As demand for programmers has increased overseas, this has driven up foreign wages, making "offshoring" jobs less attractive.

Myth #3: *You've got three professional certifications . . . you're ready to work.* Many freshly minted technical school graduates sporting IT certifications feel ready to jump into a job. But employers routinely cite experience as being more desirable than certification. Experience earned through an internship or a part-time job will make you much more marketable when your certification program is complete.

Myth #4: *Women are at a disadvantage in an IT career.* Currently, women make up less than 25 percent of the IT workforce. This presents an opportunity for women with IT training because many IT departments are actively seeking to diversify their workforce. Also, although a salary gender gap (difference between what men and women earn for the same job) exists in IT careers, it's smaller than in any other profession.

Myth #5: *People skills don't matter in IT jobs.* Despite what many people think, IT professionals are not locked in lightless cubicles, basking in the glow of their monitors. Most IT jobs require constant interaction with others, often in team settings. People skills are important, even when you work with computers.

Myth #6: *Mathematically impaired people need not apply.* It is true that a career in programming involves a fair bit of math, but even if you're not mathematically inclined, you can explore other IT careers. IT positions also value such attributes as teamwork, creativity, leadership ability, and artistic style.

Myth #7: *Working in IT means working for a computer company or in an IT department.* Computers and information systems are used across all industries and in most job functions. As an accounting major, if you minor in IT, employers may be more willing to consider hiring you because working in accounting today means constantly interfacing with management information systems and manipulating data.

Resolving myths is an important step toward considering a job in IT. But you need to consider other issues related to IT careers before you decide to pursue a particular path.

How Much Will I Make?

IT salaries vary widely depending on experience level and the geographic location of the job. To obtain the most accurate information, research salaries yourself. Job posting sites such as Monster.com can provide guidance, but a better site is Salary.com. As shown in Figure 2, you can use the salary wizard on this site to determine what IT professionals in your town are making compared with national averages. Hundreds of IT job titles are listed so that you can fine-tune your search to the specific job you're interested in.

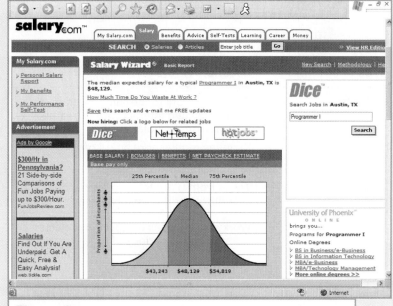

Figure 2

The salary wizard at Salary.com shows that for an entry-level programming position (programmer I) in Austin, Texas, you could expect to earn a median salary of $48,129. The wizard is easy to tailor to your location and job preferences.

Is an IT Career Right for You?

A career in IT can be a difficult path. Before preparing yourself for an IT career, consider the following:

1. **Salary range.** What affects your salary in an IT position? Your skill set and experience level are obvious answers. However, the size of your employer and geographic location are also factors. Large companies tend to pay more, so if you're pursuing a high salary, set your sights on a large corporation. But remember that making a lot of money isn't everything. There are other quality-of-life issues to consider, such as job satisfaction.

2. **Possibility of gender bias.** Many women view IT departments as Dilbert-like microcosms of antisocial geeks and don't feel they would fit in. Unfortunately, some mostly male IT departments do suffer from varying degrees of gender bias. Although some women may thrive on the challenge of enlightening these "male enclaves" and bringing them forward to the 21st century, others find such environments difficult to work in.

3. **Location.** Location in this case refers to the setting in which you work. IT jobs can be office-based, field-based, project-based, or home-based. Not every situation is perfect for every individual. Figure 3 summarizes the major job types and their locations.

4. **A changing workplace.** In IT, the playing field is always changing. New software and hardware are constantly being developed. It's almost a full-time job to keep your skills up-to-date. You can expect to spend a lot of time in training and self-study trying to learn new systems and techniques to keep your skills current.

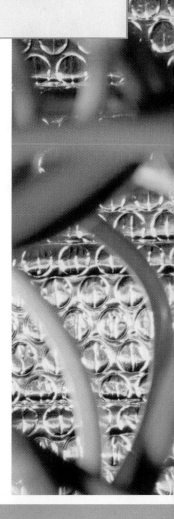

Figure 3

Where Do You Want to Work?

Type of Job	Location/Hours	Special Considerations
Office-based	Report for work to the same location each day and interact with the same people on a regular basis Requires regular core hours of attendance (such as 9 to 5)	May require working beyond "normal" working hours Some positions require workers to be on call 24/7
Field-based	Travel from place to place, as needed, and perform short-term jobs at each location	Involves a great deal of travel and working independently
Project-based	Work at client sites on specific projects for extended periods of time (weeks or months) Contractors and consultants fall into this area	Can be very attractive to individuals who like workplace situations that vary on a regular basis
Home-based (Telecommuting)	Work from home	Involves very little day-to-day supervision and requires an individual who is self-disciplined

5. **Stress.** Whereas the average American works 42 hours a week, a survey by *InformationWeek* shows that the average IT staff person works 45 hours a week and is on call for another 24 hours. On-call time (hours an employee must be available to work in the event of a problem) has been increasing in recent years because more IT systems (such as e-commerce systems) require 24/7 availability.

The good news is that despite the stress and changing nature of the IT environment, most computing skills are portable from industry to industry. A networking job in the clothing manufacturing industry uses the same primary skill set as a networking job for a supermarket chain. So, if something disastrous happens to the industry you're in, you should be able to transition to another industry with little trouble.

Figure 4

Stress comes from multiple directions in IT jobs.

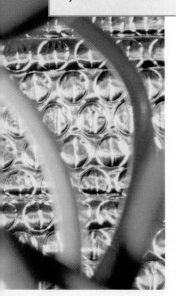

What Realm of IT Should You Work In?

Figure 5 provides an organizational chart for a modern IT department that should help you understand the careers currently available. The chief information officer (CIO) has overall responsibility for the development, implementation, and maintenance of information systems and infrastructure. Usually the CIO reports to the chief operating officer (COO).

The responsibilities below the CIO are usually grouped into two units: development and integration, and technical services. The development and integration unit is responsible for the development of systems and Web sites. The technical services unit is responsible for the day-to-day operations of the company's information systems, including all hardware and software deployed.

In large organizations, responsibilities are distinct and jobs are more narrowly defined. In medium-sized organizations, there can be overlap between position responsibilities. At a small shop, you might be the network administrator, database administrator, computer support technician, and help-desk analyst all at the same time. Let's look at each department and explore typical jobs found in them.

Working in Development and Integration

Two distinct paths exist in this division: Web development and systems development. Because everything involves the Web today, there is often a great deal of overlap between these departments.

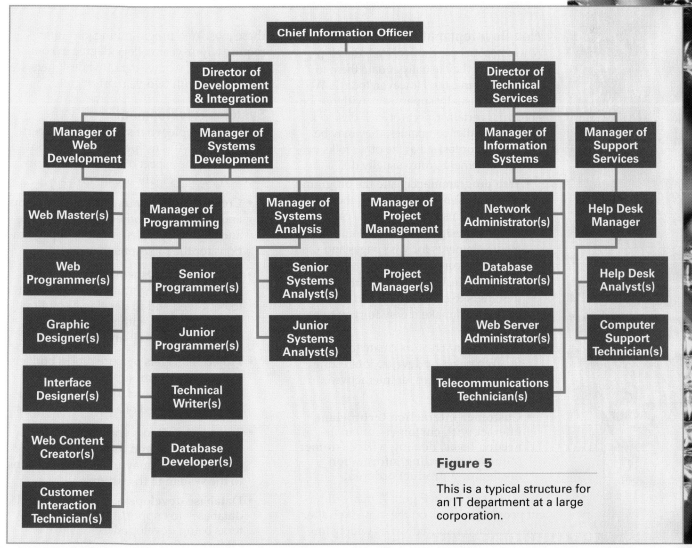

Figure 5

This is a typical structure for an IT department at a large corporation.

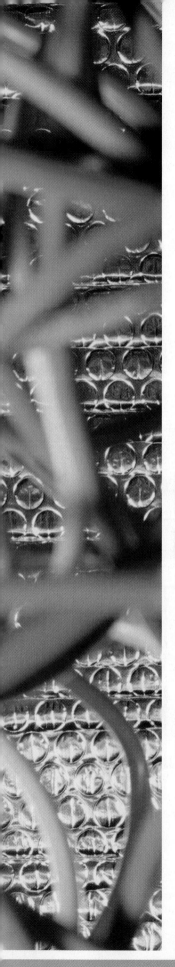

Totally unsure about what career (IT or otherwise) you would like to pursue? There are many online tools such as the ISEEK Skills Assessment (**www.iseek.org**) that can help you identify careers based on your skills. This tool has you fill out a skills matrix (see Figure 6) rating your skills in a variety of categories. The program then evaluates the skills matrix and suggests job titles for you to explore.

Assessments - ISEEK Skills Assessment

Click on the skill name to display a detailed description of the skill you are rating.

Rate your skills as follows:

+2 It is very important to me that this skill is part of my career.
+1 It is somewhat important to me that this skill is part of my career.
 0 I don't care if this skill is part of my career.
-1 It is somewhat important to me that this skill is NOT part of my career.
-2 It is very important to me that this skill is NOT part of my career.

When you have completed rating skills in this category, click the "Continue" button.

Interpersonal Skills	+2	+1	0	-1	-2
Adjusting to Others' Actions	○	○	⊙	○	○
Awareness of Others	○	○	⊙	○	○
Helping or Serving Others	○	○	⊙	○	○
Instructing	○	○	⊙	○	○
Negotiating	○	○	⊙	○	○
Persuading	○	○	⊙	○	○

Continue

Figure 6

Here you see one of 10 categories on the ISEEK skills matrix that you can complete to help you assess which career paths match your talents.

Web Development

When most people think of Web development careers they usually equate them to being a **Web master**. However, today's Web masters are usually supervisors with responsibility for certain aspects of Web development. At smaller companies, they may be responsible for tasks that the other folks in a Web development group usually do:

- **Web programmers** create the programming for Web pages and link them to other systems such as databases.
- **Graphic designers** create art and multimedia elements for Web pages and often do page layout.
- **Interface designers** work with graphic designers to create a look and feel for the site and make it easy for you to navigate a site.
- **Web content creators** create the content for Web pages or develop interesting animations, games, or interactive information pieces.
- **Customer interaction technicians** interact with customers on an as-needed basis, dealing with customer inquiries regarding information needed or a product ordered.

As you can see in Figure 7, many different people can work on the same Web site. The education required varies widely for these jobs. Web programming jobs often require a four-year college degree in computer science, whereas graphic designers are often hired with two-year art degrees.

Systems Development

Ask most people what systems developers do and they will say "programming," but this is only one aspect of systems development. A variety of jobs are involved:

- **Computer programmers** write programs and interact with other team members and end users to determine the specifications for the programs they create.
- **Systems analysts** work with end users to determine the nature of the problem to be solved and to develop a solution. They then work with programmers to get the system built and tested.
- **Project managers** prepare project budgets, assemble the team, supervise the work, and generate reports to keep upper management informed of a project's progress.
- **Technical writers** generate systems documentation for end users and for programmers who may make modifications to the system in the future.
- **Database developers** design and build databases to support the software systems being developed.

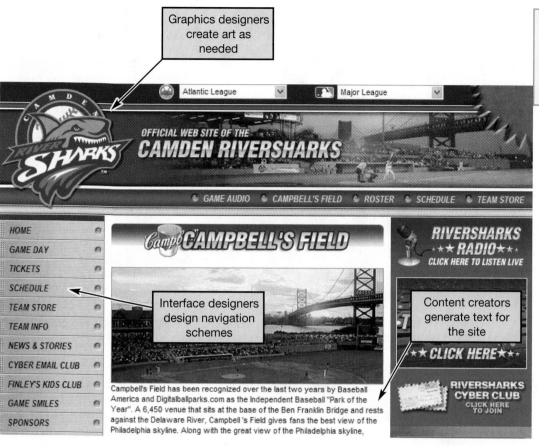

Graphics designers create art as needed

Figure 7

As you can see, it takes a "village" to create and maintain a Web site.

OFFICIAL WEB SITE OF THE
CAMDEN RIVERSHARKS

Atlantic League   Major League

⚫ GAME AUDIO ⚫ CAMPBELL'S FIELD ⚫ ROSTER ⚫ SCHEDULE ⚫ TEAM STORE

HOME
GAME DAY
TICKETS
SCHEDULE
TEAM STORE
TEAM INFO
NEWS & STORIES
CYBER EMAIL CLUB
FINLEY'S KIDS CLUB
GAME SMILES
SPONSORS

Camp **CAMPBELL'S FIELD**

Interface designers design navigation schemes

RIVERSHARKS
★★★ RADIO ★★★
CLICK HERE TO LISTEN LIVE

Content creators generate text for the site

★★ CLICK HERE ★★

RIVERSHARKS CYBER CLUB
CLICK HERE TO JOIN

Campbell's Field has been recognized over the last two years by Baseball America and Digitalballparks.com as the Independent Baseball "Park of the Year". A 6,450 venue that sits at the base of the Ben Franklin Bridge and rests against the Delaware River, Campbell 's Field gives fans the best view of the Philadelphia skyline. Along with the great view of the Philadelphia skyline,

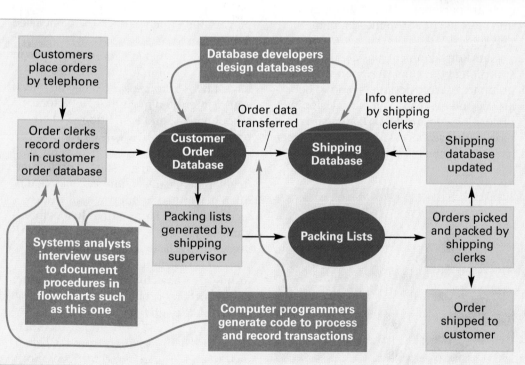

Customers place orders by telephone

Database developers design databases

Order clerks record orders in customer order database

Customer Order Database

Order data transferred

Info entered by shipping clerks

Shipping Database

Shipping database updated

Packing lists generated by shipping supervisor

Packing Lists

Orders picked and packed by shipping clerks

Systems analysts interview users to document procedures in flowcharts such as this one

Computer programmers generate code to process and record transactions

Order shipped to customer

Figure 8

Here you see a flow-chart of an order-processing system. Each member of the systems development team performs functions critical to the development process (as shown in the red boxes).

Large development projects may have all of these team members on the project. Smaller projects may require an overlap of positions (such as a programmer also acting as a systems analyst). The majority of these jobs require four-year college degrees in computer science or Management Information Systems (MIS). As shown in Figure 8, team members work together to build a system.

Get in the Game: Careers in Game Development

The video gaming industry in the United States has surpassed the earning power of the Hollywood movie industry to become a $10 billion per year behemoth. Although some aspects of game development such as scenery design and certain aspects of programming are being sent offshore, the majority of game development requires a creative team that needs to work in close proximity to each other. Therefore, it is anticipated that most game development jobs will stay in the United States. And with the release of the Xbox 360 and PlayStation 3 consoles, development budgets for games are expected to double since the new consoles can support more sophisticated games. As the majority of development costs are personnel-related, this translates into more job opportunities for game developers.

Game development jobs are usually split along two paths: designers and programmers. Game designers tend to be artistic and are responsible for designing or creating 2-D and 3-D art, game interfaces, video sequences, and special effects as well as game levels and scenarios.

Game designers must master software packages such as 3D Studio Max, Maya, Lightwave, PhotoShop, and Flash (see Figure 9). Programmers are then responsible for coding the scenarios developed by these designers. Using languages such as C, C++, Assembly, and Java, programmers build the game and ensure that it plays accurately.

Aside from programmers and designers, playtesters and quality assurance professionals play the games with the intent of breaking them or discovering bugs within the game interfaces or worlds. Playtesting is an essential part of the game development process because it assists designers in determining which aspects of the game are most intriguing to players and which parts of the game need to be repaired or enhanced.

No matter what job you may pursue in the realm of gaming, you will need to have a two- or four-year college degree. If you're interested in gaming, look for a school with a solid animation/3-D art program or computer game programming curriculum.

So, how can you get started on a game development career? One key task that is often performed by high school and college students is beta testing. Just before a game is ready to go to market, the "beta version" (the last version tested before release) is distributed to volunteers for testing. The objective is to play the game and report any problems in game play or design. Although beta testing is an unpaid job, playtesters (who are compensated) are often recruited from the beta testers who provide good feedback. So, contact your favorite game manufacturer and get on their beta testing squad. It might help you get your foot in the door for a paying job in the future.

Figure 9

Lightwave is a popular package that is used to create realistic graphics for games such as the one shown here.

Working in Technical Services

Technical services jobs are vital to keeping IT systems running. The people in these jobs install and maintain the infrastructure behind the IT systems and work with end users to make sure they can effectively interact with the systems. The two major categories of technical services careers are information systems and support services.

Information Systems

The information systems department keeps the networks and telecommunications up and running at all times. Within the department, you'll find a variety of positions:

- **Network administrators** (sometimes called network engineers) install and configure servers, design and plan networks, and test new networking equipment.

- **Database administrators (DBAs)** install and configure database servers and ensure that the servers provide an adequate level of access to all users.

- **Web server administrators** install, configure, and maintain Web servers and ensure that the company maintains Internet connectivity at all times.

- **Telecommunications technicians** oversee the communications infrastructure, including training employees to use telecommunications equipment. They are often on call 24 hours a day.

Support Services

As a member of the support services team, you interface with users (external customers or employees) and troubleshoot their computer problems. These positions include the following:

- **Helpdesk analysts** staff the phone (or e-mail) and solve problems for customers or employees, either remotely or in person. Often, helpdesk personnel are called on to train users on the latest software and hardware.

- **Computer support technicians** go to a user's physical location and fix software and hardware problems. They also often have to chase down faults in the network infrastructure and repair them.

As important as these people are, they often receive a great deal of abuse by angry

So You Want to Be a Network Administrator?

You know that network administrators are the people who design, install, and maintain the network equipment and infrastructure. But what *exactly* do they do?

Network administrators are involved in every stage of network planning and deployment. They decide what equipment to buy and what type of media to use, and they determine the correct topology for the network. They also often develop policies regarding network usage, security measures, and hardware and software standards.

After the planning is complete, network administrators help install the network (either by supervising third-party contractors or by doing the work themselves). Typical installation tasks include configuring and installing client computers and peripherals, running cable, and installing wireless media devices. Installing and configuring security devices and software are also critical jobs.

As equipment and cables break, network administrators must locate the source of the trouble and fix the problem. They also obtain and install updates to network software. Network administrators also evaluate new equipment to determine whether they should upgrade the network. In addition, they monitor the network performance to ensure that users' needs are met.

Given the importance of the Internet to most organizations, network administrators also ensure that the Internet connection is maintained at all times. Problems with Internet connectivity are usually a high priority on the network administrator's to-do list. Finally, network administrators plan disaster recovery strategies (such as what to do if a fire destroys the server room).

So, if you like to troubleshoot problems, plan complex systems, and explore new ideas, a career in network administration might be for you.

users whose computers are not working. When working in support services, you need to be patient and have a "thick skin."

Technical services jobs often require two-year college degrees or training at trade schools or technical institutes. At smaller companies, job duties tend to overlap between the help desk and technician jobs. And these jobs are in demand. A recent survey of 1,400 Chief Information Officers sponsored by Robert Half Technology identified Windows administration, wireless network management, and database management (SQL) as the top skills needed by U. S. IT departments.

How Should You Prepare for a Job in IT?

A job in IT requires a robust skill set and formal training and preparation. Most employers today have an entry-level requirement of

a college degree, a technical institute diploma, appropriate professional certifications, and/or experience in the field. How can you prepare for a job in IT?

1. **Get educated.** Two- and four-year colleges and universities normally offer three degrees to prepare students for IT careers: computer science, MIS, and computer engineering (although titles vary). Alternatives to colleges and universities are privately licensed technical (or trade) schools. Generally, these programs focus on building skill sets rapidly and obtaining a job in a specific field, such as Web development or network administration. The main advantage of trade schools is that their programs usually take less time to complete than college degrees. However, to have a realistic chance of employment in IT fields other than networking or Web development, you should attend a degree-granting college or university.

2. **Investigate professional certifications.** Certifications attempt to provide a consistent method of measuring a level of skill in a particular area of IT. There are hundreds of IT certifications, most of which you get by passing a written exam. Software and hardware vendors (such as Microsoft and Cisco) and professional organizations (such as the Computing Technology Industry Association) often establish certification standards. (Visit **www.microsoft.com**, **www.cisco.com**, **www.comptia.org**, and **www.sun.com** for more information on certifications.)

    Employees with certifications generally earn more than employees who aren't certified. However, most employers don't view a certification as a substitute for a college degree or a trade school program. You should think of certifications as an extra edge beyond your formal education that will make you more attractive to employers. To ensure you're pursuing the right certification, ask employers which certifications they respect or explore online job sites for job postings in your field and see which certifications are listed as desirable or required.

3. **Get experience.** Aside from education, employers want you to have experi-

Figure 10

At smaller companies, you may be fixing a user's computer in the morning, installing and configuring a new network operating system in the afternoon, and troubleshooting a router problem in the evening (as shown here).

ence, even for entry-level jobs. As you're completing your education, consider getting an internship or part-time job in your field of study. Many colleges will help you find internships and allow you to earn credit toward your degree through internship programs.

4. **Do Research.** Find out as much as you can about the company and the industry it is in before going on an interview. Start with the company's Web site and then expand your search to business and trade publications (such as Business Week and CIO Magazine).

How DO You Find a Job in IT?

Training for a career is not useful unless you can find a job at the end of your training. Here are some tips on getting a job:

1. **Visit your school's placement office.** Many employers recruit at schools, and most schools maintain a placement office to help students find jobs. Early in your college career, visit the placement office. Employees there can help you with résumé preparation and job interviewing skills and can provide you with leads for internships and jobs.

Figure 11

Online IT Career Resources

www.computerjobs.com

www.jobcircle.com

www.computeruser.com

www.justtechjobs.com

www.computerwork.com

www.tech-engine.com

www.dice.com

www.gamasutra.com

2. **Visit online employment sites.** Most IT jobs are advertised online at sites such as Monster.com and CareerBuilder.com (see Figures 11 and 12). Begin searching for jobs on these sites early in your education because the job listings detail the skill sets employers require. Focusing on coursework that will provide you with desirable skill sets will make you more marketable when you graduate.

3. **Start networking.** Many jobs are never advertised but are filled by word of mouth. Seek out contacts in your field and discuss job prospects with them.

Figure 12

Employment sites, such as CareerBuilder.com, enable you to search for specific jobs within a defined geographic area. These sites also allow you to store your résumé at the site and apply for positions with one click.

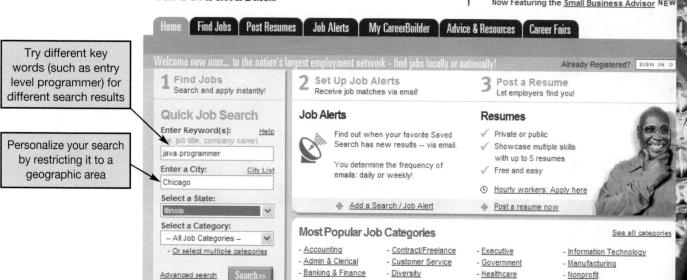

Try different key words (such as entry level programmer) for different search results

Personalize your search by restricting it to a geographic area

Figure 13

Professional Organizations

Organization Name	Purpose	Web Site
Association for Computing Machinery (ACM)	Oldest scientific computing society. Maintains a strong focus on programming and systems development.	www.acm.org
Association of Internet Professionals (AIP)	Formed by the merger of smaller organizations, this is the largest professional group supporting Web developers.	www.association.org
Institute of Electrical and Electronics Engineers (IEEE)	Provides leadership and sets engineering standards for all types of network computing devices and protocols.	www.ieee.org
Association of Information Technology Professionals (AITP)	Heavy focus on IT education and development of seminars and learning materials.	www.aitp.org

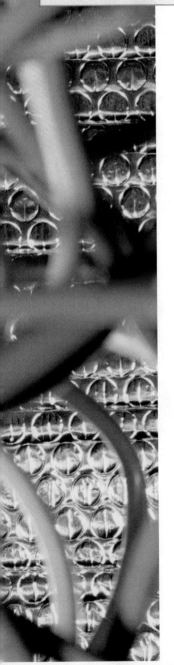

Find out what skills are needed and ask them to recommend others in the industry with whom you can speak. Professional organizations such as the Association for Computing Machinery (ACM) are one way to network. These organizations often have chapters on college campuses and offer reduced membership rates for students. The contacts you make there could lead to your next job. Figure 13 lists major pro-fessional organizations you should consider investigating.

4. **Check corporate Web sites for jobs.** Many corporate Web sites list current job opportunities. For example, the Campbell Soup Company features a searchable site (see Figure 14) you can tailor to a specific geographic area or job type. Check company sites you're interested in working for.

Campbell's — Campbell Soup Company

Home   About Us   Around the World   Media Relations   Investor Center   Career Center   Contact Campbell

Careers
Diversity
Development Programs
Campus Connection
Job Search

Career Center

Careers

▸ New Search

Click Job Title for Details.

Job Title	Requisition Number	Company	Job Type	City	State
Information Systems Auditor	1173	Campbell Soup Company	Information Technology	Cherry Hill	NJ
Program Manager	1294	Campbell Soup Company	Information Technology	Camden	NJ
Security Data Engineer	1373	Campbell Soup Company	Information Technology	Camden	NJ

Figure 14

Corporate Web sites often list available jobs. The Campbell Soup Company site offers a number of methods to tailor a search, such as information technology jobs available in New Jersey, shown here. You can often send a resume to apply for a job with one click of the mouse.

You've spent four years getting a college degree. You've been on numerous interviews and you now have an employer making you a job offer. Don't fall into the trap that over 50 percent of Americans fall into: failure to negotiate salary and benefits. The vast majority of employers make offers to prospective employees that are less than they are willing to pay. Yet many people never try to negotiate with a prospective employer due to fear:

1. **Fear of employer perception:** People think that if they ask for more money, they'll appear greedy or ungrateful.
2. **Fear of the employer's superior power:** You need a job and they are the ones making the decision whether to give it to you, so asking for more money can seem daunting.
3. **Fear of losing the offer:** Many people fear that they will lose an offer if they try to negotiate. However, employers rarely withdraw an offer just because an employee attempts to negotiate.

When an employer has made you a job offer, the employer has taken a lot of time, effort, and money to search for employees and they've decided on you. They are most likely willing to make some compromises to ensure you take the job. So here are a few tips on negotiation:

1. **Don't start talking about compensation too early in the interview process.** Let the employer quote a salary figure first. And, consider carefully before you jump at the first offer.
2. **Consider the entire compensation package when negotiating.** Don't be afraid to ask for alternatives to salary if the employer is unwilling to give you more money. An extra week of vacation or a signing bonus can be just as valuable as an increase in the weekly paycheck.
3. **Don't reveal your salary expectations at the start of a negotiation.** If you make statements like "I can't take this job for less than $50,000 per year," the person on the other side of the negotiation may feel pressured or trapped. Talk in general terms and ease them toward the salary you want.
4. **Never negotiate issues one at a time.** A successful negotiation is a give and take proposition. For instance, you may not need the medical plan that the prospective employer offers because your spouse's plan already covers you. Therefore, when you ask for more salary and an extra week's vacation, suggest that you would be willing to give up the medical coverage to get what you want. This way, both sides win.

For more information, visit the IT Career Builder's Toolkit Web site (**www.cbtoolkit.com**). The *IT Career Builder's Toolkit* features not only advice on preparing to start an IT career, it also provides suggestions for advancing your IT career.

The outlook for IT jobs should continue to be positive in the future. We wish you luck with your education and job search.

Glossary

3-D sound card An expansion card that enables a computer to produce sounds that are omnidirectional or three-dimensional.

802.11 standard A wireless standard established in 1997 by the Institute of Electrical and Electronics Engineers; also known as Wi-Fi (short for Wireless Fidelity), it enables wireless network devices to work seamlessly with other networks and devices.

A

academic fair use A provision that gives teachers and students special consideration regarding copyright violations. As long as the material is being used for educational purposes, limited copying and distribution are allowed.

Accelerated Graphics Port (AGP) bus The AGP bus design was specialized to help move three-dimensional graphics data quickly. It establishes a direct pathway between the graphics card and main memory so that data does not have to travel on the Peripheral Component Interconnect (PCI) bus, which already handles transferring a great deal of system data being moved through the computer.

access method A program or hardware mechanism that controls which computer is allowed to use the transmission media in a network at a certain time.

access time The time it takes a storage device to locate its stored data.

accounting software An application program that helps small business owners manage their finances more efficiently by providing tools for tracking accounting transactions such as sales, accounts receivable, inventory purchases, and accounts payable.

active-matrix displays With an LCD monitor using active-matrix technology, each pixel is charged individually, as needed. The result is that an active-matrix display produces a clearer, brighter image than a passive-matrix display.

Active Server Pages (ASP) A scripting environment in which users combine Hypertext Markup Language (HTML), scripts and reusable Microsoft ActiveX server components to create dynamic Web pages.

active topology A network topology in which each node on the network is responsible for retransmitting the token, or the data, to other nodes.

Advanced Research Products Agency Network (ARPANET) A U.S. government-funded project for the military in the 1960s, ARPANET was the first attempt to enable computers to communicate over vast distances in a reliable manner.

algorithm A set of specific, sequential steps that describe in natural language exactly what a computer program must do to complete its task.

alphabetic check Confirms that only textual characters are entered in a database field.

alphanumeric pagers Devices that display numbers and text messages on their screens. Like numeric pagers, alphanumeric pagers do not allow the user to send messages.

Alt key One of the keys on a standard PC computer keyboard used in conjunction with other keys for shortcuts and special tasks.

American Standard Code for Information Interchange (ASCII) A format for representing each letter or character as an 8-bit (or 1-byte) binary code.

analog-to-digital converter chip Converts analog signals into digital signals.

antivirus software Software that is specifically designed to detect viruses and protect a computer and files from harm.

APIs *See application programming interfaces (APIs)*

applet A small program designed to be run from within another application. Java applets are often run on your computer by your browser through the Java Virtual Machine (an application built into current browsers).

application programming interfaces (APIs) Blocks of code in the operating system that software applications need to interact with it.

application server A server that acts as a repository for application software.

application software The set of programs on a computer that helps a user carry out tasks such as word processing, sending e-mail, balancing a budget, creating presentations, editing photos, taking an online course, and playing games.

arithmetic logic unit (ALU) Part of the central processing unit (CPU) that is designed to perform mathematical operations such as addition, subtraction, multiplication, and division and to perform comparison operations such as greater than, less than, and equal to.

artificial intelligence (AI) The science that attempts to produce computers that display the same type of reasoning and intelligence that humans do.

ASCII *See American Standard Code for Information Interchange (ASCII)*

ASP *See Active Server Pages (ASP)*

assembly languages Languages that enable programmers to write their programs using a set of short, English-like commands that speak directly to the central processing unit (CPU) and give the programmer very direct control of hardware resources.

Asymmetrical Digital Subscriber Line (ADSL) A typical Digital Subscriber Line (DSL) transmission that downloads (or receives) data from the Internet faster than it uploads (or sends) data.

authentication The process of identifying a computer user, based on a login or username and password. The computer system determines whether the computer user is authorized and what level of access is to be granted on the network.

authentication servers Servers that keep track of who is logging on to the network and which services on the network are available to each user.

B

Back button A button on a Web browser used to return to the previously viewed Web page.

backdoor program A program that enables a hacker to take complete control of a computer without the legitimate user's knowledge or permission.

backup utility A software application that creates a duplicate copy of selected data on the hard disk and copies it to another storage device.

bandwidth (or data transfer rate) The maximum speed at which data can be transmitted between two nodes on a network, usually measured in megabits per second (Mbps).

base class The original object class.

base 2 number system (or binary system) A number system that uses two digits, 0 and 1, to represent any value. Also called the binary number system.

base 10 number system (or decimal notation) A number system that uses 10 digits, 0 through 9, to represent any value.

base transceiver station A large communications tower with antennas, amplifiers, and receivers/transmitters.

basic input/output system (BIOS) A program that manages the data between the operating system and all the input and output devices attached to the computer system. BIOS is also responsible for loading the operating system (OS) from its permanent location on the hard drive to random access memory (RAM).

bastion host A heavily secured server located on a special perimeter network between the company's secure internal network and the firewall.

batch processing Accumulating transaction data until a certain point is reached, then processing those transactions all at once.

benchmarking A process used to measure performance in which two devices or systems run the same task and the times are compared.

beta versions Early versions of software programs that are still under development. Beta versions are usually provided free of charge in return for user feedback.

binary decisions Decision points that can be answered in one of only two ways: yes (true) or no (false).

binary digit (or bit) A digit that corresponds to the on and off states of a computer's switches. A bit contains either a value of 0 or 1.

binary language The language computers use to process information, consisting of only the values 0 and 1.

binary number system The number system used by computers to represent all data. Because it includes only two digits (0 and 1), the binary number system is also referred to as the base 2 number system.

biometric access devices Devices that use some unique characteristic of human biology to identify authorized users.

BIOS *See basic input/output system (BIOS)*

bistable display A display that has the ability to retain its image even when the power is turned off.

bit depth The number of bits the video card uses to store data about each pixel on the monitor.

black-hat hackers Hackers who use their knowledge to destroy information or for illegal gain.

blog *See Weblog (blog)*

BlueBoard An application developed by Colligo Networks that enables a personal digital assistant (PDA) display to be used as a drawing board and be instantly connected with up to four other PDAs.

Bluetooth Technology that uses radio waves to transmit data over short distances.

Bookmark A feature in some browsers that places a marker of a Web site's Uniform Resource Locator (URL) in an easily retrievable list (called Favorites in Microsoft Internet Explorer).

Boolean operators Words used to refine Internet searches. These words—AND, NOT, and OR—describe the relationships between keywords in a search.

boot process (or start-up process) Process for loading the operating system into random access memory (RAM) when the computer is turned on.

boot-sector viruses Viruses that replicate themselves into the Master Boot Record of a floppy or hard drive.

breadcrumb list A list that shows the hierarchy of previously viewed Web pages within the Web site that you are currently visiting. Shown at the top of some Web pages, it provides an aid to Web site navigation.

bridges Network devices that are used to send data between two different local area networks (LANs) or two segments of the same LAN.

broadband connections High-speed Internet connections, including cable, satellite, and Digital Subscriber Line (DSL).

browsing (1) Viewing database records. (2) "Surfing" the Web.

brute force attacks Attacks delivered by specialized hacking software that try many combinations of letters, numbers, and pieces of a user ID in an attempt to discover a user password.

bus A group of electrical pathways inside a computer that provide communications between various parts of a computer and the central processing unit (CPU) and main memory.

bus (or linear bus) topology Networking topology in which all devices are connected to a central cable called the bus (or backbone).

bus width How many bits of data can be transferred along the data pathway at one time.

business-to-business (B2B) E-commerce transactions between businesses.

business-to-consumer (B2C) E-commerce transactions between businesses and consumers.

byte Eight binary digits (or bits).

C

C The predecessor language of C++, developed originally for system programmers by Brian Kernighan and Dennis Ritchie of AT&T Bell Laboratories in 1978. It provides higher-level programming language features (such as if statements and for loops) but still allows programmers to manipulate the system memory and central processing unit (CPU) registers directly.

C++ The successor language to C, developed by Bjarne Stroustrup. It uses all of the same symbols and keywords as C but extends the language with additional keywords, better security, and more support for the reuse of existing code through object-oriented design.

cable modem A device that enables a computer to send data over cable lines. A modem modulates and demodulates the signal into digital data and back again.

cache memory Small blocks of memory located directly on and next to the central processing unit (CPU) chip that act as holding places for recently or frequently used instructions or data that the CPU accesses the most. When these instructions or data are stored in cache memory, the CPU can more quickly retrieve them than

if it had to access the instructions or data from random access memory (RAM).

CAD *See computer-aided design (CAD)*

Carrier Sense Multiple Access with Collision Detection (CSMA/CD) A protocol that nodes on a network can use. With CSMA/CD, a node connected to the network listens (that is, has carrier sense) to determine that no other nodes are currently transmitting data signals. If the node doesn't hear any other signals, it assumes it is safe to transmit data. All devices on the network have the same right (that is, they have multiple access) to transmit data when they deem it safe. It is therefore possible for two devices to begin transmitting data signals at the same time. If this happens, the two signals collide. When signals collide, a node on the network alerts the other nodes.

cathode-ray tube (CRT) A picture tube device in a computer monitor; very similar to the picture tube in a conventional television set. A CRT screen is a grid made up of millions of pixels, or tiny dots. The pixels are illuminated by an electron beam that passes back and forth across the back of the screen very quickly so that the pixels appear to glow continuously.

CD-R (Compact Disc-Recordable) disc A portable, optical storage device that can be written to once and can be used with either a CD-R drive or a CD-RW drive.

CD-R drive A drive for reading and writing CD-R discs.

CD-ROM A portable, read-only optical storage device.

CD-ROM drive A drive for reading compact discs (CDs).

CD-RW (Compact Disc-Read/Writable) disc A portable, optical storage device that can be written and rewritten to many times.

CD-RW drive A drive that can both read and write data to CDs.

cell phones Telephones that operate over a wireless network. Cell phones can also offer Internet access, text messaging, personal information management (PIM) features, and more.

cells Individual boxes formed by the columns and rows in a spreadsheet. Each cell can be uniquely identified according to its column and row position.

central processing unit (CPU) The part of the system unit of a computer that is responsible for data processing (or the "brains" of the computer); it is the largest and most important chip in the computer. It controls all the functions performed by the computer's other components and processes all the commands issued to it by software instructions.

centralized A type of network design in which users are neither responsible for creating their own data backups nor for providing security for their computers; instead, those tasks are handled by a centralized server, software, and a system administrator.

chat room An area on the Web where people come together to communicate online. The conversations are in real time and are visible to everyone in the chat room.

cgi-bin A directory where Common Gateway Interface (CGI) scripts are normally placed.

CGI scripts Computer programs that conform to the Common Gateway Interface (CGI) specification, which provides a method for sending data between end users (using browsers) and Web servers.

circuit switching A method of communication in which a dedicated connection is formed between two points (such as two people on telephones) and the connection remains active for the duration of the transmission.

classes Categories of objects that define the common properties of all objects belonging to the class.

click-and-brick businesses Traditional stores that have an online presence.

clickstream data Information captured about each click that users make as they navigate a Web site.

client A computer that requests information from a server in a client server network (such as your computer when you are connected to the Internet).

client-based e-mail E-mail that is dependent on an e-mail account provided by an Internet service provider (ISP) and a client software program, such as Microsoft Outlook or Eudora.

client/server network A network that consists of client and server computers, in which the clients make requests of the server and the server returns the response.

client-side application A computer program that runs on the client computer and requires no interaction with a Web server.

clip art A gallery of images that is often included with software packages.

clock cycle The "ticks" of the system clock. One cycle equals one "tick."

clock speed The steady and constant pace at which a computer goes through machine cycles, measured in hertz (Hz).

coaxial cable A single copper wire surrounded by layers of plastic insulation and sheathing used mainly in cable television and cable Internet.

code editing The step in which programmers actually type the code into the computer.

coding Translating an algorithm into a programming language.

cold boot Starting a computer from a powered down or off state.

command-driven interface The interface between user and computer in which the user enters commands to communicate with the computer system.

comments (or remarks) Plain English notations inserted into program code for documentation. The comments are not ever seen by the compiler.

commerce servers Computers that host software that enables consumers to purchase goods and services over the Web. These servers generally use special security protocols to protect sensitive information (such as credit card numbers) from being intercepted.

Common Gateway Interface (CGI) Provides a methodology by which a browser can request that a program file be executed (or run) instead of just being delivered to the browser.

communications server A server that handles all communications between the network and other networks, including managing Internet connectivity.

Compact Flash Memory cards about the size of a matchbook that can hold between 64 megabytes (MB) and 8 gigabytes (GB) of data.

compilation The process by which code is converted into machine language, the language the central processing unit (CPU) can understand.

compiler The program that understands both the syntax of the programming language and the exact structure of the central processing unit (CPU) and its machine language. It can "read" the source code and translate the source code directly into machine language.

completeness check Ensures that all database fields defined as "required" have data entered into them.

computed field (or computational field) A numeric field in a database that is filled as the result of a computation.

computer A data processing device that gathers, processes, outputs, and stores data and information.

computer-aided design (CAD) 3-D modeling programs used to create automated designs, technical drawings, and model visualizations.

computer fluent Describes a person who understands the capabilities and limitations of computers and knows how to use them to accomplish tasks.

computer forensics The application of computer systems and techniques to gather potential legal evidence; a law enforcement specialty used to fight high-tech crime.

computer network Two or more computers that are connected by software and communications media so that they can communicate with each other.

computer protocol A set of rules for accomplishing electronic information exchange. If the Internet is the information superhighway, protocols are the driving rules.

computer virus A computer program that attaches itself to another computer program (known as the host program) or pretends to be an innocuous program and attempts to spread itself to other computers when files are exchanged.

connectionless protocol A protocol that a host computer can use to send data over the network without establishing a direct connection with any specific recipient computer.

connection-oriented protocol A protocol that requires two computers to exchange control packets, which set up the parameters of the data exchange session, before sending packets that contain data.

connectivity port A port that enables the computer (or other device) to be connected to other devices or systems such as networks, modems, and the Internet.

consistency check Comparing the value of data in a database field against established parameters to determine whether the value is reasonable.

consumer-to-consumer (C2C) E-commerce transactions between consumers through online sites such as eBay.com.

Control (Ctrl) key One of the keys on a PC computer keyboard that is used in combination with other keys to perform shortcuts and special tasks.

control unit A component that controls the switches inside the central processing unit (CPU).

cookies Small text files that some Web sites automatically store on a client computer's hard drive when a user visits the site.

copyright violation When one person uses another person's material for their own personal economic benefit, or when someone diminishes the economic benefits of the originator.

course management software Programs that provide traditional classroom tools such as calendars and grade books over the Internet, as well as areas for students to exchange ideas and information in chat rooms, discussion forums, and using e-mail.

CPU *See central processing unit (CPU)*

CPU usage The percentage of time a central processing unit (CPU) is working.

cradle Connects a personal digital assistant (PDA) to a computer using either a universal serial bus (USB) port or a serial port.

CRT *See cathode-ray tube (CRT)*

cursor The flashing | symbol on a computer monitor that indicates where the next character will be inserted.

cursor control keys The set of special keys on a keyboard, generally marked by arrows, that move the cursor one space at a time, either up, down, left, or right. Other cursor control keys move the cursor up or down one full page or to the beginning or end of a line.

custom installation Installing only those features of a software program that a user wants on the hard drive, thereby saving space on the hard drive.

customer relationship management (CRM) software A business program used for storing sales and client contact information in one central database.

cybercrime Any criminal action perpetrated primarily through the use of a computer.

cybercriminals Individuals who use computers, networks, and the Internet to perpetrate crime.

cyberterrorists Terrorists who use computers to accomplish their goals.

D

data Numbers, words, pictures, or sounds that represent facts or ideas.

data collisions When two computers send data at the same time and the sets of data collide somewhere in the media.

data dictionary (or database schema) Defines the name, data type, and length of each field in the database.

data inconsistency Differences in data in lists caused when data exists in multiple lists and not all lists are updated when a piece of data changes.

data integrity When data contained in a database is accurate and reliable.

data marts Small slices of a data warehouse.

data mining The process by which great amounts of data are analyzed and investigated to spot significant patterns or trends within the data that would otherwise not be obvious.

data redundancy When the same data exists in more than one place in a database.

data staging A three-step process: extracting data from source databases, transforming (reformatting) the data, and storing the data in a data warehouse.

data transfer rate (or bandwidth) The maximum speed at which data can be transmitted between two nodes on a network, usually measured in megabits per second (Mbps).

data type (or field type) Indicates what type of data can be stored in the database field or memory location.

data warehouse A large-scale electronic repository of data that contains and organizes in one place all the data related to an organization.

database Electronic collections of related data that are organized and searchable.

database administrator (or database designer) An individual trained in the design, construction, and maintenance of databases.

database management system (DBMS) Specially designed application software (such as Oracle or Microsoft Access) that interacts with the user, other applications, and the database to capture and analyze data.

database query An inquiry the user poses to the database to extract a meaningful subset of data.

database server A server that provides client computers with access to information stored in a database.

database software An electronic filing system best used for larger and more complicated groups of data that require more than one table, and where it's necessary to group, sort, and retrieve data, and to generate reports.

date fields Fields in a database that hold date data such as birthdays, due dates, and so on.

debugger A tool that helps programmers step through a program as it runs to locate errors.

debugging The process of running the program over and over to find errors and to make sure the program behaves in the way it should.

decentralized A type of network in which users are responsible for creating their own data backups and for providing security for their computers.

decision points Points at which a computer program must choose from an array of different actions based on the value of its current inputs.

decision support system (DSS) A system designed to help managers develop solutions for specific problems.

dedicated servers Servers used to fulfill one specific function (such as handling e-mail).

default values The values a database will use for fields unless the user enters another value.

denial of service (DoS) attack An attack that occurs when legitimate users are denied access to a computer system because a hacker is repeatedly making requests of that computer system to tie up its resources and deny legitimate users access.

derived class A class created based on a previously existing class (i.e., base class). Derived classes inherit all of the member variables and methods of the base class from which they are derived.

desktop As its name implies, your computer's desktop puts at your fingertips all of the elements necessary for a productive work session that are typically found on or near the top of a traditional desk, such as files and folders.

desktop box A style of system unit for desktop computers that sits horizontally on top of a desk.

desktop publishing (DTP) software Programs for incorporating and arranging graphics and text to produce creative documents.

detail report A report generated with data from a database that shows the individual transactions that occurred during a certain time period.

device driver Software that facilitates the communication between a device and the operating system.

dial-up connection A connection to the Internet using a standard telephone line.

digital ink An extension of the text-entry systems used on personal digital assistant (PDA) devices.

digital pen A device for drawing images and entering text in a tablet PC.

digital signal processor A specialized chip that processes digital information and transmits signals very quickly.

Digital Subscriber Line (DSL) A technology that uses telephone lines to connect your computer to the Internet and provides high bandwidth throughput. DSL enables phone and data transmission to share the same telephone line.

Digital Subscriber Line (DSL) modem A modem that uses modulation techniques to separate the types of signals into voice and data signals so they can travel in the right "lane" on the twisted pair wiring. Voice data is sent at the lower speed, whereas digital data is sent at frequencies ranging from 128 kilobits per second (Kbps) to 1.5 megabits per second (Mbps).

digital video-editing software Programs for editing digital video.

directories Hierarchical structures that include files, folders, and drives, used to create a more organized and efficient computer.

Disk Cleanup A Windows utility that removes unnecessary files from your hard drive.

disk defragmenter utilities Utilities that regroup related pieces of files together on the hard disk, enabling faster retrieval of the data.

distributed denial of service (DDoS) attacks Automated attacks that are launched from more than one zombie computer at the same time.

docking station Hardware for connecting a portable computing device to printers, scanners, full-size monitors, mice, and other peripherals.

documentation A description of the development and technical details of a computer program, including how the code works and how the user interacts with the program.

domain name Part of a Uniform Resource Locator (URL). Domain names consist of two parts: The first part indicates the site's host; the second part is a three-letter suffix that indicates the type of organization. (Example: popsci.com)

Domain Name System (DNS) server A server that contains location information for domains on the Internet and functions like a phone book for the Internet.

DoS attack *See denial of service (DoS) attack*

dot-matrix printer The first type of computer printer, which has tiny hammer-like keys that strike the paper through an inked ribbon.

dot pitch The diagonal distance, measured in millimeters, between pixels on the screen. A smaller dot pitch means that there is less blank space between pixels, and thus a sharper, clearer image.

dotted decimal numbers The numbers in an Internet Protocol (IP) address.

double data rate synchronous DRAM (DDR SDRAM) Memory chips that are faster than SDRAM but not as fast as RDRAM.

drawing software (or illustration software) Programs for creating or editing two-dimensional line-based drawings.

drive bays Special shelves inside computers designed to hold storage devices.

DSL *See Digital Subscriber Line (DSL)*

DSL/cable routers Routers that are specifically designed to connect to Digital Subscriber Line (DSL) or cable modems.

DSL modem *See Digital Subscriber Line (DSL) modem*

dual processor A design that has two separate central processing unit (CPU) chips installed on the same system.

DVD drive A drive that enables the computer to read digital video discs (DVDs). A DVD±R/RW drive can write DVDs as well as read them.

DVD-RW drive A drive that enables the computer to read and write to DVDs.

Dvorak keyboard A leading alternative keyboard that puts the most commonly used letters in the English language on "home keys," the keys in the middle row of the keyboard. It is designed to reduce the distance your fingers travel for most keystrokes, increasing typing speed.

dynamic addressing The process of assigning Internet Protocol (IP) addresses when users log on using their Internet service provider (ISP). The computer is assigned an address from an available pool of IP addresses.

Dynamic Host Configuration Protocol (DHCP) Handles dynamic addressing. Part of the Transmission Control Protocol/Internet Protocol (TCP/IP) protocol suite, DHCP takes a pool of IP addresses and shares them with hosts on the network on an as-needed basis.

dynamic RAM (DRAM) The most basic type of random access memory (RAM); used in older systems or in systems for which cost is an important factor. DRAM offers access times on the order of 60 nanoseconds.

E

editor A tool that helps programmers as they enter code, highlighting keywords and alerting the programmers to typos.

educational software Applications that offer some form of instruction or training.

edutainment Software that both educates and entertains the user.

electronic commerce (e-commerce) Conducting business online.

electronic switches Devices inside the computer that can be flipped between two states: 1 or 0, on or off.

elements In Hypertext Markup Language (HTML), elements are the tags and the text between the tags.

e-mail (electronic mail) Internet-based communication in which senders and recipients correspond.

e-mail server A server that processes and delivers incoming and outgoing e-mail.

e-mail virus A virus transmitted by e-mail that often uses the address book in the victim's e-mail system to distribute itself.

encryption The process of encoding data (ciphering) so that only the person with a corresponding decryption key (the intended recipient) can decode (or decipher) and read the message.

entertainment software Programs designed to provide users with entertainment; computer games make up the vast majority of entertainment software.

ergonomics Refers to how a user sets up his or her computer and other equipment to minimize risk of injury or discomfort.

error handling In programming, the instructions that the program runs if the input data is incorrect or another error is encountered.

Ethernet networks Networks that use the Ethernet protocol as the means (or standard) by which the nodes on the network communicate.

Ethernet port A port that is slightly larger than a standard phone jack and transfers data at speeds of up to 1,000 megabits per second (Mbps). It is used to connect a computer to a cable modem or a network.

event Every keystroke, every mouse click, and each signal to the printer creates an action, or event, in the respective device (keyboard, mouse, or printer) to which the operating system responds.

exception reports Reports that show conditions that are unusual or that need attention by users of a system.

executable program The binary sequence (code) that instructs the central processing unit (CPU) to perform certain calculations.

expansion bus An electrical pathway that expands the capabilities of a computer by enabling a range of different expansion cards (such as video cards and sound cards) to communicate with the motherboard.

expansion cards (or adapter cards) Circuit boards with specific functions that augment the computer's basic functions as well as provide connections to other devices.

expansion hub A device that connects to one port, such as a universal serial bus (USB) port, to provide additional new ports, similar to a multiplug extension cord for electrical appliances.

expert system Designed to replicate the decision-making processes of human experts to solve specific problems.

export Putting data into an electronic file in a format that another application can understand.

Extended Industry Standard Architecture (EISA) bus An older expansion bus for connecting devices such as the mouse, modem, and sound cards.

Extensible Hypertext Markup Language (XHTML) A new standard recently released by the World Wide Web Consortium (WC3) that combines elements from both Extensible Markup Language (XML) and Hypertext Markup Language (HTML). XHTML has much more stringent rules than HTML does regarding tagging (for instance, all elements require an end tag in XHTML).

Extensible Markup Language (XML) A language that enables designers to define their own tags, making it much easier to transfer data between Web sites and Web servers.

extension (or file type) In a filename, the three letters that follow the user-supplied filename after the dot (.) ; the extension identifies what kind of family of files the file belongs to or which application should be used to read the file.

extranets Pieces of intranets that only certain corporations or individuals can access. The owner of the extranet decides who will be permitted to access it.

F

Favorites A feature in Microsoft Internet Explorer that places a marker of a Web site's Uniform Resource Locator (URL) in an easily retrievable list in the browser's toolbar. (Called Bookmarks in some browsers.)

fiber-optic line (or cable) Lines that transmit data at close to the speed of light along glass or plastic fibers.

field Where a category of information in a database is stored. Fields are displayed in columns.

field constraints Properties that must be satisfied for an entry to be accepted into the database field.

field name An identifying name assigned to each field in a database.

field size The maximum number of characters (or numbers) that a field in a database can contain.

fifth-generation languages (5GLs) Considered the most "natural" of languages. With 5GLs, instructions closely resemble human speech or are visual in nature so that little programming knowledge is necessary.

file A collection of related pieces of information stored together for easy reference.

file allocation table (FAT) An index of all sector numbers that the hard drive stores in a table to keep track of which sectors hold which files.

file compression utility A program that takes out redundancies in a file to reduce the file size.

file management Providing organizational structure to the computer's contents.

file path Identifies the exact location of a file, starting with the drive in which the file is located, and including all folders, subfolders (if any), the filename, and

extension. (Example: C:\My Documents\Spring 2005\ English Comp\Term Paper\Illustrations\ EBronte.jpg)

file servers Computers deployed to provide remote storage space or to act as a repository for files that users can access.

File Transfer Protocol (FTP) A protocol used to upload and download files from one computer to another over the Internet.

filename The first part of the label applied to a file, similar to our first names; it is generally the name a user assigns to the file when saving it.

financial and business-related software Software used by businesses or individuals that helps them perform specific or general business tasks.

financial planning software Programs for managing finances, such as Intuit's Quicken and Microsoft Money, which include electronic checkbook registers and automatic bill payment tools.

firewalls Software programs or hardware devices designed to prevent unauthorized access to computers or networks.

FireWire 800 One of the fastest ports available, moving data at 800 megabits per second (Mbps).

FireWire port (previously called the IEEE 1394 port) A port based on a standard developed by the Institute of Electrical and Electronics Engineers (IEEE), with a transfer rate of 400 megabits per second (Mbps). Today, it is most commonly used to connect digital video devices such as digital cameras to the computer.

first-generation languages (1GLs) The actual machine languages of a central processing unit (CPU), the sequence of bits— 1s and 0s—that the CPU understands.

flash drive Drives that plug into a universal serial bus (USB) port on a computer and store data digitally. Also called USB drives.

flash memory Portable, nonvolatile memory.

flash memory card A form of portable storage. This removable memory card is often used in digital cameras, MP3 players, and personal digital assistants (PDAs).

floppy disk A portable 3.5-inch storage format, with a storage capacity of 1.44 megabytes (MB).

floppy disk drive A drive bay for a floppy disk.

flowcharts Visual representations of the patterns an algorithm comprises.

folder A collection of files stored on a computer.

footprint The amount of physical space on the desk a computer takes up.

For and Next Keywords in Visual Basic to implement a loop.

foreign key The primary key of another database table that is included for purposes of establishing relationships with that other table.

format To design or change the appearance of a document by changing fonts, font styles, or sizes; adding colors to text; adjusting the margins; adding borders to portions of text or whole pages; inserting bulleted and numbered lists; organizing text into columns, and so forth.

formula An equation a spreadsheet user builds using addition, subtraction, multiplication, and division, as well as values and cell references.

Forward button A button on a Web browser toolbar that enables you to return to a Web page after going back using the Back button.

fourth-generation languages (4GLs) Computer languages that are nonprocedural: They specify what is to be accomplished without determining how. Many database query languages and report generators are 4GLs.

frames Containers designed to hold multiple data packets.

freeware Any copyrighted software that can be used for free.

frequently asked questions (FAQs) A list of answers to the most common questions.

FTP *See File Transfer Protocol (FTP)*

full installation Installing all the files and programs from the distribution CD to the computer's hard drive.

function keys Act as shortcut keys to perform special tasks; they are sometimes referred to as the "F" keys because they start with the letter F followed by a number.

fuzzy logic Allows the interjection of experiential learning into the equation by considering probabilities.

gigabyte (GB) About a billion bytes.

gigahertz (GHz) One billion hertz.

Global Positioning System (GPS) A system of 21 satellites (plus three working spares), built and operated by the U.S. military, that constantly orbit the earth. They provide information to GPS-capable devices to pinpoint locations on the earth.

Graffiti One of the more popular notation systems for entering data into a personal digital assistant (PDA).

graphical user interface (or GUI, pronounced "gooey") Unlike the command- and menu-driven interfaces used earlier, GUIs display graphics and use the point-and-click technology of the mouse and cursor, making them much more user-friendly.

graphics and multimedia software Programs to design and create attractive documents, images, illustrations, and Web pages, as well as three-dimensional models and drawings.

grid computing A form of networking that enables linked computers to use idle processors of other networked computers for complex calculations.

groupware Software that helps people who are in different locations work together using tools such as e-mail, threaded messaging, and online scheduling.

hacker (or cracker) Anyone who breaks into a computer system (whether an individual computer or a network) unlawfully.

handshaking The process of two computers exchanging control packets that set up the parameters of a data exchange.

hard disk drive (or hard drive) Holds all permanently stored programs and data; is located inside the system unit.

hardware Any part of the computer you can physically touch.

head crash Impact of read/write head with magnetic platter of the hard disk drive that often results in data loss.

hexadecimal notation A number system that uses 16 digits to represent numbers; also called a base 16 number system.

hibernation When a computer is in a state of deeper sleep. Pushing the power button awakens the computer from hibernation, at which time the computer reloads everything to the desktop exactly as it was before it went into hibernation.

high-level languages Third-, fourth-, and fifth-generation computer languages.

historical data Data that shows trends over time.

History list A feature on a browser's toolbar that shows all the Web sites and pages visited over a certain period of time.

hits A list of sites (or results) that match an Internet search.

home page The main or opening page of a Web site.

home phoneline network adapter (also HPNA adapter) A device that attaches to computers and peripherals on a phoneline network to enable them to communicate using phone lines.

host Organization that maintains the Web server on which a particular Web site is stored.

hot-swappable bays Bays that provide the ability to remove one drive and exchange it with another drive while the computer is running.

HTML *See Hypertext Markup Language (HTML)*

HTML embedded scripting language A language used to embed programming language code directly within the Hypertext Markup Language (HTML) code of a Web page.

HTTP *See Hypertext Transfer Protocol (HTTP)*

hubs Simple amplification devices that receive data packets and retransmit them to all nodes on the same network (not between different networks).

hyperlink fields Fields in a database that store hyperlinks to Web pages.

hyperlinks Specially coded text that, when clicked, enables a user to jump from one location, or Web page, to another within the Web site or to another Web site altogether.

hypertext Text that is linked to other documents or media (such as video clips, pictures, and so on).

Hypertext Markup Language (HTML) A set of rules for marking up blocks of text so that a Web browser knows how to display them. It uses a series of tags that define the display of text on a Web page.

Hypertext Transfer Protocol (HTTP) The protocol a browser uses to send requests to a Web server; created especially for the transfer of hypertext documents over the Internet.

icons Pictures on the desktop that represent an object such as a software application or a file or folder.

identity theft Occurs when someone uses personal information about someone else (such as the victim's name, address, and social security number) to assume the victim's identity for the purpose of defrauding others.

if else Keywords in the programming language C++; used for binary decisions.

image-editing software (sometimes called photo-editing software) Programs for editing photographs and other images.

impact printers Printers that have tiny hammer-like keys that strike the paper through an inked ribbon, thus making a mark on the paper. The most common impact printer is the dot-matrix printer.

import To bring data into an application from another source.

indexer A program in a search engine that organizes into a large database the information a spider collects on the Internet.

Industry Standard Architecture (ISA) bus An older expansion bus used for connecting devices such as the mouse, modem, and sound cards.

information Data that has been organized or presented in a meaningful fashion.

information system A system that includes data, people, procedures, hardware, and software and is used to gather and analyze information.

inheritance The ability of a new class of object to automatically pick up all of the data and methods of an existing class, and then extend and customize those to fit its own specific needs.

initial value A beginning point in a loop.

ink-jet printer A nonimpact printer that sprays tiny drops of ink onto paper.

input device Hardware device used to enter, or input, data (text, images, and sounds) and instructions (user responses and commands) into a computer; input devices include keyboards, mice, scanners, microphones, and digital cameras.

input form Provides a view of the data fields to be filled in a database, with appropriate labels to assist database users in populating the database.

instant messaging (IM) services Programs that enable users to communicate in real time with others who are also online.

instruction set The collection of commands a specific central processing unit (CPU) can run.

instructions The steps and tasks the computer needs to process data into usable information.

integrated circuits (or chips) Very small regions of semiconductor material, such as silicon, that support a huge number of transistors.

integrated development environment (IDE) A developmental tool that helps programmers write, compile, and test their programs.

integrated software application A single software program that incorporates the most commonly used tools of many productivity software programs into one integrated stand-alone program.

Internet A network of networks and the largest network in the world, connecting millions of computers from more than 65 countries.

Internet2 An ongoing project sponsored by more than 200 universities (supported by government and industry partners) to develop new Internet technologies and disseminate them as rapidly as possible to the rest of the Internet community. The Internet2 backbone supports extremely high-speed communications (up to 9.6 gigabits per second [Gbps]).

Internet backbone The main pathway of high-speed communications lines over which all Internet traffic flows.

Internet Explorer (IE) A popular graphical browser from Microsoft Corporation for displaying different Web sites, or locations, on the Web; it can display pictures (graphics) in addition to text, as well as other forms of multimedia, such as sound and video.

Internet hoaxes E-mail messages that contain information that is untrue.

Internet Protocol (IP) A protocol for sending data between computers on the Internet.

Internet Protocol address (IP address) The means by which all computers connected to the Internet identify each other. It consists of a unique set of four numbers separated by dots, such as 123.45.178.91.

Internet Protocol version 4 (IPv4) The original IP addressing scheme.

Internet Protocol version 6 (IPv6) A proposed IP addressing scheme that makes IP addresses longer, thereby providing more available IP addresses. It uses eight groups of 16-bit numbers.

Internet service providers (ISPs) National, regional, or local companies that connect individuals, groups, and other companies to the Internet.

Internet telephony Hardware and software that enables people to use the Internet to transmit telephone calls.

interpreter Translates source code into an intermediate form, line by line. Each line is then executed as it is translated.

interrupt A signal that tells the operating system that it is in need of immediate attention.

interrupt handler A special numerical code that prioritizes requests to the operating system.

interrupt table A place in the computer's primary memory (or random access memory, RAM) where interrupt requests are placed.

intranet A private corporate network that is used exclusively by company employees to facilitate information sharing, database access, group scheduling, videoconferencing, or other employee collaboration.

IP *See Internet Protocol (IP)*

IP address *See Internet Protocol address (IP address)*

IrDA port A port based on a standard developed by the Infrared Data Association for transmitting data. IrDA ports transmit data between two devices using infrared light waves, similar to a TV remote control. IrDA ports have a maximum throughput of 4 megabits per second (Mbps) and require that a line of sight be maintained between the two ports.

J

jam signal A special signal sent to all network nodes, alerting them that a collision has occurred.

Java A platform-independent programming language that Sun Microsystems introduced in the early 1990s. It quickly became popular because its object-oriented model enables Java programmers to benefit from its set of existing classes.

Java applets Small Java-based programs.

Java Server Pages (JSP) An extension of the Java servlet technology with dynamic scripting capability.

JavaScript A programming language often used to add interactivity to Web pages. JavaScript is not as full-featured as Java, but its syntax, keywords, data types, and operators are a subset of Java's.

join query A database query that links (or joins) two database tables using a common field in both tables and extracts the relevant data from each.

K

kernel (or supervisor program) The essential component of the operating system, responsible for managing the processor and all other components of the computer system. Because it stays in random access memory (RAM) the entire time your computer is powered on, the kernel is called memory resident.

kernel memory The memory that the computer's operating system uses.

key pair A public and a private key used for coding and decoding messages.

keyboard Used to enter typed data and commands into a computer.

keywords (1) Specific words a user wishes to query (or look for) in an Internet search. (2) The set of specific words that have pre-defined meanings for a particular programming language.

kilobyte (KB) Approximately 1,000 bytes.

knowledge-based system A support system that provides additional intelligence that supplements the user's own intellect and makes the decision support system (DSS) more effective.

L

label Descriptive text that identifies the components of a spreadsheet.

LANs *See local area networks (LANs)*

laptop computer (or notebook computer) A portable computer that offers a large display and all of the computing capabilities of a full desktop system.

Large Scale Networking (LSN) A program created by the U.S. government, the objective of which is to fund the research and development of cutting-edge networking technologies. Major goals of the program are the development of enhanced wireless technologies and increased network throughput.

laser printer A nonimpact printer known for quick and quiet production and high-quality printouts; it uses laser beams to make marks on paper.

latency (or rotational delay) Occurs after the read/write head of the hard drive locates the correct track, then waits for the correct sector to spin to the read/write head.

Level 1 cache A block of memory that is built onto the central processing unit (CPU) chip for the storage of data or commands that have just been used.

Level 2 cache A block of memory that is located either on the central processing unit (CPU) chip or on a separate chip near the CPU. It takes somewhat longer to access than the CPU registers. Level 2 cache contains more storage area than Level 1 cache.

Level 3 cache On computers with Level 3 cache, the central processing unit (CPU) checks this area for instructions and data after it looks in Level 1 and Level 2 cache, but before it looks in to random access memory (RAM). The Level 3 cache is often

designed to hold between 2 megabytes (MB) and 4 MB of data.

Linux An open-source operating system based on UNIX. Because of the stable nature of this operating system, it is often used on Web servers.

liquid crystal display (LCD) Technology used in flat-panel computer monitors.

local area networks (LANs) Networks in which the nodes are located within a small geographic area.

local buses Located on the motherboard, these buses run between the central processing unit (CPU) and the main system memory.

logic bombs Computer viruses that run when a certain set of conditions is met, such as specific dates keyed off of the computer's internal clock.

logical port A virtual communications gateway or path that enables a computer to organize requests for information (such as Web page downloads, e-mail routing, and so on) from other networks or computers.

logical port blocking When a firewall is configured to ignore all incoming packets that request access to a certain port so no unwanted requests will get through to the computer.

loop An algorithm that performs a repeating set of actions. A logical yes/no expression is evaluated. As long as the expression evaluates to TRUE (yes), the algorithm will perform the same set of actions and continue to loop around. When the answer to the question is no, the algorithm breaks free of the looping structure and moves on to the next step.

M

Mac OS Apple Computer's operating system. In 1984, Mac OS became the first operating system to incorporate the user-friendly point-and-click technology in a commercially affordable computer. The most recent version of the Mac operating system, Mac OS X, is based on the UNIX operating system. Previous Mac operating systems had been based on Apple's own proprietary program.

machine cycle (or processing cycle) The time it takes to fetch and execute a single machine level instruction by the central processing unit (CPU).

machine language Long strings of binary code used by the control unit to set up the hardware in the central processing unit (CPU) for the rest of the operations it needs to perform.

macro viruses Viruses that are distributed by hiding them inside a macro.

Macromedia Flash A software product from Macromedia for developing Web-based multimedia.

macros Small programs that group a series of commands to run as a single command.

magnetic card readers Devices that read information from a magnetic strip on the back of a credit card–like access card (such as a student ID card). The card reader, which can control the lock on a door, is programmed to admit only authorized personnel to the area.

magnetic media Portable storage devices, such as floppy disks and Zip disks, that use a magnetized film to store data.

mainframes Large, expensive computers that support hundreds or thousands of users simultaneously.

management information system (MIS) A system that provides timely and accurate information that enables managers to make critical business decisions.

mapping programs Software that provides street maps and written directions to locations.

Master Boot Record A program that runs whenever a computer boots up.

Media Access Control (MAC) address A physical address similar to a serial number on an appliance that is assigned to each network adapter; it is made up of six 2-digit numbers such as 01:40:87:44:79:A5.

megabyte (MB) About a million bytes.

megahertz (MHz) One million hertz; hertz is the unit of measure for processor speed, or machine cycles per second.

memo fields Text fields in a database that are used to hold long pieces of text.

memory A component inside the system unit that helps process data into information; memory chips hold (or store) the instructions or data that the central processing unit (CPU) processes.

memory bound A system that is limited in how fast it can send data to the central processing unit (CPU) because there's not enough random access memory (RAM) installed.

memory card reader An external device for reading flash memory cards.

memory effect The result of a laptop battery needing to be completely used up before it is recharged or it won't hold as much charge as it originally did.

memory modules (or memory cards) Small circuit boards that hold a series of random access memory (RAM) chips.

Memory Stick Sony's brand of flash memory; the cards measure just 2 inches by 1 inch and weigh a fraction of an ounce.

menu-driven interface A user interface in which the user chooses a command from menus displayed on the screen.

menus Lists of commands that appear on the screen.

meta search engine A search engine that searches other search engines rather than individual Web sites.

metadata Data that describes other data.

methods (or behaviors) Actions associated with a class of objects.

metropolitan area networks (MANs) Wide area networks (WANs) that link users in a specific geographic area (such as within a city or county).

microbrowser Software that makes it possible to access the Internet from a cell phone or personal digital assistant (PDA).

microphone A device for capturing sound waves (such as voice) and transferring them to digital format on a computer.

microprocessors Chips that contain a central processing unit (CPU).

Microsoft Disk Operating System (MS-DOS) A single-user, single-task operating system created by Microsoft. MS-DOS was the first widely installed operating system in personal computers.

Microsoft Visual Basic (VB) A powerful programming language used to build a wide range of Windows applications. VB's strengths include a simple, quick interface that is easy for a programmer to learn and use. It has grown from its roots in the lan-guage BASIC to become a sophisticated and full-featured object-oriented language.

Microsoft Windows The most popular operating system for desktop computers.

MIME *See Multipurpose Internet Mail Extensions (MIME)*

mobile computing devices Portable electronic tools such as cell phones, personal digital assistants (PDAs), and laptops.

mobile switching center A central location that receives cell phone requests for service from a base station.

model management system Software that assists in building management models in decision support systems (DSSs).

modem A device that converts the digital signals the computer understands to the analog signals that can travel over phone lines.

modem card A device that provides the computer with a connection to the Internet.

modem port A port that uses a traditional telephone signal to connect two computers.

monitor (or display screen) A common output device that displays text, graphics, and video as "soft copies" (copies that can be seen only on-screen).

Moore's Law A mathematical rule, named after Gordon Moore, the cofounder of the central processing unit (CPU) chip manufacturer Intel, that predicts that the number of transistors inside a CPU will increase so fast that CPU capacity will double every 18 months.

motherboard A special circuit board in the system unit that contains the central processing unit (CPU), the memory (RAM) chips, and the slots available for expansion cards. It is the largest printed circuit board; all of the other boards (video cards, sound cards, and so on) connect to it to receive power and to communicate.

mouse A device used to enter user responses and commands into a computer.

MP3 player A small portable device for storing MP3 files (digital music).

MS Transcriber A notation system for personal digital assistants (PDAs) that doesn't require special strokes and can recognize both printed and cursive writing with fairly decent accuracy.

multifunction printer A device that combines the functions of a printer, scanner, fax machine, and copier into one machine.

multimedia Anything that involves one or more forms of media plus text.

multimedia cards (MMCs) Thin, small, rugged cards used as portable memory that can hold up to 128 megabytes (MB) of data.

Multimedia Message Service (MMS) An extension of Short Message Service (SMS) that enables messages that include text, sound, images, and video clips to be sent from a cell phone or PDA to other phones or e-mail addresses.

multipartite viruses Literally meaning "multipart" viruses, this type of computer virus attempts to infect both the boot sector and executable files at the same time.

Multipurpose Internet Mail Extensions (MIME) A specification that was introduced in 1991 to simplify attachments to e-mail messages. All e-mail client software now uses this protocol for attaching files.

multitasking When the operating system allows a user to perform more than one task at a time.

multiuser operating system (or network operating system) Enables more than one user to access the computer system at one time by efficiently juggling all the requests from multiple users.

Musical Instrument Digital Interface (MIDI) port A port for connecting electronic musical instruments (such as synthesizers) to a computer.

N

nanoscience The study of molecules and nanostructures whose size ranges from 1 to 100 nanometers.

nanotechnology The science revolving around the use of nanostructures to build devices on an extremely small scale.

Napster The most well-known file-exchange site for digital music. Peer-to-peer sharing technology previously allowed users to exchange files, rather than downloading from a public server. Napster was purchased, shut down, and then reopened for downloading music that a user purchases, in compliance with copyright provisions.

natural language processing (NLP) system A system that enables users to communicate with computer systems using a natural spoken or written language as opposed to using computer programming languages.

negative acknowledgment (nack) What computer Y sends to computer X if a packet is unreadable, indicating the packet was not received in understandable form.

netiquette General rules of etiquette for Internet chat rooms and other online forums.

Netscape Navigator A popular graphical browser from Netscape Communications for displaying different Web sites, or locations, on the Web; it can display pictures (graphics) in addition to text, as well as other forms of multimedia, such as sound and video.

network A group of two or more computers (or nodes) that are configured to share information and resources such as printers, files, and databases.

network access points (NAPs) The points of connection between Internet service providers (ISPs).

network adapters Adapters that enable the computer (or peripheral) to communicate with the network using a common data communication language, or protocol.

Network Address Translation (NAT) A process firewalls use to assign internal Internet Protocol (IP) addresses on a network.

network administrator Someone who has training in computer and peripheral maintenance and repair, network design, and the installation of network software.

network architecture The design of a network.

network interface card (NIC) An expansion (or adapter) card that enables a computer to connect with a network.

network navigation devices Devices on a network such as routers, hubs, and switches that move data signals around the network.

network operating system (NOS) Software that handles requests for information, Internet access, and the use of peripherals for the rest of the network nodes.

network topology The layout and structure of the network.

New Technology File System (NTFS) A file system in Windows XP that differs from File Allocation Table (FAT). NTFS was developed with the Windows NT version and has been used in Windows 2000 and Windows XP.

newsgroup (or discussion group) An online discussion forum in which people "post" messages and read and reply to messages from other members of the newsgroup.

NIC *See network interface card (NIC)*

nodes Devices connected to a network, such as a computer, a peripheral (such as a printer), or a communications device (such as a modem).

nonimpact printers Printers that spray ink or use laser beams to make marks on the paper. The most common nonimpact printers are ink-jet and laser printers.

nonvolatile storage Permanent storage, as in read-only memory (ROM).

normalization The process of recording data only once in a database to reduce data redundancy.

number system An organized plan for representing a number.

numeric check Confirms that only numbers are entered in a database field.

numeric fields Fields in a database that store numbers.

numeric keypad Section of a keyboard that enables a user to enter numbers quickly.

numeric pagers Paging devices that display only numbers on their screens, telling the user that he or she has received a page and providing the number to call. Numeric pagers do not allow the user to send a response.

object A variable in a program that is an example of a class. Each object in a specific class is constructed from similar data and methods.

object fields Fields in a database that hold objects such as pictures, video clips, or entire documents.

object-oriented analysis An approach to software design that differs from the tradi-

tional "top-down" design. In OO analysis, programmers first identify all of the classes (collections of data and methods) that are required to completely describe the problem the program is trying to solve.

object-oriented database A database that stores data in objects, not in tables.

object-relational database A hybrid between a relational and an object-oriented database. It is based primarily on the relational database model, but it is better able to store and manipulate unstructured data such as audio and video clips.

octet Eight bits. For example, each of the four numbers in the dotted decimal notation of an Internet Protocol (IP) address is represented with an octet.

office support system (OSS) A system (such as Microsoft Office) designed to assist employees in accomplishing their day-to-day tasks and to improve communications.

online service providers (OSPs) Internet access providers such as America Online (AOL) that have their own proprietary online content and often offer special services and areas that only their subscribers can access.

online transaction processing (OLTP) The immediate processing of user requests or transactions.

open-source program A program that is available for developers to use or modify as they wish; it is typically free of charge.

open systems Systems whose designs are public, enabling access by any interested party.

operating system (OS) System software that controls the way in which a computer system functions, including the management of hardware, peripherals, and software.

operators The coding symbols that represent the fundamental actions of a computer language.

optical media Portable storage devices that use a laser to read and write data, such as CDs and DVDs.

optical mouse A mouse that uses an internal sensor or laser to control the mouse's movement. The sensor sends signals to the computer, telling it where to move the pointer on the screen.

organic light-emitting displays (OLEDs) These displays, currently used in some Kodak cameras, use organic compounds that produce light when exposed to an electrical current.

output device A device that sends processed data and information out of a computer in the form of text, pictures (graphics), sounds (audio), or video.

P

packet A small segment of data that is bundled to be sent over transmission media. Each packet contains the address of the computer or peripheral device to which it is being sent.

packet filtering A process firewalls perform to filter out packets sent to specific logical ports.

packet screening Involves examining incoming data packets to ensure they originated from or are authorized by valid users on the internal network.

packet sniffer A program that looks at (or sniffs) each data packet as it travels on the Internet.

packet switching A communications methodology in which data is broken into small chunks (called packets) and sent over various routes at the same time. When the packets reach their destination, they are reassembled by the receiving computer.

page file The file the operating system builds on the hard drive when it is using virtual memory to enable processing to continue.

paging If the data or instructions that have been placed in the swap file are needed later, the operating system swaps them back into active random access memory (RAM) and replaces them in the hard drive's swap file with less active data or instructions.

paging device (or pager) A small wireless device that enables a user to receive and sometimes send numeric (and sometimes text) messages on a small display screen.

painting software Programs for developing bit-mapped graphics.

Palm OS One of the two main operating systems for personal digital assistants (PDAs), made by 3Com.

parallel port A port that sends data between devices in groups of bits at

speeds of 92 kilobits per second (Kbps). Parallel ports were commonly used to connect printers to computers.

parallel processing A network computer environment in which each computer works on a portion of the same problem simultaneously.

Parcel Transfer Protocol (PTP) A new transmission protocol under development by a team of scientists and computer professionals. The protocol must be designed to keep running even if packets are lost in transmission and to block out noise that can be picked up while data is traversing millions of miles. PTP stores data at the receiver until all data is received and accounted for, then transmits it to the proper destination.

Pascal The only modern computer language that was specifically designed as a teaching language; it is seldom taught at the college level any longer.

passive-matrix displays Computer monitor technology in which electrical current passes through a liquid crystal solution and charges groups of pixels, either in a row or a column. This causes the screen to brighten with each pass of electrical current and subsequently to fade.

passive topology When data merely travels the entire length of the communications medium and is received by all network devices.

path (or subdirectory) The information following the slash or colon in a Uniform Resource Locator (URL).

path separators The backslash marks (\) used by Microsoft Windows and DOS in file names. Mac files use a colon (:), and UNIX and Linux use the forward slash (/) as the path separator.

patient simulator A computer-controlled mannequin that simulates human body functions and reactions. Patient simulators are used in training doctors, nurses, and emergency services personnel to simulate dangerous situations that would normally put live patients at risk.

PC cards (or PCMCIA, short for Personal Computer Memory Card International Association) Credit card–sized cards that enable users to add fax modems, network connections, wireless adapters, USB 2.0 and FireWire ports, and other capabilities primarily to laptops.

PDA *See personal digital assistant (PDA)*

peer-to-peer (P2P) network A network in which each node connected to the network can communicate directly with every other node on the network.

peer-to-peer (P2P) sharing The process of users transferring files between computers.

Peripheral Component Interconnect (PCI) buses Expansion buses that connect directly to the central processing unit (CPU) and support such devices as network cards and sound cards. They have been the standard bus for much of the past decade and continue to be redesigned to increase their performance.

peripheral devices Devices such as monitors, printers, and keyboards that connect to the system unit through ports.

personal area networks (PANs) Networks used to connect wireless devices (such as Bluetooth-enabled devices) in close proximity to each other.

personal digital assistant (PDA) A small device that enables a user to carry digital information. Often called palm computers or handhelds, PDAs are about the size of a hand and usually weigh less than five ounces.

personal firewalls Firewalls specifically designed for home networks.

personal information manager (PIM) software Programs such as Microsoft Outlook or Lotus Organizer that strive to replace the various management tools found on a traditional desk, such as a calendar, address book, notepad, and to-do lists.

phoneline networks Networks that use conventional phone lines to connect the nodes in a network.

physical memory The amount of random access memory (RAM) that is installed in a computer.

pipelining A technique that enables the central processing unit (CPU) to work on more than one instruction (or stage of processing) at a time, thereby boosting CPU performance.

pixels Illuminated, tiny dots that create the images you see on a computer monitor. Pixels are illuminated by an electron beam that passes back and forth across the back of the screen very quickly so that the pixels appear to glow continuously.

plagiarism When someone uses someone else's ideas or words and represents them as his or her own.

platform The combination of a computer's operating system and processor. The two most common platform types are the PC and the Apple Macintosh.

platter Thin, round metallic plates stacked onto the hard disk drive spindle.

plotters Large printers that use a computer-controlled pen to produce oversize pictures that require precise continuous lines to be drawn, such as in maps or architectural plans.

Plug and Play Technology that enables the operating system, once the system is booted up, to recognize automatically any new peripherals and configure them to work with the system.

plug-in (or player) A small software program that "plugs in" to a Web browser to enable a specific function; for example, to view and hear some multimedia files on the Web.

Pocket PC (formerly Windows CE) One of the two main operating systems for personal digital assistants (PDAs), made by Microsoft.

point of presence (POP) A bank of modems through which many users can connect to an Internet service provider (ISP) simultaneously.

pointer The I-beam or arrow that appears on the computer screen.

polymorphic viruses A virus that changes its virus signature (the binary pattern that makes the virus identifiable) every time it infects a new file. This makes it more difficult for antivirus programs to detect the virus.

port An interface through which external devices are connected to the computer.

portability The capability to move a completed solution easily from one type of computer to another.

portal A subject directory on the Internet that is part of a larger Web site that focuses on offering its visitors a variety of information, such as the weather, news, sports, and shopping guides.

positive acknowledgment (ack) What computer Y sends when it receives a data packet that it can read from computer X.

powerline network Network that uses the electrical wiring in a home to connect the nodes in the network.

powerline network adapter An adapter that is attached to each computer or peripheral that is part of a powerline network.

power-on self-test (POST) The first job the basic input/output system (BIOS) performs, ensuring that essential peripheral devices are attached and operational. This process consists of a test on the video card and video memory, a BIOS identification process (during which the BIOS version, manufacturer, and data are displayed on the monitor), and a memory test to ensure memory chips are working properly.

power supply Used to regulate the wall voltage to the voltages required by computer chips; it is housed inside the system unit.

presentation software An application program for creating dynamic slide shows, such as Microsoft PowerPoint or Corel Presentations.

Pretty Good Privacy (PGP) A public-key encryption package.

primary key (or key field) The unique field that each database record must have.

print server A server that manages all client-requested printing jobs for all printers on the network.

printer A common output device that creates tangible or hard copies of text and graphics.

private key One-half of a pair of binary files that is needed to decrypt an encrypted message. The private key is kept only by the individual who created the key pair and is never distributed to anyone else. The private key is used to decrypt messages created with the corresponding public key.

private-key encryption A procedure in which only the two parties involved in sending a message have the code. This could be a simple shift code where letters of the alphabet are shifted to a new position.

problem statement A very clear description of which tasks the computer program must accomplish and how the program will execute these tasks and respond to unusual situations. It is the starting point of programming work.

processor speed The number of operations (or cycles) the processor completes each second, measured in hertz (Hz).

productivity software Programs that enable a user to perform various tasks generally required in home, school, and business. This category includes word processing, spreadsheet, presentation, personal information management (PIM), and database programs.

program Instruction set that provides a means for users to interact with and use the computer, all without specialized computer programming skills.

program development life cycle (PDLC) A number of stages, from conception to final deployment, a programming project follows.

programming The process of translating a task into a series of commands a computer will use to perform that task.

programming language A kind of "code" for the set of instructions the central processing unit (CPU) knows how to perform.

project management software An application program such as Microsoft Project that helps project managers easily create and modify project management scheduling charts.

proprietary software A program that is owned and controlled by the company it is created by or for.

proprietary (or private) systems Systems whose design is not made available for public access.

protocol (1) A set of rules for exchanging data and communication. (2) The first part of the Uniform Resource Locator (URL) indicating the set of rules used to retrieve the specified document. The protocol is generally followed by a colon, two forward slashes, www (indicating World Wide Web), and then the domain name.

prototype A small model of a computer program, often built at the beginning of a large project.

proxy server Acts as a go-between for computers on the internal network and the external network (the Internet).

pseudocode A text-based approach to documenting an algorithm.

public key One half of a pair of binary files that is needed to decrypt an encrypted

message. After creating the keys, the user distributes the public key to anyone he wishes to send him encrypted messages. A message encrypted with a public key can be unencrypted only using the corresponding private key.

public-key encryption A procedure in which the key for coding is generally distributed as a public key that may be placed on a Web site. Anyone wishing to send a message codes it using the public key. The recipient decodes the message with a private key.

 Q

query The process of requesting information from a database.

query language Language used to retrieve and display records. A query language consists of its own vocabulary and sentence structure, used to frame the requests.

QWERTY keyboard A keyboard that gets its name from the first six letters on the top-left row of alphabetic keys on the keyboard.

R

Rambus DRAM (RDRAM) The fastest and the most recent type of RAM on the market. RDRAM is found on multimedia machines because its speed is necessary to transfer large multimedia files efficiently.

random access memory (RAM) The computer's temporary storage space or short-term memory. It is located as a set of chips on the system unit's motherboard, and its capacity is measured in megabytes.

range checks A type of data validation used in databases to ensure that a value entered falls within a specified range (such as requiring a person's age to fall in a range of between 1 and 120).

rapid application development (RAD) A method of system development in which developers create a prototype first and generate system documents as they use and remodel the product.

read-only memory (ROM) A set of memory chips located on the motherboard that stores data and instructions that cannot be changed or erased; it holds all the instructions the computer needs to start up.

read/write heads The read/write heads move from the outer edge of the spinning platters to the center, up to 50 times per second, to retrieve (read) and record (write) the magnetic data to and from the hard disk.

real-time operating system (RTOS) A program with a specific purpose that must guarantee certain response times for particular computing tasks, or the machine's application is useless. Real-time operating systems are found in many types of robotic equipment.

real-time processing The process of updating a database (or information system) immediately as changes are made.

record A collection of related fields in a database.

recycle bin A folder on a Windows desktop where deleted files from the hard drive reside until permanently purged from the system.

reference software A software application that acts as a source for reference materials, such as standard atlases, dictionaries, and thesauri.

referential integrity For each value in the foreign key of one table, there is a corresponding value in the primary key of the related table.

refresh rate (or vertical refresh rate) The number of times per second an electron beam scans the monitor and recharges the illumination of each pixel.

registers Special memory storage areas built into the central processing unit (CPU).

registry Contains all the different configurations (settings) used by the operating system (OS) as well as by other applications.

relational algebra The use of English-like expressions that have variables and operations, much like algebraic equations.

relational database Organizes data in table format by logically grouping similar data into relations (or tables) that contain related data.

relations Database tables that contain related data.

relationships In relational databases, the links between tables that define how the data are related.

repeaters Devices that are installed on long cable runs to amplify a signal.

resolution The clearness or sharpness of an image, which is controlled by the number of pixels displayed on the screen.

restore point The snapshot of the entire system's settings that Windows XP creates every time the computer is started, or when a new application or driver is installed.

reusability The ability to reuse existing classes of objects from other projects, enabling programmers to produce new code quickly.

ring (or loop) topology Networked computers and peripherals that are laid out in a logical circle. Data flows around the circle from device to device in one direction only.

ROM *See read-only memory (ROM)*

root directory The top level of the filing structure in a computer system. In Windows computers, the root directory of the hard drive is represented as C:\.

root domain name servers Servers that know the location of all the computers hosting all domains for an entire top-level domain.

routers Devices that route packets of data between two or more networks.

runtime (or logic) errors The kinds of errors in the problem logic that are only caught when the program executes.

S

Safe mode A special diagnostic mode designed for troubleshooting errors that occur during the boot process.

sampling rate The number of times per second a signal is measured and converted to a digital value. Sampling rates are measured in kilobits per second.

satellite Internet A way to connect to the Internet using a small satellite dish, which is placed outside the home and connects to a computer with coaxial cable. The satellite company then sends the data to a satellite orbiting the earth. The satellite, in turn, sends the data back to the satellite dish and to the computer.

scalable network A type of network that enables the easy addition of users without affecting the performance of the other network nodes (computers or peripherals).

ScanDisk (or Error-Checking) A Windows utility that checks for lost files and fragments as well as physical errors on the hard drive.

screen savers Animated images that appear on a computer monitor when no user activity has been sensed for a certain time.

script kiddies Amateur hackers without sophisticated computer skills; typically teenagers, who don't create programs used to hack into computer systems but instead use tools created by skilled hackers that enable unskilled novices to wreak the same havoc as professional hackers.

scripts Lists of commands (mini-programs or macros) that can be executed on a computer without user interaction.

scrollbars On the desktop, bars that appear at the side or bottom of the screen that control which part of the information is displayed on the screen.

search engine A set of programs that searches the Web for specific words (or keywords) you wish to query (or look for) and then returns a list of the Web sites on which those keywords are found.

second-generation languages (2GLs) Also known as assembly languages. 2GLs deal directly with system hardware but provide acronyms which are easier for human programmers to work with.

second-level domains Domains that fall within top-level domains of the Internet. Each second-level domain needs to be unique within that particular domain, but not necessarily unique to all top-level domains.

sectors A section of a hard disk drive platter, wedge-shaped from the center of the platter to the edge.

Secure Digital A newer type of memory card that is faster and offers encryption capabilities so data is secure even if the user loses the card. The stamp-sized Secure Digital cards can hold up to 4 gigabytes (GB) of data.

Secure Sockets Layer (SSL) A protocol that provides for the encryption of data transmitted using the Intenet. The current versions of all major Web browsers support SSL.

seek time The time it takes for the hard drive's read/write heads to move over the surface of the disk, between tracks, to the correct track.

select query A query that displays a subset of data from a table based on the criteria the user specifies.

semiconductor Any material that can be controlled to either conduct electricity or act as an insulator (not allowing electricity to pass through).

serial port A port that enables the transfer of data, one bit at a time, over a single wire at speeds of up to 56 kilobits per second (Kbps); it is often used to connect external modems to the computer.

server A computer that provides resources to other computers on a network.

server-side application A program that runs on the Web server as opposed to running inside a browser on a client computer.

shareware Software that enables users to "test" the software by running it for a limited time free of charge.

shielded twisted pair (STP) cable Twisted pair cable that contains a layer of foil shielding to reduce interference.

Short Message Service (SMS) (or text messaging) Technology that enables short text messages (up to 160 characters) to be sent over mobile networks.

Simple Mail Transfer Protocol (SMTP) A protocol for sending e-mail along the Internet to its destination.

single-user, multitask operating system An operating system that allows only one person to work on a computer at a time, but the system can perform a variety of tasks simultaneously.

single-user, single-task operating system An operating system that allows only one user to work on a computer at a time to perform just one task at a time.

smart battery A rechargeable lithium ion battery used in mobile computing devices that can report the number of minutes of battery life remaining.

SmartMedia A type of flash memory card that is especially thin and light. SmartMedia cards can hold up to 128 megabytes (MB) of data.

SMTP *See Simple Mail Transfer Protocol (SMTP)*

software The set of computer programs or instructions that tells the computer what to do and enables it to perform different tasks.

software licenses Agreements between the user and the software developer that must be accepted prior to installing the software on a computer.

software piracy Violating a software license agreement by copying an application onto more computers than the license agreement permits.

software suite A collection of software programs that have been bundled together as a package.

software updates (or service packs) Small downloadable software modules that repair errors identified in commercial program code.

sort (or index) The process of organizing a database into a particular order.

sound card An expansion card that attaches to the motherboard inside the system unit that enables the computer to produce sounds.

source code The instructions programmers write in a higher-level language.

spam Unwanted or junk e-mail.

speech-recognition software (or voice-recognition software) Software that translates spoken words into typed text.

speech-recognition system A computer that can be operated through a microphone, with a user telling the computer to perform specific commands (such as to open a file) or to translate spoken words into data input.

spider (or crawler or bot) A program that constantly collects information on the Web, following links in Web sites and reading Web pages. Spiders got their name because they crawl over the Web using multiple "legs" to visit many sites simultaneously.

spreadsheet software An application program such as Microsoft Excel or Lotus 1-2-3 that enables a user to do calculations and numerical analyses easily.

SSL *See Secure Sockets Layer (SSL)*

standby mode When a computer's more power-hungry components, such as the monitor and hard drive, are powered down to save energy.

star topology The most widely deployed client/server network layout in businesses. In a star topology, the nodes connect to a central communications device called a switch. The switch receives a signal from

the sending node and retransmits it to the node which should receive it. Because the switch retransmits data signals, a star topology is an active topology.

statements Sentences in programming code.

static addressing Assigning an Internet Protocol (IP) address for a computer that never changes and is most likely assigned manually by a network administrator.

static RAM (SRAM) A type of random access memory that is faster than DRAM. In SRAM, more transistors are used to store a single bit, but no capacitor is needed.

stealth viruses Viruses that temporarily erase their code from the files where they reside and hide in the active memory of the computer.

storage devices Devices such as hard disk drives, floppy disk drives, and CD drives used for storing data and information.

streaming audio Technology that enables audio files to be fed to a browser continuously. This avoids users having to download the entire file before listening to it.

streaming video Technology that enables video files to be fed to a browser continuously. This avoids users having to download the entire file before viewing it.

structured (analytical) data Data that can be identified and classified as discrete bits of information (such as a name or phone number). Unstructured data includes non-traditional data such as audio clips (including MP3 files), video clips, and pictures that must be viewed in their entirety as opposed to discrete segments.

Structured Query Language (SQL) The most popular database query language today.

stylus A device used to tap or write on touch-sensitive screens.

subject directory A structured outline of Web sites organized by topics and subtopics. Yahoo! is a popular subject directory.

subnotebook computers Portable computers that are smaller and weigh less than normal notebook computers. Usually, these feature smaller displays and keyboards.

subwoofer A special type of speaker designed to more faithfully reproduce low-frequency sounds.

summary data reports *See summary reports*

summary reports A report that summarizes data in some fashion (such as a total of the day's concession sales at an amusement park).

supercomputers Specially designed computers that can perform complex calculations extremely rapidly. They are used in situations in which complex models requiring intensive mathematical calculations are needed (such as weather forecasting or atomic energy research).

swap file (or page file) A temporary storage area on the hard drive where the operating system "swaps out" or moves the data or instructions from random access memory (RAM) that have not recently been used. This process takes place when more RAM space is needed.

switch A device for trasmitting data on a network. A switch makes decisions, based on the Media Access Control (MAC) address of the data, as to where the data is to be sent.

Symbian OS A popular operating system for full-featured cell phones.

Symmetrical Digital Subscriber Line (SDSL) A Digital Subscriber Line (DSL) transmission that uploads and downloads data at the same speed.

synchronizing The process of updating data so the files on different systems are the same.

synchronous DRAM (SDRAM) Much faster than DRAM, it is the current memory standard and provides the level of performance most home users require.

syntax An agreed-upon set of rules defining how a programming language must be structured.

syntax errors Violations of the strict, precise set of rules that define a programming language.

system clock A computer's internal clock.

system development life cycle (SDLC) An organized process (or set of steps) for developing an information processing system.

system evaluation The process of looking at a computer's subsystems, what they do, and how they perform to determine whether the computer system has the right hardware components to do what the user ultimately wants it to do.

system files The main files of the operating system.

system requirements Minimum storage, memory capacity, and processing standards recommended by the software manufacturer to ensure proper operation of a software application.

System Restore A utility in Windows XP that lets you restore your system settings to a specific previous date when everything was working properly.

system software The set of programs that enables a computer's hardware devices and application software to work together; it includes the operating system and utility programs.

system unit The metal or plastic case that holds all the physical parts of the computer together, including the computer's processor (its brains), its memory, and the many circuit boards that help the computer function.

T

T lines High-speed fiber-optic communications lines that are designed to provide much higher throughput than conventional voice (telephone) and data (DSL) lines.

T-1 lines High-speed fiber-optic communications lines that can support 24 simultaneous voice or data channels and achieve a maximum throughput of 1.544 megabits per second (Mbps).

T-2 lines High-speed fiber-optic communications lines composed of four T-1 lines that deliver a throughput of approximately 6.3 megabits per second (Mbps).

T-3 lines Fiber-optic communications lines often used by Tier 1 and Tier 2 Internet service providers (ISPs) and very large businesses; they consist of a bundle of 28 T-1 lines. T-3 lines deliver 44.736 megabits per second (Mbps) of bandwidth.

T-4 lines Fiber-optic communications lines that contain 168 T-1 lines and provide 274.176 megabits per second (Mbps) of throughput.

table In database terminology, a group of related records.

tablet PC A portable computer designed specifically to work with handwriting recognition technology.

tags In Hypertext Markup Language (HTML), a way to indicate how the text should look (such as <b> and </b> to indicate boldface text).

Task Manager A Windows utility that shows programs currently running and permits you to exit nonresponding programs when you click End Task.

Task Scheduler A Windows utility that enables you to schedule tasks to run automatically at predetermined times, with no interaction necessary on your part.

tax-preparation software An application program such as Intuit's TurboTax and H&R Block's TaxCut for preparing state and federal taxes. Each program offers a complete set of tax forms and instructions as well as expert advice on how to complete each form.

TCP/IP *See Transmission Control Protocol/Internet Protocol (TCP/IP)*

telephony software Software that, combined with the Internet, speakers, and a microphone, turns a computer into a high-tech phone and answering service.

Telnet Both a protocol for connecting to a remote computer and a Transmission Control Protocol/Internet Protocol (TCP/IP) service that runs on a remote computer to make it accessible to other computers.

templates Forms included in many productivity applications that provide the basic structure for a particular kind of document, spreadsheet, or presentation.

terminator A device that absorbs a signal so it is not reflected back onto parts of the network that have already received it.

test condition A check to see whether a loop is completed.

testing plan In the problem statement, a plan that lists specific input numbers the program would typically expect the user to enter. It then lists the precise output values that a perfect program would return for those input values.

text fields Fields in a database that can hold any combination of alphanumeric data (letters or numbers) and are most often used to hold text.

thermal printer A printer that works by either melting wax-based ink onto ordinary paper (in a process called thermal wax transfer printing) or by burning dots onto specially coated paper (in a process called direct thermal printing).

third-generation languages (3GLs, or high-level languages) Computer languages that use symbols and commands to help programmers tell the computer what to do, making 3GL languages easier to read and remember. Programmers are relieved of the burden of having to understand everything about the hardware of the computer to give it directions. In addition, 3GLs enable programmers to name storage locations in memory with their own names so they are more meaningful to them.

thrashing A condition of excessive paging in which the operating system becomes sluggish.

three-way handshake A process the Transmission Control Protocol (TCP) uses to establish a connection.

throughput The actual speed of data transfer that is achieved. It is usually less than the data transfer rate and is measured in megabits per second (Mbps).

Tier 1 ISPs Internet service providers that route a large percentage of the traffic on the Internet and have extremely high-speed connections with other ISPs, sometimes in the 2.5 to 10 gigabits per second (Gbps) range.

Tier 2 ISPs Internet service providers that usually have a regional or national focus. Therefore, to enable their customers to reach any possible point on the global Internet, Tier 2 ISPs must route at least a portion of their traffic through the global Tier 1 ISPs.

Tier 3 ISPs Internet service providers that provide Internet access to homes or to small to medium-size businesses. These ISPs normally cover a local geographical area. All Tier 3 ISPs need to be connected to at least one Tier 2 ISP.

time-variant data Data that doesn't all pertain to one period in time, such as data in a data warehouse.

toggle key A keyboard key whose function changes each time it's pressed; it "toggles" between two functions.

token A special data packet used to pass data in a token-ring network.

token method The access method that ring networks use to avoid data collisions.

token-ring topology A network layout in which data is passed using a special data packet called a token.

toolbars On the desktop, groups of icons collected together in a small box.

top-down design A systematic approach in which a programming problem is broken down into a series of high-level tasks.

top-level domain (TLD) The three-letter suffix in the domain name (such as .com or .edu) that indicates the kind of organization the host is.

touchpad A small, touch-sensitive screen at the base of the keyboard. To use the touchpad, you simply move your finger across the pad to direct the cursor.

tower configuration A style of system unit on a desktop computer that typically sits vertically on the floor below a desk.

trackball mouse A mouse with a rollerball on top instead of on the bottom. Because you move the trackball with your fingers, it doesn't require much wrist motion, so it's considered healthier for your wrists than a traditional mouse.

trackpoint A small, joystick-like nub that enables you to move the cursor with the tip of your finger.

tracks Concentric circles on a hard disk drive platter.

transaction processing system (TPS) A system used to keep track of everyday business activities (such as sales of products).

transceiver In a wireless network, a device that translates the electronic data that needs to be sent along the network into radio waves and then broadcasts these radio waves to other network nodes.

transistors Electrical switches that are built out of layers of a special type of material called a semiconductor.

Transmission Control Protocol (TCP) A protocol for preparing data for transmission; it provides for error checking and resending lost data.

Transmission Control Protocol/Internet Protocol (TCP/IP) The main suite of protocols used on the Internet.

transmission media The radio waves or cable that transport data on a network.

Trojan horse A computer program that appears to be something useful or desirable (such as a game or a screen saver), but at the same time does something malicious in the background without the user's knowledge.

twisted pair wiring (or twisted pair cable) Cables made of copper wires that are twisted around each other and surrounded by a plastic jacket (such as traditional home phone wire).

two-way pagers Devices that support both receiving and sending text messages.

U

Unicode An encoding scheme that uses 16 bits instead of the 8 bits used in ASCII. Unicode can represent more than 65,000 unique character symbols, enabling it to represent the alphabets of all modern languages and all historic languages and notational systems.

Uniform Resource Locator (URL) A Web site's unique address, such as **www.microsoft.com**.

universal serial bus (USB) port A port that can connect a wide variety of peripherals to the computer, including keyboards, printers, Zip drives, and digital cameras. USB 2.0 transfers data at 480 megabits per second (Mbps) and is approximately 40 times faster than the original USB port.

UNIX An operating system originally conceived in 1969 by Ken Thompson and Dennis Ritchie of AT&T's Bell Labs. In 1974, the UNIX code was rewritten in the standard programming language C. Today there are various commercial versions of UNIX.

unshielded twisted pair (UTP) cable The most popular transmission media option for Ethernet networks. UTP cable is composed of four pairs of wires that are twisted around each other to reduce electrical interference.

unstructured data Nontraditional database data such as audio clips (including MP3 files), video clips, pictures, and extremely large documents. Data of this type is known as a binary large object (BLOB) because it is actually encoded in binary form.

URL *See Uniform Resource Locator (URL)*

USB *See universal serial port (USB)*

USB 2.0 External bus that supports a data throughput of 480 megabits per second (Mbps). These buses are backward compatible with buses using the original universal serial bus (USB) standard.

User Datagram Protocol (UDP) A protocol that prepares data for transmission but has no re-sending capabilities.

user interface Part of the operating system that enables you to interact with your computer.

Utility Manager A utility in the Accessories folder of Windows XP that enables you to magnify the screen image; you can also have screen contents read out loud or display an on-screen keyboard.

utility programs Small programs that perform many of the general housekeeping tasks for the computer, such as system maintenance and file compression.

V

vacuum tubes Used in early computers, vacuum tubes act as computer switches by allowing or blocking the flow of electrical current.

validation The process of ensuring that data entered into a database is correct (or at least reasonable) and complete.

validation rules Rules that are set up in a database to alert the user to possible wrong entries.

value Numeric data either entered in to a spreadsheet directly or as a result of a calculation.

variable declaration Alerts the operating system that the program needs to allocate storage space in random access memory (RAM) for the variable.

variables A name or symbol that stands for a value.

VBScript A subset of Visual Basic; also used to introduce interactivity to Web pages.

video card (or video adapter) An expansion card that is installed inside a system unit to translate binary data (the 1s and 0s your computer uses) into the images viewed on the monitor.

video RAM (VRAM) The random access memory included with a video card.

videoconferencing Technology that enables a person sitting at a computer and equipped with a personal video camera and a microphone to transmit video and audio across the Internet (or other communications medium). All computers participating in a videoconference need to have a microphone and speakers installed so that participants can hear one another.

virtual memory The space on the hard drive that the operating system stores data to if you don't have enough random access memory (RAM) to hold all of the programs you're currently trying to run.

virtual private network (VPN) Utilizes the public Internet communications infrastructure to build a secure, private network between various locations.

virtual reality programs Software that turns an artificial environment into a realistic experience.

virus signatures Portions of the virus code that are unique to a particular computer virus and make it identifiable by antivirus software.

visual programming A technique for automatically writing code when the programmer says the layout is complete. It helps programmers produce a final application much more quickly.

Voice over IP (VoIP) The transmission of phone calls over the same data lines and networks that make up the Internet. Also called Internet telephony.

voice pager A device that offers all the features of a numeric pager but also enables the user to receive voice messages.

volatile storage Temporary storage, such as in random access memory (RAM); when the power is off, the data in volatile storage is cleared out.

VPN *See virtual private network (VPN)*

W

WAN *See wide area network (WAN)*

WAP *See Wireless Application Protocol (WAP)*

warm boot The process of restarting the system while it's powered on.

Web-based e-mail E-mail that uses the Internet as the client; therefore, a user can access a Web-based e-mail account from

any computer that has access to the Web—no special client software is needed.

Web browser Software that enables a user to access the Web and display Web pages.

Web clipping Technology for extracting the information from a Web site and formatting it so it is more useful on smaller personal digital assistant (PDA) displays.

Web-enabled The capability of a device, such as a desktop computer, laptop, or mobile device, to access the Internet.

Web page authoring software Programs you can use to design interactive Web pages without knowing any Hypertext Markup Language (HTML) code.

Web server A computer running a specialized operating system that enables it to host Web pages (and other information) and provide requested Web pages to clients.

Web site A location on the Web.

Weblog (blog) Personal logs or journal entries posted on the Web.

"what-if" analysis Testing the effects that different variable values have on a spreadsheet analysis, using the recalculation feature.

white-hat hackers Hackers who break into systems just for the challenge of it (and who don't wish to steal or wreak havoc on the systems). They tout themselves as experts who are performing a needed service for society by helping companies realize the vulnerabilities that exist in their systems.

wide area network (WAN) A network made up of local area networks (LANs) connected over long distances.

Wi-Fi (Wireless Fidelity) The 802.11 standard for wireless data transmissions established by the Institute of Electrical and Electronics Engineers (IEEE).

wildcards Symbols used in an Internet search when the user is unsure of the keyword's spelling or when a word can be spelled in different ways or can contain different endings. The asterisk (*) is used to replace a series of letters and the percent sign (%) to replace a single letter in a word.

windows In a graphical user interface, rectangular boxes that contain programs displayed on the screen.

Windows Explorer The program in Microsoft Windows that helps a user manage files and folders by showing the location and contents of every drive, folder, and file on the computer.

Windows key A function key specific to the Windows operating system. Used alone, it brings up the Start menu; however, it's used most often in combination with other keys as shortcuts.

wireless access point A device similar to a switch in an Ethernet network. It takes the place of a wireless network adapter and helps to relay data between network nodes.

Wireless Application Protocol (WAP) The standard that dictates how handheld devices will access information on the Internet.

wireless DSL/cable router A device that enables wireless and wired nodes to be connected to the same network and share an Internet connection.

wireless Internet service provider Providers such as Verizon or T-Mobile that offer their subscribers wireless access to the Internet.

Wireless Markup Language (WML) A format for writing content viewed on a cellular phone or personal digital assistant (PDA) that is text-based and contains no graphics.

wireless media Communications media that do not use cables but instead rely on radio waves to communicate.

wireless network A network that uses radio waves instead of wires or cable as its transmission medium.

wireless network adapter Devices that are required for each node on a wireless network for the node to be able to communicate with other nodes on the network.

wireless network interface cards (wireless NICs) Cards installed in a system that connect with wireless access points on the network.

wizards Step-by-step guides that walk you through the necessary steps to complete a complicated task.

WML *See Wireless Markup Language (WML)*

word processing software Programs used to create and edit written documents such as papers, letters, and résumés.

word size The number of bits a computer can work with at a time.

worksheet The basic element in a spreadsheet program; it is a grid consisting of columns and rows.

World Wide Web (WWW or Web) The part of the Internet used the most. What distinguishes the Web from the rest of the Internet is (1) its use of common communication protocols (such as Transmission Control Protocol/Internet Protocol, or TCP/IP) and special languages (such as the Hypertext Markup Language, or HTML) that enable different computers to talk to each other and display information in compatible formats, and (2) its use of special links (called hyperlinks) that enable users to jump from one place to another in the Web.

worm A program that attempts to travel between systems through network connections to spread infections. Worms can run independently of host file execution and are active in spreading themselves.

WWW *See World Wide Web (WWW or Web)*

 X

XML *See Extensible Markup Language (XML)*

 Z

Zip disk A portable storage medium with storage capacities ranging from 100 megabytes (MB) to 750 MB.

Zip disk drive A storage drive that uses Zip disk media.

zombies Computers that are controlled by hackers who use them to launch attacks on other computer systems.

Index

Third Edition

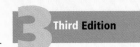

Credits

Chapter 1

Chapter Opener	© Mendola/Doug/Chezem/Corbis
Figure 1.3	Courtesy of Hewlett Packard/tablet pc
Figure 1.3	Courtesy of Nokia/cell phone
Figure 1.3	Courtesy of Sandisk/ USB flash drive
Figure 1.3	Courtesy of Linksy/ router
Figure 1.4	© Lynn Goldsmith/Corbis
Figure 1.5b	This images is reproduced with permission of United Parcel Service of America, Inc., © United Parcel Service of America, Inc. All rights reserved.
Figure 1.5c	Courtesy of Symbol Corporation
Figure 1.6	© 1997–2005, Ryan Bliss, all rights reserved.
Figure 1.7	Copyright 2003 Georgia Tech, Credit: Stanley Leary
Figure 1.8	'Liquid Time Series Tokyo' (2001) interactive installation by Camille Utterback
Figure 1.9	Cyberkinetics Neurotechnology Systems, Inc.
Figure 1.10	Medical Technologies, Inc., © 2003
Figure 1.11	Reprinted by permission of Meryn Tawhai, Physiome Project.
Figure 1.12	Courtesy of Intuitive Surgical da Vinci Surgical Systems.
Figure 1.13	Courtesy of Rhino Parking Systems, Inc., Oakland, CA.
Figure 1.14	Courtesy of the Florida Ninth Judicial Court/Mark Yarn.
Figure 1.15	© Michael Darden/Corbis
Figure 1.16	© 2004 Antenna Audio
Figure 1.17	Reprinted by permission of NCSA University of Illinois.
Figure 1.18	University of Ferrara, Dept. of Architecture-Cy-Ark Foundation Pompeii
Figure 1.20	© 2006 Autodesk, Inc. All rights reserved.
Figure 1.21a	Courtesy of White Box Robotics.
Figure 1.21b	Friendly Robotics® and Robomower® are registered trademarks of F. Robotics Acquisitions Ltd.
Figure 1.21c	© I-Robot
Figure 1.22	Cambridge University/Ghim Wei Ho
Figure 1.23	© Dr. Peter Harris/Photo Researchers
Figure 1.24	© MPI Bio Chemistry/Volker Stegar/Photo Researchers
Figure 1.25	Image of VeriChip courtesy of Applied Digital Solutions.
Figure 1.26	NASA
Figure 1.27	TBO Technology
Figure 1.28	© P. Wood/H. Sulton/Corbis
Figure 1.29	© Chuck Savage/Corbis (face on card)
Figure 1.31	Courtesy of International Business Machines Corporation. Unauthorized used not permitted. (inside of computer)
Figure 1.32	Adobe Illustrator box shot and Adobe Photoshop box shot reprinted with permission of Adobe Systems, Inc.
Figure 1.32	Microsoft box shot reprinted with permission of Microsoft Corporation.
Figure 1.32	Dreamweaver box shot reprinted with permission of Dreamweaver.
Figure 1.32	MacOffice box shot reprinted with permission of Microsoft Corporation.
Figure 1.32	Dungeon Siege box shot reprinted with permission of Microsoft Corporation.
Figure 1.34	Courtesy of Panasonic/TV.
Figure 1.34	Courtesy of Hewlett Packard/digital entertainment center.
Figure 1.34	Courtesy of Microsoft Corporation/ wireless keyboard and trackball.
Figure 1.34	Phillips/TST remote control
Figure 1.35	Screen shot(s) reprinted by permission from Microsoft Corporation.

Chapter 2

Chapter Opener	© Randy Farris/Corbis
Figure 2.1	Linksys/router
Figure 2.4a	Courtesy of Hewlett Packard.
Figure 2.4b	Courtesy of Datadesk Technologies, Inc.
Figure 2.8	Courtesy of Maples Communications/Targus.
Figure 2.16	Pentax Technology
Figure 2.17	Courtesy of Hewlett Packard.
Figure 2.20b	Photo courtesy of Apple Computers, Inc.
Figure 2.23	Screen shot(s) reprinted by permission from Microsoft Corporation.
Figure 2.25	Courtesy of Lexar/USB drive.
Figure 2.27	Courtesy of International Business Machines Corporation. Unauthorized use not permitted.
Figure 2.28	Courtesy of International Business Machines Corporation. Unauthorized use not permitted
Figure 2.30a	Courtesy of Datadesk Technologies, Inc.
Figure 2.30b	Courtesy of Kensington.
Figure 2.32	Courtesy of Universal Display Corp.
Figure 2.33	Micro Optical Corp.

Technology in Focus: The History of the PC

Figure 1	Courtesy of apple2history.org
Figure 2a	Getty Images
Figure 2b	© Roger Ressmeyer/Corbis
Figure 3	Photo courtesy of Apple Computer, Inc.
Figure 4	Photo courtesy of Apple Computer, Inc.
Figure 6	© Jerry Mason/Photo Researchers, Inc.
Figure 7	© The Computer History Museum
Figure 8	© The Computer History Museum
Figure 9	Time Magazine, Copyright Time, Inc.
Figure 10	© David Wilson/Corbis
Figure 11	Courtesy of Dan Bricklin and Bob Frankston.
Figure 13	© The Computer History Museum
Figure 14	Photo courtesy of Apple Computer, Inc.
Figure 15	Photo courtesy of Apple Computer, Inc.
Figure 16	© The Computer History Museum
Figure 17	© The Computer History Museum
Figure 18	Courtesy of Ames Laboratory.
Figure 19	Naval Historical Center
Figure 20	© The Computer History Museum

Chapter 3

Chapter Opener	© Larry Williams/Corbis
Figure 3.2a	MuVo is a registered trademark of Creative Technology Ltd. in the United States and /or others countries. NOMAD is a registered trademark of Aonix and is used by Creative Technology Ltd. and /or its affiliates under license.
Figure 3.3	© IEI03
Figure 3.8	Screen shot(s) reprinted by permission from Microsoft Corporation.
Figure 3.11	Reproduced with permission of Yahoo! Inc. © 2005 by Yahoo! Inc. YAHOO! and the YAHOO! logo are trademarks of Yahoo! Inc.
Figure 3.12	Screen shot(s) reprinted by permission from Microsoft Corporation.
Figure 3.13a	© 1998–2006 The Mozilla Organization
Figure 3.13b	© 2005 Google. All rights reserved
Figure 3.15a	© 2005 Google.
Figure 3.15b	© Reproduced with the permission of Overture Services, Inc. All rights reserved.

Figure 3.17	© 2005 Google. All rights reserved.
Figure 3.18	© 2004, Librarians' Index to the Internet, lii.org. All rights reserved.
Figure 3.19	Screen shot(s) reprinted by permission from Microsoft Corporation.
Figure 3.20	© 2005 Gawker Media. All rights reserved.
Figure 3.21	Courtesy of Childnet International
Figure 3.22	The AOL Instant Messenger Logo, AOL, AIM and Buddy List are registered trademarks of America Online, Inc. The AIM Instant Messenger browser frame is © 2005 by America Online, Inc. The America Online content, name, icons and trademarks are used with permission.
Figure 3.23	Reproduced with permission of Yahoo! Inc. © 2005 by Yahoo! Inc. YAHOO! and the YAHOO! logo are trademarks of Yahoo! Inc.
Figure 3.24	© 2005 Montgomery County Community College. All rights reserved.

	Screen shot(s) reprinted by permission from Microsoft Corporation.
Figure 3.25	Screen shot(s) reprinted by permission from Microsoft Corporation.
Figure 3.26	© 2002–2004 PestPatrol, Inc.All rights reserved.
Figure 3.28a	Adobe product icon(s) reprinted with permission from Adobe Systems Incorporated.
Figure 3.28 b, c, f	© 1995-2005 Macromedia, Inc. All rights reserved.
Figure 3.28e	© 1995-2004 RealNetworks, Inc. All rights reserved. RealNetworks, Real.com, RealAudio, RealVideo, RealSystem, RealPlayer, RealJukebox, and RealMedia are trademarks or registered trademarks of RealNetworks, Inc.
Figure 3.28g	Logo reprinted by permission from Microsoft Corporation.

Chapter 4

Chapter Opener	© Sanford/Agliolo/Corbis
Figure 4.2	Screen shot(s) reprinted by permission from Microsoft Corporation.
Figure 4.3	© 2006 Sun Microsystems, Inc. All rights reserved.
Figure 4.4	Screen shot(s) reprinted by permission from Microsoft Corporation.
Figure 4.5	Screen shot(s) reprinted by permission from Microsoft Corporation.
Figure 4.6	Screen shot(s) reprinted by permission from Microsoft Corporation.
Figure 4.7	Screen shot(s) reprinted by permission from Microsoft Corporation.
Figure 4.8	Screen shot(s) reprinted by permission from Microsoft Corporation.
Figure 4.9	Screen shot(s) reprinted by permission from Microsoft Corporation.
Figure 4.10	Microsoft Office box shot reprinted with permission from Microsoft Corporation.
Figure 4.10	Lotus Smart Suite box shot courtesy of International Business Machines

	Corporation. Unauthorized use not permitted.
Figure 4.10	Adobe Creative Suite courtesy of Adobe.
Figure 4.10	WordPerfect box shot reprinted with permission of Corel Corporation.
Figure 4.10	StarOffice box shot © Sun Microsystems 2003.
Figure 4.10	Vcom SystemSuite box shot courtesy of vcom SystemsSuite.
Figure 4.11	© Michael Keller/Corbis
Figure 4.12b	Screen shot(s) reprinted by permission from Microsoft Corporation.
Figure 4.13	Screen shots © Intuit Inc. All rights reserved.
Figure 4.14	Screen shots © Intuit Inc. All rights reserved.
Figure 4.15	Screen shot(s) reprinted by permission from Microsoft Corporation.
Figure 4.17	© 2004 Quark, Inc. and Quark Media House Sàrl, Switzerland. All rights reserved.

Figure 4.18	Screen shot(s) reprinted by permission from Microsoft Corporation. Adobe product screen shot(s) reprinted with permission from Adobe Systems Incorporated.
Figure 4.19	Adobe product screen shot(s) reprinted with permission from Adobe Systems Incorporated.
Figure 4.20	Screen shot(s) reprinted by permission from Microsoft Corporation.
Figure 4.22	© Blackboard Inc. All rights reserved.
Figure 4.23	Courtesy of the Entertainment Software Association. Used with permission.
Figure 4.24	Reprinted with permission of Logitech (joystick).
Figure 4.24	I-Scaptes II (goggles)
Figure 4.26	AP/Wide World Photos
Figure 4.27	© 2004 Linktivity. All rights reserved.
Figure 4.27b	©2005 SMART Technologies
Figure 4.28	Screen shot(s) reprinted by permission from Microsoft Corporation.
Figure 4.29	Copyright 2004, PlayFirst, Inc. All Rights Reserved. Reproduced with permission of Yahoo! Inc. © 2005 by Yahoo! Inc. YAHOO! and the YAHOO! logo are trademarks of Yahoo! Inc.
Figure 4.30	Screen shot(s) reprinted by permission from Microsoft Corporation.
Figure 4.31a	Screen shot(s) reprinted by permission from Microsoft Corporation.
Figure 4.31b	The AOL Instant Messenger Logo, AOL, AIM and Buddy List are registered trademarks of America Online, Inc. The AIM Instant Messenger browser frame is © 2005 by America Online, Inc. The America Online content, name, icons and trademarks are used with permission.

Technology in Focus: Digital Entertainment

Figure 2a-b	Screen shot(s) reprinted by permission from Microsoft Corporation.
Figure 5	Photo of Nikon Coolpix SQ coutesy of MWW Group.
Figure 5	Photo © Konica Minolta Photo Imaging U. S. A., Inc.
Figure 5	Image courtesy of © Kodak.
Figure 5	CANON, the Canon logo, Canon EOS Rebel are trademarks of Canon, Inc. All rights reserved. Used by permission.
Figure 8	Courtesy of Sandisk.
Figure 9	Courtesy of Hewlett Packard.
Figure 10	Copyright © 1995–2003, Jasc Software, Inc.
Figure 11a	CANON the Canon logo, Powershot and Elura are trademarks of Canon, Inc. All rights reserved. Used by permission.
Figure 11b	Sony Corporation
Figure 13a	RCA camcorder photo courtesy of Thomson.
Figure 13b	JVC Corporation
Figure 14a	Courtesy of Pinnacle
Figure 14b	© Iomega
Figure 15a-b	Screen shot(s) reprinted by permission from Microsoft Corporation.
Figure 16	Adobe product screen shot(s) reprinted with permission from Adobe Systems Incorporated.

Chapter 5

Chapter Opener	© Mendola/Jeff Mangiat/Corbis
Figure 5.2	© Henry Ray Adams/Corbis (car)
Figure 5.2	Courtesy of Nokia (cell phone).
Figure 5.2	NASA (space shuttle)
Figure 5.5	Copyright © 2006 Apple Computer, Inc. All rights reserved.
Figure 5.6	The Linux 2.0 Penguin, "Tux," was created by Larry Ewing (lewign@isc.tamu.edu) using the GIMP Software.

Figure 5.7	Courtesy of Intel Corporation (chip).
Figure 5.8	Screen shot(s) reprinted by permission from Microsoft Corporation.
Figure 5.9	Screen shot(s) reprinted by permission from Microsoft Corporation.
Figure 5.11	Screen shot(s) reprinted by permission from Microsoft Corporation.
Figure 5.12h	Screen shot(s) reprinted by permission from Microsoft Corporation.
Figure 5.13	Screen shot(s) reprinted by permission from Microsoft Corporation.
Figure 5.14	Screen shot(s) reprinted by permission from Microsoft Corporation.
Figure 5.15	Screen shot(s) reprinted by permission from Microsoft Corporation.
Figure 5.16a	Screen shot(s) reprinted by permission from Microsoft Corporation.
Figure 5.16b	Reproduced with permission of Yahoo! Inc.© 2005 by Yahoo! Inc. YAHOO! and the YAHOO! logo are trademarks of Yahoo! Inc.
Figure 5.17	Screen shot(s) reprinted by permission from Microsoft Corporation.

Figure 5.18	Screen shot(s) reprinted by permission from Microsoft Corporation.
Figure 5.19	Screen shot(s) reprinted by permission from Microsoft Corporation.
Figure 5.21	Screen shot(s) reprinted by permission from Microsoft Corporation.
Figure 5.23	Screen shot(s) reprinted by permission from Microsoft Corporation.
Figure 5.26	Screen shot(s) reprinted by permission from Microsoft Corporation.
Figure 5.27	Screen shot(s) reprinted by permission from Microsoft Corporation.
Figure 5.28	Screen shot(s) reprinted by permission from Microsoft Corporation.
Figure 5.31	Screen shot(s) reprinted by permission from Microsoft Corporation.
Figure 5.32	Screen shot(s) reprinted by permission from Microsoft Corporation.
Figure 5.33	Screen shot(s) reprinted by permission from Microsoft Corporation.

Chapter 6

Chapter Opener	© Colin Anderson/Brand X Pictures/ Picture Quest
Figure 6.4	Courtesy of Intel Corporation.
Figure 6.5	Screen shot(s) reprinted by permission from Microsoft Corporation.
Figure 6.6	Screen shot(s) reprinted by permission from Microsoft Corporation.
Figure 6.11	Screen shot(s) reprinted by permission from Microsoft Corporation.
Figure 6.13	Screen shot(s) reprinted by permission from Microsoft Corporation.
Figure 6.14	© Terra Nova Designs
Figure 6.16	Courtesy of International Business Machines Corporation. Unauthorized used not permitted.
Figure 6.18	Screen shot(s) reprinted by permission from Microsoft Corporation.
Figure 6.21a	Courtesy of Victorinox.

Figure 6.21b	Courtesy of EdgeTech Corporation.
Figure 6.21c	Courtesy of Kensington
Figure 6.21d	Courtesy of EdgeTech Corporation.
Figure 6.21e	Courtesy of Archos.
Figure 6.21f	Courtesy of Lexar.
Figure 6.23	Courtesy of Archos.
Figure 6.24	Courtesy of Sandisk.
Figure 6.28	Screen shot(s) reprinted by permission from Microsoft Corporation.
Figure 6.29	Screen shot(s) reprinted by permission from Microsoft Corporation.
Figure 6.31	Klipsch Audio Technologies
Figure 6.33	© Creative Technology Ltd., © 2003
Figure 6.35a-i	Courtesy of Hack In The Box, www.hackinthbox.org
Figure 6.41	Courtesy of Koutech.

Technology in Focus: Computing Alternatives

Chapter 7

Chapter 8

Figure 8.10a-b	Courtesy of Sandisk.		Figure 8.21b	Courtesy of Blackberry.
Figure 8.10c	Courtesy of Sony Corporation		Figure 8.25	© Reuters NewMedia/Corbis
Figure 8.11	AP/Wide World Photos		Figure 8.28	© Microsoft Corporation
Figure 8.12b	AP/Wide World Photos		Figure 8.29	Laboratory for Communications Engineering, Cambridge
Figure 8.14a	Image used with permission of Palm, Inc. Palm is a trademark of Palm, Inc.		Figure 8.32	AP/Wide World Photos
Figure 8.17	Courtesy of Hitachi Global Storage Technologies.		Figure 8.33a	Brother UK Ltd.
			Figure 8.33b	Infocus
Figure 8.19	Courtesy of Linksys.		Figure 8.35	Photo Researchers
Figure 8.21a	Image used with permission of Palm, Inc. Palm is a trademark of Palm, Inc.			

Technology in Focus: Protecting Your Computer and Backing Up Your Data

Figure 4	Image courtesy of American Power Conversion Corporation.		Figure 12	Screen shot(s) reprinted by permission from Microsoft Corporation.
Figure 8	Screen shot(s) reprinted by permission from Microsoft Corporation.		Figure 15a	© 2005 Cloudmark, Inc. All rights reserved.
Figure 10	© 2003 Rhodes Software Pty Ltd. All Rights Reserved. www.accountlogon.com		Figure 15b	© 2005 FMR Corp. All rights reserved.
			Figure 15c	These materials have been reproduced with the permission of PayPal, Inc. Copyright © 2005 PayPal, Inc. All rights reserved.
Figure 11	The AOL Instant Messenger Logo, AOL, AIM and Buddy List are registered trademarks of America Online, Inc. The AIM Instant Messenger browser frame is © 2005 by America Online, Inc. The America Online content, name, icons and trademarks are used with permission.		Figure 16	Screen shot(s) reprinted by permission from Microsoft Corporation.
			Figure 17	© 2005 StompSoft, Inc. All rights reserved.

Chapter 9

Chapter Opener	© Denis Scott/Corbis		Figure 9.5b	Reprinted by permission of International Business Machines Corporation. Unauthorized use not permitted.
Figure 9.2c	© Ferranti Electronics/A. Sternberg/Photo Researchers		Figure 9.15	Reprinted by permission Kobi Benson.
Figure 9.5a	Courtesy of Intel Corporation.			

Chapter 10

Chapter Opener	© Paul Cooklin/Brand X Pictures/ Picture Quest	**Figure 10.19**	Screen shot(s) reprinted by permission from Microsoft Corporation.
Figure 10.16	Screen shot(s) reprinted by permission from Microsoft Corporation.	**Figure 10.22**	© 1995–2005 Macromedia, Inc. All rights reserved.
Figure 10.18	Screen shot(s) reprinted by permission from Microsoft Corporation.		

Chapter 11

Chapter Opener	© Boden/Ledingham/Master File	**Figure 11.16 a-b**	Screen shot(s) reprinted by permission from Microsoft Corporation.
Figure 11.1	Screen shot(s) reprinted by permission from Microsoft Corporation.	**Figure 11.17**	Screen shot(s) reprinted by permission from Microsoft Corporation.
Figure 11.2a-b	Screen shot(s) reprinted by permission from Microsoft Corporation.	**Figure 11.18**	Courtesy of the Federal Bureau of Investigation.
Figure 11.3	(financial aid office) Corbis/Royalty Free	**Figure 11.19 a-b**	Screen shot(s) reprinted by permission from Microsoft Corporation.
Figure 11.3	(teacher) © John Henley/Corbis		
Figure 11.3	(student registration) © Jose Luis Palaez, Inc/Corbis	**Figure 11.20**	Screen shot(s) reprinted by permission from Microsoft Corporation.
Figure 11.3	(student housing officer) © John Feingersh/Corbis	**Figure 11.21**	Screen shot(s) reprinted by permission from Microsoft Corporation.
Figure 11.3	(parent) © Bill Varie/Corbis	**Figure 11.22**	Screen shot(s) reprinted by permission from Microsoft Corporation.
Figure 11.4	Screen shot(s) reprinted by permission from Microsoft Corporation.	**Figure 11.23**	Screen shot(s) reprinted by permission from Microsoft Corporation.
Figure 11.6	Screen shot(s) reprinted by permission from Microsoft Corporation.	**Figure 11.24**	Screen shot(s) reprinted by permission from Microsoft Corporation.
Figure 11.7	© 2005, Oracle. All rights reserved.	**Figure 11.25**	Screen shot(s) reprinted by permission from Microsoft Corporation.
Figure 11.8a-b	Screen shot(s) reprinted by permission from Microsoft Corporation.	**Figure 11.26**	© 2004 California State Controller's Office. All rights reserved.
Figure 11.9	Screen shot(s) reprinted by permission from Microsoft Corporation.	**Figure 11.28**	(web user) © Reed Kaestner/Corbis
Figure 11.10	Screen shot(s) reprinted by permission from Microsoft Corporation.	**Figure 11.28**	(information systems) © LWA-JDC/Corbis
Figure 11.11	© 1997–2004 The Vermont Teddy Bear Company, Inc.	**Figure 11.29**	(tele-salesperson) © R. W. Jones/Corbis
		Figure 11.29	(supplier shipments) © R. W. Jones/Corbis
Figure 11.12	Screen shot(s) reprinted by permission from Microsoft Corporation.	**Figure 11.29**	(online shipping) © Paul Burton/Corbis
Figure 11.13 a-b	Screen shot(s) reprinted by permission from Microsoft Corporation.	**Figure 11.29**	(data retrieval) © Tom & Dee McCarthy/Corbis
Figure 11.14 a-c	Screen shot(s) reprinted by permission from Microsoft Corporation.	**Figure 11.30**	(step 1) © Norbert Schaefer/Corbis
		Figure 11.30	(step 5) © Corbis
Figure 11.15 a-c	Screen shot(s) reprinted by permission from Microsoft Corporation.	**Figure 11.31 a-c**	Screen shot(s) reprinted by permission from Microsoft Corporation.

Chapter 12

Chapter Opener	© Chris McElcheran/Masterfile	**Figure 12.24**	Screen shot(s) reprinted by permission from Microsoft Corporation.
Figure 12.15	© 2005 RealVNC Ltd. All rights reserved. www.realvnc.com	**Figure 12.26**	Courtesy of ShakeMap Working Group.

Chapter 13

Chapter Opener	© Didier Bodet/Brand X Pictures/ Picture Quest	**Figure 13.15**	© 1997–2005 Barnesandnoble.com llc. All rights reserved.
Figure 13.10	Screen shot(s) reprinted by permission from Microsoft Corporation.	**Figure 13.23a**	© 2005 by Yahoo! Inc. YAHOO! and the YAHOO! logo are trademarks of Yahoo! Inc.
Figure 13.11b	© Jose Luis Palaez/Corbis		
Figure 13.14	Screen shot(s) reprinted by permission from Microsoft Corporation.		

Technology in Focus: Careers in IT

Figure 2	© 2000–2004 Salary.com, Inc. All rights reserved.	**Figure 7**	© 1999–2001 FutureFiction.com All rights reserved worldwide
Figure 5	© 1999–2005 iSeek Solutions Version 3.0	**Figure 9**	© 2005 Digital Animations. All rights reserved.
Figure 5	(marketing dept.) © LWA-JDC/Corbis		
Figure 5	(golfer) © Mark A Johnson/Corbis	**Figure 12**	© 2005 CareerBuilder LLC. All rights reserved.
Figure 5	(supervisor) © Gabe Palmer/Corbis		
Figure 5	(customer) © Larry Williams/Corbis	**Figure 14**	© 2005 Campbell Soup Company. All rights reserved.
Figure 5	(stressed worker) © Jon Feingersh/Corbis		